Detail in Contemporary Residential Architecture

Virginia McLeod

Published in 2007 by
Laurence King Publishing Ltd
361-373 City Road
London EC1V 1LR
e-mail: enquiries@laurenceking.co.uk
www.laurenceking.co.uk

A catalogue record for this book is
available from the British Library

ISBN-13: 978 1 85669 482 7
ISBN-10: 1 85669 482 8
1005416083
Designed by Hamish Muir
Picture Research by Sophia Gibb
Printed in China

Detail in Contemporary Residential Architecture

Virginia McLeod

Laurence King Publishing

Contents

Introduction

The private house occupies a unique position in architecture and in the history of human culture. The house is the domain of the family, of domestic activities and is used for living, working, eating and sleeping, and as a private place where individuals and families enjoy their personal lives. However, the house in its traditional form – a series of common rooms and separate sleeping areas – has undergone a number of radical changes over the last century in which the possibilities for self-expression in the domestic environment have revealed a new platform for architectural experiment. Shifts in social patterns have also fuelled this experimentation. Architects now design houses for many different types of households – single parent families, couples without children, multi-generational families, and so on. Along with social change, the pace with which technology has developed over the past 50 years, in particular computer and construction technologies, have combined to offer more and more possibilities for what a house contains, what it looks like and to whom it caters.

Construction details are as vital a part of architecture as its external form and interior layout. Whether so subtle as to be invisible, or revealed as extraordinarily complex, details determine the quality and character of a building. Good detailing entails exercising the utmost care and attention at the junctions between materials, between the different elements of a building and where a material changes direction. Through details, the myriad parts that make up a building come together to form a whole – joints, connections, seams, openings and surfaces are transformed via a combination of technology and invention into a building.

We are accustomed to being presented with photographic representations of architecture in books, magazines and on-line, with the inspiring image continuing to be the focus of the two-dimensional representation of architecture. Increasingly these images are now often accompanied by floor plans to provide a better understanding of the way a building works. The availability of floor plans is, of course, of enormous assistance in helping us to understand the spatial sequences, the extent and scale of a building, however it is not inherent in the purpose of a plan or a photograph, even if accompanied by a section, to reveal the individual elements – literally the nuts and bolts – that go together to make up a wall, a floor, a roof, a window, a staircase, a kitchen, and so on. Construction details, however, do just this, and this book unites the photograph, the plan and section, as well as the details to bring to the reader a comprehensive insight into the true workings of the building.

Architects draw details specifically to reveal the inner workings of a building – primarily, of course, they are used by the builder in order to put the building together. Readers of architectural publications, however, are all too rarely given the opportunity to examine the details – the 'real' representation of how a building is put together. This book aims to remedy that situation and provides a guide to the inner workings of over 50 of the most inspiring examples of contemporary domestic architecture. This book brings to the reader what has previously been hidden behind the façade, what had previously remained invisible. These details reveal not only an 'x-ray' of the houses presented, but an insight into the cognitive processes of the architects who brought the houses into being.

Architectural details make up to 95 per cent of the sometimes hundreds of drawings produced to describe the way a building is put together. They act as the means by which architects communicate their intent to builders, engineers and other participants in the building process.

They also act as one of the most challenging intellectual and technical exercises for any architect, producing as they must, a series of what are essentially graphic representations of every single junction and connection in a building. Almost exclusively made up of two-dimensional representations (plan and sectional drawings), the challenge resides in the architect's ability to imagine the most complex of junctions, assemblies and components in three dimensions – as they will actually be built on site – and transfer them on to paper, or on screen, into two dimensions, into the conventional drawn representations that have been used in the construction industry for decades, even centuries.

While the selection of details presented for each of the houses in this book is necessarily limited by space, they nonetheless go a long way towards deconstructing the image of the finished building. They not only inspire, they also help us to understand the thought that went into the making of the building and perhaps the technical problems that were solved along the way.

Details also reveal the preoccupations and specialties of an individual architect. Each of the architects in this book were asked to provide their personal selection of the details that they felt best represented the house in question. As a result, a focus on the way glazing is put together with the materials that hold it in place may be revealed in some projects, while the sculptural qualities of a balustrade or even a recessed light fitting may come into focus through the details in others.

In many cases, details also reveal cultural differences as well as commonalities. The scope of this book covers five continents – Europe, North America, South America, Asia and Australia. Many of the houses appear to have aesthetic qualities in common, perhaps revealing similarities in the way architecture is taught at universities around the world, as well as the contemporary cultural influences that cross geographical boundaries. However, many differences are revealed in the details. The climate or economics in one country or region may make concrete inappropriate or too expensive to use in a domestic context. Timber or stone may, instead, be the most available, affordable material.

Similarly, differences in the traditions of the building trades are also revealed in the details. For example, bamboo is used as an every day necessity in the building industry in China where it has been used for centuries, most notably for scaffolding. The familiarity and expertise with which Chinese builders are able to manipulate this inexpensive and readily available material is virtually unknown in the west. This expertise is brilliantly utilized by contemporary architects working in China who relish the opportunity to take advantage of the consummate ease with which Chinese builders work with bamboo. This can be seen in projects such as Kengo Kuma's Bamboo Wall House and MADA s.p.a.m.'s Father's House, both in China. In the former, bamboo has been used for almost the entire building, interior and exterior, horizontal and vertical surfaces, and in the latter the beauty and versatility of the material is revealed in the polished bamboo matting that is employed as a surface treatment for interior walls and floors.

In Australia, a 200 year tradition of building with timber is illustrated in the work of Peter Stutchbury (the Verandah House), Drew Heath (the Zig Zag Cabin) and Sean Godsell (the Peninsula House). Over time, the level of sophistication with which this ubiquitous building material is used has reached a level of artistry that goes well beyond what might ordinarily be thought of as a timber construction. Like bamboo in Chinese construction, and indeed concrete in Japanese architecture, timber is used by these architects as the primary medium with which to express an architectural intention, which is again manifested in the quality of the detailing.

This volume also reveals some of the most surprising and perhaps even bewildering houses of recent times. For example, the Natural Ellipse in Tokyo by Masaki Endoh + Masahiro Ikeda, constructed from fibre reinforced polymer, Kengo Kuma's Plastic House in Japan constructed almost entirely from white plastic, and Simon Conder's Black Rubber Beach House clad in ethylene propylene diene monomer (EPDM). In houses such as these, the image of the building has quickly become iconic, made, as they are from materials rarely, if ever, used in domestic construction. The construction details, however, reveal the creative thinking behind the icon, as well as the reality of designing the components and junctions that make such unusual materials useful as weather-proof domestic shelters.

Another important aspect of contemporary house design is the emergence of environmentally responsive architecture. Many innovative approaches to designing appropriately for climate and to reduce the amount of energy used both in the construction and operation of buildings have found expression in domestic architecture. While this book is presented in chapters based on the main construction material, examples of environmentally responsive houses appear throughout the book. Here, we see some of the most unusual materials in detail, including straw bales in Sarah Wigglesworth's Stock Orchard Street House in London, solar panels in Pugh + Scarpa's Solar Umbrella in California and Georg Driendl's Solar Tube in Austria that employs a central atrium to act as a heat sink in winter and ventilator in summer. Again, the mechanics, the junctions, the materials and their importance to the way the house as a whole works, is revealed in the details.

Despite the effects of social, cultural and technological change, the houses in this book reveal that the typical brief for a house, large or small, remains relatively unchanged. But perhaps because it is so thoroughly known, both by the clients who commission them, the architects who design them and the builders who construct them, it has proven again and again to be fertile ground for experimentation and the search for perfection. Free from the inhibiting control of developers, and often inspired by adventurous and free-thinking clients, architects have embraced the opportunities presented by domestic architecture. Here, this creativity and insight are revealed in the details – just as important in contemporary architecture as site orientation, façade composition and the disposition of the rooms. It is in the details that the architect is free to approach every door, every window, every stair, in fact every screw, bolt, connection and assembly, with the same degree of attention that we might ordinarily associate with product design or sculpture. It seems fitting, therefore, that this book bridges the gap between two dimensions and three, and between images and reality to reveal the true nature of architectural detailing.

Virginia McLeod

Notes

Imperial and Metric Measurements
Dimensions have been provided by the architects in metric and converted to imperial, except in case of projects in the USA in which imperial dimensions have been converted to metric.

Terminology
An attempt has been made to standardize terminology to aid understanding across readerships, for example 'wood' is generally referred to as 'timber' and 'aluminum' as 'aluminium'. However materials or processes that are peculiar to a country, region or architectural practice that have no direct correspondence are presented in the original.

Floor Plans
Throughout the book, the following convention of hierarchy has been used – ground floor, first floor, second floor, and so on. In certain contexts, terms such as basement level or upper level have been used for clarity.

Scale
All floor plans, sections and elevations are presented at conventional architectural metric scales, typically 1:50, 1:100 or 1:200 as appropriate. An accurate graphic scale is included on the second page near the floor plans of every project to aid in the understanding of scale. Details are also presented at conventional architectural scales, typically 1:1, 1:5 and 1:10.

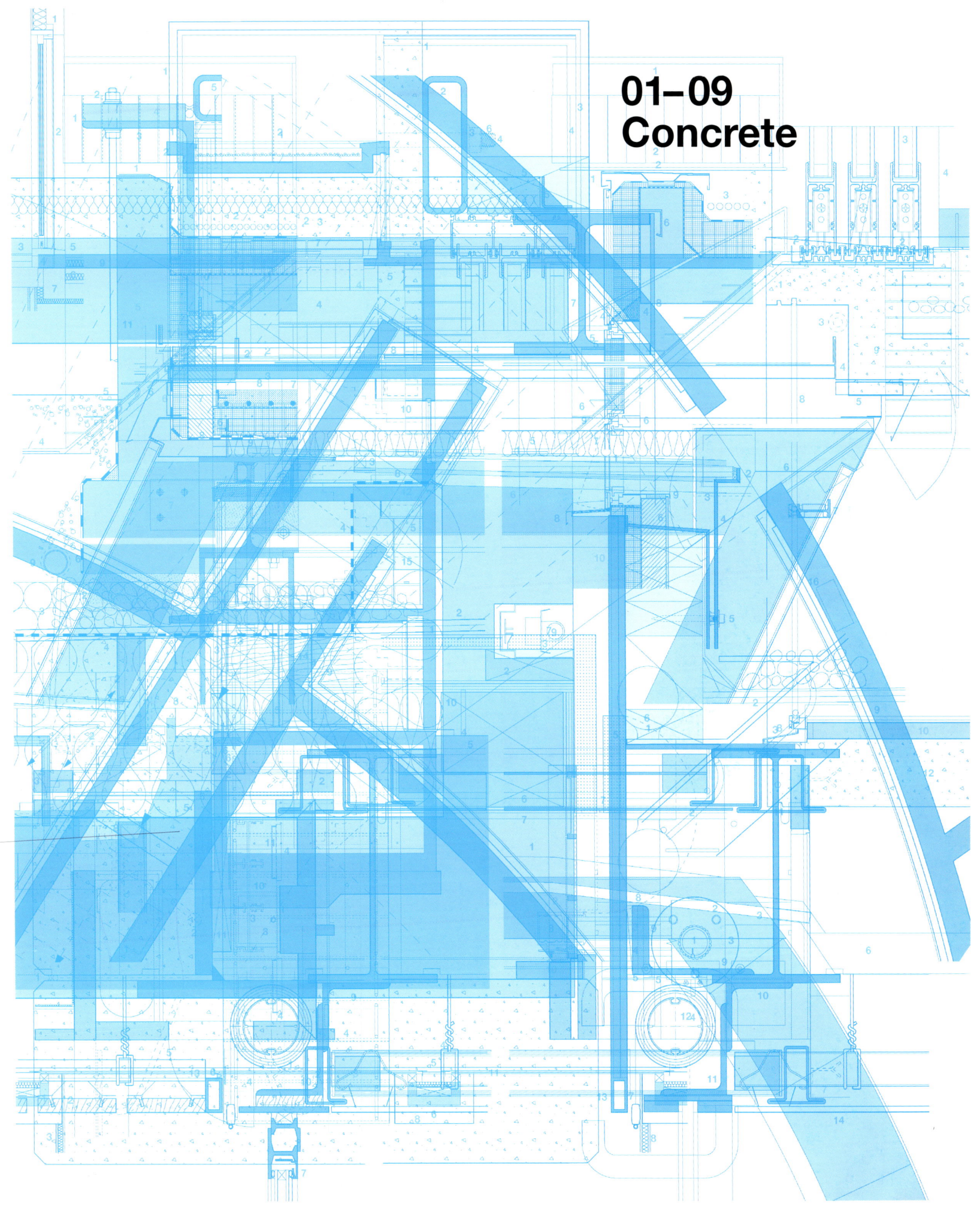

01–09 Concrete

Alberto Campo Baeza

De Blas House
Madrid, Spain

Client
Francisco de Blas

Area
200 square metres (2,150 square feet)

Project Team
Alberto Campo Baeza, Raúl del Valle
González

Structural Engineer
Mª Concepción Pérez Gutiérrez

Clerk of Works
Francisco Melchor

Builder
Juan Sáinz, Siete Encinas

The house is located on the top of
a north-facing hill on the outskirts of
Madrid, overlooking a tranquil village
in a valley with a mountain range
visible on the horizon. The concept for
the house was to strip the brief down
to the essentials, resulting in a
composition of only two elements: a
solid concrete box and a transparent
enclosure, the former acting as a
plinth on which the latter is placed.
The box rises inscrutably out of the
ground with only a few punctured
openings in the walls indicating its
habitability. Its upper surface is
pierced by a staircase descending
into the main volume of the house,
and by the swimming pool.

   Sitting lightly on top of the box, a
slender steel structure frames a glass
enclosure. This unconventional
arrangement allows for spaces of
great contrast. The glass enclosure
is designed as a place for the quiet
contemplation of the landscape, the
seasons and the changing light
throughout the day. In contrast, the
spaces in the concrete box are far
more intimate and cellular, relying
on the punctured windows for light
and ventilation. The plan is rigorously
orthogonal and centred around the
communal spaces such as the living
and dining areas below and the
contemplation space above. On
either side are bedrooms, bathrooms,
a study and the plant room for the
pool. Manipulating solid and void,
transparent and opaque, the house
sits happily in the landscape: both
entrenched in it and sitting lightly
on its surface.

1 The bipartite
composition of solid
base and transparent
box sit inscrutably in
the landscape.
2 The house is
surrounded by the
hardy vegetation of
the Spanish interior –
the subject of
contemplation from
the transparent
enclosure.
3 The platform
on which the glass
enclosure sits is
punctured only by a
staircase to the spaces
below and the swim-
ming pool to
the west.
4 A simple door, visually inseparable from
the in-situ concrete
walls allows access
directly from the lower
level spaces to the
exterior.
5 In contrast to the
light-filled upper level
enclosure, the spaces
below are intimate
and cellular in nature.

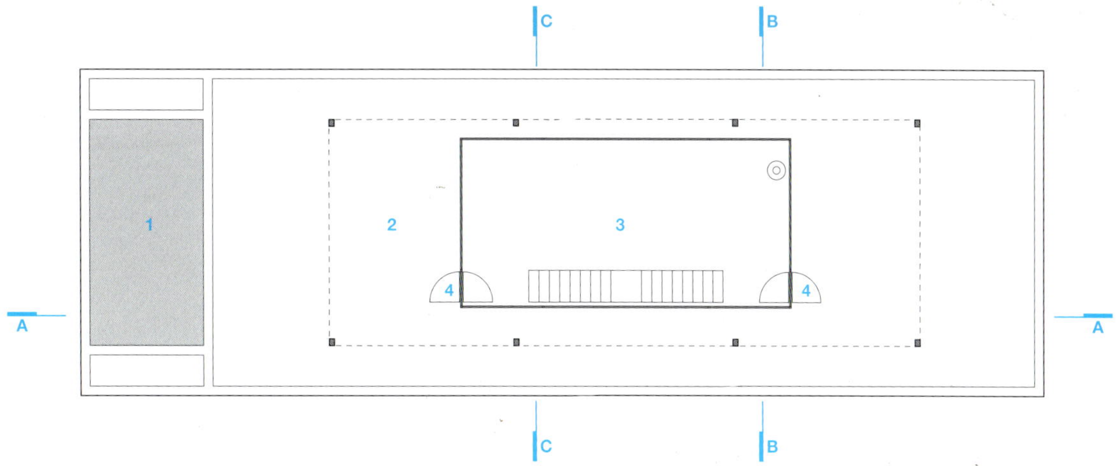

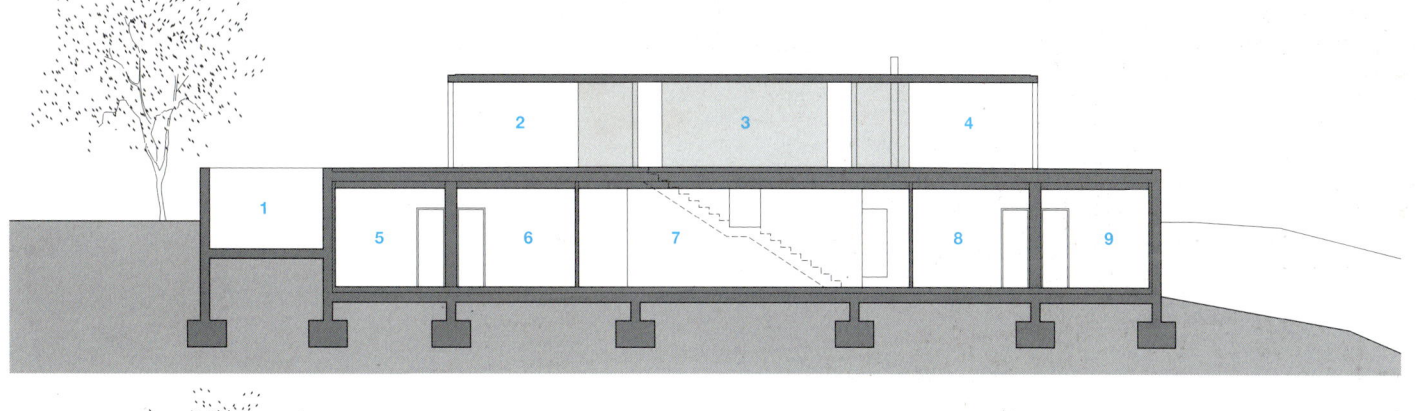

01.01
Upper Level Floor Plan
1:200
1 Pool
2 Line of roof over
3 Contemplation pavilion
4 Entry

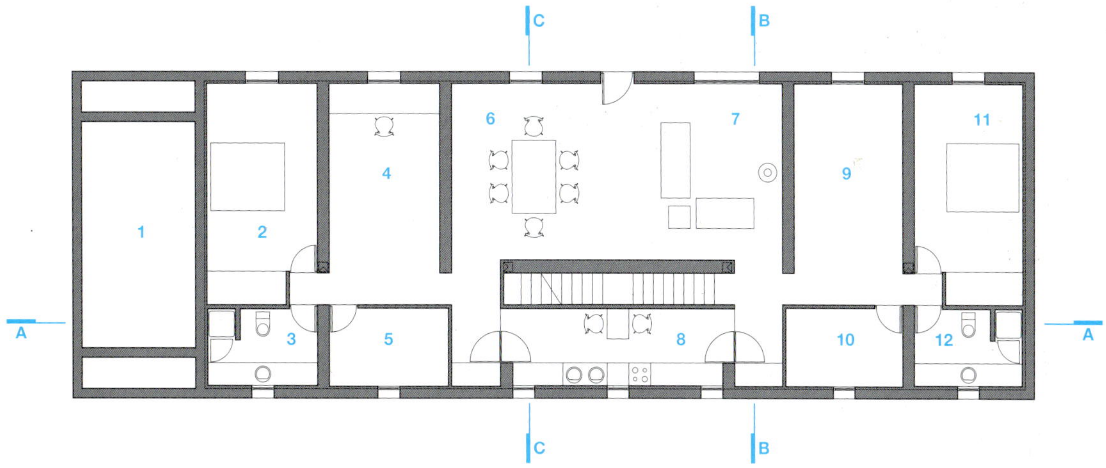

01.02
Lower Level Floor Plan
1:200
1 Pool plant
2 Bedroom 1
3 Bathroom 1
4 Study
5 Utility room
6 Dining
7 Living
8 Kitchen
9 Dressing room
10 Store
11 Bedroom 2
12 Bathroom 2

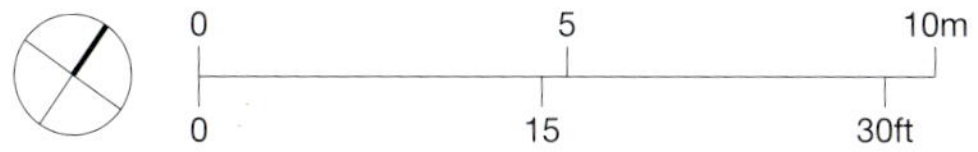

0 5 10m

0 15 30ft

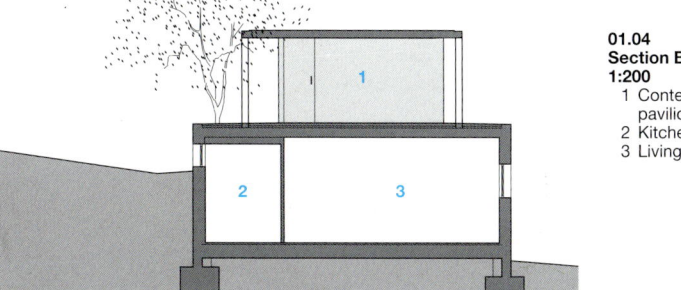

01.03
Section A–A
1:200
1 Pool
2 Terrace
3 Contemplation pavilion
4 Terrace
5 Bathroom 1
6 Utility store
7 Kitchen
8 Dressing room
9 Bathroom 2

01.04
Section B–B
1:200
1 Contemplation pavilion
2 Kitchen lobby
3 Living room

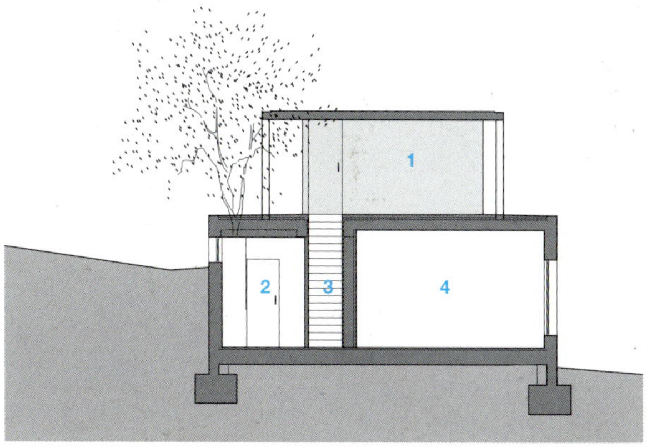

01.05
Section C–C
1:200
1 Contemplation pavilion
2 Kitchen
3 Staircase
4 Dining room

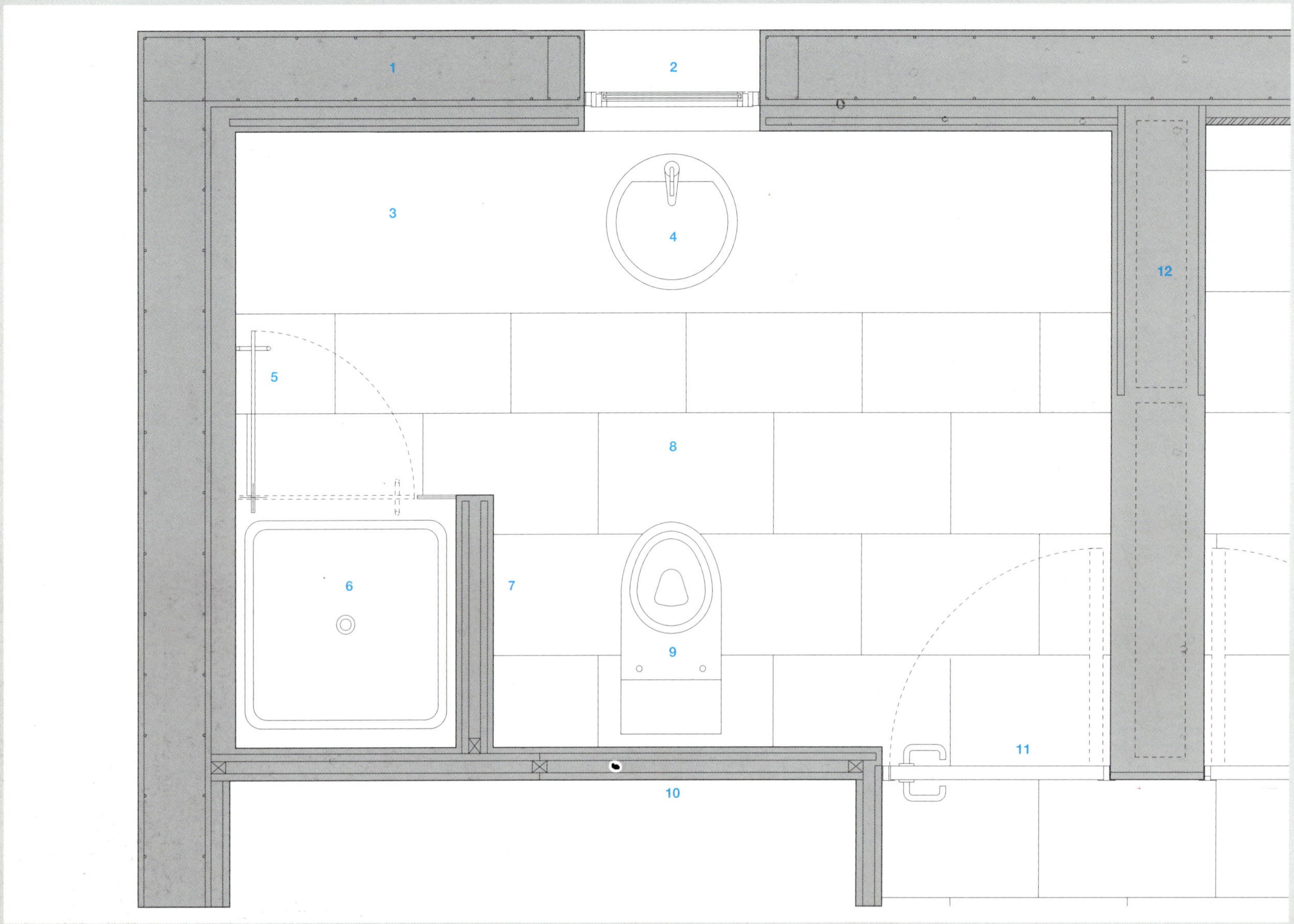

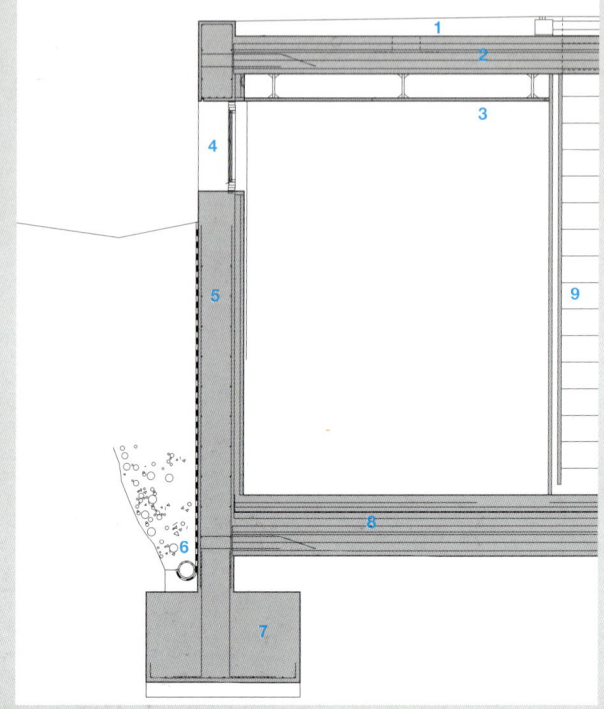

01.06
Bathroom Detail Plan
1:20
1 Cast in-situ
reinforced concrete
wall
2 Thermal glass
pivoting window
3 Limestone counter
4 Hand basin
5 Translucent glass
door
6 Limestone lined
shower
7 Limestone wall
8 Limestone paving
slabs
9 WC
10 Plasterboard wall
11 Steel-framed white
painted timber door
12 Plasterboard wall

01.07
Detail Wall Section
1:50
1 Concrete paving
2 Reinforced
concrete slab
3 Painted
plasterboard ceiling
4 Thermal glass
pivoting window
5 Cast in-situ
reinforced concrete
wall
6 Subterranean
drainage
7 Reinforced
concrete foundation
8 Reinforced
concrete slab
9 Plasterboard wall

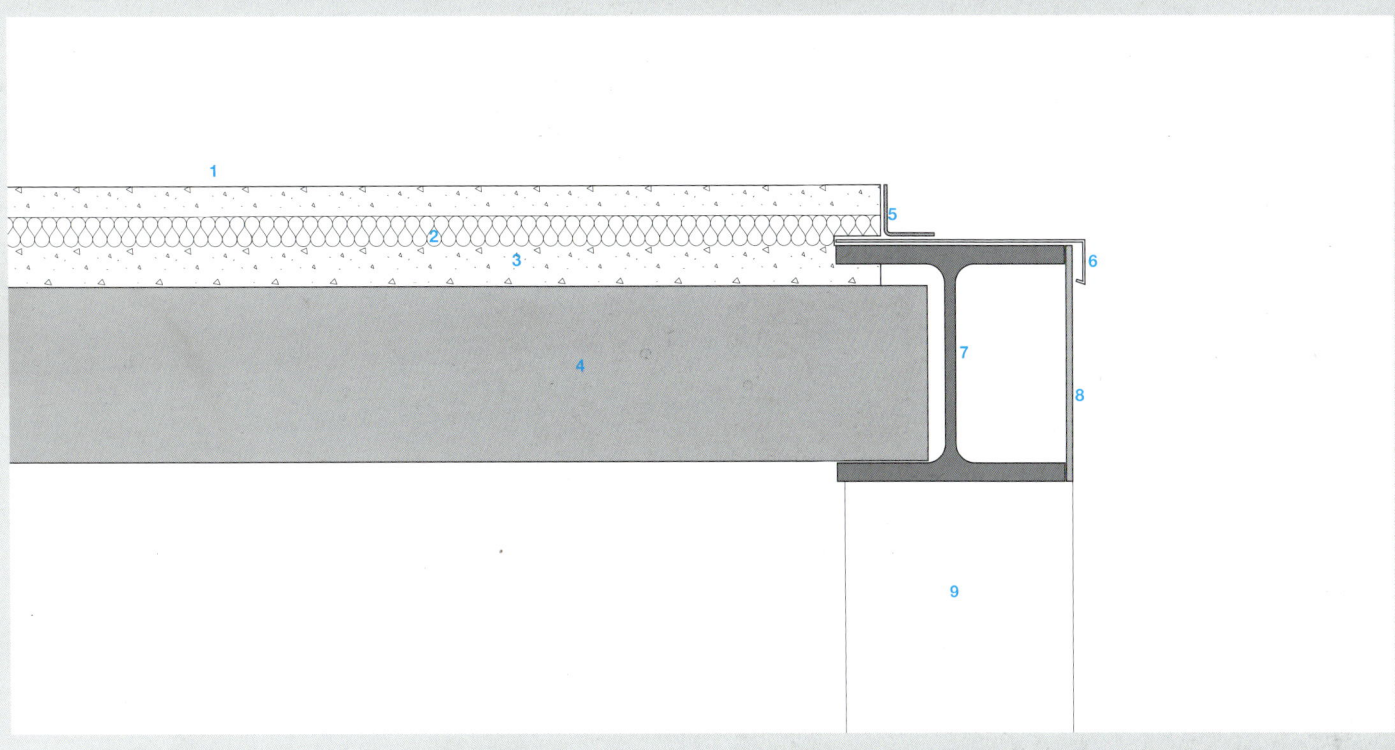

01.08
Roof Detail
1:5
 1 Concrete screed to roof
 2 Thermal insulation and waterproofing
 3 Reinforced concrete slab
 4 Pre-cast concrete slab
 5 White painted galvanized steel angle
 6 Sealed drip groove in flashing
 7 Steel beam
 8 Steel plate
 9 Welded column

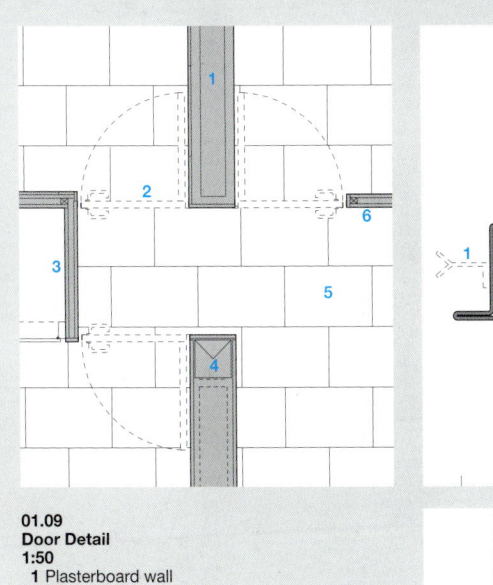

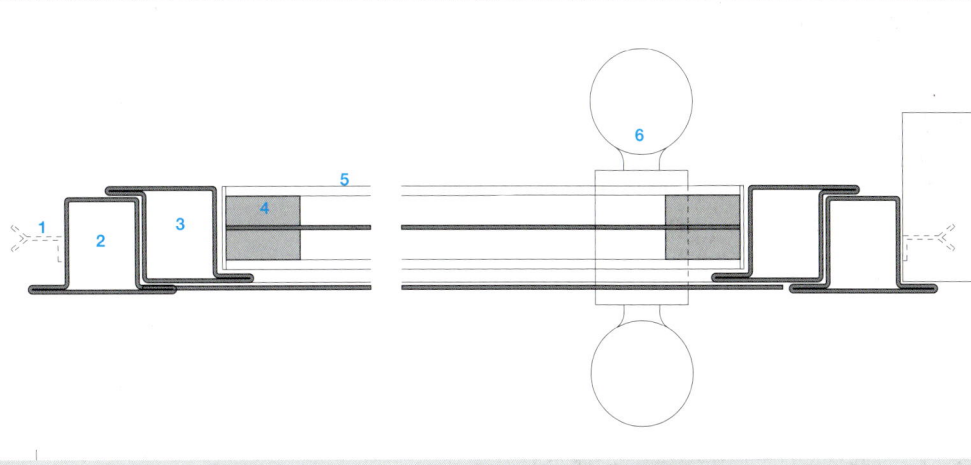

01.10
Door Detail
1:5
 1 Steel anchorage
 2 White painted steel door frame
 3 White painted steel door architrave
 4 Timber door framing
 5 White painted damp-proof membrane board
 6 Stainless steel door handle

01.09
Door Detail
1:50
 1 Plasterboard wall
 2 Timber door
 3 Closet
 4 Steel column
 5 Limestone floor
 6 Plasterboard wall

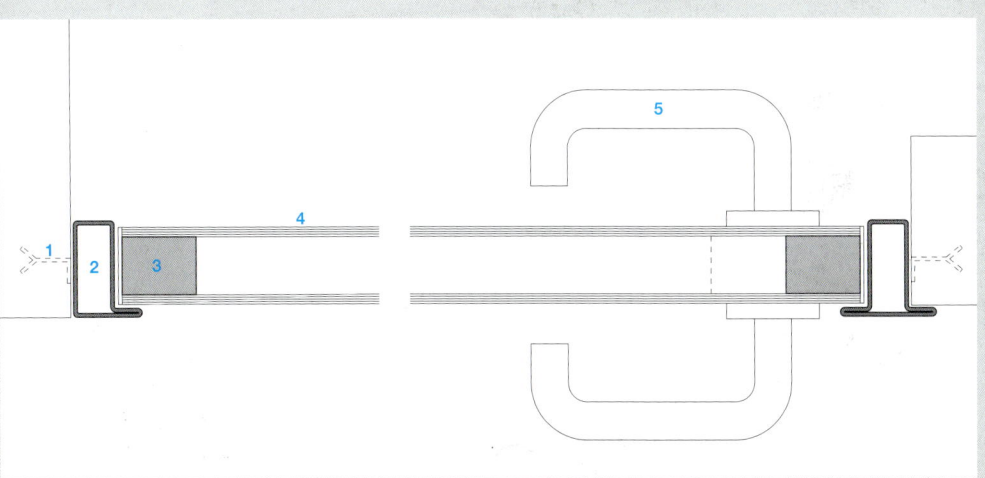

01.11
Door Detail
1:5
 1 Steel anchorage
 2 White painted steel door frame
 3 Timber door framing
 4 White painted damp-proof membrane board
 5 Stainless steel door handle

13

Flatz House
Schaan, Liechtenstein

Client
Dr. Dietmar Flatz

Area
277 square metres (2,980 square feet)

Project Team
Marlies Sofia, Paul Martin, Eckehard
Loidolt, Christian Tabernigg

Structural Engineer
Ferdy Kaiser

Landscape Architect
Vogt Landschaftsarchitekten

Mechanical Engineer
GMI Gasser & Messner Ingenieure

This house for a doctor and his family of five stands on a west-facing slope overlooking the small town of Schaan, with its back to the imposing presence of a range of craggy mountains. In contrast to the surrounding country-style villas, the Flatz House is uncompromisingly modern, the stacked cubic volumes appearing as a minimalist sculpture in the suburban landscape. Addressing the brief for a larger than average family home, the house nevertheless conceals its extent partly because of the way it is embedded in the slope, and partly because of the way the four levels are notched, cantilevered and locked into one another to create a series of private, semi-private, open and closed spaces.

A large rectangular basement containing an independent apartment, a cellar and garage, creates a platform on which the L-shaped ground floor stands, housing the kitchen and living spaces. On the first floor, the parents' quarters, a narrower block with a large terrace, acts as a hinge from which the cantilevered children's areas on the top floor are accessed. From the upper levels distant views stretch from the valley of the Rhine to the Swiss mountains, while the living spaces open up to the immediate landscape. The construction materials emphasize the simplicity of the arrangement. Yellow pigmented concrete on the exterior, white plaster for the interior, plane tree wood and green stone, are all detailed with the utmost restraint.

1 Viewed from the north, the four level house appears as a series of cubist elements stacked and cantilevered one from the other.
2 The childrens' bedroom block at the top of the house cantilevers over an expansive terrace accessed from the parents' bedroom.
3 On the first floor, a small swimming pool occupies the space created by the L-shaped kitchen, living and dining room.
4 View of the kitchen and dining area which have direct views out over the garden.
5 The upper levels are characterized by simple white plaster walls, detailed with concealed lighting that makes the flat plane of the ceiling appear to float.

02.01
Second Floor Plan
1:250
1 Terrace below
2 Bedroom 1
3 Bedroom 2
4 Bathroom
5 Bedroom 3
6 Terrace

02.02
First Floor Plan
1:250
1 Terrace
2 Bathroom
3 Master bedroom

02.03
Ground Floor Plan
1:250
1 Terrace
2 Living Room
3 Kitchen
4 Dining room
5 Pool

02.04
Basement Floor Plan
1:250
1 Terrace
2 Cellar
3 Bathroom
4 Bedroom
5 Kitchenette
6 Bathroom
7 Store
8 Garage
9 Store
10 Store

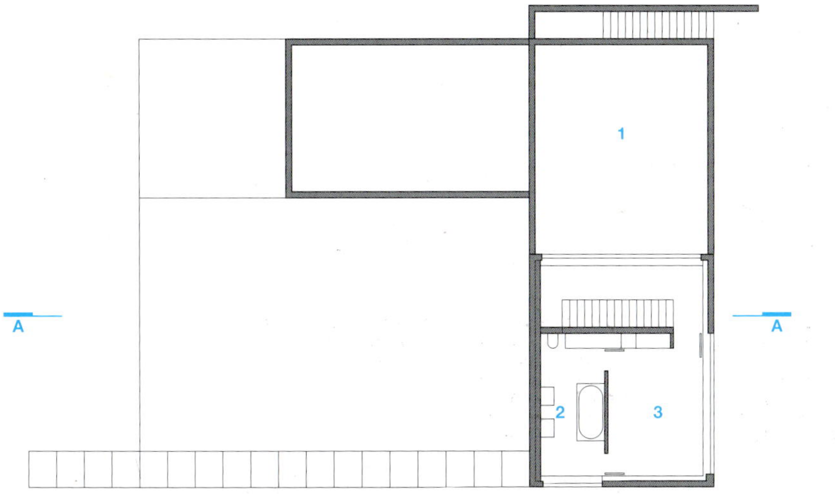

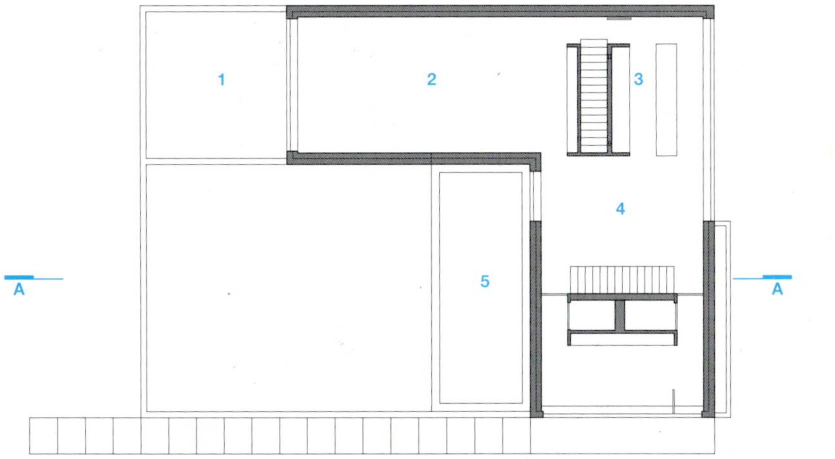

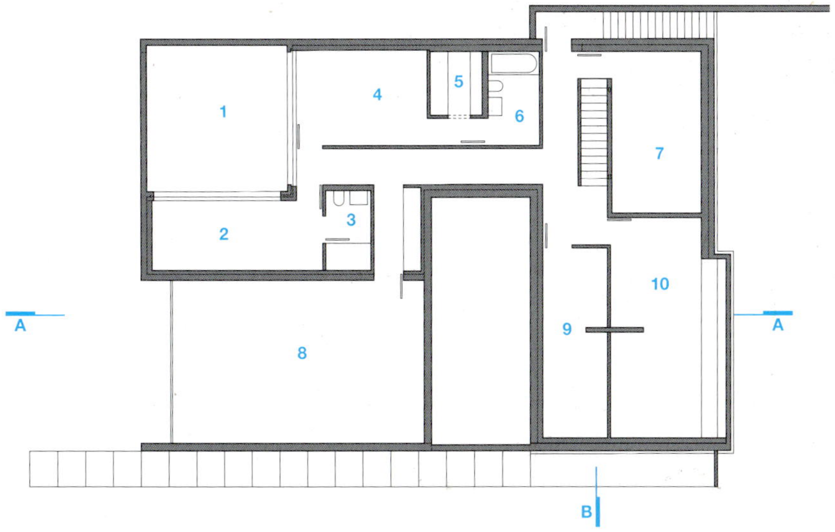

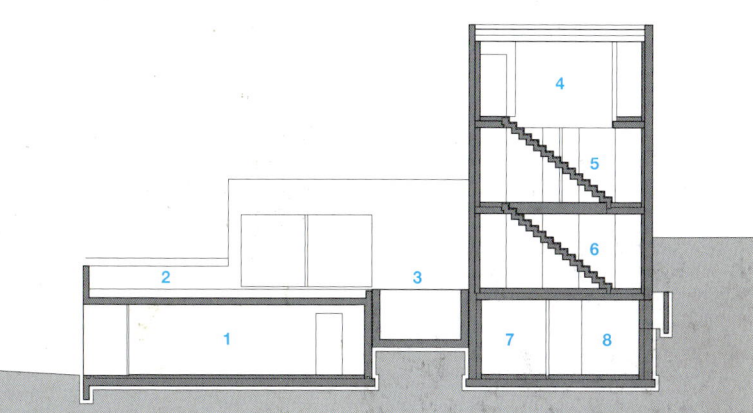

02.05
Section A–A
1:250
1 Garage
2 Terrace
3 Pool
4 Childrens'
  bedrooms
5 Parents' bedroom
6 Dining room
7 Store
8 Store

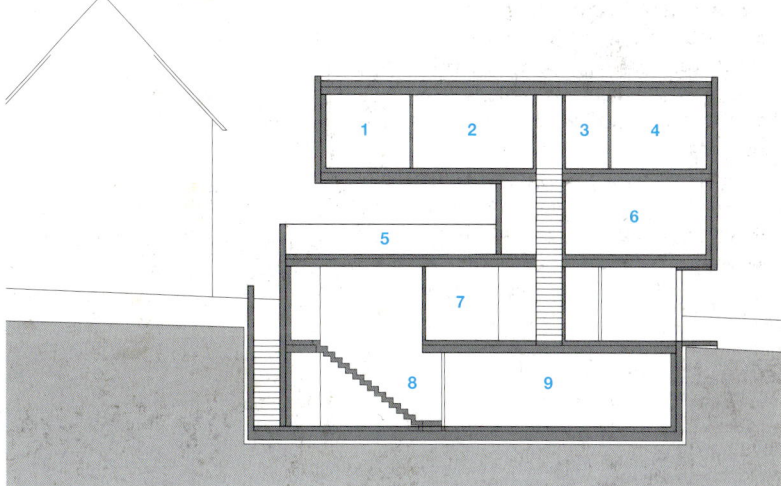

02.06
Section B–B
1:250
1 Bedroom 1
2 Bedroom 2
3 Bathroom
4 Bedroom 3
5 Terrace
6 Bathroom
7 Dining room
8 Store
9 Store

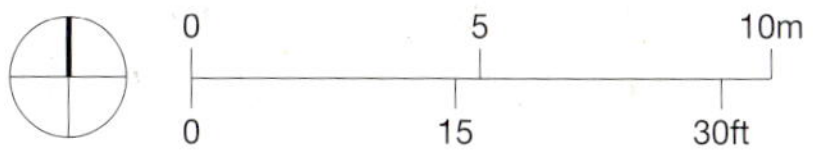

0   5   10m

0   15   30ft

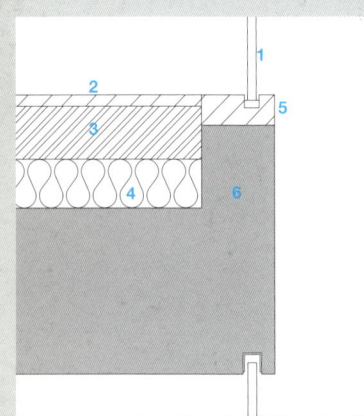

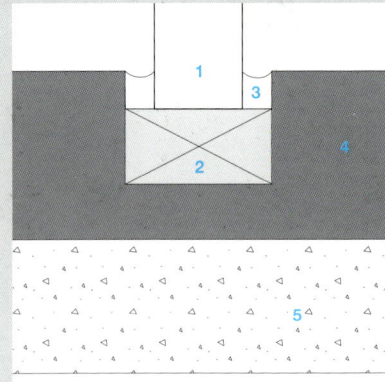

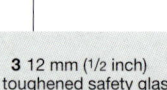

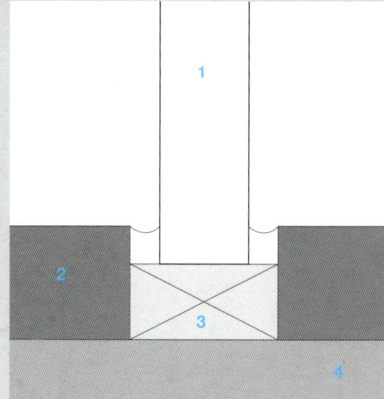

02.07
Floor Detail
1:10
1 12 mm (1/2 inch) toughened safety glass
2 Solid larch flooring

3 Floating floor
4 Insulation
5 40 mm (11/2 inch) larch wood sill
6 Reinforced concrete

02.08
Glazing Detail 1
1:1
1 12 mm (1/2 inch) toughened safety glass
2 Timber frame

3 Black neoprene
4 Larch wood sill
5 Reinforced concrete upturn beam

02.09
Glazing Detail 2
1:1
1 Concrete
2 25 x 25 mm (1 inch) steel U-profile

3 12 mm (1/2 inch) toughened safety glass
4 Silicone groove

02.10
Glazing Detail 3
1:1
1 12 mm (1/2 inch) toughened safety glass
2 Solid larch wood

floor
3 Timber framing
4 Floating floor

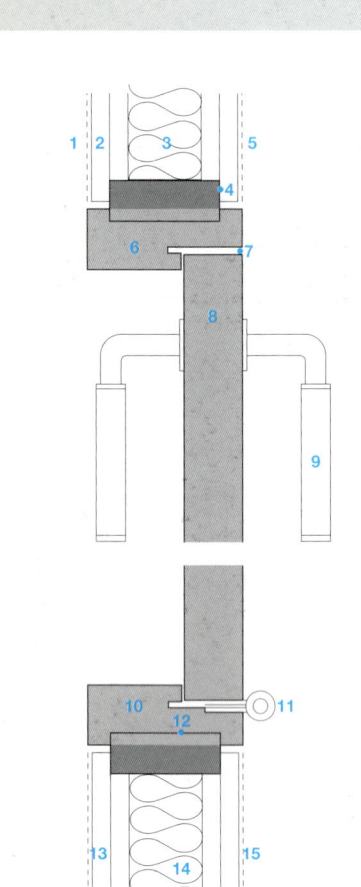

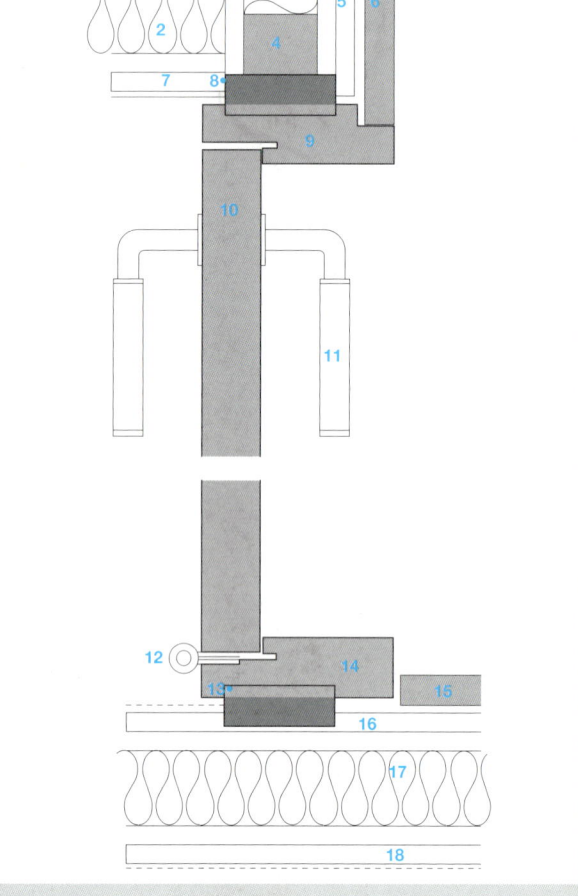

02.11
Door Detail 1
1:5
  1 Gypsum board wall, primed
  2 Gysum board wall
  3 Heat insulation
  4 75 x 27 mm (3 x 1 inch) intermediate timber blocking
  5 Gypsum board wall, primed
  6 Timber door frame
  7 5 mm (1/5 inch) shadow gap
  8 Door leaf

9 Door handle
10 Timber door frame
11 Door hinge
12 75 x 27 mm (3 x 1 inch) intermediate timber blocking
13 Gypsum board wall, primed
14 Heat insulation
15 Gypsum board wall, primed

02.12
Door Detail 2
1:5
  1 Granite stone facing
  2 Gypsum board wall
  3 Heat insulation
  4 50 x 20 mm (2 x 3/4 inch) timber profile
  5 Gypsum board wall, primed
  6 75 x 27 mm (3 x 1 inch) intermediate timber blocking
  7 Timber door frame
  8 Door leaf

9 Door handle
10 Door hinge
11 Timber door frame
12 75 x 27 mm (3 x 1 inch) intermediate timber blocking
13 Granite stone facing
14 Gypsum board wall
15 50 x 50 mm (2 inch) timber profile
16 Heat insulation
17 Gypsum board wall, primed

02.13
Door Detail 3
1:5
  1 Gypsum board
  2 Heat insulation
  3 Heat insulation
  4 Timber profile
  5 Gypsum board
  6 Granite facing
  7 Gypsum board wall, primed
  8 75 x 27 mm (3 x 1 inch) intermediate timber blocking
  9 Timber door frame
  10 Door leaf

11 Door handle
12 Door hinge
13 75 x 27 mm (3 x 1 inch) intermediate timber blocking
14 Timber door frame
15 Granite facing
16 Gypsum backer board, primed
17 Heat insulation
18 Gypsum backer board, primed

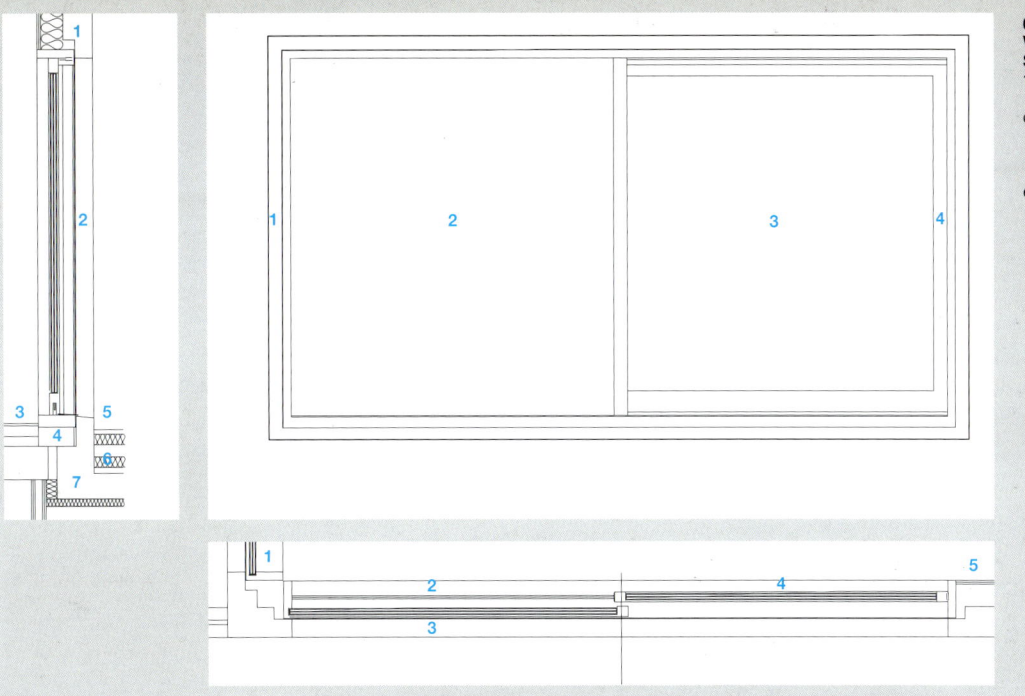

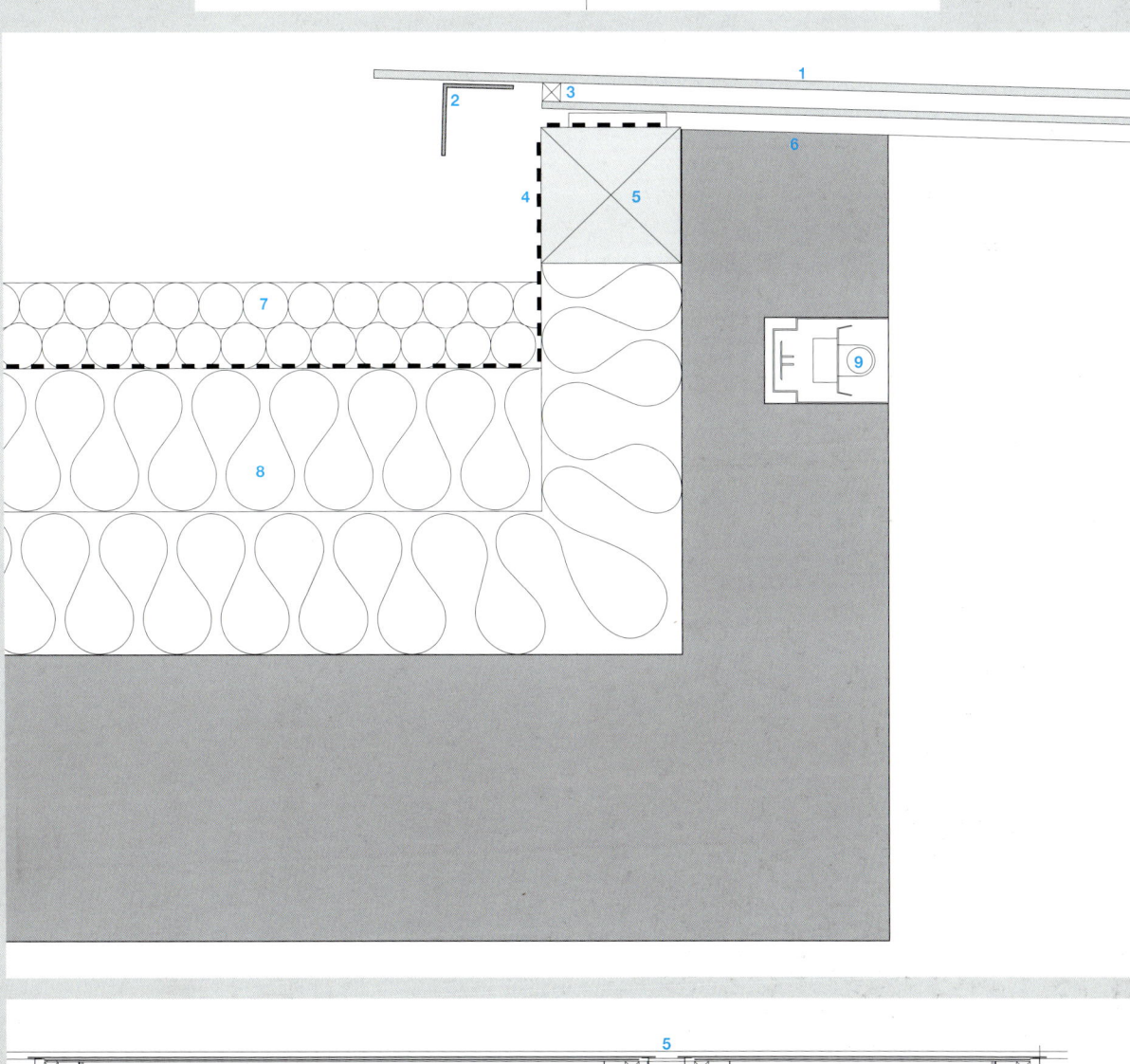

02.14
**Window Detail
Section**
1:50
 1 Reinforced
concrete
 2 Guide bar
 3 Balcony
 4 Embrasure
extension
 5 Timber floor
 6 Heat insulation
 7 Ferro-concrete

02.15
**Window Detail
Elevation**
1:50
 1 Natural oak finish
window frame
 2 Fixed part of
window
 3 Moveable part of
window
 4 Natural oak finish
window frame

02.16
Window Detail Plan
1:50
 1 Glazing
 2 Guide rail
 3 Fixed part of
window
 4 Moveable part of
window
 5 Gypsum board wall,
primed

02.17
Roof Detail 1
1:2
 1 Sealed double-
glazed unit
 2 Steel angle
 3 Filler
 4 Neoprene bearing
 5 Square section
timber
 6 Reinforced
concrete
 7 Grit filler
 8 Insulation
 9 Block out lighting

02.18
Roof Detail 2
1:50
 1 Heat insulation
 2 Gypsum board
sheeting
 3 Gypsum board wall,
primed
 4 Overhead lighting
 5 Roof system
incorporating overhead
lighting
 6 Ferro-concrete
 7 Gypsum board
sheeting
 8 Gypsum board wall

03
Studio Daniel Libeskind

Studio Weil
Port d'Andratx, Mallorca, Spain

Client
Barbara Weil

Area
430 square metres (4,630 square feet)

Project Team
Daniel Libeskind, Johannes Hucke,
Wendy James

Structural Engineer
Gracia Lopez Pationo

Local Architect
Jaime Vidal Contesi

Studio Weil is an exhibition space and workshop for the American painter and sculptor Barbara Weil. Daniel Libeskind has worked closely with the artist with the intention of creating a building that not only responds to the surrounding landscape, but also forms a space which complements the artist's work. Studio Weil, located at Port d'Andratx in Mallorca, is Libeskind's first small-scale work and explores the connections between the intimate and the grand, between the domestic and the cultural and, in doing so, develops a space for contemplation, domestic reverie and the presentation of art. Rather than drawing on the Mediterranean landscape as a background for the art, the studio is introspective, avoiding the typical Mallorcan profusion of terraces, balconies, picture windows and sea views.

The building takes the form of a concrete arc, cut in half by a pair of stairs, one leading to a viewing point at the top of the building and the other leading from the garden to the ground floor gallery. Both stairs offer glimpses into the studios through windows that slash through the envelope at abrupt angles in which the glass lies flush with the wall surface. The interior is monastic in nature with limited views into and out of the building. Instead, the artist and visitors are invited to reflect on the brightly coloured, animated art works that contrast so brilliantly with the stark white geometry of the building.

1 The white concrete form wraps around the gallery allowing only a few glimpses into the interior. Elsewhere, the smooth surface is slashed with slit-like openings allowing day-light into the gallery spaces.
2 Away from the street facade, the sculptural building reposes in a white-gravelled Mediterranean land-scape. The steel mesh-balustraded stair leads from the garden to a roof terrace.
3 The gallery spaces are completely white, relieved only by light-ing and by the art works themselves.
4 The windows, with glazing that lies flush with the interior wall surfaces, cast dramat-ic shafts of light across the interior.

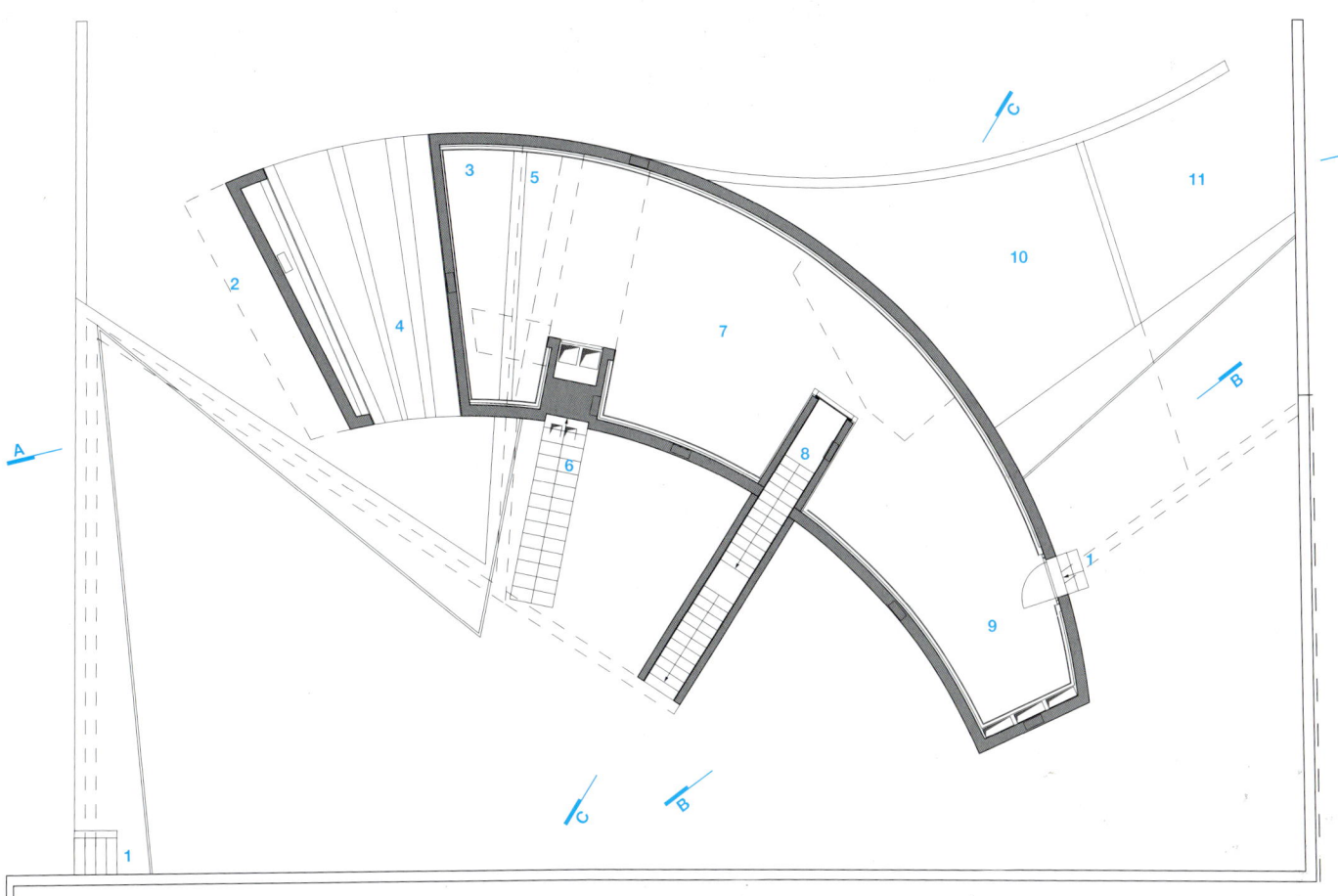

03.01
First Floor Plan
1:200
1 Garden entrance
2 Line of roof
3 Void to ground floor
4 Open gallery
5 Balustrade to roof terrace
6 Stair to roof (west stair)
7 Upper gallery
8 Stair to garden (east stair)
9 Gallery
10 Roof to workshop
11 Void to delivery area

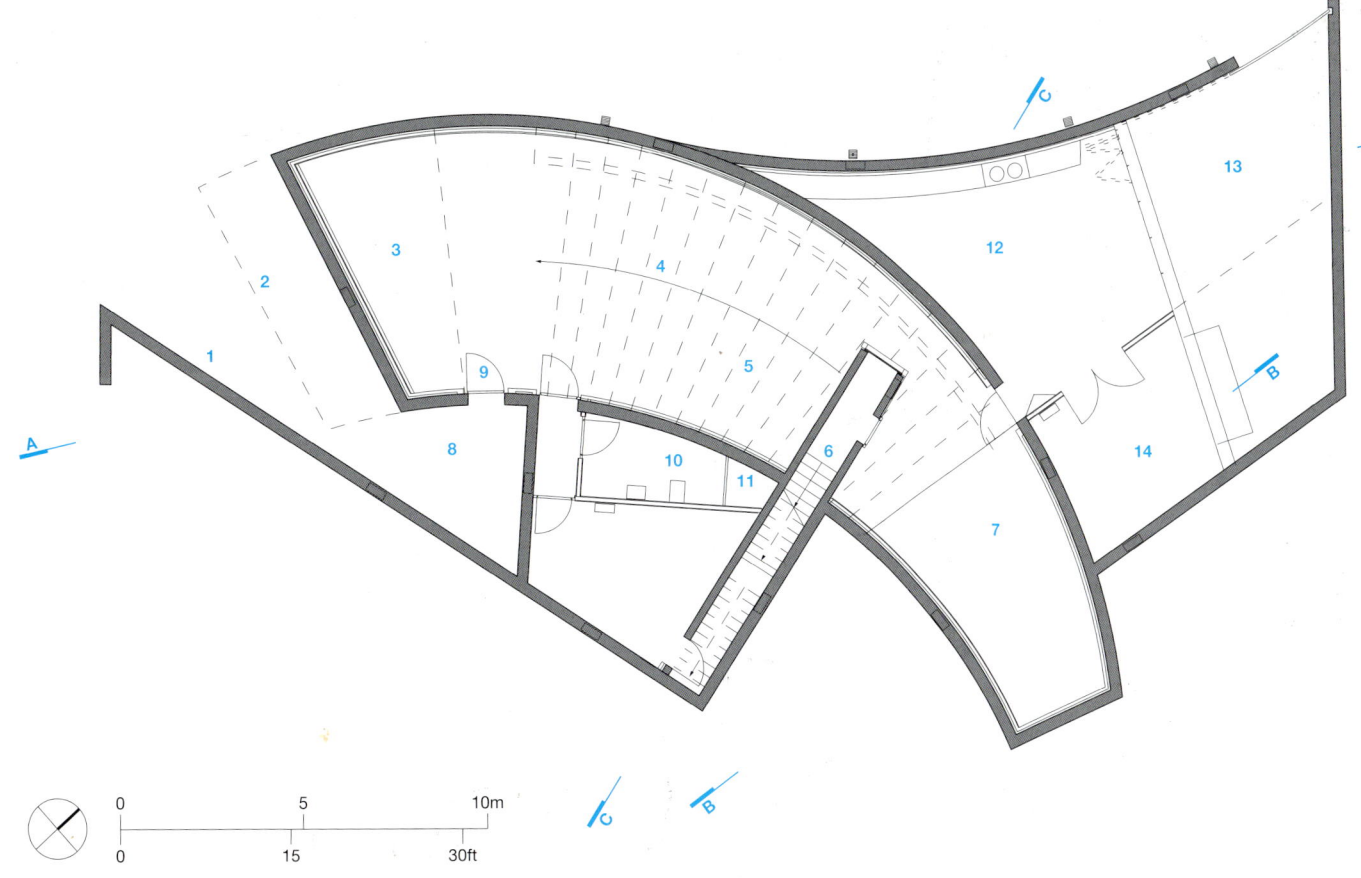

03.02
Ground Floor Plan
1:200
1 Reused stone drywall
2 Line of roof over
3 Void to open gallery above
4 Ramp
5 Lower gallery
6 Stair to garden (east stair)
7 Gallery
8 Entrance platform
9 Entrance
10 WC
11 Shower
12 Workshop
13 Delivery courtyard
14 Spray room

0   5   10m
0   15   30ft

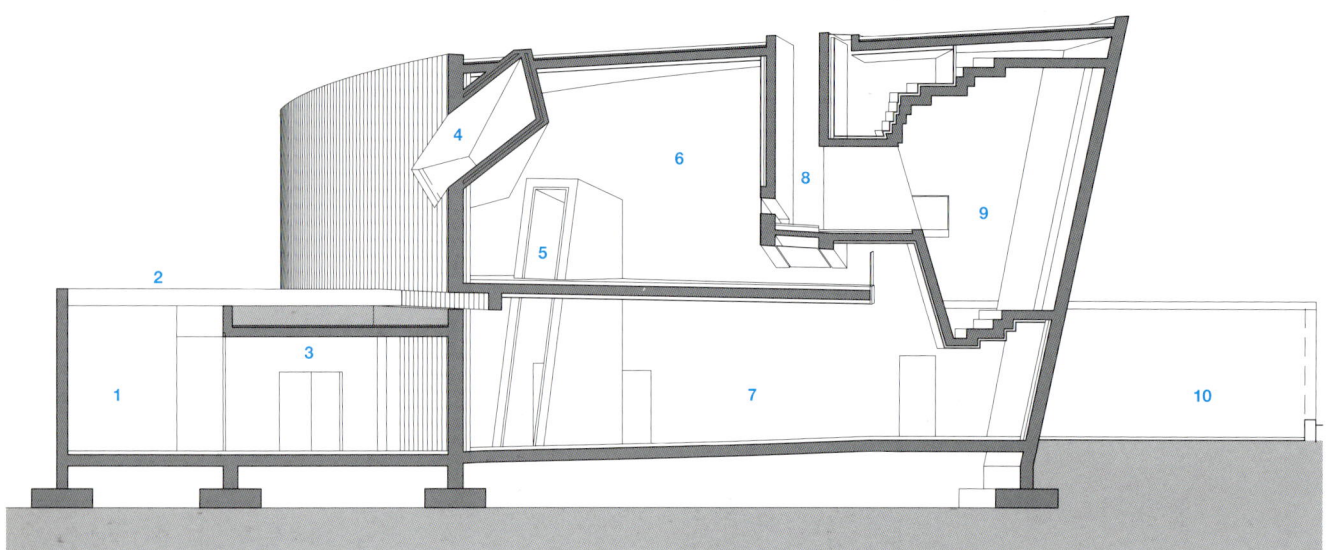

03.03
Gallery Section A–A
1:200
1 Delivery courtyard
2 Upper terrace
3 Workshop
4 Roof cut window
5 East stair
6 Upper gallery
7 Lower gallery
8 West stair
9 Open gallery
10 Entrance courtyard

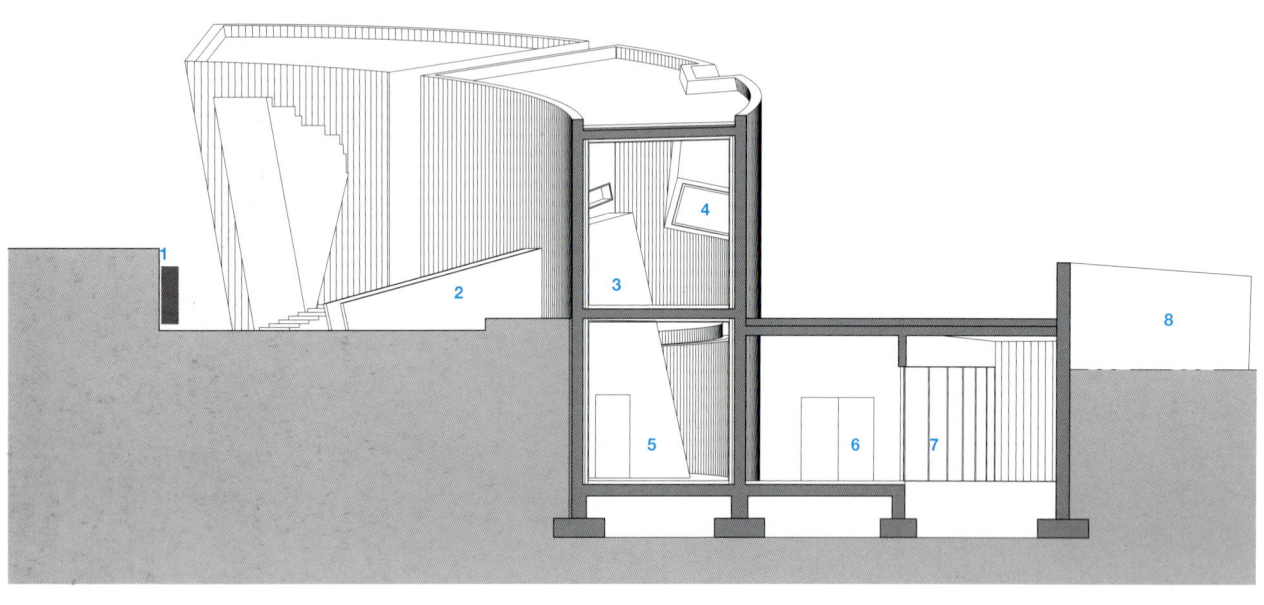

03.04
Workshop Section
B–B
1:200
1 Existing retaining
   wall
2 East stair
3 Upper gallery
4 Roof cut window
5 Lower gallery
6 Spray room
7 Delivery courtyard
8 Retaining wall

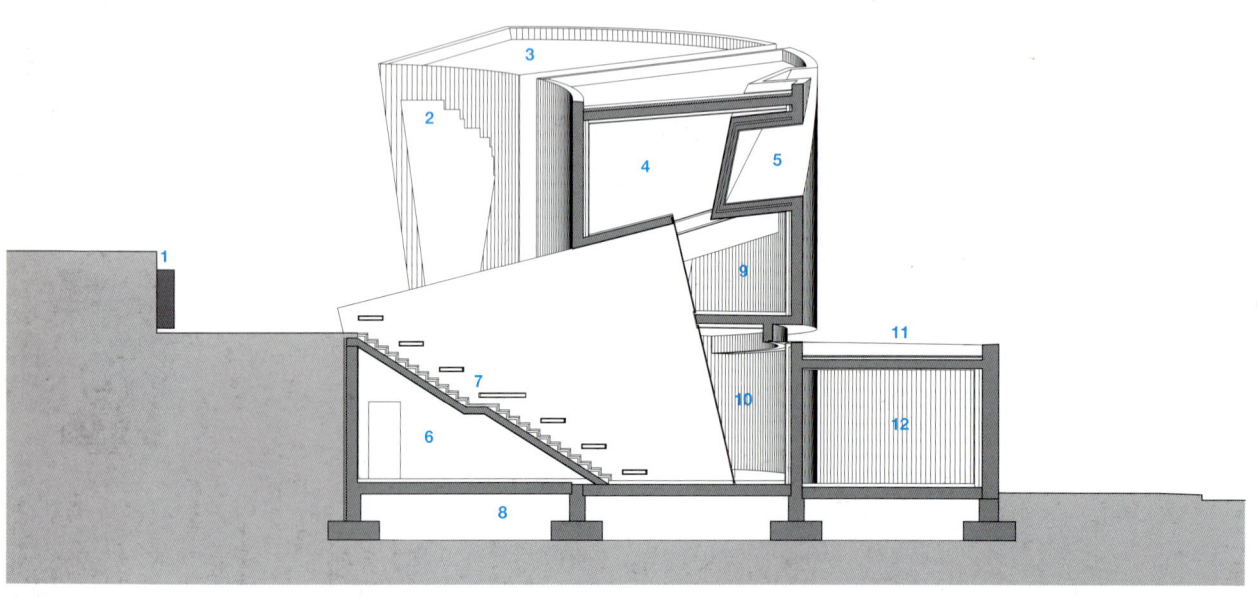

03.05
East Stair Section
C–C
1:200
1 Existing retaining
   wall
2 Open gallery
3 Roof
4 Upper gallery
5 Roof cut window
6 Storage
7 East stair
8 Ventilated under-
   floor area
9 First floor gallery
10 Ground floor
    gallery
11 Gravel roof to
    workshop
12 Workshop

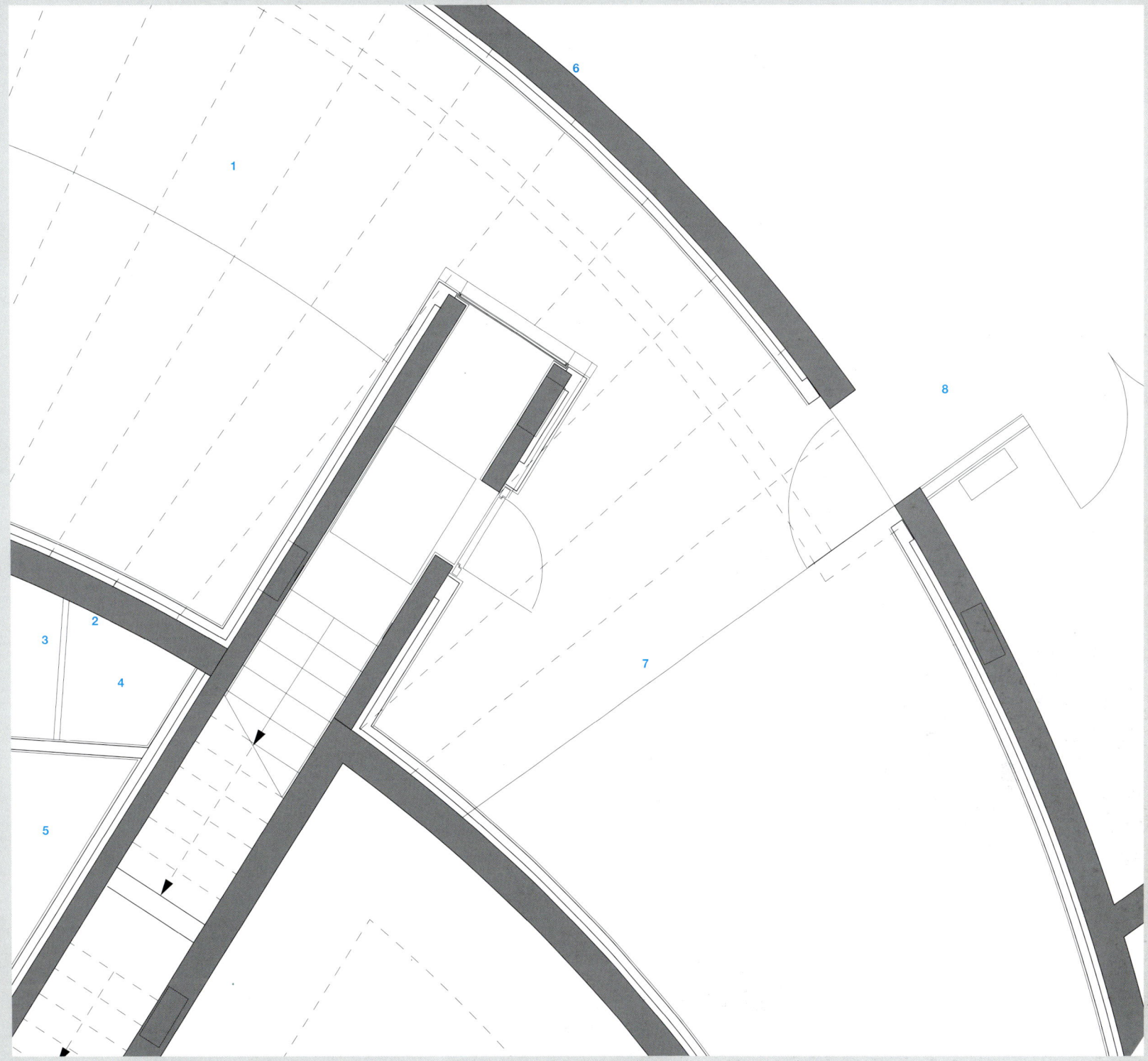

03.06
Ground Floor Plan
Detail
1:50
1 Lower gallery with
hardtop screed to floor
and rendered, painted
ceiling
2 Rendered and
painted exterior wall
3 WC with tiled floor
and rendered, painted
ceiling
4 Shower with tiled
walls and floor
5 Service and storage
area with screed to
floor and rendered,
painted ceiling
6 Rendered and
painted exterior wall
7 3% slope to ramp
8 Workshop

04
Georg Driendl

Solar Tube
Vienna, Austria

Area
308 square metres (3,315 square feet)

Project Team
Reinhard Weber, Martina Ziesel,
Franz Driendl

Structural Engineer
Ernst Illetschko

Mechanical Engineer
Ing. Franz Bergles

Solar Tube is located in the north-western outskirts of Vienna, in a quiet residential area consisting mostly of single family homes. Situated on a steep slope, the house is organized around a fully glazed atrium that accommodates the vertical circulation, connecting all five levels. Entry from the street, which is at the same level as the terrace, is via a ramped bridge straight into the galleried living room. Alternatively, access can also be gained by traversing a staircase along the boundary to the other end of the house, ten metres below street level. Within the house, the concept of transparency that is apparent from the large expanses of glazing on the exterior, continues.

A series of levels and galleries create views throughout the house and out into the landscape beyond. The entire structure is designed to be a light and heat collector. The wooded site, which generates plenty of shade, allows the use of generously glazed facades. The roof and floors are also partly transparent, so that the atrium acts as a passive distributor of light and ventilation throughout the house. In summer, the atrium allows unwanted heat to travel upwards to be expelled at roof level through an opening panel, much like a chimney. In winter, heating costs are minimized by allowing solar energy to penetrate the swathes of glazing. Solar Tube was built in just five months, which was possible due to the use of primarily prefabricated or proprietary components and materials. The black-painted steel structure is visible on the interior, framing sections of timber panelling, stone and glass which characterize the cubic aesthetic of the design.

1 Stands of established trees on the site allow the use of floor to ceiling glazing without the risk of overheating the interior. The glass facade also allows views right through the house.
2 From the garden, the full extent of the house becomes apparent. Sloped and curved glazing is designed to trap sun in winter to warm the interior.
3 Glazing details

continue on the interior. Here, secondary panels of etched glass define a bathroom with spectacular views into the tree canopy.
4 A central atrium accommodating the

main circulation through the house acts as a passive environmental device to distribute natural light throughout the house.

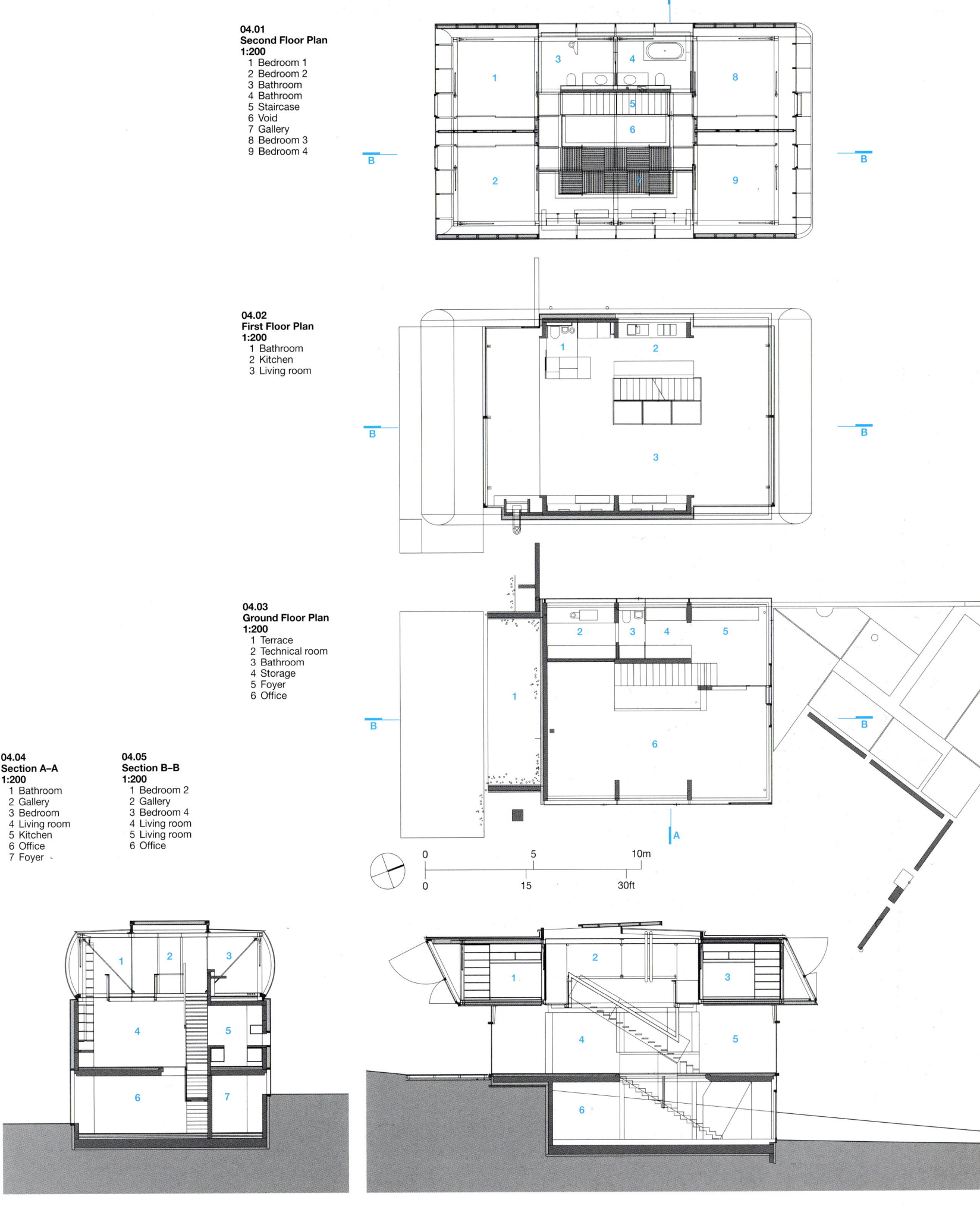

04.01
Second Floor Plan
1:200
1 Bedroom 1
2 Bedroom 2
3 Bathroom
4 Bathroom
5 Staircase
6 Void
7 Gallery
8 Bedroom 3
9 Bedroom 4

04.02
First Floor Plan
1:200
1 Bathroom
2 Kitchen
3 Living room

04.03
Ground Floor Plan
1:200
1 Terrace
2 Technical room
3 Bathroom
4 Storage
5 Foyer
6 Office

04.04
Section A–A
1:200
1 Bathroom
2 Gallery
3 Bedroom
4 Living room
5 Kitchen
6 Office
7 Foyer

04.05
Section B–B
1:200
1 Bedroom 2
2 Gallery
3 Bedroom 4
4 Living room
5 Living room
6 Office

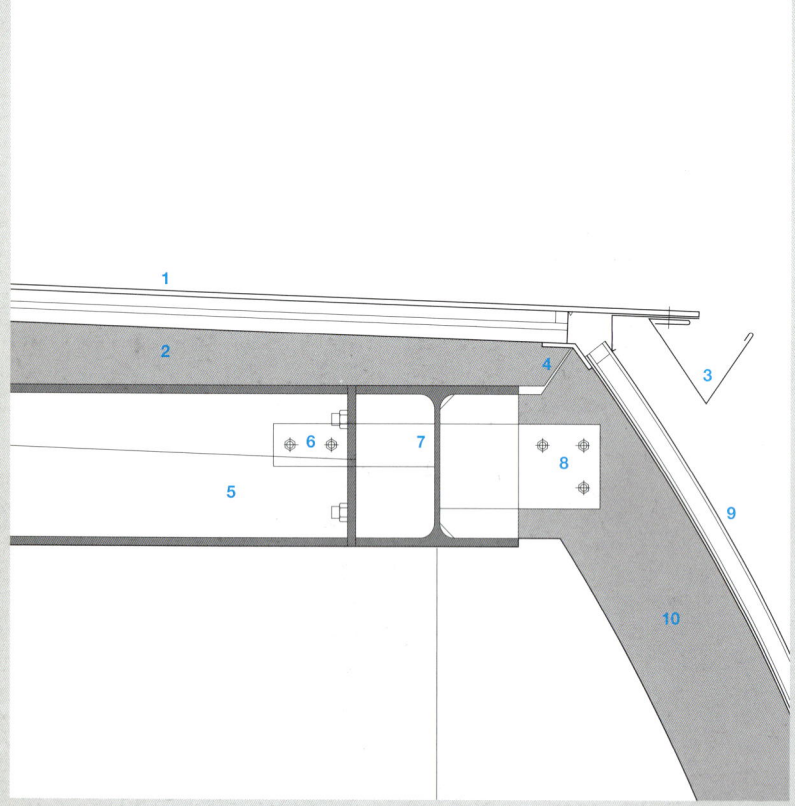

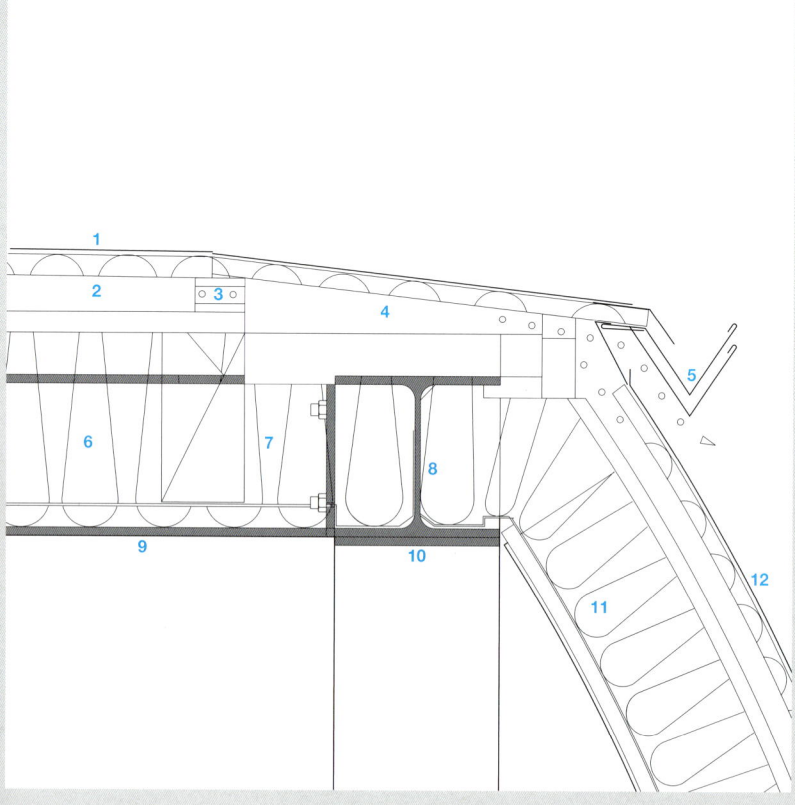

04.06
Fixed Glazing Detail 1
1:10
 1 Insulated glazing
 2 Glulam beam
 3 Gutter
 4 Angle iron
 5 Steel beam
 6 Steel flange
 7 Steel beam
 8 Steel flange
 9 Curved insulated
glass
10 Curved glulam
beam

04.07
Fixed Glazing Detail 2
1:10
 1 Timber roof
structure with rubber
sheet finish
 2 Ventilation gap
 3 Steel angle
 4 Substructure and
ventilation
 5 Gutter
 6 Thermal insulation
 7 Thermal insulation
 8 Insulation over steel
structure
 9 Plywood soffit
10 Steel structure
11 Timber beam and
thermal insulation
12 Timber cladding
with Uginox sheet
finish

04.08
Fixed Glazing Detail 3
1:10
 1 Rubber over steel
sheet
 2 Steel-framed roof
glazing
 3 Uginox sheet finish
 4 Timber panels
 5 Steel structure
 6 Gutter
 7 Uginox sheet finish

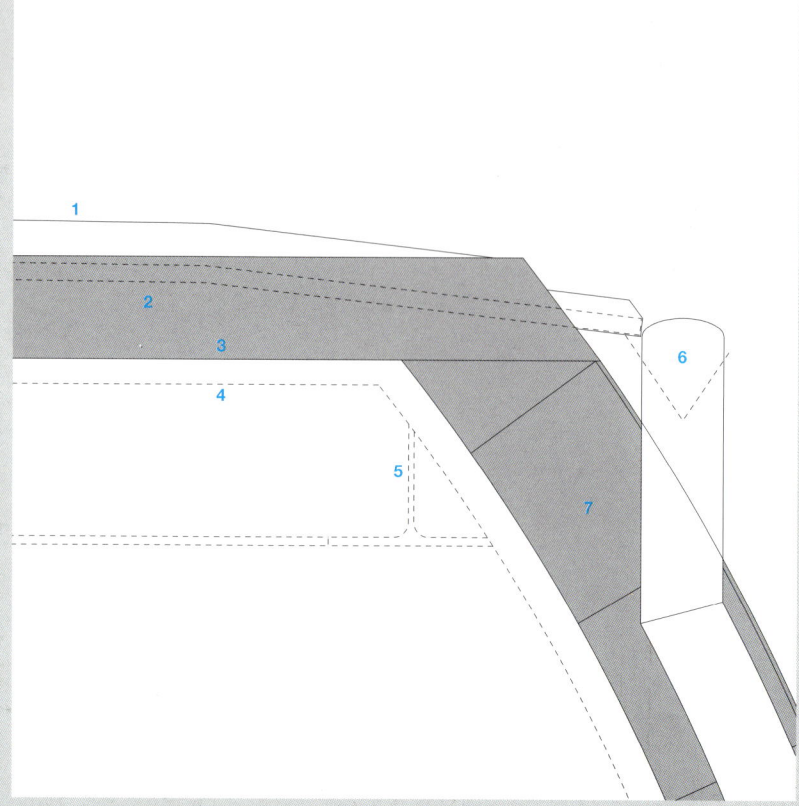

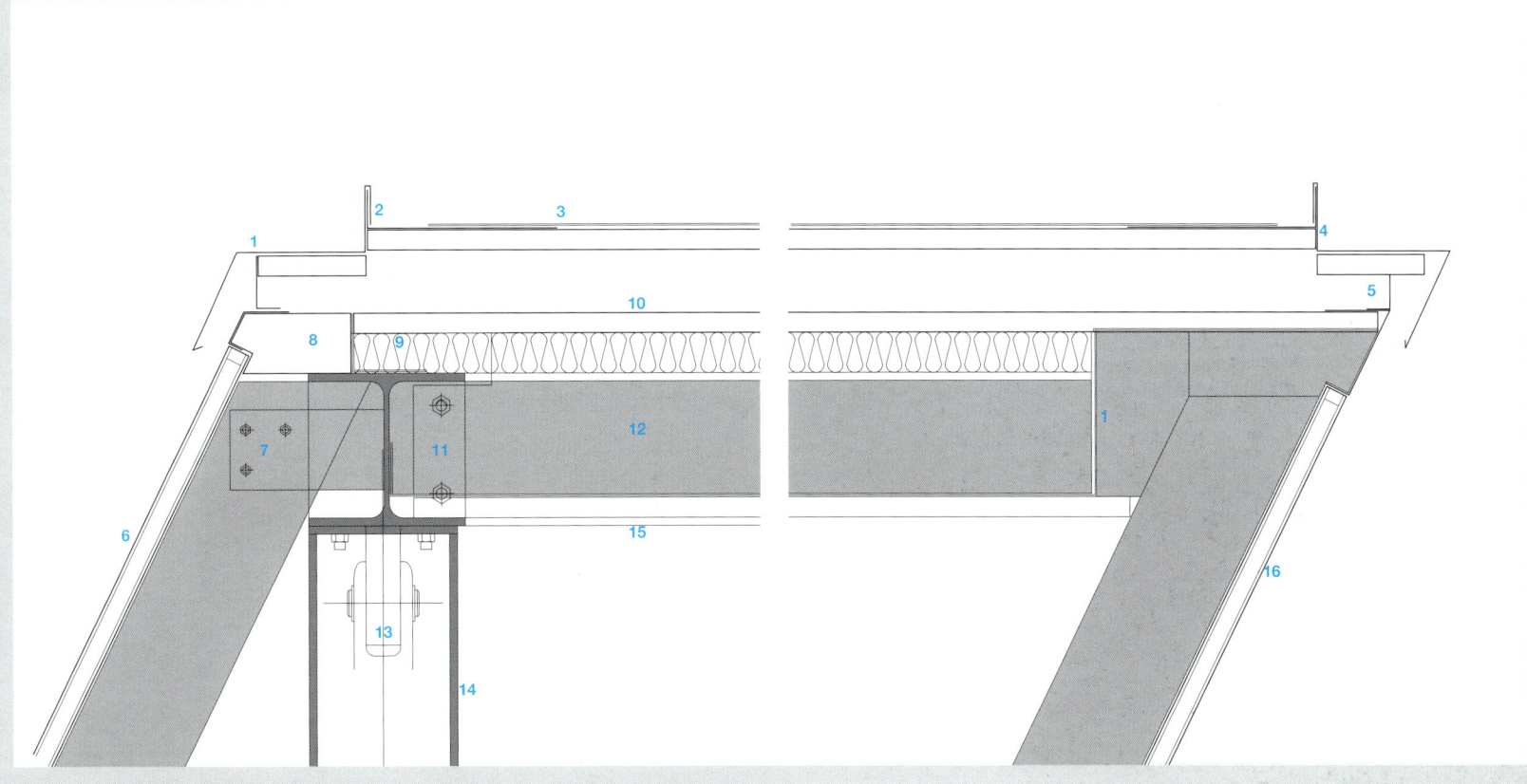

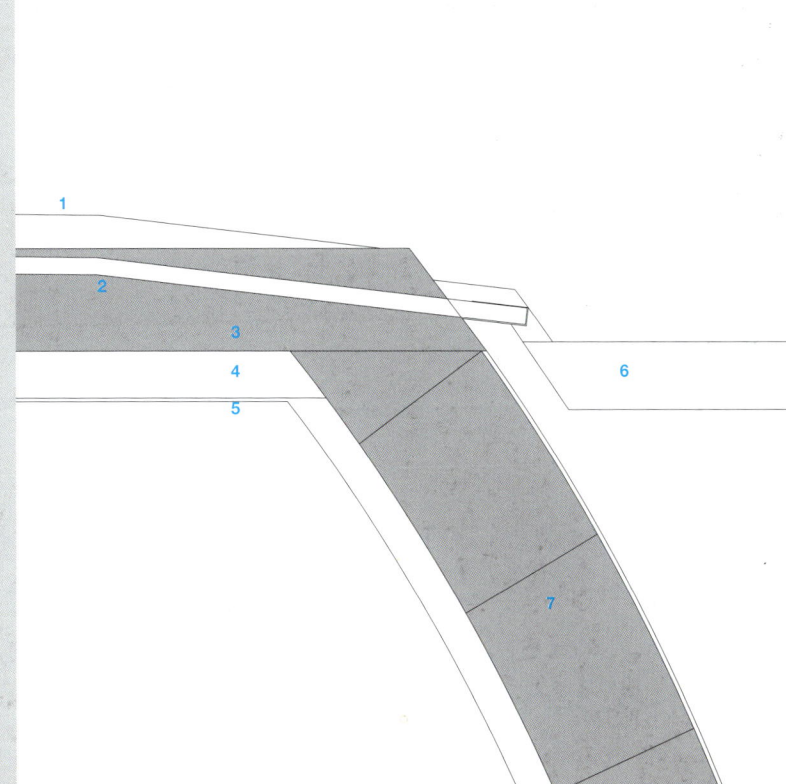

04.09
Fixed Glazing Detail 4
1:10
 1 Metal flashing
 2 Welded sheet steel
 3 Rubber outer layer roofing
 4 Metal flashing
 5 Ventilation gap
 6 Insulated glazing
 7 Steel flange
 8 Thermal insulation
 9 Thermal insulation
10 Plywood structure
11 Steel flange
12 Steel structure
13 Tension rod
14 Steel structure
15 Plywood
16 Insulated glazing

04.10
Fixed Glazing Detail 5
1:10
 1 Rubber over sheet steel
 2 Steel framed roof glazing
 3 Uginox sheet
 4 Timber panels
 5 Steel structure
 6 Gutter
 7 Uginox sheet

Jim Jennings Architecture

Visiting Artists' House
Geyserville, California, USA

Client
Oliver Ranch – Steven and Nancy
Oliver

Area
348 square metres (3,745 square feet)

Project Team
Jim Jennings, Cheri Fraser, Troy
Schaum, Paul Burgin, Les Taylor, May
Fung, Michael Lin

Consulting Architect
Tim Perks

Structural Engineer
Kevin Clinch

Electrical and Lighting Consultant
Dan Dodt

Landscape Architect
Andrea Cochran

The building is located on the crest
of a hill at a former Sonoma County
sheep ranch that is now home to
commissioned sculptures by Richard
Serra, Bruce Nauman, Martin Puryear
and others. Itself designed as site-
specific sculpture, the house is
defined by two massive in-situ
concrete blade walls that cut through
the hill. The walls appear to be
parallel, however they actually diverge
at one end and converge at the
other along the length of the building
to accentuate the perceived
elongation and foreshortening of
space. When looking out to the
converging end, objects in the
landscape appear larger and closer
than they actually are. At the diverging
end, the opposite occurs.

Throughout the length of the
building, the floor steps to create a
constantly shifting section. A site-
specific sculpture is carved directly
into the inward-facing surfaces of the
concrete walls, in dialogue with the
architecture. A maple ceiling floats
between the parallel walls, allowing
light to wash down the walls and
highlight the incised carving. The
glass slots between the ceiling and
the walls are detailed so that
the recesses pass uninterrupted to
the wall's outer boundaries. All of
the details of the project were
developed with the purpose of
expressing the architectural concept
in its purest form.

1 An open terrace at
each end of the
building allows private
contemplation of
the landscape and
expansive views over
the ranch where
sculptures commis-
sioned specifically for
the ranch stand
sentinel among the
mature trees.
2 Each of the two
living pavilions is a
simple arrangement of
glass curtain walls,
steel cross beams and
metal roof decking,
all set between in-situ
concrete walls. A stair
slotted between two
concrete blade walls
(left) opens out onto
the shared central
courtyard that sepa-
rates and connects
the two living suites.
A pair of Donald Judd
chairs are the only
addition to the con-
crete walled space.

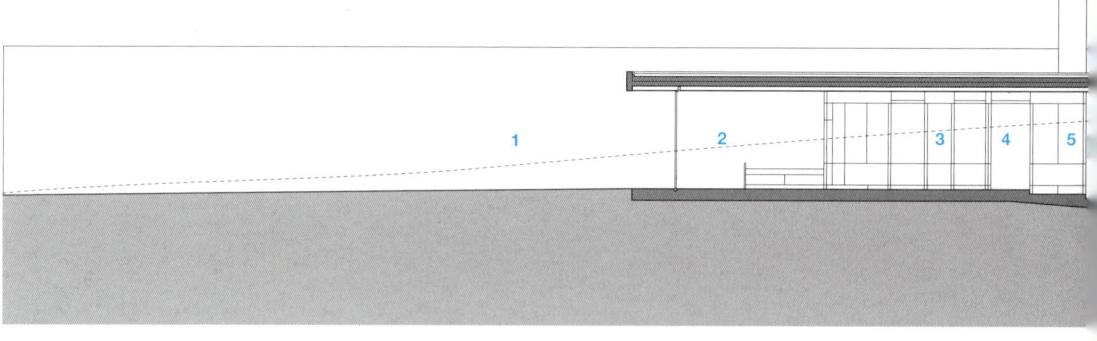

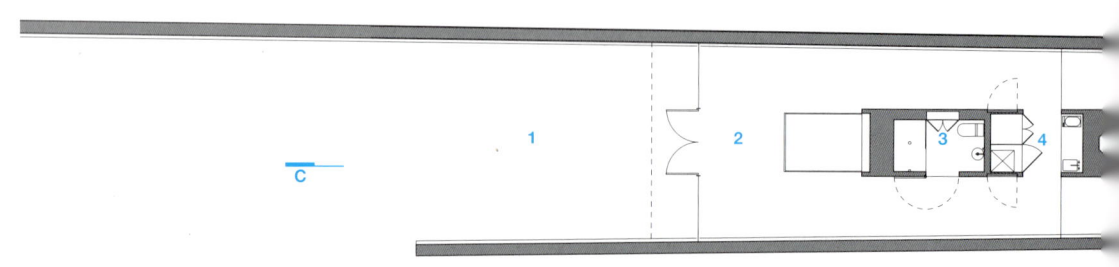

3 To accommodate David Rabinowitch's art work, a fine aggregate was added to the concrete and a 10 centimetre (4 inch) thick screed surface was added to the reinforced concrete wall. This allowed the artist to cut into the surface of the wall without compromising the structure. Slots of glazing on either side of the floating ceiling wash the surface of the concrete walls with natural light.

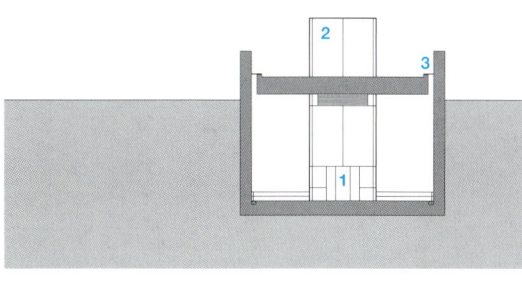

05.01
Section A–A
1:200
1 Fireplace
2 Chimney
3 Glazing slot

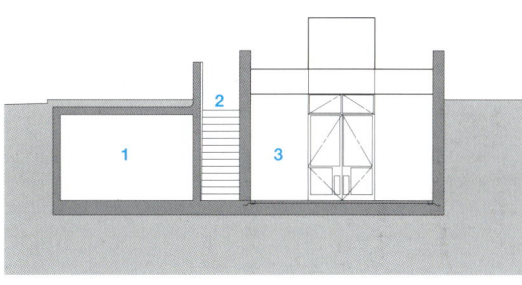

05.02
Section B–B
1:200
1 Utility room
2 External access stair
3 Glazed courtyard facade

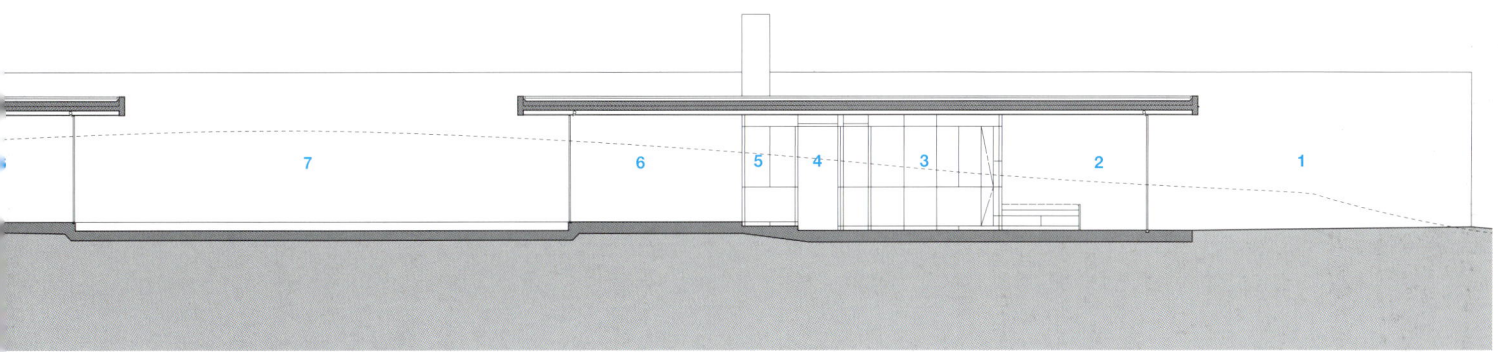

05.03
Section C–C
1:200
1 Terrace
2 Bedroom
3 Bathroom
4 Kitchen
5 Fireplace
6 Living room
7 Central courtyard

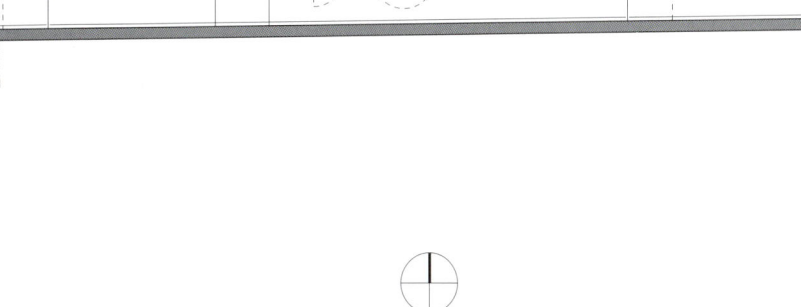

05.04
Floor Plan
1:200
1 Terrace
2 Bedroom
3 Bathroom
4 Kitchen
5 Fireplace
6 Living room
7 Central courtyard

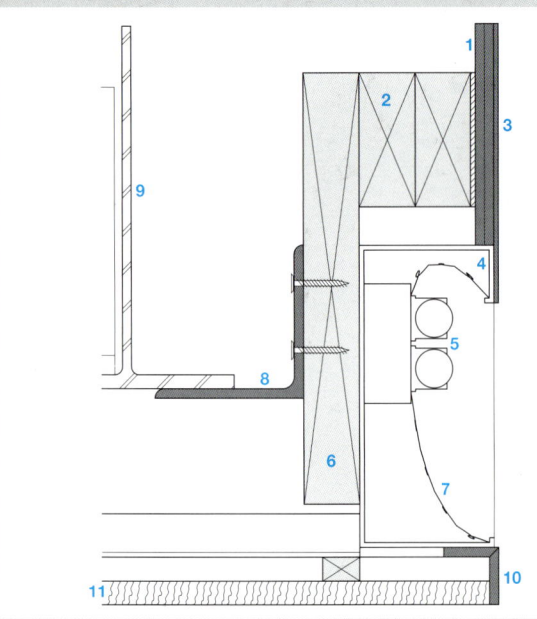

05.05
**Concealed Lighting
Detail**
1:5
1 12.5 mm ($^1/_2$ inch)
plywood sheeting
2 Two timber
blocking pieces
3 Aluminium panel
4 Custom sheet
metal housing
5 Staggered linear
lamp fittings
6 Timber blocking
7 Custom light
reflector
8 100 x 100 mm
(4 x 4 inch) steel angle
9 Suspended steel
I-beam
10 37 x 37 x 6 mm
(1$^1/_2$ x 1$^1/_2$ x $^1/_4$ inch)
anodized aluminium
angle
11 Linear timber
ceiling system

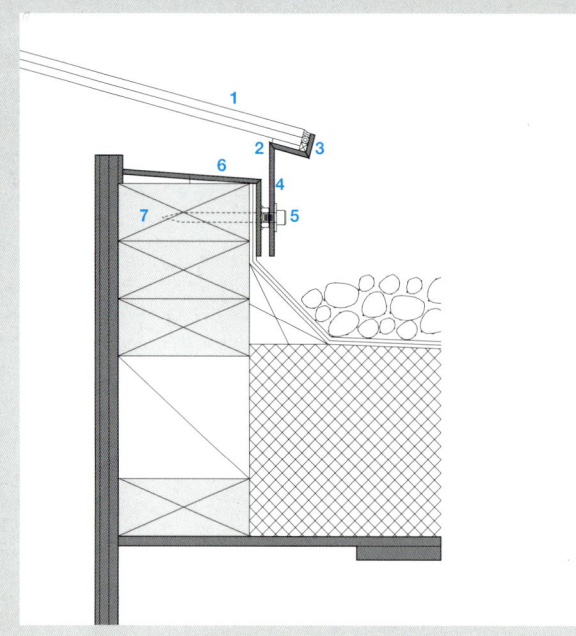

05.08
Skylight Frame Detail
1:5
1 7 mm ($^3/_8$ inch)
tempered laminated
glass
2 Glazing tape
3 Backer rod and
sealant
4 2 mm ($^1/_8$ inch)
stainless steel plate
custom fabricated
glazing container
5 6 mm ($^1/_4$ inch)
stainless steel
hexagonal socket head
cap screw at 305 mm
(12 inch) centres with
banded sealing washer
6 Custom fabricated
2 mm ($^1/_8$ inch)
stainless steel plate
curb frame
7 Lag bolt through
curb frame

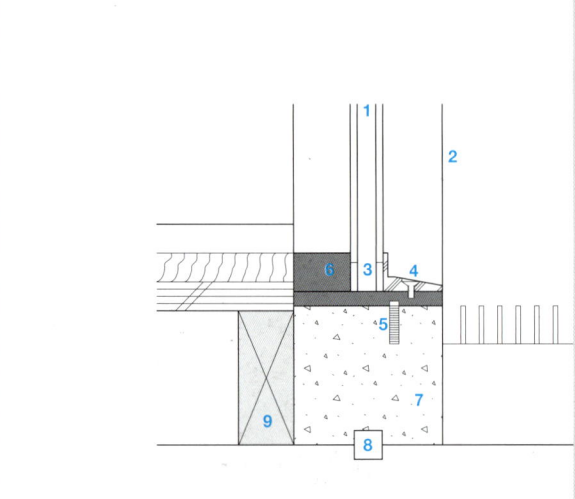

05.06
Window Sill Detail
1:5
1 5 mm ($^1/_4$ inch)
tempered glass
2 Stainless steel door
jambs
3 2 x 5 mm ($^1/_8$ x $^3/_8$
inch) glazing tape
4 Milled aluminium
glass stop
5 Drilled and epoxy
set studs set into curb
at 305 mm (12 inch)
centres
6 5 mm ($^1/_4$ inch)
continuous stainless
steel threshold
7 Concrete curb
8 Waterstop
9 Pressure treated
timber blocking

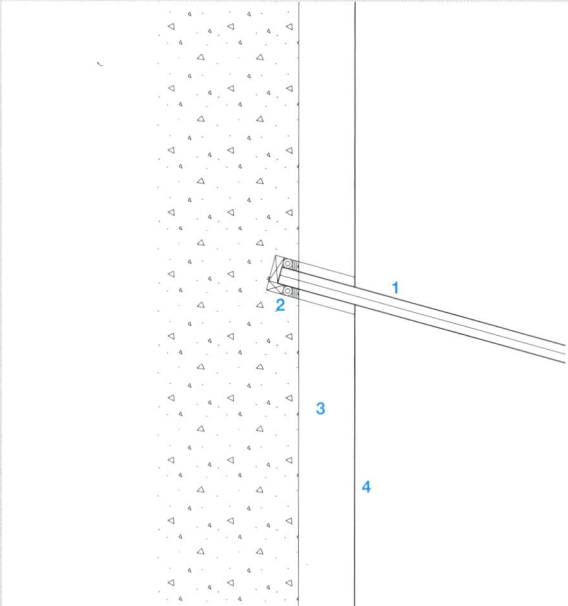

05.09
**Saw Cut at Concrete
Wall For Skylight
Detail**
1:5
1 Tempered
laminated glass
2 Backer rod and
sealant
3 Unreinforced area
of concrete to allow for
saw cut
4 Line of inside face
of concrete

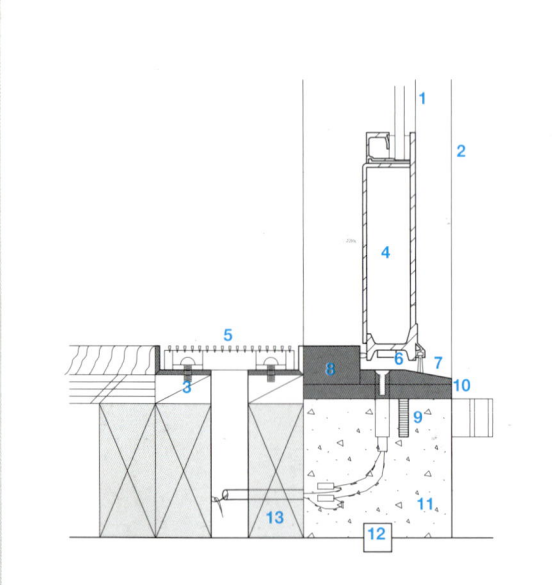

05.07
Door Sill Detail
1:5
1 Window system
2 Stainless steel door
jambs
3 Stainless steel
angle welded to grate
support rods
4 Custom built
windows and frames
5 8 mm ($^3/_8$ inch)
stainless steel grating
6 Magnet isolated in
rubber seal
7 5 mm ($^1/_4$ inch)
milled aluminium sill
plate
8 Alarm or 'reed
contact' at door sill
9 Drilled and epoxy
set studs set into curb
at 305 mm (12 inch)
centres
10 5 mm ($^1/_4$ inch)
continuous stainless
steel threshold
11 Concrete curb
12 Water stop
13 Pressure treated
timber blocking

05.10
**Step at Fireplace
Detail**
1:5
1 Tongue and groove
timber floor
2 12.5 mm ($^1/_2$ inch)
stainless steel plate
3 Epoxy set stud
4 18 mm ($^3/_4$ inch)
plywood subfloor
5 Reinforced
concrete floor slab

05.11
Window and
Doorhead Detail
1:5
1 Gravel roof cover
2 Roof
3 Steel beam
4 Roller operated
window blind
5 Suspended linear
timber ceiling system
6 37 x 18 mm
(1 1/2 x 2/3 inch) clear
anodized aluminium
section
7 Glazed door and
window system
8 Suspended
aluminium soffit
9 100 x 75 x 6 mm
(4 x 3 x 1/4 inch)
stainless steel angle
10 100 x 75 x 6 mm
(4 x 3 x 1/4 inch)
stainless steel angle

05.12
Skylight Detail
1:5
1 7 mm (3/8 inch)
tempered laminated
glass
2 Backer rod and
sealant
3 Glazing tape
4 2 mm (1/8 inch)
stainless steel plate
custom fabricated
glazing container
5 6 mm (1/4 inch)
stainless steel
hexagonal socket
head cap screw at 305
mm (12 inch) centres
6 Custom fabricated
2 mm (1/8 inch)
stainless steel plate
curb frame
7 Aluminium panel
over 12 mm (1/2 inch)
plywood substrate
8 Timber shims

9 125 x 75 x 6 mm
(5 x 3 x 1/4 inch)
stainless steel angle
10 75 x 75 x 6 mm
(3 x 3 x 1/4 inch)
stainless steel angle
11 100 x 75 x 6 mm
(4 x 3 x 1/4 inch)
stainless steel angle
12 Roller operated
window shade
13 37 x 18 mm
(1 1/2 x 3/4 inch) clear
anodized aluminium
section
14 Suspended
aluminium soffit

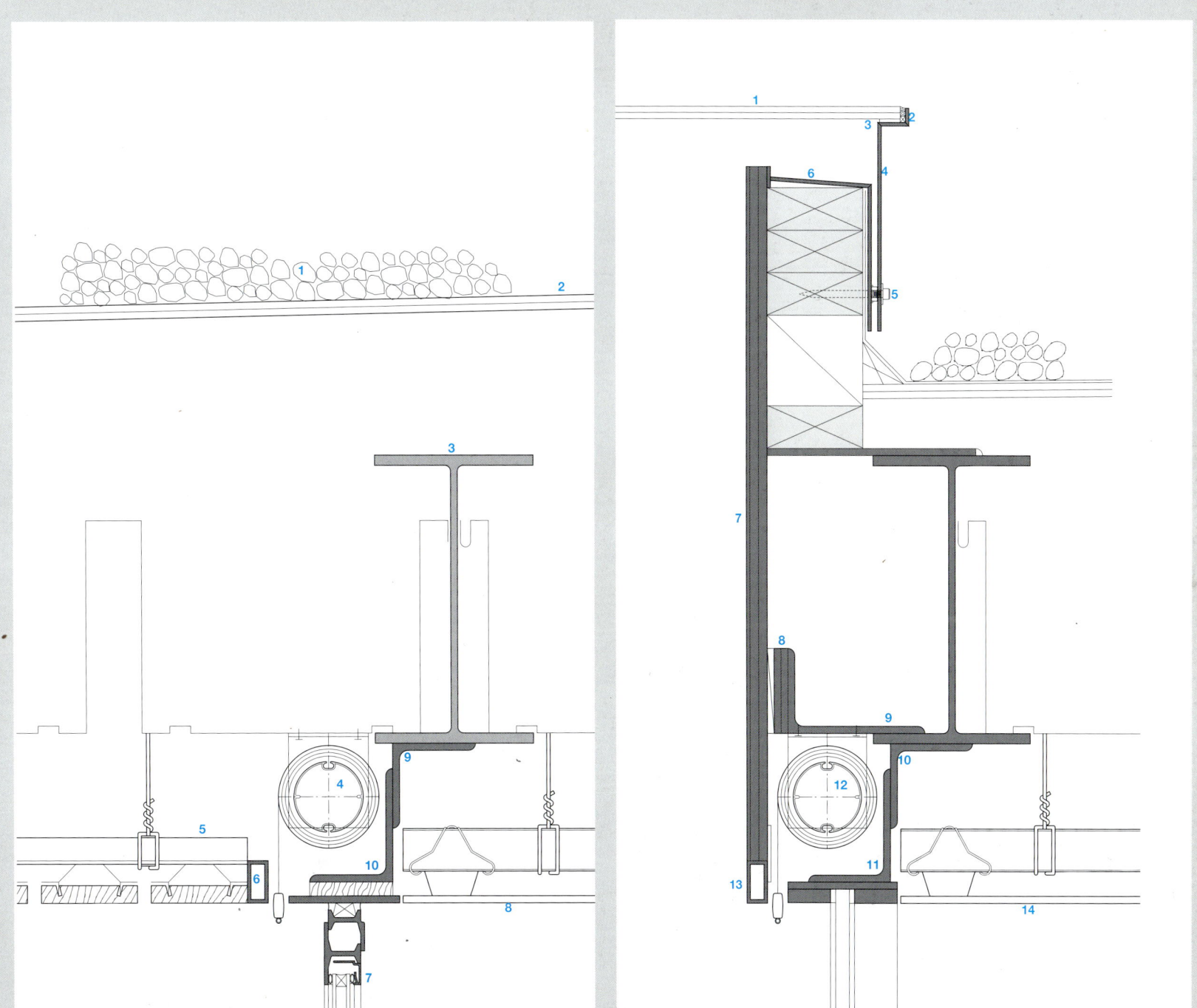

Kei'ichi Irie + Power Unit Studio

Y House
Chita, Aichi, Japan

Area
136 square metres (1,400 square feet)

Project Team
Kei'ichi Irie, Keiko Yoshida

Structural Engineer
MIAS/Masahiro Ikeda, Akira Suzuki,
Shin Yokoo

General Contractor
Maeda Construction Company

Y house is an architectural protest against the destruction of the Japanese urban landscape – a phenomenon the architect refers to as 'hideous violence'. The architect recognizes that pre-modern Japanese towns and cities co-existed with nature – a situation so often missing in the swathe of development that has engulfed large tracts of modern cities. This striking house is located in a row of modern houses that exemplify the contemporary urban condition. While the architect acknowledges that it is impossible to implement meaningful change in such a context, the design nevertheless intends to be neither a destructive nor 'violent' architectural intervention.

The envelope of the house creates an environment that isolates the interior from the outside. Once inside the building, the floor slopes to follow the topography, terminating in a large cantilevered floor that opens directly onto a stand of mature trees. The doors onto the cantilevered terrace are the only significant opening in the envelope, and are used to frame views of the forest via large sliding doors. In contrast, the openings to the street serve only to introduce light through translucent glass, with the single exception of one black-rimmed window which frames a small view of the town. The walls to the cantilevered space are slightly battered to avoid assimilating the house into the retaining walls that were imposed on the landscape to facilitate the construction of the new neighbourhood. These slanted concrete surfaces also create an isolated acoustic space, further serving to isolate the house from its context.

1 Appearing to hover above the ground, the 'hull' of the house is anchored back into the site where private spaces are accommodated.
2 The concept of isolation is clearly expressed in this view in which the solid flanking walls serve to block out the neighbouring houses.
3 The materiality of the house is dominated by in-situ concrete. Super-slim elements of black steel are lightly dropped into place.
4 The battered concrete walls intersect to create living spaces on various levels, located to reflect the existing topography of the site.
5 The glazed wall onto the terrace contains a black steel-framed door, emphasizing a framed view.

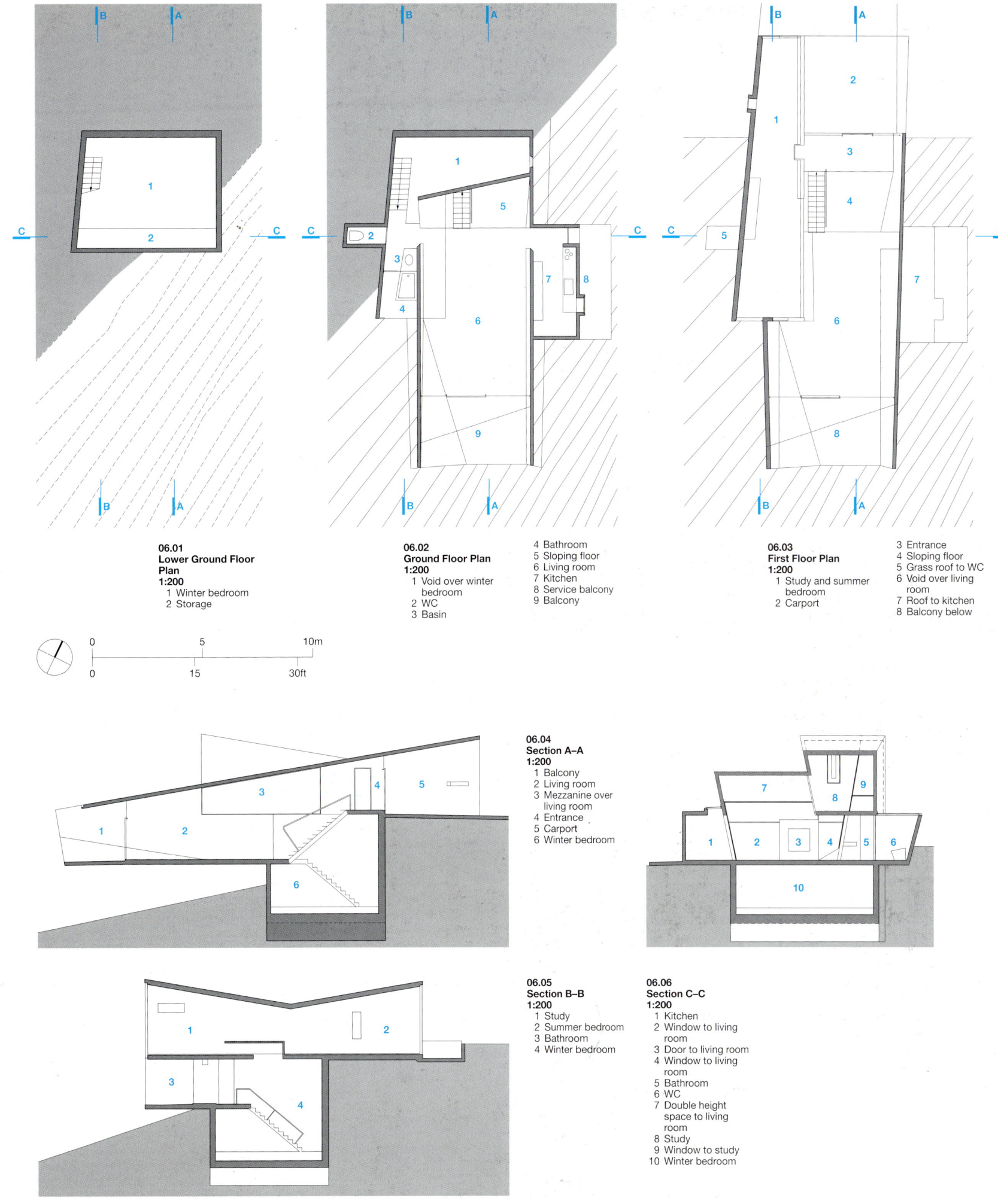

06.01
**Lower Ground Floor
Plan**
1:200
1 Winter bedroom
2 Storage

06.02
Ground Floor Plan
1:200
1 Void over winter
   bedroom
2 WC
3 Basin

4 Bathroom
5 Sloping floor
6 Living room
7 Kitchen
8 Service balcony
9 Balcony

06.03
First Floor Plan
1:200
1 Study and summer
   bedroom
2 Carport

3 Entrance
4 Sloping floor
5 Grass roof to WC
6 Void over living
   room
7 Roof to kitchen
8 Balcony below

0   5   10m
0   15   30ft

06.04
Section A–A
1:200
1 Balcony
2 Living room
3 Mezzanine over
   living room
4 Entrance
5 Carport
6 Winter bedroom

06.05
Section B–B
1:200
1 Study
2 Summer bedroom
3 Bathroom
4 Winter bedroom

06.06
Section C–C
1:200
1 Kitchen
2 Window to living
   room
3 Door to living room
4 Window to living
   room
5 Bathroom
6 WC
7 Double height
   space to living
   room
8 Study
9 Window to study
10 Winter bedroom

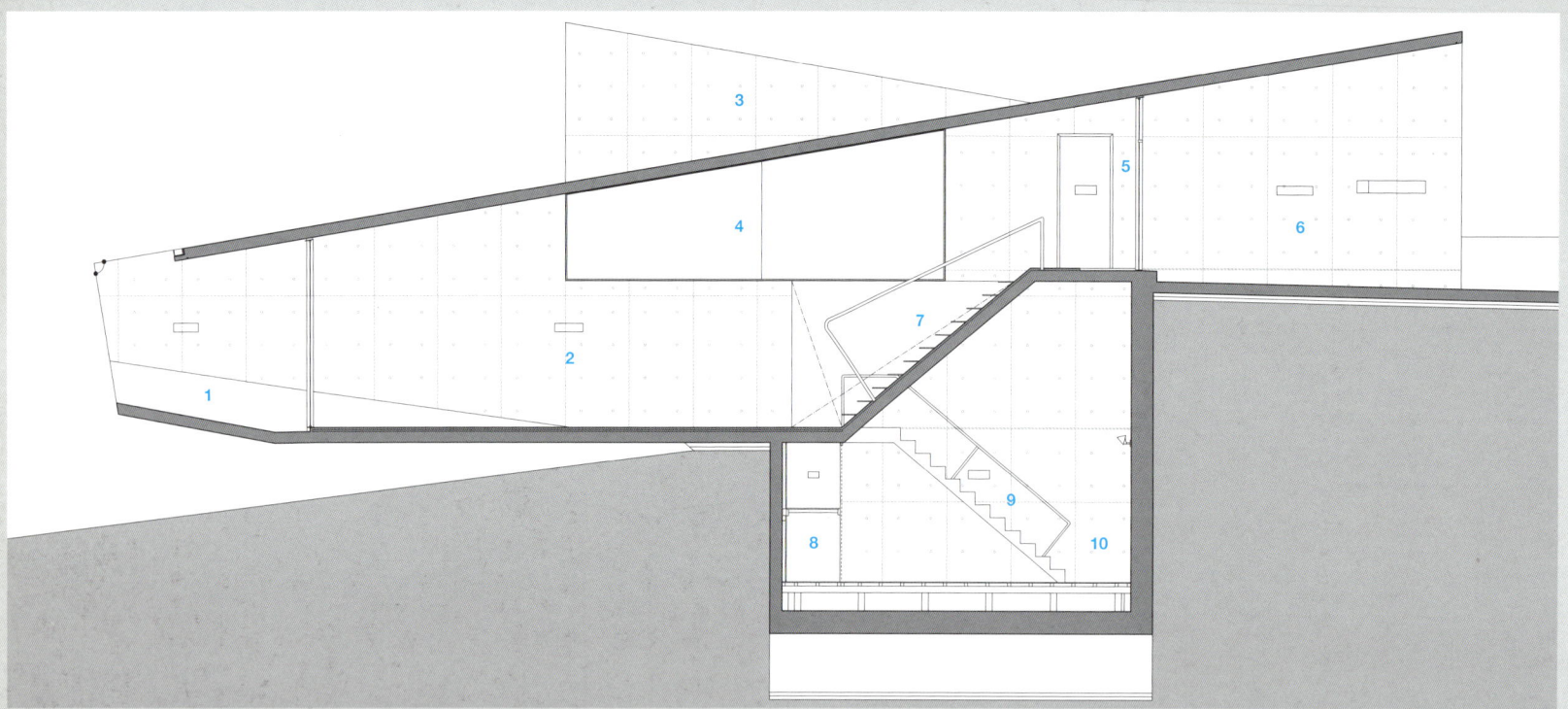

06.07
Detail Section
1:100
1 Balcony
2 Living room
3 Roof to kitchen

beyond
4 Mezzanine over
living room
5 Entrance
6 Carport
7 Staircase
8 Storage

9 Staircase
10 Winter bedroom

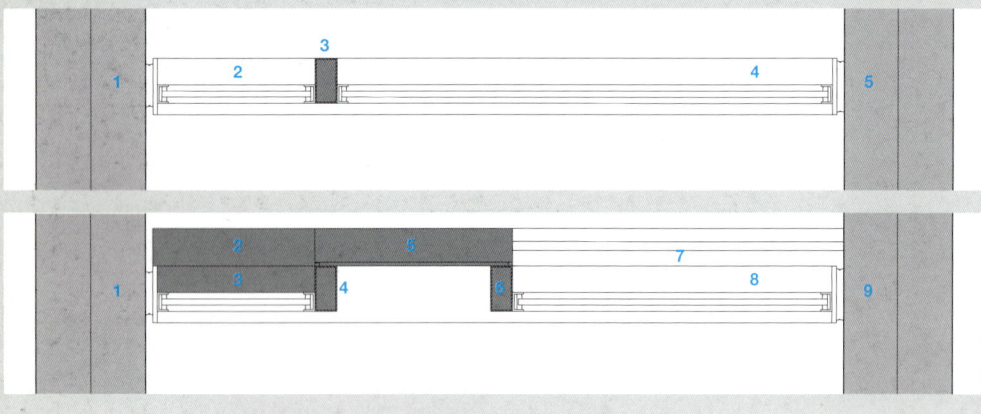

06.08
Window Sash Detail 1
1:10
1 150 mm (6 inch)
concrete wall
2 Fixed glass
3 30 x 60 mm (1¹/₅ x
2¹/₃ inch) steel box
section
4 Fixed glass
5 150 mm (6 inch)
concrete wall

06.09
Window Sash Detail 2
1:10
1 150 mm (6 inch)
concrete wall
2 Steel baseplate
3 Fixed glass
4 30 x 60 mm (1¹/₅ x
2¹/₃ inch) steel box
section
5 Steel framed sliding
door
6 30 x 60 mm (1¹/₅ x
2¹/₃ inch) steel box
section
7 Slide rail
8 Fixed glass
9 150 mm (6 inch)
concrete wall

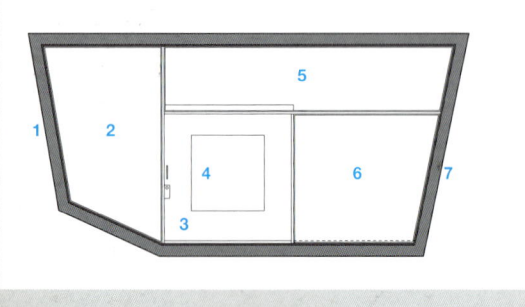

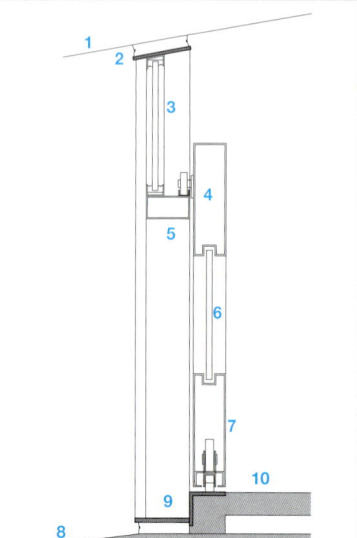

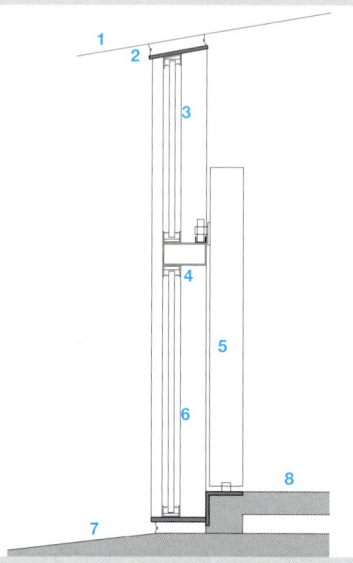

06.10
Balcony Detail
1:100
1 150 mm (6 inch)
concrete wall
2 Fixed glass
3 Steel-framed
sliding door
4 Glass sliding door
5 Fixed glass

6 Fixed glass
7 150 mm (6 inch)
concrete wall

06.11
Window Detail 1
1:10
1 Concrete ceiling
2 Steel flat bar
3 Fixed glass
4 Steel-framed door
5 Hanger rail
6 Sliding glass door
7 Steel-framed door
8 Concrete slab to
balcony
9 Steel flat bar
10 Concrete slab

06.12
Window Detail 2
1:10
1 Concrete ceiling
2 Steel flat bar
3 Fixed glass
4 Hanger rail
5 Sliding door
6 Fixed glass
7 Concrete slab to
balcony
8 Concrete slab

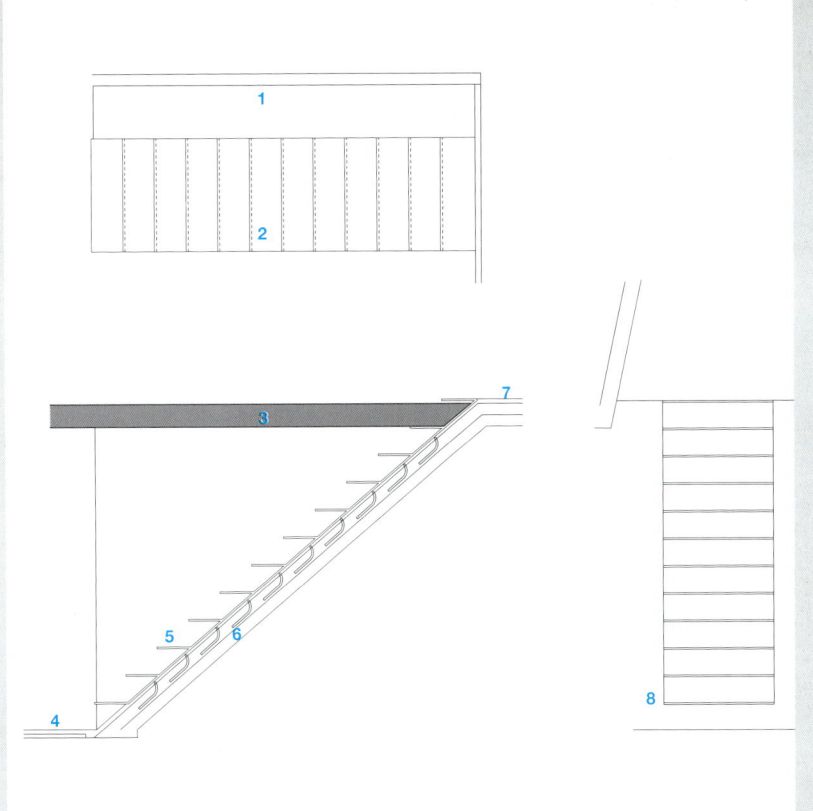

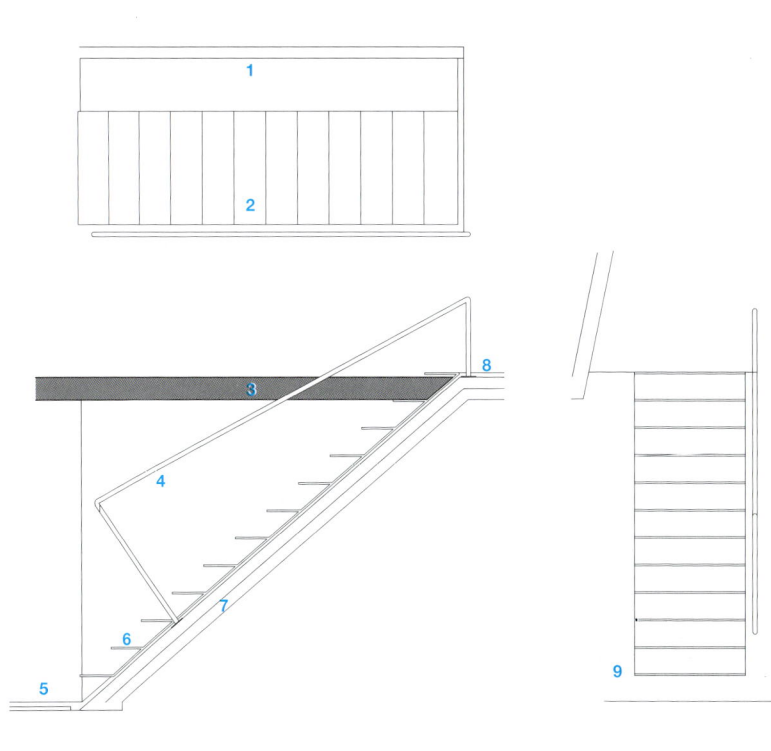

06.13
Stair Plan, Section and Elevation 1
1:50
1 Concrete slope
2 Plan view of steel staircase
3 150 mm (6 inch) concrete slab
4 Concrete floor
5 Steel treads attached to stringer with steel anchor rods
6 Steel stringer
7 150 mm (6 inch) concrete slab
8 Staircase elevation

06.14
Stair Plan, Section and Elevation 2
1:50
1 Concrete slope
2 Plan view of steel staircase
3 Concrete floor slab beyond
4 Steel pipe handrail
5 Concrete floor
6 Steel treads attached to stringer with steel anchor rods
7 Steel stringer
8 Concrete slab
9 Staircase elevation

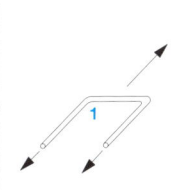

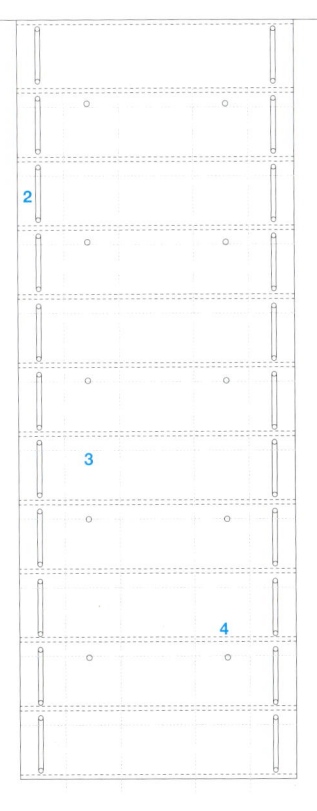

06.15
Elevational Stair Detail
1:20
1 Steel anchor rod
2 Steel anchor rod
3 Structural steel grid
4 Steel plate tread

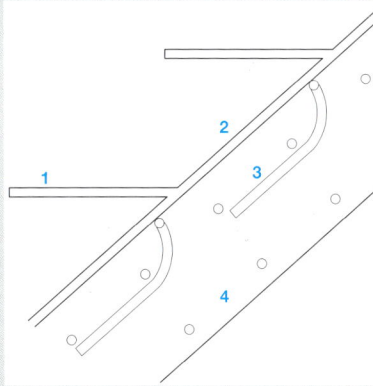

06.16
Sectional Stair Detail
1:10
1 Steel plate tread
2 Steel base plate
3 Steel anchor rod
4 Steel stringer and structural grid

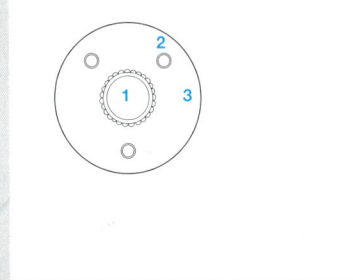

06.17
Stair Handrail Detail
1:5
1 Steel pipe handrail
2 Anchor bolt
3 Steel plate

Léon Wohlhage Wernik Architekten

House Voss
Münsterland, Germany

Client
Karin and Reinhold Voss

Area
300 square metres (3,230 square feet)

Project Team
Professor Hilde Léon, Konrad
Wohlhage, Siegfried Wernik, Peter
Deluse, Ulrich Vetter, Peter Czekay,
Werner Mayer-Biela, Bettina Zalenga

Structural Engineer
Pichler Ingenieure

Landscape Design
S.A.L. Planungsgruppe/Heinz Günther
Schulten

Builder
Manfred Bukowski

Bordered to the south and west by the
course of a small stream and a stand
of established trees, and to the north
by newly built homes, this house
reacts to its context with two
markedly different faces. The north
facade is all but impenetrable, while to
the south, the building opens up to
the landscape. Consisting of a simple
two-storey box, the design takes
advantage of the natural landscape by
creating a series of visual layers
between interior and exterior with two
high-walled atria. The exterior walls
are punctuated with windows and
portals enabling those inside the
house to see first into the protected
environment of the atria and then out
onto the landscape beyond.

This ambivalence – between
openness and introspection, closure
and penetration – characterizes the
house. Sophisticated materials and
finishes enhance these qualities.
In particular, the concrete of the outer
shell, with no adornment other than
the markings of the casting process,
is a canvas on which trees throw
their shadows in ever-changing
patterns. Material consistency is
echoed in the pre-cast concrete
paving slabs and window frames
of dark grey aluminium. Interior
masonry is simply rendered, the
ceilings painted white, the floors
covered with black parquetry, while a
straight flight of folded steel stairs
connects the two floors.

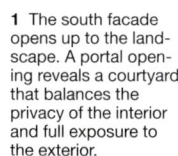

1 The south facade
opens up to the land-
scape. A portal open-
ing reveals a courtyard
that balances the
privacy of the interior
and full exposure to
the exterior.
2 The north facade
presents a closed face
to the world. The entry
is semi-concealed in
a recessed opening to
the left.
3 Full height glazed
sliding doors with
anodized aluminium
frames slide away
to open up the living
spaces to the court-
yard.
4 A minimal palette
of interior colours and
finishes, primarily
white walls and black
timber floors, comple-
ments the unadorned
concrete of the
exterior.
5 A strip window at
the top of the house
brings north light down
through the staircase
slot into the ground
floor.

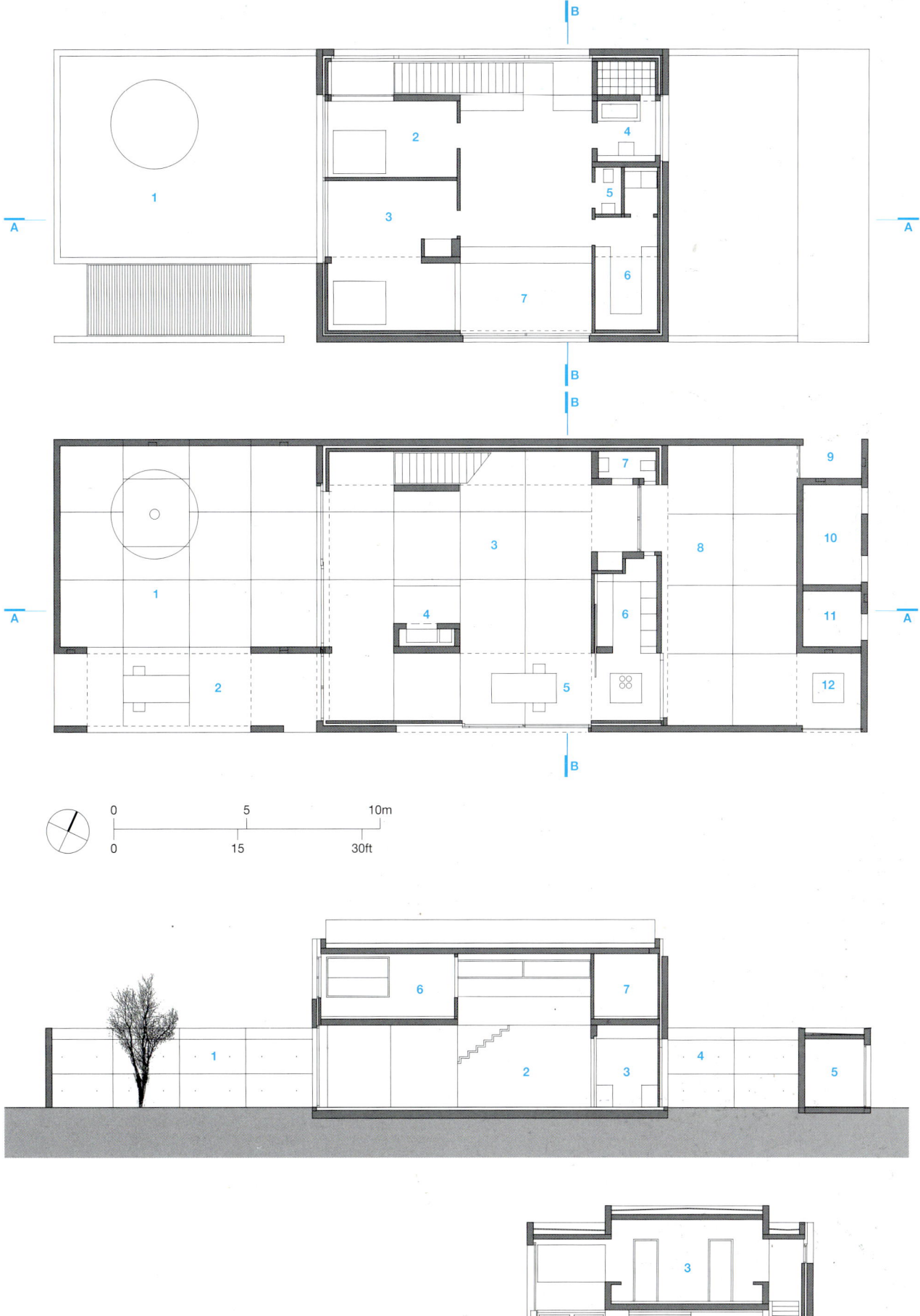

07.01
First Floor Plan
1:200
1 Courtyard
2 Bedroom
3 Bedroom
4 Bathroom
5 WC
6 Dressing room
7 Void

07.02
Ground Floor Plan
1:200
1 Courtyard
2 Outdoor dining
3 Living room
4 Fireplace
5 Dining room
6 Kitchen
7 WC
8 Entry court
9 Entry
10 Utility room 1
11 Utility room 2
12 Utility room 3

07.03
Section A–A
1:200
1 Courtyard
2 Living room
3 Kitchen
4 Entry court
5 Utility room
6 Bedroom
7 WC

07.04
Section B–B
1:200
1 Dining room
2 Living room
3 Bedroom lobby

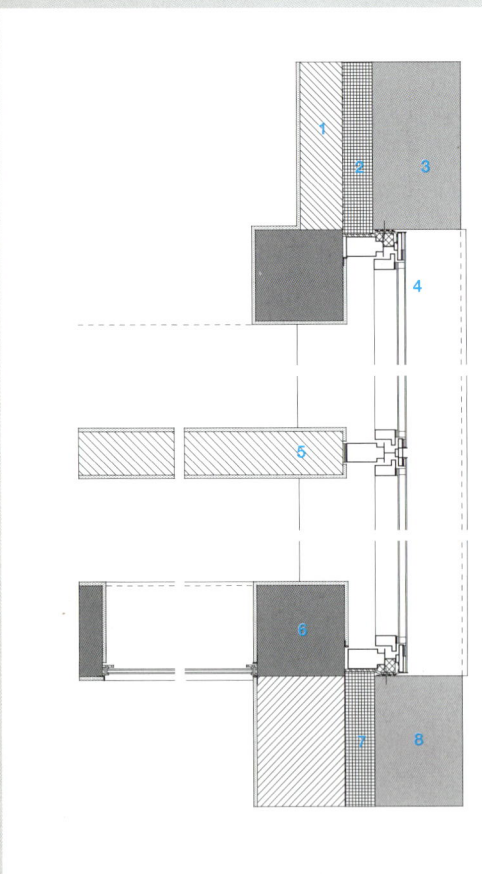

07.05
Fixed Glazing Detail
1:20
1 115 mm (4¹/2 inch) vertically cored brickwork with 15 mm (³/5 inch) thick plaster finish
2 80 mm (3 inch) core insulation with vapour barrier
3 240 mm (9¹/2 inch) exposed reinforced concrete wall
4 Double glazing in thermally divided powder-coated aluminium frame
5 Wall in lightwall construction
6 240 mm (9¹/2 inch) exposed reinforced concrete wall
7 80 mm (3 inch) core insulation with vapour barrier
8 240 mm (9¹/2 inch) exposed reinforced concrete wall

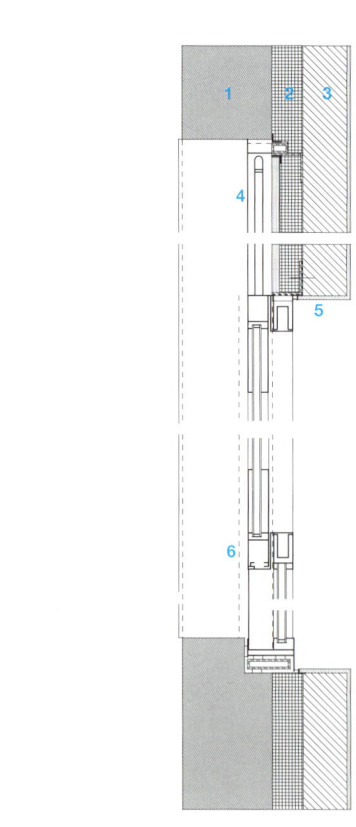

07.06
Sliding Glass Door Detail 1
1:20
1 240 mm (9¹/2 inch) exposed reinforced concrete wall
2 80 mm (3 inch) core insulation with vapour barrier
3 115 mm (4¹/2 inch) vertically cored brickwork with 15 mm (³/5 inch) thick plaster finish
4 Slide rail
5 U-profile aluminium
6 Sliding element

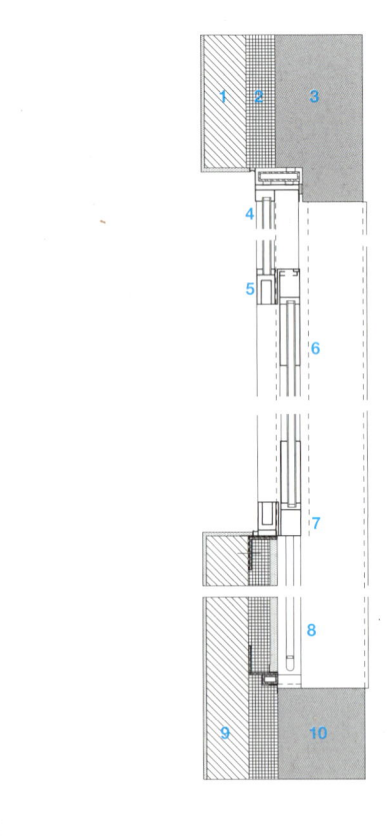

07.07
Sliding Glass Door Detail 2
1:20
1 115 mm (4¹/2 inch) vertically cored brickwork with 15 mm (³/5 inch) thick plaster finish
2 80 mm (3 inch) core insulation with vapour barrier
3 240 mm (9¹/2 inch) exposed reinforced concrete wall
4 Fixed glazing
5 U-profile
6 Sliding element
7 Aluminium profile
8 Slide rail
9 115 mm (4¹/2 inch) vertically cored brickwork with 15 mm (³/5 inch) thick plaster finish
10 240 mm (9¹/2 inch) exposed reinforced concrete wall

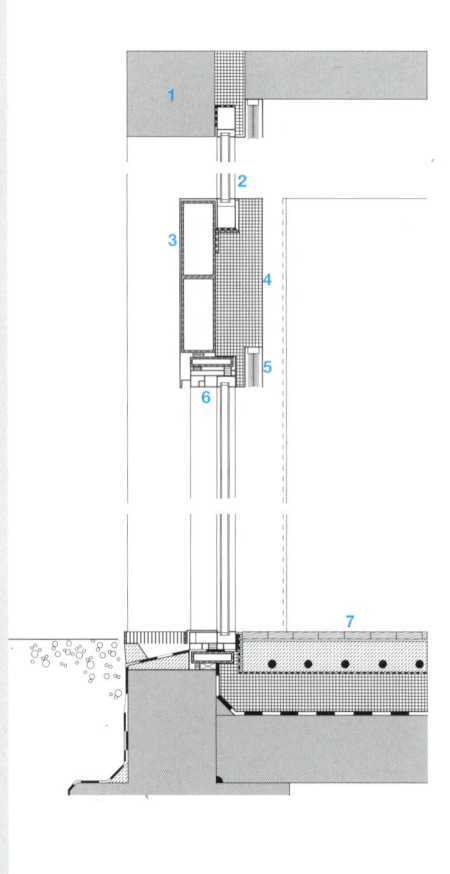

07.08
Sliding Glass Door Detail 3
1:20
1 Concrete wall
2 Fixed glazing
3 Steel profile
4 Insulated aluminium panelling
5 Integrated sun protection
6 Double glazing in thermally divided powder-coated aluminium frame
7 Ground floor construction comprised of 20 mm (³/4 inch) wenge parquet flooring over 90 mm (3¹/2 inch) coated screed around underfloor heating, then polythene sheet separating layer over 180 mm (7 inch) reinforced concrete floor slab

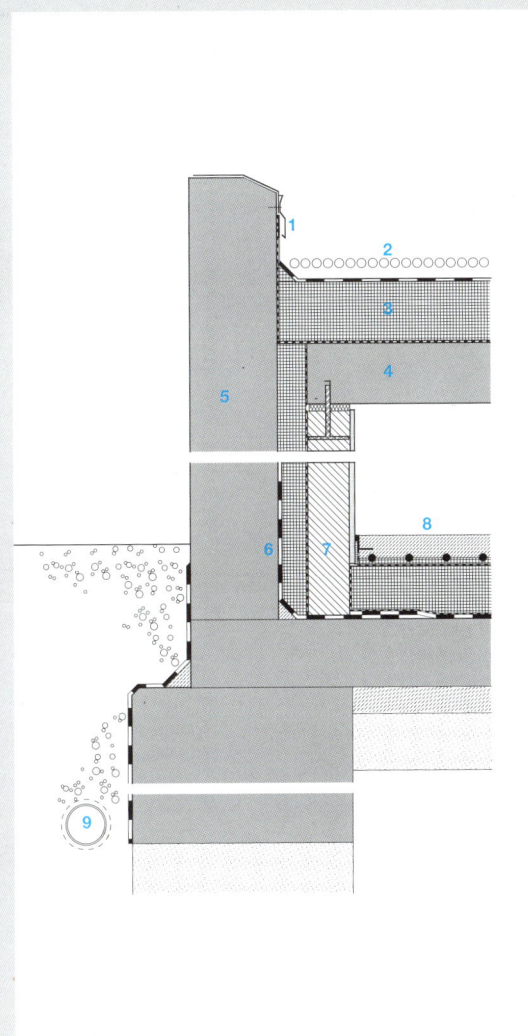

07.09
**External Concrete
Wall Detail**
1:20
  1 Aluminium sheet
  2 Roof construction
comprised of a 50 mm
(2 inch) layer of gravel
over plastic waterproof
membrane
  3 120–220 mm (4³/4 –
8¹/2 inch) polystyrene
insulation to falls and
back-up to sealing
layer over 180 mm (7
inch) reinforced
concrete roof slab
  4 Exposed concrete
roof slab
  5 240 mm (9¹/2 inch)
exposed concrete wall
  6 80 mm (3 inch) core
insulation with vapour
barrier
  7 115 mm (4¹/2 inch)
vertically cored
brickwork with 15 mm
(3/5 inch) plaster finish
  8 Ground floor
construction
comprised of 20 mm
(3/4 inch) wenge
parquet flooring over
90 mm (3¹/2 inch)
coated screed around
underfloor heating
then polythene sheet
separating layer over
180 mm (7 inch) thick
reinforced concrete
slab
  9 Drainage back filled
with rubble

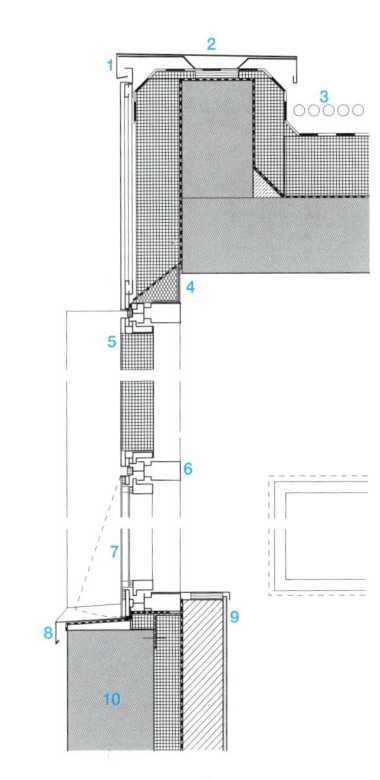

07.10
**Upper Level Slot
Window Detail**
1:20
  1 Aluminium capping
  2 Aluminium sheet
cover to parapet
  3 Roof construction
comprised of a 50 mm
(2 inch) layer of gravel
over plastic waterproof
membrane with
120–220 mm (4³/4 –
8¹/2 inch) polystyrene
insulation to falls and
back-up sealing layer
and reinforced
concrete roof slab
  4 Insulated aluminium
sandwich panelling
  5 Insulated aluminium
sandwich panelling
  6 Aluminium profile
  7 Double glazing in
thermally divided
powder-coated
aluminium frame
  8 Aluminium sheet
  9 Aluminium sheet
  10 240 mm (9¹/2 inch)
exposed concrete wall
with 80 mm (3 inch)
core insulation, vapour
barrier and 115 mm
(4¹/2 inch) vertically
cored brickwork
with 15 mm (3/5 inch)
plaster finish

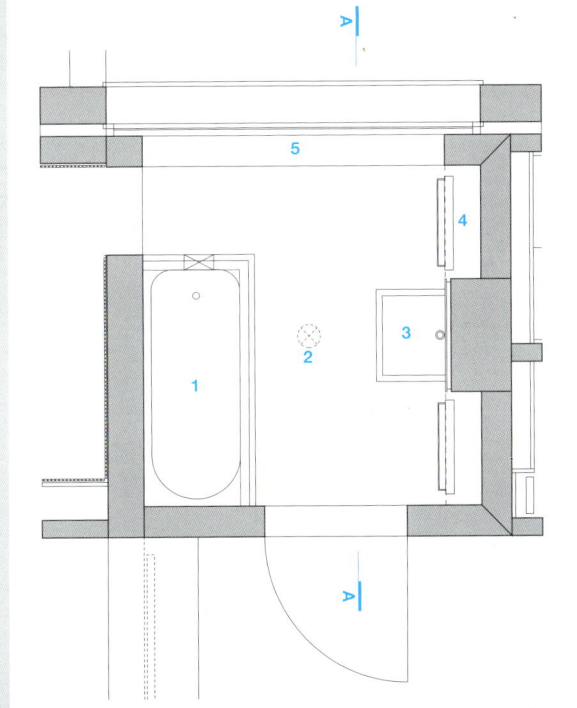

07.11
Bathroom Plan
1:50
  1 Solid cedarwood
bathtub
  2 Ceiling light
  3 Washbasin
  4 Built-in closet
  5 Clipboard wall
system

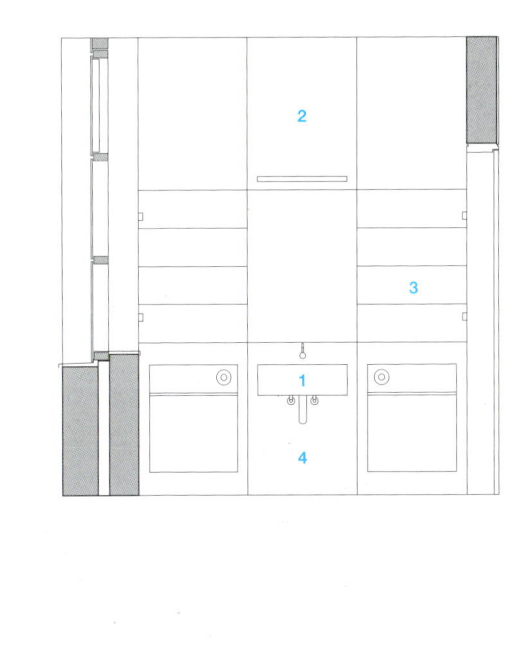

07.12
**Bathroom Elevation
A–A**
1:50
  1 Washbasin
  2 Integrated light
  3 Integrated built-in
storage
  4 Fairfaced concrete
wall

Solar Umbrella
Los Angeles, California, USA

Client
Angela Brooks and Lawrence Scarpa

Area
176 square metres (1,900 square feet)

Project Team
Lawrence Scarpa, Angela Brooks,
Anne Burke, Vanessa Hardy, Ching
Luk, Gwynne Pugh

Main Contractor
Above Board Construction

Located in a neighbourhood of single storey bungalows, the Solar Umbrella boldly establishes a precedent for the next generation of California modernist architecture. A striking addition transforms an existing bungalow. What was formerly the front becomes the back as the new design reorganizes the residence towards the south, optimizing exposure to sunlight. Solar panels wrapping around the south-west elevation and roof define the formal expression of the residence. Conceived as a solar canopy, these panels protect the house from thermal gain by screening it from direct exposure to the sun, and transforming sunlight into usable energy.

The addition includes a new entry, living area, master suite and utility room. The kitchen now opens into a large living area which, in turn, opens out to the garden where an operable wall of glass defines the edge between interior and exterior. The new entry sequence features a pool that cascades into a lower tier of water that penetrates and interlocks with the geometry of the residence. Located directly above the living area, the bedroom opens onto a covered patio overlooking the garden. A series of stepped roofs, glazed walls, and clerestory windows broadcast light from multiple directions. Light and shadow become palpable elements that enliven the more permanent elements of the design. The programme integrates passive and active solar design strategies, making the residence 100 per cent energy neutral. Recycled, renewable, and high performance materials are specified throughout.

1 A view of the south-east facade reveals the importance of the 'solar umbrella' – the panels wrap the roof and south-west facade, helping to create a 100 per cent energy neutral house. The living room and master suite open up to the elegant garden. **2** A generous covered terrace on the first floor creates a private place for relaxation with views over the neighbourhood. This outdoor room creates strong visual and physical links between outside and inside, interlocking with interior spaces. **3 and 4** The living room is anchored by a large custom-made, built-in sofa and fireplace and given dynamism by the floating, folded plate steel stairs.

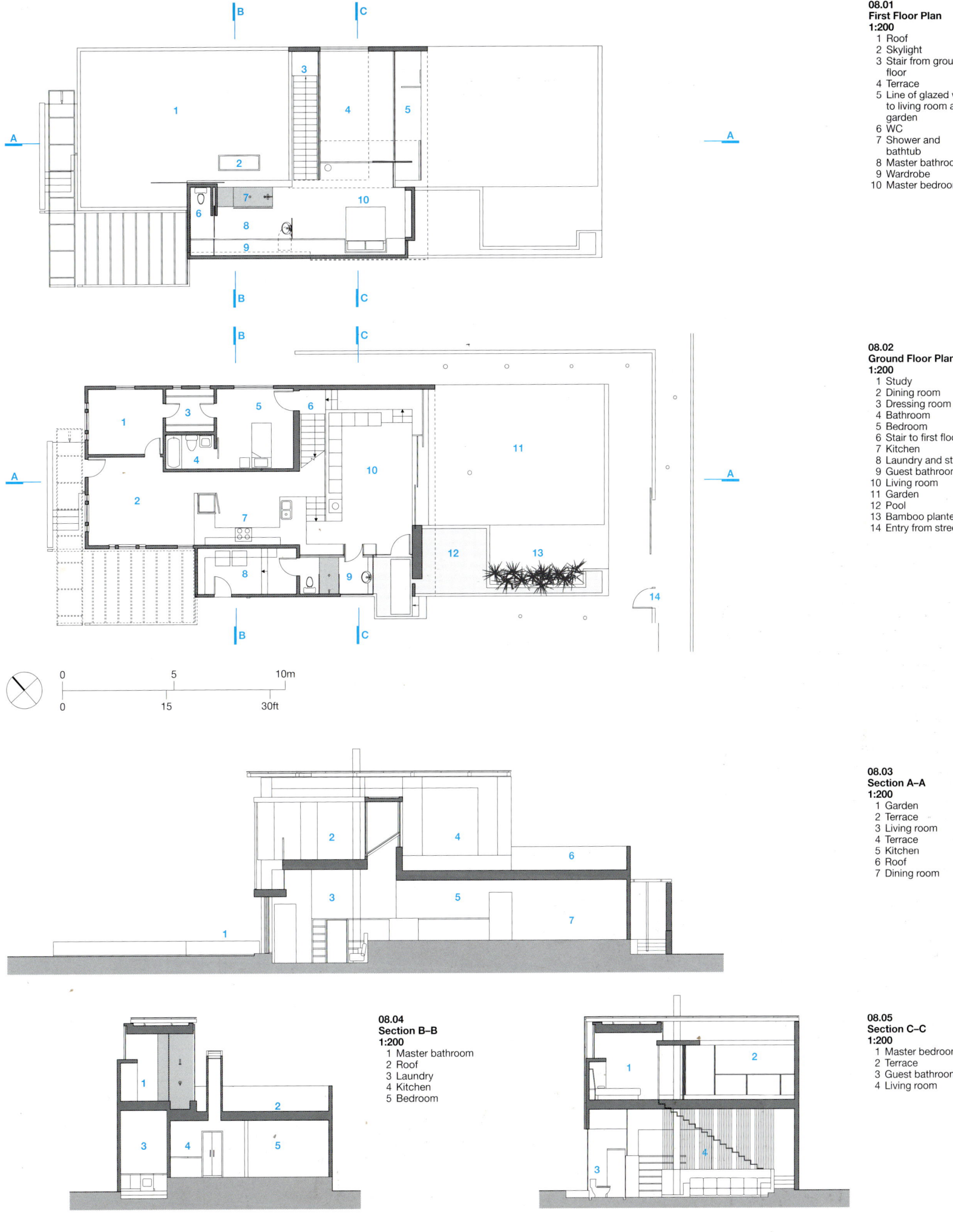

  1 Roof
  2 Skylight
  3 Stair from ground
     floor
  4 Terrace
  5 Line of glazed wall
     to living room and
     garden
  6 WC
  7 Shower and
     bathtub
  8 Master bathroom
  9 Wardrobe
 10 Master bedroom

08.02
Ground Floor Plan
1:200
  1 Study
  2 Dining room
  3 Dressing room
  4 Bathroom
  5 Bedroom
  6 Stair to first floor
  7 Kitchen
  8 Laundry and store
  9 Guest bathroom
 10 Living room
 11 Garden
 12 Pool
 13 Bamboo planter
 14 Entry from street

08.03
Section A–A
1:200
  1 Garden
  2 Terrace
  3 Living room
  4 Terrace
  5 Kitchen
  6 Roof
  7 Dining room

08.04
Section B–B
1:200
  1 Master bathroom
  2 Roof
  3 Laundry
  4 Kitchen
  5 Bedroom

08.05
Section C–C
1:200
  1 Master bedroom
  2 Terrace
  3 Guest bathroom
  4 Living room

0   5   10m
0   15   30ft

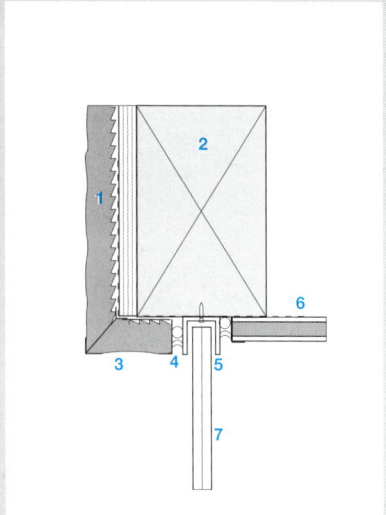

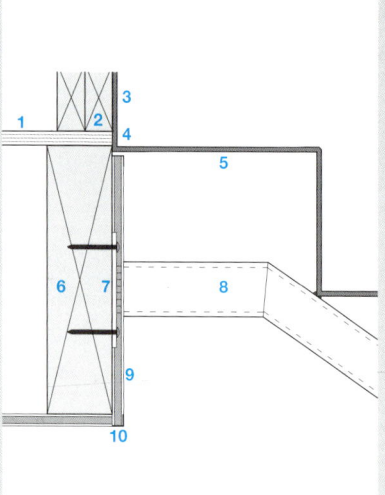

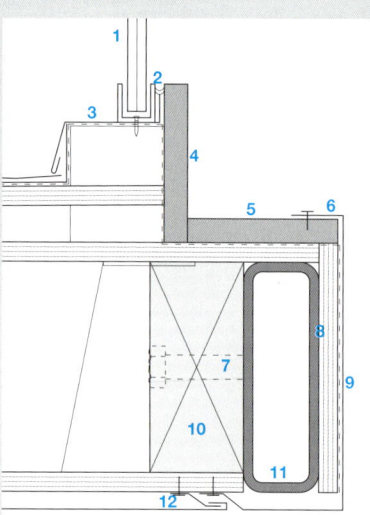

08.06
Window Head Detail
1:5
 1 Plaster screed to external surface
 2 Timber header
 3 Plaster corner screed
 4 Continuous caulking with backer rod both sides
 5 Continuous aluminium channel
 6 Continuous water proofing membrane under flashing with minimum 100 mm

(4 inch) overlap
 7 12 mm (1/2 inch) laminated glass

08.07
Detail at Top Landing Stair Stringer Connection
1:10
 1 19 mm (3/4 inch) plywood floor sheeting
 2 Two timber furring joists
 3 6 mm (1/4 inch) steel plate at last riser
 4 J-angle corner trim
 5 Steel plate treads and risers
 6 Timber beam
 7 150 x 150 x 6 mm (6 x 6 x 1/4 inch)

concealed steel plate
 8 Steel pipe stringer
 9 Gypsum wall board
 10 Corner trim

08.08
Window Sill Detail
1:5
 1 12 mm (1/2 inch) laminated glass
 2 Continuous caulking
 3 24 gauge flashing to match window frame
 4 14 mm (5/8 inch) medium density fibre board
 5 14 mm (5/8 inch) medium density fibre board
 6 20 gauge sheet

metal siding with patina finish
 7 12 mm (1/2 inch) diameter stud bolts at 610 mm (24 inch) centres
 8 12 mm (1/2 inch) plywood sheet
 9 Continuous waterproof membrane
 10 Timber blocking
 11 Steel edge beam
 12 Cleats at 610 mm (24 inch) centres

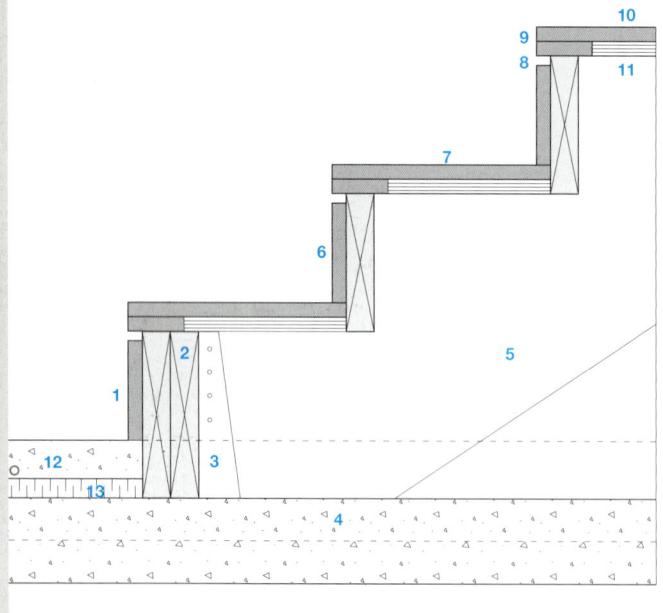

08.09
Detail at Stair Landing to Kitchen
1:10
 1 19 mm (3/4 inch) chipboard to last riser
 2 Timber blocking
 3 Face mounted steel hanger
 4 Reinforced concrete floor
 5 50 x 355 mm (2 x 14 inch) steel stringer
 6 19 mm (3/4 inch) cherry riser
 7 19 mm (3/4 inch) cherry stair tread

8 6 mm (1/4 inch) shadow gap
9 38 mm (11/2 inch) cherry nosing
10 19 mm (3/4 inch) cherry flooring
11 19 mm (3/4 inch) cherry plywood subfloor
12 Finished concrete floor with radiant heating
13 25 mm (1 inch) fibre insulation

08.10
Door Jamb Detail 1
1:5
 1 Corner screed
 2 24 mm (7/8 inch) external plaster
 3 24 gauge flashing
 4 12 mm (1/2 inch) laminated glass
 5 10 mm (3/8 inch) continuous caulking both sides
 6 Timber blocking
 7 Wood furring
 8 Waterproof membrane
 9 Plaster screed

10 Continuous caulking
11 12 mm (1/2 inch) plywood sheet
12 Waterproof membrane
13 12 mm (1/2 inch) diameter bolt with epoxy grout
14 Waterproof membrane
15 Reinforced concrete wall

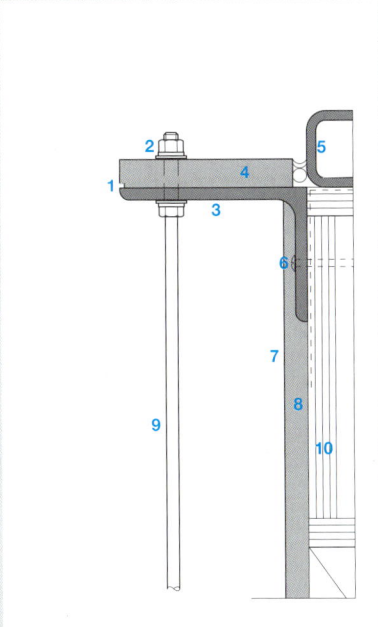

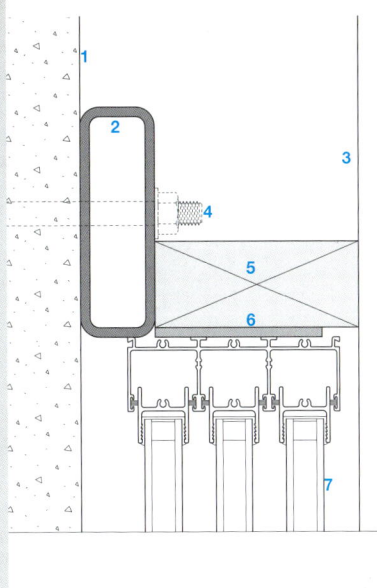

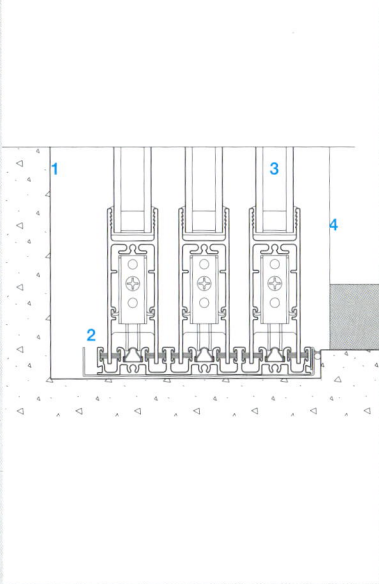

08.11
Detail at Open Patio Curb
1:5
  1 5 mm (1/4 inch) saw cut
  2 Stainless steel flat nuts with washers top and bottom
  3 127 x 76 x 10 mm (5 x 3 x 3/8 inch) steel angle
  4 19 mm (3/4 inch) MDP point to match wall
  5 Steel window frame
  6 6 mm (1/4 inch) screws at 300 mm (12 inch) centres
  7 Gypsum plasterboard
  8 Continuous waterproof membrane
  9 Threaded steel rod
  10 19 mm (3/4 inch) plywood

08.12
Door Head Detail at Pocket
1:5
  1 Fair face concrete wall
  2 Steel rectangular hollow section
  3 Face of timber stud
  4 15 mm (5/8 inch) diameter epoxy bolt
  5 Timber blocking
  6 Shim as necessary
  7 Multi-slide door

08.13
Door Sill Detail at Pocket
1:5
  1 Face of concrete
  2 Sill pan
  3 Multi-slide door
  4 Face of stud

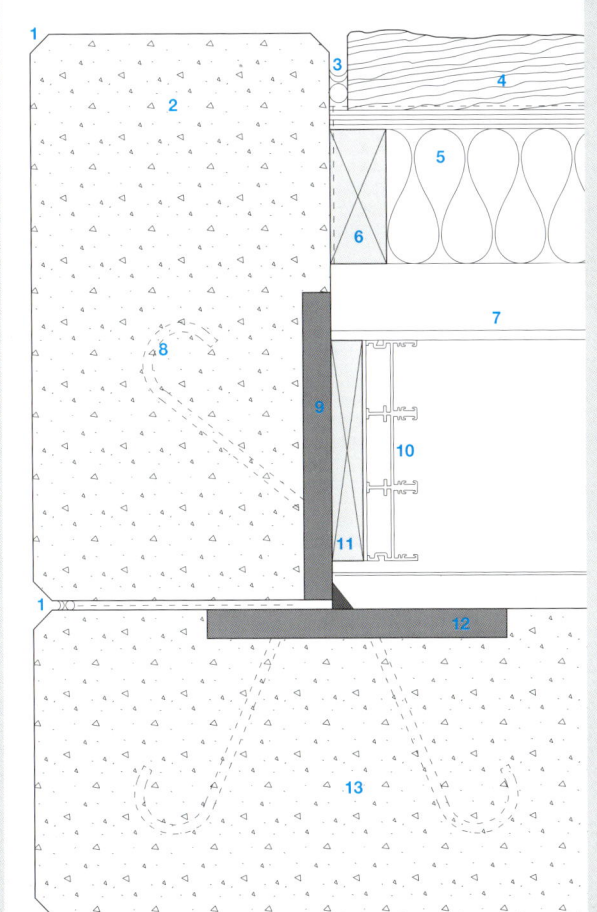

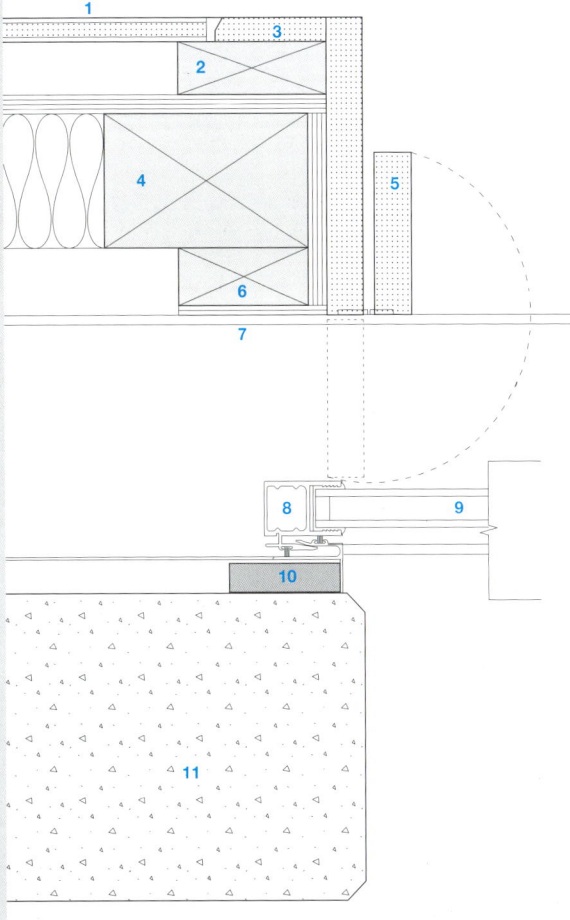

08.14
Door Jamb Detail 2
1:5
  1 Chamfered corner to concrete
  2 Reinforced concrete
  3 Continuous caulking
  4 50 mm (2 inch) routed cherrywood panels
  5 Ultra touch insulation
  6 50 x 100 mm (2 x 4 inch) timber framing
  7 6 mm (1/4 inch) plywood
  8 12 mm (1/2 inch) diameter welded rods embedded into tilt-up concrete panels
  9 19 x 200 mm (3/4 x 8 inch) steel plate
  10 Multi-slide jamb pocket
  11 Timber blocking
  12 19 x 200 mm (3/4 x 8 inch) steel plate
  13 200 mm (8 inch) thick tilt-up concrete wall panels

08.15
Door Jamb Detail 3
1:5
  1 15 mm (5/8 inch) gypsum board
  2 Timber furring
  3 14 x 76 mm (5/8 x 3 inch) medium density fibreboard with flat tape and mud to gypsum board
  4 Timber post
  5 Door leaf pocket concealer panel – 25 mm (1 inch) medium density fibreboard painted to match gypsum board with magnetic catch at top and bottom
  6 Timber blocking
  7 6 mm (1/4 inch) plywood
  8 Sliding glass door jamb
  9 Argon-filled dual glazed sliding pocket glass doors
  10 19 mm (3/4 inch) aluminium bar
  11 200 mm (8 inch) thick tilt-up concrete wall panels

4 x 4 House
Kobe, Hyogo, Japan

Area
118 square metres (1,270 square feet)

Project Team
Tadao Ando, Masataka Yano,
Tatsuhito Ono

Structural Engineer
Ascoral Engineering Associates

Main Contractor
Nakata Construction Co. Ltd

This house is located on a beachfront overlooking the Seto Inland Sea. On the opposite shore lies Hokudan, on Awaji Island, the epicentre of the devastating Great Hanshin Earthquake in 1995. To the east stretches the Akashi Strait Bridge, the longest suspension bridge in the world. The site is subject to erosion and over the past years a great deal of the land has been transformed into a beach, leaving a slim stretch of dry land remaining safe beyond the breakwater. So despite the relative generosity of space compared to other Japanese urban locations, the considerable geotechnical limitations had a direct impact on the architectural solution.

The house is a four-storey tower, each level made up of a four-by-four metre plan. On the uppermost level is a four-metre cube that protrudes from the face of the building, shifted across from the main vertical axis by a metre in order to create space for the stair. The landscape, framed by full-height glazing within this spectacular double-height cube, is a panorama sweeping over the sea, Awaji Island and the Akashi Bridge, where, for the client who makes his living in the area, memories of the earthquake are embedded. Constrained by the limitations of the site, each of the four levels houses a distinct function. On the ground level are the entrance and bathroom, the first floor the bedroom, the second floor the study and the top floor the kitchen, living and dining areas. The concrete exterior is alleviated at the upper levels where the concrete gives way to serve as a frame to great sheets of clear glazing that acknowledge the unique qualities of the waterfront location.

1 The house overlooks the Seto Inland Sea and Awaji Island. A double-height, four metre cube that accommodates the living, dining and kitchen spaces allows the bay to become the focus for the inhabitants.
2 The cube at the top of the house is offset by one metre to allow a stair to traverse the full height of the house without compromising the space available to the living quarters.
3 The kitchen stands as a free-standing timber unit in the double-height living space. The concrete walls, cast in-situ are left unpainted, creating a stark contrast with the massive panes of clear glazing overlooking the bay.
4 View of the kitchen and dining area with dramatic views overlooking the sea and Awaji Island in the distance.

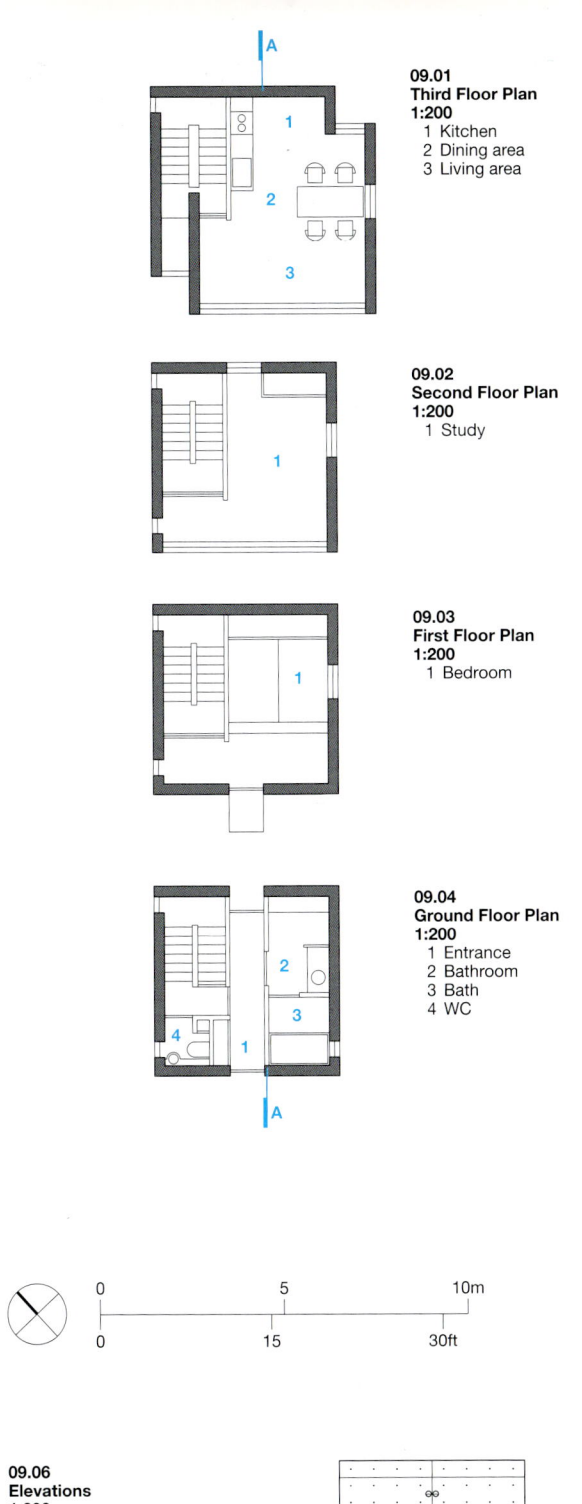

09.01
Third Floor Plan
1:200
1 Kitchen
2 Dining area
3 Living area

09.02
Second Floor Plan
1:200
1 Study

09.03
First Floor Plan
1:200
1 Bedroom

09.04
Ground Floor Plan
1:200
1 Entrance
2 Bathroom
3 Bath
4 WC

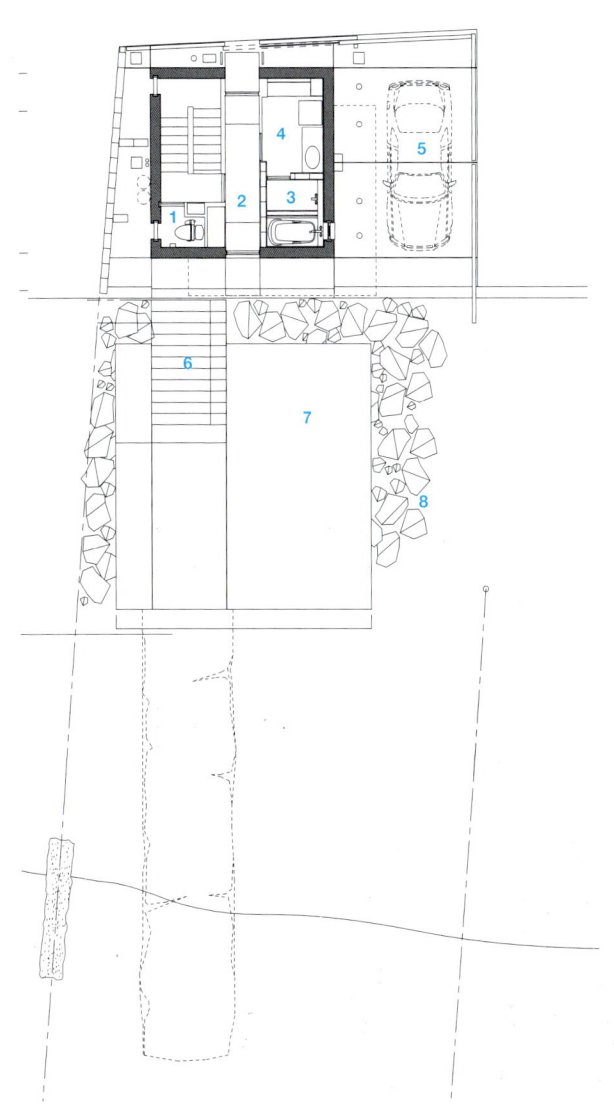

09.05
Site Plan
1:200
1 WC
2 Entrance
3 Bath
4 Bathroom
5 Carport
6 Concrete stair to entrance
7 Concrete deck
8 Crushed granite border

0		5		10m
0	15		30ft	

09.06
Elevations
1:200
1 East
2 North
3 West
4 South

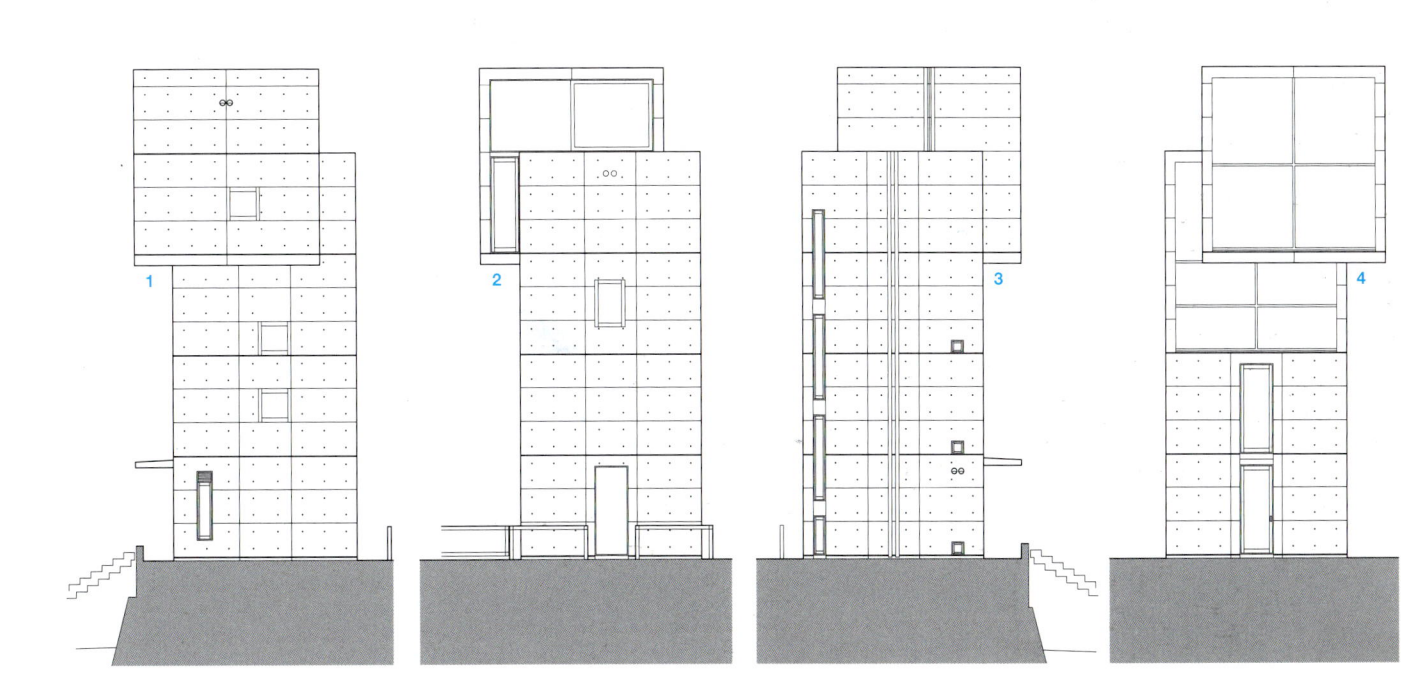

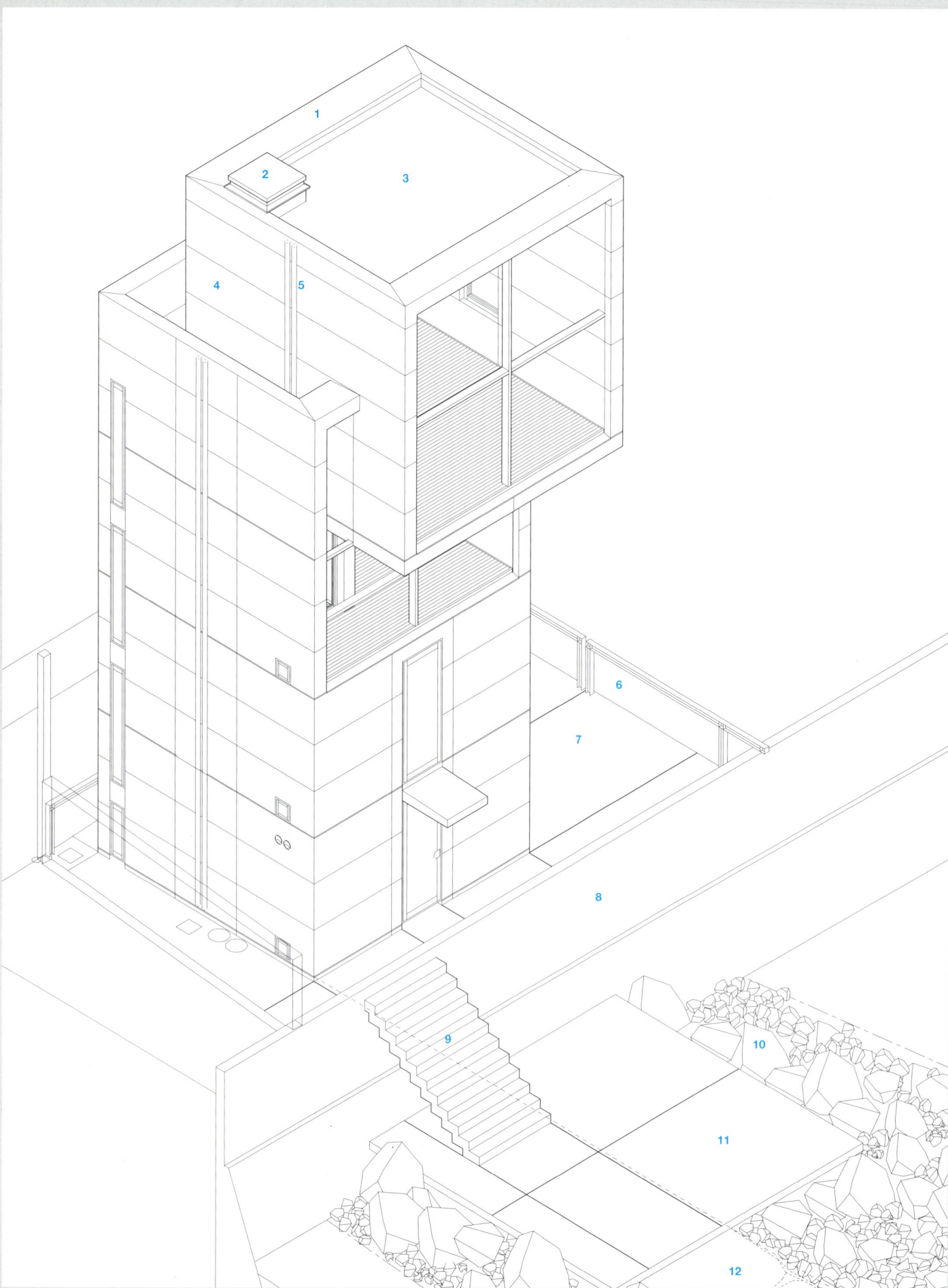

09.07
Axonometric
1 Trowel finished concrete with waterproofing to top of parapet
2 Acrylic plate skylight
3 Roof of bituminous membrane with waterproofing layer, cinder concrete and gravel finish
4 Exterior walls of exposed concrete with fluoropolymer paint finish
5 Steel rainwater pipe
6 100 x 100 x 6 x 8 mm (4 x 4 x 1/5 x 1/3 inch) H-section steel fence with galvanized finish
7 Trowel finished concrete parking area
8 Existing tide embankment
9 Trowel finished concrete stair
10 Crushed granite border
11 Trowel finished concrete deck
12 Existing concrete

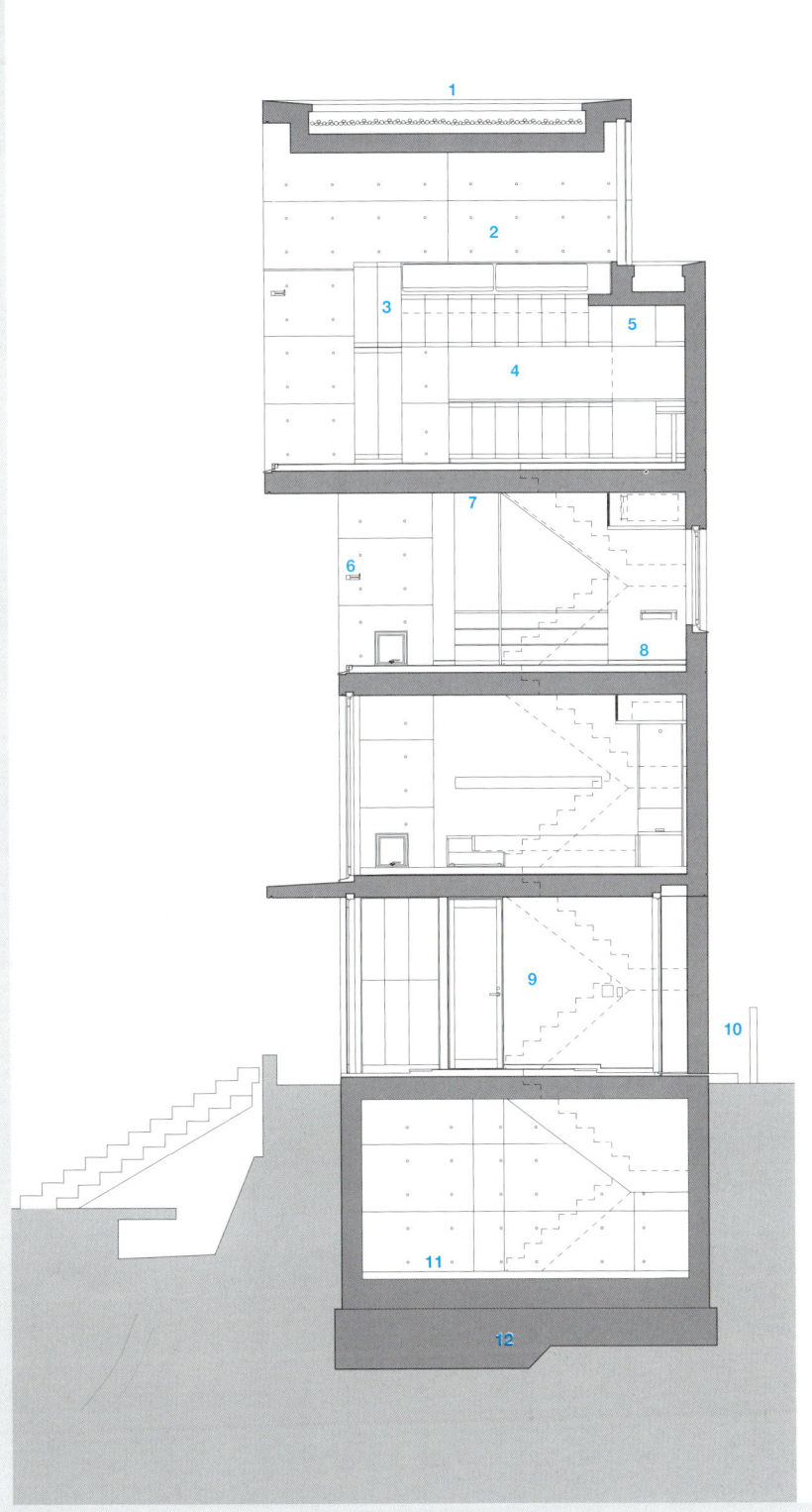

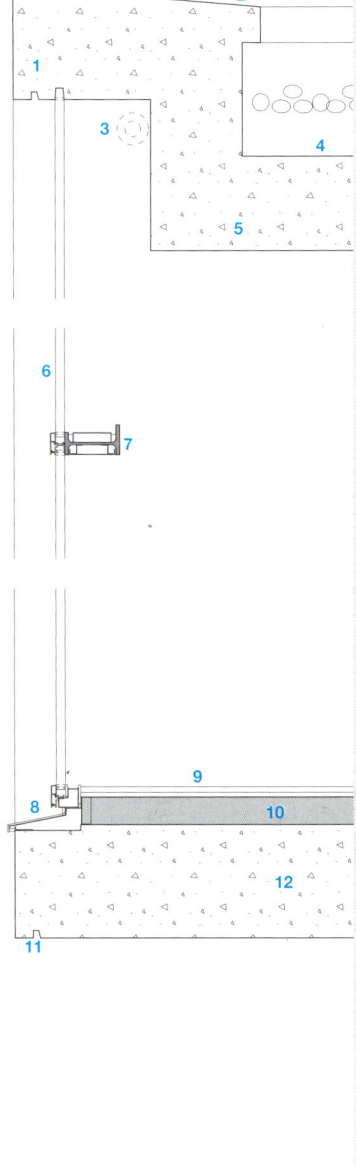

09.08
Section A–A
1:100
1 Roof of bituminous
membrane with
waterproofing layer,
cinder concrete and
gravel finish
2 Interior wall of
exposed concrete
3 Kitchen joinery from
oak on plywood
substrate
4 Stainless steel
splashback
5 Stainless steel
range hood
6 Timber shelves

7 Exposed concrete
ceiling
8 Oak flooring
9 Interior walls of
painted plasterboard
10 100 x 100 x 6 x 8
mm (4 x 4 x ⅕ x ⅓
inch) H-section steel
fence with galvanized
finish
11 Tiles and carpeting
to floor
12 Reinforced
concrete footings

09.09
Parapet Detail
1:20
1 Exposed concrete
parapet
2 Top of parapet from
trowel finished
concrete with
waterproofing layer
3 Roller blind
4 Bituminous
membrane to roof with
cinder concrete and
gravel
5 Exposed concrete
ceiling
6 Clear glazing
7 H-section steel

glazing bar
8 Steel sill with
baking paint finish
9 Plywood substrate
floor with oak boards
10 Plywood and
insulation to joists
11 Drip groove to
concrete
12 Exposed concrete
eaves soffit

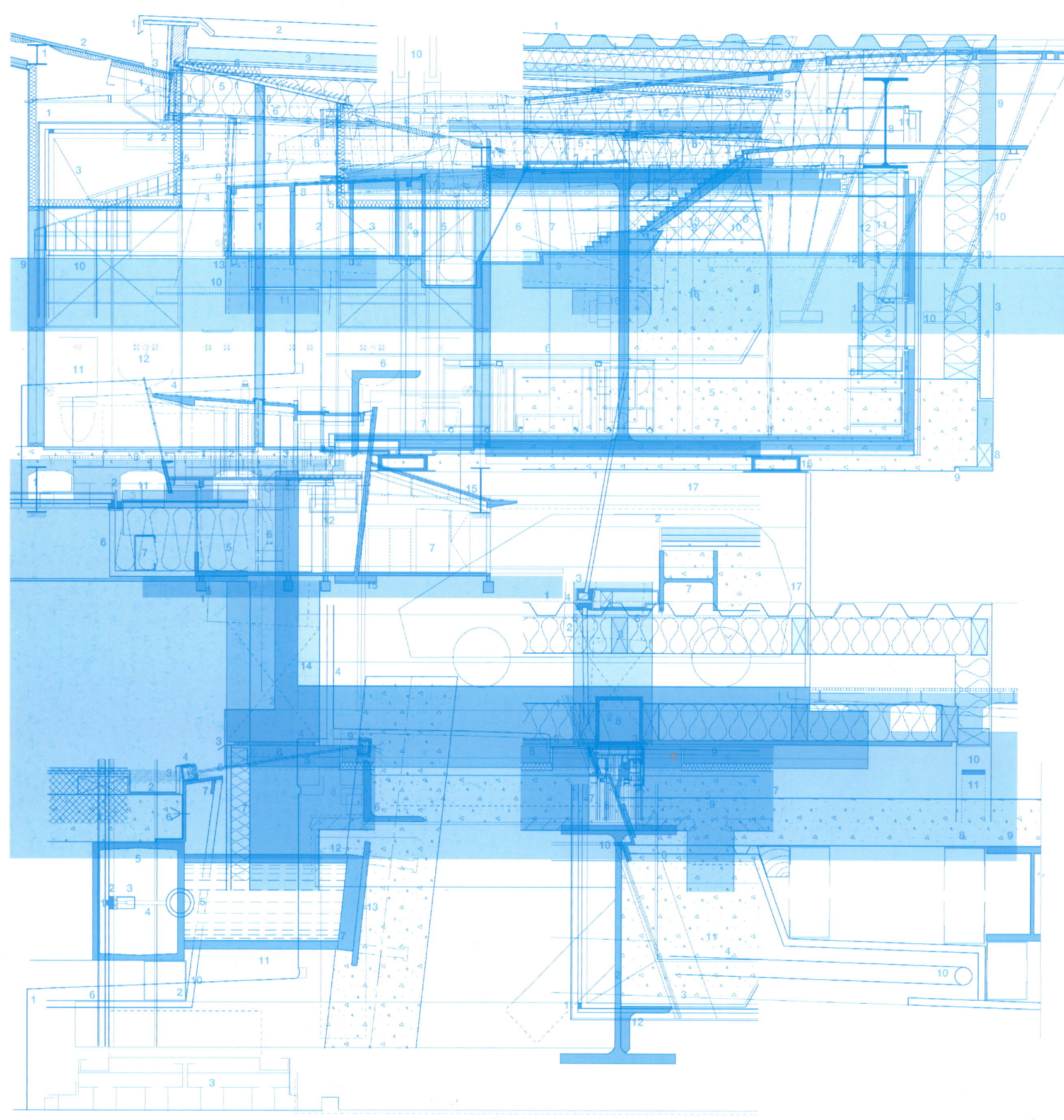

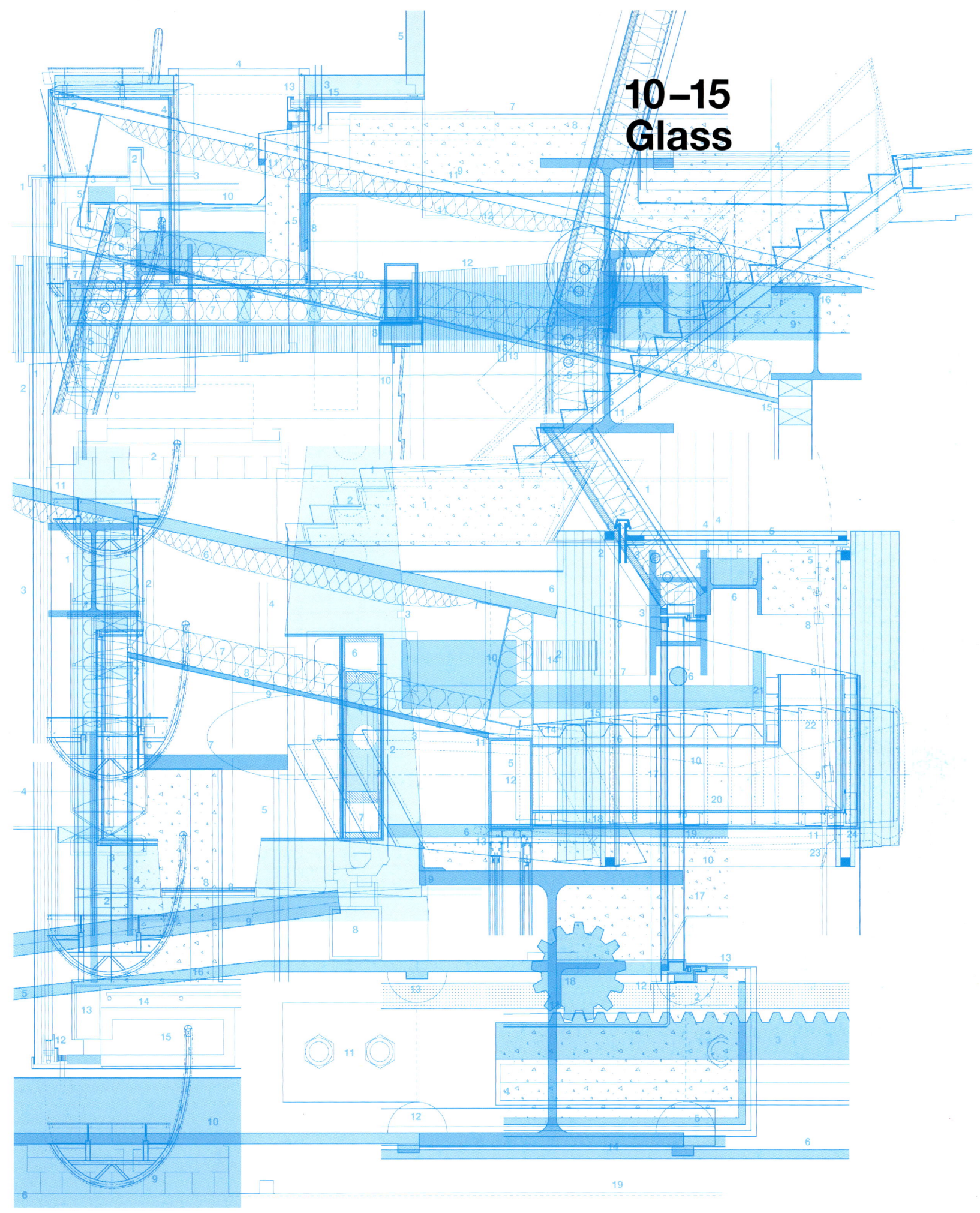

M-Lidia House
Girona, Spain

Client
Miquel Subiràs and Lídia Casado

Area
170 square metres (1,830 square feet)

Project Team
Miquel Subiràs, A. Sáez, A. Planagumà, M. Sánchez

Main Contractor
Metàl-liques Olot

The M-Lidia House in Montagut, Girona is located in a range of low hills, inland from the Costa Brava on the east coast of Spain. The design concept is a purification of a typical domestic programme, arranged as three simple rectlinear zones in a symmetrical arrangement. In the centre, a fully glazed living and dining area opens out onto a timber deck. This volume is flanked by two bedroom wings, accessed via a strip of service functions ranged along the north-west facade, and separated from the living space by a sliver of courtyard on one side and a stair rising up from the garage below on the other.

The two bedroom wings are fully glazed on the courtyard facades serving to focus attention on the communal spaces. However, they are distinguished and protected from neighbouring houses by stainless steel sheet cladding to the other facades. This screen is mimicked in the interior where the kitchen can be separated from the living space by a sculptural sliding screen of linear steel strips which provides a textural contrast to the expanse of glazing on the opposite wall overlooking the landscape. Completely hidden from view, a basement level accommodates a garage and storage area, as well as a stair that leads up into the house. Here, an enclosed glazed bridge at ground floor level enables uninterrupted access from the living spaces to the children's bedroom. The simplicity of the form and the way in which the building is focused on the landscape suggests a classical villa. However, the materials and spatial sequences make it clear that this is a house designed for uncompromised contemporary living.

1 and 2 At night, the expanses of clear glazing to the living room (centre) and the bedroom wings either side reveal the level of transparency that is the key to the way the inhabitants are able to interract with the landscape. To the rear of the living space, the stainless steel sliding screen hides the kitchen from view.
3 A staircase rises up from the garage below, where a bridge at ground level makes the connection between the living room and the bedroom.
4 View of the living room with the steel screen in the open position revealing the linear kitchen that runs the length of the north-west wall. A slot of glazing to a clerestory window illuminates the kitchen, while a horizontal band of windows above the work top allows views out over the garden.
5 View of the living room with the screen closed.

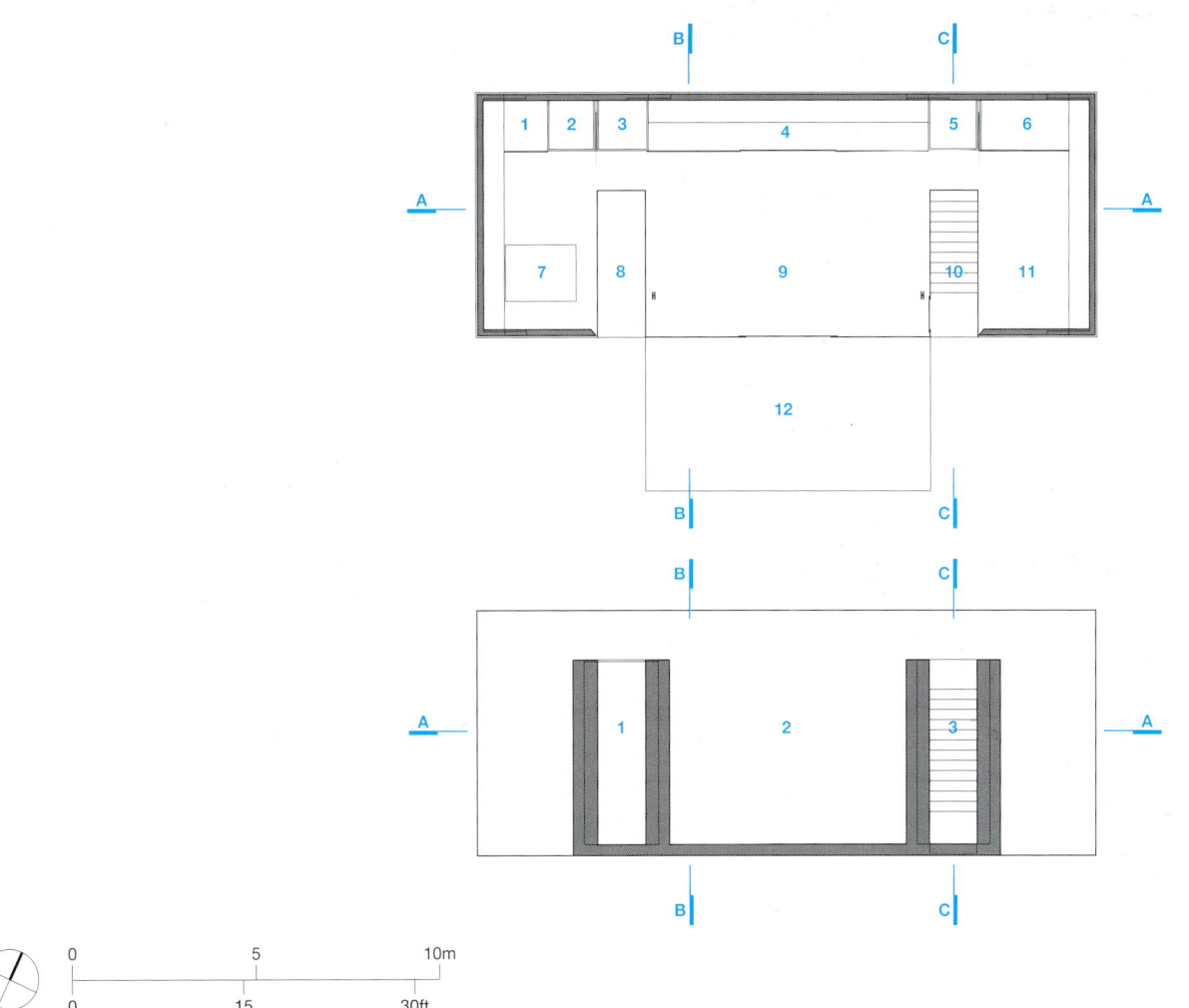

10.01
Ground Floor Plan
1:200
1 Bathroom
2 Shower
3 WC
4 Kitchen
5 Laundry
6 Study
7 Bedroom
8 Patio
9 Living and dining room
10 Entrance
11 Children's bedroom
12 Terrace

10.02
Basement Plan
1:200
1 Storage
2 Garage
3 Stair up to ground floor

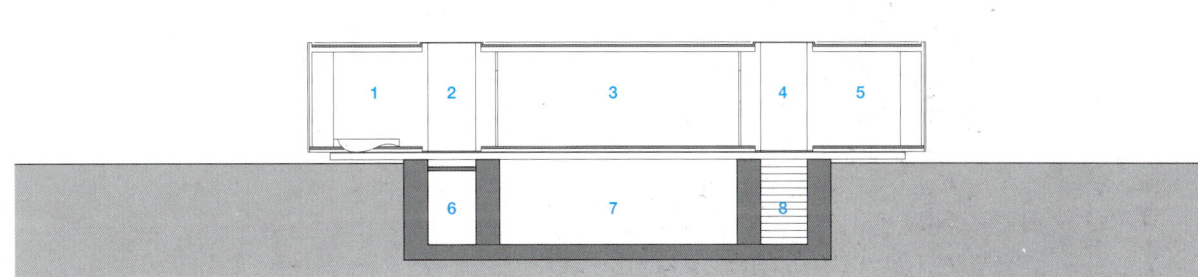

10.03
Section A–A
1:200
1 Bedroom
2 Patio
3 Living and dining room
4 Void over stair
5 Children's bedroom
6 Storage
7 Garage
8 Stair from garage to house

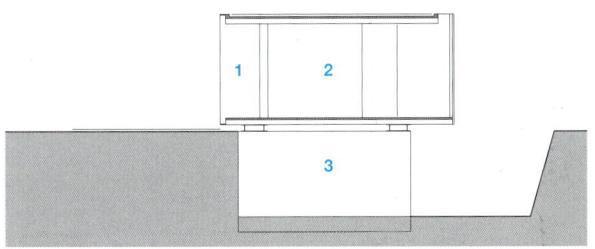

10.04
Section B–B
1:200
1 Kitchen
2 Living and dining room
3 Garage

10.05
Section C–C
1:200
1 Laundry
2 Children's bedroom
3 Garage

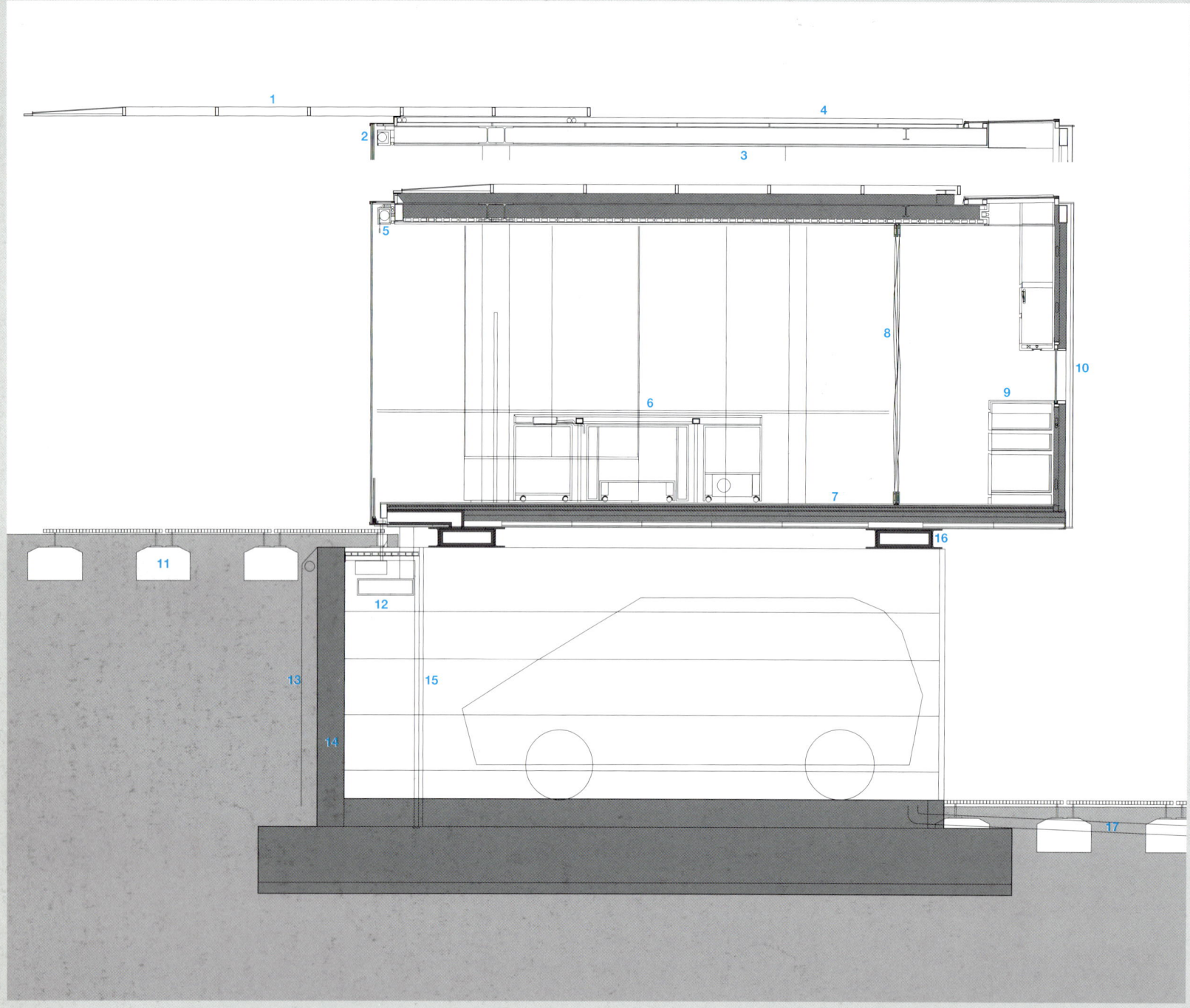

10.06
Detail Section
1:50
1 Extendable porch roof
2 Laminated glass sliding door
3 Plaster finish to ceiling
4 Fixed porch roof
5 Roller blind
6 Extendable table
7 Timber decking
8 Sliding partition
9 Lacquered finish to kitchen carcasses, with Corian work top
10 Galvanized steel panels to exterior surface
11 Concrete footing
12 Motorized sliding door to garage
13 Drainage screen
14 Reinforced concrete wall
15 Steel sheet finish to storage wall doors
16 Steel horizontal structure with air-conditioning system
17 Waste pipe

10.07
Sliding Glass Door Detail
1:10
1 5 mm (1/5 inch) thick steel sheet
2 80 x 25 x 2 mm (3 x 1 x 1/10 inch) roof upstand
3 Impermeable roofing membrane
4 Steel sheet cover to roller blind assembly
5 Timber blocking
6 Roller blind
7 Timber panel to conceal blind and enable maintenance access
8 Continuous line of fluorescent light fittings
9 Plaster finishing angle
10 Plaster finish to ceiling
11 Laminated glass sliding door
12 Glass support and stainless steel window assembly
13 Steel box beam structure to floor edge
14 Concrete reinforcing to floor structure
15 Air-conditioning duct
16 Timber decking

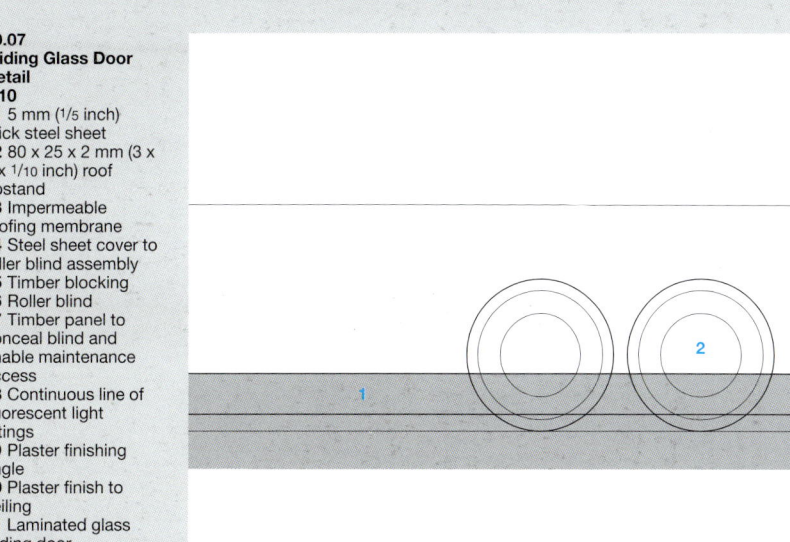

10.08
Sliding Door Detail 1
1:2
1 25 x 4 mm (1 x 1/5 inch) steel sheet
2 Steel guide rail
3 8 mm (1/3 inch) diameter stainless steel lane
4 15 mm (3/5 inch) laminated glass

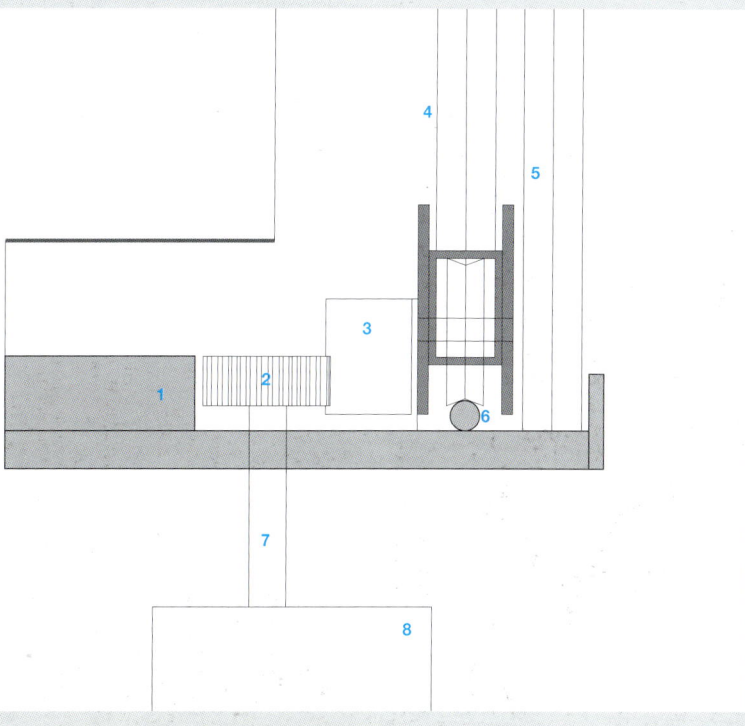

10.09
Sliding Door Detail 2
1:2
1 Timber blocking
2 Gear wheel
3 Connector zip
4 Glass support and stainless steel window assembly
5 Laminated glass sliding door
6 8 mm (1/3 inch) diameter stainless steel lane
7 Axle
8 Motor

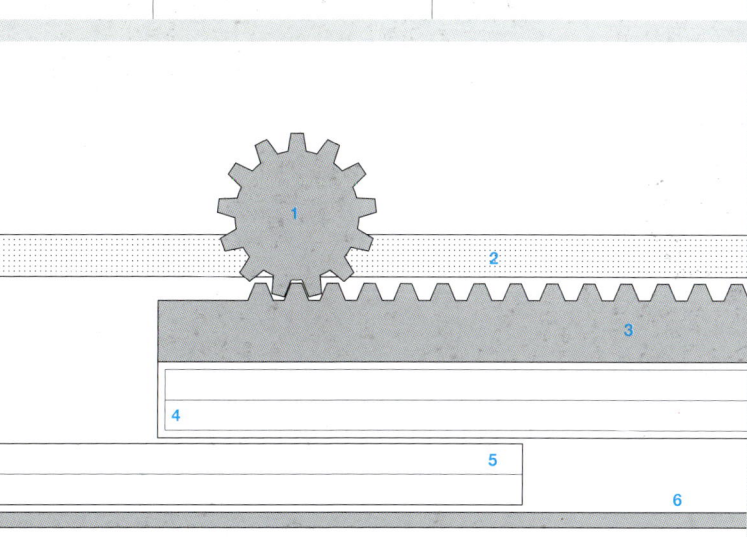

10.10
Sliding Door Detail 3
1:2
1 Gear wheel
2 Line of floor beyond
3 Connector zip
4 Laminated glass (moving part)
5 Laminated glass (fixed part)
6 25 x 4 mm (1 x 1/5 inch) steel sheet exterior wall finish

Rose House
Saddleback Mountain, Kiama, NSW, Australia

Client
Peter and Maria Rose

Area
218 square metres (2,350 square feet)

Project Team
Ian Moore, Dua Cox, Claire Meller, Sterrin O'Shea

Structural Engineer
Peter Chan and Partners

Geotechnical Engineer
Cottier + Associates

Builder
Phillip C. Young

Located south of Sydney on the southern face of Saddleback Mountain, this family house enjoys dramatic views in all directions. In order to maximize the views and minimize the impact of building on a steep slope, the house has been sited on a gentle slope, centred on a north–south ridge to take advantage of an almost symmetrical fall to both east and west. The simple rectangular plan is divided into three equal zones, separated by service cores. The central kitchen, living and dining area is flanked by bedroom, bathroom and dressing areas for the parents at one end and two children's bedrooms, each with ensuite bathroom, at the other.

By centralizing the living spaces and pulling the service cores back from the external envelope, views are opened up in all directions. Verandahs run the length of the house on both long facades, providing sun protection to the full height glass walls. The glass doors to the living space slide completely away, opening up the whole house and providing exceptional cross ventilation. In order to minimize the impact of the structure on the pristine mountain site, a lightweight steel structure consisting of two vierendeel trusses runs the length of the house, sitting on two reinforced concrete block store rooms that provide the primary bracing to the structure. The trusses allow the building to cantilever to the east and west, further emphasizng the impression of a light-weight structure.

1 A canopy broaches the gap between the carport and the house, where sliding glass doors and a panel of glass louvres bring south light into the interior.
2 The south facade consists of full width glazing, allowing indirect south light, and ventilation via the operable louvres, into the house.
3 Night view of the dining and living room at the centre of the house. Electrically operated blinds preserve privacy.
4 During the day the blinds are reduced to a minimal strip above the windows, and the fully glazed north and south facades open up to the views.

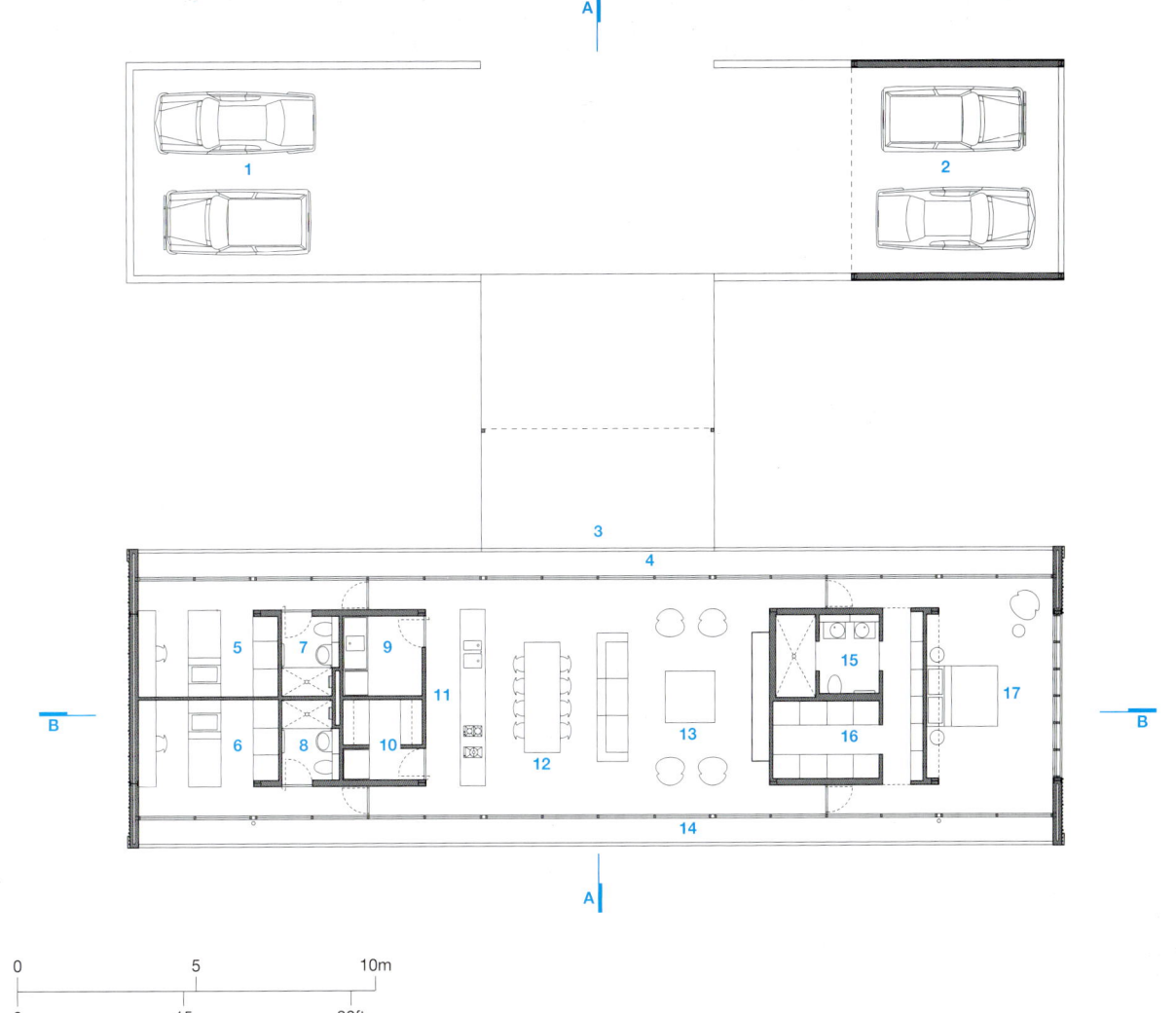

11.01
Floor Plan
1:200
1 Visitor car parking
2 Carport
3 Entrance
4 Terrace
5 Bedroom 1
6 Bedroom 2
7 Bathroom 1
8 Bathroom 2
9 Laundry
10 Pantry
11 Kitchen
12 Dining room
13 Living room
14 Terrace
15 Master bathroom
16 Dressing room
17 Master bedroom

0 ——— 5 ——— 10m
0 ——— 15 ——— 30ft

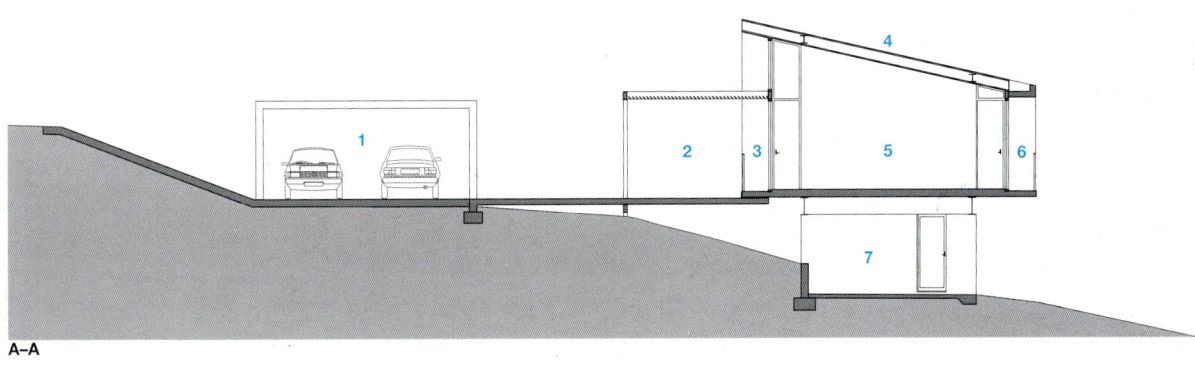

A–A

11.02
Section A–A
1:200
1 Carport
2 Entrance
3 Terrace
4 Steel-framed metal sheet roof
5 Living room
6 Terrace
7 Basement store

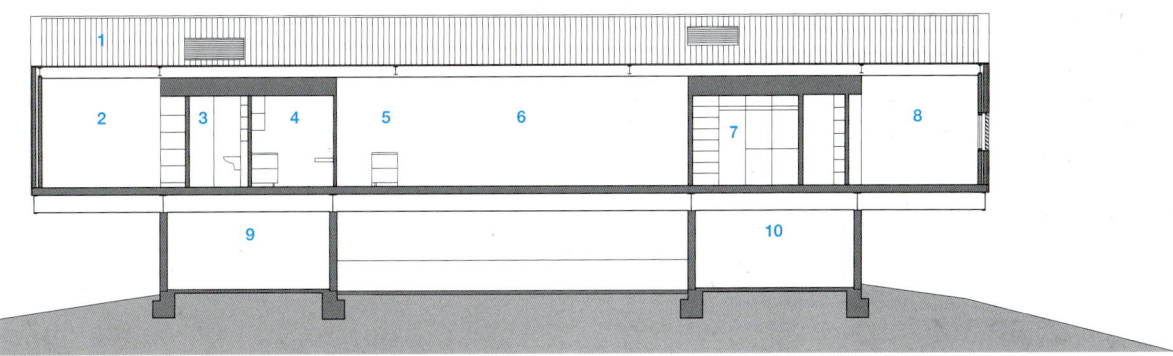

B–B

11.03
Section B–B
1:200
1 Steel-framed metal sheet roof
2 Bedroom
3 Bathroom
4 Pantry
5 Kitchen
6 Living room
7 Dressing room
8 Master bedoom
9 Basement store
10 Basement store

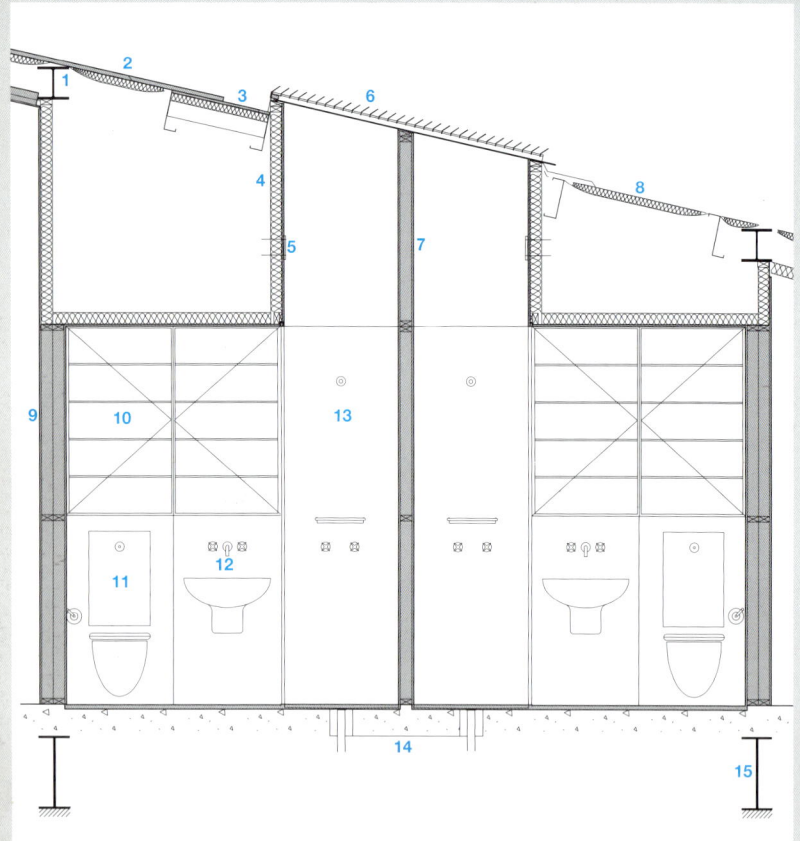

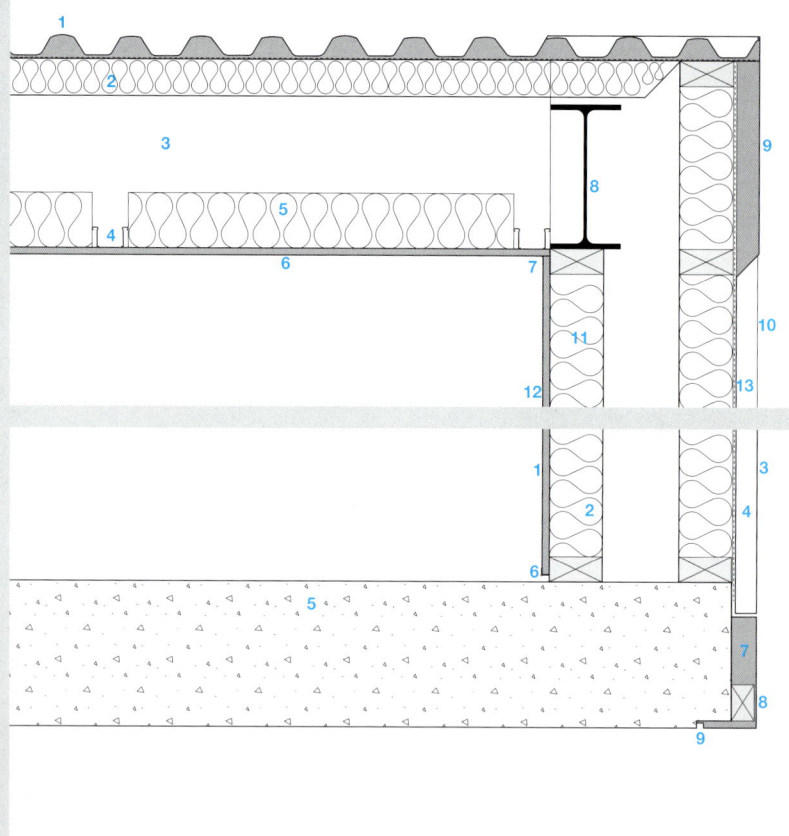

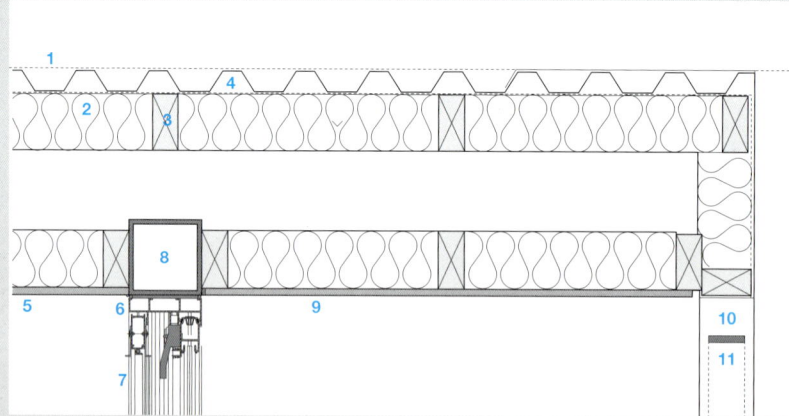

11.04
Bathroom Section
Detail
1:50
 1 Steel beam
 2 50 mm (2 inch)
insulation blanket with
double-sided
aluminium foil sarking
 3 Gutter
 4 75 mm (3 inch)
thick insulation batts
between studs and
ceiling frame
 5 Exhaust fan
 6 Skylight with
aluminium louvres
 7 Plasterboard wall
 8 Metal deck roof
 9 Plasterboard wall
10 Mirrored cabinet
with glass shelves
11 Wall hung WC with
concealed cistern
behind
12 Wall hung basin
13 Aluminium cladding
panel
14 Concrete floor
15 Steel beam

11.05
Roof Cladding Detail
1:10
 1 Longspan roof
sheeting
 2 50 mm (2 inch)
insulation blanket
 3 250 mm (10 inch) Z-
purlin
 4 Rondo 129 furring
channel at 450 mm (18
inch) centres
 5 75 mm (3 inch)
thick insulation batts
 6 10 mm (1/3 inch)
thick plasterboard
 7 Rondo P157
 8 200 mm (8 inch)
universal beam
 9 Armour grey steel
sheet capping
10 Long span cladding
11 75 mm (3 inch)
thick insulation batts
12 10 mm (1/3 inch)
thick plasterboard
13 Building paper

11.06
Wall Cladding Detail 1
1:10
 1 10 mm (1/3 inch)
thick plasterboard
 2 75 mm (3 inch)
thick insulation batts
 3 Long span cladding
 4 Building paper
 5 Concrete screed
 6 Rondo P50
 7 Armour grey sheet
steel cladding
 8 Timber framing
 9 10 mm (1/3 inch)
drip groove

11.07
Wall Cladding Detail 2
1:10
 1 Stramit long span
cladding
 2 75 mm (3 inch)
thick insulation batts
 3 Timber stud
 4 Building paper
 5 10 mm (1/3 inch)
thick plasterboard
 6 Aluminium window
frame
 7 Flyscreen
 8 100 x 100 x 6 mm
(4 x 4 x 1/4 inch) square
steel section
 9 Fibre cement sheet
10 50 x 12 mm (2 x 1/2
inch) flat steel bar
11 150 x 75 mm (6 x 3
inch) steel channel

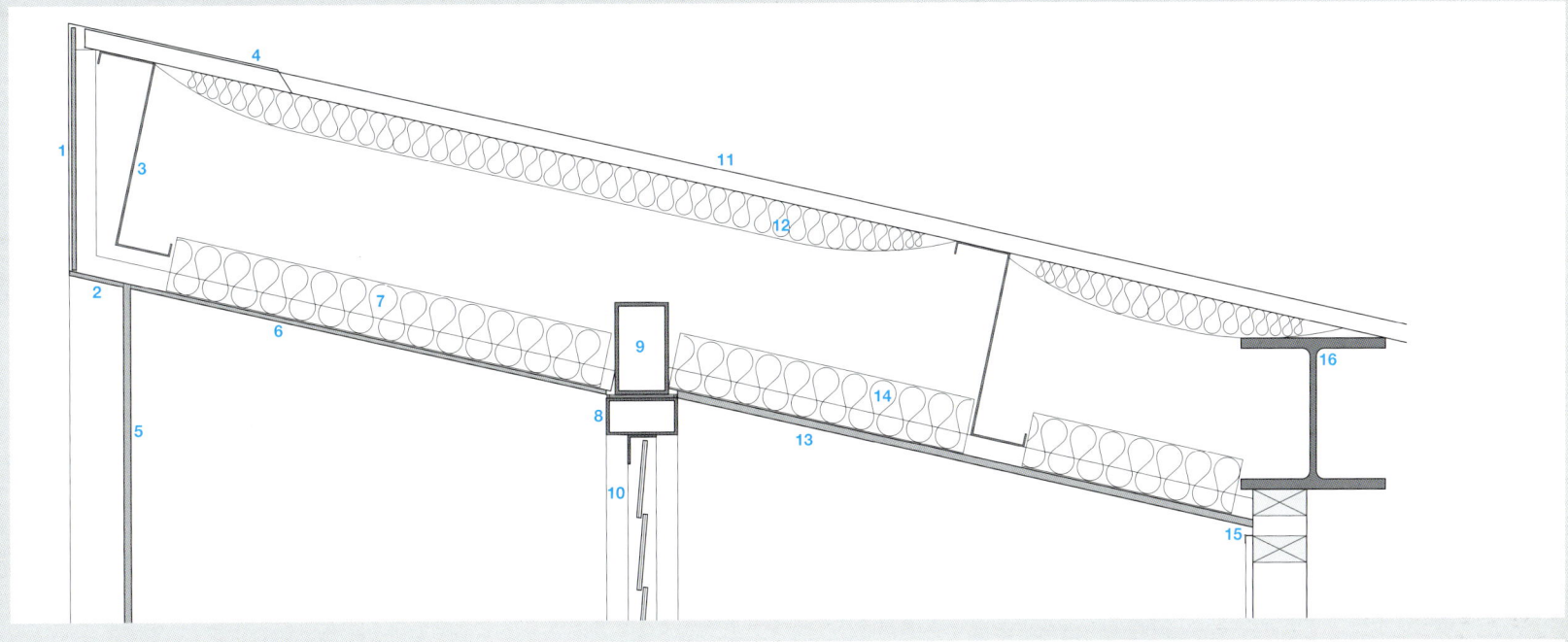

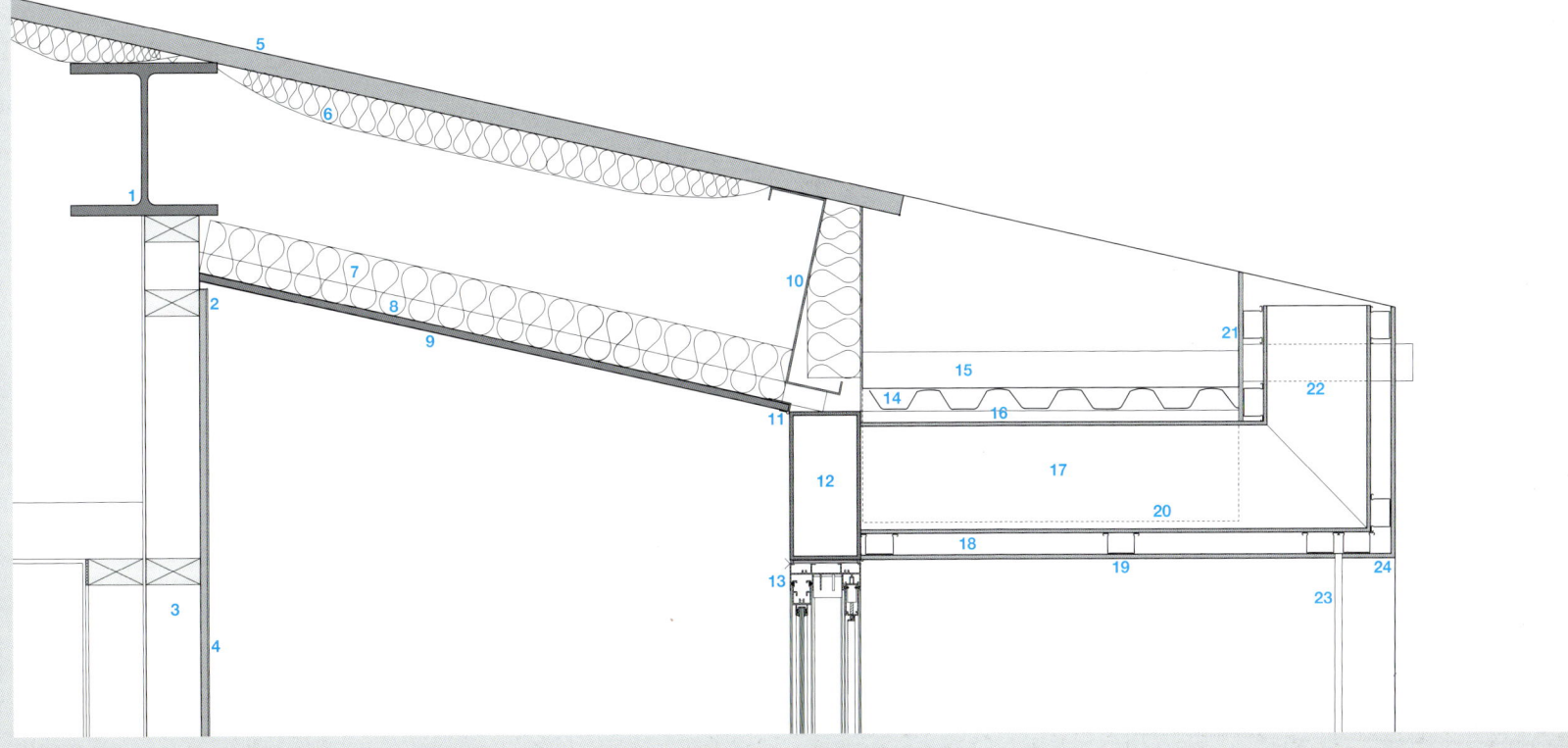

11.08
Eave Detail
1:10
 1 Glass fibre cement fascia
 2 Armour grey steel sheet fascia capping
 3 250 mm (10 inch) Z-purlin
 4 Armour grey steel sheet folded fascia capping
 5 10 mm (1/3 inch) shadow line
 6 Glass fibre cement soffit lining
 7 Rondo 129 furring channel at 450 mm (18 inch) centres
 8 Aluminium window frame
 9 125 x 75 x 5 mm (5 x 3 x 1/4 inch)

rectangular steel section
10 Glass louvres
11 Stramit long span roof sheeting
12 50 mm (2 inch) thick insulation blanket
13 10 mm (1/3 inch) thick plasterboard
14 75 mm (3 inch) thick insulation batts
15 Rondo P50 channel
16 200 mm (8 inch) steel beam

11.09
Box Gutter Detail
1:10
 1 200 mm (8 inch) steel beam
 2 Rondo P50
 3 Steel stud
 4 10 mm (1/3 inch) thick plasterboard
 5 Stramit long span roof sheeting
 6 50 mm (2 inch) thick insulation blanket with double-sided aluminium foil sarking
 7 75 mm (3 inch) thick insulation batts
 8 Rondo 129 furring channel
 9 10 mm (1/3 inch) thick plasterboard
10 250 mm (10 inch) Z-purlin

11 Rondo P12 stopping bead
12 200 x 100 mm (8 x 4 inch) rectangular steel section
13 Aluminium sliding door
14 Stramit long span gutter support
15 Armour grey Colorbond sheet steel box gutter lining
16 Packer to suit fall
17 150 mm (6 inch) steel outrigger
18 Fibre cement sheet soffit lining
19 Rondo 129 furring channel
20 Line of sump
21 Armour grey Colorbond sheet steel box gutter lining

22 300 x 50 mm (12 x 2 inch) overflows from sumps
23 10 mm (1/3 inch) shadow line
24 Armour grey folded steel sheet capping

Small House
Tokyo, Japan

Area
77 square metres (830 square feet)

Structural Engineer
Sasaki Structural Consultants

This tiny house is located in the centre of Tokyo and has been designed for a family consisting of a single parent and three children. The client requested a terrace, a bathroom, spacious living and dining areas, bedrooms and family room. It was also important for the family to be able to engage, via the house, with the landscape outside. With a very limited site, the architect first determined how much space would be needed for the function of each room, so that each space would have a different character. The spatial and formal response was to pile up four different volumes, rather than carving up a single homogenous volume. After the stacking process, connections were made between the floors, which are all out of alignment, to create the exterior form. This overall volume was then adjusted to allow for car parking, to create a suitable level of privacy from neighbours, and to manipulate the position of the core of spiral stairs according to the uses on each floor.

The house also embraces the different relationships between inside and outside. The angle of the outside walls, for example, which is determined by the floor plan and ceiling height, opens upward towards the sky, and downward like an observatory to take in views of the neighbour's cherry blossom tree. Because each room is small and independent, relationships with the outside have a significant effect on the interior. By shifting the centre of gravity of each room, each floor benefits from different distances from the exterior and from the spiral stairs. Thus, various places for play, work and general domestic activities are able to develop naturally throughout the house. As a result, comfort and enjoyment are brought about through the very smallness of the house.

1 A view at dusk reveals the difference in floor-plate dimensions and ceiling heights between the four levels of the house, generated to accommodate different functions and to create varying spaces for use by the members of the family.
2 On the street facade, panels of aluminium and sheets of translucent glass protect the family's privacy while allowing natural light into the interior spaces.
3 The steel-framed stair, fabricated from folded steel plate, comprises the centre of gravity for the house, linking all four small levels.

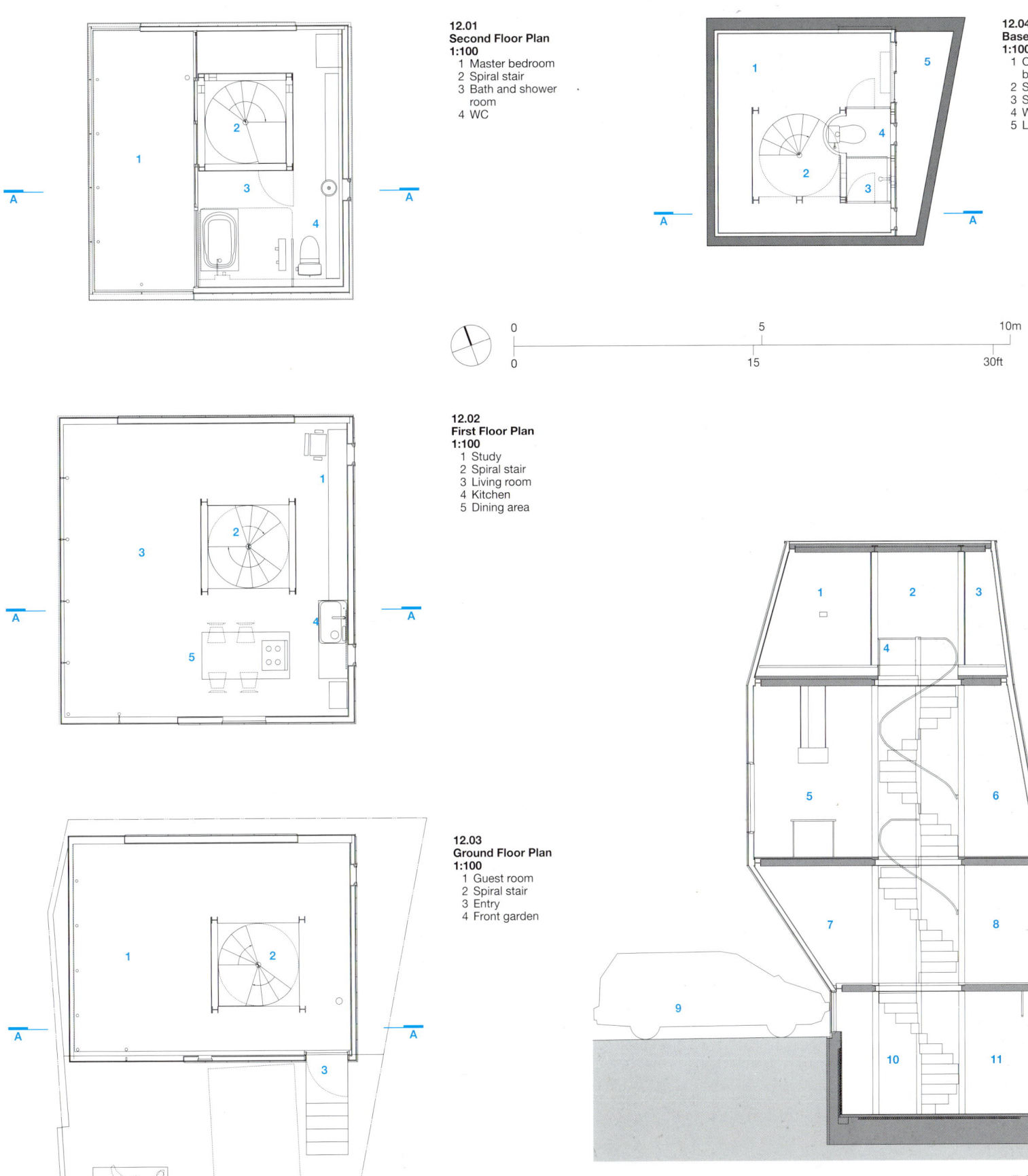

12.01
Second Floor Plan
1:100
1 Master bedroom
2 Spiral stair
3 Bath and shower room
4 WC

12.04
Basement Floor Plan
1:100
1 Children's bedroom
2 Spiral stair
3 Shower
4 WC
5 Light well

12.02
First Floor Plan
1:100
1 Study
2 Spiral stair
3 Living room
4 Kitchen
5 Dining area

12.03
Ground Floor Plan
1:100
1 Guest room
2 Spiral stair
3 Entry
4 Front garden

12.05
Section A–A
1:100
1 Master bedroom
2 Stairwell
3 WC
4 Spiral stair
5 Living room
6 Kitchen
7 Guest room
8 Guest room
9 Car parking
10 Children's bedroom
11 Shower
12 Light well

0   5   10m
0   15   30ft

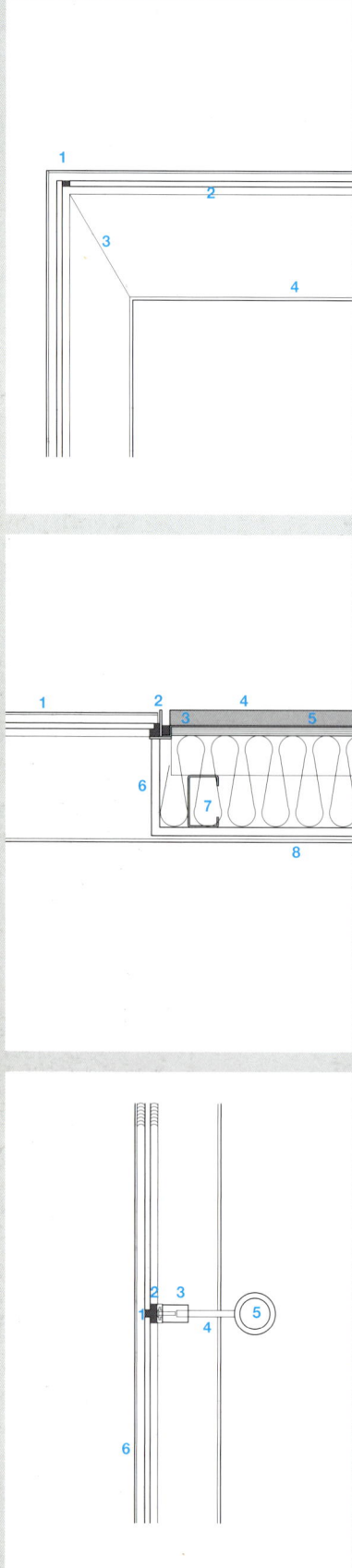

12.06
Exterior Corner Wall Detail
1:10
1 Silicon seal
2 8 mm (1/3 inch) glass in PVC frame
3 Steel frame
4 Steel plate sill to floor edge

12.08
Glazing Detail 2
1:10
1 8 mm (1/3 inch) glass in PVC frame
2 38 mm (1 1/2 inch) stainless steel glass frame
3 Silicone seal
4 Galvanized and aluminium coated sheet steel flashing
5 Exterior wall comprised of galvanized and aluminiuim coated sheet steel roofing, asphalt roofing and 12 mm (1/2 inch) structural plywood board
6 Timber sill
7 Steel channel wall framing
8 Interior wall comprised of 12.5 mm (1/2 inch) plasterboard with synthetic resin paint finish and 130 mm (5 1/10 inch) glass wool thermal insulation

12.10
Glazing Detail 4
1:10
1 Silicone seal
2 Silicone gasket
3 38 mm (1 1/5 inch) steel flat mullion with synthetic resin paint finish
4 38 mm (1 1/5 inch) steel flat with synthetic resin paint finish at 500 mm (19 2/3 inch) centres
5 60.5 mm (2 4/5 inch) diameter tubular steel column with synthetic resin paint finish
6 8 mm (1/3 inch) glass in PVC frame

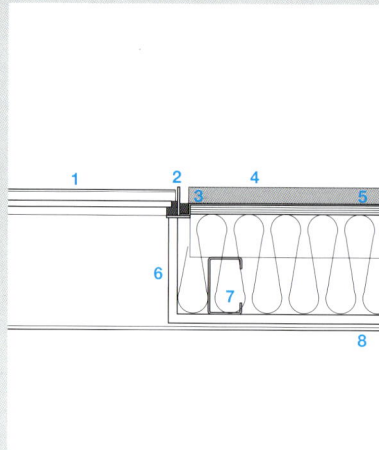

12.07
Glazing Detail 1
1:10
1 8 mm (1/3 inch) glass in PVC frame
2 38 mm (1 1/2 inch) stainless steel glass frame
3 Silicone seal
4 Galvanized and aluminium coated sheet steel flashing
5 Exterior wall comprised of galvanized and aluminium coated sheet steel roofing, asphalt roofing and 12 mm (1/2 inch) structural plywood board
6 Timber frame
7 Steel channel wall framing
8 Interior wall comprised of 12.5 mm (1/2 inch) plasterboard with synthetic resin paint finish and 130 mm (5 1/10 inch) glass wool thermal insulation

12.09
Glazing Detail 3
1:10
1 8 mm (1/3 inch) glass in PVC frame
2 47 mm (1 3/4 inch) steel flat with synthetic resin paint finish
3 Silicone seal
4 45 mm (1 3/4 inch) stainless steel glass frame
5 6 mm (1/5 inch) stainless steel dead load support
6 Glass frame with synthetic resin paint finish
7 H-section steel beam with synthetic resin paint finish

12.11
Glazing Detail 5
1:10
1 Silicon seal
2 8 mm (1/3 inch) glass in PVC frame
3 Steel frame
4 Steel plate sill to floor edge

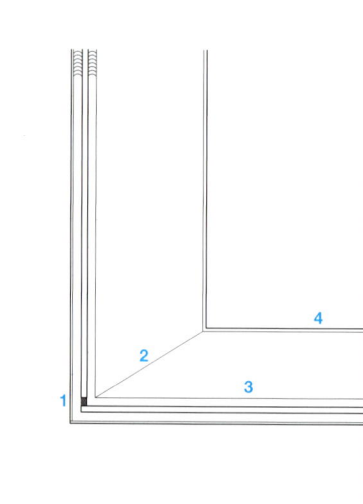

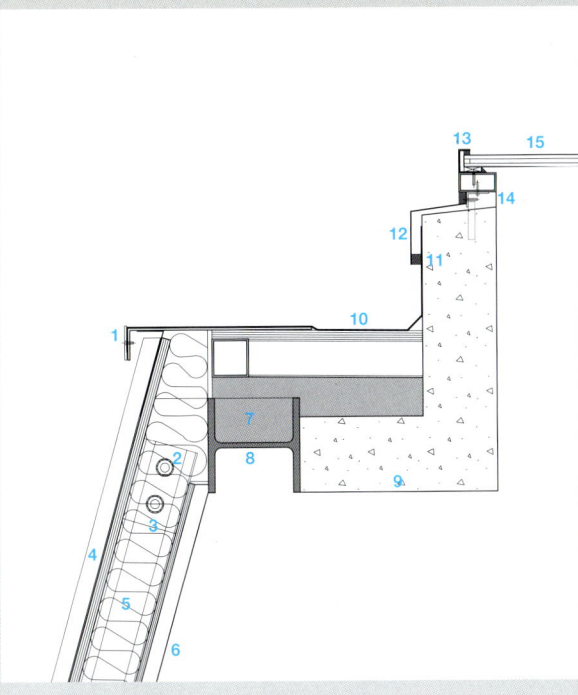

12.12
Parapet Detail
1:10
  1 45 mm (1³/₄ inch) aluminium flat
  2 9 mm (1/3 inch) steel gusset plate
  3 9 mm (1/3 inch) diameter high tension bolt
  4 Exterior wall comprised of galvanized and aluminium coated sheet steel roofing, asphalt roofing and 12 mm (1/2 inch) structural plywood board
  5 Insulation
  6 Interior wall comprised of 20 mm (3/4 inch) waterproof mortar with synthetic resin paint finish, timber lathe board and 75 mm (3 inch) glass wool thermal insulation
  7 9 mm (1/3 inch) steel stiffener
  8 Steel H-section beam with synthetic resin paint finish
  9 Exposed concrete
  10 Roof comprised of vulcanized rubber membrane waterproofing, 12 mm (1/2 inch) plywood board and 40 mm (1¹/₂ inch) thermal insulation
  11 Silicone seal
  12 Galvanized and aluminium coated sheet flashing
  13 Aluminium glazing frame
  14 Mortar joint
  15 Glazing

12.13
Exterior Wall Detail
1:10
  1 Exterior wall comprised of galvanized and aluminium coated sheet steel roofing, asphalt roofing and 12 mm (1/2 inch) structural plywood board
  2 Floor comprised of floating timber boards with corrosion-proof treatment, waterproof mortar, waterproof membrane, light-weight concrete and 12 mm (1/2 inch) structural plywood board
  3 Galvanized and aluminium coated sheet flashing
  4 Steel gusset plate
  5 9 mm (1/3 inch) diameter high tension bolt
  6 Interior wall comprised of 20 mm (3/4 inch) waterproof mortar with synthetic resin paint finish, timber lathe board and glass wool thermal insulation
  7 9 mm (1/3 inch) steel stiffener
  8 Steel H-section beam with synthetic resin paint finish
  9 Exposed concrete

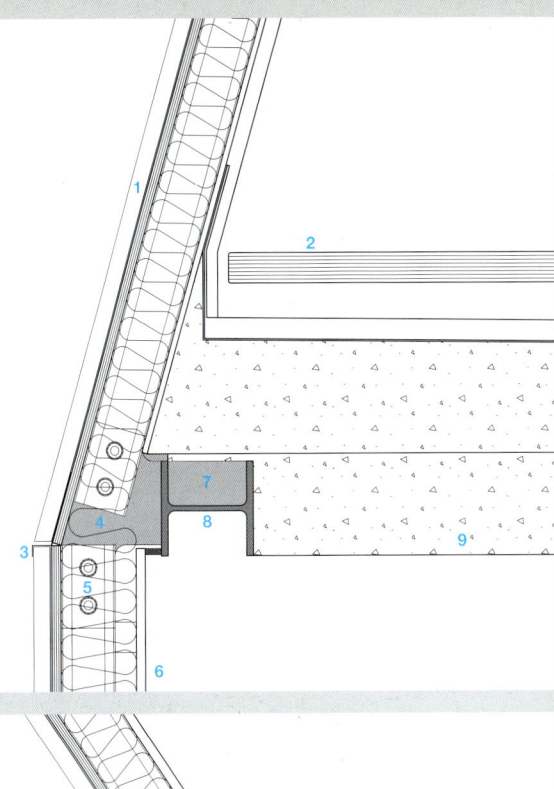

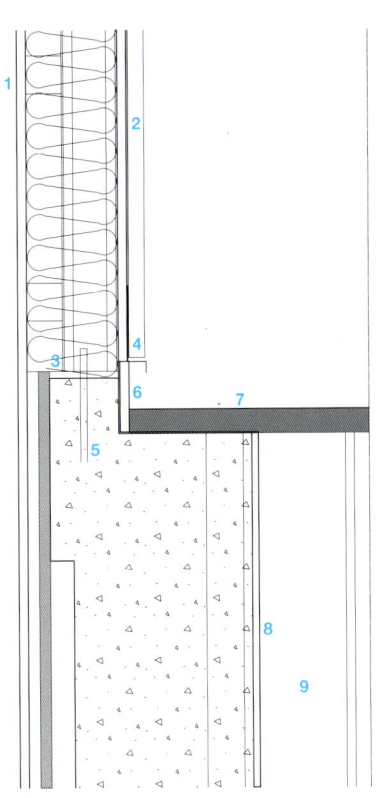

12.14
Retaining Wall Detail
1:10
  1 Interior wall comprised of 20 mm (3/4 inch) waterproof mortar with synthetic resin paint finish, timber lathe board and glass wool thermal insulation
  2 Exterior wall comprised of galvanized and aluminium coated sheet steel roofing, asphalt roofing and 12 mm (1/2 inch) structural plywood board
  3 9 mm (1/3 inch) steel anchor plate
  4 Galvanized and aluminium coated sheet flashing
  5 9 mm (1/3 inch) steel anchor bolt
  6 Waterproof mortar
  7 Paving stone floor with waterproof membrane coating
  8 Sheet pile
  9 Steel H-section retaining wall

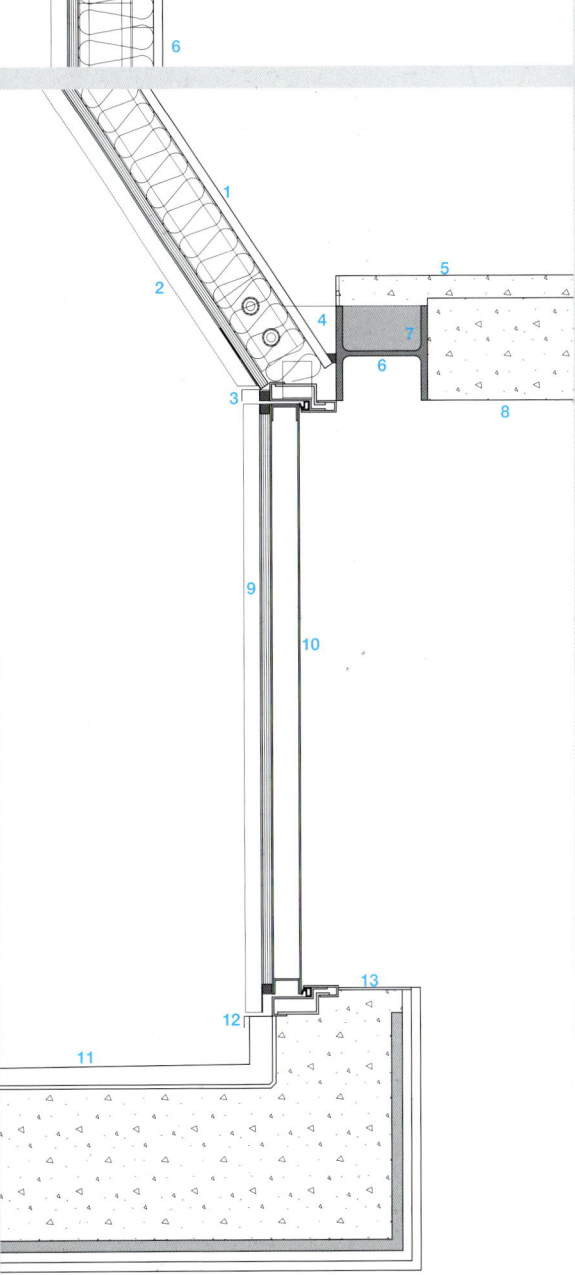

12.15
Window Detail
1:10
  1 Interior walll comprised of 20 mm (3/4 inch) waterproof mortar with synthetic resin paint finish, timber lathe board and 75 mm (3 inch) glass wool thermal insulation
  2 Exterior wall comprised of galvanized and aluminium coated sheet steel roofing, asphalt roofing and 12 mm (1/2 inch) structural plywood board
  3 Galvanized and aluminium coated sheet flashing
  4 9 mm (1/3 inch) steel gusset plate
  5 30 mm (1¹/₅ inch) self-levelling mortar floor
  6 Steel H-section beam with synthetic resin paint finish
  7 9 mm (1/3 inch) steel stiffener
  8 Exposed concrete
  9 Exterior wall finish comprised of galvanized and aluminium coated sheet steel roofing, asphalt roofing and 12 mm (1/2 inch) structural plywood board
  10 40 mm (1¹/₂ inch) flush steel window with synthetic resin paint finish
  11 Waterproof mortar to floor with waterproof membrane coating
  12 Galvanized and aluminium coated flashing
  13 Cement plastering with synthetic resin paint finish
  14 12.5 mm (1/2 inch) plasterboard with synthetic resin paint finish

13
Kruunenberg Van der Erve

Laminata, House of Glass
Leerdam, The Netherlands

Client
CWL Koopwoningen

Area
400 square metres (4,305 square feet)

Glass Consultant
Saint-Gobain Glass Netherlands

Structural Consultant
Van Rijn Partners

Main Contractor
Radix + Veerman

This project was an initiative of the Leerdam housing association which sponsored a competition to explore new ways of using glass in construction. The resulting house totally redefines the use of glass as a building material. The concept involved a massive rectangular block formed by 2,000 sheets of plate glass. In reality, the construction involved pre-cutting to size 13,000 sheets of glass, then painstakingly cleaning and gluing each plate into place on site. The resulting massive walls of laminated glass rest on a concrete structure, with a plywood roof resting on top.

Extensive research was carried out to investigate the suitability of glass as a primary building material. Although the glass itself is naturally brittle, this inflexibility is countered by a special two-component silicon glue that is UV-resistant and permanently flexible. Despite its apparent delicacy, the laminated glass is as strong as concrete. To address environmental concerns, the massive glass walls, combined with a central floor-heating system, are capable of economically maintaining a constant temperature in winter and are thick enough to absorb and dissipate summer heat without transferring it to the interior. Programmatically, a meandering cut through the massive block of glass organises the house, creating a central hallway with living spaces and secondary spaces hollowed out of the masses on either side. More private rooms are accommodated in a concrete base, while a private courtyard in the centre extends through both levels, bringing in natural light and fresh air.

1 From afar the house appears as a conventional domestic structure, however on closer inspection, all of the slightly reflective external wall surfaces are the result of the thin ends of the laminated glass panels, which together form the facades.
2 Detail view of an interior wall – timber doors, concrete floors and clear glazing contrast with the walls of laminated glass.
3 Slots of clear glazing are set into the laminated walls to provide carefully framed views out over the landscape.
4 The central corridor is apparently carved out of a massive block of glass. The mass of glass allows finely filtered light into the centre of the house.

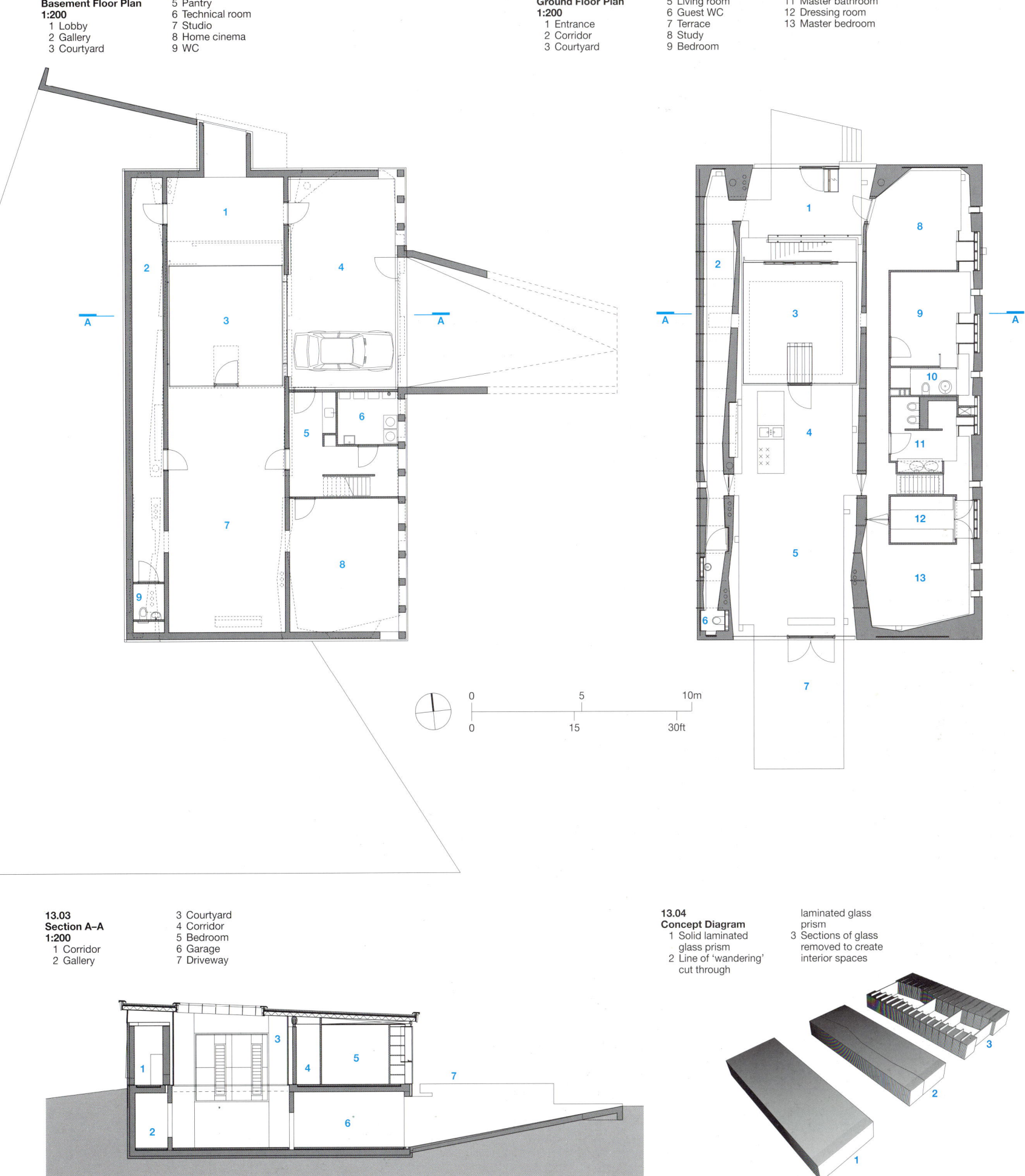

13.01
Basement Floor Plan
1:200
1 Lobby
2 Gallery
3 Courtyard
4 Garage
5 Pantry
6 Technical room
7 Studio
8 Home cinema
9 WC

13.02
Ground Floor Plan
1:200
1 Entrance
2 Corridor
3 Courtyard
4 Kitchen
5 Living room
6 Guest WC
7 Terrace
8 Study
9 Bedroom
10 Bathroom
11 Master bathroom
12 Dressing room
13 Master bedroom

13.03
Section A–A
1:200
1 Corridor
2 Gallery
3 Courtyard
4 Corridor
5 Bedroom
6 Garage
7 Driveway

13.04
Concept Diagram
1 Solid laminated glass prism
2 Line of 'wandering' cut through
laminated glass prism
3 Sections of glass removed to create interior spaces

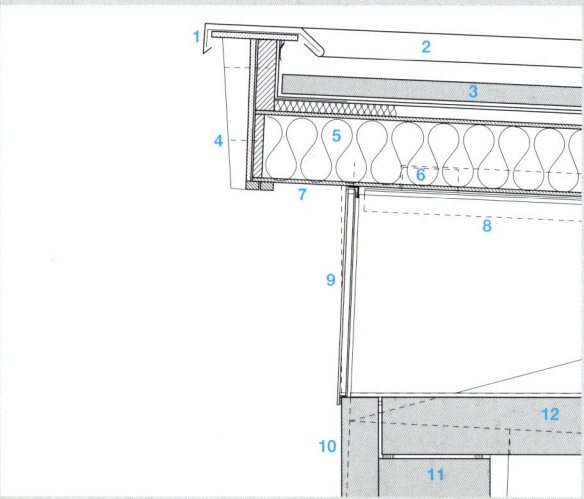

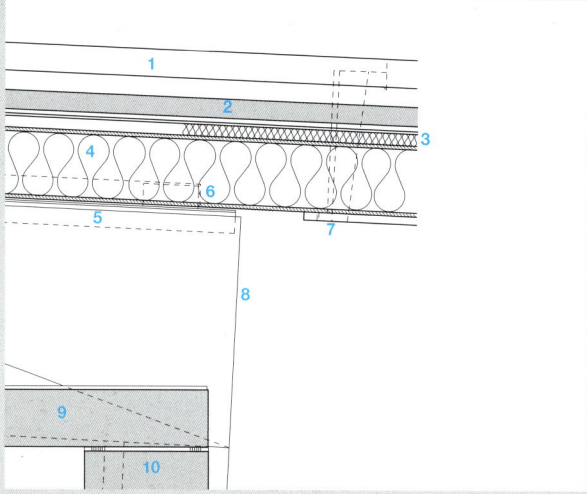

13.05
Roof and External Wall Detail 1
1:20
 1 Zinc capping to roof edge
 2 Zinc capping
 3 Ballast layer of gravel
 4 Western red cedar support
 5 Insulation
 6 Anodized aluminium roof anchor
 7 Timber stressed skin panels

 8 Roof support of prefabricated structural float glass
 9 Structural glazed isolation glass
 10 Layers of 10 mm (2/5 inch) laminated structural float glass
 11 Layers of 10 mm (2/5 inch) laminated structural float glass
 12 Layers of 10 mm (2/5 inch) laminated structural float glass

13.06
Roof and External Wall Detail 2
1:20
 1 Zinc capping
 2 Ballast layer of gravel
 3 Insulation with integral electrical installation
 4 Insulation
 5 Anodized aluminium roof anchor
 6 Anodized aluminium roof anchor
 7 Roof edge to

courtyard
 8 Roof support of prefabricated structural float glass
 9 Layers of 10 mm (2/5 inch) laminated structural float glass
 10 Layers of 10 mm (2/5 inch) laminated structural float glass

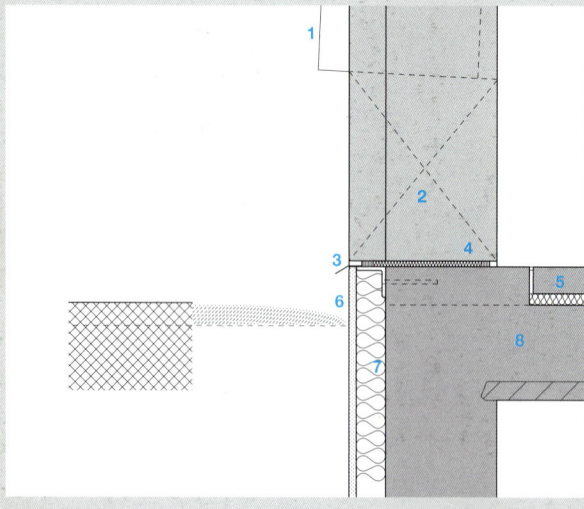

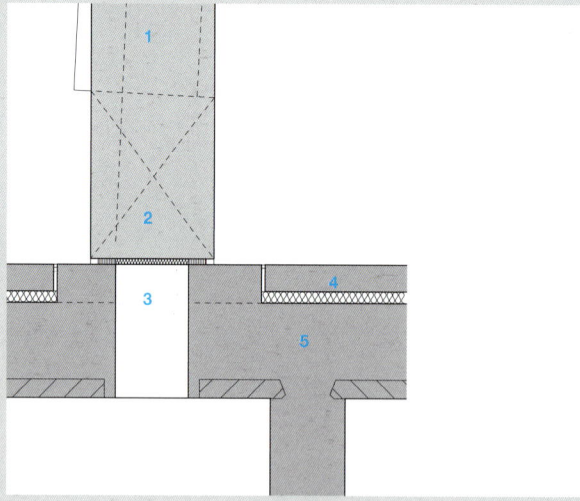

13.07
Glazing and Concrete Detail at Ground Floor
1:20
 1 Prefabricated structural float glass in line with roof support
 2 Coloured float glass filling
 3 Anodized aluminium profile
 4 80 x 80 x 10 mm (31/10 x 31/10 x 2/5 inch) Inox profile
 5 Underfloor heating

 6 Stucco finished facade isolation
 7 80 mm (3 inch) insulation
 8 250 mm (94/5 inch) reinforced concrete slab

13.08
Glazing Detail at Ground Floor
1:20
 1 Layers of 10 mm (2/5 inch) laminated structural float glass
 2 Coloured float glass filling
 3 Opening to provide daylight to basement
 4 Underfloor heating
 5 250 mm (94/5 inch) thick reinforced concrete

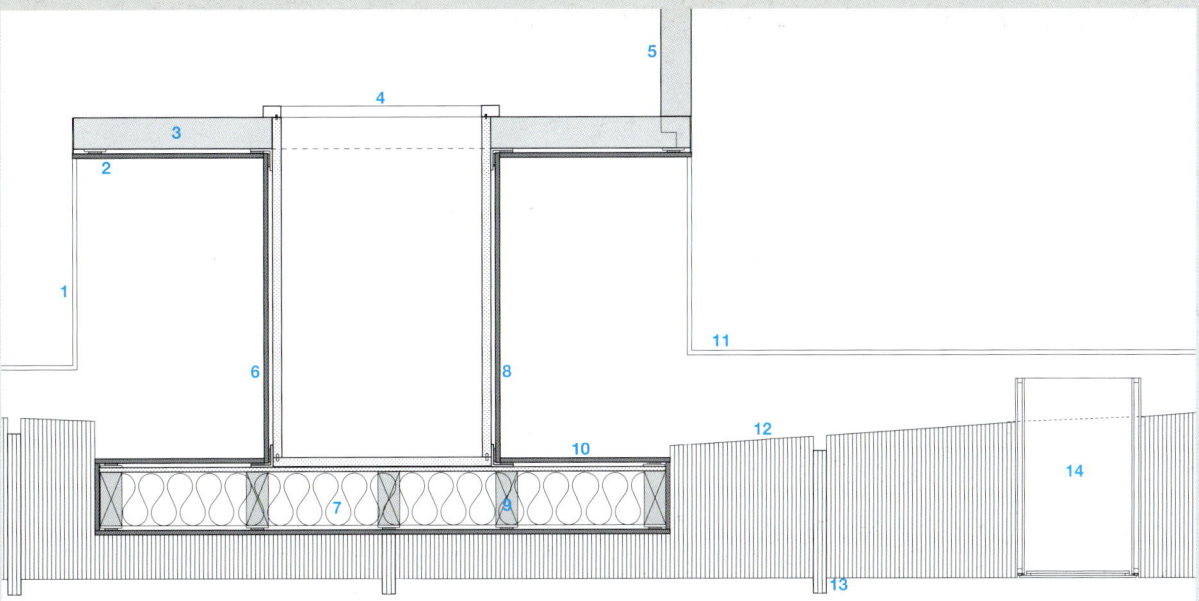

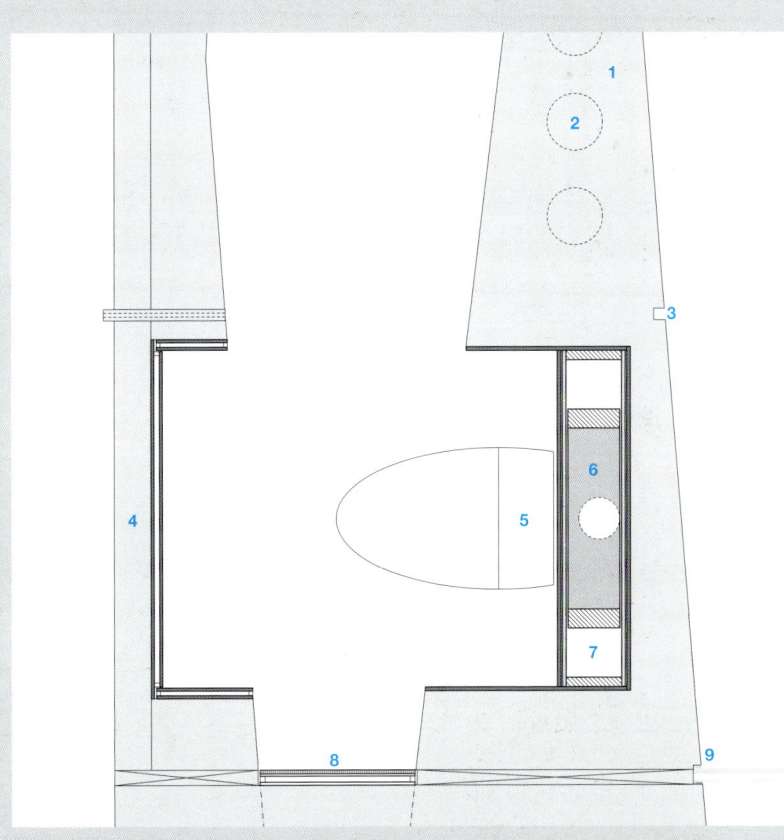

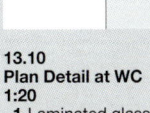

Picture Window House
Shizuoka Prefecture, Japan

Area
274 square metres (2,950 square feet)

Project Team
Shigeru Ban, Nobutaka Hiraga, Jun Yashiki

Structural Engineer
Hoshino Architect and Engineer

Main Contractor
Daido Kogyo

Located 96 kilometres (60 miles) south of Tokyo on the Izu Peninsula, this family house enjoys the rare commodity of open views of the sea and sky. Taking the desire to open the house as much as possible to uninterrupted views of the Pacific Ocean, the entire house, in effect, becomes an enormous window. The ground floor consists of a huge open volume containing the living room, dining room and kitchen. Here, large glass doors on both long facades slide open on tracks recessed into the floor, and stack away at either end to create an integral indoor-outdoor space.

On the first floor is a double-height studio at one end of the long bar and a storage area at the other. In between are four bedrooms with floor to ceiling windows overlooking the sea. Behind the bedrooms, along the north elevation, is an uncommonly long bathroom that also acts as a circulation space to the sleeping areas. The bathroom contains a bathtub, two toilets and five sinks, with only glass doors separating the three areas within the whole. One area contains a sink, tub and toilet, another larger space with three sinks, and a third with a toilet and sink. The material palette consists primarily of white-painted steel and glass. The steel structure functions as a bridge, with the braced two-storey spaces on either end anchoring the column-free span of the bedrooms and living area. Diagonal steel bracing is visible in front of the bedroom windows. On the first floor, large banks of aluminium louvres accentuate the horizontal lines of the house, but can be retracted to create a completely transparent facade.

1 The living room on the lower level is protected from the sun by a large cantilevered awning. Both sides of the space open completely – one side to the forest and the other to the sea. The diagonal bracing is visible on the upper level across the run of bedrooms that also overlook the sea.
2 View of the main living space where the timber floor extends out onto the deck. The full-height glass doors slide away and stack at either end of the space.

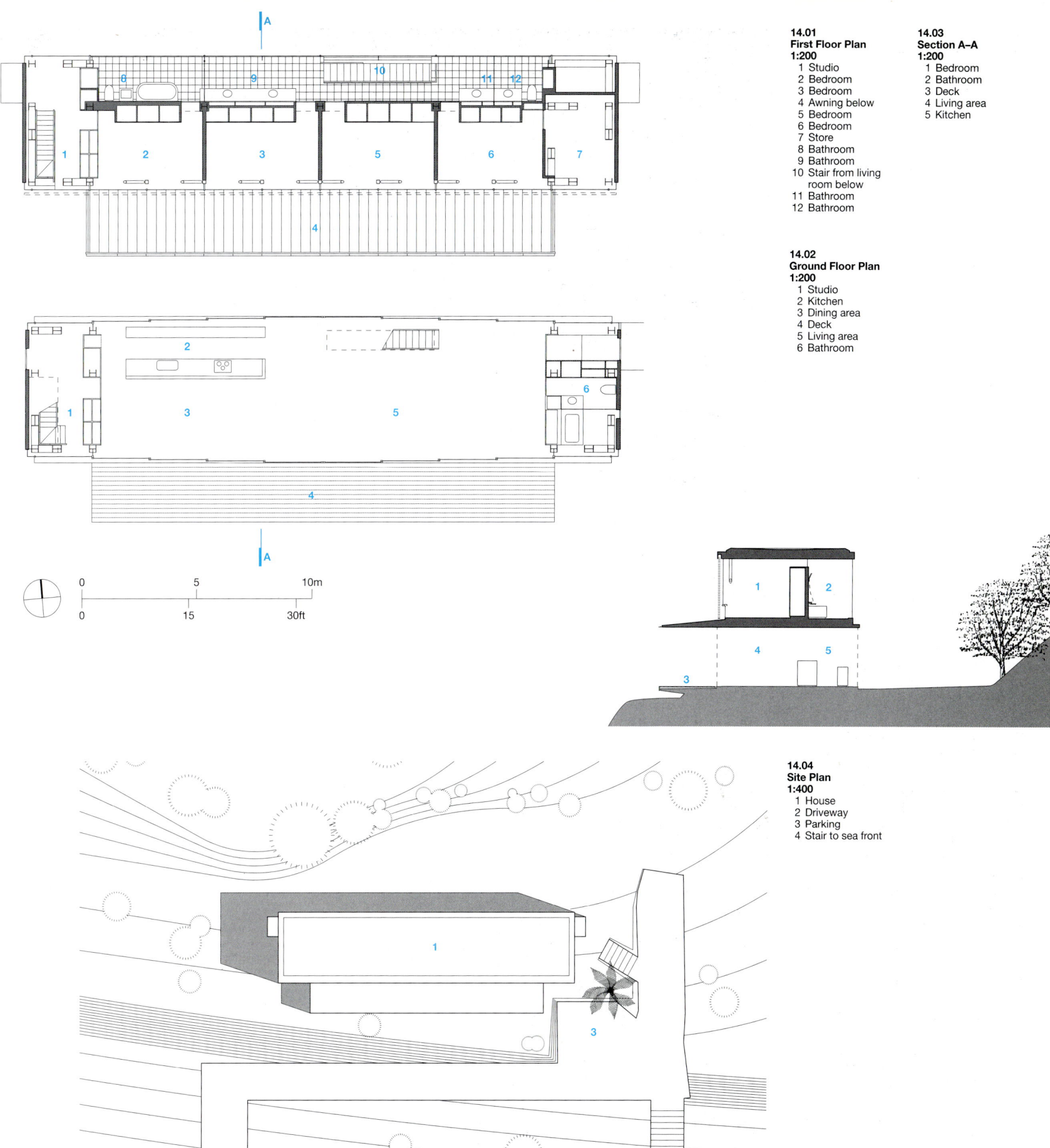

14.01
First Floor Plan
1:200
1 Studio
2 Bedroom
3 Bedroom
4 Awning below
5 Bedroom
6 Bedroom
7 Store
8 Bathroom
9 Bathroom
10 Stair from living
   room below
11 Bathroom
12 Bathroom

14.03
Section A–A
1:200
1 Bedroom
2 Bathroom
3 Deck
4 Living area
5 Kitchen

14.02
Ground Floor Plan
1:200
1 Studio
2 Kitchen
3 Dining area
4 Deck
5 Living area
6 Bathroom

14.04
Site Plan
1:400
1 House
2 Driveway
3 Parking
4 Stair to sea front

14.05
Glazing Detail 1
1:5
1 Aluminium external blind
2 Aluminium frame to blind assembly
3 Double sliding aluminium window
4 Threshold
5 60 x 60 mm (2¹/₃ x 2¹/₃ inch) square hollow section
6 Steel L-angle
7 Roller blind box
8 Glabellum sheet steel cladding
9 60 x 60 mm (2¹/₃ x 2¹/₃ inch) square hollow section
10 Double sliding aluminium window
11 Steel L-angle
12 12 mm (¹/₂ inch) thick cherry parquet flooring
13 300 x 300 mm (11³/₄ inch x 11³/₄ inch) steel I-beam
14 Steel connecting plate
15 Insulation
16 130 mm (5¹/₄ inch) concrete slab
17 8 mm (¹/₃ inch) thick flexible board ceiling

14.06
Glazing Detail 2
1:5
1 Glabellum sheet steel cladding
2 Threshold
3 Double sliding aluminium window
4 Fixed glass
5 Aluminium sash
6 Steel L-angle
7 Structural steel section
8 150 x 150 mm (6 x 6 inch) porcelain tiles
9 130 mm (5¹/₄ inch) concrete slab
10 250 x 120 mm (9⁴/₅ x 4³/₄ inch) steel beam
11 130 mm (5¹/₄ inch) concrete slab
12 Steel L-angle

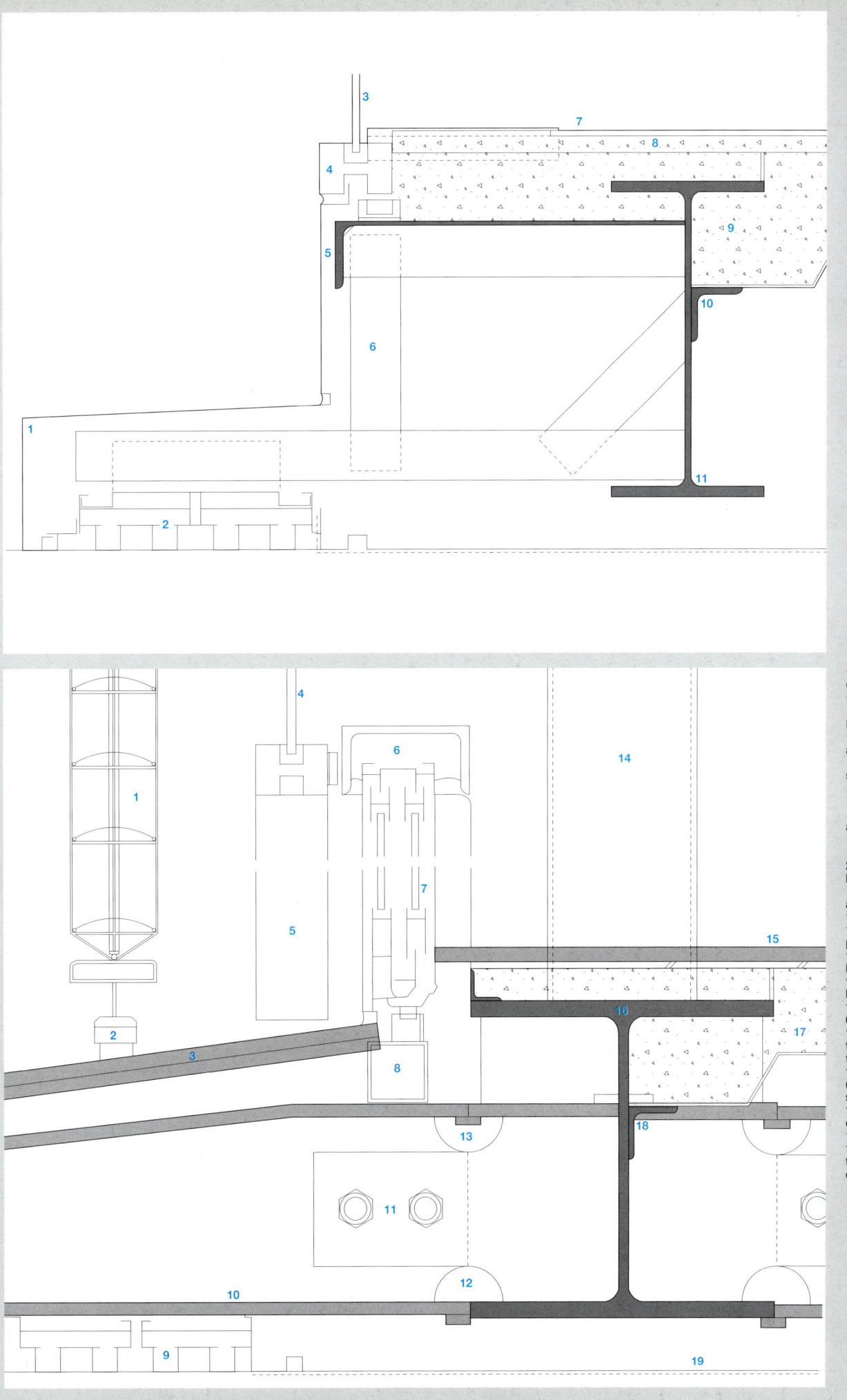

14.07
Glazing Detail 3
1:5
1 Glabellum sheet steel cladding
2 Double sliding aluminium window
3 Fixed glass
4 Aluminium sash
5 Steel angle
6 Structural steel
7 150 x 150 mm (6 x 6 inch) porcelain tiles
8 Levelling mortar bed
9 Concrete slab
10 Steel L-angle
11 300 x 150 mm (12 x 6 inch) steel beam

14.08
Glazing Detail 4
1:5
1 Aluminium exterior blind
2 Aluminium blind anchor
3 Glabellum sheet steel cladding
4 Fixed glass
5 Aluminium sash
6 Double sliding aluminium window
7 Glazing
8 60 x 60 mm (2^{1}/3 x 2^{1}/3 inch) square hollow section
9 Double sliding aluminium window
10 Steel beam
11 Steel connecting plate
12 Connector weld between beams
13 Connector weld between beams
14 150 x 150 mm (6 x 6 inch) steel column
15 12 mm (^{1}/2 inch) thick cherry parquet flooring
16 300 x 300 mm (11^{3}/4 x 11^{3}/4 inch) steel I-beam
17 130 mm (5^{1}/4 inch) concrete slab
18 Steel L-angle
19 8 mm (^{1}/3 inch) thick flexible board ceiling

15
Carlos Zapata Studio

**Private House
Quito, Ecuador**

Area
800 square metres (8,610 square feet)

Project Team
Carlos Zapata, Rolando Mendoza,
Pamela Torres

Structural Engineer
Luis Roggiero Gil, Moncayo &
Roggiero

Contractor
Luis Roggiero Gil, Moncayo &
Roggiero

Landscape Architect
Stephen Christopher Haus, Suzana
Perez

This house for a young couple and
their two children is located just
outside Quito on the edge of an
inclined site with sweeping views of
Cotopaxi Mountain, one of Central
America's tallest active volcanoes.
The house appears as a tangled
profusion of angles and fragments
that fuse with the terrain and
accentuate its natural contours.
Despite the almost windowless
curved armature of the concrete wall
which presents a closed, protective
shield towards the street, the two
wings of the house reach out, opening
up on the other facade with double-
height battered green-tinted glazing
to embrace uninterrupted views of
the valley.

Inside, views of the surrounding
housing development are excluded in
favour of a vista of the mountains.
The design conscientiously avoids
90 degree angles in the horizontal
and vertical plane, instead favouring
the juxtaposition of shallow curves
with straight lines and tight angles
to create a dynamism that is
seemingly incompatible with a static
structure. The house includes all the
customary spaces of a domestic
environment, arranged conventionally
with living, dining and kitchen spaces
on the ground floor level, with
bedrooms and bathrooms above.
A luxurious addition to this
programme, however, is a lap pool
that originates inside the house,
continuing outside where swimmers
enjoy spectacular views.

1 The two arms of the
house wrap around to
embrace views of the
Andes in the distance.
A deck with reflecting
pool cantilevers out
over the sloping site.
2 Full height green-
tinted glazing reflects
the landscape and
minimizes the visual
impact of the building
as seen from below.
3 Banks of curved
timber characterize the
interior, where expan-
sive curves and
shallow angles create
dynamic interstitial
spaces.

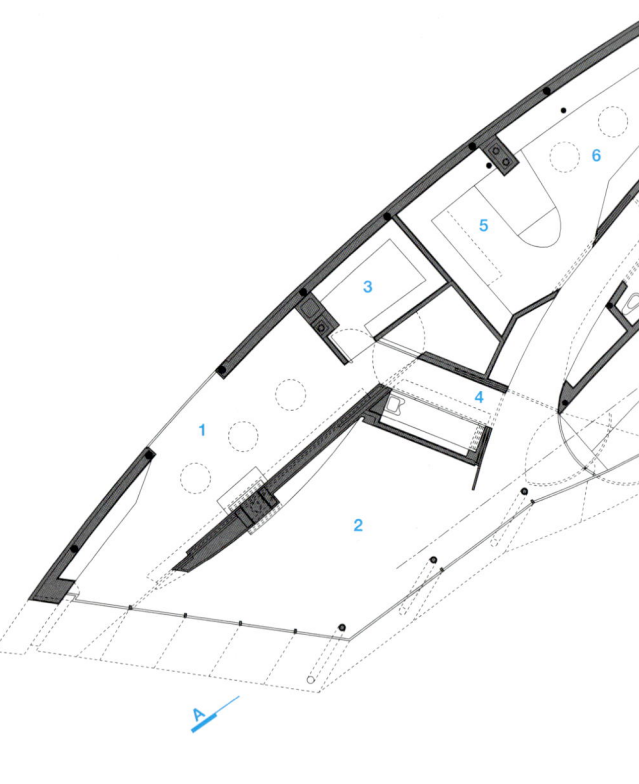

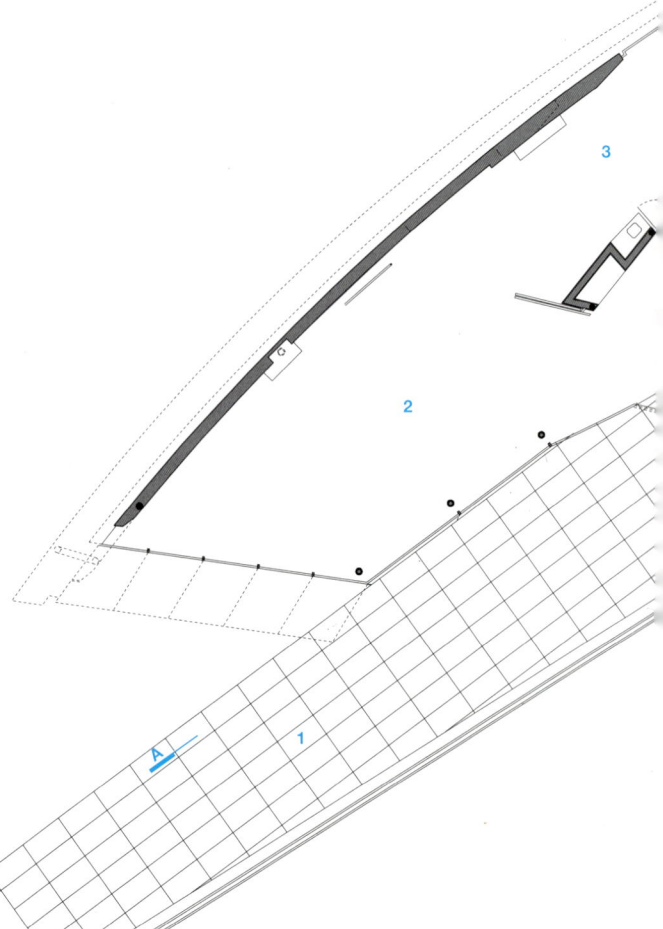

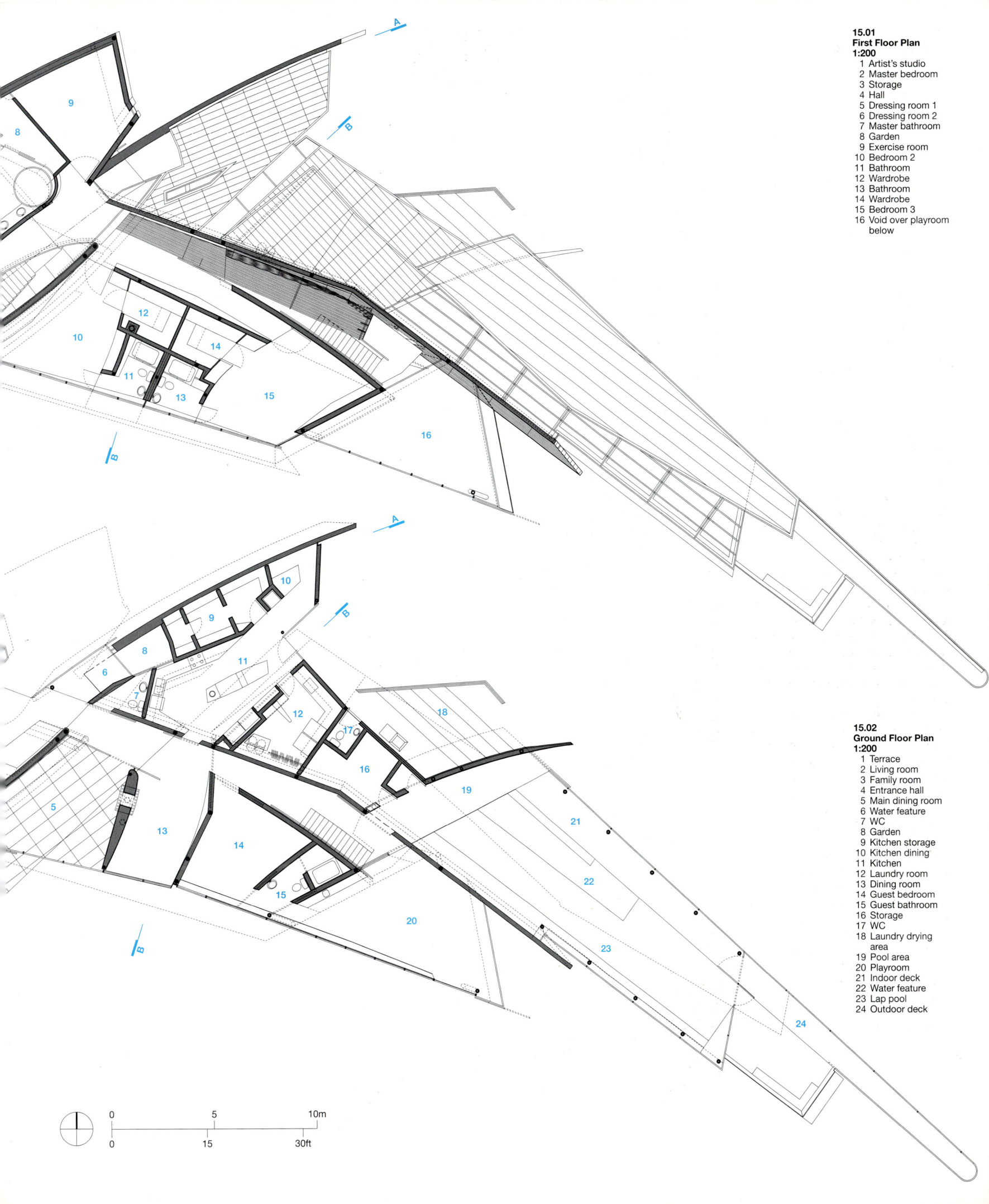

15.01
First Floor Plan
1:200
1 Artist's studio
2 Master bedroom
3 Storage
4 Hall
5 Dressing room 1
6 Dressing room 2
7 Master bathroom
8 Garden
9 Exercise room
10 Bedroom 2
11 Bathroom
12 Wardrobe
13 Bathroom
14 Wardrobe
15 Bedroom 3
16 Void over playroom
   below

15.02
Ground Floor Plan
1:200
1 Terrace
2 Living room
3 Family room
4 Entrance hall
5 Main dining room
6 Water feature
7 WC
8 Garden
9 Kitchen storage
10 Kitchen dining
11 Kitchen
12 Laundry room
13 Dining room
14 Guest bedroom
15 Guest bathroom
16 Storage
17 WC
18 Laundry drying
   area
19 Pool area
20 Playroom
21 Indoor deck
22 Water feature
23 Lap pool
24 Outdoor deck

0   5   10m

0   15   30ft

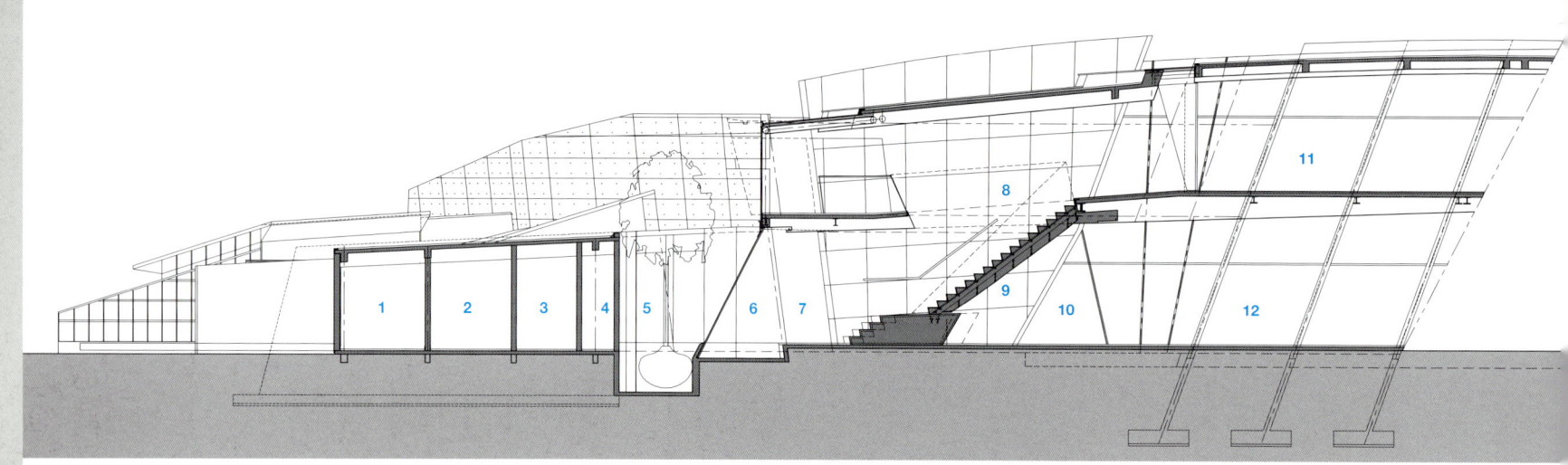

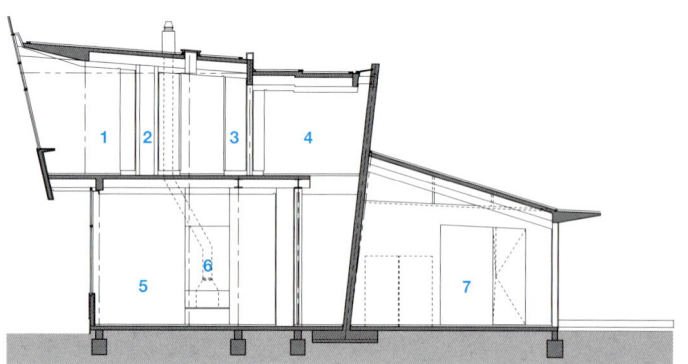

15.03
Section A–A
1:200
1 Kitchen dining area
2 Storage
3 Storage
4 Locked store
5 Garden
6 Water feature
7 Rear hall
8 Central hall
9 Entry hall
10 Entry to main dining room
11 Master bedroom
12 Living room

15.04
Section B–B
1:200
1 Bathroom
2 Wardrobe
3 Wardrobe
4 Rear stair hall
5 Dining room
6 Fireplace
7 Kitchen

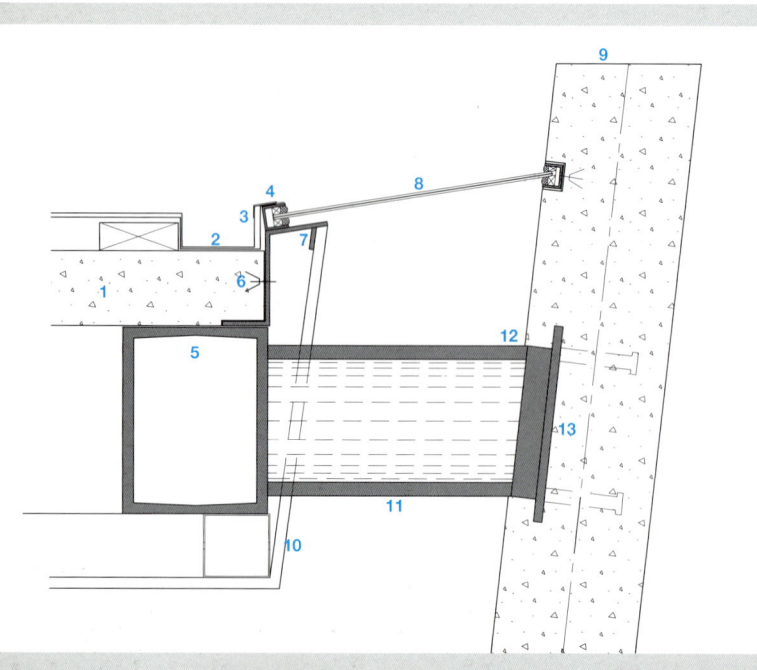

15.05
Skylight Detail
1:10
1 100 mm (4 inch) thick concrete slab
2 Lead-lined gutter with counter flashing anchored to top of steel channel
3 Channel welded to Z-angle

4 Structural silicone with neoprene setting block
5 Box beam
6 65 x 125 x 85 mm (2¹/2 x 5 x 3¹/3 inch) continuous Z-angle welded to box beam and anchored to edge of concrete slab
7 Continuous steel

bar welded to Z-angle
8 6 mm (1/4 inch) thick laminated tempered glass
9 Top of concrete wall
10 15 mm (2/3 inch) plywood with veneer finish
11 200 mm (8 inch) diameter steel tube welded to box beam

and weld plate
12 Welded steel tube 3 mm (1/8 inch) inside of face of wall
13 Embedded weld plate

15.06
Wall Detail
1:10
1 6 mm (1/4 inch) thick tempered glass
2 Steel heater grate screwed to metal angles
3 Steel angle anchored to sub floor
4 Baseboard heating

elements centred between vertical mullions
5 Steel channel anchored to embedded steel plate with allen bolts
6 Plywood ceiling with timber veneer finish anchored to framing with allen bolts

7 Finished floor level
8 Metal channel ceiling frame
9 Steel beam
10 Continuous light cove with fluorescent fixture

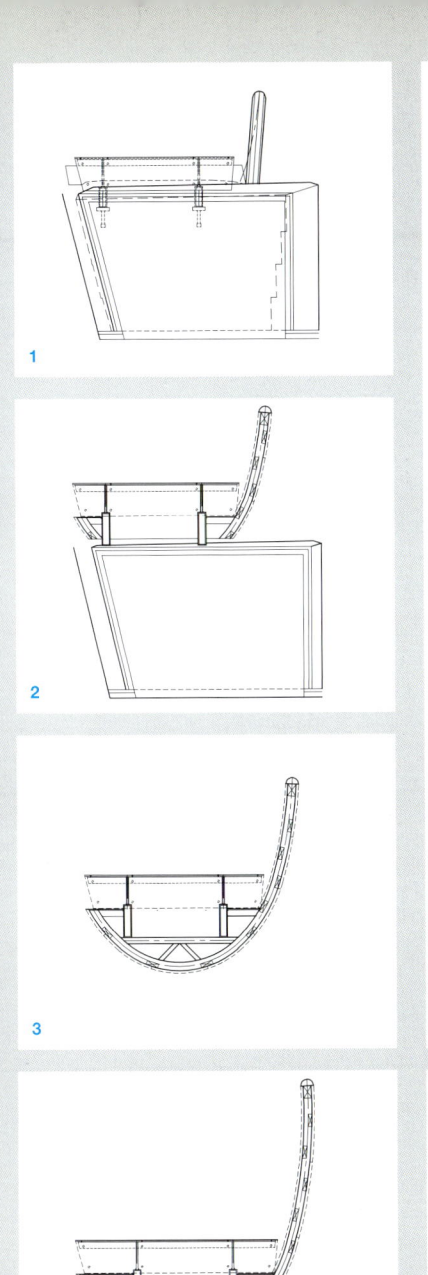

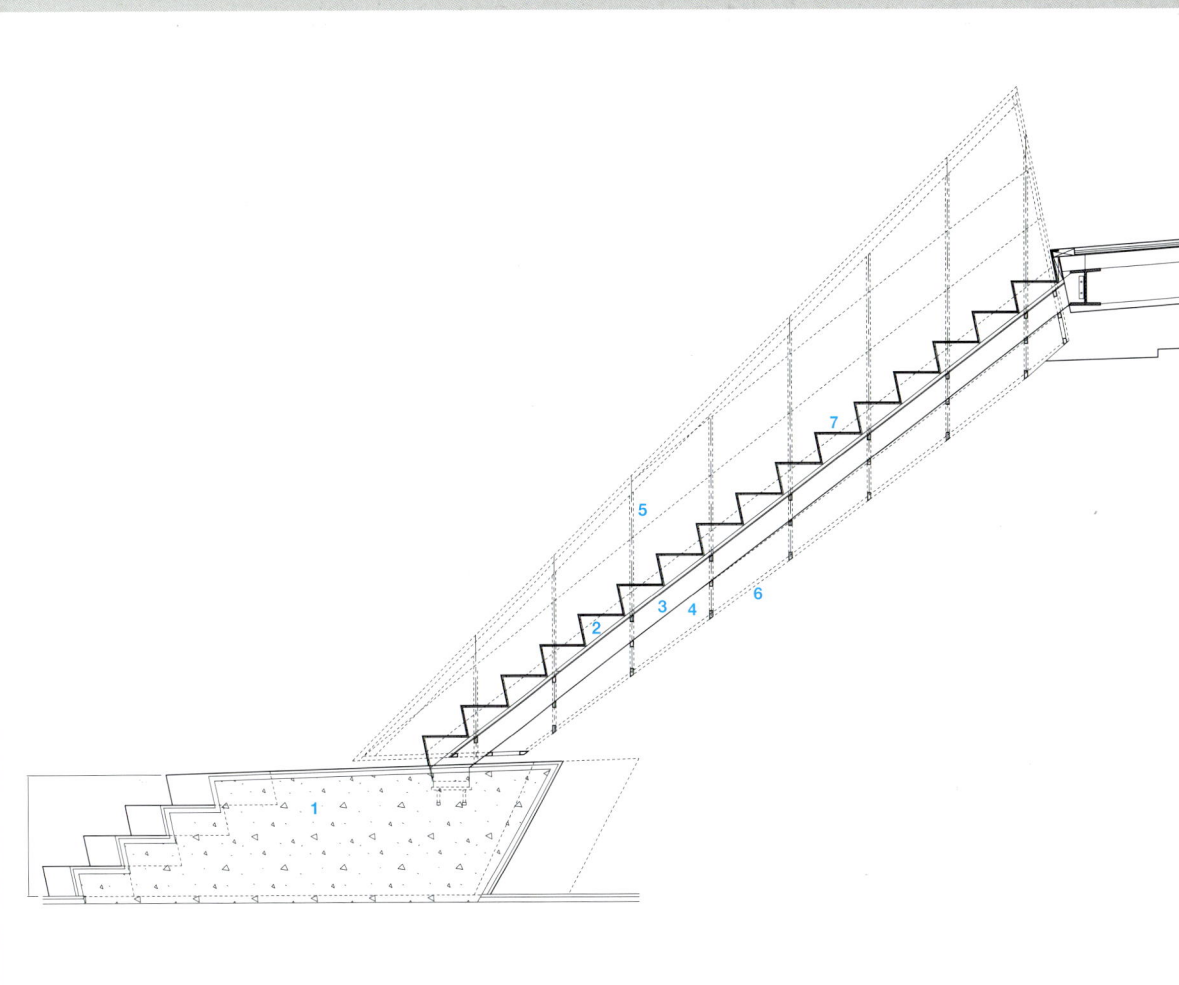

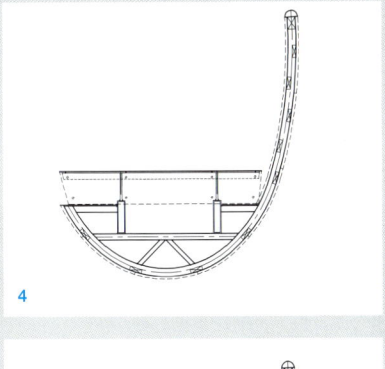

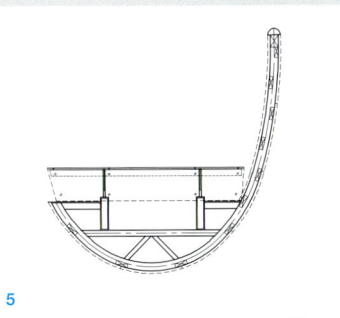

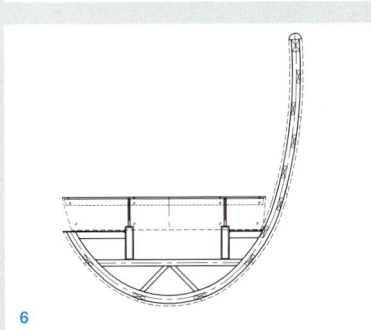

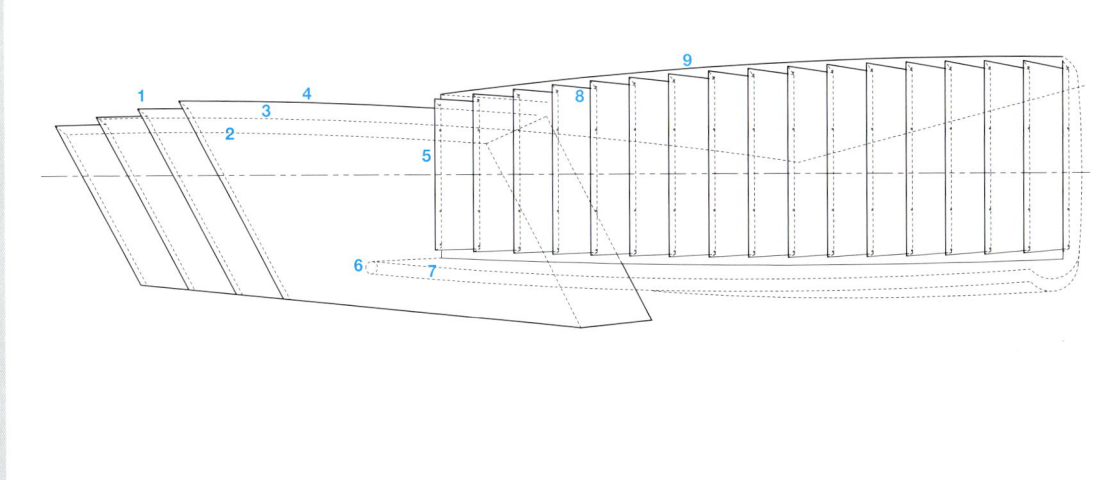

15.07
Stair Tread Details
1:50
  1 Tread 4
  2 Tread 6
  3 Tread 8
  4 Tread 12
  5 Tread 14
  6 Tread 20

15.08
Stair Elevation
1:50
  1 Stone finish on concrete base
  2 12.5 mm (1/2 inch) thick triangular metal plate welded to box beam
  3 12.5 mm (1/2 inch) thick stainless steel plate
  4 200 x 50 mm (8 x 2 inch) steel box beam
  5 Metal ribs
  6 Line of lateral studs

  7 6 mm (1/4 inch) thick beaded stainless steel finish folded metal treads and risers

15.09
Stair Plan
1:50
  1 Line of wall at tread elevation
  2 Line of stair at first floor
  3 Line of floor at first floor
  4 Line of floor at first floor
  5 6 mm (1/4 inch) thick stainless steel finish folded metal treads and risers
  6 6 mm (1/4 inch)

thick stainless steel plate
  7 Timber sheathing
  8 6 mm (1/4 inch) thick stainless steel
  9 Line of wall at tread elevation

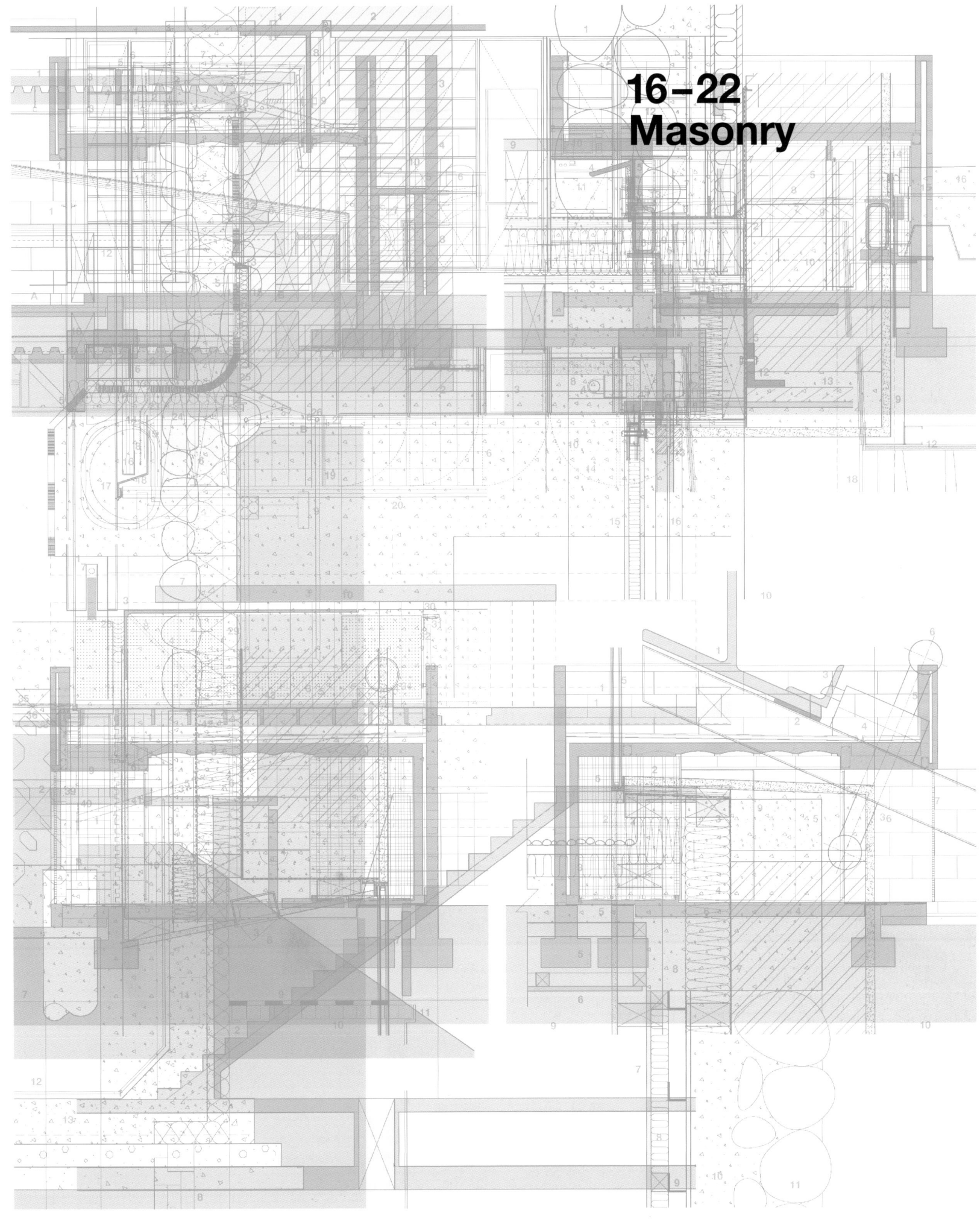

House in the Landscape
Bärnau, Germany

Client
Sabine and Andreas Rösch

Area
295 square metres (3,175 square feet)

Project Team
Christian Brückner, Peter Brückner,
Robert Reith, Wolfgang Herrmann

Structural Engineer
Klaus-Peter Brückner

Located in Bavaria, close to the Czech border, Brückner & Brückner have designed a compact house above the small town of Bärnau. As a response to the destruction of traditional villages and towns over recent decades, the architects traced the last remnants of a local building tradition which had, for the most part, been lost. Aware that contemporary regional building is often in danger of lapsing into cliché, the Brückner brothers have successfully developed a formal architectural language that is contemporary as well as authentic. Here, the severely defined form has a gable roof without overhanging eaves – a reference to traditional Oberpfalz building. No decorative shrubs or fences separate it from the meadow that is bordered to the north by woodland.

The two cladding materials for the double cavity external walls are from local sources: the yellowish-grey, granite from a nearby quarry, and the larch from the owners' woodland. The building reveals itself to be a dwelling via the glazed joint that vertically and horizontally separates the stone plinth from the timber element placed above it. The building's compact expression is strengthened through the timber cladding which continues homogeneously from the walls to form the roof, with only a metal edge to indicate the rainwater drainage behind the facade. To the west this generously organized house – the same materials are employed in the interior – responds to the water meadows in the valley below. The glazed joint here broadens to become a two-storey window in the stair well whereas for the living room, a wide, gateway-like opening was cut into the stone shell.

1 Located amongst lush meadows and forests, this simple house utilizes only material available in the near vicinity, including locally quarried granite and larch from the owners' woodland.
2 A hardy granite carapace protects the lower levels of the house.
3 A continuous slot of glazing running both horizontally and vertically separates the two main construction materials – granite and timber.
4 The same materials continue on the interior. Rough cut granite and horizontal timber boards for vertical surfaces, and polished granite for the floors. Elsewhere, white-painted plasterboard provides light-reflecting surfaces.

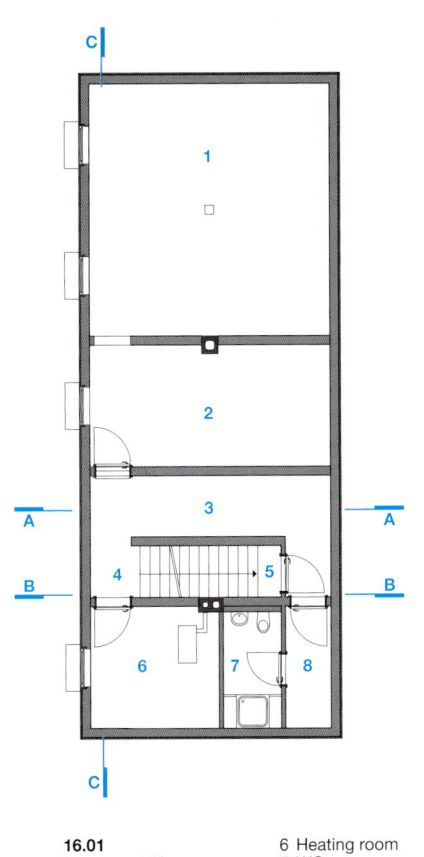

16.01
Basement Plan
1:200
1 Storeroom 1
2 Storeroom 2
3 Corridor
4 Stair to upper level
5 Store
6 Heating room
7 WC
8 Dressing room

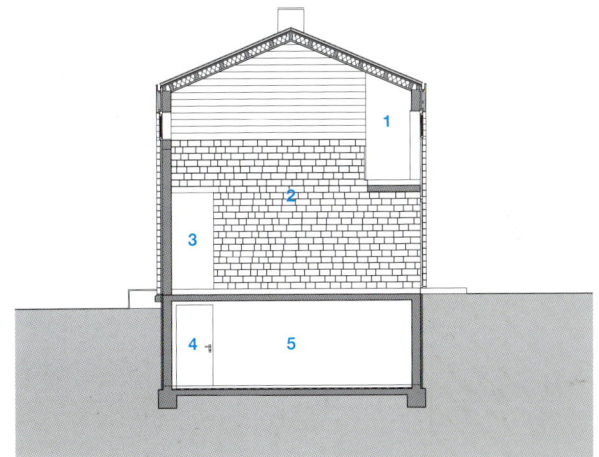

16.02
Ground Floor Plan
1:200
1 Reading room
2 Living and dining room
3 Kitchen
4 Timber deck
5 Corridor
6 Dressing room
7 Guest bathroom
8 Pantry
9 Corridor
10 Main entry
11 Stair to upper level
12 Office 1

16.03
First Floor Plan
1:200
1 Master bedroom
2 Bathroom
3 Dressing room
4 Bedroom
5 Corridor
6 Void over ground floor below
7 Office 2

16.04
Section A–A
1:200
1 Corridor
2 Void over entrance
3 Corridor to living and dining room
4 Door to storeroom
5 Corridor

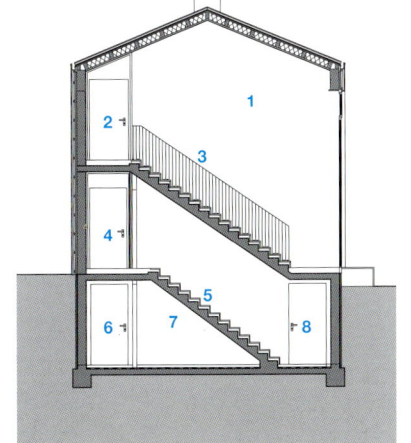

16.05
Section B–B
1:200
1 Void over stair
2 Door to office 2
3 Stair
4 Door to office 1
5 Stair
6 Door to dressing room
7 WC
8 Door to heating room

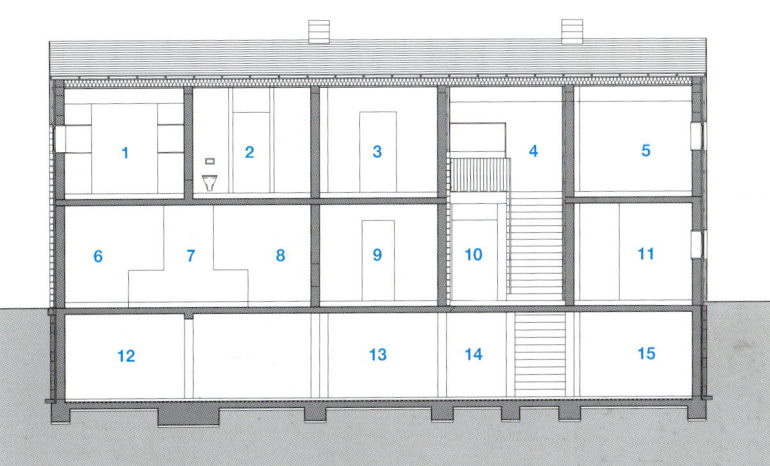

16.06
Section C–C
1:200
1 Master bedroom
2 Bathroom
3 Bedroom 2
4 Staircase
5 Office 2
6 Reading room
7 Living and dining room
8 Kitchen
9 Door to dressing room
10 Entrance
11 Office 1
12 Storeroom 1
13 Storeroom 2
14 Corridor
15 Heating room

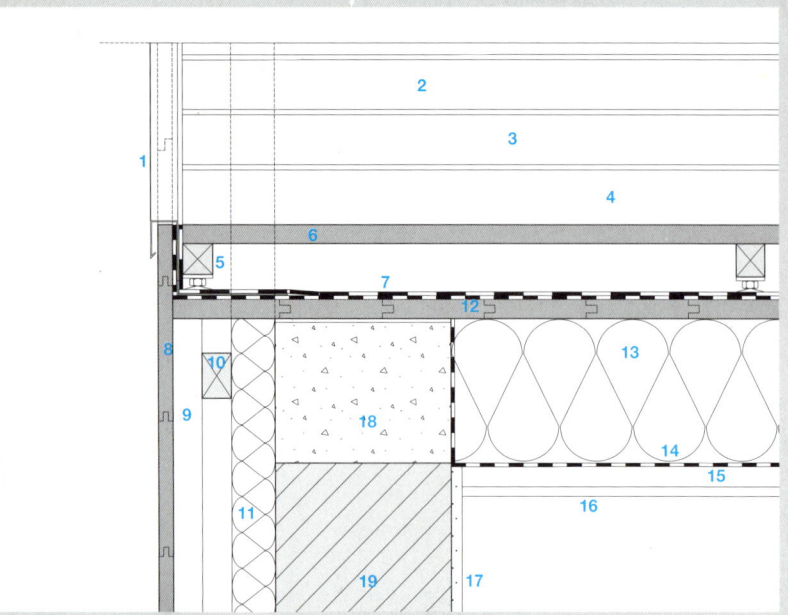

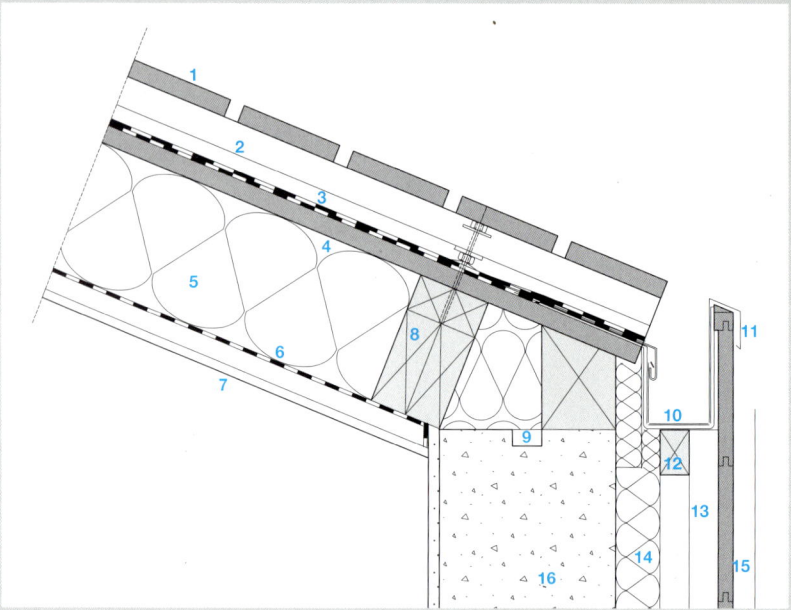

16.07
Roof and External
Wall Detail
1:10
 1 Titanium zinc metal
cladding
 2 Larchwood plank
 3 Larchwood plank
 4 Larchwood plank
 5 40 x 40 mm (1½ x
1½ inch) rafter
 6 Larchwood planks
 7 Asphalt sheeting
 8 Larchwood external
cladding
 9 40 x 60 mm (1½ x

2⅓ inch) timber batten
10 40 x 60 mm (1½ x
2⅓ inch) timber batten
11 60 mm (2⅓ inch)
insulation
12 Spigot and groove
formboards
13 180 mm (7 inch)
insulation
14 Purlin rafter behind
15 Asphalt sheeting
with moisture barrier
16 Gypsum plaster
ceiling
17 Painted
plasterboard wall

18 Reinforced
concrete
19 Brick wall

16.08
Eaves Detail
1:10
 1 Larchwood planks
 2 Air break
 3 Asphalt sheeting
 4 Spigot and groove
formboards
 5 180 mm (7 inch)
insulation
 6 Timber batten
 7 Gypsum
plasterboard ceiling
 8 Rafter purlin
 9 Halfen channel
10 Concealed steel

gutter
11 Titanium zinc metal
gutter flashing
12 40 x 60 mm (1½ x
2⅓ inch) batten
13 40 x 60 mm (1½ x
2⅓ inch) batten
14 60 mm (2⅓ inch)
insulation
15 Larchwood external
cladding
16 Reinforced
concrete

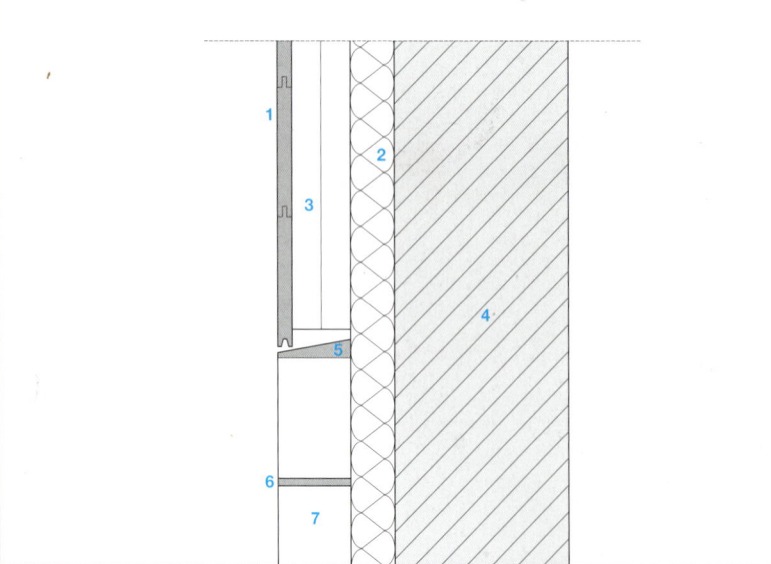

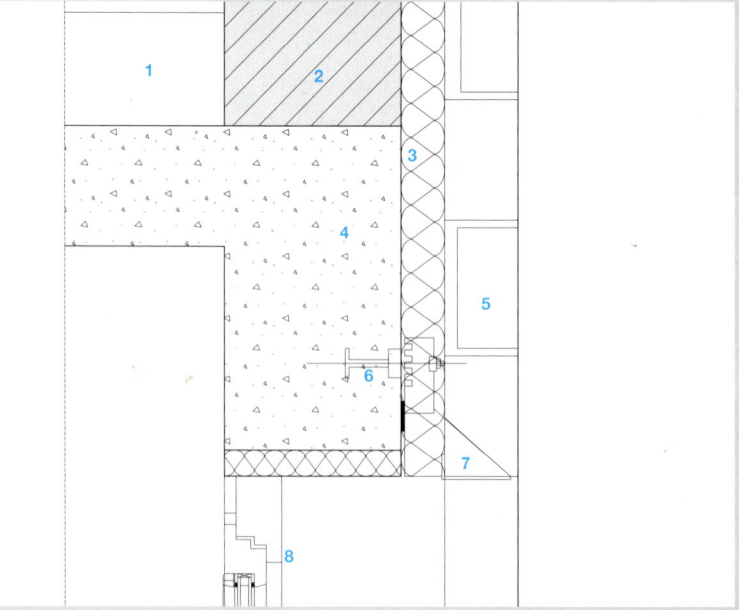

16.09
Gable Detail – Timber
to Stone Transition
1:10
 1 Larchwood external
cladding
 2 60 mm (2⅓ inch)
thick insulation
 3 40 x 60 mm (1½ x
2⅓ inch) timber batten
 4 Brick wall
 5 Mortar joint
 6 Mortar joint
 7 Granite cladding

16.10
Footing Detail
1:10
 1 Floor board
 2 Brick wall
 3 60 mm (2⅓ inch)
thick insulation
 4 Reinforced
concrete
 5 Granite cladding
 6 Cladding anchor
 7 Steel angle lintel
 8 Timber window
frame

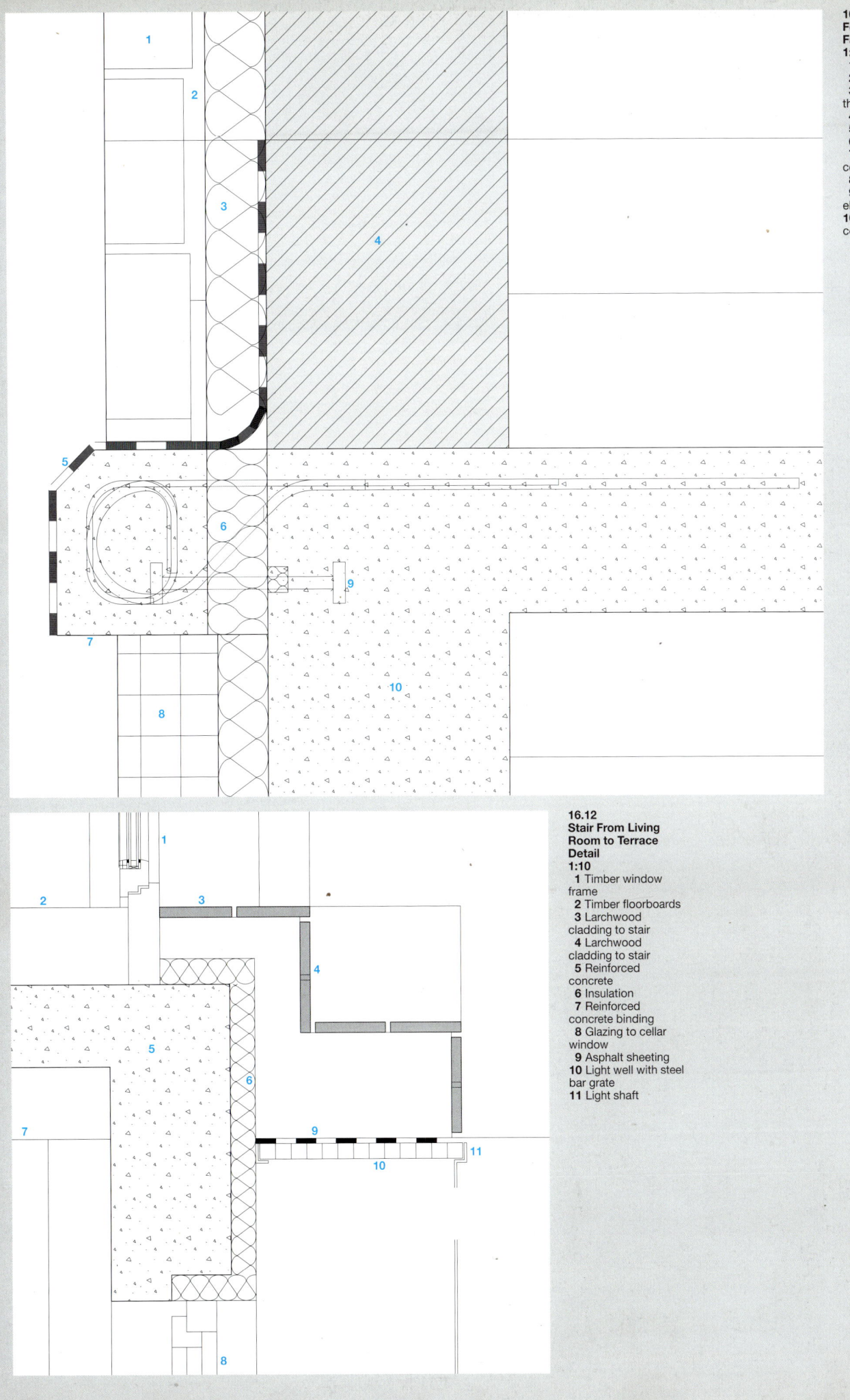

16.11
Footing and Stone Facade Detail
1:5
  1 Granite cladding
  2 Mortar joint
  3 60 mm (2¹⁄₃ inch) thick insulation
  4 Brick wall
  5 Asphalt sheeting
  6 Thermal insulation
  7 Reinforced concrete footing
  8 Concrete filter layer
  9 Thermal break element
10 Reinforced concrete

16.12
Stair From Living Room to Terrace Detail
1:10
  1 Timber window frame
  2 Timber floorboards
  3 Larchwood cladding to stair
  4 Larchwood cladding to stair
  5 Reinforced concrete
  6 Insulation
  7 Reinforced concrete binding
  8 Glazing to cellar window
  9 Asphalt sheeting
10 Light well with steel bar grate
11 Light shaft

Dirty House
London, England, UK

Client
Tim Noble and Sue Webster

Area
465 square metres (5,000 square feet)

Project Team
David Adjaye, Josh Carver, Aimee Lau

Structural Engineer
Techniker

Main Contractor
R. J. Parry

The brief for the Dirty House was to design a studio, office and home for two contemporary artists in a turn-of-the-century timber factory in London's East End. The concept was to transform the factory into a new urban dwelling and to celebrate the site's prominent corner position. Spatially, the concept is comprised of two parts: the working spaces below and the living spaces above. Upon entering the building, a 5.5 metre (18 feet) high hallway provides three points of entry: a stairwell which rises to the top floor residential space; a doorway leading to the office via a lobby; and at the end of the corridor, a narrow passageway which opens onto the larger of the two double-height studios. This studio caters for the intricate work requiring north light, while large scale works are created in the more generally lit studio to the south.

The top floor is conceived as a glass pavilion with panoramic views of the East End and the emerging cluster of towers on the city skyline. The building has a dark base with mirror tinted windows and is covered in a resin pigment. The top floor pavilion has an over sailing roof which fits exactly to the original plan of the existing building, providing a covered outdoor terrace. The white roof is lit from below, which, in the evening, creates the impression that the roof is floating. Through the live/work nature of the brief, the project explores a new type of domestic architecture that represents an emerging demographic in contemporary society, creating spaces and facilities that stimulate and shelter the occupants for a full 24 hours a day.

1 The house appears as a solid black box with a floating white roof. At street level, mirror glass windows provide an intriguingly reflective surface for passers by.

2 The kitchen in the upper level living space is lit from above with a skylight cut into the flat roof.

3 A series of skylights cut into the pure white volume light the bedroom and open bathing space.

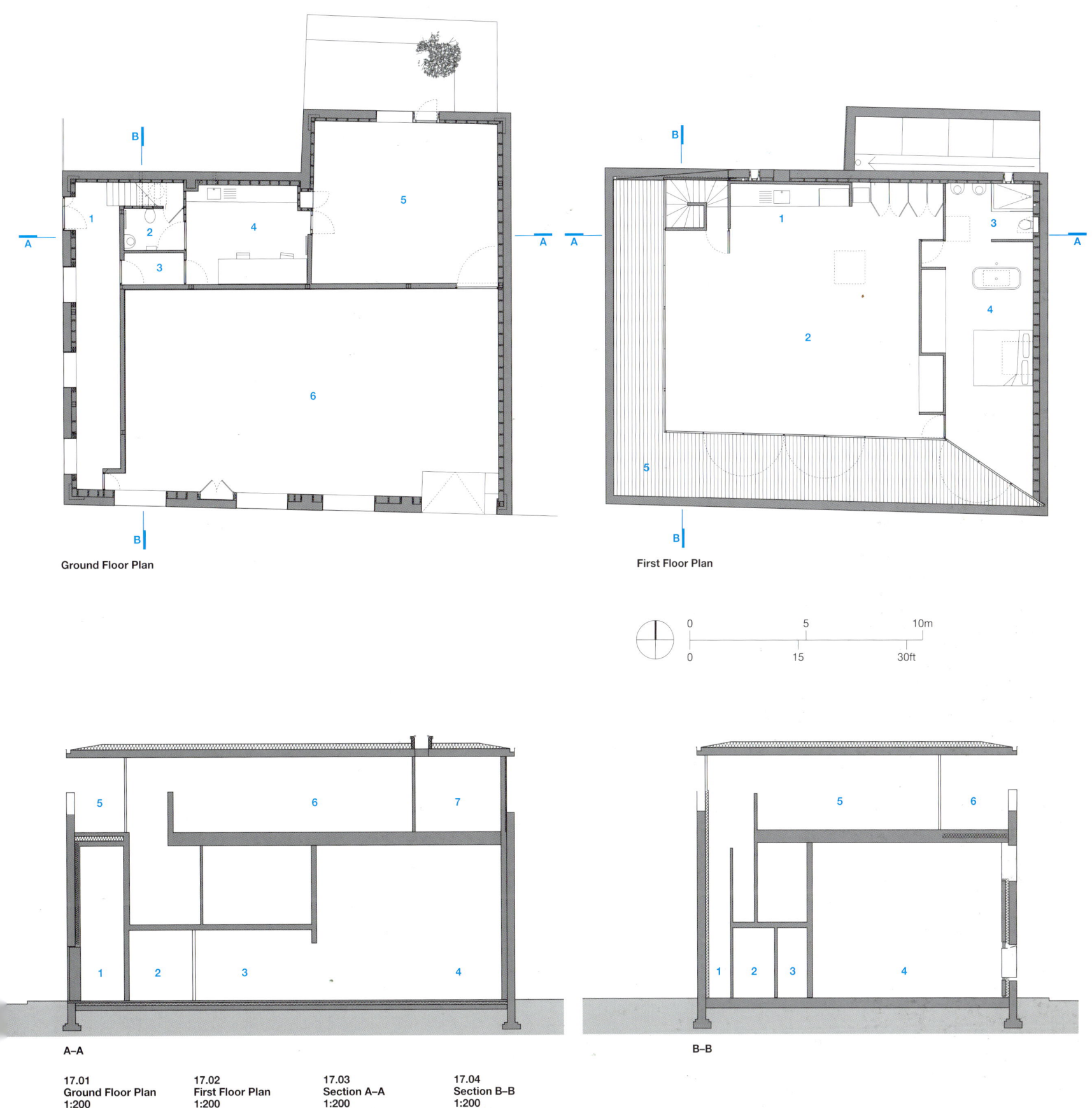

Ground Floor Plan

First Floor Plan

0   5   10m
0   15   30ft

A–A

B–B

17.01
Ground Floor Plan
1:200
  1 Entry Space
  2 WC
  3 Office lobby
  4 Office
  5 Studio 1
  6 Studio 2

17.02
First Floor Plan
1:200
  1 Kitchen
  2 Living and dining
  3 Bathroom
  4 Bedroom
  5 Terrace

17.03
Section A–A
1:200
  1 Entry Space
  2 WC
  3 Office
  4 Studio 1
  5 Terrace
  6 Kitchen
  7 Bathroom

17.04
Section B–B
1:200
  1 Stair
  2 WC
  3 Office Lobby
  4 Studio 2
  5 Living and dining
  6 Terrace

17.05
Detail Cross Section
1:50
1 175 mm (7 inch) insulation cut to fall
2 Plywood deck
3 Single ply EPDM membrane fully adhered to 18 ply substrate laid to fall
4 Ring gutter formed in plywood and bonded with rubber membrane
5 Breather membrane
6 Vapour barrier
7 Painted external grade mineral board to terrace soffit
8 Floor to ceiling double-glazed units with structural galvanized mullions
9 New masonry wall to raise terrace balustrade to 1,400 mm (4½ feet) above finished floor level
10 Terrace wall overclad with painted and treated softwood timber decking
11 External painted and treated softwood timber decking
12 Terrace sealed with rubber membrane
13 Ceiling formed in Gyprock Plank and outer layer of 12.5 mm (½ inch) Gyproc Sound Bloc on Gyprock Resilient Bars at 450 mm (17½ inch) centres with 100 mm (4 inch) Isowool 1,000 in cavity for one hour fire protection and 53 decibel sound isolation between studio and apartment
14 Double-glazed unit flush with internal wall finish
15 External window coated with anti-vandal paint
16 Existing brick wall repaired and retained
17 External walls coated with anti-vandal paint
18 12.5 mm (½ inch) Gyproc wall board
19 Dimmable downlight to all ground floor windows
20 Double-glazed unit flush with external wall with internal sand blasted pane and external mirror finish pane
21 Internal window reveal formed with 12.5 mm (½ inch) Gyprock wall board
22 Vapour barrier
23 New concrete screed to form level surface throughout with underfloor heating over insulation and damp proof membrane
24 Breather membrane
25 Chemical damp proof course injected into existing external wall

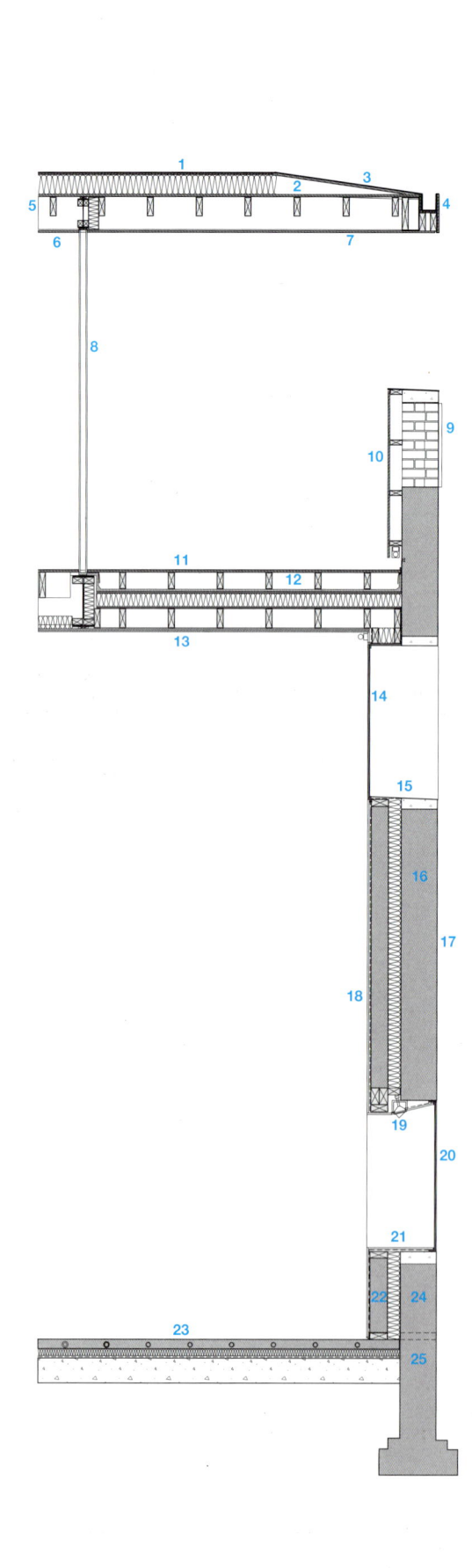

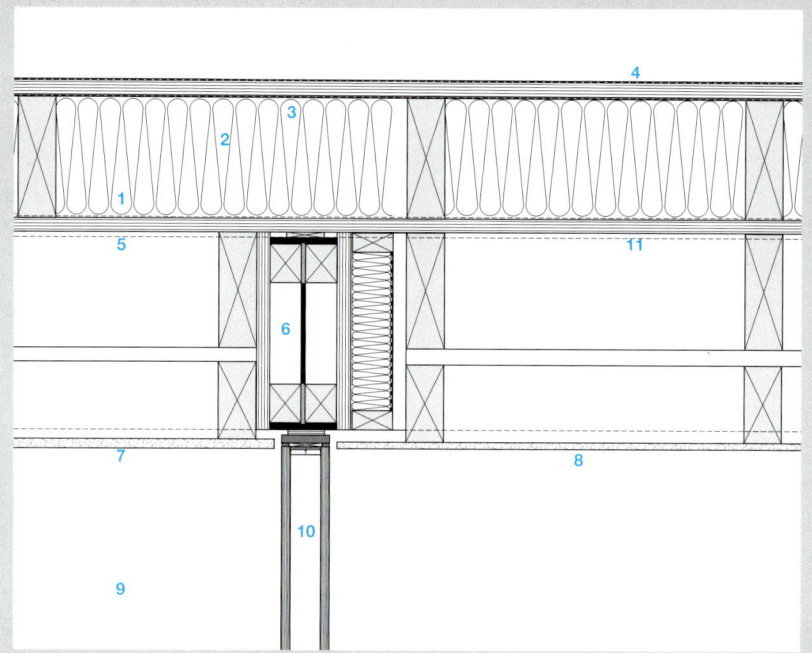

17.06
Terrace Glazing Head Detail
1:10
1 Vapour barrier
2 Insulation
3 Breather membrane
4 Single ply EPDM membrane fully adhered to 18 ply substrate on graded joists laid at minimum 1 in 80 fall
5 Edge of steel beam

dotted beyond
6 Primary roof steel supported on glazing mullions
7 Painted 12.5 mm (½ inch) plasterboard ceiling
8 Painted fibre cement sheet soffit
9 Living room
10 Toughened double glazed unit held in galvanized steel structural mullions

11 18 mm (¾ inch) plywood

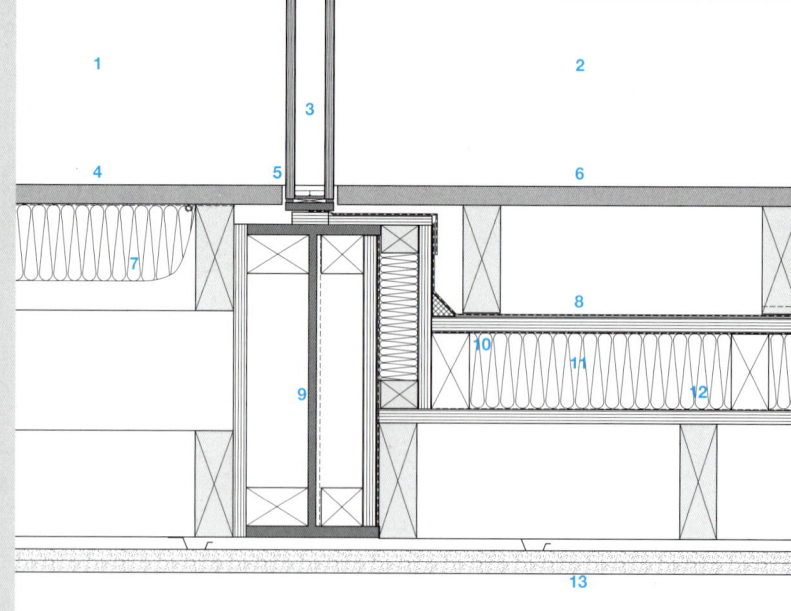

17.07
Terrace Glazing Detail
1:10
1 Living room
2 Terrace
3 Toughened double glazed unit held in galvanized steel structural mullions
4 Painted internal timber decking
5 T-bar to base of galvanized structural

mullion
6 Painted external decking timber
7 Underfloor heating fixed to topside of floor joists
8 Single ply EPDM membrane laid on 18 ply to fall to floor waste
9 Primary steel beam
10 Breather membrane
11 Insulation
12 Vapour barrier
13 Two layers of fire

resistant plasterboard on acoustic resilient bars

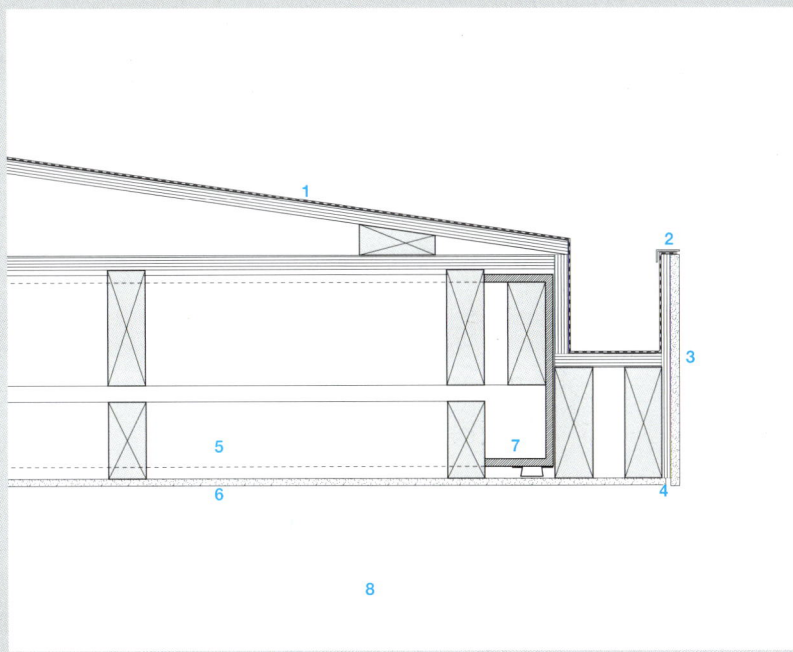

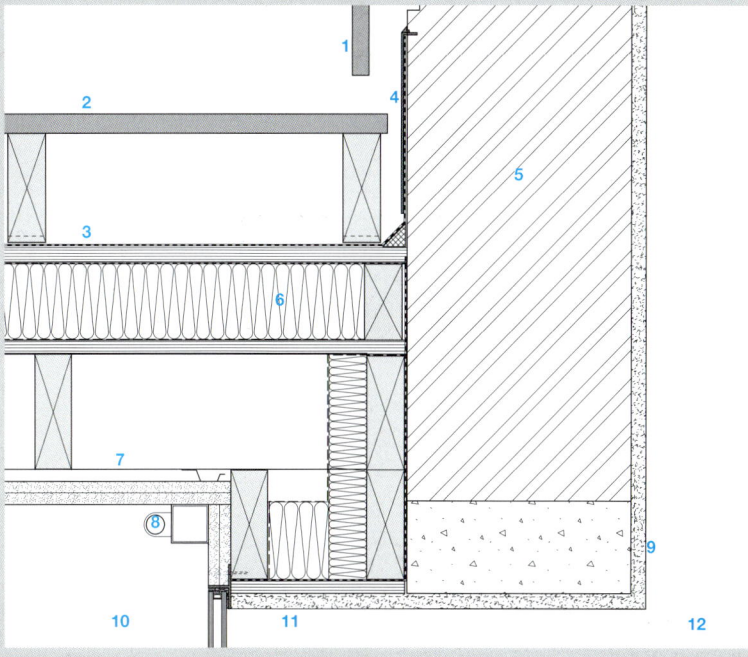

17.08
Fascia Detail
1:10
1 Single ply EPDM membrane fully adhered to 18 ply substrate laid to fall
2 Aluminium capping trim to fascia panel
3 Painted 12 mm (^{1}/$_2$ inch) fibre cement fascia panel
4 5 mm (^{1}/$_5$ inch) shadow gap
5 Line of steel beam dotted beyond
6 9 mm (^{1}/$_3$ inch) painted fibre cement sheet soffit liner
7 Steel perimeter beam
8 Terrace

17.09
Windowhead Detail
1:10
1 Painted external decking boards to match terrace flooring
2 Painted external timber decking laid over joists with slotted bases
3 Single ply EPDM membrane laid over 18 ply substrate
4 Painted lead flashing chased into existing brickwork and lapped with single ply membrane
5 Existing brickwork wall
6 Insulation with breather membrane and vapour barrier
7 Two layers of 15 mm (^{1}/$_2$ inch) fire resistant plasterboard fixed to acoustic resilient bars
8 Fluorescent luminaire
9 20 mm (^{3}/$_4$ inch) anti-billposter high build paint treatment to brickwork and window reveal with fine mesh reinforcement window reveal edge
10 Studio
11 Translucent double-glazed unit fixed into steel section with structural silicon
12 Exterior

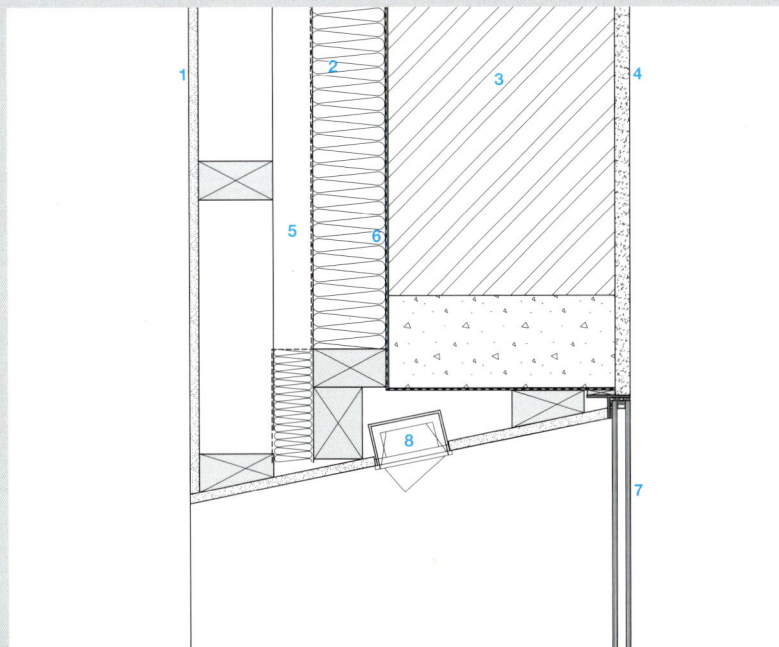

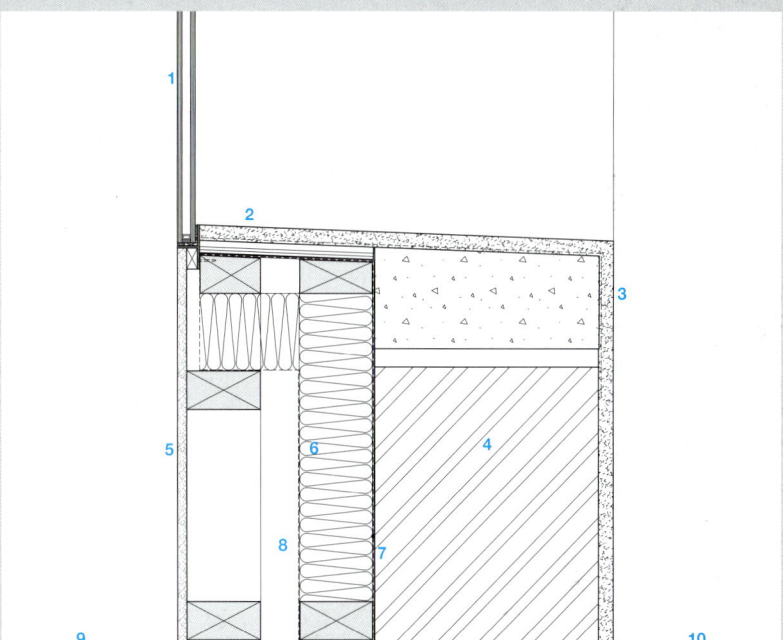

17.10
Flush Windowhead Detail
1:10
1 Painted 12.5 mm (^{1}/$_2$ inch) plasterboard
2 Insulation
3 Existing brickwork wall
4 20 mm (^{3}/$_4$ inch) anti-bill poster high build paint treatment to brickwork
5 Vapour barrier
6 Breather membrane
7 Double-glazed unit fixed with internal sandblasted pane and external pane with mirror film on internal face fixed into steel section with structural silicon
8 Adjustable downlight

17.11
Window Sill Detail
1:10
1 Translucent double-glazed unit fixed into steel section with structural silicon
2 18 ply substrate laid to fall
3 20 mm (^{3}/$_4$ inch) anti-bill poster high build paint treatment to brickwork and window reveal with fine mesh reinforcement to window reveal edge
4 Existing brickwork wall
5 Painted 12.5 mm (^{1}/$_2$ inch) plasterboard
6 Insulation
7 Breather membrane
8 Vapour barrier
9 Studio
10 Exterior

81

**Tagomago House
San Carlos, Ibiza, Spain**

Client
Enrique Vives

Area
483 square metres (5,200 square feet)

Project Team
Carlos Ferrater

Structural Engineer
Jordi Bernuz

Quantity Surveyor
Construcciones Collado

The house is situated in the north-east area of the island of Ibiza in a typical Mediterranean landscape of pine and juniper trees, facing the sea and the island of Tagomago. Used as a holiday home, the design is based on a central nucleus comprised of the main house, surrounded by a number of small autonomous buildings. The house is articulated along a longitudinal axis to provide each pavilion with the optimum orientation and privacy, as well as allowing sufficient flexibility to allow for differing numbers of guests. The design places great importance on the spatial and environmental sequences in terms of the sun and the Mediterranean light.

Recalling southern Mediterranean architecture, the house offers a serene atmosphere almost akin to a monastic environment. Materials, principally limestone, white concrete and timber, are used in a pure and non-manipulated state, and wherever possible pertain to the vernacular architecture of the island. Secondary materials include stone facades and walls, traditional decking, concrete beams, ceramic floors, timber door and window frames, and stone, concrete and timber paving. The programme features a series of open spaces, patios, porches and terraces that establish imprecise boundaries between inside and outside. The living room opens onto an extended timber terrace that acts as a spatial link with the landscape and a place to enjoy the views. Adjacent to the main living spaces are four small outbuildings, which can be adapted in the future should family numbers increase.

1 View of the independent guest houses – private terraces and patios are created for each pavilion.
2 The main house features an expansive timber deck accessed via large sliding timber-framed doors. A swimming pool recessed into the deck enjoys dramatic views over the island.
3 View to the rear of the guest pavilions

where the bathrooms are located.
4 View of the north facade of the guest pavilions – a black-framed glazed panel is repeated in each pavilion, allowing a

framed view from one end of the house to the other.
5 The dazzling white limestone contrasts with the intense blue of the Mediterranean sky.
6 View from the living

room of the main house to the deck and beyond to the Mediterranean.

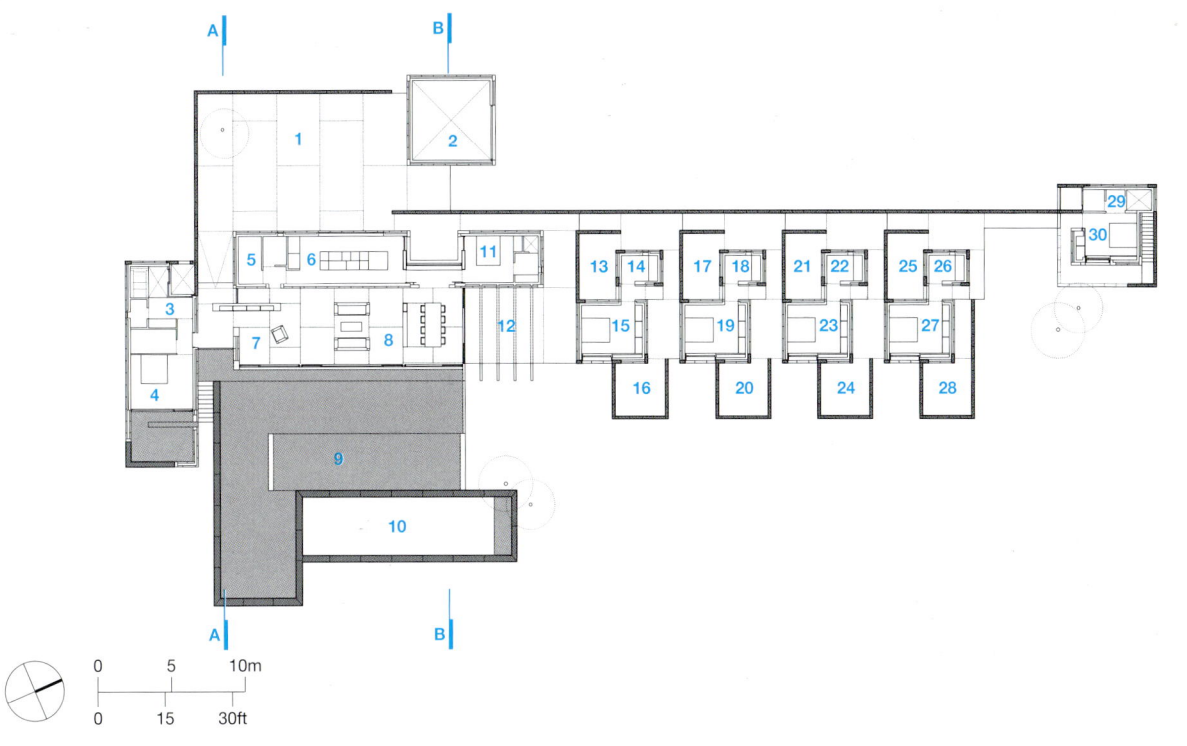

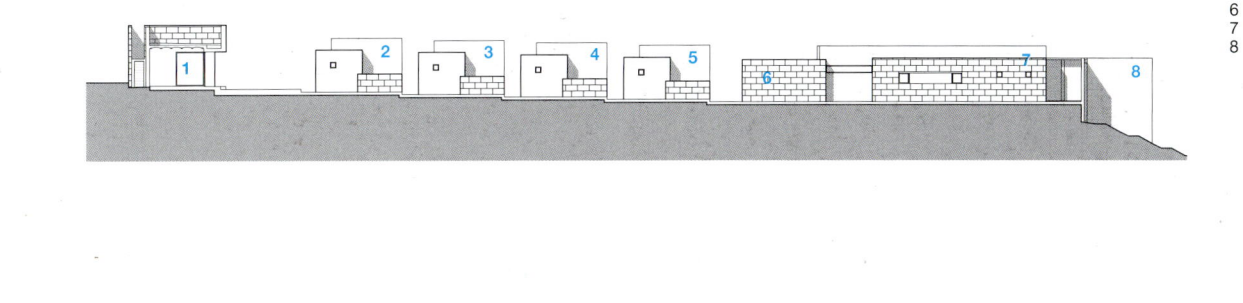

18.02
East Elevation
1:500
1 Master bedroom
2 Living room
3 Covered deck
4 Pavilion 1
5 Pavilion 2
6 Pavilion 3
7 Pavilion 4
8 Guest pavilion

18.03
West Elevation
1:500
1 Guest pavilion
2 Pavilion 4
3 Pavilion 3
4 Pavilion 2
5 Pavilion 1
6 Guest bedroom
and bathroom
7 Kitchen
8 Master bathroom

18.04
Section A–A
1:200
1 Mechanical store
2 Kitchen
3 Dining room
4 Covered area of
timber deck
5 Swimming pool

18.05
Section B–B
1:200
1 Mechanical store
2 Living room
3 Covered timber
deck
4 Swimming pool

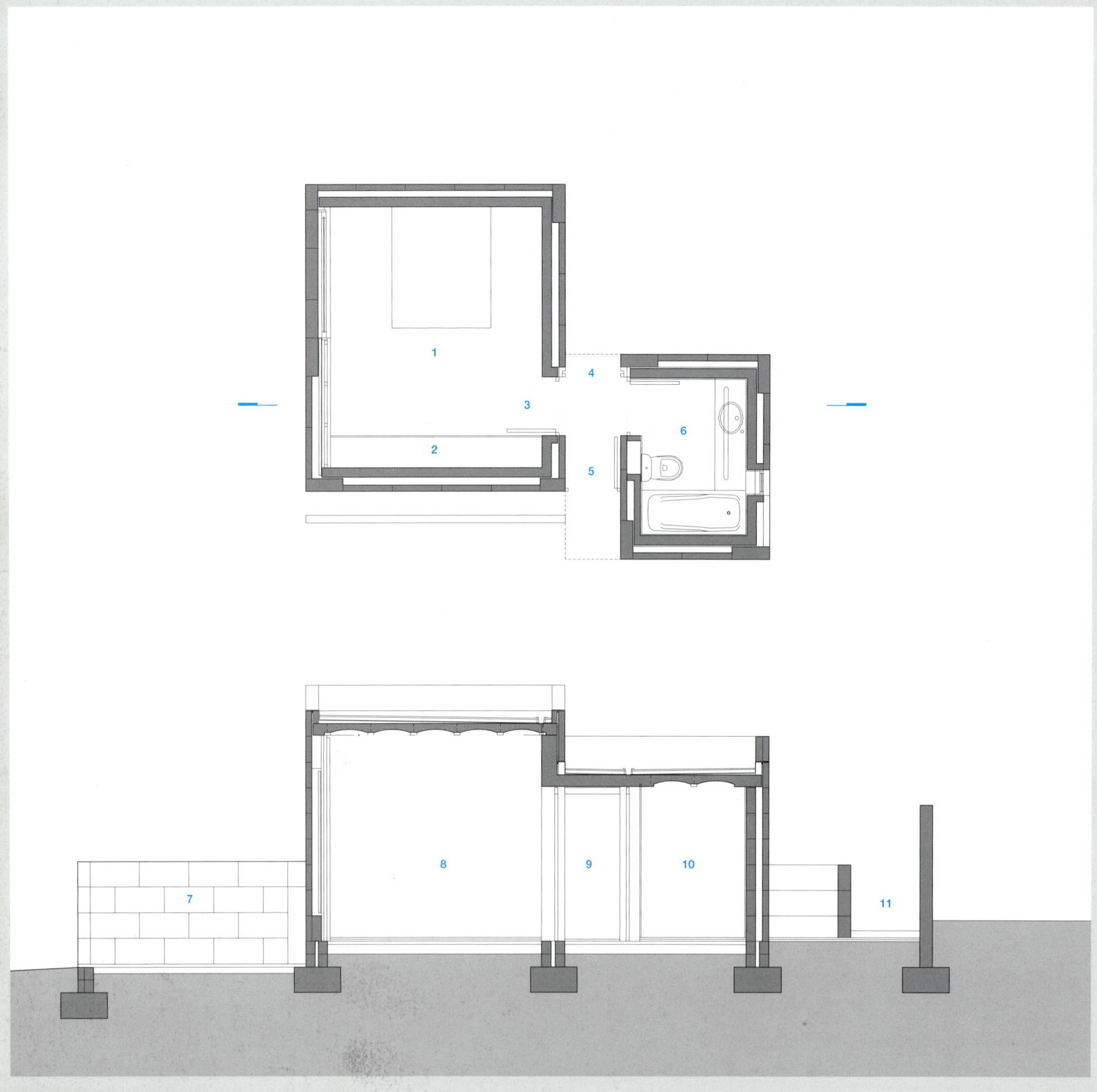

18.06
Guest Pavilion Detail
Plan and Section
1:75
1 Bedroom
2 Storage
3 Bedroom entry
4 Glazed link
between bedroom and
bathroom
5 Pavilion entry
6 Bathroom
7 Stone terrace wall
8 Bedroom
9 Glazed link
10 Bathroom
11 Terrace

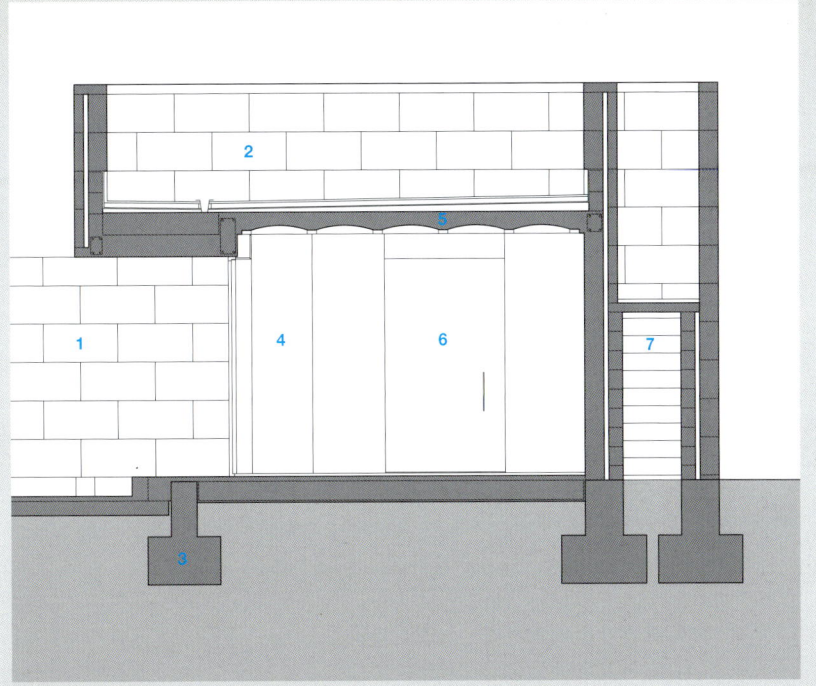

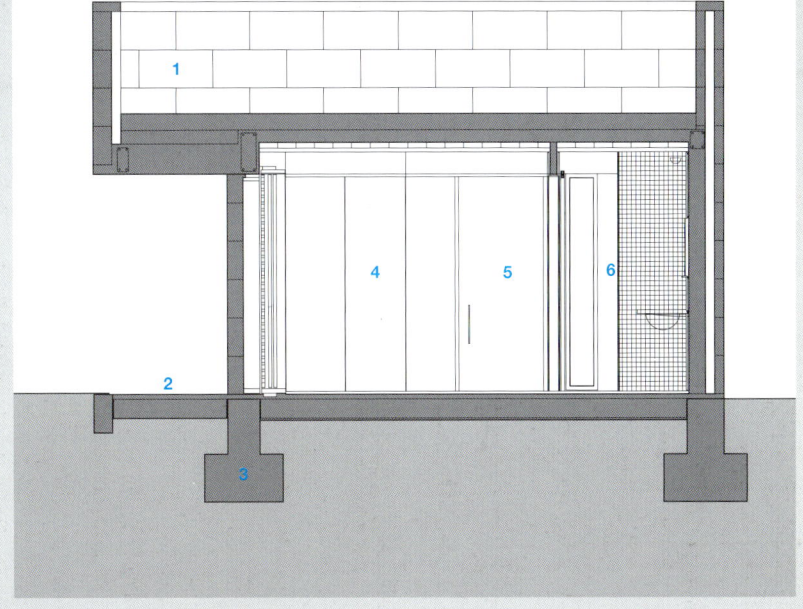

18.07
Guest Pavilion Detail
Section 1
1:75
  1 Mares stone wall
  2 Mares stone wall
  3 Concrete pad
footing
  4 Iroco timber
panelling
  5 Ceramic tiled
vaulted roof
  6 Timber door
  7 Air chamber

18.08
Guest Pavilion Detail
Section 2
1:75
  1 Mares stone wall
  2 Reinforced
concrete slab
  3 Concrete pad
footing
  4 Iroco timber
panelling
  5 Timber door
  6 Ceramic tiled
bathroom

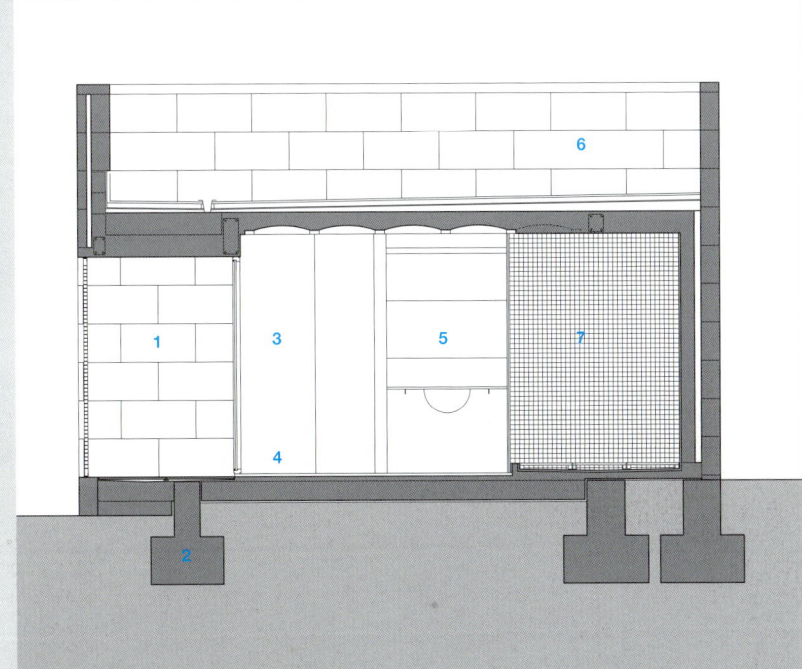

18.09
Guest Pavilion Detail
Section 3
1:75
  1 Mares stone wall
  2 Concrete pad
footing
  3 Iroco timber
panelling
  4 Continuous
concrete slab with
terrazzo finish to
pavement
  5 Mirror above
bathroom bench
  6 Mares stone wall
  7 Tesselated tiling to
shower

18.10
Guest Pavilion Detail
Section 4
1:75
  1 Mares stone wall
  2 Tesselated tiling to
shower
  3 Timber door
  4 Continuous
concrete slab with
terrazzo finish to
pavement
  5 Iroco timber
panelling
  6 Mares stone wall
  7 Concrete pad
footing

19
John Pawson

Tetsuka House
Tokyo, Japan

Client
Katsuhiko and Yumiko Tetsuka

Area
181 square metres (1,950 square feet)

Project Team
John Pawson, Vishwa Kaushal,
Shingo Ozawa

General Contractor
Nakajima Corporation

This minimalist house is located on a constricted site in a suburb to the south-west of Tokyo. Extremely high land values and demanding building regulations to cope with the risk of earthquakes have not dampened a design that expresses traditional and contemporary aspects of Japanese domestic life. The elegant two-storey box turns its back on its surroundings, creating instead a tranquil inner calm. Constructed from rendered and painted concrete, the box is pierced by only a few glazed openings in order to edit out the outside world. Spaces for living, dining and cooking are located on the ground floor, while sleeping, bathing and dressing areas upstairs are reached by a single flight of stairs.

A secluded courtyard with a single Japanese maple forms the focus for the entire house. The main living space faces directly onto the courtyard, as does a tea ceremony room with traditional tatami mat floor. The boundary between the internal spaces and the courtyard are blurred via panes of full-height glazing and a stone bench that seamlessly traverses the length of the house. While the courtyard has the prosaic function of filtering out the nondescript suburban context, more importantly it serves to frame elements of the landscape – a trace of sky, branches of the tree – in the manner of traditional Japanese landscape design. Similarly, windows are located to define alternative views, with those that are hemmed in by adjacent buildings infilled with translucent glass to preserve the internal environment of calm and privacy. A limited palette of materials – limestone, plaster, concrete, timber and glass – reinforces the formal rigour of the architecture.

1 A blade wall guides people towards the entrance at the south-west corner. Punctures in the external skin are avoided in favour of an internal light-filled courtyard.

2 The living area dissolves seamlessly into the courtyard via a full-height wall of glass. This is emphasized by a stone bench that traverses the length of the house.

3 The kitchen is in keeping with the calm asceticism that characterizes the entire house. A single stainless steel spout rises from the stone work top.

4 A concrete staircase links the living spaces downstairs and the bedroom, bathroom and dressing room upstairs.

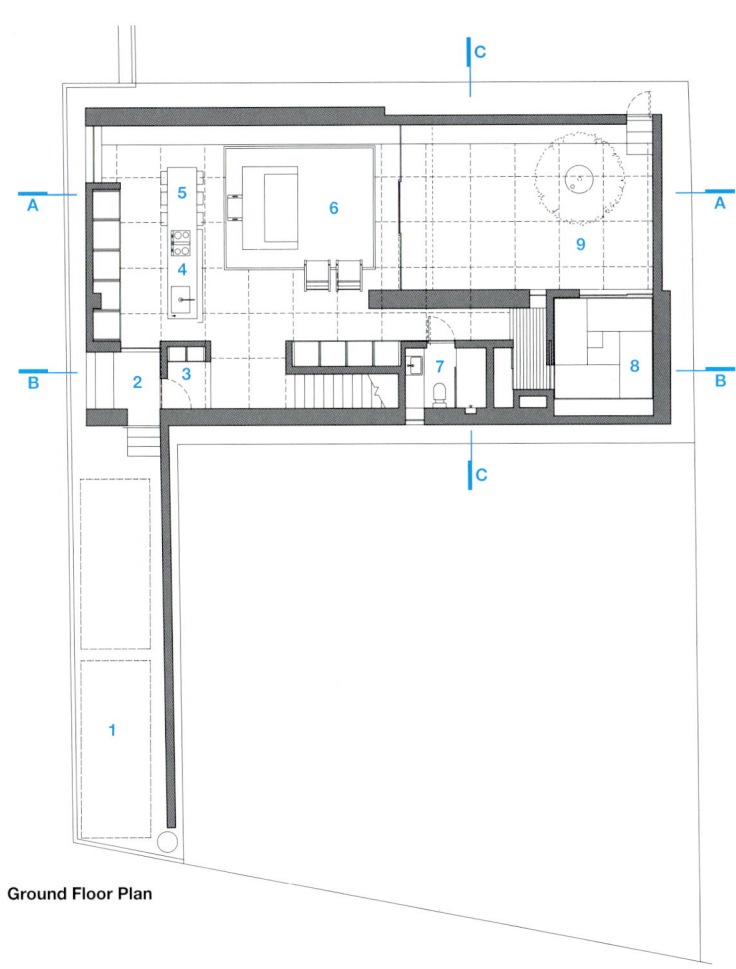

Ground Floor Plan

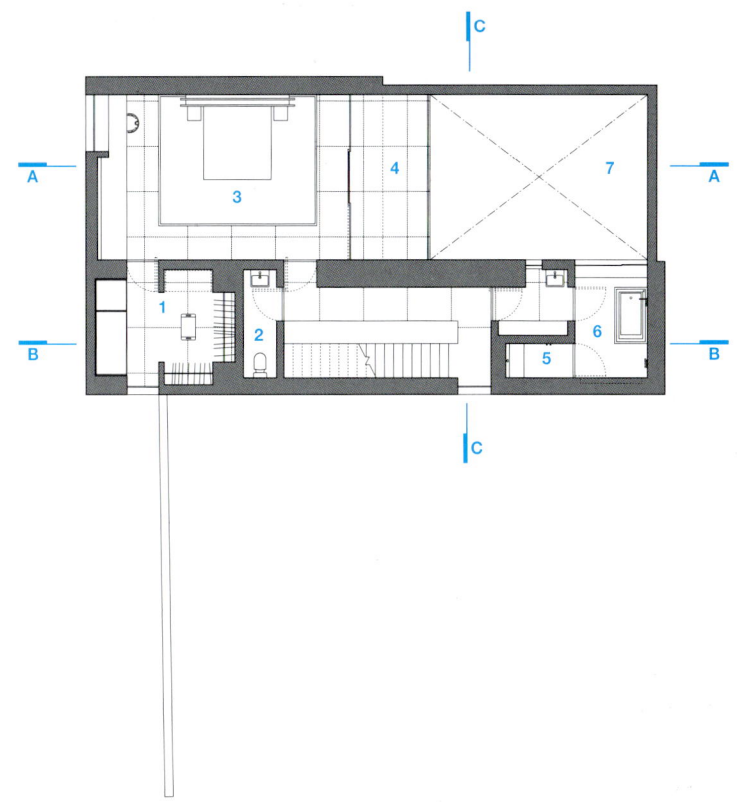

First Floor Plan

0   5   10m

0   15   30ft

19.01
Ground Floor Plan
1:200
  1 Parking
  2 Entrance
  3 Entrance lobby
  4 Kitchen
  5 Dining
  6 Living room
  7 WC
  8 Tea room
  9 Courtyard

19.02
First Floor Plan
1:200
  1 Dressing room
  2 WC
  3 Bedroom
  4 Terrace
  5 Shower
  6 Bathroom
  7 Courtyard below

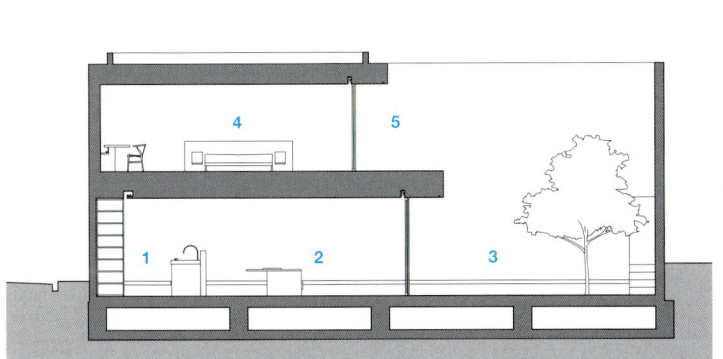

Section A–A

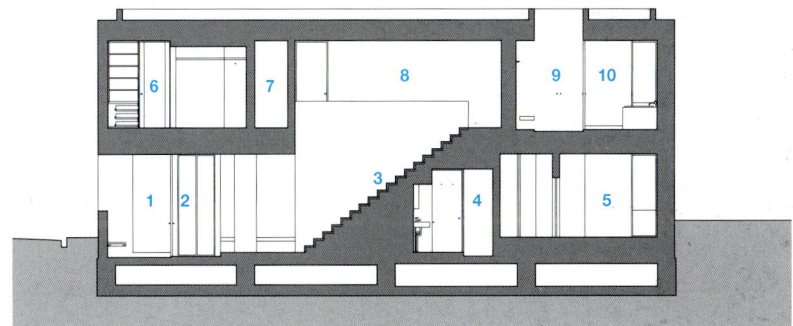

Section B–B

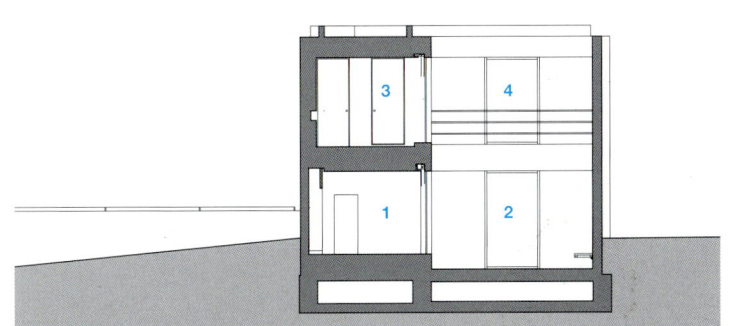

Section C–C

19.03
Section A–A
1:200
  1 Kitchen
  2 Living room
  3 Courtyard
  4 Bedroom
  5 Terrace

19.04
Section B–B
1:200
  1 Entrance
  2 Entrance lobby
  3 Staircase
  4 WC
  5 Tea room
  6 Dressing room
  7 WC
  8 Hall
  9 Shower
  10 Bathroom

19.05
Section C–C
1:200
  1 Tea room
  2 Courtyard
  3 Bathroom
  4 Terrace

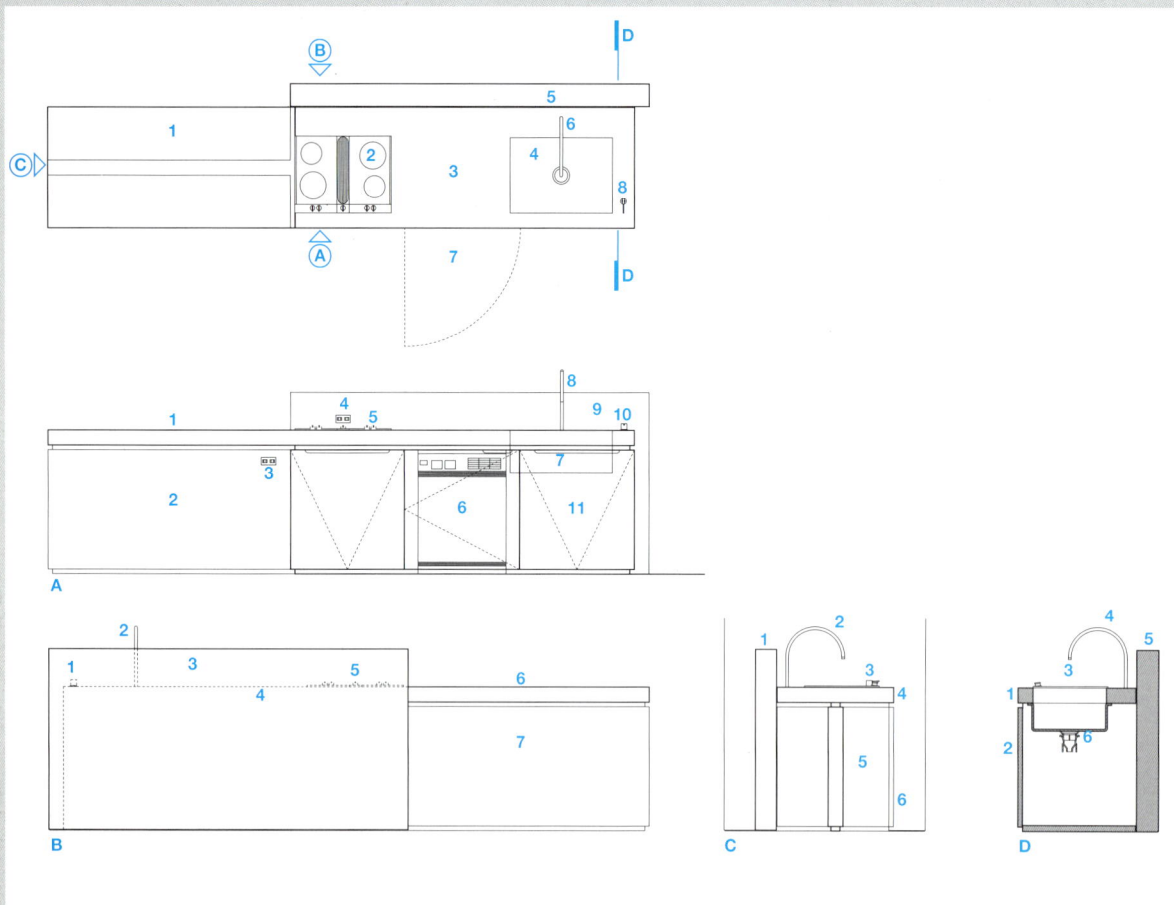

19.06
Kitchen Details
1:50

Plan
1 Limestone countertop
2 Hotplates
3 Limestone worktop
4 Stainless steel sink
5 Low wall between kitchen and living room
6 Stainless steel spout
7 Integrated dishwasher
8 Stainless steel tap

Elevation A
1 Limestone countertop
2 White-painted MDF panel
3 Power point
4 Power point
5 Hotplates
6 Dishwasher
7 Stainless steel sink behind
8 Stainless steel spout
9 Stone-clad splashback
10 Stainless steel tap
11 White-painted MDF panel

Elevation B
1 Stainless steel tap behind
2 Stainless steel spout behind
3 Low wall
4 Line of counter behind
5 Hotplates behind
6 Limestone countertop
7 Line of under-bench structure

Elevation C
1 Low wall between kitchen and dining room
2 Stainless steel spout
3 Stainless steel tap
4 Limestone countertop
5 End panel
6 White-painted MDF panel to front

Section D–D
1 Limestone counter-top
2 White-painted MDF panel to front
3 Stainless steel sink
4 Stainless steel spout
5 Low wall between kitchen and dining room
6 Waste disposal unit

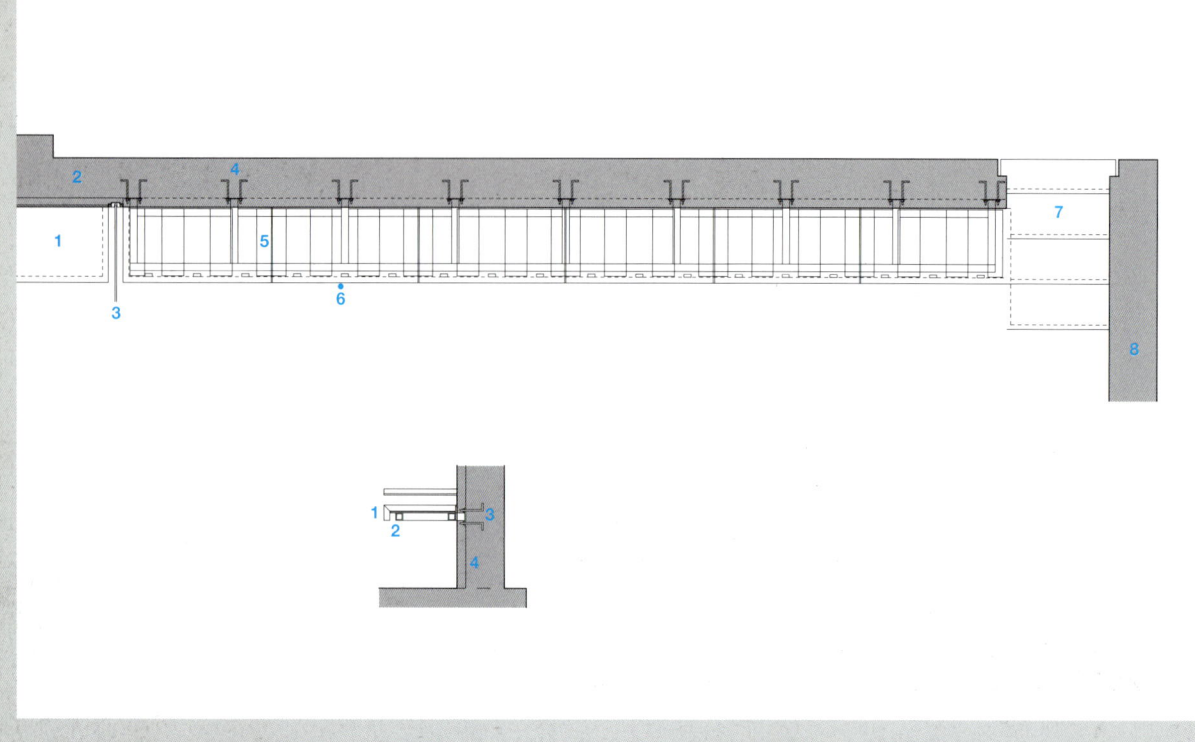

19.07
Stone Bench Details
1:50

Plan
1 Limestone bench
2 Concrete wall
3 Glass wall
4 Anchor
5 Steel plate
6 50 x 50 mm (2 x 2 inch) steel frame
7 Limestone stair
8 Concrete wall

Section
1 Limestone bench
2 50 x 50 mm (2 x 2 inch) steel frame
3 Anchor
4 Concrete wall

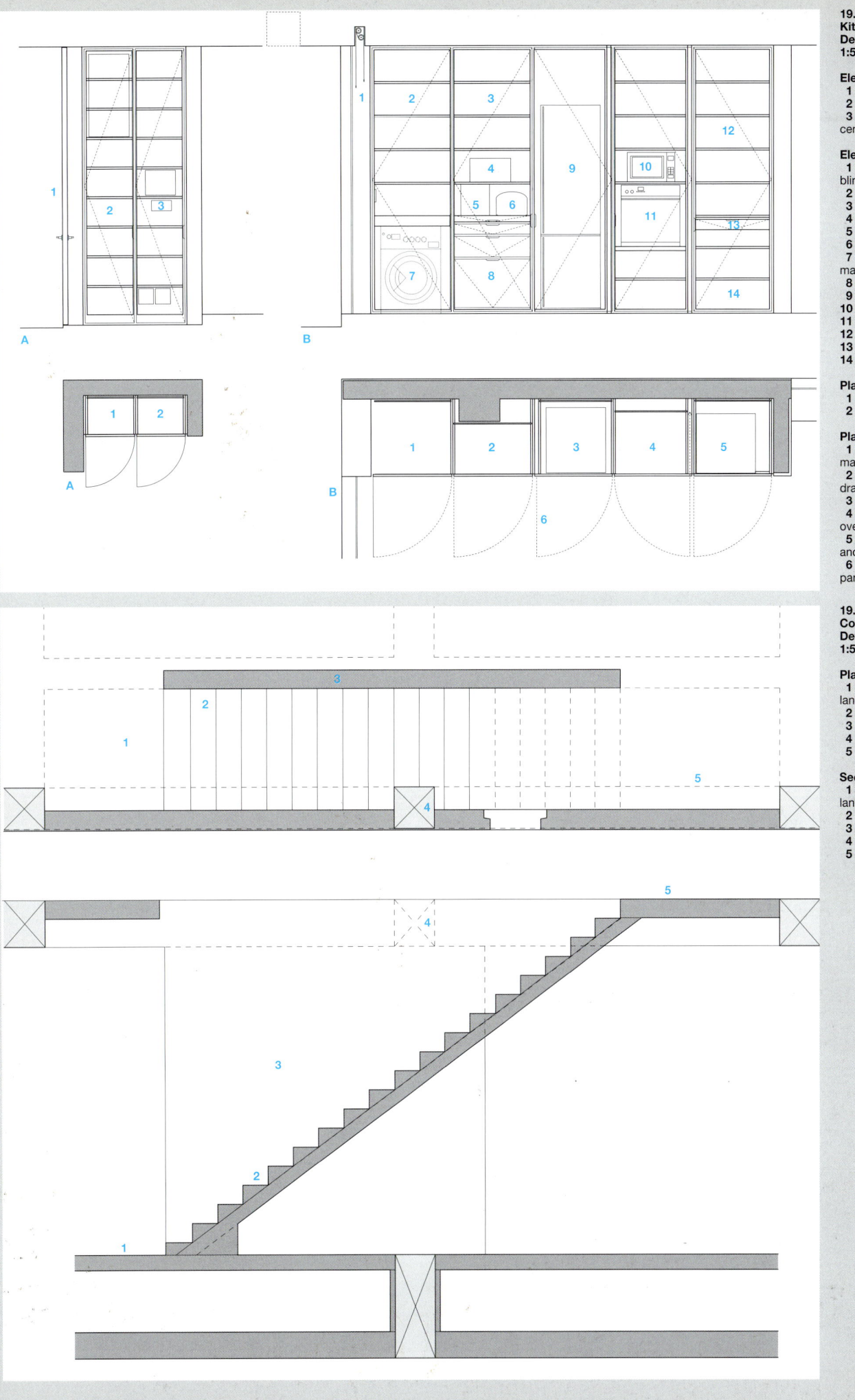

19.08
Kitchen Cupboard
Details
1:50

Elevation A
1 Entry door
2 Adjustable shelves
3 Floor heating
central panel

Elevation B
1 Recessed roller
blind
2 Adjustable shelves
3 Adjustable shelves
4 Toaster
5 Coffee maker
6 Rice cooker
7 Washing and drying
machine
8 Drawers
9 Fridge freezer
10 Microwave
11 Oven
12 Adjustable shelves
13 Drawer
14 Adjustable shelves

Plan A
1 Adjustable shelves
2 Adjustable shelves

Plan B
1 Washing and drying
machine
2 Appliances and
drawer
3 Fridge freezer
4 Microwave and
oven
5 Adjustable shelves
and drawer
6 Folding sliding
panel

19.09
Concrete Staircase
Details
1:50

Plan
1 Ground floor
landing
2 Treads
3 Structural wall
4 Column
5 First floor landing

Section
1 Ground floor
landing
2 Treads and risers
3 Wall beyond
4 Beam
5 First floor landing

Father's House
Lantian, China

Area
385 square metres (4,144 square feet)

Project Team
Qingyun Ma, Weihang Chen, Peter
Knutson, Yinghui Wang, Satoko Saeki,
James Macgill

Landscape Architect
MADA s.p.a.m.

Structural Engineer
MADA s.p.a.m.

Main Contractor (Exterior)
Zongqi Fan

Main Contractor (Interior)
Shanghai Dumiao Interior Decoration
Co. Ltd.

This house is situated in a river valley
at the foot of Quinlin Mountain in
north-west China. The valley has been
carved out of the Shan Xi plateau by
waters running down from the
mountain over many thousands of
years. Arranged over two levels with
kichen, dining and living spaces on
the ground floor and bedrooms and
bathroom above, the house is entered
via a gate that leads to an L-shaped
walled garden with a reflection
pool. The house is made up of three
main components. The structural
frame is of reinforced concrete, wall
infill panels are of local river
stones, and interior walls, ceilings and
shutters are of bamboo board.

The structural frame remains
a consistent dimension for all beams
and columns. The river stones were
collected over a period of two years
by local villagers and sorted by colour,
so that each wall panel has a specific
colour tone. Four types of wall make
up the construction. The retaining wall
around the site is constructed in the
vernacular fashion traditionally used
by local villagers. At the perimeter
wall, the stones are exposed on both
sides, fixed within the structure with
cement and imbedded tie bars.
The interior walls are of local bamboo
board typically used for concrete
formwork, polished and varnished.
All openings are floor to ceiling with
metal frame windows. The wall to
the courtyard is fully openable,
protected by movable bamboo board
shutters.

1 The concrete frame
is infilled with river
stones along the
perimeter wall and
full-height glazing with
bamboo shutters on
the courtyard facade.
2 The river stones that
characterise the
aesthetic of the house
were gathered and
sorted by colour by
local villagers and
arranged so that each
panel has a specific
colour tone.
3 A reflecting pool
occupies the space
between the perimeter
wall and the house.
Here, the quality and
texture of the stone
walls is most apparent.
4 The bamboo panels
lend a warmth and
texture to the interior
spaces as well as
introducing another
traditional material into
this otherwise contem-
porary structure.

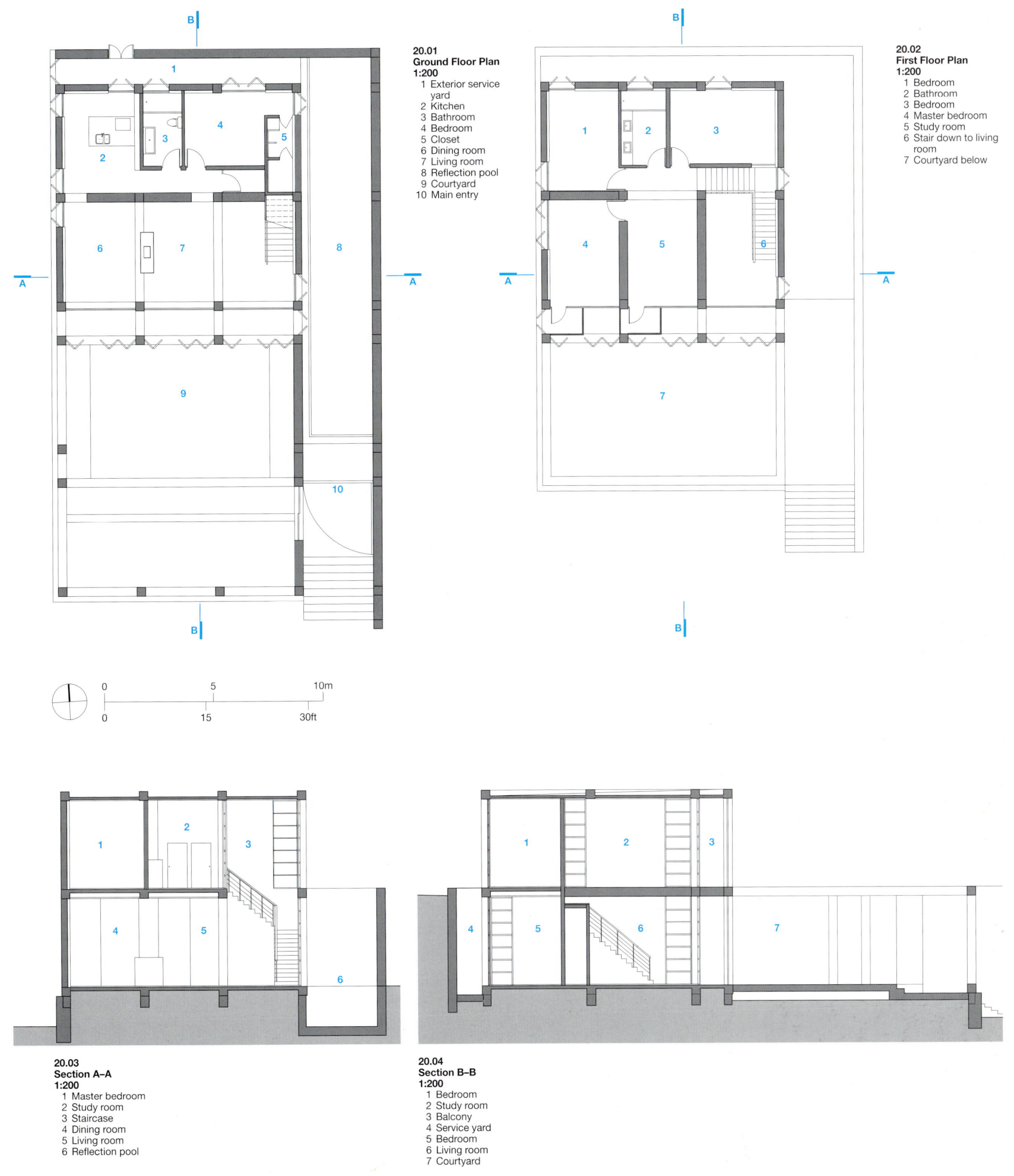

20.01
Ground Floor Plan
1:200
1 Exterior service yard
2 Kitchen
3 Bathroom
4 Bedroom
5 Closet
6 Dining room
7 Living room
8 Reflection pool
9 Courtyard
10 Main entry

20.02
First Floor Plan
1:200
1 Bedroom
2 Bathroom
3 Bedroom
4 Master bedroom
5 Study room
6 Stair down to living room
7 Courtyard below

20.03
Section A–A
1:200
1 Master bedroom
2 Study room
3 Staircase
4 Dining room
5 Living room
6 Reflection pool

20.04
Section B–B
1:200
1 Bedroom
2 Study room
3 Balcony
4 Service yard
5 Bedroom
6 Living room
7 Courtyard

91

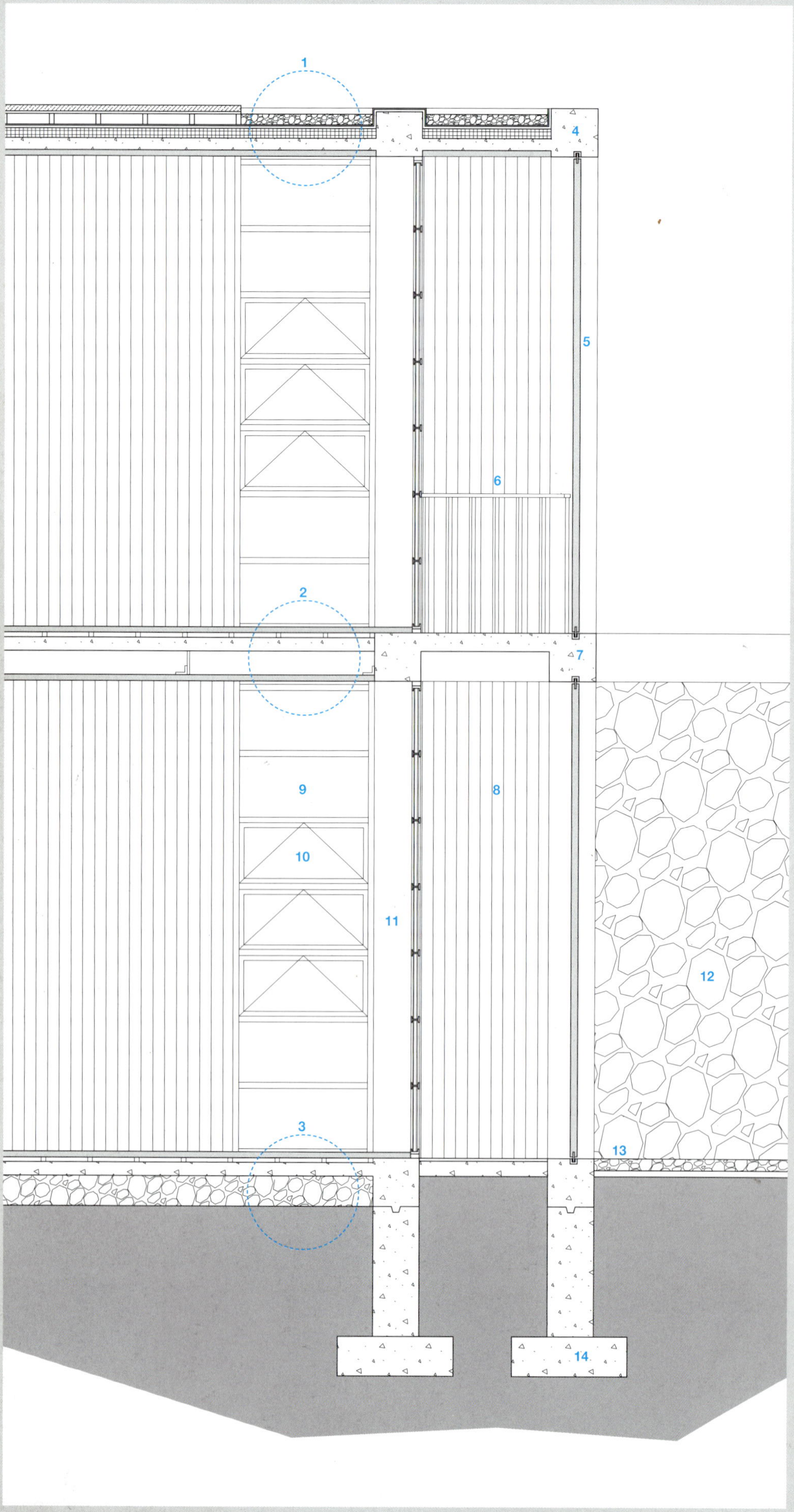

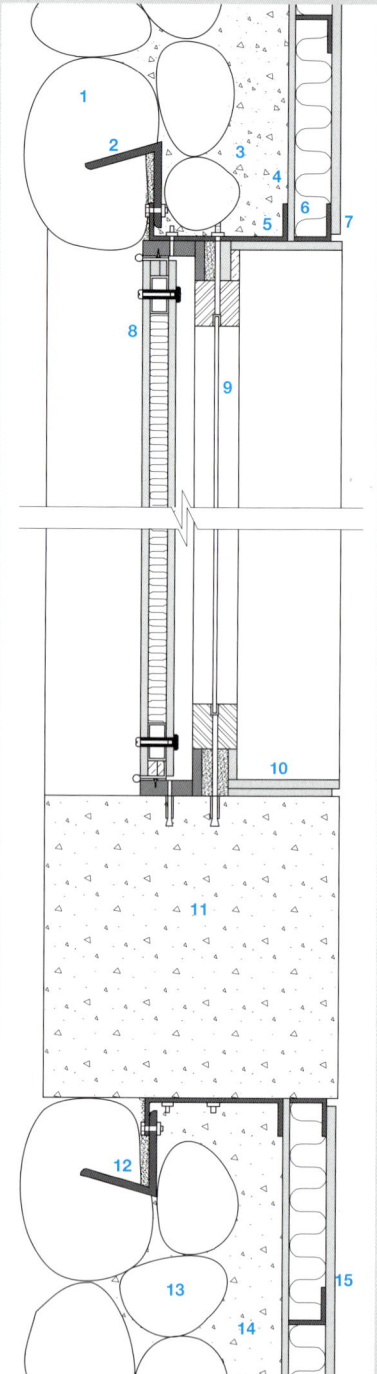

20.05
Detail Wall Section 1
1:50
  1 Reinforced
concrete roof slab
covered with rigid
insulation, PVC
membrane and gravel,
and lined with bamboo
panels
  2 Polished bamboo
flooring over reinforced
concrete slab floor,
lined with suspended
ceiling framing and
polished bamboo
ceiling panels
  3 Polished bamboo
board flooring on
reinforced concrete
floor slab over
waterproof membrane,
vapour barrier, gravel
bed and compacted
soil
  4 Reinforced
concrete structural
frame
  5 Polished bamboo
board folding shutters
  6 Aluminium handrail
with matt black finish
  7 Polished reinforced
concrete floor slab
  8 Polished bamboo
board door behind
  9 Fixed clear glazed
window panel
10 Operable clear
glazed window panel
11 Aluminium
storefront window
system
12 River stone external
wall
13 Polished finish river
stone paving
14 Reinforced
concrete footings

20.06
Wall Plan Detail
1:10
  1 River stone external
wall
  2 Steel angle tie back
  3 Cement mortar bed
  4 Vapour barrier over
bamboo formwork
  5 Steel angle bolted
to wall
  6 Batt insulation
  7 Polished bamboo
board to interior wall
  8 Polished bamboo
board folding door
  9 Fixed clear glazed
window
10 Polished bamboo
board flooring
11 Reinforced
concrete column
12 Steel angle tie back
13 River stone external
wall

14 Cement mortar bed
15 Polished bamboo
wall panels

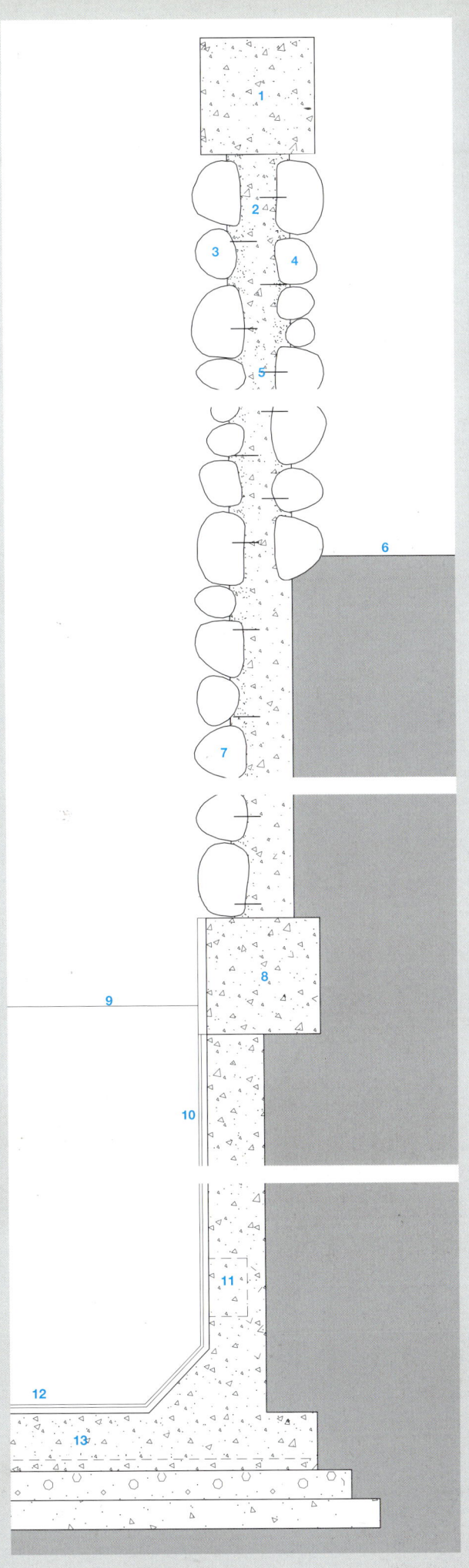

20.07
Detail Wall Section 2
1:20
1 Reinforced concrete wall cast in-situ
2 Cement mortar for fixing stones in place
3 Local river stone to interior wall of courtyard
4 Local river stones to exterior wall
5 Non-corrosive steel wall tie back
6 Finished level to top soil
7 Local river stone to interior wall of courtyard
8 Reinforced concrete wall to pool
9 Water level
10 Ceramic tiles to pool wall
11 Recessed underwater lighting
12 Ceramic tile finish on 10 mm (1/3 inch) mortar bed over elastic waterproofing membrane
13 Reinforced concrete slab over gravel bed

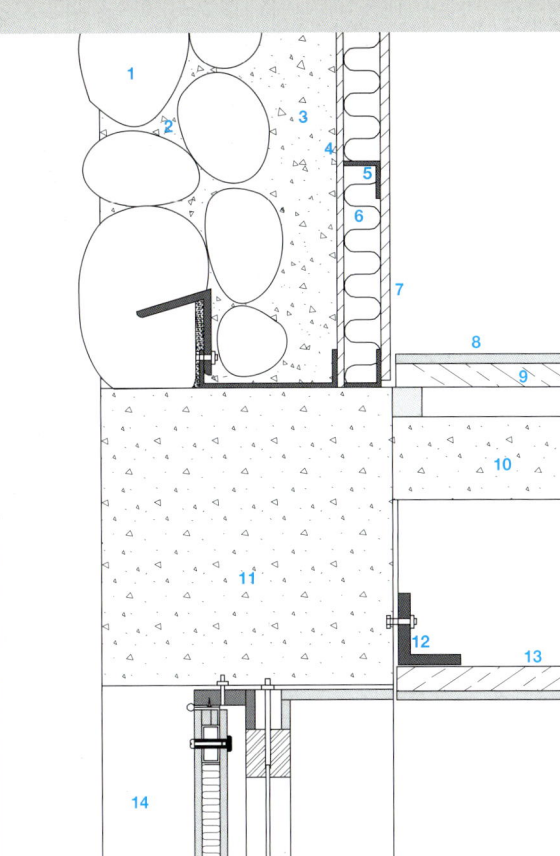

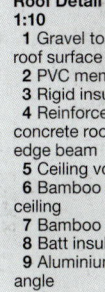

20.08
Detail Wall Section 3
1:10
1 River stone
2 Cement mortar
3 Reinforced concrete wall, cast in-situ
4 Vapour barrier
5 Bamboo formwork
6 Batt insulation
7 Polished bamboo board to wall
8 Polished bamboo board to floor
9 Plywood subfloor
10 Reinforced concrete floor slab
11 Reinforced concrete beam and lintel
12 Steel angle bolted to concrete structure
13 Ceiling duct space
14 Reinforced concrete column behind
15 Bamboo window shutter
16 Glazed door

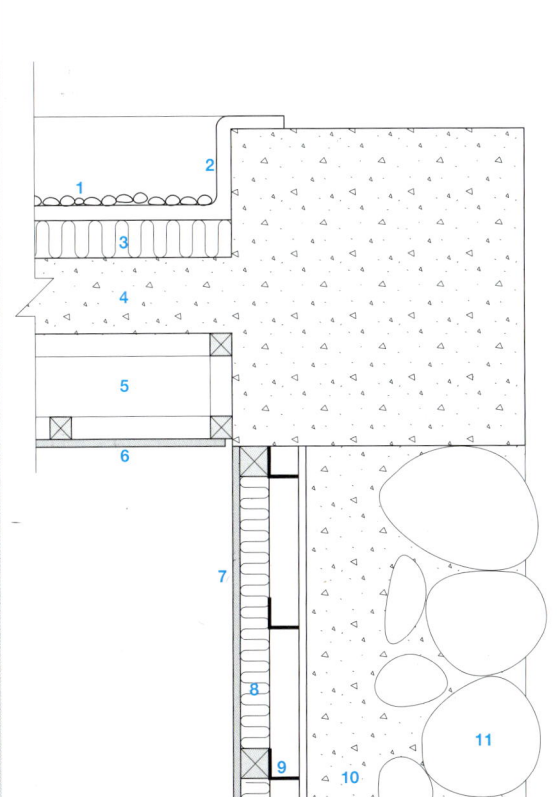

20.09
Roof Detail
1:10
1 Gravel to finished roof surface
2 PVC membrane
3 Rigid insulation
4 Reinforced concrete roof and edge beam
5 Ceiling void
6 Bamboo panel ceiling
7 Bamboo panel wall
8 Batt insulation
9 Aluminium fixing angle
10 Cement mortar
11 River stones to exterior wall

21
Olson Sundberg Kundig Allen Architects

Chicken Point Cabin
Chicken Point, Idaho, USA

Area
292 square metres (3,145 square feet)

Project Team
Tom Kundig, Steven Rainville, Debbie Kennedy

Structural Engineer
Monte Clark Engineering

Main Contractor
MC Construction

Mechanical Fabrication
Turner Exhibits

The idea for this simple, yet sophisticated cabin, was to create a lakeside shelter in the woods – a small box with a correspondingly giant window that opens to the surrounding landscape. The cabin's window-wall opens up the entire living space to the forest and lake. The cabin is large enough to accommodate a typical domestic programme and sleep ten people, and yet retains an intimate quality appropriate to the natural setting. The design concept is essentially composed of three parts: a concrete-block box, a plywood insert and a 1.2 metre (4 foot) diameter steel fireplace.

Materials are deliberately low maintenance to take account of the occasional occupation – concrete block, steel, concrete floors and plywood – in keeping with the notion of a cabin, and left unfinished to age naturally and acquire a patina that complements the idyllic setting. Open, interior spaces are intended to be a seamless extension to the outdoors. The concrete floor continues outside to become a terrace with a built-in hot tub. The steel entry door is exaggerated in height to easily accommodate long skis. Once inside, the concrete block volume is punctuated by relatively few distractions: a steel fireplace, a bridge that spans the main space and the master sleeping alcove that floats above the kitchen area. The dramatic window-wall pivots on an off-centre axis, its speed regulated by a fly-ball governor, referred to by the owners and architects alike as the 'gizmo'.

1 A massive roof shelters the cabin while a giant window-wall pivots open via a mechanical fly wheel, opening up the living spaces to the landscape.
2 The three formal components of the composition are seen here in the concrete block container, the plywood insert with double-height door and the fireplace.
3 The window-wall opens up the house to views of Hayden Lake and the Reservoir Mountains beyond.
4 View of the dramatic double-height entry door on the west facade.
5 Detail view of the 'gizmo' operated window-wall.
6 The dining area features a massive timber dining table.

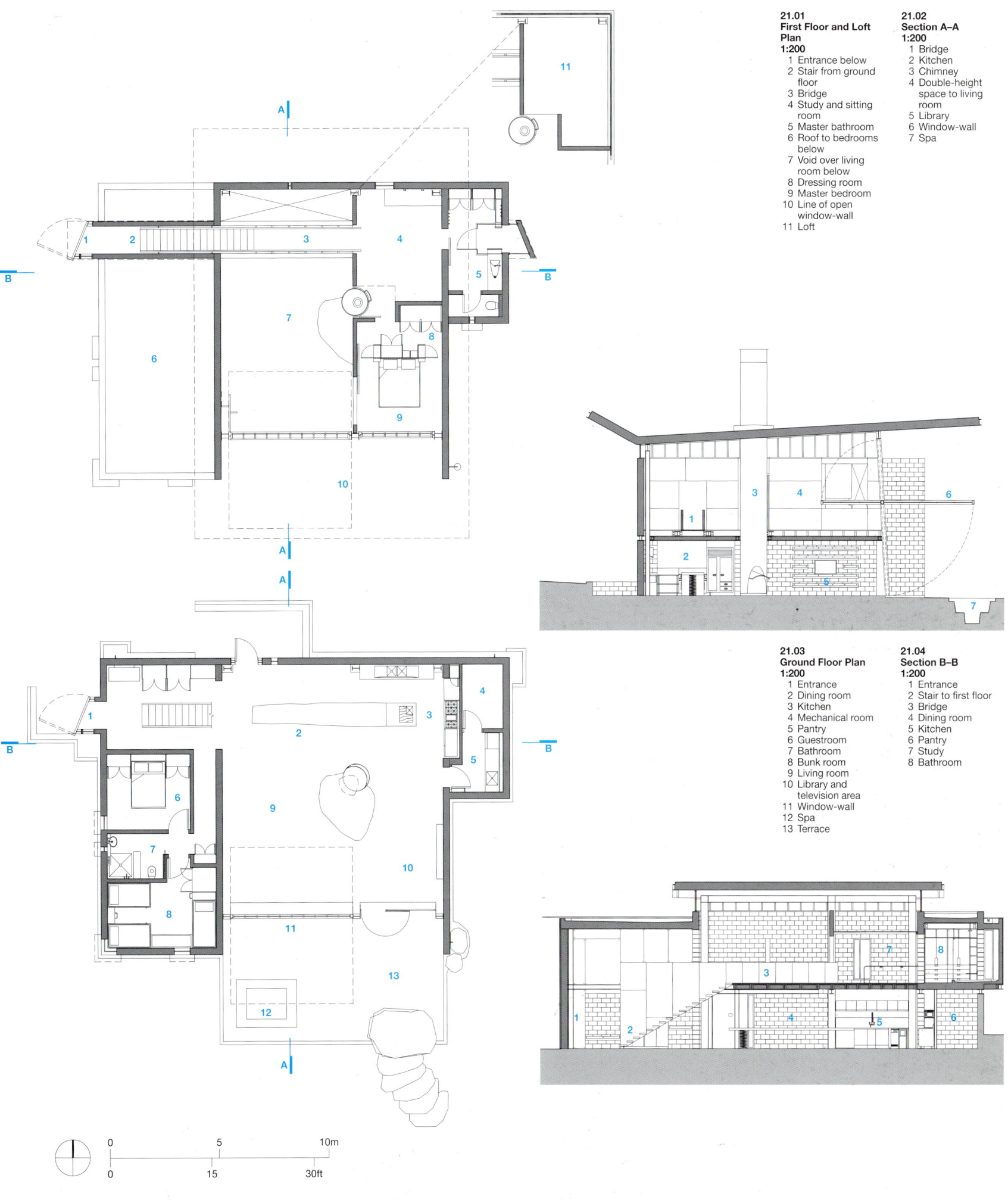

21.01
First Floor and Loft Plan
1:200
1 Entrance below
2 Stair from ground floor
3 Bridge
4 Study and sitting room
5 Master bathroom
6 Roof to bedrooms below
7 Void over living room below
8 Dressing room
9 Master bedroom
10 Line of open window-wall
11 Loft

21.02
Section A–A
1:200
1 Bridge
2 Kitchen
3 Chimney
4 Double-height space to living room
5 Library
6 Window-wall
7 Spa

21.03
Ground Floor Plan
1:200
1 Entrance
2 Dining room
3 Kitchen
4 Mechanical room
5 Pantry
6 Guestroom
7 Bathroom
8 Bunk room
9 Living room
10 Library and television area
11 Window-wall
12 Spa
13 Terrace

21.04
Section B–B
1:200
1 Entrance
2 Stair to first floor
3 Bridge
4 Dining room
5 Kitchen
6 Pantry
7 Study
8 Bathroom

0   5   10m

0   15   30ft

95

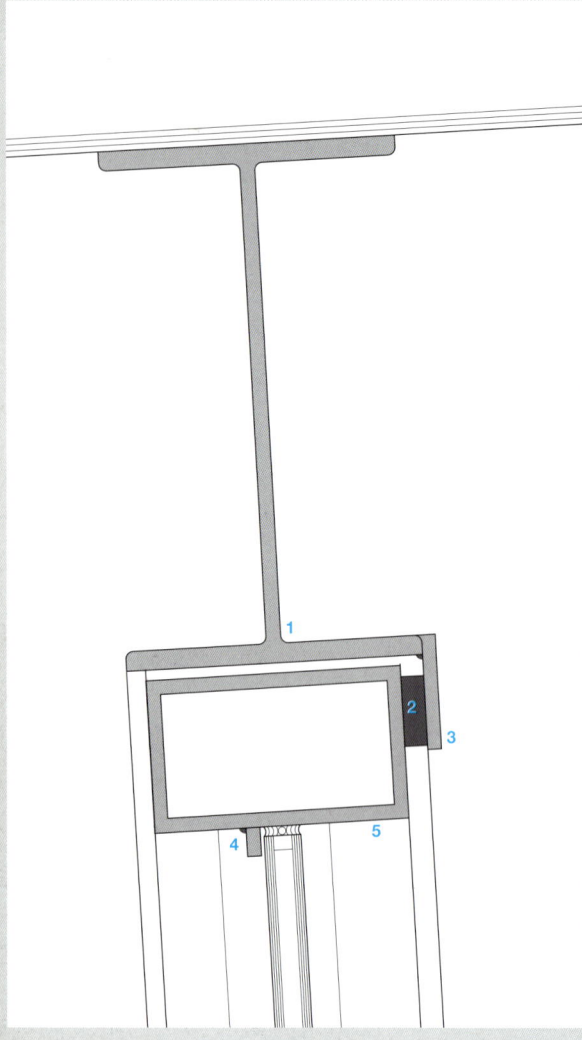

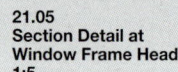

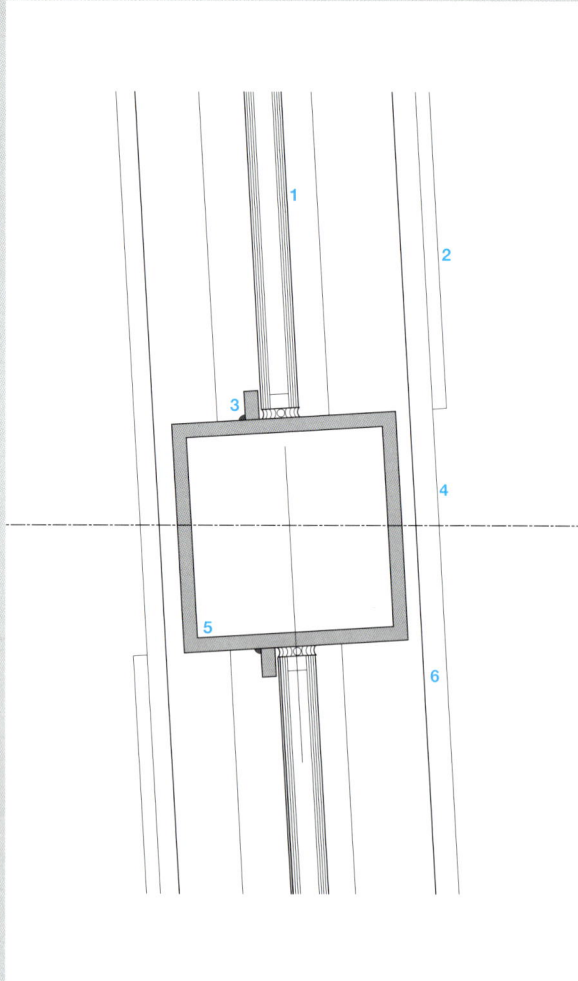

21.05
Section Detail at Window Frame Head
1:5
1 Fixed steel beam
2 Weather strip secure to strike plate
3 Steel strike plate with continuous fillet weld to top
4 Continuous welded steel glass stop
5 Steel window wall frame

21.06
Section Detail at Window Axle
1:5
1 Glazing assembly
2 Line of strike plate beyond
3 Continuous welded steel glass stop
4 Line of window frame beyond
5 Steel square section horizontally centred on window frame
6 Line of door frame beyond

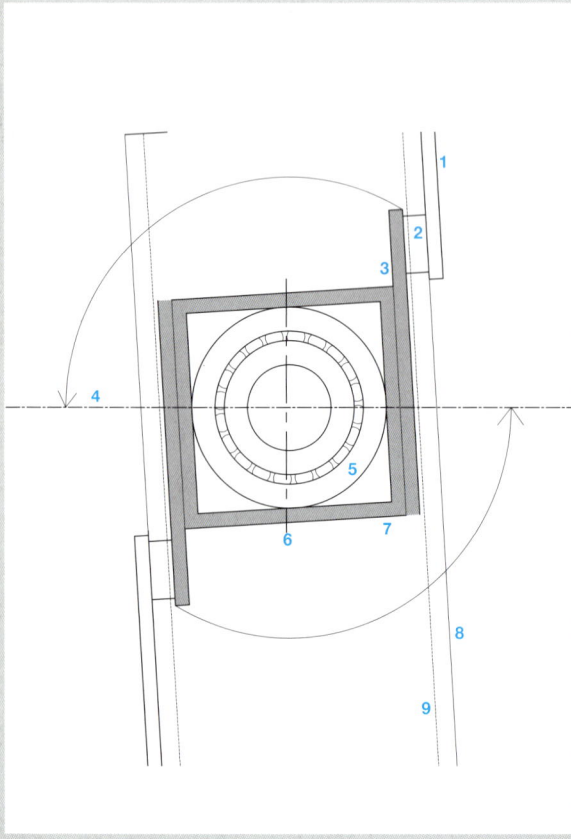

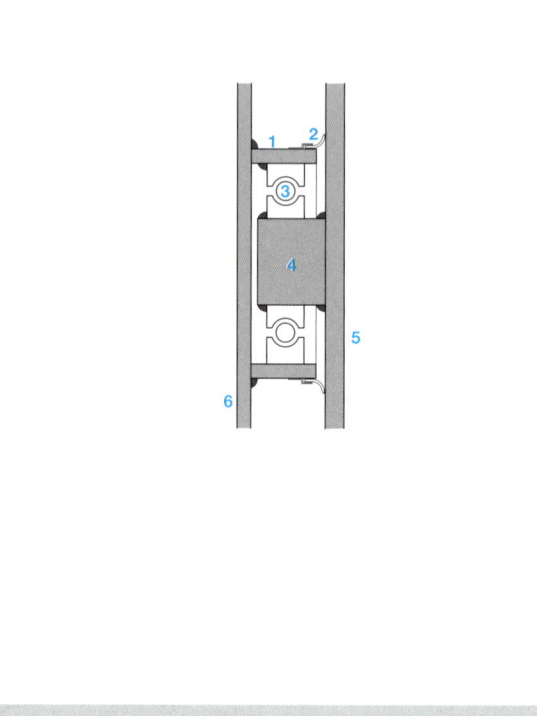

21.07
Section Detail at Bearing Mechanism
1:5
1 Strike plate beyond
2 Weather stripping secure to plate
3 Steel plate secured to steel section with fillet weld
4 Centre line of axle
5 Bearing mechanism
6 Line of continuous gasket
7 Steel square section enclosure
8 Line of window frame beyond
9 Line of steel frame

21.08
Bearing Mechanism Detail
1:5
1 Steel plate
2 Continuous gasket
3 Bearing mechanism
4 Bearing mechanism
5 Wide flange
6 Steel window frame

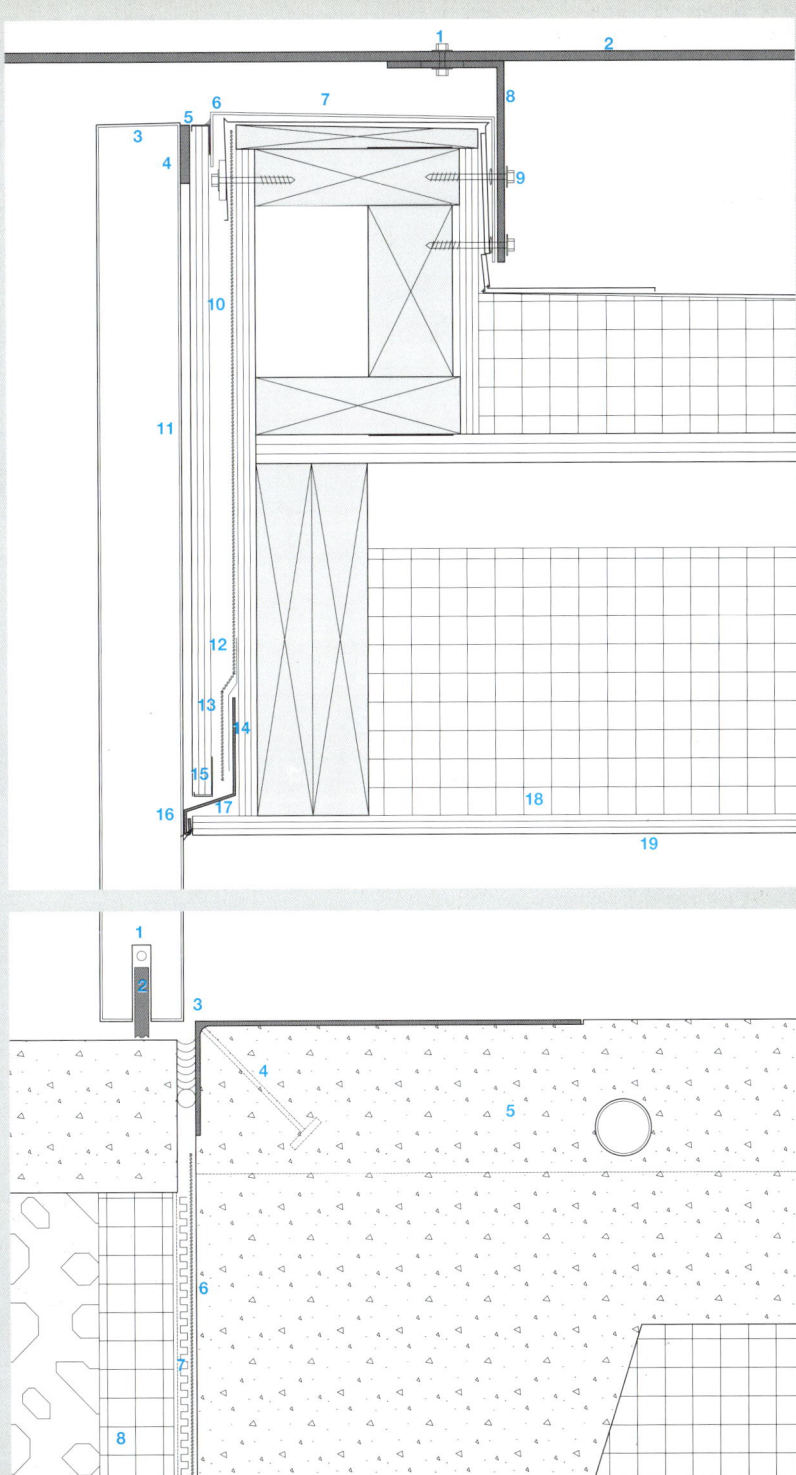

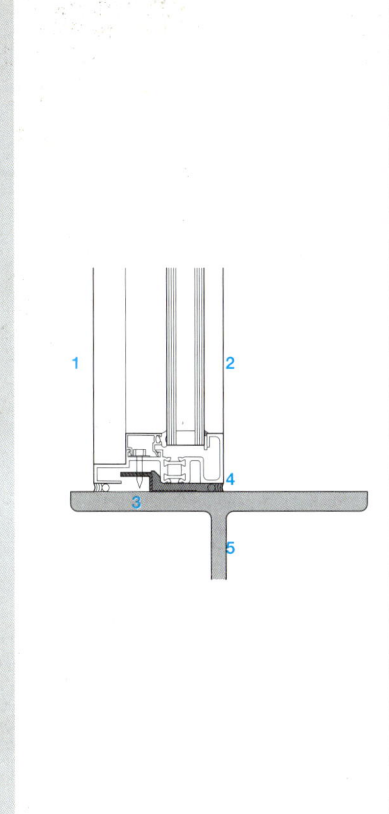

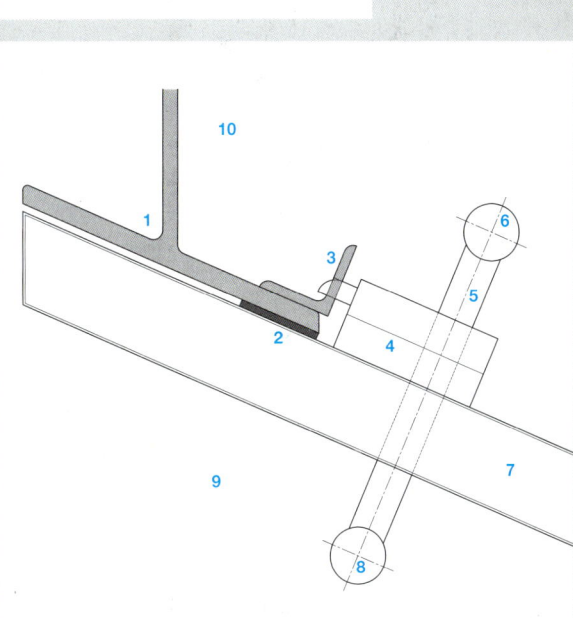

Sky Arc House
Marin County, California, USA

Area
595 square metres (6,400 square feet)

Project Team
Will Bruder, Ben Nesbeitt, Eric Weber, Dominique Price, John Puhr, Jeff Densic, Rob Gaspard, Michael Crooks, Tom Cheney, Joe Herzog, Richard Jensen, Katie Jones, Dwayne Smyth, Troy Strange, Greg Packham

Structural Engineer
Rudow + Berry, Inc

Main Contractor
Van Acker Construction Associates

This house is located on a forested hillside with dramatic views to the bay and Mount Tamalpais. The steep eastern part of the site was chosen for a new residence for a young family, while the western part accommodates a play area and garden, as well as a recording studio. An open-air stair links the residence through a tunnel under the driveway. The simple volumes, clad in pre-weathered pewter-grey zinc, recede into the texture of the landscape, with vertical standing seams in the cladding. The glazing is 'solex green' for visual harmony with the landscape, with operable windows in mahogany, and in lieu of overhangs, shade is provided by translucent fibreglass awnings.

The process of arrival begins as the driveway widens into a forecourt of ripple-textured concrete. A rhythm of translucent slots lead to the entryway, where the warm glow of a resin lantern-wall indicates the timber entry door. Children's bedrooms and a modest guest suite with bay views are located on the entry level. A switchback stair leads down to the main living level where expansive panoramas of the bay and mountains are revealed. Outwardly, the room expands seamlessly through glass and sliding partitions to a timber deck and lawn terrace. From the living room, the gallery tunnel connects to the garden stair and then to the studio. The studio and control room are shaped by acoustic considerations, their volumes sized and tuned for quality of sound, and built of in-situ concrete to minimize sound transmission.

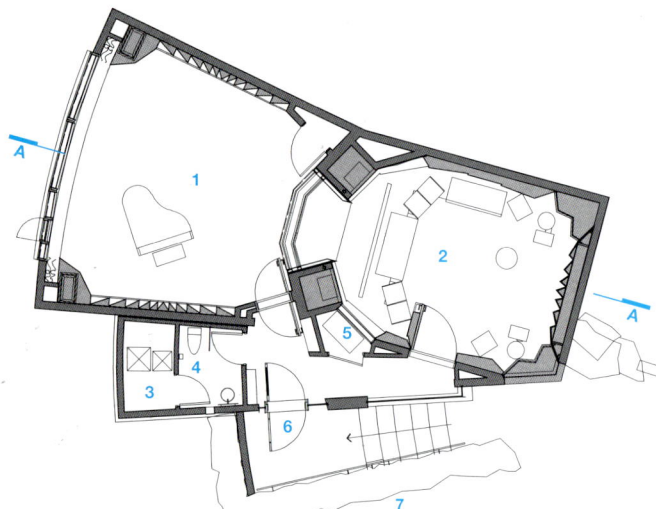

22.01
Studio Floor Plan
1:200
1 Recording studio
2 Control room
3 Utility and store
4 WC
5 Machine room
6 Entry
7 Garden

1 Backing onto a steep hillside, the house curves with the topography to embrace dramatic views of the forest.
2 Stepping up along the hill, the verticality of the facades is reinforced by standing seam zinc cladding, interrupted with slots of glazing to take in the views.
3 The south-east facade is shaded by translucent fibreglass awnings.
4 The music studio echoes the form of the house, tucked away to the west of the house, and connected to it via a tunnel that also acts as a gallery.
5 View of the main entry where a wall of resin glows in welcome.
6 The interior of the studio is designed to maximize the acoustic performance of the space while connecting the musician with the landscape outside with panels of clear glazing.

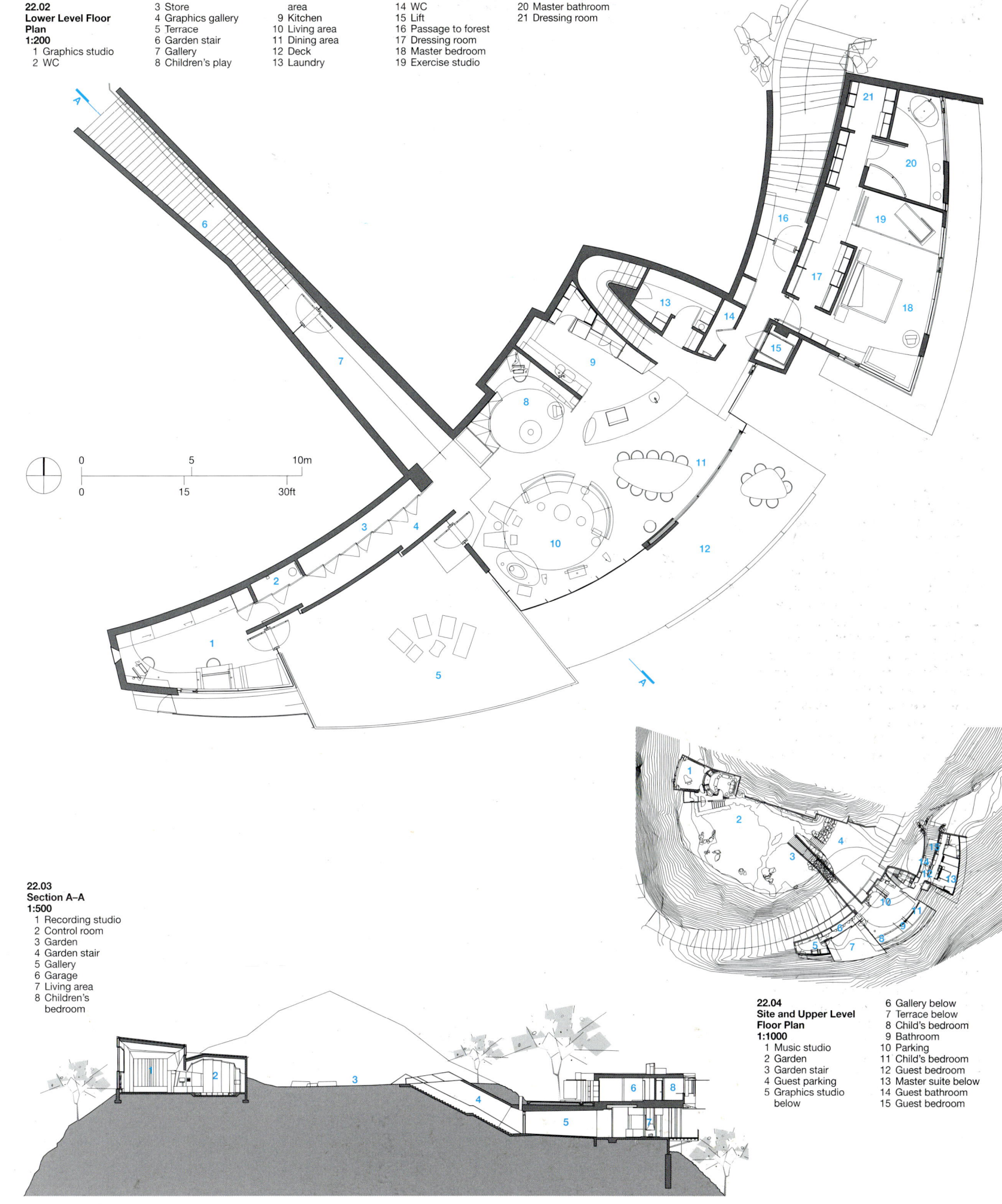

22.02
Lower Level Floor Plan
1:200
1 Graphics studio
2 WC
3 Store
4 Graphics gallery
5 Terrace
6 Garden stair
7 Gallery
8 Children's play
area
9 Kitchen
10 Living area
11 Dining area
12 Deck
13 Laundry
14 WC
15 Lift
16 Passage to forest
17 Dressing room
18 Master bedroom
19 Exercise studio
20 Master bathroom
21 Dressing room

0   5   10m
0   15   30ft

22.03
Section A–A
1:500
1 Recording studio
2 Control room
3 Garden
4 Garden stair
5 Gallery
6 Garage
7 Living area
8 Children's
bedroom

22.04
Site and Upper Level Floor Plan
1:1000
1 Music studio
2 Garden
3 Garden stair
4 Guest parking
5 Graphics studio
below
6 Gallery below
7 Terrace below
8 Child's bedroom
9 Bathroom
10 Parking
11 Child's bedroom
12 Guest bedroom
13 Master suite below
14 Guest bathroom
15 Guest bedroom

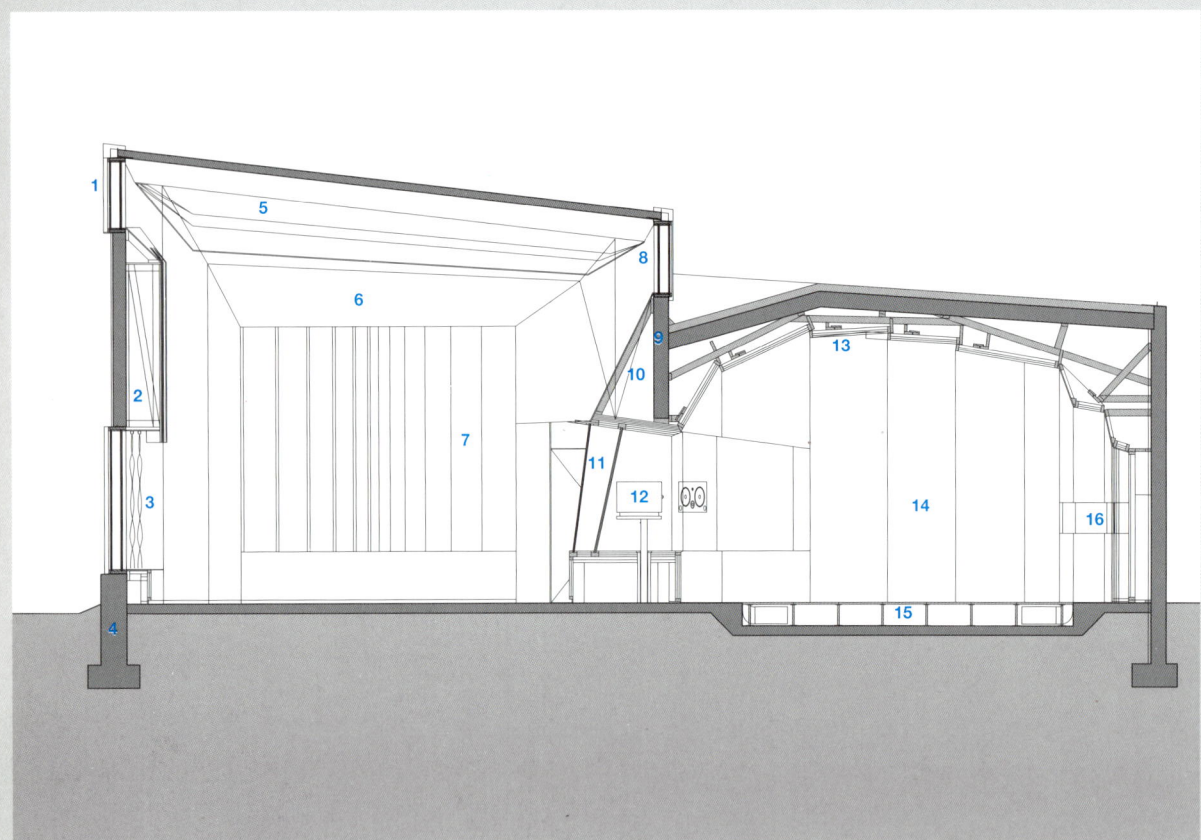

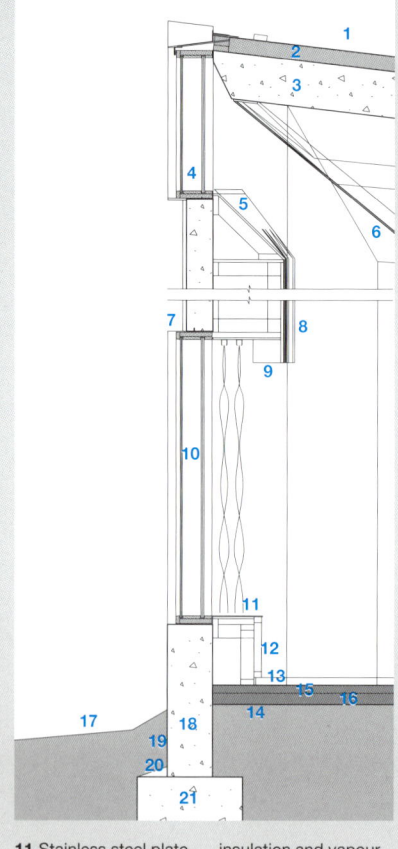

22.05
Studio Section
1:100
1 Timber window and zinc flashing assembly
2 Gypsum board over 50 x 100 mm (2 x 4 inch) timber framed acoustic reflector
3 Insulated timber frame window assembly with laminated solex glazing
4 Reinforced concrete wall

5 Gypsum board over 50 x 100 mm (2 x 4 inch) timber framed acoustic reflector
6 Gypsum board over 50 x 100 mm (2 x 4 inch) timber framed acoustic reflector
7 50 mm (2 inch) rigid insulation soak panel on timber frame
8 Timber window and zinc flashing assembly
9 Reinforced concrete wall
10 Gypsum board over

50 x 100 mm (2 x 4 inch) timber framed acoustic reflector
11 Laminated glass acoustic glazing assembly
12 Removeable aluminium centre speaker
13 50 mm (2 inch) rigid insulation soak panel on timber frame
14 50 mm (2 inch) rigid insulation soak panel on timber frame
15 Acoustically

isolated raised access floor and plenum
16 Translucent laminated glazing over internal lighting (clear laminated glazing to opposite end)

22.06
Studio Wall Section
1:50
1 Class A fully adhered membrane roof
2 100 mm (4 inch) rigid insulation board
3 Concrete roof deck
4 Timber window and zinc flashing assembly
5 Gypsum board to be flush with removeable stop to facilitate glazing replacement

6 Gypsum board on timber frame acoustical reflector system
7 Flat seam zinc flashing
8 Gypsum board on timber frame acoustical reflector system
9 Return finish at edge
10 Insulated timber window assembly with laminated solex glazing

11 Stainless steel plate with non-directional finish on plywood substrate and support frame
12 Rigid fibreglass soak panel with glued cloth covering on timber frame
13 Recessed aluminium base
14 Aggregate base course
15 100 mm (4 inch) concrete slab
16 50 mm (2 inch) rigid

insulation and vapour barrier
17 Finished grade
18 Reinforced concrete wall
19 Composite perimeter drain
20 Mortar wash
21 Reinforced concrete foundation

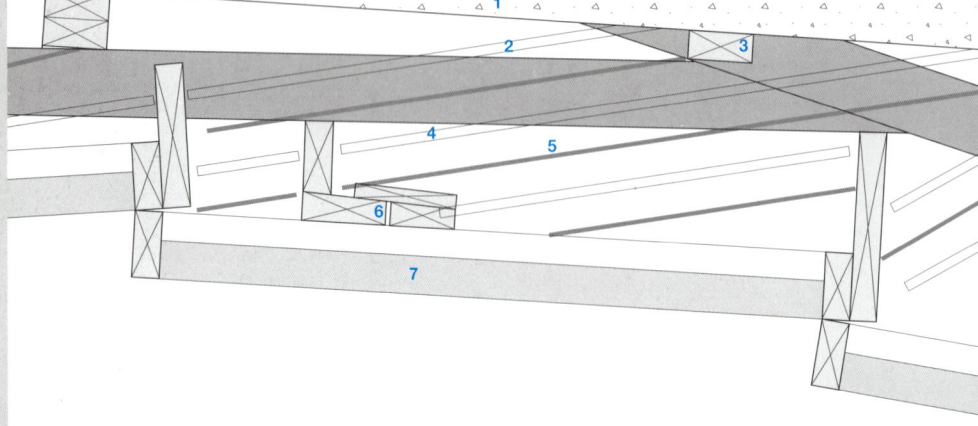

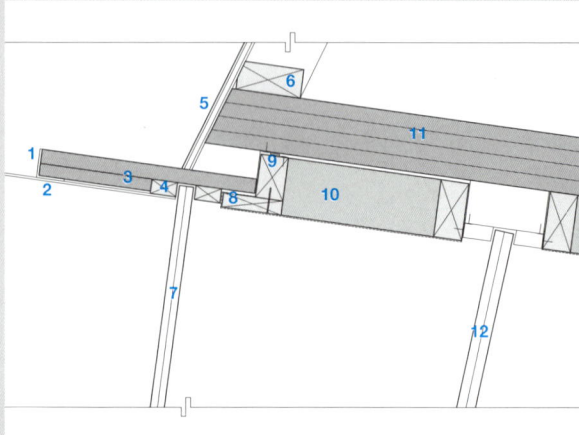

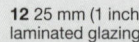

22.07
Control Room Ceiling Detail
1:10
1 Reinforced concrete roof
2 50 x 100 mm (2 x 4 inch) timber acoustic panel framing beyond
3 50 x 100 mm (2 x 4 inch) timber nailer with 'tapcon' anchors at

405 mm (16 inch) centres
4 Alternating layers of 12 mm (1/2 inch) sound deadening board and batt insulation to fill cavity completely
5 Alternating layers of 12 mm (1/2 inch) sound deadening board and batt insulation to fill cavity completely

6 Taper cut timber panel support clips
7 50 mm (2 inch) rigid insulation soak panel on timber frame

22.08
Window Head at Control Room View Portal Detail
1:10
1 Stainless steel angle with polished finish
2 Stainless steel head plate with non-uniform finish to both faces and polished edge
3 38 mm (1 1/2 inch) plywood head plate support
4 Completely filled cavity with acoustic caulk airtight seal
5 Veneer plaster over gypsum board
6 50 x 100 mm (2 x 4 inch) timber reflector panel framing
7 19 mm (3/4 inch)

3 38 mm (1 1/2 inch) plywood head plate support
8 Fabric wrapped soak panel trim board
9 Galvanized Z-clip soak panel support
10 76 mm (3 inch) rigid insulation soak panel on timber frame
11 19 mm (3/4 inch) plywood portal head assembly to 76 mm (3 inch) total thickness

laminated glazing
12 25 mm (1 inch) laminated glazing

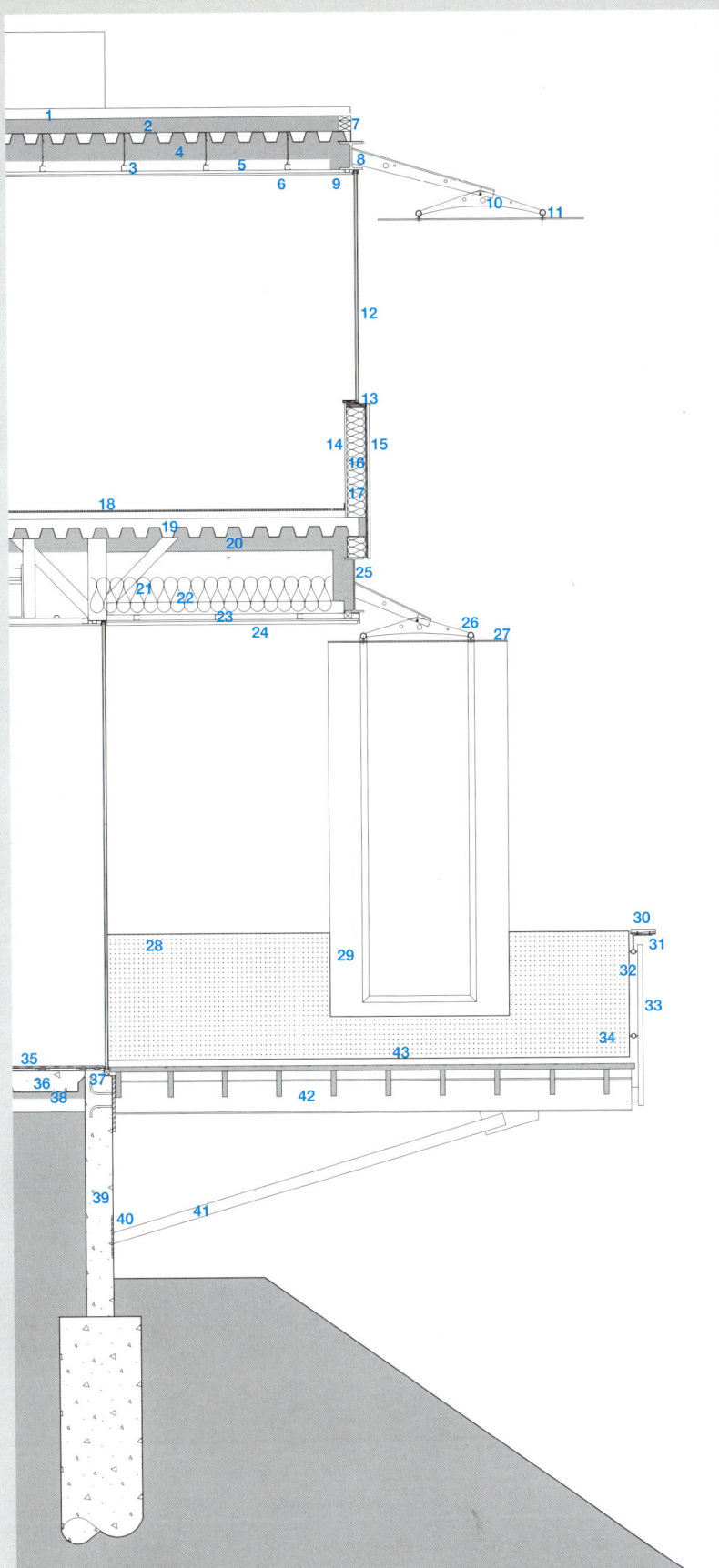

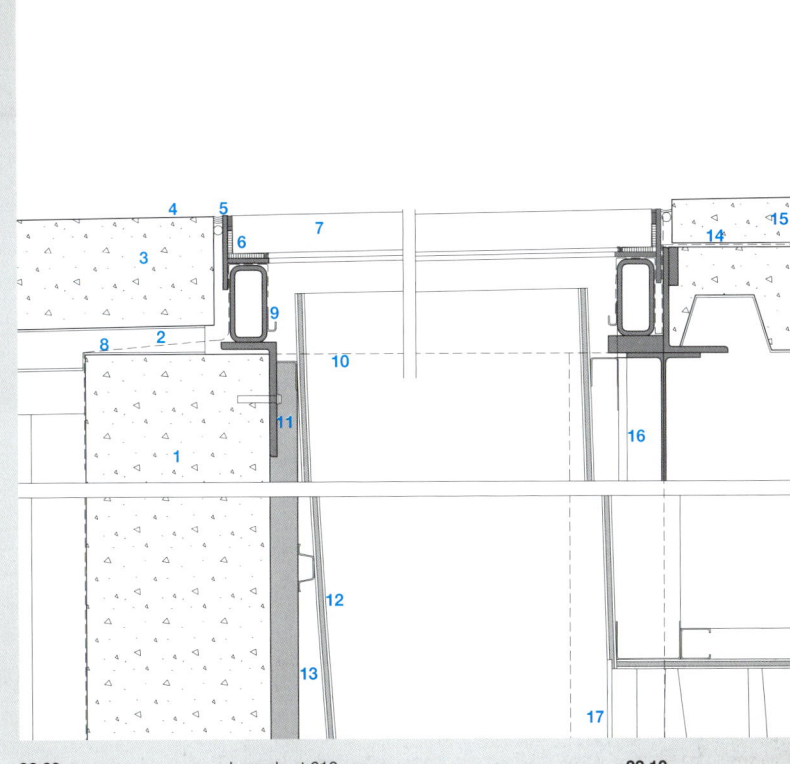

22.09
Wall Section
1:50
 1 Class A single ply membrane roof
 2 Tapered roof insulation
 3 Runner mains at 610 mm (24 inch) centres
 4 Spray on foam insulation
 5 Hat channels at 610 mm (24 inch) centres
 6 12 mm (1/2 inch) gypsum board ceiling
 7 Flat lock zinc fascia
 8 Beam with mill markings concealed on inside of beam
 9 22 mm (7/8 inch) hat channel welded to bottom flange of beam
 10 Steel bracket arm and continuous pipe frame
 11 9 mm (3/8 inch) thick translucent fibreglass awning
 12 Insulated glazing
 13 Sill flashing
 14 Gypsum board wall lining
 15 Standing seam zinc cladding over air infiltration barrier on plywood sheathing
 16 Metal framing
 17 Foil faced batt insulation with foil tape seams
 18 Carpet
 19 Topping slab with radiant heat system
 20 Spray-on foam insulation
 21 Batt insulation
 22 Metal framing
 23 Metal furring

channels at 610 mm (24 inch) centres
 24 Cement plaster ceiling
 25 Steel beam with mill markings concealed on inside of beam
 26 Steel bracket arm and continuous pipe frame
 27 10 mm (3/8 inch) thick translucent fibreglass awning
 28 Perforated stainless steel guardrail beyond
 29 Fibreglass vertical panel beyond
 30 Cedar handrail fixed to steel angle with stainless steel wood screws
 31 Steel angle welded to pipe rail
 32 Steel pipe rail with steel spacers
 33 Steel pipe stanchion
 34 Perforated stainless steel plate with sandblast finish
 35 Hardwood flooring over asphalt primer
 36 Concrete slab with radiant heating system
 37 Pressure treated sleepers set in mastic
 38 Rigid insulation board and vapour barrier
 39 Concrete stem wall
 40 Embedded steel plate
 41 Steel strut
 42 Steel beam
 43 Timber decking on timber joists

22.10
Skylight Detail
1:10
 1 250 mm (9 3/4 inch) reinforced concrete shoring wall
 2 Steel bearing plate beyond and behind, weld to pipe
 3 Steel drainage pipe to trench drain beyond
 4 Concrete driveway
 5 Silicon sealant to completely fill joint
 6 Continuous neoprene shim spacer
 7 Fibreglass panel
 8 Waterproofing membrane
 9 Continuous J-bead tack welded to tube frame
 10 Line of concrete beyond
 11 Steel anchors with paint finish
 12 Gypsum board
 13 Z-furring channels with rigid insulation
 14 Waterproof membrane
 15 Concrete topping
 16 Steel stiffener plate
 17 Glass at kitchen and line of casework beyond

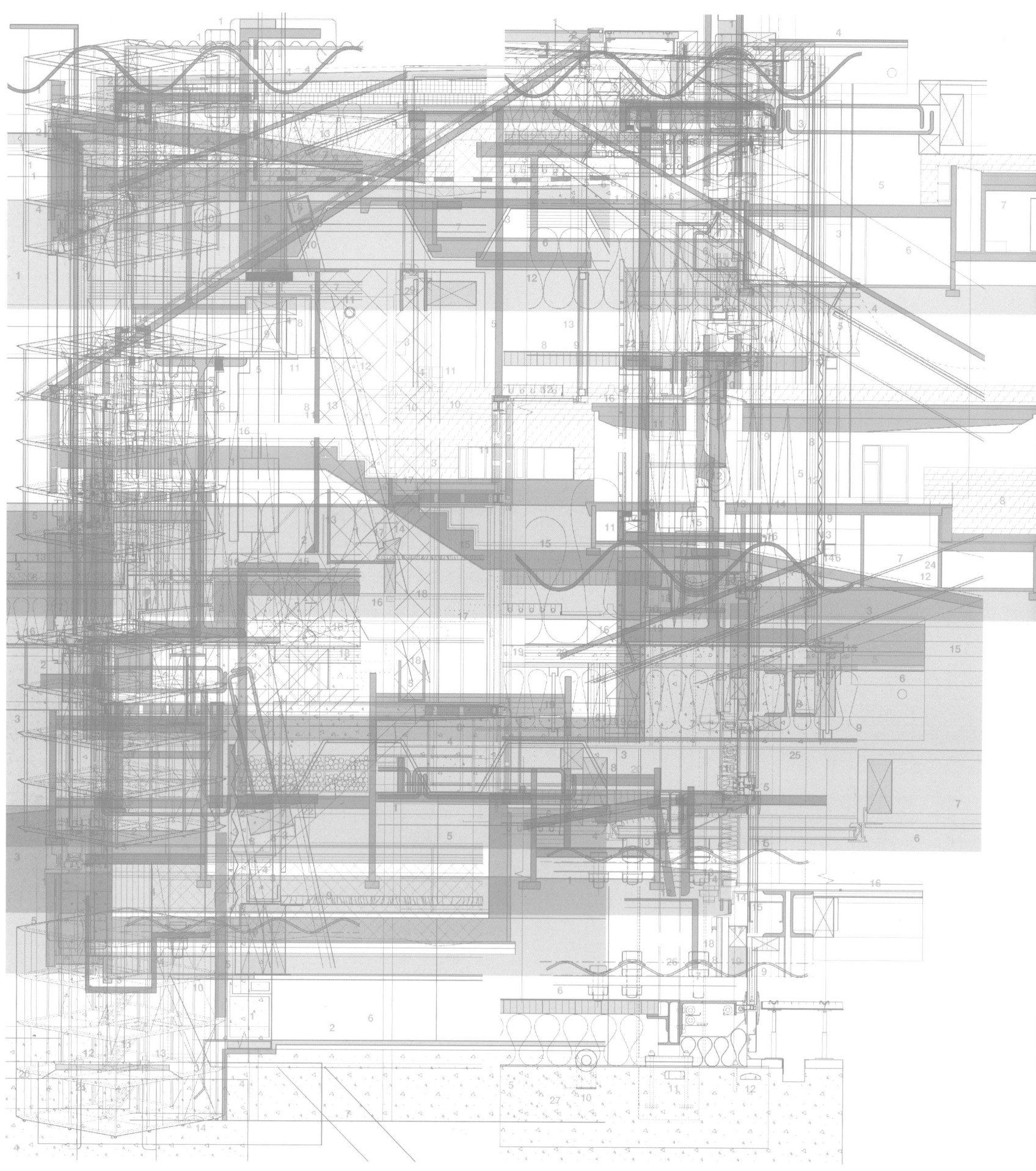

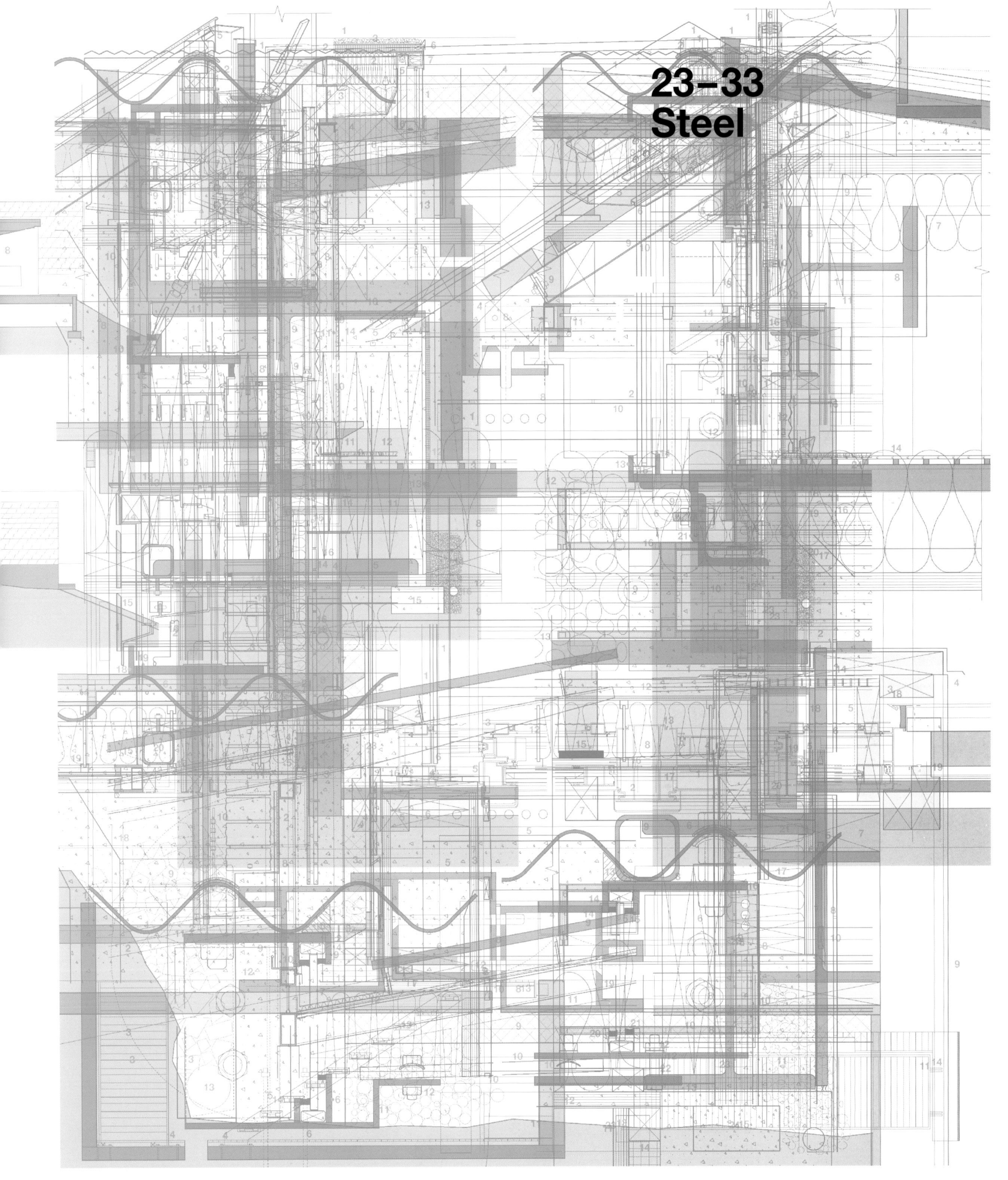

23
Aranda Pigem Vilalta

Bellows House
Girona, Spain

Client
Ramon Danés and Lídia Coma

Area
260 square metres (2,798 square feet)

Main Contractor
Josep Massegur

This elegant and apparently inscrutable house is located in the suburb of Bosc de Tosca, not far from a highway. The form and the position of the house respond directly to the orientation of this small 350 square metre (3,767 square feet) parcel of land. The graceful curve of the facade reflects the curve of the highway that runs parallel to the site, which is then fragmented into four sections. The facade that faces the street is deliberately opaque to protect it from noise and give it privacy, however four vertical slits allow views out to the north-east. In contrast, the south-west facade features four equal generously glazed windows that open the interior up to views of the mountainous landscape. In addition, thin strips of glazing at clerestory level introduce additional south light.

The interior of the house is arranged as a continuous space. Running three quarters of the length of the upper floor, the living room opens up to the terrace and the landscape beyond. To one side, the dining area and kitchen are separated by the intrusion of the entrance, while on the other are the master bedroom and bathroom. Concealed at basement level are a garage, as well as a studio accessed via a stair leading down from the living room. The stark clean geometry of the house is reinforced by smooth, near-white limestone cladding which contrasts with the lush green landscape of the garden. Lighting, both natural and artificial, is a key aspect of the design. The stone-clad form is raised above the ground where a recessed shadow gap houses a strip of lighting which, at night, makes the house appear to float above the ground.

1 View of the north-east facade at night when a strip of concealed lighting at ground floor level makes the house appear to float. Four vertical slots of glazing indicate (from left to right) the entrance, bedroom and bathroom.
2 The house protects itself from the noise of the nearby highway by restricting the openings in the north-east facade. Limestone cladding reinforces the impression of impregnability.
3 The south-west facade features large expanses of clear glazing that open the house up to views of the landscape. High level horizontal bands of glazing admit natural light even when the blinds on the main windows are drawn.

23.01
Basement Floor Plan
1:200
1 Garage
2 WC
3 Store
4 Studio

23.02
Ground Floor Plan
1:200
1 Bedroom
2 Ensuite bathroom
3 Bathroom
4 Living room
5 Bedroom
6 Entry to bedroom
7 Pedestrian
   entrance
8 Terrace
9 Dining area
10 Kitchen

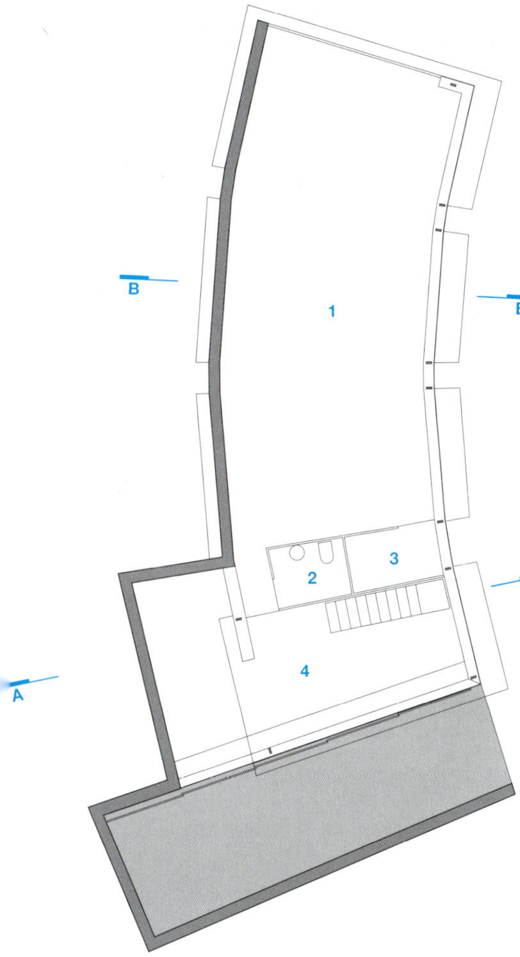

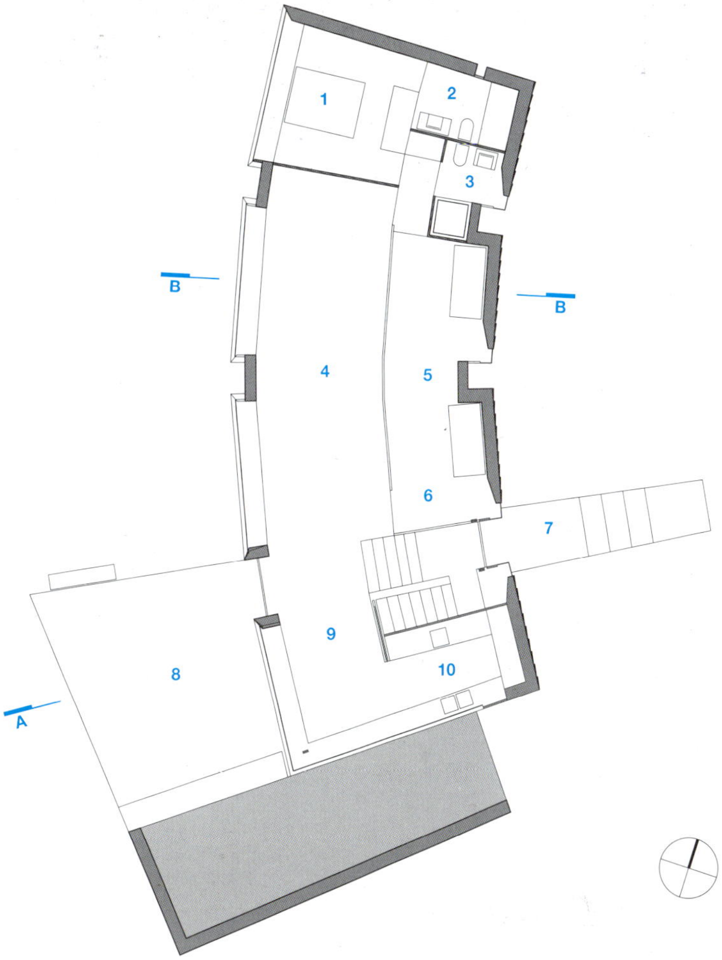

23.03
North-East Elevation
1:200
1 Window to kitchen
2 Entrance ramp
3 Pedestrian
   entrance
4 Bedroom window
5 Bathroom window

23.04
South-West Elevation
1:200
1 Window to
   bedroom
2 Living room
   window
3 Door to terrace
4 Window to dining
   room
5 Terrace
6 Garden

23.05
Section A–A
1:200
1 Dining room
2 Entrance
3 Studio
4 Exterior facade
5 Entrance ramp

23.06
Section B–B
1:200
1 Living room
2 Bedroom
3 Garage

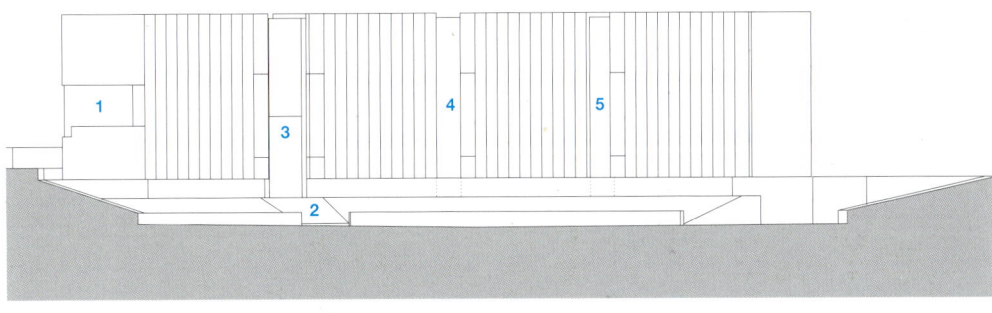

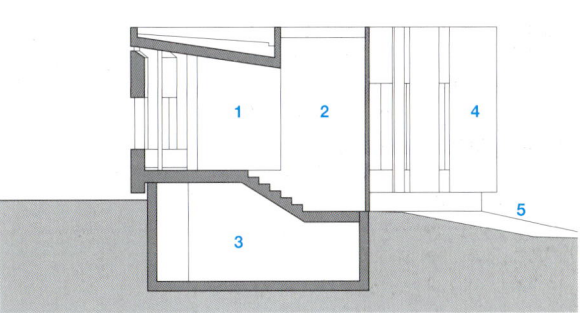

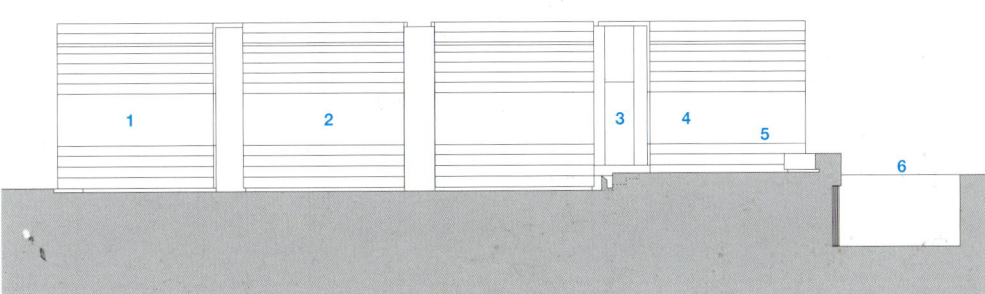

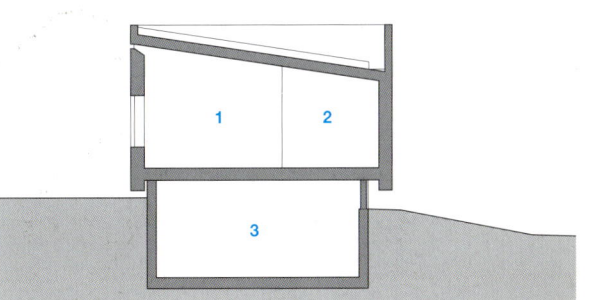

105

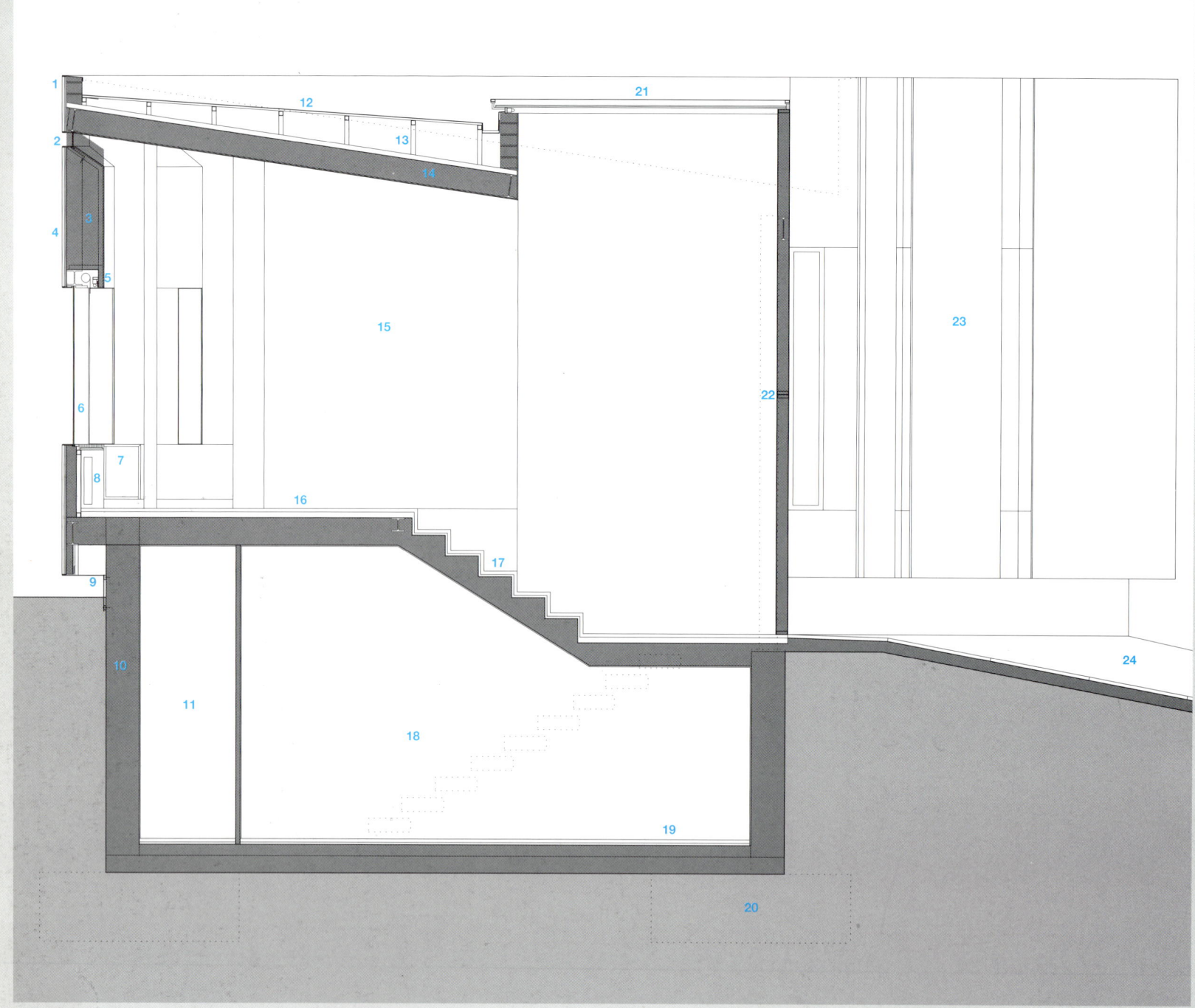

23.07
Sectional Detail
1:50
1 20 mm (3/4 inch) thick limestone cladding
2 Clear laminated glass
3 Masonry wall
4 20 mm (3/4 inch) thick limestone cladding
5 Fluorescent light fitting
6 Clear laminated glass
7 Built-in timber framed storage below window sill
8 Concealed radiator
9 Steel cover panel with lacquered finish
10 300 mm (113/4 inch) thick reinforced concrete wall
11 Garage access

12 Sandwich panel fascia
13 Steel roof substructure
14 Ceiling slab and pre-cast beams
15 Living room
16 30 mm (11/5 inch) thick parquet floor
17 Parquet finish to stair
18 Store room
19 400 x 400 x 30 mm (113/4 x 113/4 x 11/5 inch) terrazzo tiles
20 Reinforced concrete footing
21 Clear laminated glass to skylight
22 Sandwich panel cladding to entrance door
23 Sandwich panels to east facade
24 Entrance ramp

23.10
Stair Detail
1:50
1 Ceramic tiled wall
2 15 mm (3/5 inch) thick steel sheet stringer
3 22 mm (9/10 inch) thick timber to stair treads
4 15 mm (3/5 inch) thick steel sheet to landing
5 15 mm (3/5 inch) thick steel sheet stringer
6 22 mm (9/10 inch) thick timber decking
7 22 mm (9/10 inch) thick timber to stair treads
8 22 mm (9/10 inch) thick timber decking
9 3 mm (1/10 inch) thick panel with lacquered finish

10 300 mm (113/4 inch) thick reinforced concrete wall
11 15 mm (3/5 inch) thick steel sheet stringer
12 Ceramic tiled wall
13 22 mm (9/10 inch) thick timber to stair treads
14 15 mm (3/5 inch) thick steel sheet

23.08
Facade Detail
1:50
1 3 mm (1/10 inch) thick galvanized parapet cover
2 20 mm (3/4 inch) thick limestone cladding
3 Brick wall
4 Emergency roof drainage beyond
5 3 mm (1/10 inch) thick galvanized panel
6 Sandwich panel roof covering
7 Thermoceramic wall
8 PVC down pipe
9 30 mm (1 1/5 inch) thick parquet floor
10 Steel cover panel with lacquered finish
11 Plaster finish to ceiling
12 Pre-cast concrete beams and floor slab
13 Gravel filling
14 Laminated matt glass
15 400 mm (15 3/4 inch) reinforced concrete wall
16 400 x 400 x 30 mm (15 3/4 x 15 3/4 x 1 4/5 inch) terrazzo tiles

23.09
Facade Detail
1:50
1 3 mm (1/10 inch) thick galvanized panel
2 20 mm (3/4 inch) thick limestone cladding
3 Sandwich panel roof covering
4 Pre-cast concrete beams and roof slab
5 Clear laminated glass
6 Wall cavity
7 Living room wall beyond
8 Plaster wall finish
9 Roller blind
10 Clear laminated glass
11 Living room window beyond
12 20 mm (3/4 inch) thick limestone cladding
13 Built-in timber framed storage below window sill
14 30 mm (1 1/5 inch) thick parquet floor
15 Pre-cast concrete beams and floor slab
16 3 mm (1/10 inch) thick lacquered panel
17 400 mm (15 3/4 inch) reinforced concrete wall
18 Plaster finish wall beyond
19 400 x 400 x 30 mm (15 3/4 x 15 3/4 x 1 1/5 inch) terrazzo tiles

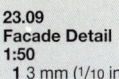
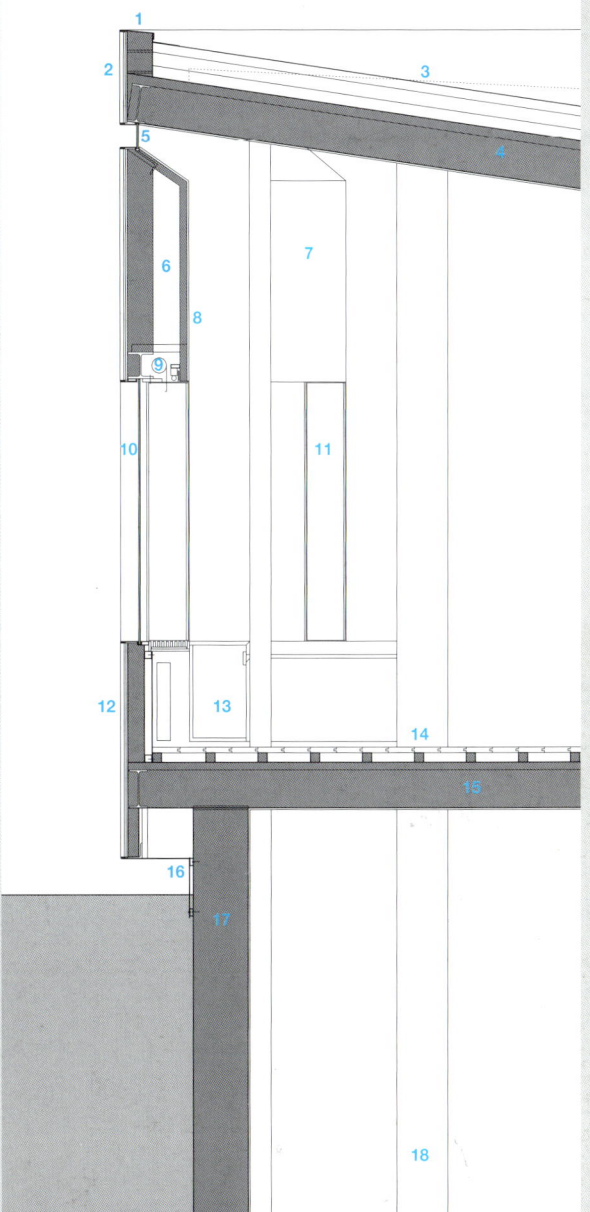
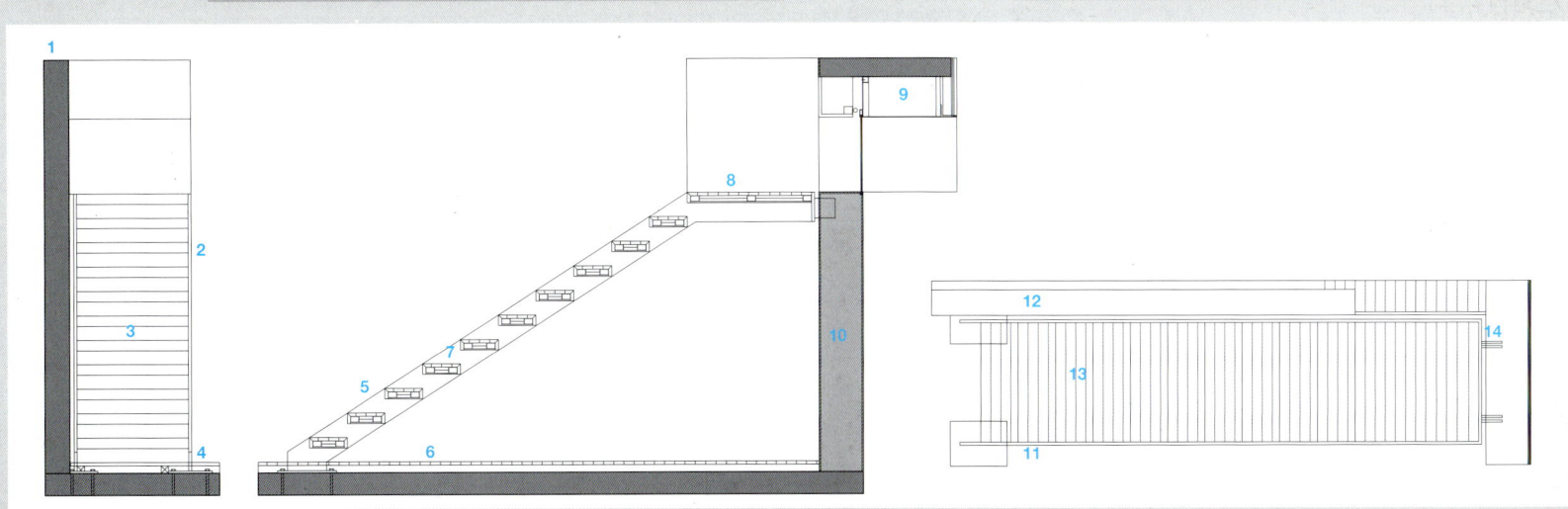

Colorado House
Telluride, Colorado, USA

Area
930 square metres (10,000 square feet)

Project Team
Stephen Cassell, Adam Yarinsky, John Quale, Scott Abrahams, Matt Azen, Tom Jenkinson, Monica Rivera, Martha Skinner, Kim Yao, Innes Yates

Structural Engineer
Buckhorn Geotech Engineers

Services Engineer
Burggraaf & Associates

Construction Manager
Fortenberry Construction

Landscape Architect
Mathews/Nielsen

Lighting Consultant
Richard J. Shaver

Concrete Consultant
Reginald Hough

Situated on a remote site in the San Juan mountains, the Colorado House is conceived as a frame for the landscape. The house is located on a small rise at the edge of a meadow surrounded by aspen trees. A series of Cor-Ten-clad parallel retaining walls are oriented towards views of two distant mountain ranges. Stepping down the hill, the walls weave the house into the site.

The design balances a desire for large living spaces as well as for areas for personal contemplation. The kitchen, located in the centre of the house, is the hub of activity, while bedrooms are pushed to the periphery. The bedrooms open onto the landscape with walls of glass, giving each a specific view that encompasses the foreground and the mountains. The materials, detail and construction reinforce its connection to the landscape. Exterior walls of reddish brown Cor-Ten shingles rest on sandblasted concrete foundations, the colour recalling historical mining structures found in the local vicinity.

1 A series of parallel walls organizes the layout, creating frames for spectacular views. The living room (right) is dominated by a fireplace arranged perpendicular to the shingled walls.
2 The exterior walls are clad in Cor-Ten shingles, designed so that the pattern varies depending on the amount of overlap between each row and the orientation of the shingle. Windows are carefully placed to frame views of the distant mountains.
3 and 4 Inside, the steel walls appear as cool grey surfaces. Interior finishes and detailing are confined to a simple and sophisticated palette of neutral colours with timber and steel accents.

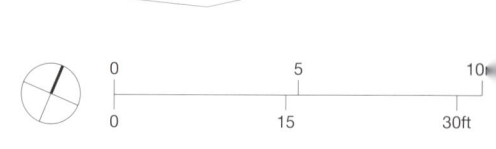

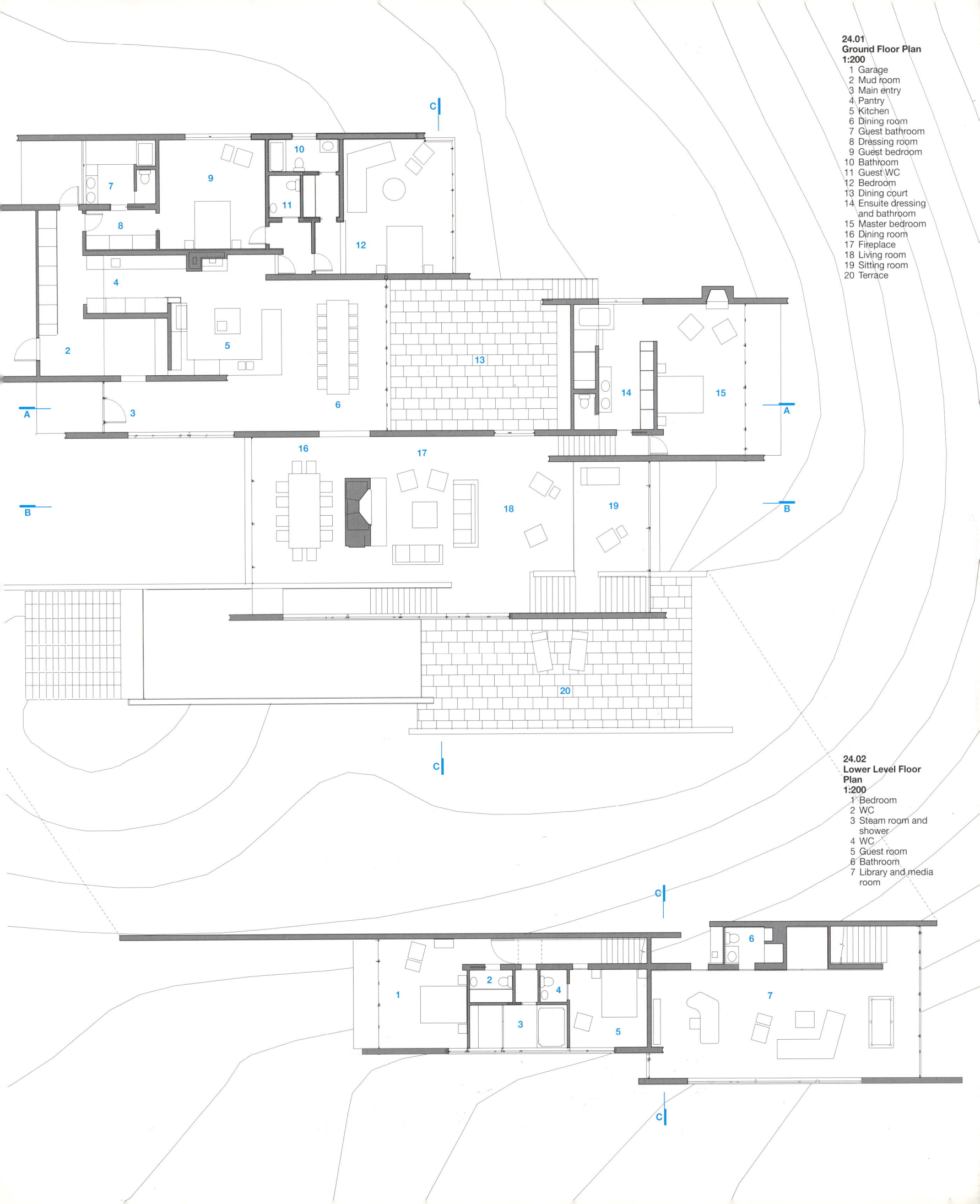

24.01
Ground Floor Plan
1:200
1 Garage
2 Mud room
3 Main entry
4 Pantry
5 Kitchen
6 Dining room
7 Guest bathroom
8 Dressing room
9 Guest bedroom
10 Bathroom
11 Guest WC
12 Bedroom
13 Dining court
14 Ensuite dressing and bathroom
15 Master bedroom
16 Dining room
17 Fireplace
18 Living room
19 Sitting room
20 Terrace

24.02
Lower Level Floor Plan
1:200
1 Bedroom
2 WC
3 Steam room and shower
4 WC
5 Guest room
6 Bathroom
7 Library and media room

24.03
Section A–A
1:200
1 Entry path
2 Entry porch
3 Kitchen
4 Dining room
5 Dining courtyard
6 Mechanical room
7 Master bathroom
8 Master bedroom

24.04
Section B–B
1:200
1 Entry path
2 Entry porch
3 Sculpture courtyard
4 Dining room
5 Living room
6 Guest room
7 Library and media room
8 Sitting room

24.05
Section C–C
1:200
1 Bedroom
2 Dining courtyard
3 Mechanical room
4 Living room
5 Excercise room
6 Stair
7 Library and media room
8 Terrace

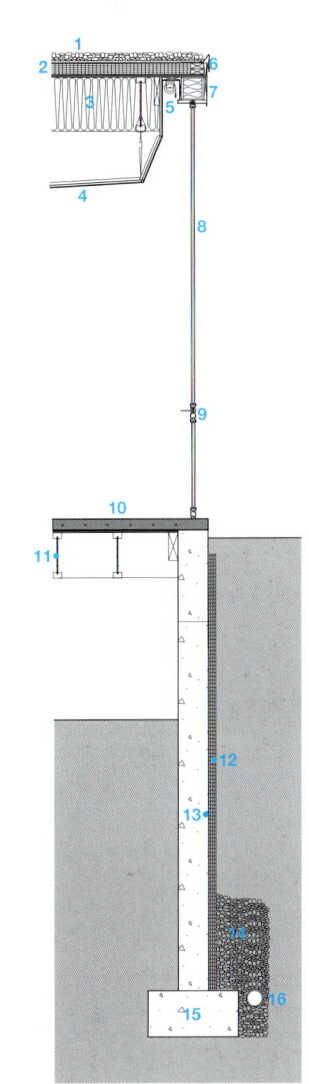

24.06
**Typical Window Wall
Section**
1:50
  1 Gravel ballast on 12
mm (1/2 inch) recovery
board
  2 Rigid insulation
  3 Batt insulation
  4 Gypsum wallboard
  5 Roller blind
  6 Stainless steel edge
flashing as gravel stop
with 25 mm (1 inch)
drip on pressure
treated timber fascia
  7 Stainless steel
flashing on pressure
treated timber fascia
  8 Clear glazing
  9 Steel glazing
mullion
  10 Concrete slab
  11 TJI structural
framing
  12 50 mm (2 inch) rigid
insulation
  13 Reinforced
concrete foundation
wall
  14 Gravel fill
  15 Reinforced
concrete footing
  16 Filter fabric over
100 mm (4 inch) tile
drain

24.07
Shingle Wall Detail 1
1:10
  1 Gravel ballast on 12
mm (1/2 inch) recovery
board
  2 Tapered extruded
polystyrene insulation
  3 Fully adhered
EPDM roofing
membrane
  4 Stainless steel
flashing
  5 18 gauge
breakform weathering
steel coping attached
with stainless steel
spring block
  6 Timber blocking
  7 19 mm (3/4 inch)
plywood
  8 18 gauge
weathering steel
shingles painted on
rear faces and
fastened to sleeper
system with 50 mm
(2 inch) overlap to
conceal steel fasteners
  9 12 mm (1/2 inch)
pressure treated
vertical sleepers
  10 12 mm (1/2 inch)
pressure treated
horizontal sleepers
wrapped in felt
  11 Roofing underlay
applied to 19 mm (3/4
inch) plywood
  12 19 mm (3/4 inch)
plywood
  13 Batt insulation

24.08
**Typical Shingle Wall
Section**
1:50
  1 Gravel ballast on 12
mm (1/2 inch) recovery
board
  2 Rigid insulation
  3 Batt insulation
  4 Vapour barrier
  5 Gypsum board
  6 18 gauge
breakform weathering
steel coping
  7 Timber blocking
  8 Plywood
  9 18 gauge
weathering steel
shingles painted on
rear faces and
fastened to sleeper
system with 50 mm (2
inch) overlap to
conceal steel fasteners
  10 Gypsum wallboard
  11 Batt insulation
  12 Reinforced
concrete wall
  13 12 mm (1/2 inch)
rigid insulation
  14 Reinforced
concrete slab
  15 TJI structural
framing
  16 Bituthene
waterproofing
membrane
  17 50 mm (2 inch) rigid
insulation
  18 Timber blocking
  19 Damp proofing
  20 Reinforced
concrete foundation
wall
  21 Gravel fill
  22 Filter fabric over
100 mm (4 inch) tile
drain
  23 Reinforced
concrete footing

24.09
Shingle Wall Detail 2
1:10
  1 Gypsum wallboard
  2 Plywood
  3 Batt insulation
  4 Plywood
  5 18 gauge
weathering steel
shingles painted on
rear faces and
fastened to sleeper
system with 50 mm (2
inch) overlap to
conceal steel fasteners
  6 12 mm (1/2 inch)
pressure treated
horizontal sleepers
wrapped in felt
  7 Stainless steel
thru-wall flashing
  8 Timber blocking
  9 89 mm (31/2 inch)
rigid insulation
  10 Embedded plate at
window supports
  11 Reinforced
concrete

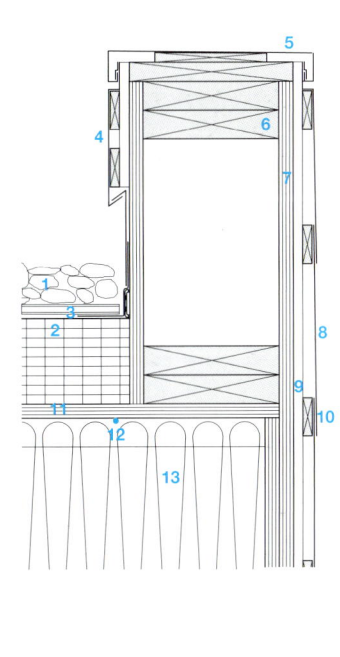

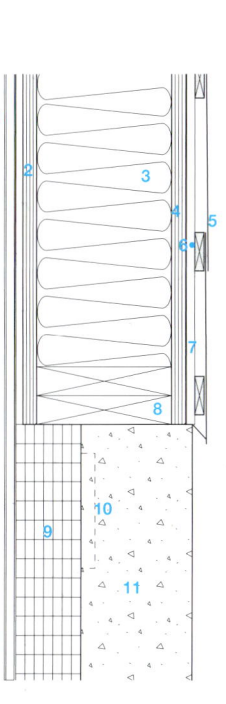

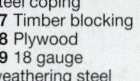

Koehler House
Bay of Fundy, New Brunswick,
Canada

Client
Mary Beth and David Koehler

Area
139 square metres (1,500 square feet)

Project Team
Julie Snow, Ben Awes, Jim Larson,
Connie Lindor, Ken McQuade, Lucas
Alm

Structural Engineer
John Johnson Engineers/Campbell
Comeau Engineering Ltd

Main Contractor
ERB Builders

The Koehler House perches on a
granite cliff sparsely populated with
spruce and pine trees overlooking the
Bay of Fundy. This unabashedly
modernist house is confident and
spare in counterbalance to the drama
of the landscape. In this isolated,
dramatic landscape, there are no
other buildngs in site. The building has
a two-level rectilinear plan aligned
along an east–west axis with one edge
delicately cantilevered over the cliff.
This strong geometry makes it seem
as though the house is simultaneously
anchored and floating on the horizon.

Glass walls frame spectacular views
in all directions, opening up on
pleasant days, or closed and covered
with translucent curtains. The open
plan living and dining area includes a
minimal kitchen consisting of two
islands with cabinets and appliances
tucked away under the counters so
that nothing obstructs the view. The
house takes some of its cues from
ship design without resorting to literal
nautical references. Sliding pocket
doors transform transparent
bedrooms into private cabins, and
everything has a place to be stored.
Outdoor spaces present different
options for viewing the landscape: a
roofless deck for star gazing, a
covered deck shielded from the rain
and a screened-in porch for protection
from insects. The house appears light
and elegant and yet is more than
appropriately robust for the
challenging climate and exposed site.

1 Walls of glass over
two levels make the
view over the cliffs and
the ocean an integral
element of the design.
2 A covered terrace
and an open roof deck
above make the most
of the dramatic loca-
tion. Slim steel struc-
ture adds to the appar-
ent weightlessness of
the house.
3 The kitchen is
reduced to two island
benches with all the
necessary storage and
equipment hidden
below to reduce any
impact on the view.
4 White painted walls
and pale timber are
complemented
through the use of the
masonry chimney
which anchors the
building to the site.

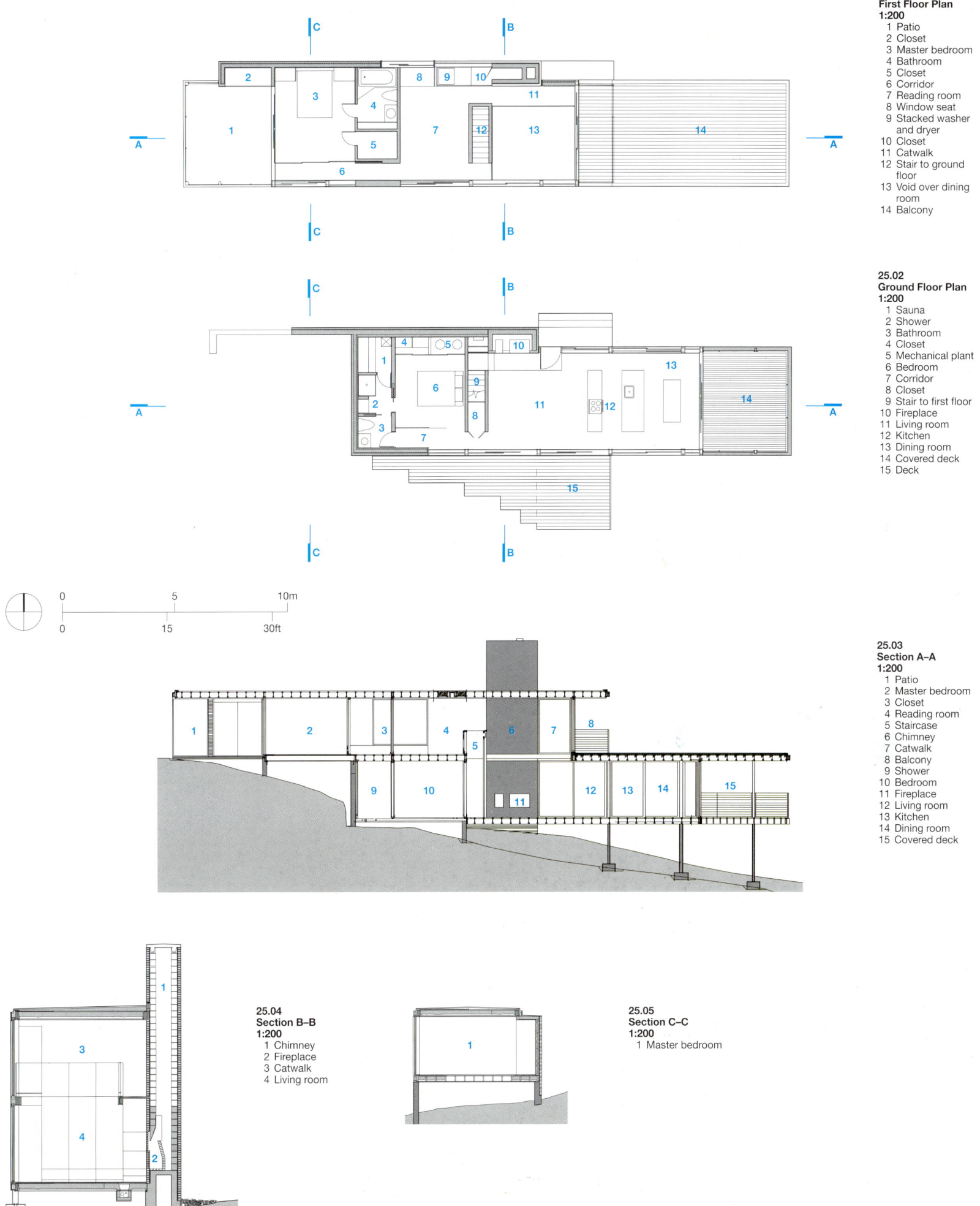

25.01
First Floor Plan
1:200
1 Patio
2 Closet
3 Master bedroom
4 Bathroom
5 Closet
6 Corridor
7 Reading room
8 Window seat
9 Stacked washer
and dryer
10 Closet
11 Catwalk
12 Stair to ground
floor
13 Void over dining
room
14 Balcony

25.02
Ground Floor Plan
1:200
1 Sauna
2 Shower
3 Bathroom
4 Closet
5 Mechanical plant
6 Bedroom
7 Corridor
8 Closet
9 Stair to first floor
10 Fireplace
11 Living room
12 Kitchen
13 Dining room
14 Covered deck
15 Deck

25.03
Section A–A
1:200
1 Patio
2 Master bedroom
3 Closet
4 Reading room
5 Staircase
6 Chimney
7 Catwalk
8 Balcony
9 Shower
10 Bedroom
11 Fireplace
12 Living room
13 Kitchen
14 Dining room
15 Covered deck

25.04
Section B–B
1:200
1 Chimney
2 Fireplace
3 Catwalk
4 Living room

25.05
Section C–C
1:200
1 Master bedroom

0 5 10m
0 15 30ft

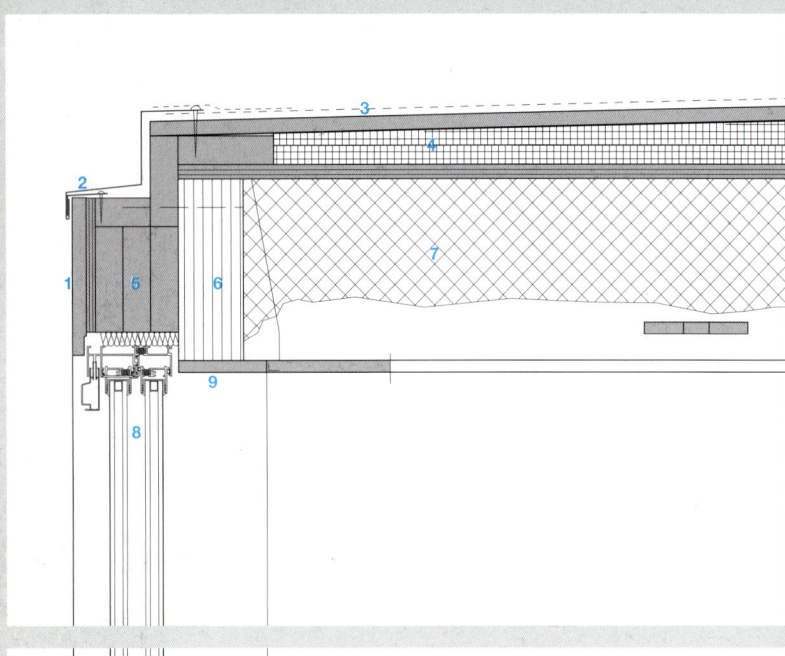

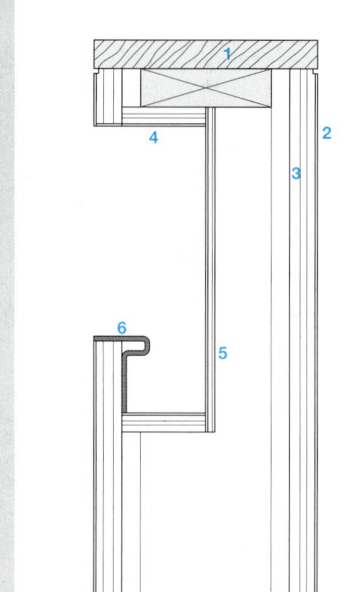

25.06
Roof Deck Detail
1:10
  1 Cedar fascia
  2 Stainless steel roof edge
  3 Single ply roof membrane
  4 Rigid insulation
  5 Timber blocking
  6 Laminated veneer lumber header
  7 Spray foam insulation
  8 Aluminium sliding door head frame
  9 Maple trim

25.09
Handrail Detail
1:5
  1 19 mm (3/4 inch) maple hardwood cap on guardrail
  2 19 mm (3/4 inch) maple veneer plywood with 3 mm (1/8 inch) reveal at all panel joints
  3 12 mm (1/2 inch) panel clips shop glued and screwed to back of wall panel and field screwed to stud
  4 12 mm (1/2 inch) maple veneer plywood top and bottom
  5 6 mm (1/4 inch) plywood back
  6 1.5 mm (1/16 inch) stainless steel handrail, seam welded, ground and sanded smooth

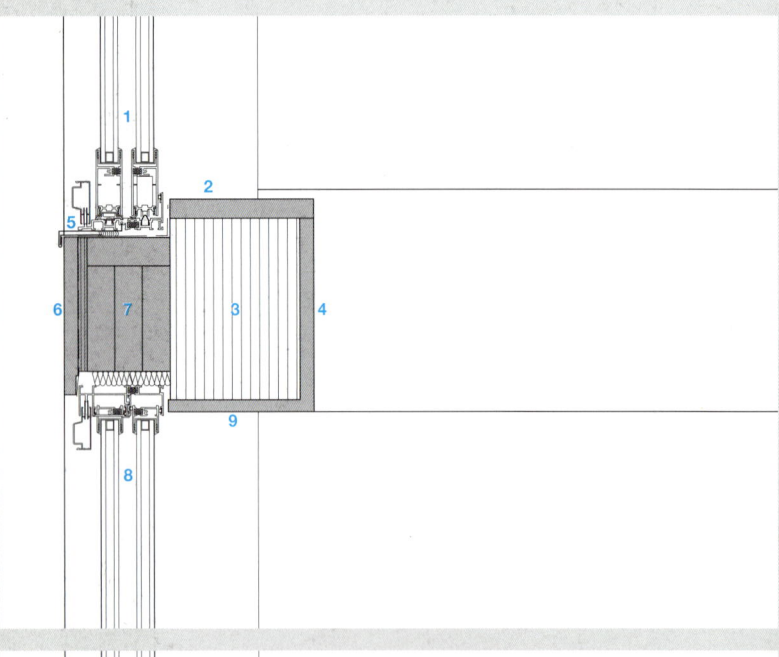

25.07
External Wall Detail
1:10
  1 Aluminium sliding door sill frame
  2 Maple trim
  3 Laminated veneer lumber header
  4 Maple trim
  5 Stainless steel flashing edging
  6 Cedar fascia
  7 Timber blocking
  8 Aluminium sliding door head frame
  9 Maple trim

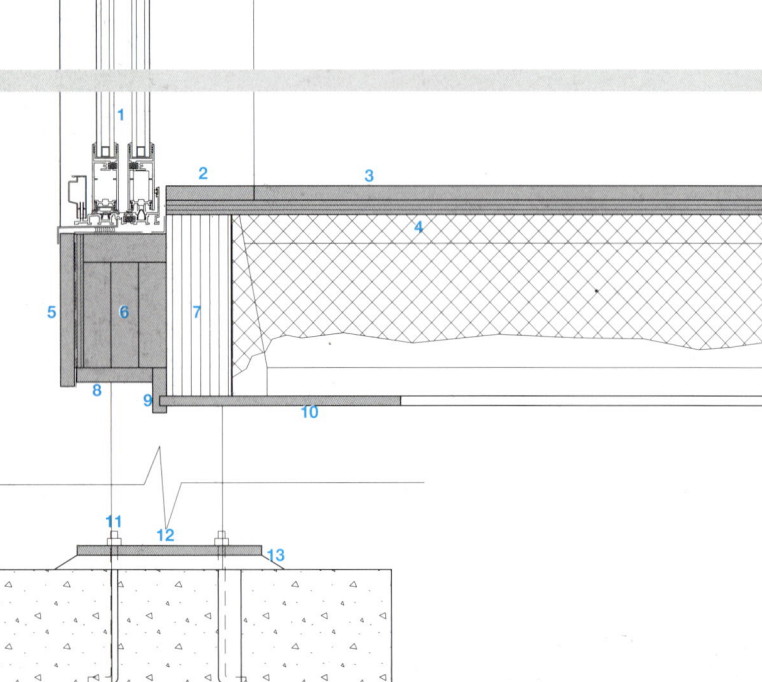

25.08
Floor Slab Detail
1:10
  1 Aluminium sliding door sill frame
  2 Maple trim
  3 Maple floor
  4 Spray insulation
  5 Cedar trim
  6 Timber blocking
  7 Laminated veneer lumber header
  8 Cedar trim
  9 Cedar trim
  10 Fibre cement panel
  11 Anchor bolts
  12 Stainless steel shoe plate
  13 Levelling concrete on competent rock

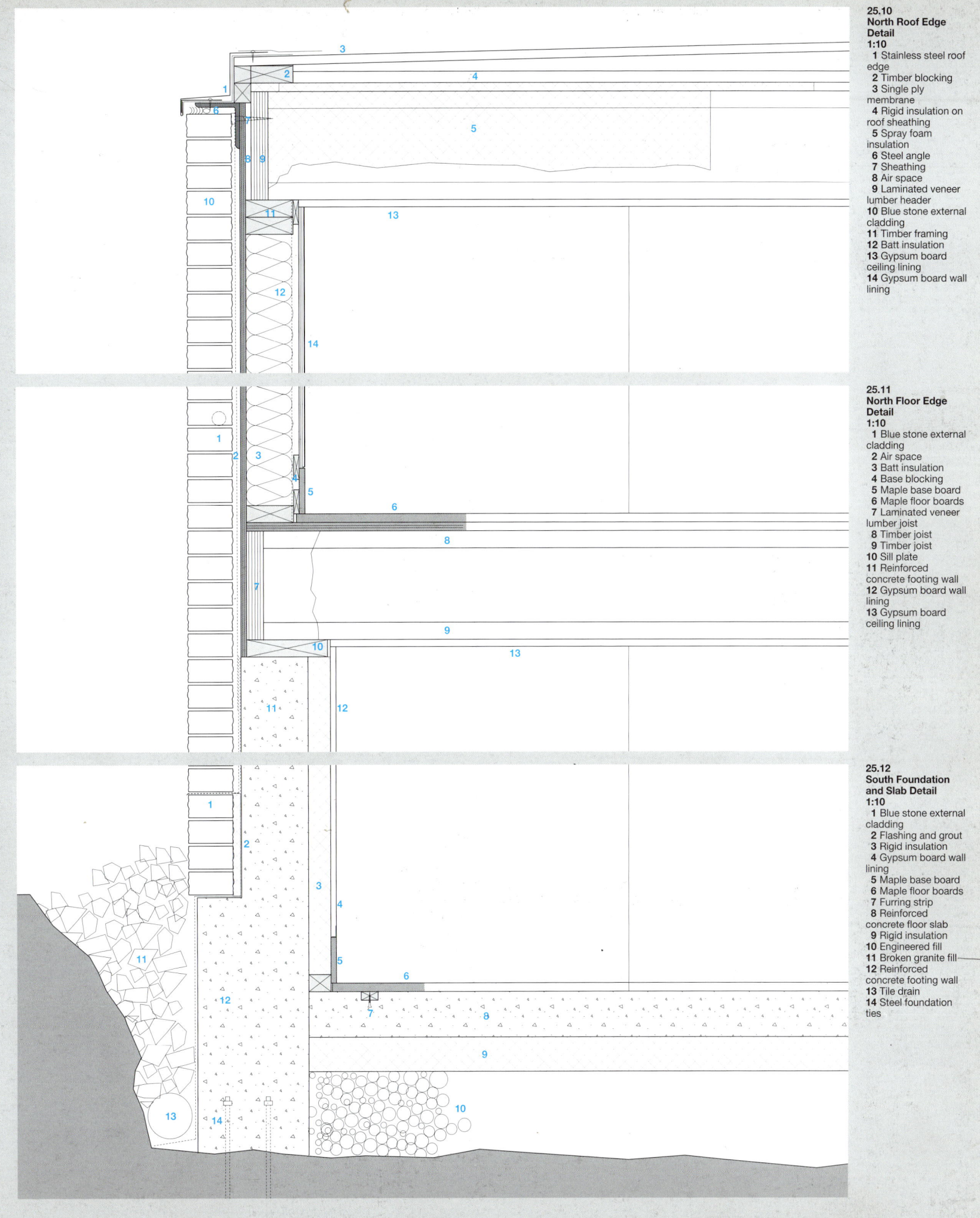

25.10
North Roof Edge Detail
1:10
1 Stainless steel roof edge
2 Timber blocking
3 Single ply membrane
4 Rigid insulation on roof sheathing
5 Spray foam insulation
6 Steel angle
7 Sheathing
8 Air space
9 Laminated veneer lumber header
10 Blue stone external cladding
11 Timber framing
12 Batt insulation
13 Gypsum board ceiling lining
14 Gypsum board wall lining

25.11
North Floor Edge Detail
1:10
1 Blue stone external cladding
2 Air space
3 Batt insulation
4 Base blocking
5 Maple base board
6 Maple floor boards
7 Laminated veneer lumber joist
8 Timber joist
9 Timber joist
10 Sill plate
11 Reinforced concrete footing wall
12 Gypsum board wall lining
13 Gypsum board ceiling lining

25.12
South Foundation and Slab Detail
1:10
1 Blue stone external cladding
2 Flashing and grout
3 Rigid insulation
4 Gypsum board wall lining
5 Maple base board
6 Maple floor boards
7 Furring strip
8 Reinforced concrete floor slab
9 Rigid insulation
10 Engineered fill
11 Broken granite fill
12 Reinforced concrete footing wall
13 Tile drain
14 Steel foundation ties

Vertical House
Los Angeles, California, USA

Client
Lorcan O'Herlihy & Cornelia Hayes
O'Herlihy

Area
223 square metres (2,400 square feet)

Project Team
Lorcan O'Herlihy, David Thompson,
Kevin Tsai

Structural Engineer
Paul Franceschi

Main Contractor
Above Board Construction

Located on a very small site, this house rejects the usual site response – the typical suburban front and back yard. Instead, space is maximized in plan and section, taking up as much of the available footprint as planning regulations allow, and increasing the height to maximize space and views. At the same time, the skin is articulated with glazing on all vertical surfaces. Here, 105 vertical slit windows constructed from three types of glazing, are positioned to frame the most desirable views. In contrast, cement fibreboard has been innovatively used as the solid component. The steel moment frame frees the skin from structural restraints, allowing an unrestricted rhythm of glazing and solid panels across the facades. This surface manipulation defines the architecture through the envelope rather than through the volume itself.

The house is arranged over four levels, with the ground floor cut away to provide a double car port and studio. The first floor accommodates the master and guest bedrooms, and the second floor contains the living, kitchen and dining rooms. Finally, a glass-walled pavilion is located on the roof terrace, serving as an outdoor room with ocean views. A core volume at the centre of the building houses the main stair and storage. The rhythmic surface treatment, which defines the conceptual expression of the house, envelopes a simple, elementary box while at the same time responding to the site restrictions and creating a comfortable, light-filled family home.

1 View of the street facade – windows are arranged across the facade regardless of the location of the floor slabs in order to capture limited views wherever they occur.
2 Three types of glazing alternate with cement fibreboard across the facades.
3 A red-painted steel spiral stair on the north facade provides an alternate means of escape and adds a sculptural element to the architectural composition.
4 Interior view of the living room on the second floor.
5 View of the master bedroom – storage walls and sliding doors maximize space.
6 A sculptural wall conceals abundant storage in the living room.

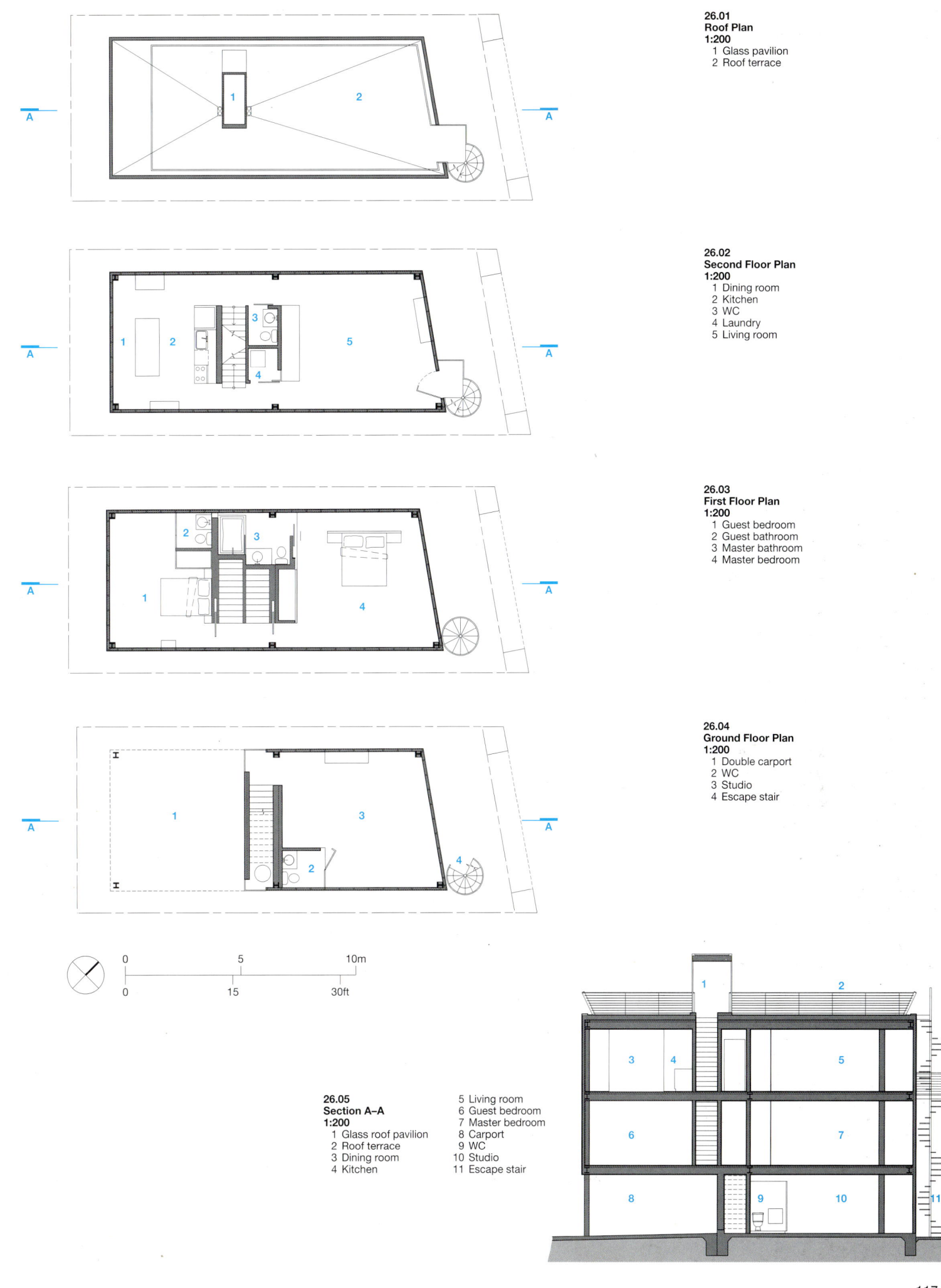

26.01
Roof Plan
1:200
1 Glass pavilion
2 Roof terrace

26.02
Second Floor Plan
1:200
1 Dining room
2 Kitchen
3 WC
4 Laundry
5 Living room

26.03
First Floor Plan
1:200
1 Guest bedroom
2 Guest bathroom
3 Master bathroom
4 Master bedroom

26.04
Ground Floor Plan
1:200
1 Double carport
2 WC
3 Studio
4 Escape stair

26.05
Section A–A
1:200
1 Glass roof pavilion
2 Roof terrace
3 Dining room
4 Kitchen
5 Living room
6 Guest bedroom
7 Master bedroom
8 Carport
9 WC
10 Studio
11 Escape stair

117

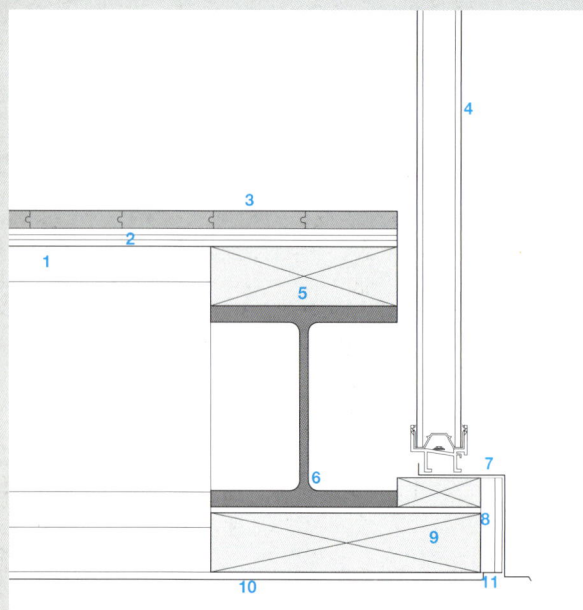

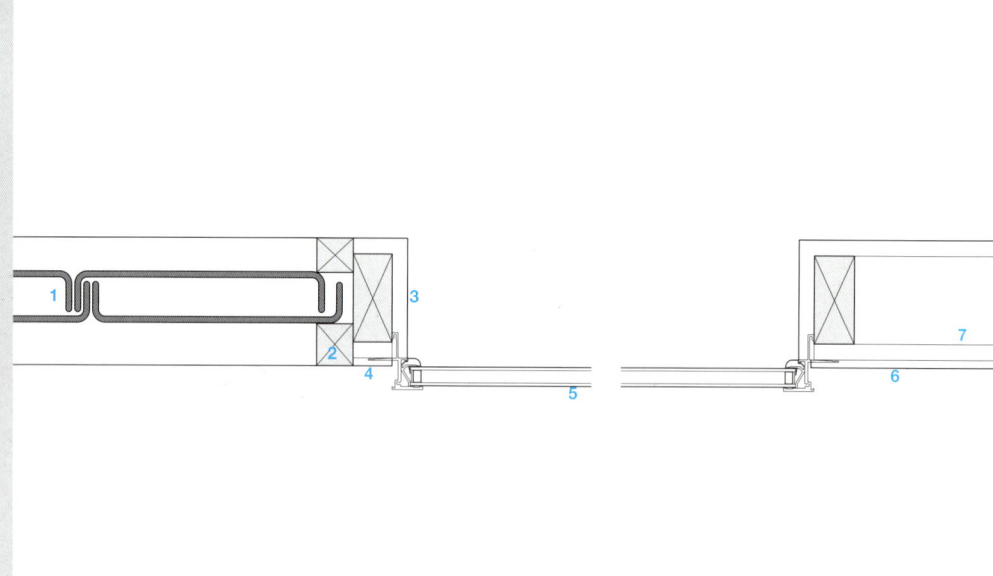

26.06
Glass at Sill Detail
1:5
 1 Timber joist
 2 Structural plywood
sub-floor
 3 Tongue and groove
hardwood flooring
 4 U-glass channel
glazing system
 5 Timber blocking
 6 Structural steel
beam
 7 Metal flashing over
building paper with

cemplank finish to
exterior surface
 8 Plywood substrate
 9 Timber blocking
10 Cemplank finish to
exterior surface
11 Z-reglit to terminate
finish

26.07
Window at Corner
Detail
1:5
 1 Milguard window
system
 2 All opening window
edges wrapped in
bituthene
 3 Cemplank finish to
exterior surface
 4 Plywood
substructure
 5 Gypsum board to
interior surface

 6 Structural steel
beam
 7 Timber blocking
 8 U-glass channel
system

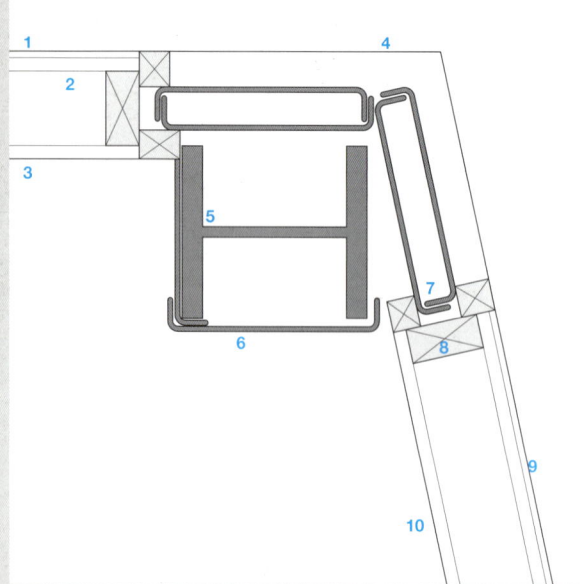

26.08
Glass at Corner
Detail
1:5
 1 Cemplank finish to
exterior surface
 2 Structural plywood
substrate
 3 Gypsum to interior
surface
 4 Line of exterior wall
below
 5 Structural steel
beam

 6 U-glass channel
system
 7 U-glass channel
system
 8 Timber blocking
 9 Cemplank finish to
exterior surface
10 Gypsum to interior
surface

26.09
Typical Wall
Assembly Detail
1:5
 1 U-glass channel
system
 2 Timber blocking
 3 Internal drywall
finish
 4 Cemplank finish to
exterior surface
 5 Milguard window
system

 6 Cemplank finish to
exterior surface
 7 Structural plywood
substrate

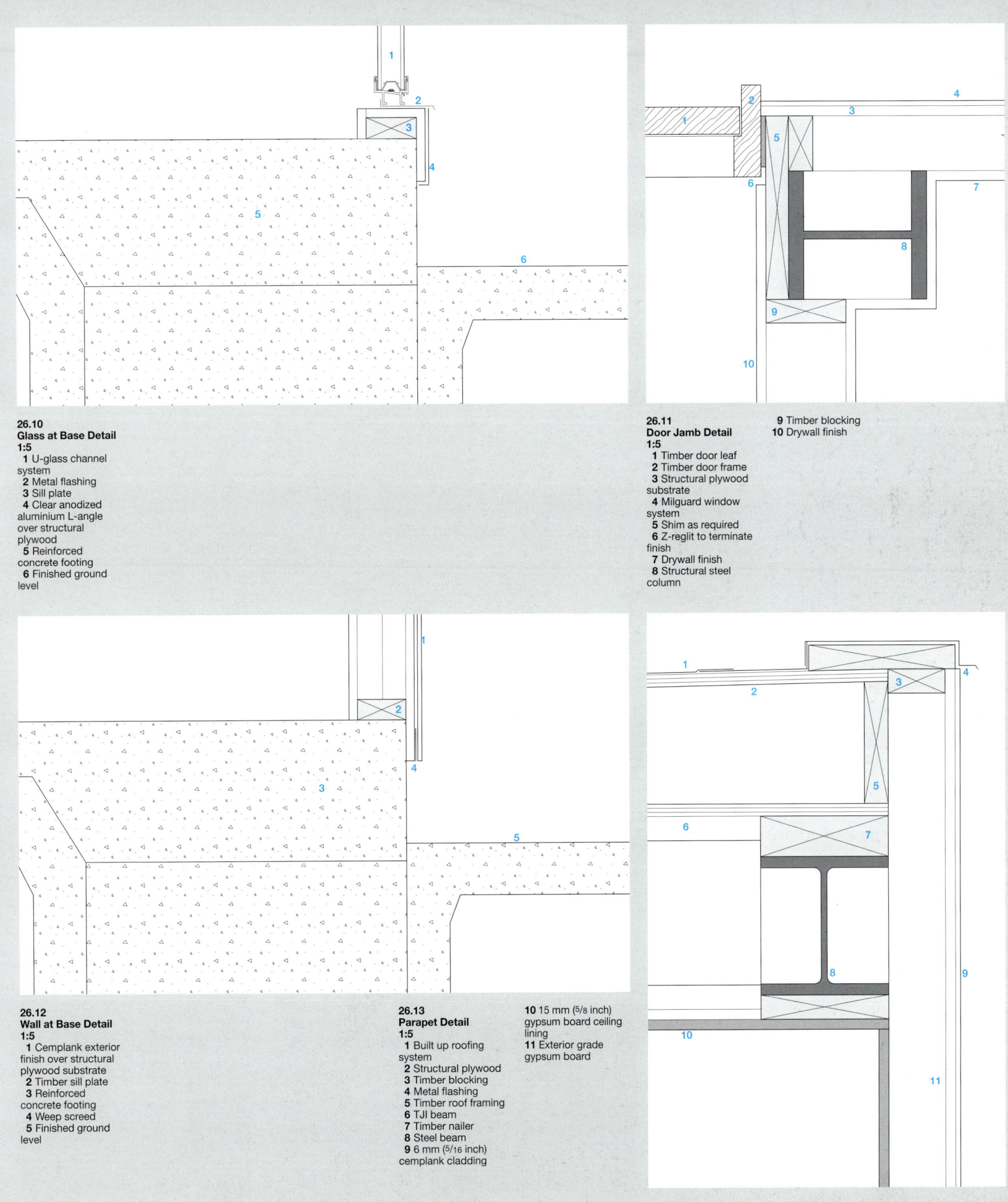

26.10
Glass at Base Detail
1:5
1 U-glass channel system
2 Metal flashing
3 Sill plate
4 Clear anodized aluminium L-angle over structural plywood
5 Reinforced concrete footing
6 Finished ground level

26.11
Door Jamb Detail
1:5
1 Timber door leaf
2 Timber door frame
3 Structural plywood substrate
4 Milguard window system
5 Shim as required
6 Z-reglit to terminate finish
7 Drywall finish
8 Structural steel column
9 Timber blocking
10 Drywall finish

26.12
Wall at Base Detail
1:5
1 Cemplank exterior finish over structural plywood substrate
2 Timber sill plate
3 Reinforced concrete footing
4 Weep screed
5 Finished ground level

26.13
Parapet Detail
1:5
1 Built up roofing system
2 Structural plywood
3 Timber blocking
4 Metal flashing
5 Timber roof framing
6 TJI beam
7 Timber nailer
8 Steel beam
9 6 mm (5/16 inch) cemplank cladding
10 15 mm (5/8 inch) gypsum board ceiling lining
11 Exterior grade gypsum board

**Mack Scogin Merrill Elam
Architects**

Mountain Tree House
Dillard, Georgia, USA

Area
186 square metres (2,000 square feet)
house and deck

Project Team
Mack Scogin, Merrill Elam, David
Yocum, Penn Ruderman, Denise
Dumais

Structural Engineer
Palmer Engineering

Landscape Architect
Marchant Martin

Lighting Designer
Ramón Noya, Ramón Luminance
Design, Atlanta, Georgia

Builder
Winfred McKay Construction

This intriguing guest house is located
on a beautiful woodland site in the
Appalachian foothills. Built as
additional accommodation to the
original house nearby, also designed
by the architect, the compact
structure accommodates a garage for
storing landscaping equipment, a
bedroom, bathroom and outdoor
living deck. A simple steel and timber
framed steel and glass volume is
cantilevered over a larger reinforced
concrete form, with a long deck
attached to one side and a ramp
descending in the opposite direction.
The simplicity of the arrangement is
transformed through a subtle balance
of solids and voids, volumes and
planes, and opaque, transparent,
matte and reflective surfaces.

Glass, Cor-Ten steel, slate and
concrete are used in an
uncompromisingly contemporary
manner, and yet the building's
relationship with the landscape is
paramount to the way the house is
perceived and inhabited. Merging
indoors and out, the ramp rises
narrowly between a wall of Cor-Ten
and a screen of translucent glass,
arriving at a slate-covered deck.
Supported on slender steel columns,
the structure echoes the rhythm of the
poplar trunks surrounding the house.
A thicket of bamboo sprouts up
through narrow holes in the deck,
making the pavilion appear to float
amongst the foliage.

1 The slim verticality
of the poplar trunks
surrounding the house
echo the dominant
repetetive vertical
elements of the struc-
ture, and contrast with
the horizontal slabs of
Cor-Ten steel.
2 View of the living
deck from the pavilion.
Slots in the floor of the
deck allow bamboo to
grow up through the
surface from below,
integrating the struc-
ture with the forest.
3 The living deck
extends into a bridge
that launches itself into
the forest. The slender
steel columns that
support it are almost
invisible among the
tree trunks and
bamboo.
4 A ramped walkway
sandwiched between
an outer screen of
translucent glass and
the solid Cor-Ten wall
of the building, brings
guests up onto the
deck, and from there
the guest quarters.
5 Detail view of the
ramp. The robustness
of the materials belies
the sophistication of
the detailing.
Junctions, joints
and surfaces are
perfectly finished,
inside and out.

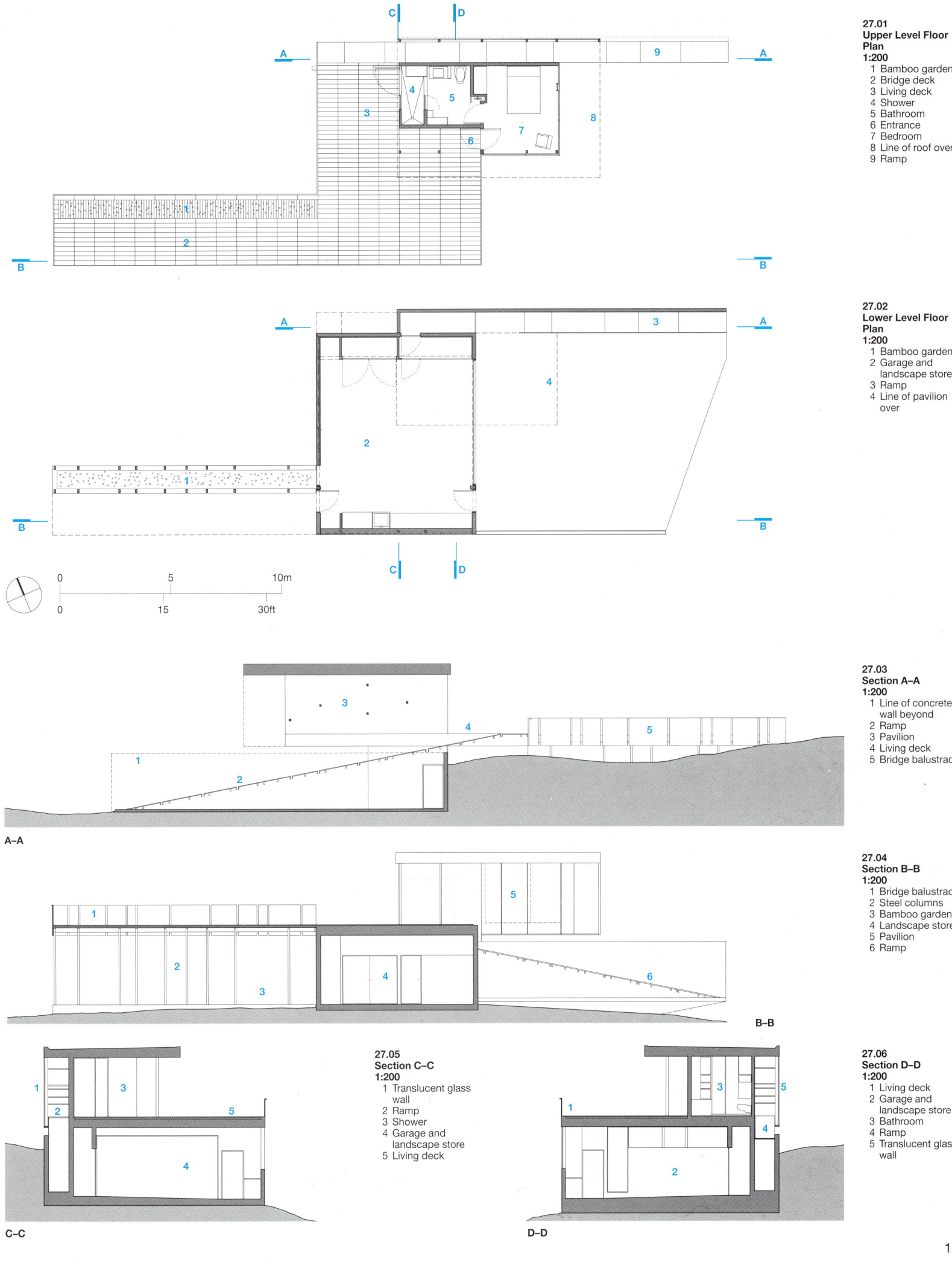

27.01
Upper Level Floor Plan
1:200
1 Bamboo garden
2 Bridge deck
3 Living deck
4 Shower
5 Bathroom
6 Entrance
7 Bedroom
8 Line of roof over
9 Ramp

27.02
Lower Level Floor Plan
1:200
1 Bamboo garden
2 Garage and landscape store
3 Ramp
4 Line of pavilion over

27.03
Section A–A
1:200
1 Line of concrete wall beyond
2 Ramp
3 Pavilion
4 Living deck
5 Bridge balustrade

A–A

27.04
Section B–B
1:200
1 Bridge balustrade
2 Steel columns
3 Bamboo garden
4 Landscape store
5 Pavilion
6 Ramp

B–B

27.05
Section C–C
1:200
1 Translucent glass wall
2 Ramp
3 Shower
4 Garage and landscape store
5 Living deck

C–C

27.06
Section D–D
1:200
1 Living deck
2 Garage and landscape store
3 Bathroom
4 Ramp
5 Translucent glass wall

D–D

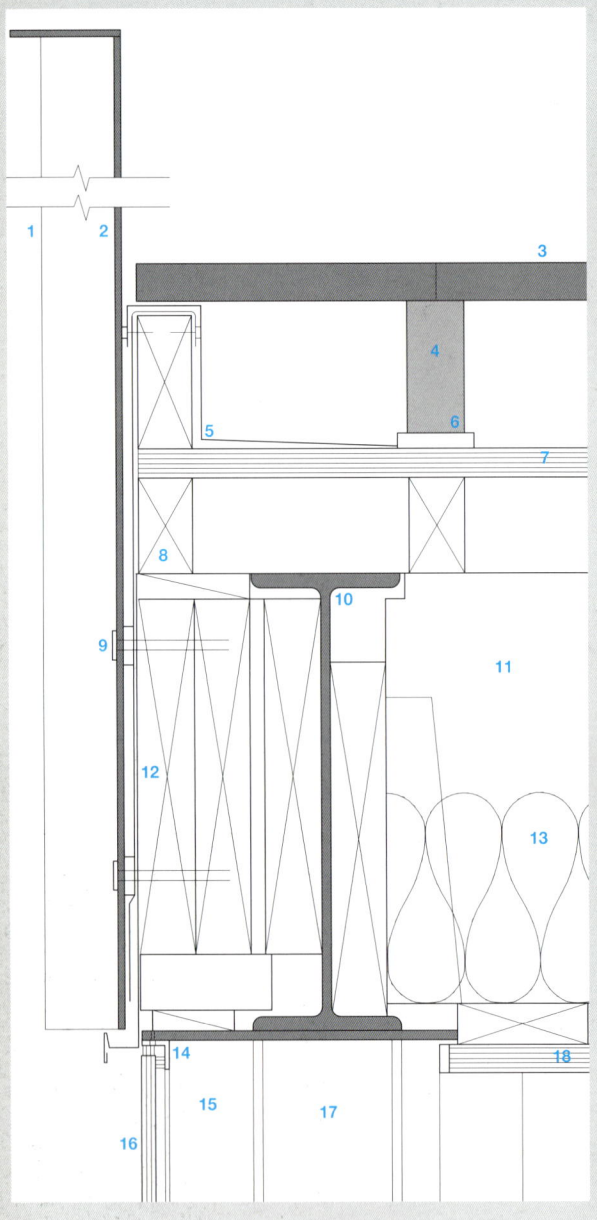

27.07
Glazing and Rail to Roof Deck Detail
1:5
  1 Line of Cor-Ten steel support
  2 Cor-Ten steel rail and support
  3 25 mm (1 inch) slate decking
  4 Sloped underside plastic lumber sleepers at 200 mm (8 inch) centres
  5 EPDM membrane with continuous flashing at edges
  6 Neoprene pads, spaced as required
  7 20 mm (3/4 inch) plywood sub-deck
  8 Timber sleepers with top edge sloped to drain
  9 Lag bolt and spacers
  10 300 x 100mm (114/5 x 4 inch) steel beam
  11 Timber deck framing
  12 Timber blocking as required
  13 Insulation batts
  14 20 mm (3/4 inch) glazing angle with sealant
  15 6 mm (1/4 inch) steel plate
  16 10 mm (1/3 inch) tempered glass
  17 100 x 100 x 6 mm (4 x 4 x 1/4 inch) HSS
  18 20 mm (3/4 inch) plywood

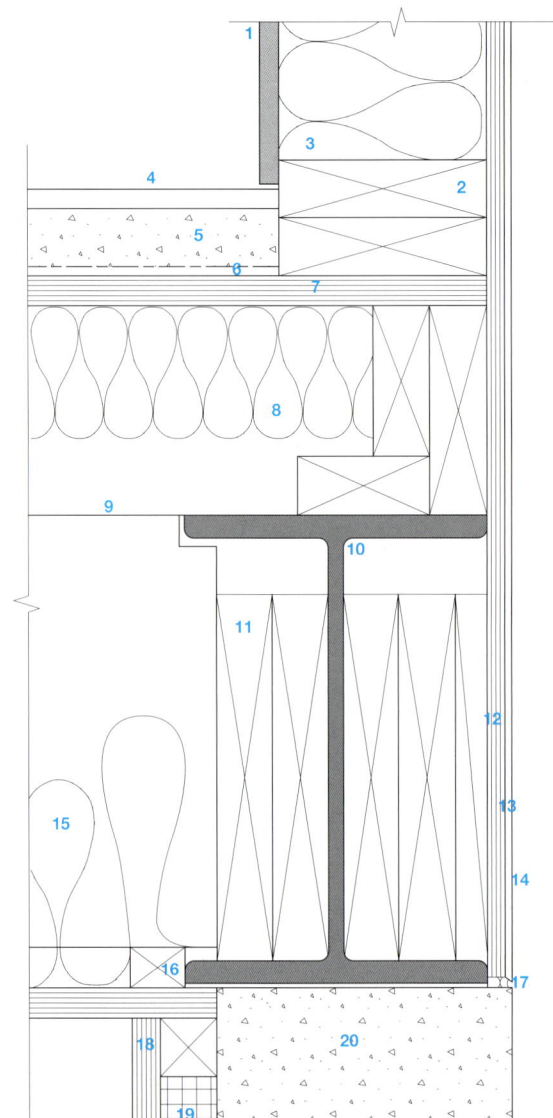

27.09
Exterior Wall Detail
1:5
  1 10 mm (1/3 inch) Gypsum wall board with W/J bead
  2 40 x 140 mm (11/2 x 51/2 inch) framing
  3 Insulation batts
  4 10 mm (1/3 inch) slate tiles
  5 45 mm (13/4 inch) mortar bed
  6 Waterproof membrane
  7 20 mm (3/4 inch) plywood sub-deck
  8 Insulation batts
  9 Line of 40 x 140 mm (11/2 x 51/2 inch) timber joist
  10 Structural steel beam
  11 40 x 250 mm (11/2 x 10 inch) timber blocking
  12 10 mm (3/4 inch) plywood
  13 Waterproof membrane
  14 16 gauge Cor-Ten cladding
  15 Insulation batts
  16 Timber blocking as required
  17 Stainless steel flashing
  18 20 mm (3/4 inch) plywood
  19 38 mm (11/2 inch) rigid insulation
  20 200 mm (8 inch) concrete wall

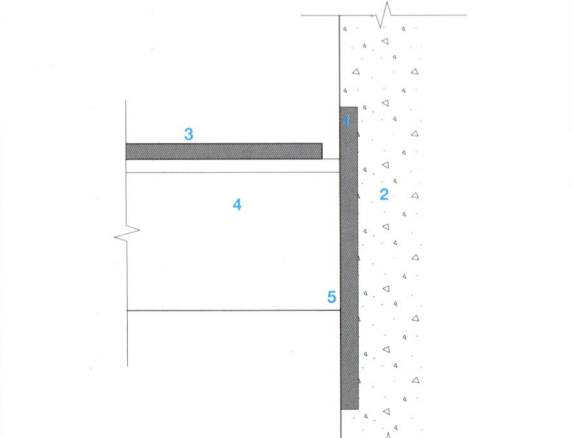
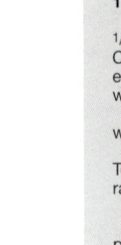

27.08
Ramp Support Detail
1
1:5
  1 200 x 10 mm (8 x 1/3 inch) continuous Cor-Ten steel plate embedded in concrete wall
  2 In-situ concrete wall
  3 8 mm (3/8 inch) Cor-Ten steel plate to form ramp surface
  4 Cor-Ten T-section
  5 Perimeter weld at plate

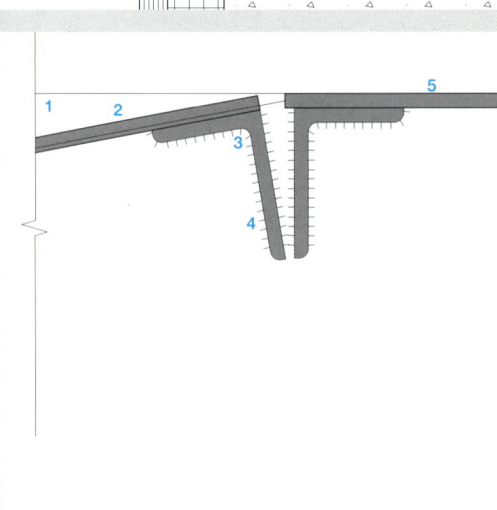

27.10
Ramp Support Detail
2
1:5
  1 16 gauge continuous Cor-Ten flashing wrapped to top of support T-section
  2 Cor-Ten steel plate to form ramp surface
  3 Cor-ten steel angle
  4 Perimeter weld at plate
  5 Continuous Cor-Ten steel plate

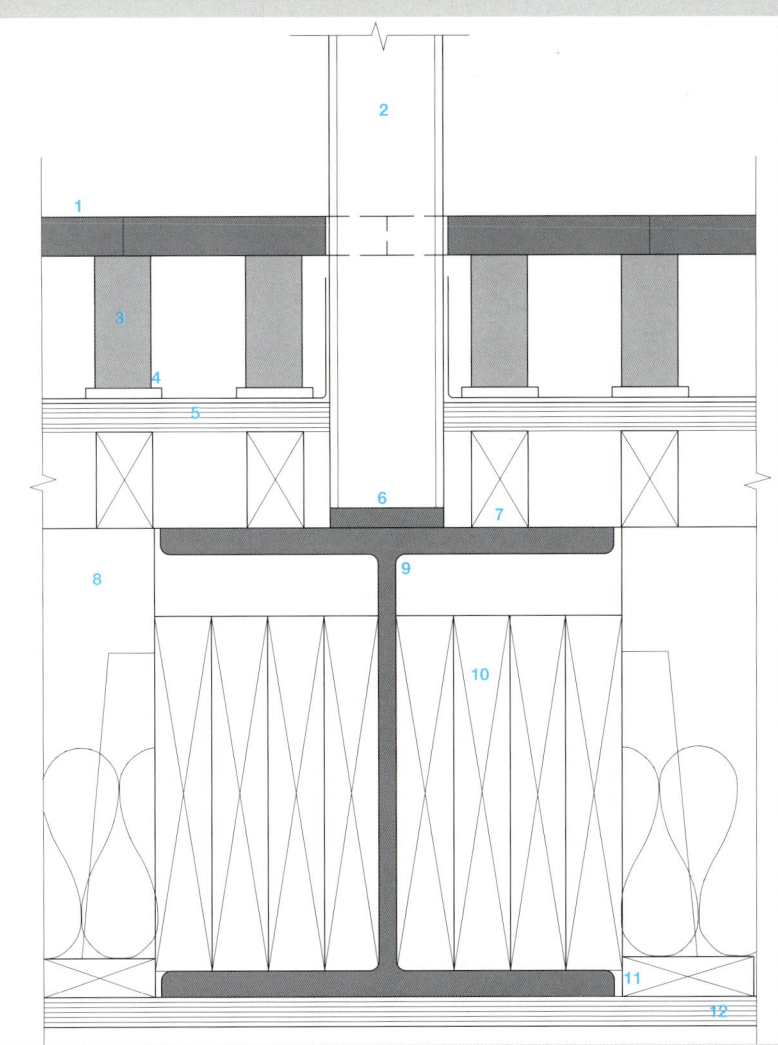

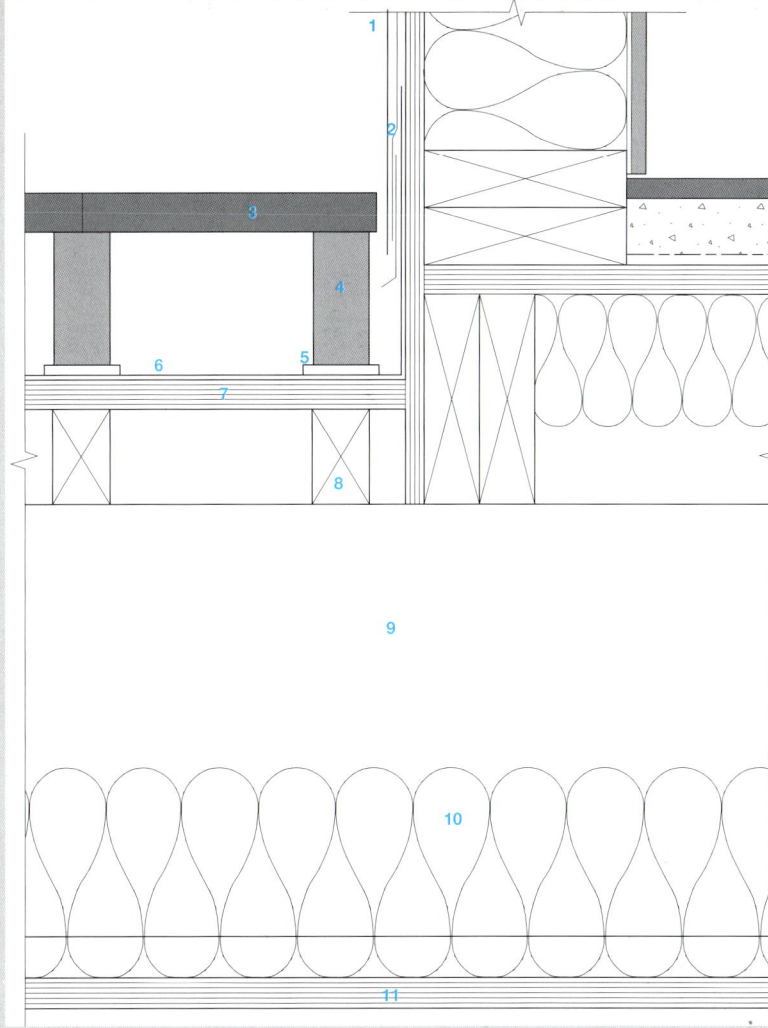

27.11
Deck and Ceiling Detail 1
1:5
 1 25 mm (1 inch) slate decking
 2 75 x 50 x 6 mm (3 x 2 x 1/4) HSS
 3 Sloped underside plastic lumber sleepers at 100 mm (4 inch) centres
 4 Neoprene pads spaced as required
 5 20 mm (3/4 inch) plywood subdeck
 6 75 x 200 x 12 mm (3 x 8 x 1/2 inch) steel plate
 7 Timber sleepers with top surface sloped to drain
 8 50 x 300 mm (2 x 12 inch) framing
 9 310 x 310 mm (121/5 x 121/5 inch) steel I-beam
 10 38 x 250 mm (11/2 x 10 inch) timber blocking
 11 20 mm (3/4 inch) finished plywood
 12 20 mm (3/4 inch) plywood

27.12
Deck and Ceiling Detail 2
1:5
 1 16 gauge Cor-Ten cladding
 2 Waterproof membrane continuous flashing to EPDM
 3 25 mm (1 inch) slate decking
 4 Sloped underside plastic lumber sleepers at 100 mm (4 inch) centres
 5 Neoprene pads spaced as required
 6 EPDM membrane with continuous flashing at edges
 7 20 mm (3/4 inch) plywood subdeck
 8 Timber sleepers
 9 50 x 300 mm (2 x 12 inch) deck framing
 10 Insulation batts
 11 20 mm (3/4 inch) plywood

27.13
Ramp Support Detail 3
1:5
 1 25 mm (1 inch) slate tiles
 2 16 gauge continuous Cor-Ten flashing wrapped to top of ramp support
 3 8 mm (3/8 inch) Cor-Ten steel plate to form ramp surface
 4 EPDM membrane on 20 mm (3/4 inch) plywood subdeck
 5 Cor-Ten T-section
 6 Perimeter weld at plate
 7 Timber sleepers
 8 Timber blocking
 9 200 x 300 mm (79/10 x 12 inch) steel I-beam
 10 500 x 10 mm (193/5 x 1/3 inch) continuous Cor-Ten steel plate
 11 Batt insulation
 12 20 mm (3/4 inch) plywood ceiling
 13 20 mm (3/4 inch) plywood wall
 14 38 mm (11/2 inch) rigid insulation
 15 200 mm (8 inch) in-situ concrete wall

**Artifice/MR House
Pompone, France**

Client
Monsieur Martin and Madame
Rodriguez

Area
140 square metres (1,505 square feet)

Project Team
David Trottin, Emmanuelle Marin-
Trottin, D. Graignic, R. Falcon

Structural Engineer
Marin + Trottin

Services Engineer
Marin + Trottin

Quantity Surveyor
Marin + Trottin

This private house was built for the price of a developer-built home to demonstrate that an architect-designed environment is an affordable option. The house stretches along a sloping strip of marshy land in the Seine and Marne region in the suburbs of Paris. The narrow, 17 metre (55 feet) wide site, generates a long narrow building that uses the length and slope of the land to unfold in half-storey changes of level as it progresses down the site. This strategy serves to integrate each of the interior spaces, from the bedrooms and private spaces at the top of the site, to the kitchen and living room embedded in the lower part of the garden, with the garden and the landscape beyond.

In addition, expanses of full height clear glazing allow a view of the garden from every room. The steel-framed structure is exposed on the interior, further emphasizing the three level changes and revealing a simple and elegant structural system of galvanized steel beams and ribbed sheet roofing. Green painted cladding panels further reinforce the connection to the landscape – the different shades of green are derived directly from the vegetation in the immediate vicinity and playfully mimic the landscape while reinforcing the design's willingness to embrace the garden as an important part of the architectural solution.

1 Stepping down the site, the house is clad in green panels of varying shades that playfully mimic, as well as reinforce, the natural elements of the landscape.

2 In addition to large expanses of glazing, solid openable panels allow the inhabitants to fine tune the ventilation and views.

3 Full height glazing is a key feature of the design. Opportunities to connect the interior with the exterior occur throughout the house.

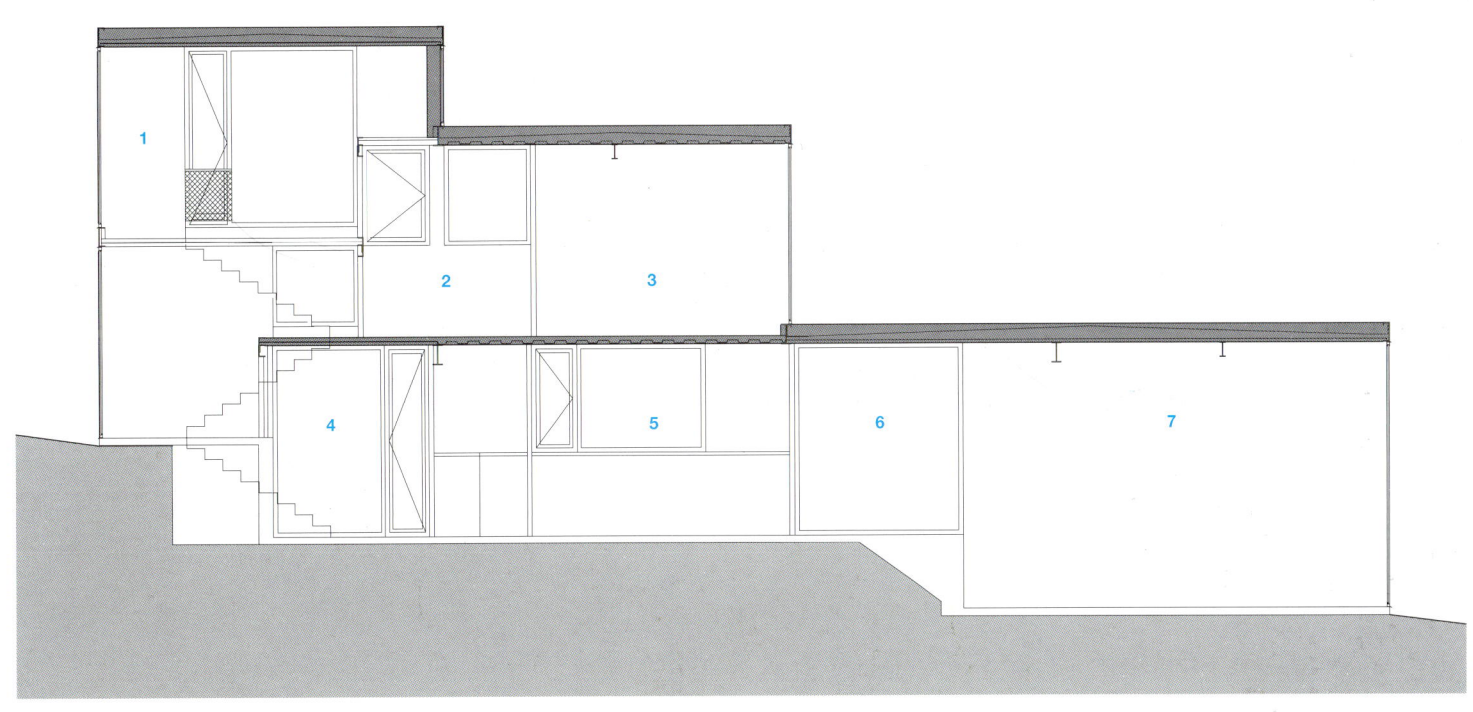

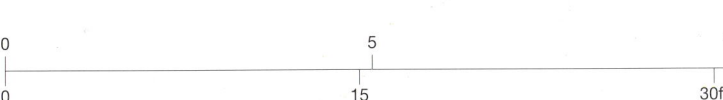

28.01
Ground Floor Plan
1:200
  1 Bedroom 1
  2 Bedroom 2
  3 WC
  4 Kitchen
  5 Dining room
  6 Living room
  7 Entry

28.02
First Floor Plan
1:200
  1 Bathroom
  2 Study
  3 Roof terrace

28.03
Second Floor Plan
1:200
  1 Bedroom 3
  2 Roof terrace

28.04
Section A–A
1:100
  1 Bedroom 3
  2 Bathroom
  3 Study
  4 Bedroom 2
  5 Kitchen
  6 Dining room
  7 Living room

28.05
Roof Parapet Detail
1:5
 1 1mm (1/24 inch) thick sheet zinc
 2 Bituminous sealing layer and thermal insulation
 3 Sealing layer
 4 Steel angle
 5 Galvanized steel section
 6 Painted fibre cement sheeting
 7 Rigid profile permanent steel formwork roofing system
 8 Waterproof membrane
 9 Aluminium U-section
 10 Insulation
 11 Painted plasterboard interior lining
 12 Line of painted plasterboard ceiling

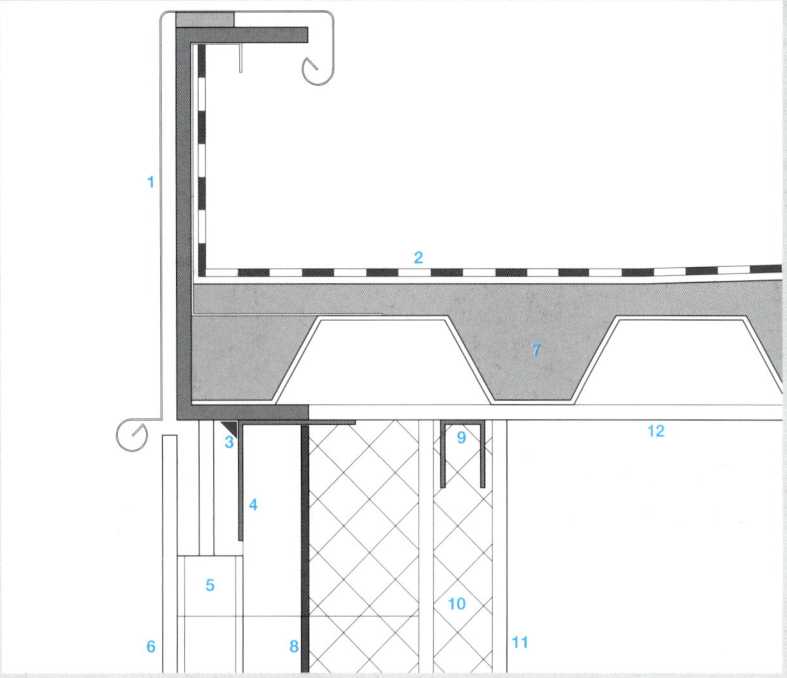

28.06
Floor and Ceiling Detail
1:5
 1 Insulation
 2 Sealing layer
 3 1mm (1/24 inch) thick sheet zinc
 4 Steel channel beyond
 5 Aluminium U-section
 6 Composite floor slab
 7 Sealing layer
 8 Steel RHS frame

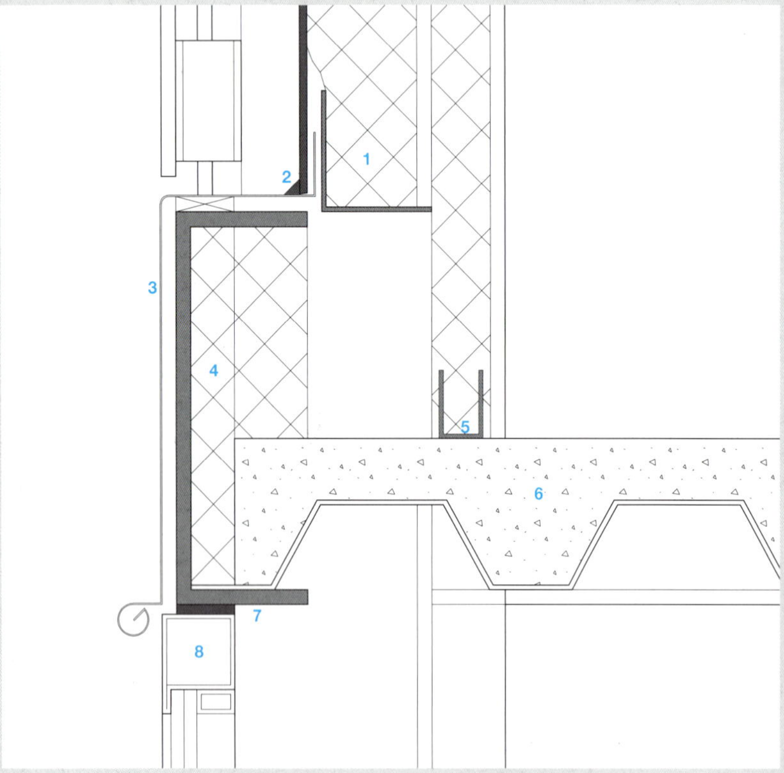

28.07
Floor and Glazing Detail
1:5
 1 Steel RHS frame
 2 Sheet flooring laid directly onto floor slab
 3 Sheet zinc drip profile
 4 Steel angle
 5 Reinforced concrete floor slab

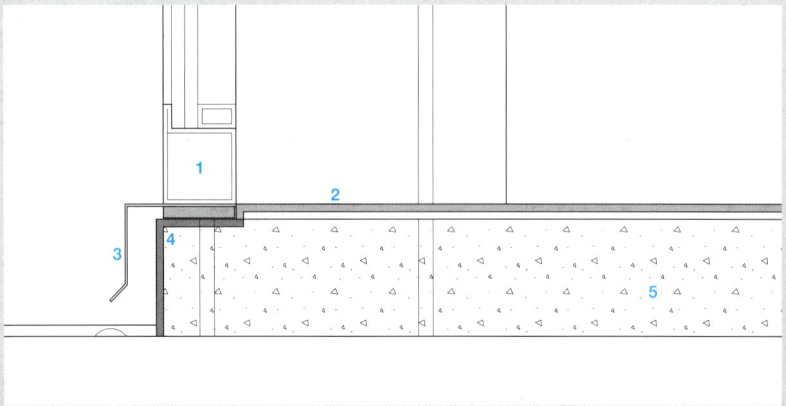

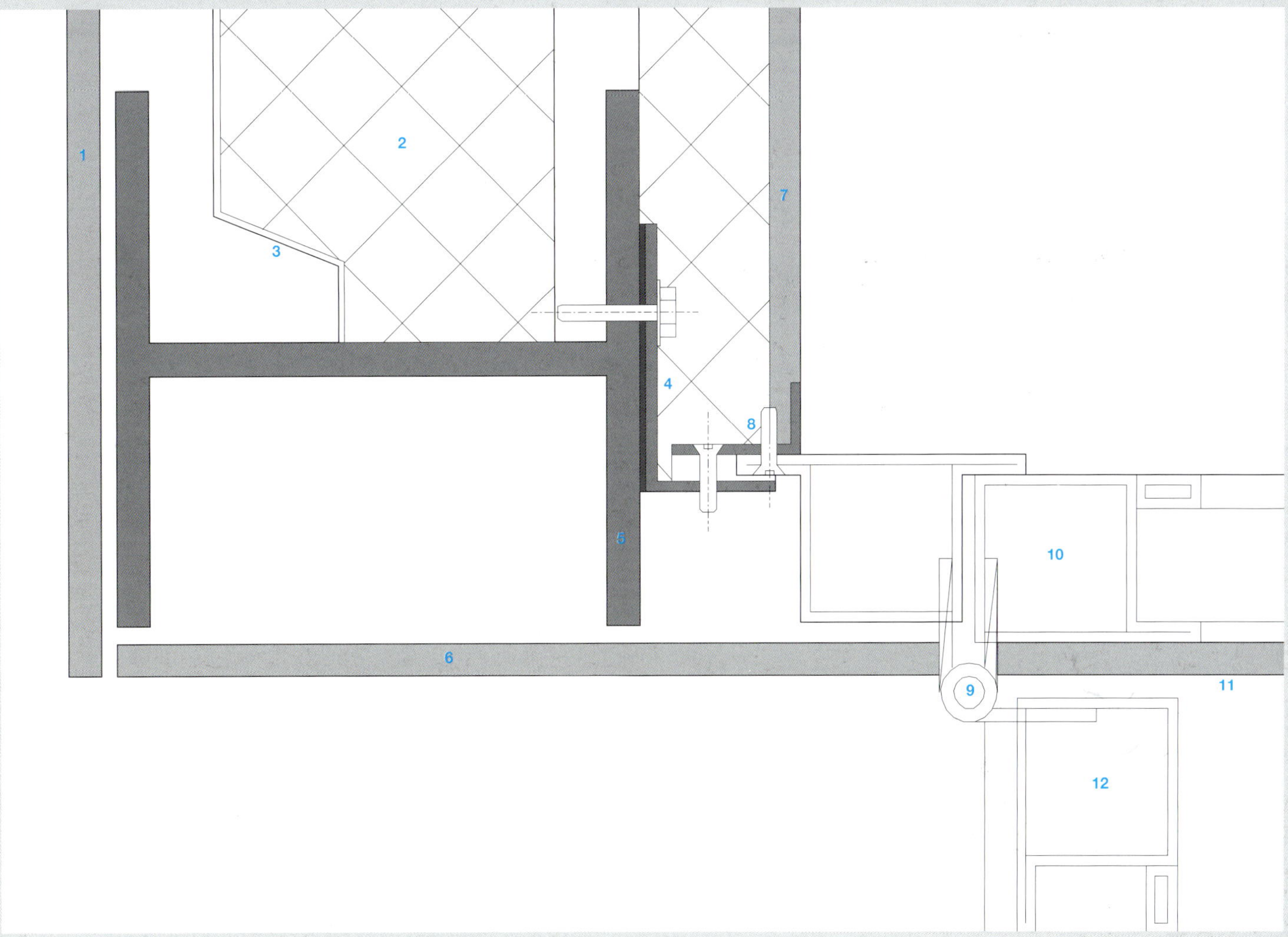

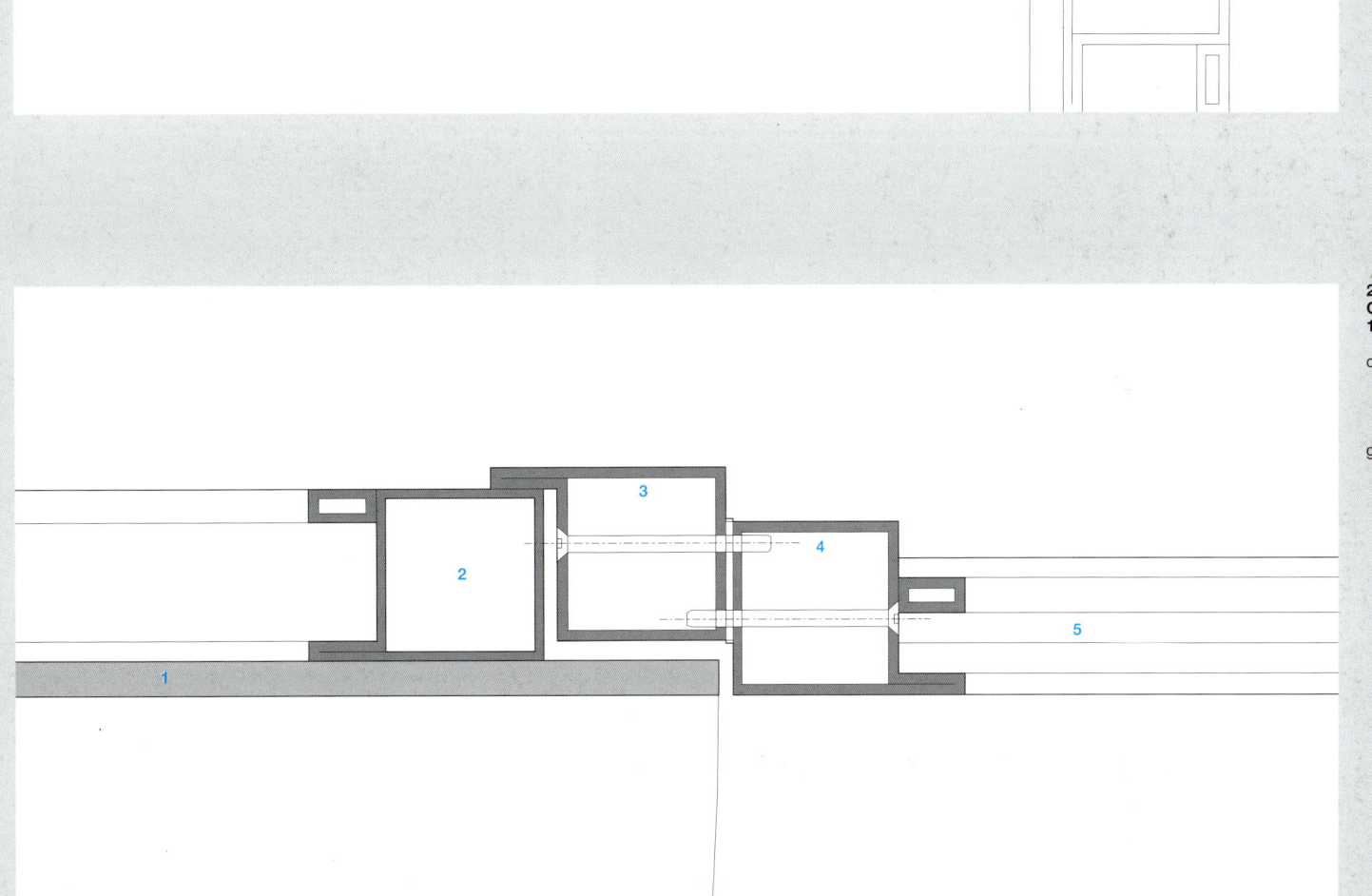

28.08
External Wall Corner Detail
1:2
 1 1mm (1/24 inch) thick sheet zinc
 2 Bituminous sealing layer and thermal insulation
 3 Sealing layer
 4 Steel angle
 5 Galvanized steel section
 6 Painted fibre cement sheeting
 7 Rigid profile permanent steel formwork cladding system
 8 Steel L-section
 9 Steel hinge
 10 Steel RHS frame
 11 Painted plasterboard interior
 12 Steel RHS frame

28.09
Glazed Wall Detail
1:2
 1 Painted fibre cement sheeting
 2 Steel RHS frame
 3 Steel window frame
 4 Steel glazing bar
 5 Proprietary double glazing assembly

127

Springtecture B
Biwa-cho, Shiga Prefecture, Japan

Client
Aoi Fujioka

Area
104 square metres (1,120 square feet)

Project Team
Keisuke Fukuma, Takashi Nabeshima

Structural Engineer
TIS + Partners

Services Engineer
Tawada Shoten

Quantity Surveyor
Shuhei Endo Architect Institute

Springtecture B is a weekend house located amidst Biwa-cho's ancient thatched roofs and their contemporary equivalents. As with the architect's other projects, naming conventions are of interest. The terms 'Rooftecture', 'Skintecture' and 'Halftecture', and in this case 'Springtecture' are used to describe projects that, while having certain preoccupations in common, take a conceptual approach that makes each unique. In this project, the concept of a continuation between interior and exterior is contrived from continuous sheets of corrugated metal that twist and turn with no obvious delineation between roof, floor and walls. The sheets of metal have apparently 'sprung' into place to create a domestic environment.

A sliding glass door and a chequered brick wall are a stark contrast to the undulating steel panels and apparently randomly-placed angled steel columns. While the blade of brick wall imposes an underlying order on the composition, the flowing ribbons of steel constantly confound an understanding of the way the building is put together. The arrangement of spaces, while conventional in content – a kitchen, dining space, living area, guest bedroom with ensuite bathroom and a terrace on the ground floor, and additional bedrooms and bathroom upstairs – is subject to the apparent vagaries of the sculptural form. The resulting interstitial spaces are given over to slices of garden, gravelled courtyards, a reflecting pool and framed views of the landscape.

1 The building appears to barely touch the ground. Right angles are avoided in favour of the undulating metal that skims the ground before rising to form the walls and roof.
2 Sheets of glazing provide sheer slices of infill between the ribbons of steel, allowing plenty of natural light into the house.
3 The raw appeal of the corrugated metal, angled steel columns and unpainted timber framing underpin the free-form nature of the architectural aesthetic.
4 Spaces of no discernible use are created as a by-product of the 'Springtecture', however even these are creatively utilized to frame views of the surrounding landscape.

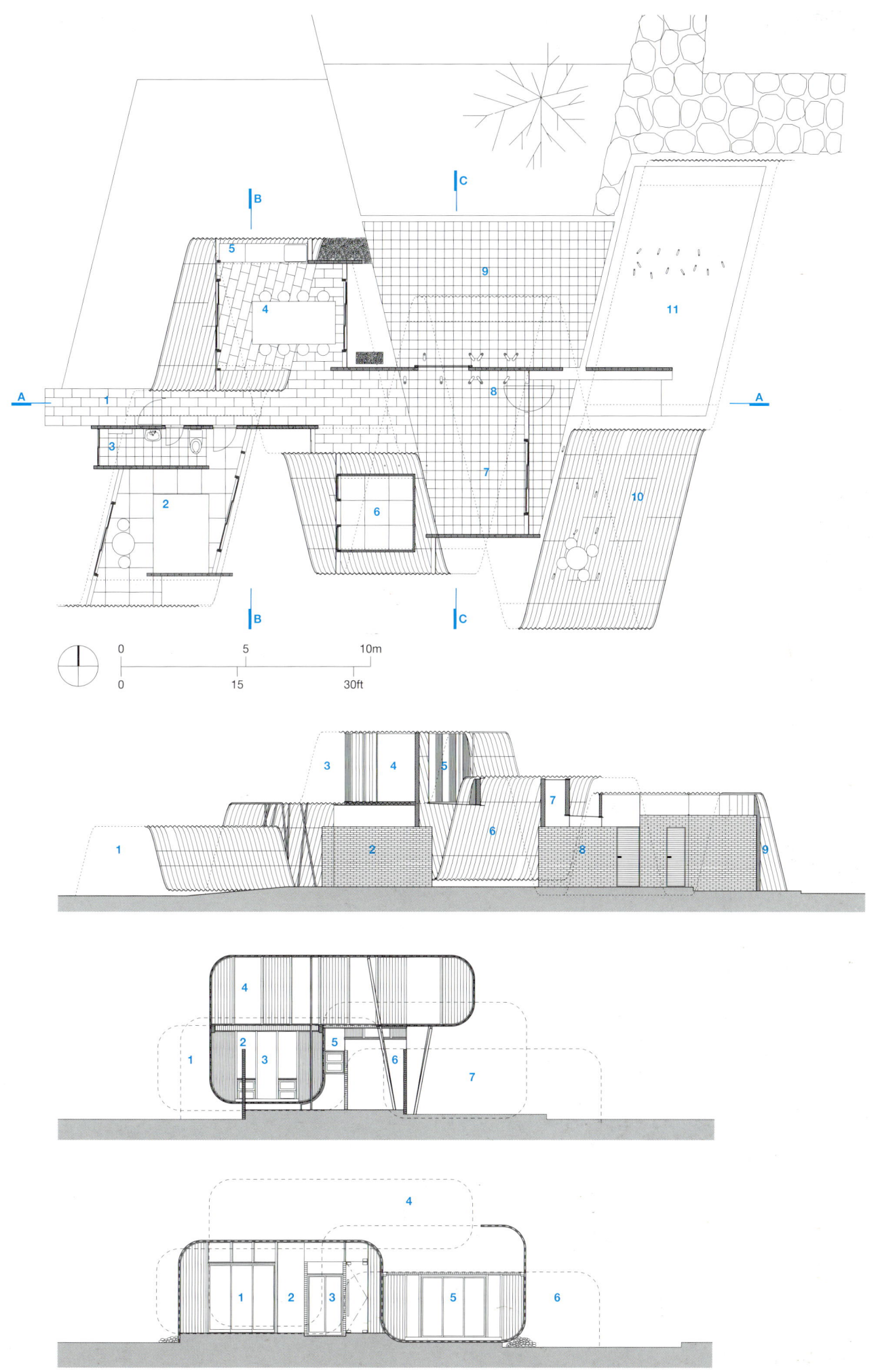

29.01
Ground Floor Plan
1:200
 1 Entrance
 2 Bedroom
 3 Bathroom
 4 Dining
 5 Kitchen
 6 Rest space
 7 Gallery
 8 Entrance
 9 Terrace
 10 Terrace
 11 Parking

0   5   10m

0   15   30ft

29.02
Section A–A
1:200
 1 Entrance
 2 Masonry wall to
    entrance corridor
 3 Line of roof
 4 Bedroom
 5 Bathroom
 6 Rest space behind
 7 Skylight over
    gallery
 8 Masonry wall to
    bedroom
 9 Terrace

29.03
Section B–B
1:200
 1 Line of terrace
    beyond
 2 Window to rest
    space
 3 Door to rest space
 4 Window to upper
    level bedroom
 5 Window to central
    circulation space
 6 Kitchen
 7 Line of terrrace
    beyond

29.04
Section C–C
1:200
 1 Gallery
 2 Entrance
 3 Doors to terrace
 4 Line of upper level
    beyond
 5 Terrace
 6 Line of parking
    area beyond

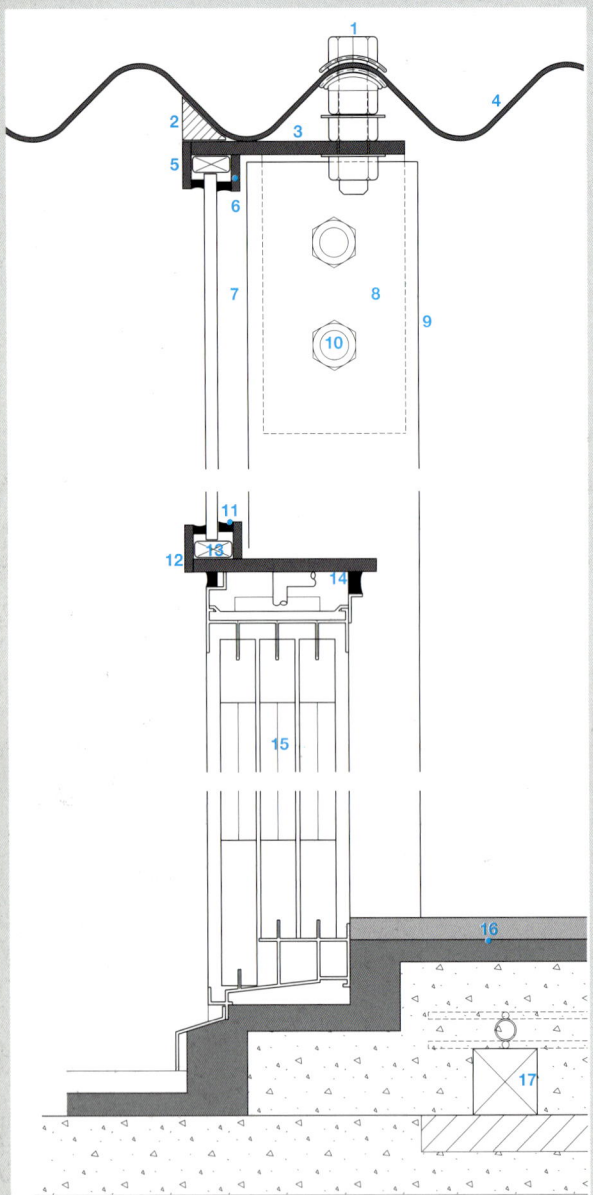

29.05
Sheet Metal Detail 1
1:5
1 Bolt and washer fixing to corrugated sheet roofing
2 Timber packing
3 150 x 9 mm (6 x 1/3 inch) flat steel bar
4 Corrugated sheet steel with hot dip galvanized finish
5 32 x 6 mm (1 1/4 x 1/3 inch) flat steel bar
6 25 x 6 mm (1 x 1/3 inch) flat steel bar
7 Fixed glass
8 Gusset steel plate
9 Japanese cypress mullion
10 Bolt fixing to mullion
11 25 x 6 mm (1 x 1/3 inch) flat steel bar
12 32 x 6 mm (1 1/4 x 1/3 inch) flat steel bar
13 Timber packing
14 125 x 9 mm (5 x 1/3 inch) flat steel bar
15 Double sliding window assembly
16 Marble flooring on setting mortar and insulation over reinforced concrete slab
17 Sub-floor structure

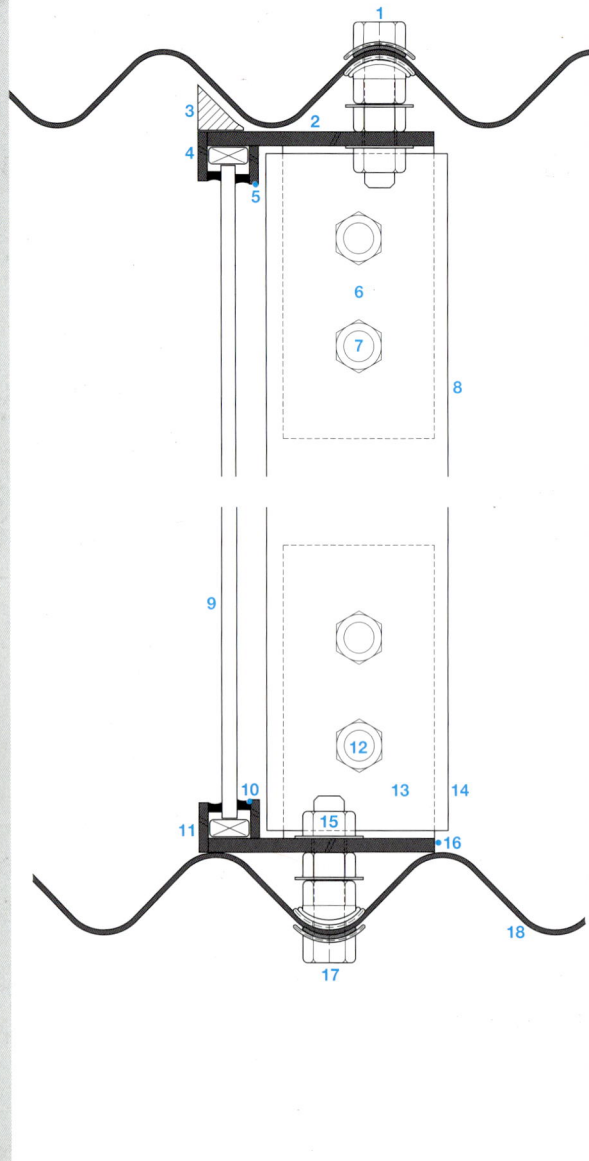

29.06
Sheet Metal Detail 2
1:5
1 Bolt and washer fixing to corrugated sheet roofing
2 150 x 9 mm (6 x 1/3 inch) flat steel bar
3 Timber packing
4 32 x 6 mm (1 1/4 x 1/3 inch) flat steel bar
5 25 x 6 mm (1 x 1/3 inch) flat steel bar
6 Gusset steel plate
7 Bolt fixing to mullion
8 Japanese cypress mullion
9 Polycarbonate sheeting
10 25 x 6 mm (1 x 1/3 inch) flat steel bar
11 32 x 6 mm (1 1/4 x 1/3 inch) flat steel bar
12 Bolt fixing to mullion
13 Gusset steel plate
14 Japanese cypress mullion
15 Bolt and washer fixing to flat steel bar
16 150 x 9 mm (6 x 1/3 inch) flat steel bar
17 Bolt and washer fixing to corrugated sheet roofing
18 Corrugated sheet steel with hot dip galvanized finish

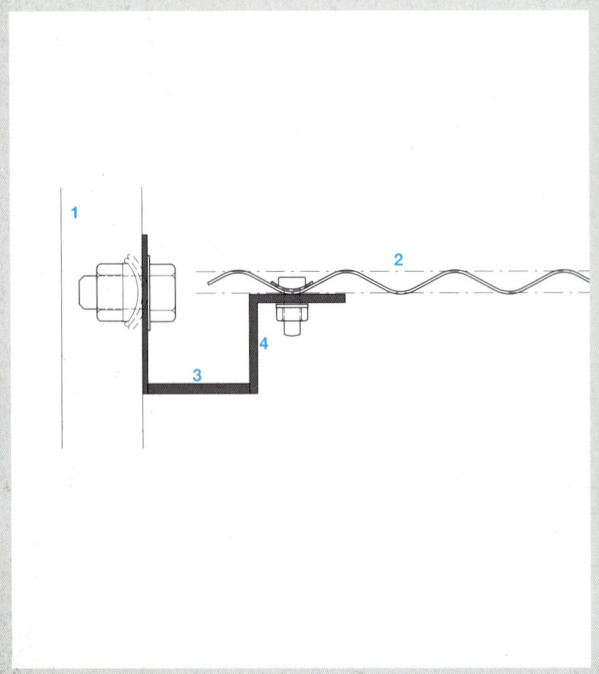

29.07
Sheet Metal Detail 3
1:10
1 Corrugated steel sheet type 2
2 Corrugated steel sheet type 1
3 Steel plate
4 Steel angle

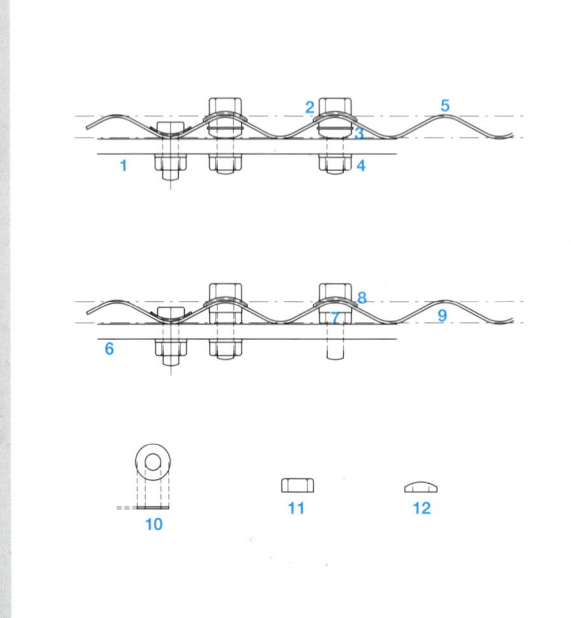

29.08
Sheet Metal Detail 4
1:10
1 Flat steel bar
2 Round washer
3 Angle washer
4 Bolt for 4 mm (1/10 inch) board
5 Corrugated sheet metal
6 Flat steel bar
7 Bolt nut
8 Angle washer
9 Bolt for 4 mm (1/10 inch) board
10 Round washer
11 Bolt nut
12 Angle washer

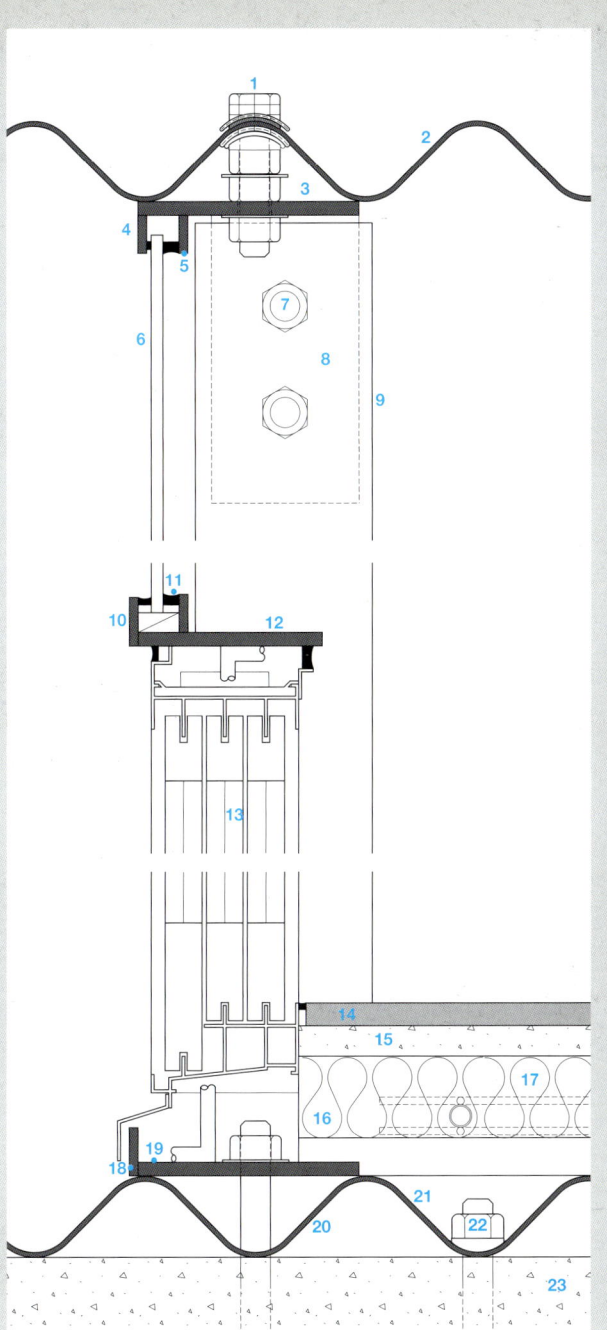

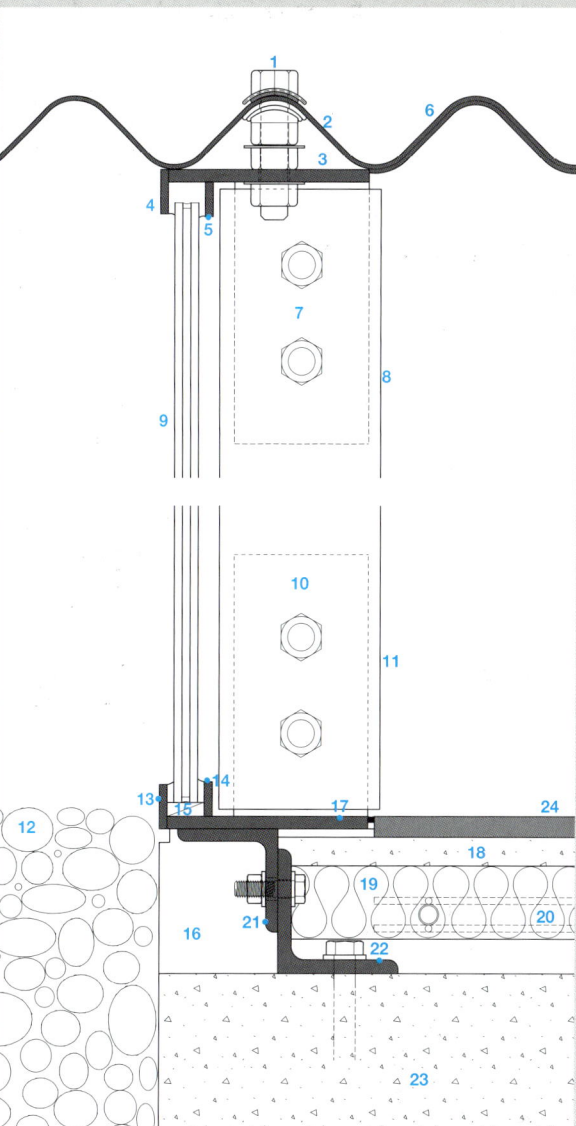

29.09
Sheet Metal Detail 5
1:5
1 Bolt and washer fixing to corrugated sheet roofing
2 Corrugated steel sheet with hot dip galvanized finish
3 Flat steel bar
4 Flat steel bar with hot dip galvanized finish
5 Flat steel bar with hot dip galvanized finish
6 Glass
7 Bolt fixing to gusset plate
8 Gusset steel plate with hot dip galvanized finish
9 Japanese cypress mullion
10 Flat steel bar with hot dip galvanized finish
11 Flat steel bar with hot dip galvanized finish
12 Flat steel bar with hot dip galvanized finish
13 Double sliding window assembly
14 Marble flooring
15 Setting mortar
16 Cinder concrete
17 Insulation
18 Flat steel bar with hot dip galvanized finish
19 Flat steel bar with hot dip galvanized finish
20 Corrugated steel sheet with hot dip galvanized finish
21 Mortar screed
22 Bolt and washer fixing to corrugated sheet roofing
23 Reinforced concrete slab

29.10
Sheet Metal Detail 6
1:5
1 Bolt and washer fixing to corrugated sheet roofing
2 Corrugated steel sheet with hot dip galvanized finish
3 Flat steel bar
4 Flat steel bar with hot dip galvanized finish
5 Flat steel bar with hot dip galvanized finish
6 Heat insulating coated film
7 Gusset steel plate with hot dip galvanized finish
8 Japanese cypress mullion
9 Insulating glass
10 Gusset steel plate with hot dip galvanized finish
11 Japanese cypress mullion
12 Gravel courtyard
13 Flat steel bar with hot dip galvanized finish
14 Flat steel bar with hot dip galvanized finish
15 Timber packing
16 Resin mortar
17 Flat steel bar with hot dip galvanized finish
18 Setting mortar
19 Cinder concrete
20 Insulation
21 75 x 75 mm (3 x 3 inch) pre-formed steel angle
22 90 x 90 mm (3¹/₂ x 3¹/₂ inch) pre-formed steel angle
23 Reinforced concrete
24 Marble flooring

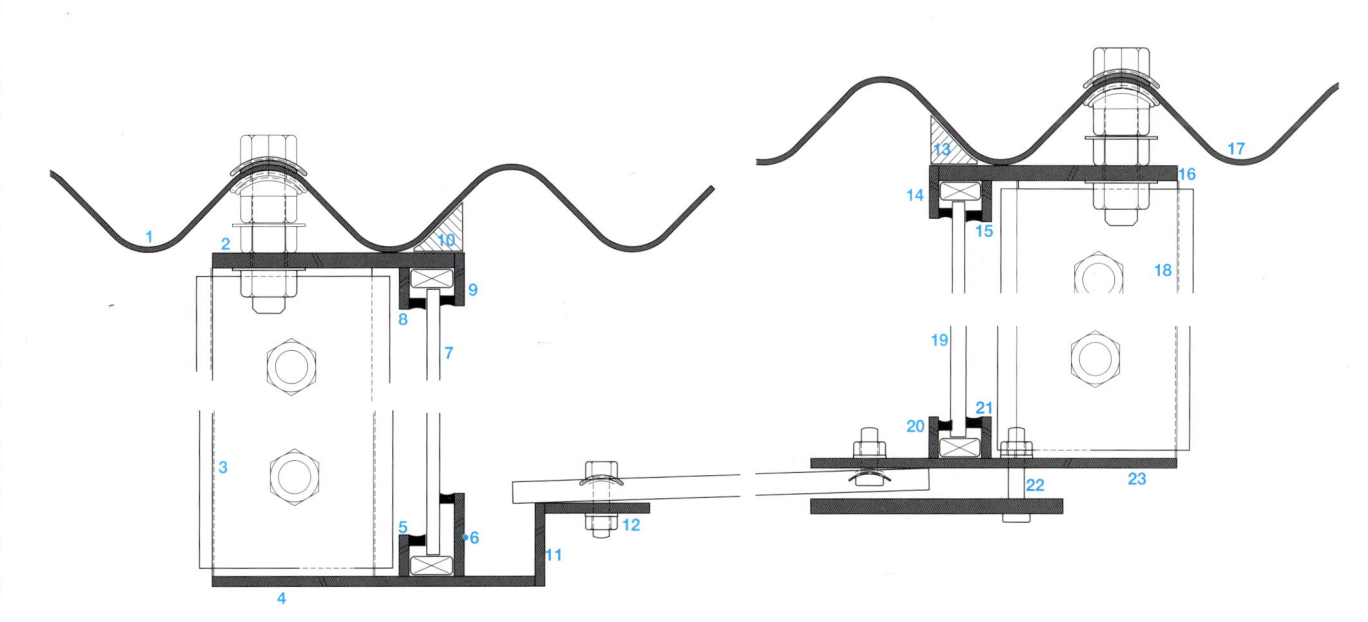

29.11
Sheet Metal Detail 7
1:5
1 Corrugated steel sheet
2 Flat steel bar
3 Japanese cypress mullion
4 Flat steel bar
5 Flat steel bar
6 Flat steel bar
7 Polycarbonate sheeting
8 Flat steel bar
9 Flat steel bar
10 Timber packing
11 Flat steel bar
12 Flat steel bar
13 Timber packing
14 Flat steel bar
15 Flat steel bar
16 Flat steel bar
17 Corrugated steel sheet
18 Japanese cypress mullion
19 Polycarbonate sheeting
20 Flat steel bar
21 Flat steel bar
22 Flat steel bar
23 Flat steel bar

Rozak House
Lake Bennett, NT, Australia

Client
Mike Rozak

Area
210 square metres (2,260 square feet)

Project Team
Joanna Rees

Structural Engineer
Colless and O'Neill

Main Contractor
Jo Tagg

The Rozak House is located on a remote site south of Darwin in the far north of Australia, at the top of an inhospitable rocky escarpment. The climate in this region is sub-tropical with high rainfall and humidity during the monsoon period. The client chose this place for its unique natural environment and wanted the design to enhance these qualities. The planning of the house consists of a series of pavilions – two bedroom 'verandahs' and a central living and dining 'verandah'. Each pavilion provides immediate contact with the surrounding landscape with direct access to light and ventilation. The whole of the floor is open-slatted timber decking to further promote ventilation.

The structural steel post and beam structure provides the required strength for protection against cyclonic winds and seasonal bush fires, however its slenderness reinforces the idea of tropical lightness. All the 'verandah' spaces are protected against insects and bush fire embers by stainless steel mesh screens. The corrugated steel sheet roof of the bedroom wings twists, like fabric stretched and draped over a frame. The steel structure is painted black, mimicking the surrounding tree trunks blackened by bush fires. The elevated form of the house protects it from heat radiating off the rocks and allows cooling breezes to sweep underneath and through the house. Constraints such as climate, the remoteness of site and cost resulted in very simple construction methods and detailing, along with the selection of low cost, lightweight and easily transportable materials.

1 The house perches lightly on the dry rocky escarpment. A plethora of screens, overhangs and other shading devices protect the inhabitants from the weather.
2 Pitched roofs are arranged as separate angled layers, overlapping to create skylights in the gaps between them and dropping down over the verandahs to shade the interior spaces.
3 Despite the challenging environmental conditions, large expanses of glazing bring light into the heart of the house.
4 The three pavilions are arranged around a pivot point of steel and polycarbonate sheeting that acts as the main entry to the house.

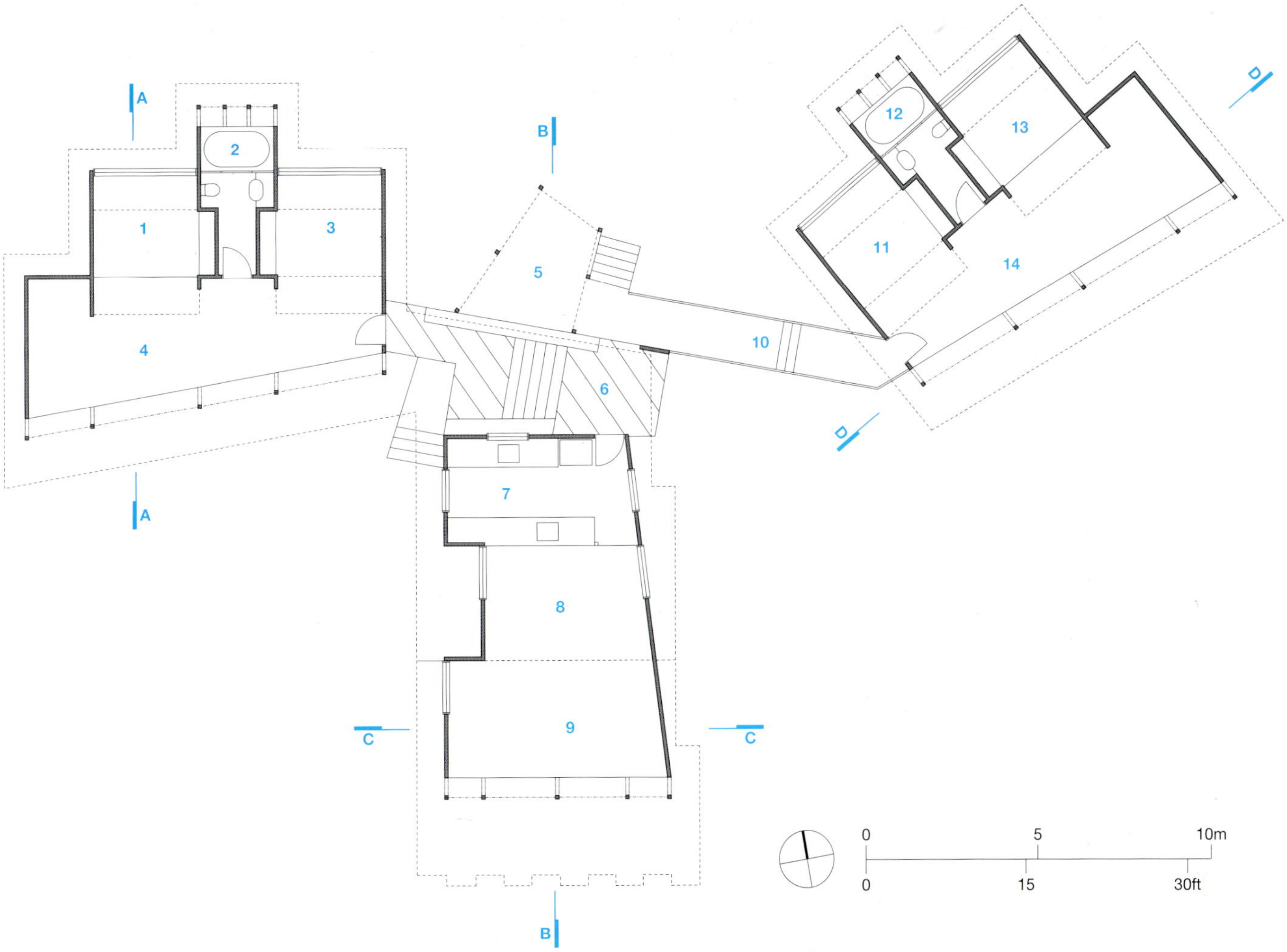

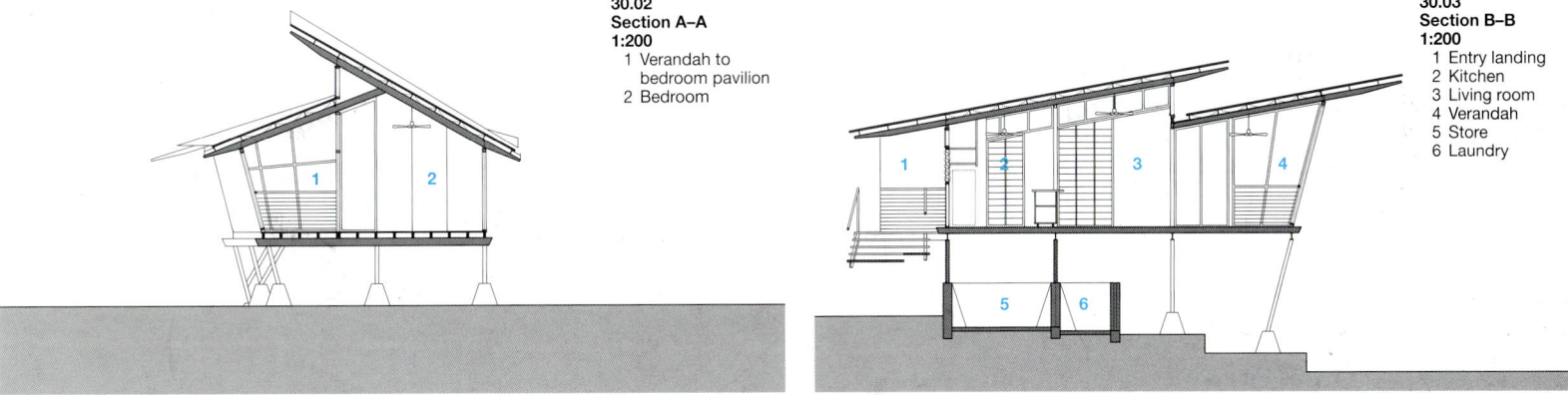

30.01
Floor Plan
1:200
1 Bedroom 1
2 Bathroom
3 Bedroom 2
4 Verandah
5 Entry tower
6 Entrance
7 Kitchen
8 Living room
9 Verandah
10 Bridge
11 Bedroom 3
12 Bathroom
13 Bedroom 4
14 Verandah

0   5   10m

0   15   30ft

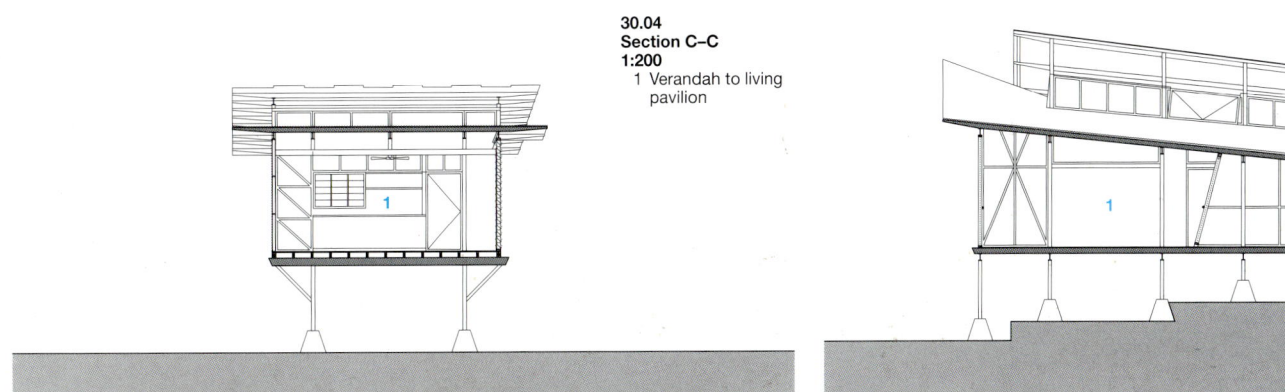

30.02
Section A–A
1:200
1 Verandah to
   bedroom pavilion
2 Bedroom

30.03
Section B–B
1:200
1 Entry landing
2 Kitchen
3 Living room
4 Verandah
5 Store
6 Laundry

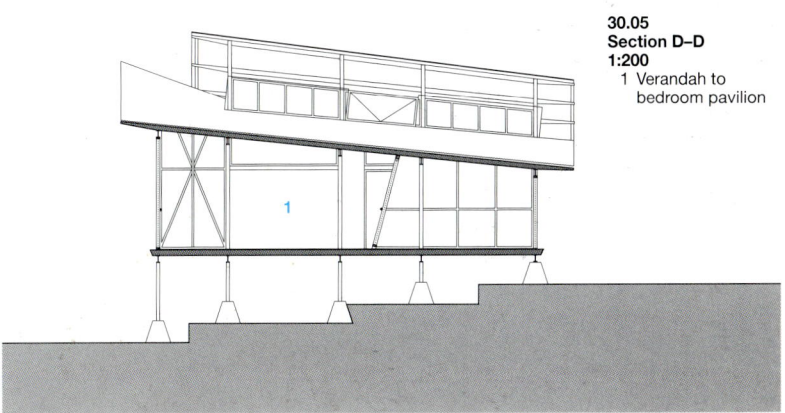

30.04
Section C–C
1:200
1 Verandah to living
   pavilion

30.05
Section D–D
1:200
1 Verandah to
   bedroom pavilion

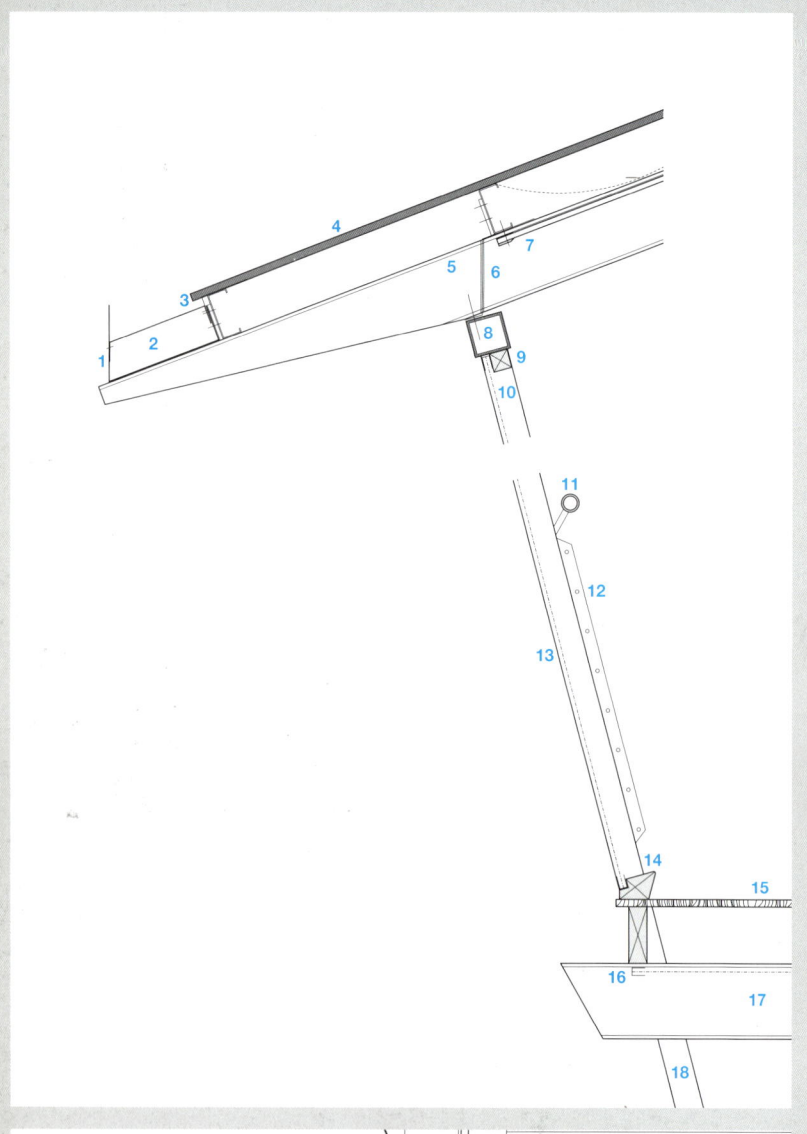

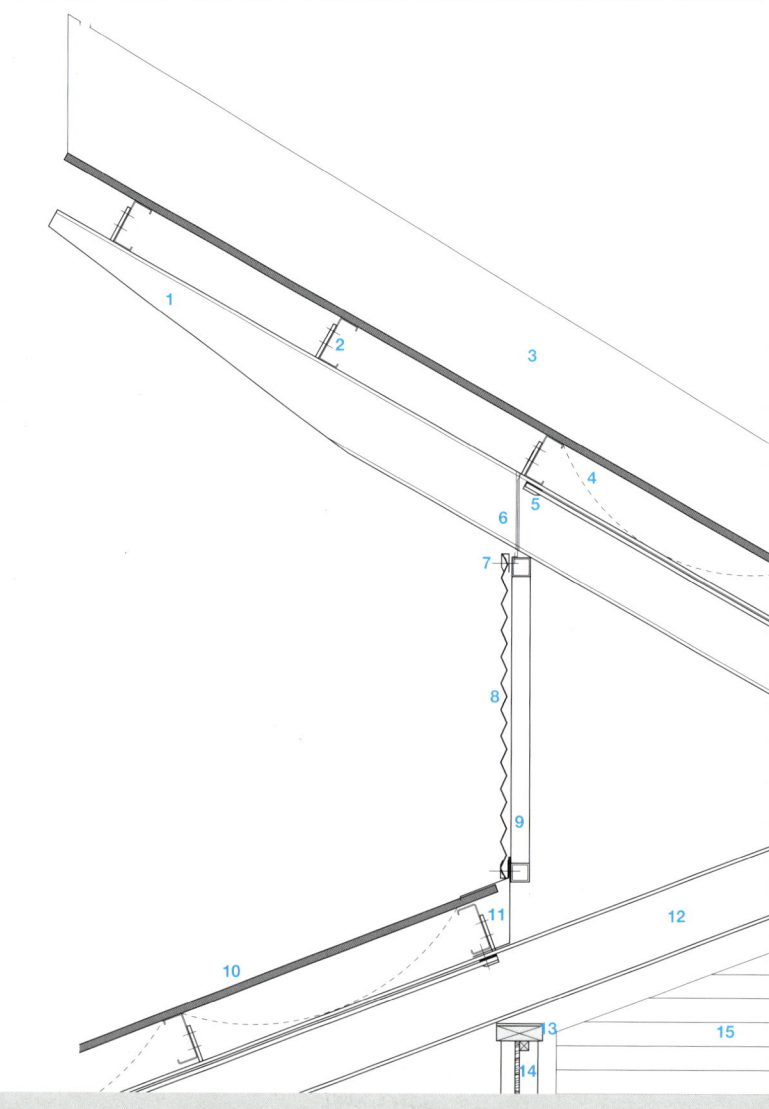

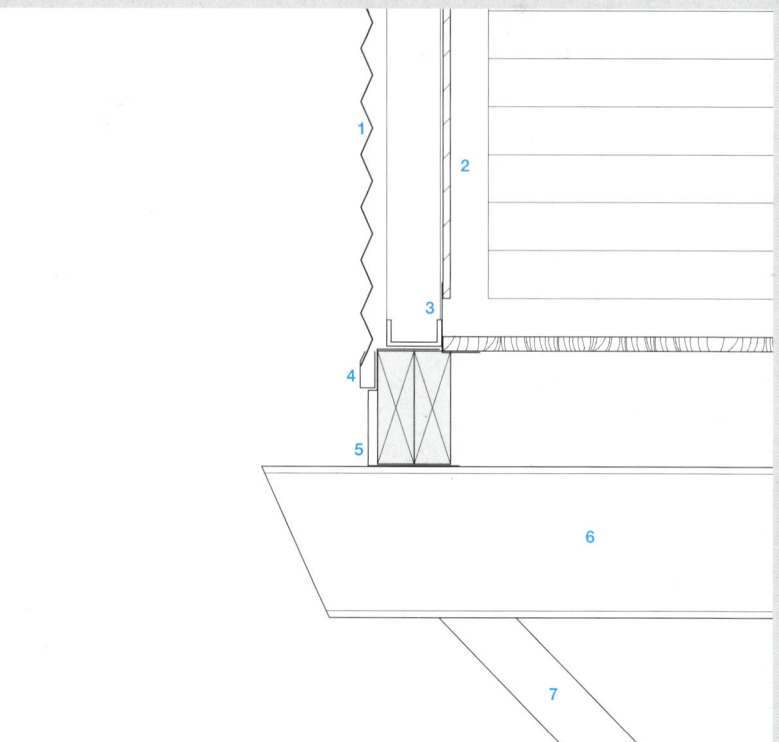

30.06
**Edge Gutter and
Screen Wall Detail
1:20**
  1 Folded zincalume
  2 Zinc strap stiffeners
  3 Zincalume flashing
  4 Zincalume Custom
Orb cladding
  5 Stiffener to rafter
beyond
  6 Perforated metal
flashing
  7 Zincalume miniorb
ceiling with U-trim to
match
  8 Steel square hollow
section
  9 Bead with clear
finish
10 Raked 75 x 5 mm (3
x 1/5 inch) square
hollow section beyond
11 Steel handrail fixed
to columns
12 Steel fin fixed to
columns and threaded
with stainless steel
cable
13 Stainless steel
mesh screen walls
screwed to aluminium
subframe
14 Profiled hardwood
skirt with clear finish
15 Timber decking
boards
16 Removeable insect
screen
17 Universal beam
18 Raked column

30.07
**Highlight to Roof
1:20**
  1 Universal I-beam
  2 C-section roof
purlin
  3 Zincalume Custom
Orb metal cladding
  4 Insulation sisalation
  5 Zincalume miniorb
ceiling with U-trim to
match
  6 Perforated metal
flashing
  7 Folded zincalume
flashing
  8 Horizontal
corrugated Suntuf
clear sheet installed
after perforated metal
flashings with clear
anodized aluminium
trim
  9 Square hollow
section mullions
10 Zincalume Custom
Orb metal cladding
11 Perforated metal
flashing folded under
purlin over miniorb
ceiling lining to
conceal edges
12 Universal I-beam
13 125 x 40 mm (5 x
1 1/2 inch) top rail with
cleat and bolt
14 Timber slats with
hard wood bead
15 Zincalume
horizontal Custom Orb
wall

30.08
**Typical Exterior Wall
Detail
1:10**
  1 Zincalume
horizontal Custom Orb
cladding
  2 Ply wall sheet with
stained trim and
zincalume trim
  3 Flat galvanized 25
mm (1 inch) shadow
edge
  4 Zincalume U-trim
  5 Zincalume flashing
to be continuous
around building –
change joist size to
suit tiled floor
  6 Universal I-beam
  7 75 x 5 mm (3 x 1/5
inch) square hollow
section prop

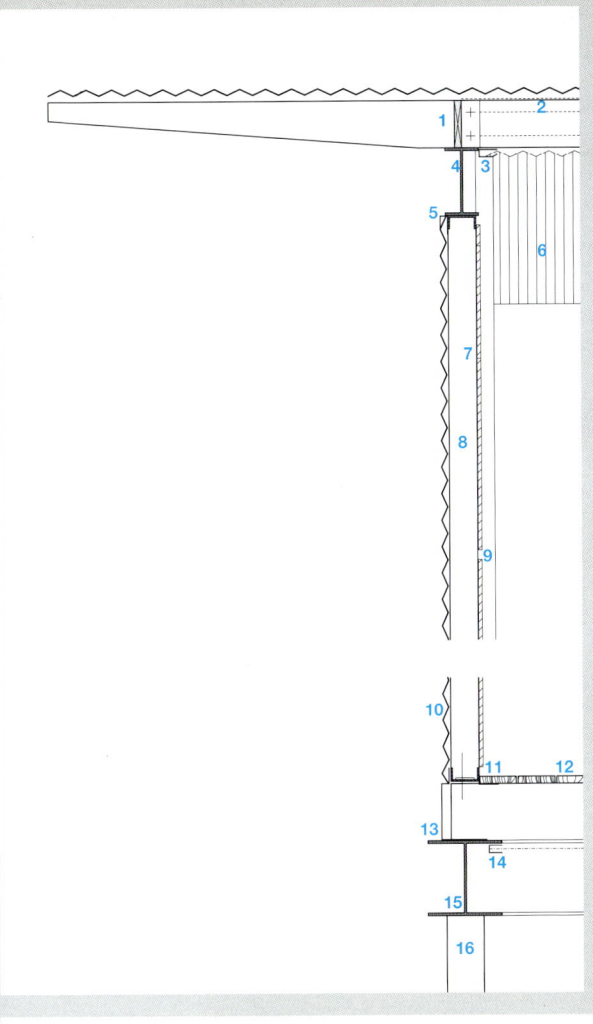

30.09
Wall Detail
1:20
1 Clear finished continuous bird board, height to suit purlins
2 Insulation sisalation
3 Zincalume J-trim to miniorb ceiling
4 Universal I-beam
5 Zincalume J-mould flashing to zincalume Custom Orb wall sheet
6 Clear polycarbonate highlight Custom Orb profile
7 Stained finish ply wall sheet
8 Pressed metal stud framed wall
9 25 mm (1 inch) shadow edge from galvanized flat
10 Zincalume Custom Orb wall sheeting
11 25 mm (1 inch) shadow edge skirting from galvanized flat
12 Timber decking boards
13 Zincalume flashing
14 Removeable insect screen
15 Paint finished bearer
16 75 x 5 mm (3 x 1/5 inch) square hollow section column

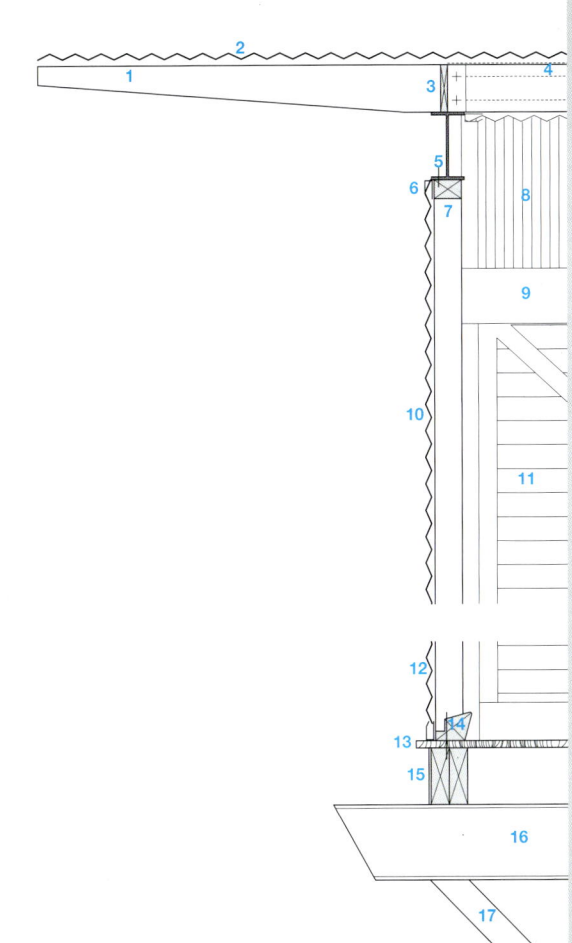
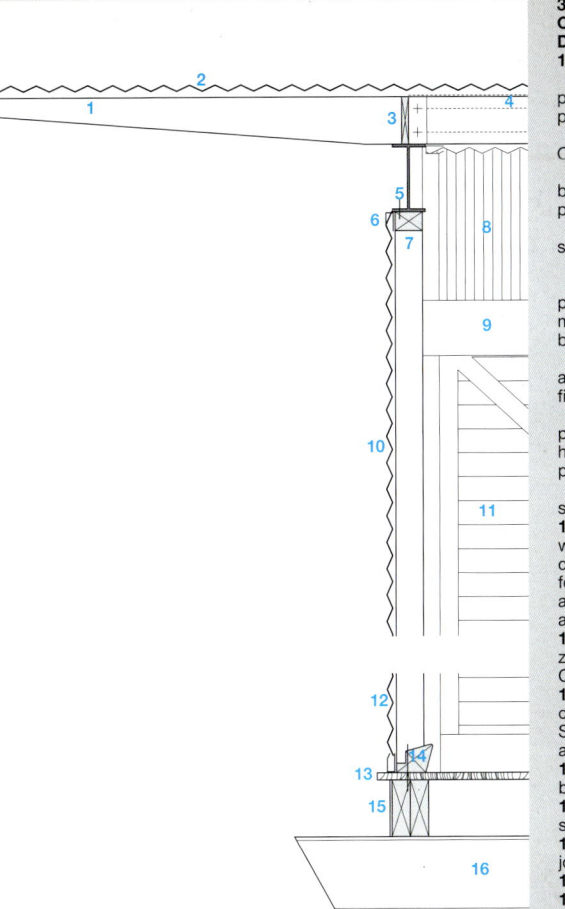
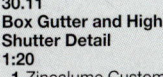

30.10
Clear Sheet Wall Detail
1:20
1 C-section roof purlin cut to tapering profile
2 Zincalume Custom Orb sheeting
3 Continuous bird board, height to suit purlins
4 Insulation sisalation
5 Universal I-beam
6 Bead to insect-proof verandah and to match screen wall behind
7 Anodized aluminium channel to finish clearsheet edges
8 Clear polycarbonate highlight Custom Orb profile
9 Rectangular hollow section beam
10 Seal clear sheet wall from insects at columns with prestite foam material to suit angle of wall sheeting and durability
11 Perforated zincalume horizontal Custom Orb wall
12 Horizontal corrugated clear sheet Suntuf finished with aluminium channel
13 Timber decking boards
14 Profiled hardwood skirt with clear finish
15 Steel fin bolted to joist
16 Universal I-beam
17 75 x 5 mm (3 x 1/5 inch) square hollow section prop

30.11
Box Gutter and High Shutter Detail
1:20
1 Zincalume Custom Orb roof cladding
2 C-section roof purlin
3 Universal I-beam
4 Zincalume miniorb ceiling with U-trim to match
5 Perforated metal flashing located close to outside edge of tie beam for fixing and maximum purlin spacing to generate maximum roof overhang
6 Location for stiffener to rafter beyond
7 Insect screen in subframe
8 Plywood shutter with clear finish
9 75 x 50 mm (3 x 2 inch) angle to support hinge and act as rain buffer
10 Zincalume flashing
11 Zincalume miniorb ceiling
12 Sisalation
13 Universal I-beam
14 Zincalume Custom Orb roof cladding

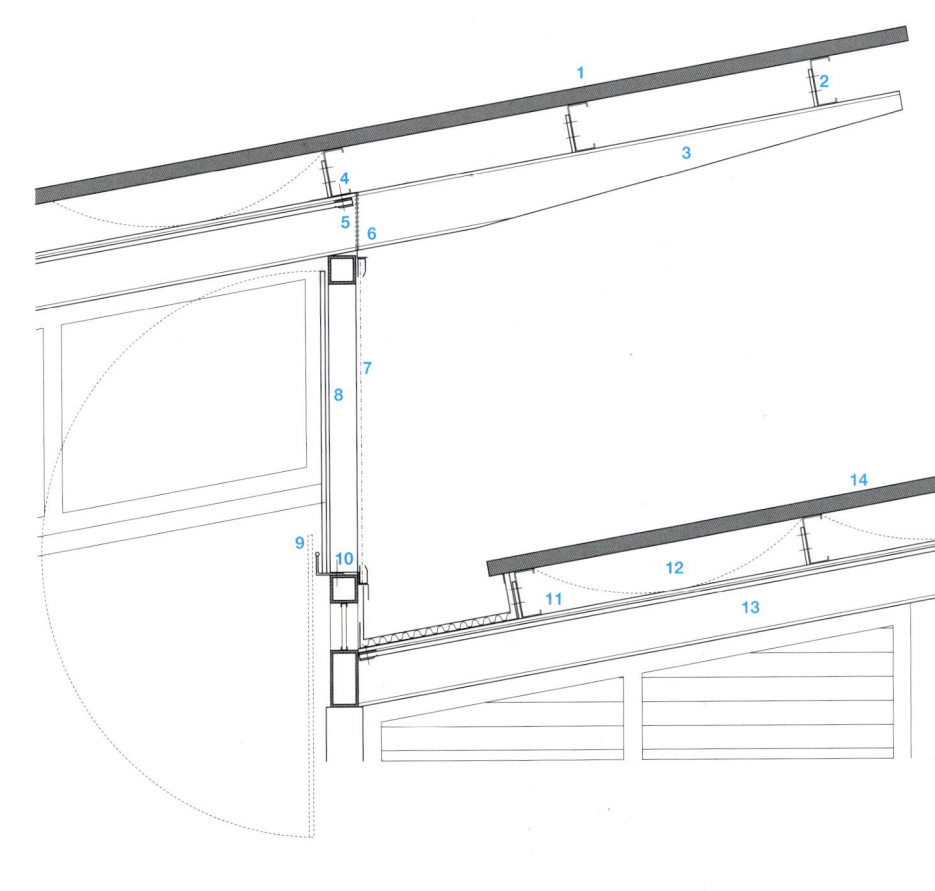

135

31
Atelier Bow-Wow + Tokyo Institute of Technology Tsukamoto Lab

Gae House
Tokyo, Japan

Area
88 square metres (950 square feet)

Project Team
Yoshiharu Tsukamoto, Momoyo Kaijima, Satoshi Saito, Daisuke Sakurai, Yuko Suzuki, Masamichi Hirabayasi, Hiroki Tominaga

Structural Engineer
Structural Design Office Oak Inc

Main Contractor
Tokyo Tekkin Concrete

Located in a residential area of Tokyo, the Gae house is situated on a typically small site. Ordinarily, small sites means that front gardens are removed and replaced with parking spaces, denigrating the landscape of the entire area. In the Gae house, however, the largest possible roof structure allows substantial setbacks at the lower levels to accommodate both a covered parking space and the reinstatement of the hedges that are typical of the area. Arranged over three levels, a lower ground level contains the bedroom and study, the roof contains the living, dining and kitchen spaces, while the ground floor accommodates the entrance and bathroom with a void over the study below.

The floor to ceiling height varies at each level according to the functions of each floor and the predetermined exterior form of the building. The floor level in the roof is only 900 millimetres (35 inches) below the eaves, leaving the opportunity to insert a horizontal window. Daylight is reflected off the white walls and is then scattered by the irregular surface of the decking to bring shadowless soft light into the interior. The facades are deliberately kept free of unnecessary openings in order to create an interior world in which the inhabitants can enjoy their private space. The slot of glazing at eaves level is complemented by two large openings in the south facade. In addition, the void between the ground and lower floors and the open tread stair serve to bring light into the lower reaches of the house.

1 The over-sized roof in fact accommodates a large part of the programme, including the living and dining areas and the kitchen. The horizontal slot of clear glazing is visible between the vertical walls of the lower level and the pitch of the roof.
2 An open tread, white steel stair links all three levels from the office in the basement, to the living space in the roof. The structure of the walls and floors, painted white, remains exposed.
3 In the living spaces, light from the horizontal window slot reflects up over the natural anodized ceiling, washing the interior in soft light.

31.01
First Floor Plan
1:100
1 Eaves glazing
2 Living and dining space
3 Roof
4 Stair from ground floor below
5 Kitchen
6 Eaves glazing

31.02
Ground Floor Plan
1:100
1 Parking
2 Storage
3 Utility area
4 Hot water boiler
5 Bathroom
6 WC
7 Laundry
8 Heating
9 Storage
10 Entrance
11 Entry foyer
12 Stair down to lower level and up to living areas
13 Void over office

31.03
Basement Floor Plan
1:100
1 Bedroom
2 Storage
3 Stair to ground floor
4 Storage
5 Closet
6 Office

31.04
Section A–A
1:100
1 Living and dining room
2 Kitchen
3 Utility area
4 Stair
5 Void over office
6 Bedroom
7 Closet
8 Office

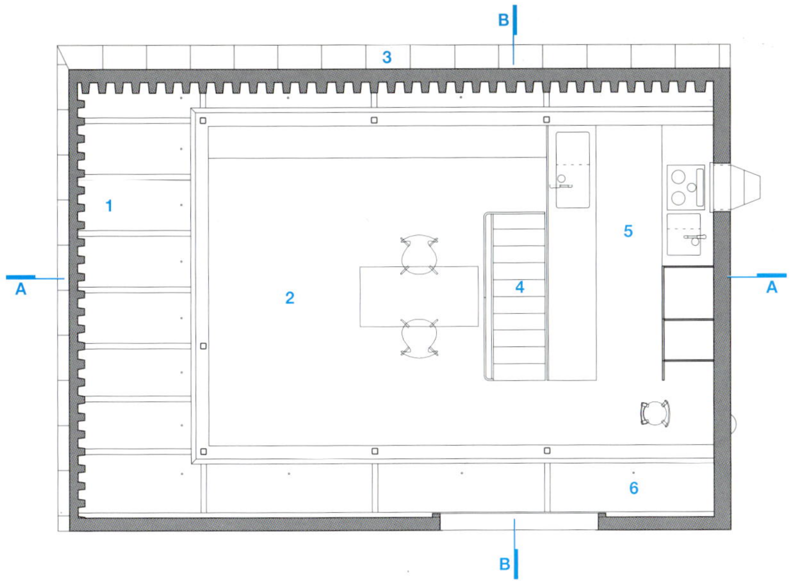

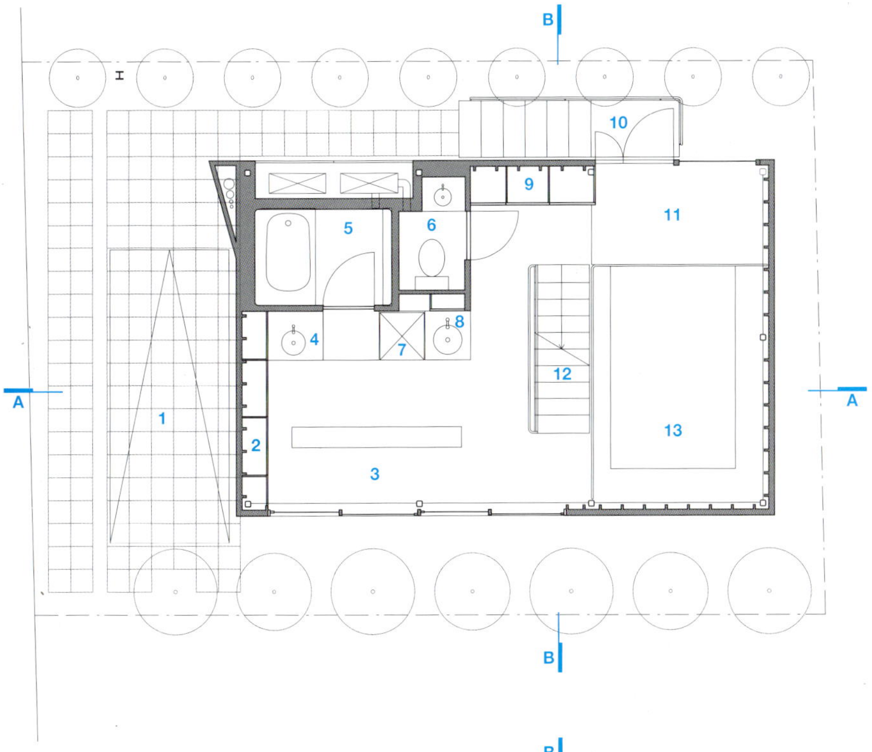

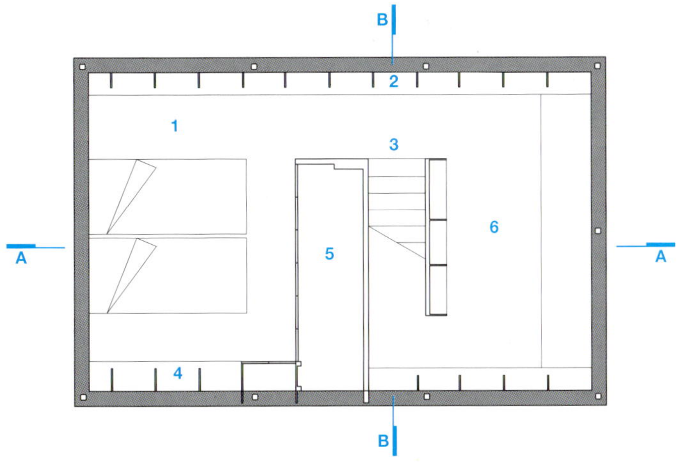

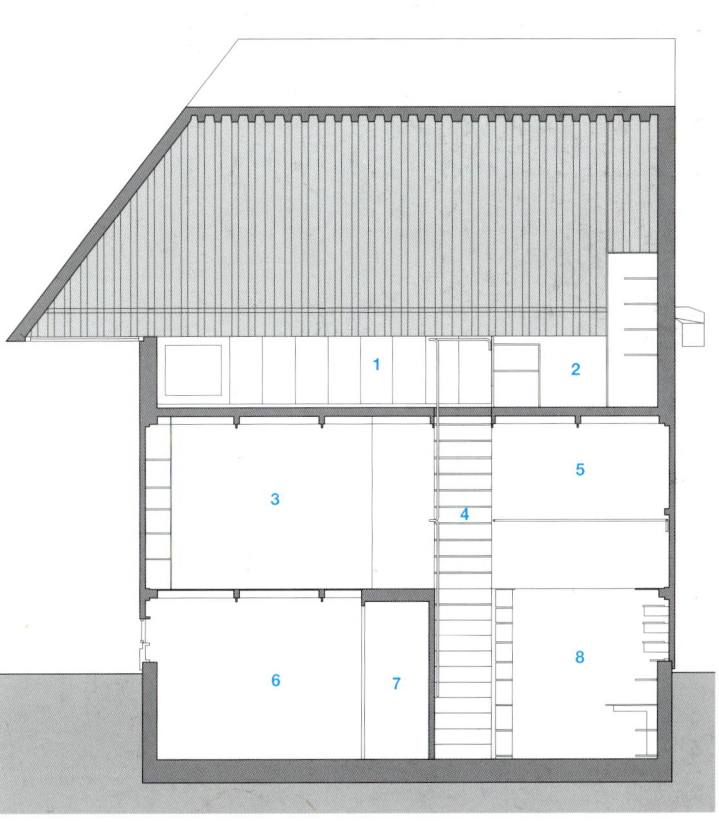

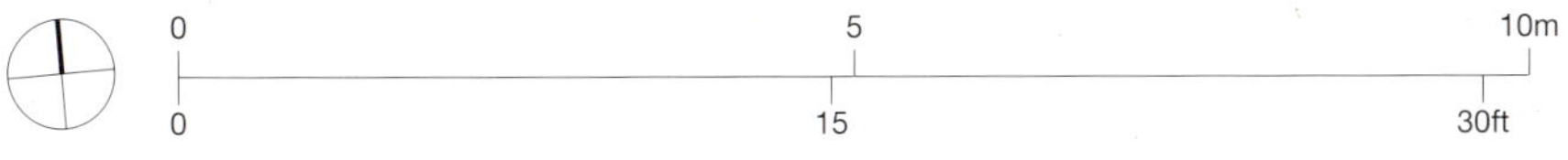

0   5   10m

0   15   30ft

137

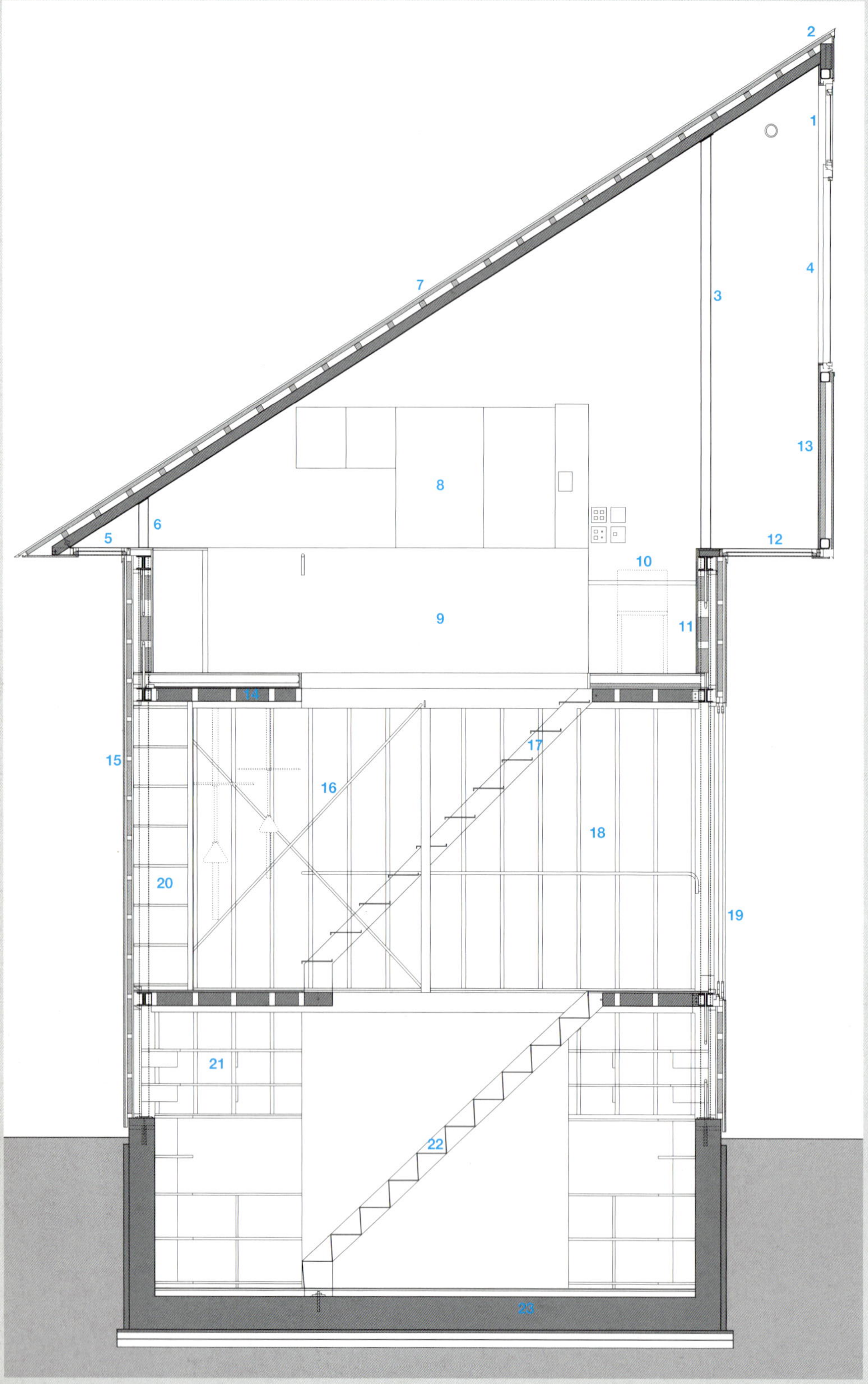

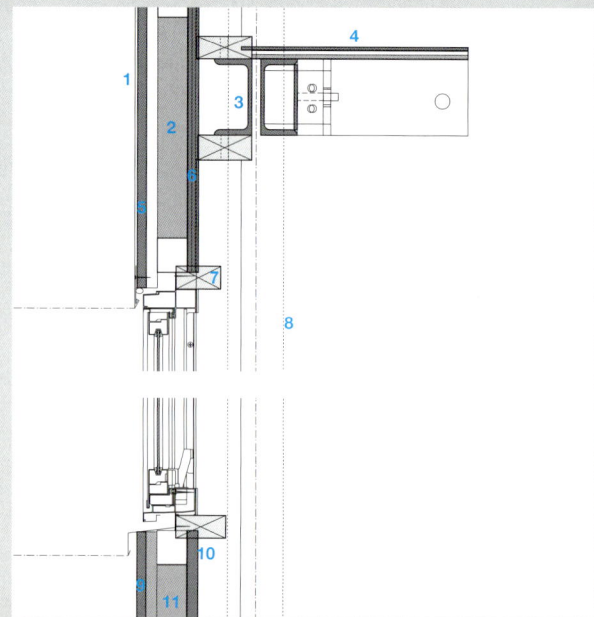

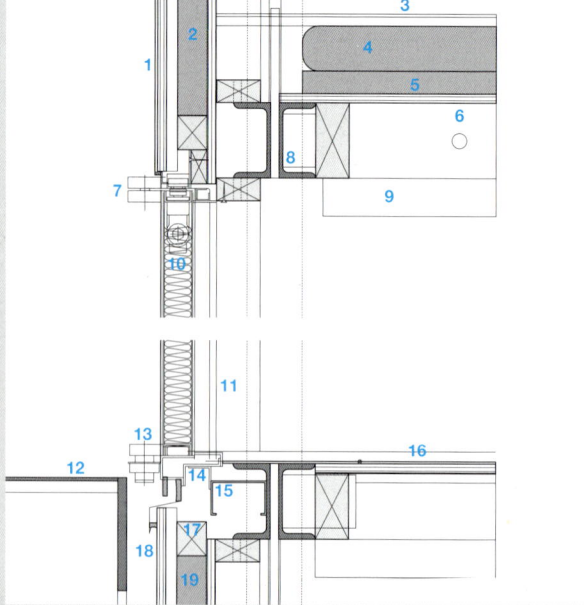

31.05
Bedroom Glazing Detail
1:10
 1 Galvanized and aluminium coated steel sheet
 2 Styrofoam insulation
 3 Two steel C-channels
 4 Larch plywood with urethane enamel paint finish
 5 Larch plywood with moisture permeable membrane waterproofing layer
 6 Larch plywood
 7 Sash support
 8 Steel square pipe column with oil paint finish
 9 Larch plywood with moisture permeable membrane waterproofing layer
 10 Larch plywood
 11 Styrofoam insulation

31.06
Section B–B
1:50
 1 Clear glazing
 2 Coloured galvanized and aluminium coated steel sheet
 3 Square steel section column
 4 Clear glazed window
 5 Galvanized and aluminium coated steel sheet to eaves
 6 Square steel section column
 7 Roof comprised of galvanized and aluminium coated steel sheet on structural plywood with sound insulation sheet over rafters, styrofoam heat insulation and ceiling joists
 8 Timber joinery to kitchen units
 9 Low wall separating kitchen from dining area
 10 Bench and seat to kitchen
 11 White birch lining over structural plywood wall
 12 Clear glazing to eaves window
 13 Wall comprised of hydrophilic coloured galvanized and aluminium coated steel sheet over plywood on furring strips and styrofoam insulation
 14 Floor comprised of white birch on plywood underlay with aqua layer and styrofoam on timber floor joists
 15 Wall comprised of hydrophilic coloured galvanized and aluminium coated steel sheet over plywood on furring strips and styrofoam insulation
 16 Steel cross bracing
 17 Steel stair
 18 Structural plywood wall lining
 19 Clear glazed windows
 20 Timber shelving
 21 Timber book shelves
 22 Steel stair
 23 Floor comprised of plywood sheet over aqua layer heating system, timber floor joists and waterproofed concrete slab

31.07
Wall and Floor Detail
1:10
 1 Galvanized and aluminium coated steel sheet
 2 Styrofoam insulation
 3 White birchwood plywood with urethane enamel paint finish
 4 Aqua heating layer
 5 Styrofoam insulation
 6 Floor joist with urethane enamel paint finish
 7 Hinge
 8 Two steel C-channels with oil paint finish
 9 Steel flat bar beam
 10 Steel door
 11 Timber window frame with urethane enamel paint finish
 12 Chequered steel plate stair tread with oil paint finish
 13 Hinge
 14 30 x 30 mm (1¹/₅ x 1¹/₅ inch) steel angle
 15 Steel C-channel
 16 Galvanized and aluminium coated steel sheet
 17 45 x 35 mm (1³/₄ x 1¹/₃ inch) furring strip
 18 Galvanized and aluminium coated steel sheet
 19 Styrofoam insulation

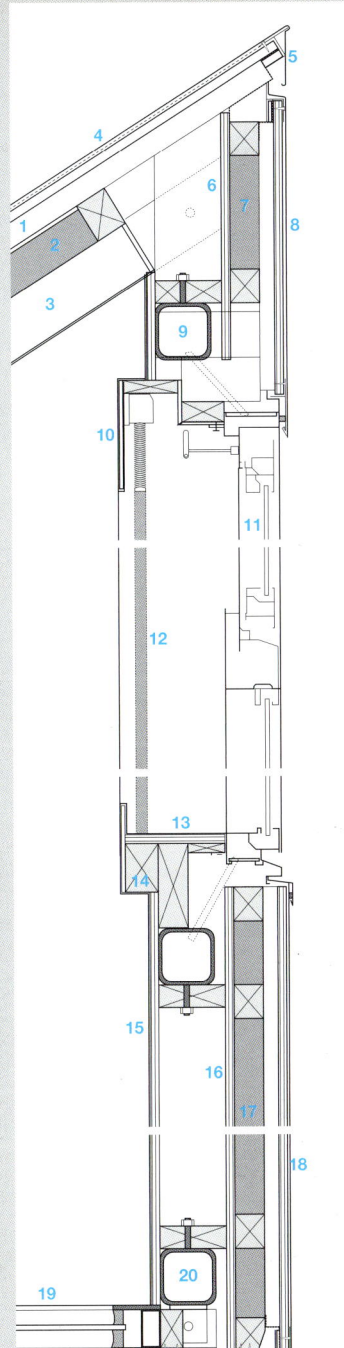

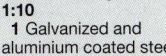

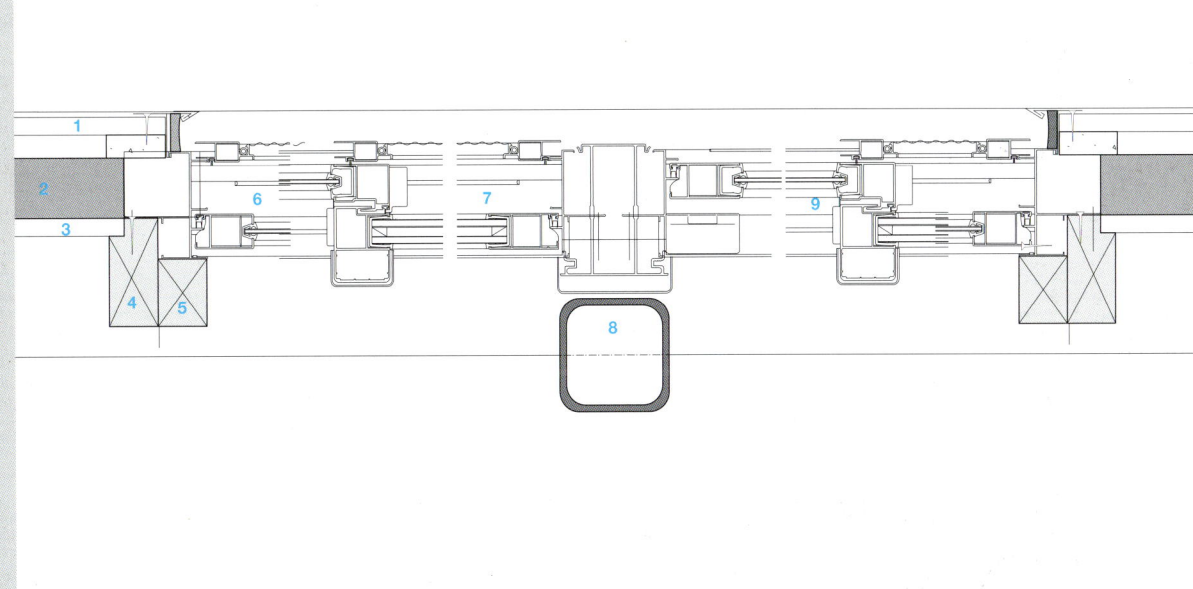

31.08
Eaves Glazing Detail
1:10
1 Galvanized and aluminium coated steel sheet
2 Styrofoam insulation
3 Bolt for tightening steel deck plate with steel flat bars
4 50 x 45 mm (2 x 1³/₄ inch) ceiling joist
5 Galvanized and aluminium coated steel

sheet
6 Timber packer
7 Void
8 Steel flat bar
9 Steel flat bar
10 Steel deck plate
11 Clear glass with shatter-prevention film
12 White birch plywood with urethane clear lacquer finish
13 Galvanized and aluminium coated steel sheet
14 Styrofoam

insulation
15 Two steel C-channels with oil paint finish
16 White birch plywood with urethane clear lacquer finish

31.09
Roof and External Wall Detail
1:10
1 30 x 40 mm (1¹/₅ x 1¹/₂ inch) timber rafter at 455 mm (18 inch) centres
2 Styrofoam insulatioin
3 Steel deck plate
4 Galvanized and aluminium coated steel sheet
5 Flashing
6 Larch plywood
7 Styrofoam insulation
8 Galvanized and aluminium coated steel sheet
9 75 x 75 mm (3 x 3 inch) steel square pipe
10 Galvanized and aluminium coated steel sheet
11 Aluminium sash
12 Aluminium blind
13 Galvanized and aluminium coated steel sheet

14 65 x 45 mm (2¹/₂ x 1³/₄ inch) timber beam
15 Galvanized and aluminium coated steel sheet
16 Larch plywood
17 Styrofoam insulation
18 Galvanized and aluminium coated steel sheet
19 Clear glass with shatter-prevention film
20 75 x 75 mm (3 x 3 inch) steel square pipe

31.10
Glazing Detail
1:5
1 15 x 40 mm (³/₅ x 1¹/₂ inch) furring strip at 300 mm (11⁴/₅ inch) centres
2 Styrofoam insulation
3 Larch plywood with urethane enamel paint finish
4 70 x 30 mm (2³/₄ x 3¹/₅ inch) timber furring strip with urethane

enamel paint finish
5 Timber window frame with urethane enamel paint finish
6 Aluminium sash
7 Aluminium sash
8 75 x 75 mm (3 x 3 inch) steel square pipe
9 Aluminium sash

House R128
Stuttgart, Germany

Client
Ursula and Werner Sobek

Area
250 square metres (2,690 square feet)

Project Team
Werner Sobek, Zheng Fei, Robert Brixner, Christoph Dengler, Jörg Kuhn, Ingo Weiss

Mechanical Engineer
Ing.-Büro F. Müller, Weissach i. T.

Control Engineer
Baumgartner GmbH

Sensor Technology
Jochen Köhnlein Gebäudeautomation

This four-storey house, designed and occupied by the architect and his family, is situated on a steep site on the edge of Stuttgart. Access to the house is via a bridge leading to the top floor kitchen and dining area. The two levels below this provide living and sleeping areas, while the bottom level accommodates a study and technical installations. Each of the four levels is defined by the concept of maximum transparency – the entire structure is clad in full height triple-glazed panels. The load-bearing structure consists of a steel frame stiffened by diagonal members and erected on a reinforced concrete raft.

All load-bearing and non-load-bearing elements, including the facade, are of modular design and assembled using easily separable jointing. The house was designed as a completely recyclable, self-sufficient, zero emissions building. All materials which may be difficult to dispose of have been avoided to ensure that the entire building is recyclable. For this reason there are no cables or pipes embedded in the walls. All supply and disposal systems are housed in metal ducts that run along the facades and are built into the floor and ceiling structures. To enable the house to function as an emission-free, zero-heating-energy building, an innovative computer-controlled energy system incorporating solar cells can be checked by telephone or computer from anywhere in the world.

1 Access to the house is via a steel bridge that continues along the length of the upper level of the house to form a terrace to the living spaces.
2 The concept of 'maximum transparency' is evident throughout the house. Floor panels are cut away to reveal vertical views from one level to another.
3 The finely detailed steel staircase with its open risers contributes to the impression of skeletal lightness which is further enforced by the glazed facades.

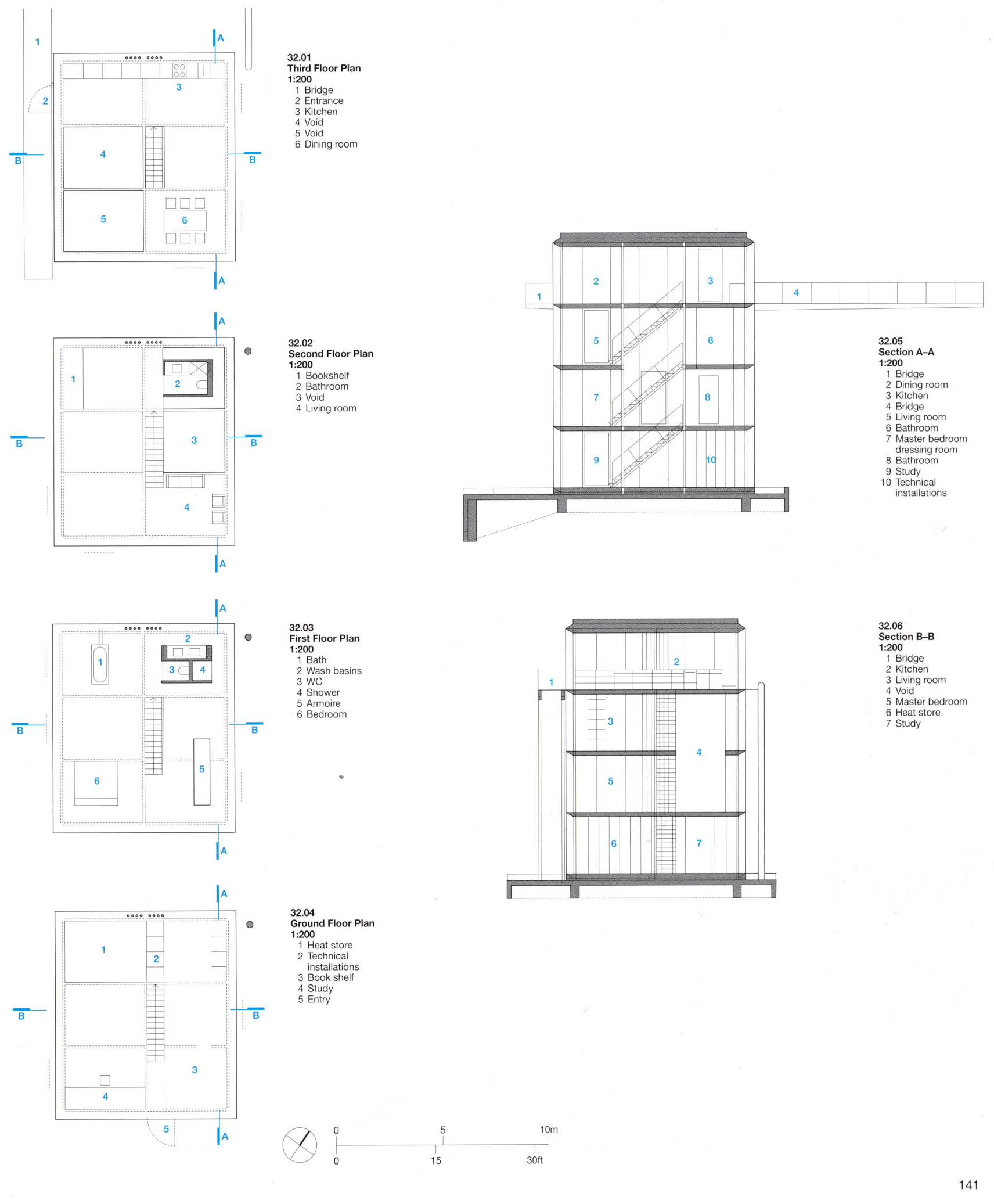

32.01
Third Floor Plan
1:200
1 Bridge
2 Entrance
3 Kitchen
4 Void
5 Void
6 Dining room

32.02
Second Floor Plan
1:200
1 Bookshelf
2 Bathroom
3 Void
4 Living room

32.03
First Floor Plan
1:200
1 Bath
2 Wash basins
3 WC
4 Shower
5 Armoire
6 Bedroom

32.04
Ground Floor Plan
1:200
1 Heat store
2 Technical
  installations
3 Book shelf
4 Study
5 Entry

32.05
Section A–A
1:200
1 Bridge
2 Dining room
3 Kitchen
4 Bridge
5 Living room
6 Bathroom
7 Master bedroom
  dressing room
8 Bathroom
9 Study
10 Technical
  installations

32.06
Section B–B
1:200
1 Bridge
2 Kitchen
3 Living room
4 Void
5 Master bedroom
6 Heat store
7 Study

0   5   10m

0   15   30ft

32.07
Steel Frame Erection Sequence
1 Main structural steel frame
2 Cross bracing to floors and walls
3 Steel staircases
4 Floor and wall panels

32.08
Facade Section 1:20
1 Solar panel
2 Roof insulation
3 Horizontal reinforcement
4 Heating and cooling panels
5 Suspended aluminium ceiling
6 Flush-mounted spotlight
7 Pipe and cable duct
8 Floor panel
9 Triple-glazed fixed window panel
10 Triple-glazed opening window panel
11 Window operating drive mechanism

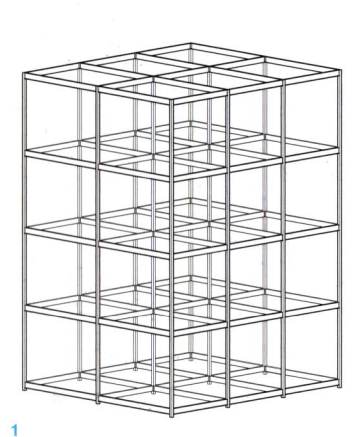

1

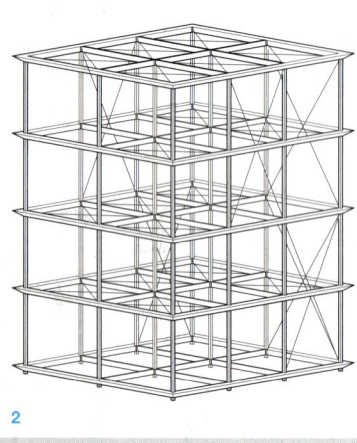

2

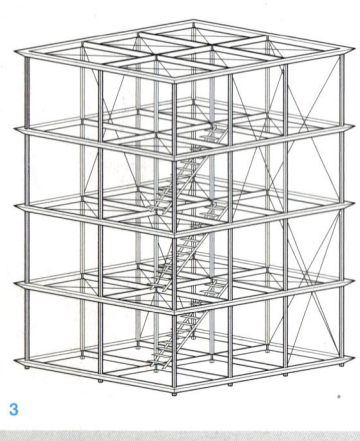

3

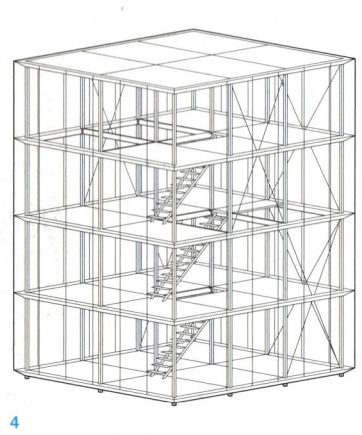

4

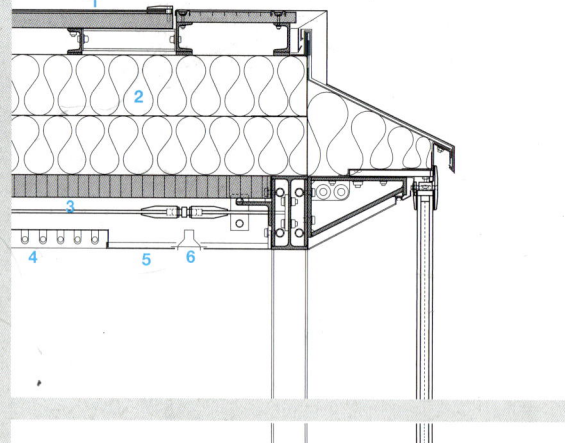

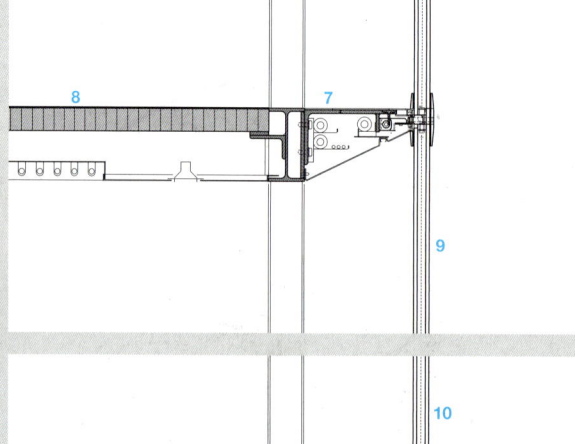

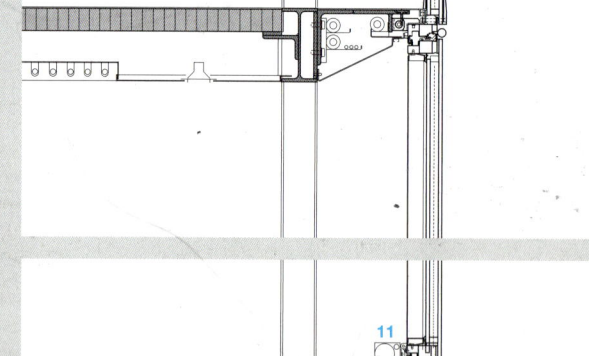

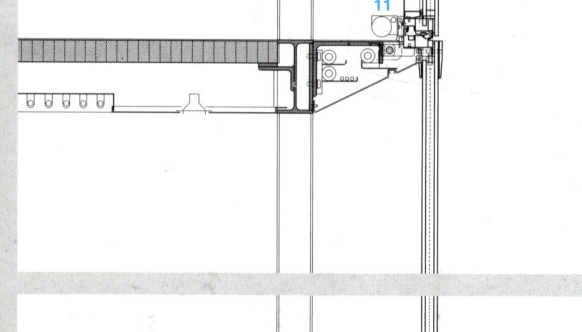

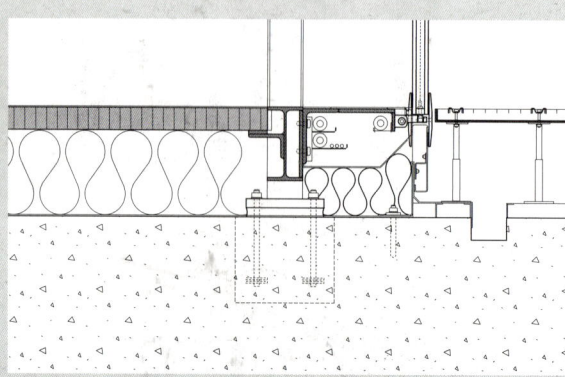

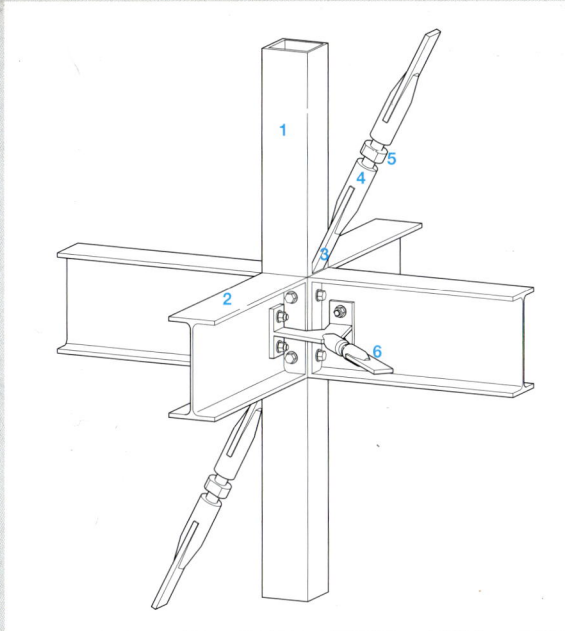

32.09
Frame Node Detail
1 Steel column
2 Steel girder
3 Tension rod
4 Bracing
5 Adjustment screw
6 Tension rod

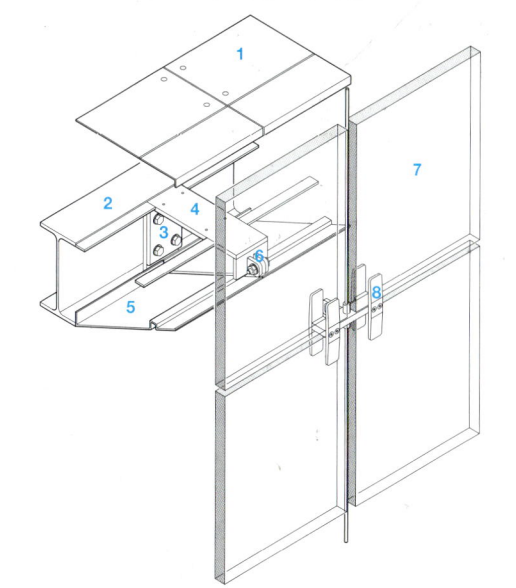

32.10
Facade Fixings Detail
1 Face plate
2 Steel girder
3 Fastening plate
4 Cantilever
5 Face plate
6 Mounting
7 Glass pane
8 Glazing clamp

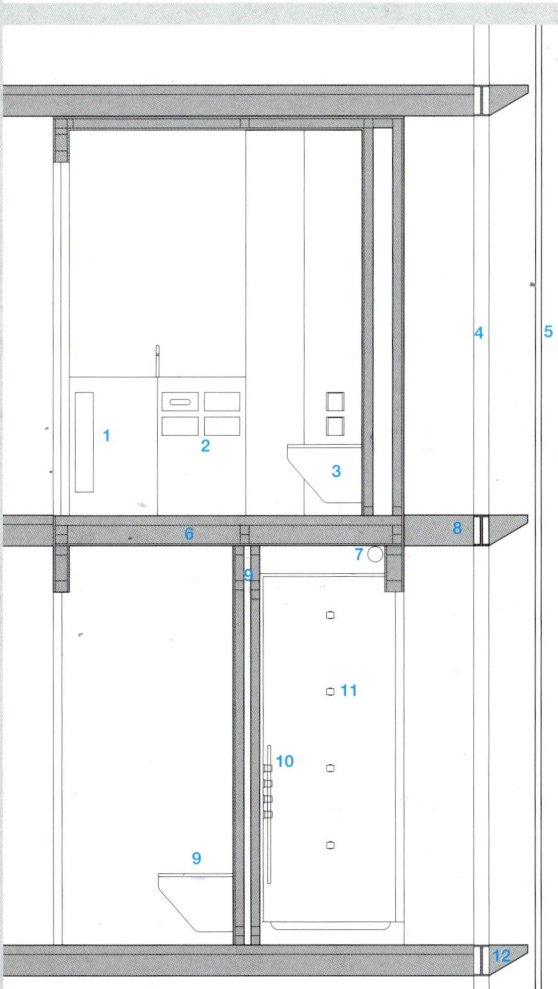

32.11
Bathroom Section
1:50
1 Towel rail
2 Drawers
3 WC
4 Steel column
5 Facade
6 Suspended ceiling
7 Water conduit
8 Steel girder
9 WC
10 Shower armature
11 Shower cabin
12 Conduit

32.12
Bathroom Plan 1
1:50
1 Conduits
2 Facade
3 Steel girder
4 Sliding door
5 Hand basin
6 Laundry shute
7 Hand basin
8 Water conduit
9 WC
10 Shower cabin
11 Floor panel
12 Stair
13 Water tank

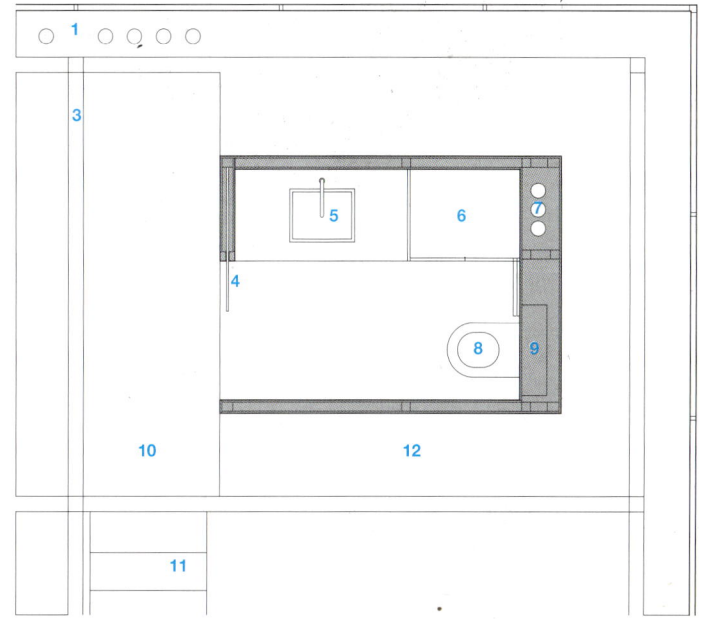

32.13
Bathroom Plan 2
1:50
1 Conduits
2 Facade
3 Steel girder
4 Sliding door
5 Hand basin
6 Technical installations
7 Water conduit
8 WC
9 Water tank
10 Floor panel
11 Stair
12 Void

33
WPA Inc.

Villa Lucy
Port Townsend, Washington, USA

Client
Kathy Wesselman and Anthony Pellecchia

Area
140 square metres (1,507 square feet)

Project Team
Anthyony Pellecchia, Anthony Goins

Structural Engineer
Dayle B Houk & Co

Main Contractor
Aran Pellecchia Construction

Villa Lucy is a weekend house on a six-acre wooded site overlooking the Strait of Juan de Fuca, off the coast of Washington State. The architect-owners had a commitment to maintaining the integrity of the site and its surrounding ecosystem. The house sits above the sloping grade to preserve the natural patterns of vegetation and rainwater. Six steel frames allow the house to float above the ground. A steel grated entry bridge hovers above grade leading to a square red timber pivot door that provides the sole graphic accent within the long flat grey-stained cedar wall. The wall acts as a rain screen – the timber is held away by vertical battens so that all sides are exposed to the air.

The house is detailed to minimize visual impact, maintaining a composition of planes and surfaces of wood, glass, concrete and metal. The exterior steel columns, beams and guardrails are left to rust naturally, developing a rich patina. The deck and bridge are made of industrial galvanized grating allowing water and plants to pass through. The house is organized into two distinct zones, opaque and transparent – the serviced and the served. The long narrow opaque zone contains all the services (bathrooms, kitchen, pantry, dressing, storage and utilities). The open, loft-like transparent zone contains the living, dining and sleeping areas, in which the furnishings are lightweight or on castors to facilitate flexibility. The house acts as a lookout, a precisely detailed observation platform designed as an antidote to the introverted routines of city living.

1 Located on a gentle slope in the midst of a wood, the house floats above the ground on slender steel columns.
2 To the south-east, a solid timber box contains all of the service elements of the house – kitchen, bathrooms and storage. The facade is interrupted by a bold red pivoting door heralding the entrance, reached via a steel bridge.
3 To the north-west two glazed pavilions on either side of an open courtyard frame uninterrupted views of the forest. Panels of windows open up to allow cross-ventilation to cool the interior during hot weather.
4 The simple linear kitchen opens up to the dining room and the courtyard.
5 View of the living room where a south-east facing clerestory window brings natural light into the house all through the day.

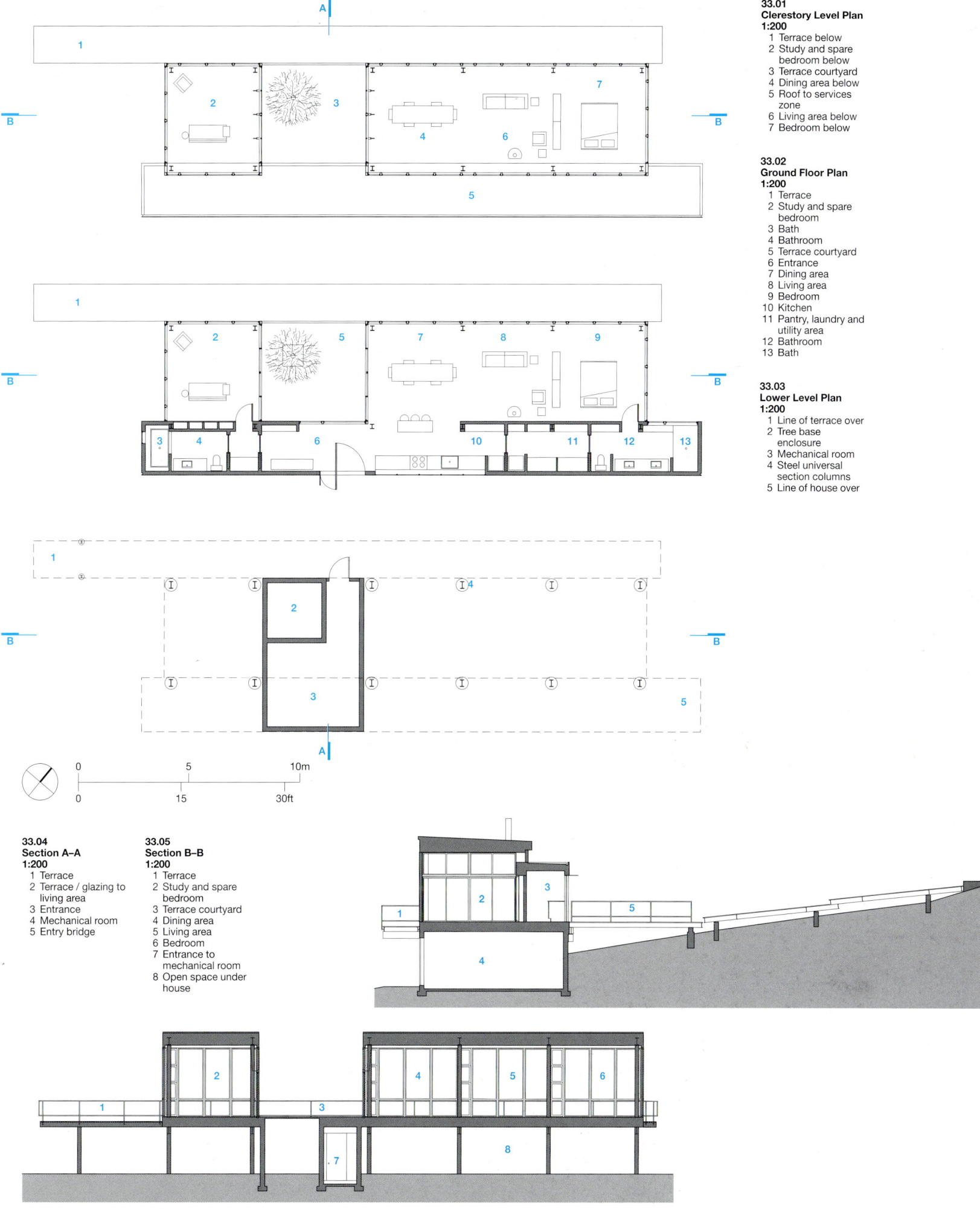

33.01
Clerestory Level Plan
1:200
1 Terrace below
2 Study and spare
 bedroom below
3 Terrace courtyard
4 Dining area below
5 Roof to services
 zone
6 Living area below
7 Bedroom below

33.02
Ground Floor Plan
1:200
1 Terrace
2 Study and spare
 bedroom
3 Bath
4 Bathroom
5 Terrace courtyard
6 Entrance
7 Dining area
8 Living area
9 Bedroom
10 Kitchen
11 Pantry, laundry and
 utility area
12 Bathroom
13 Bath

33.03
Lower Level Plan
1:200
1 Line of terrace over
2 Tree base
 enclosure
3 Mechanical room
4 Steel universal
 section columns
5 Line of house over

0   5   10m
0   15   30ft

33.04
Section A–A
1:200
1 Terrace
2 Terrace / glazing to
 living area
3 Entrance
4 Mechanical room
5 Entry bridge

33.05
Section B–B
1:200
1 Terrace
2 Study and spare
 bedroom
3 Terrace courtyard
4 Dining area
5 Living area
6 Bedroom
7 Entrance to
 mechanical room
8 Open space under
 house

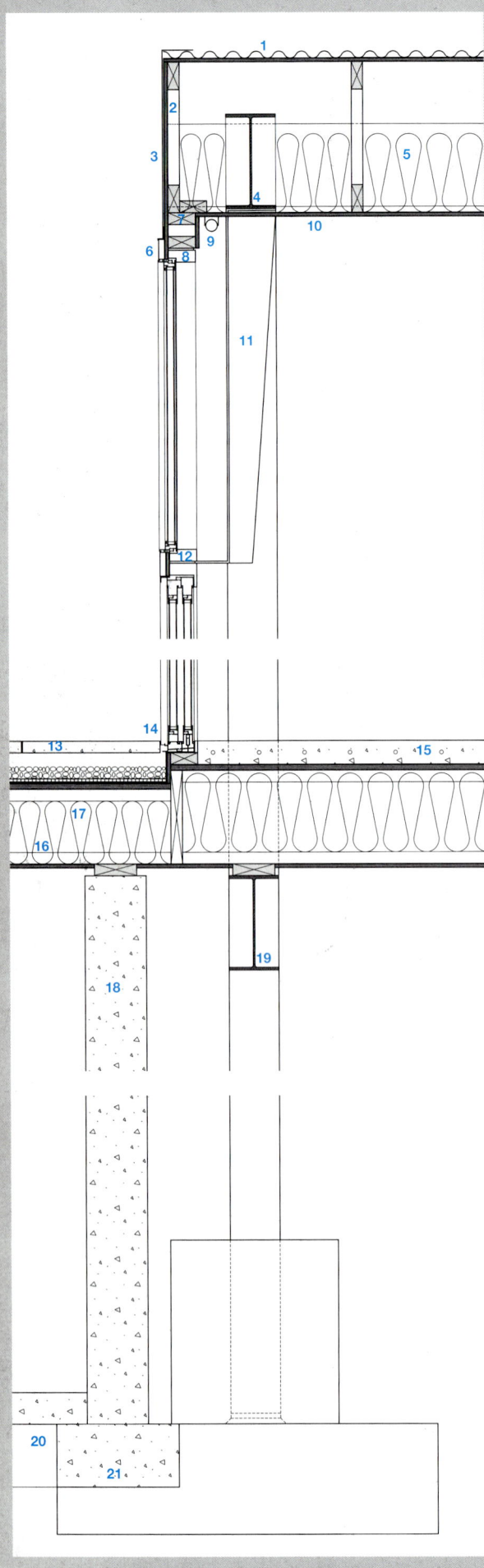

 1 Corrugated zincalume on waterproofing membrane on plywood
 2 Timber truss
 3 Zincalume cladding on waterproofing membrane on plywood
 4 Steel moment frame
 5 Insulation
 6 Cedar capping
 7 Timber blocking
 8 Alder window framing
 9 Roller shade
 10 Lite-ply ceiling
 11 Steel support bracket for sliding glass door
 12 Alder window framing
 13 Concrete pavers on sand on gravel bed on protective board on waterproofing membrane on plywood
 14 Aluminium sliding glass door
 15 Concrete floor with hydronic heating on plywood subfloor
 16 Insulation
 17 Engineered timber floor joists
 18 Cast-in-place concrete wall
 19 Steel moment frame
 20 Reinforced concrete slab
 21 Reinforced concrete footing

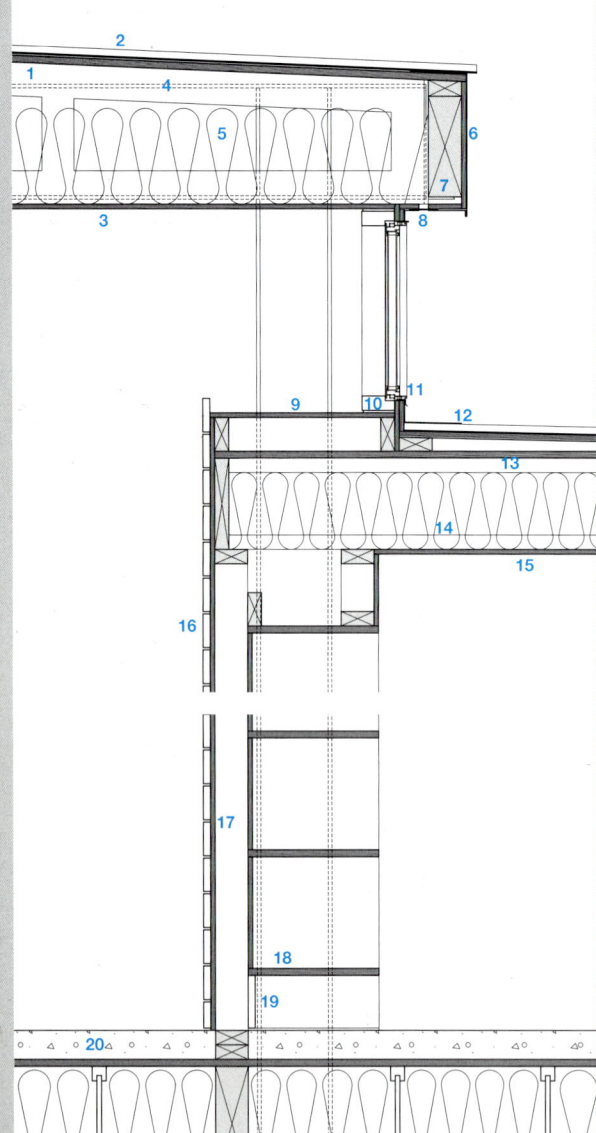

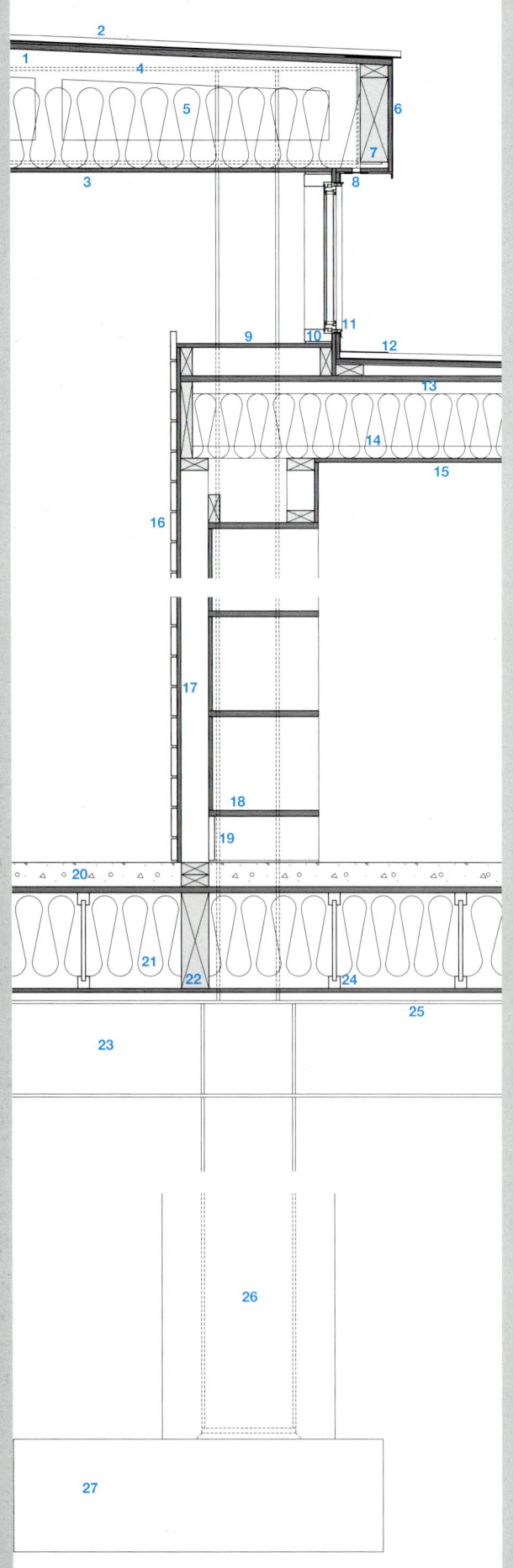

 1 Timber truss
 2 Corrugated zincalume on waterproofing membrane on plywood
 3 Lite-ply ceiling
 4 Steel moment frame
 5 Insulation
 6 Zincalume cladding on waterproofing membrane on plywood
 7 Timber beam
 8 Roof ventilation and insect screen
 9 Lite-ply finish to interior surface
 10 Alder window framing
 11 Aluminium window
 12 Corrugated zincalume on waterproofing membrane on plywood
 13 Engineered timber roof joists
 14 Insulation
 15 Lite-ply ceiling
 16 Cedar boards on plywood
 17 Timber framing
 18 Lite-ply joinery
 19 Poplar wall base
 20 Concrete floor with hydronic heating on plywood subfloor
 21 Insulation
 22 Timber beam
 23 Steel moment frame
 24 Engineered timber floor joists
 25 Exterior grade plywood
 26 Steel moment frame
 27 Reinforced concrete footing

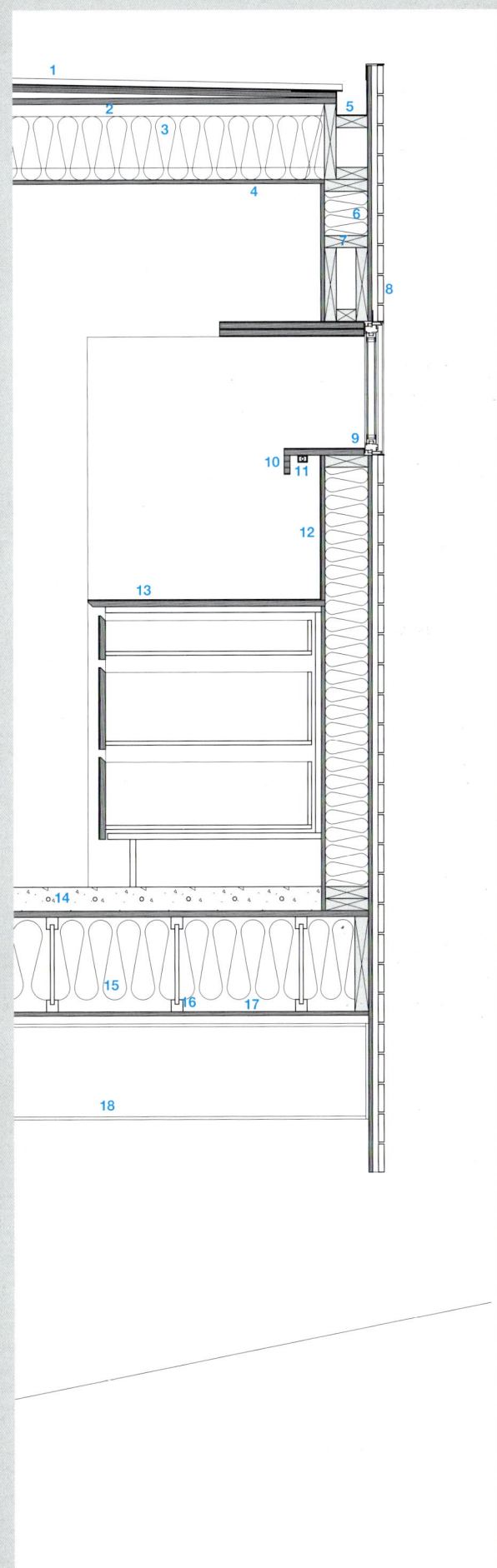

33.08
Kitchen Window Detail
1:20
 1 Corrugated zincalume on waterproofing membrane on plywood
 2 Engineered timber roof joists
 3 Insulation
 4 Lite-ply ceiling
 5 Built-in zincalume gutter
 6 Insulation
 7 Timber framing
 8 Rain screen comprised of cedar boards on timber framing on waterproofing membrane on plywood
 9 Aluminium window
 10 Lite-ply cladding to light cover
 11 Continuous linear light fixture
 12 Plastic laminate backsplash on plywood
 13 Multi-ply kitchen cabinets with plastic laminate countertop and drawer faces
 14 Concrete floor with hydronic heating on plywood subfloor
 15 Insulation
 16 Engineered timber floor joists
 17 Exterior grade plywood
 18 Steel moment frame

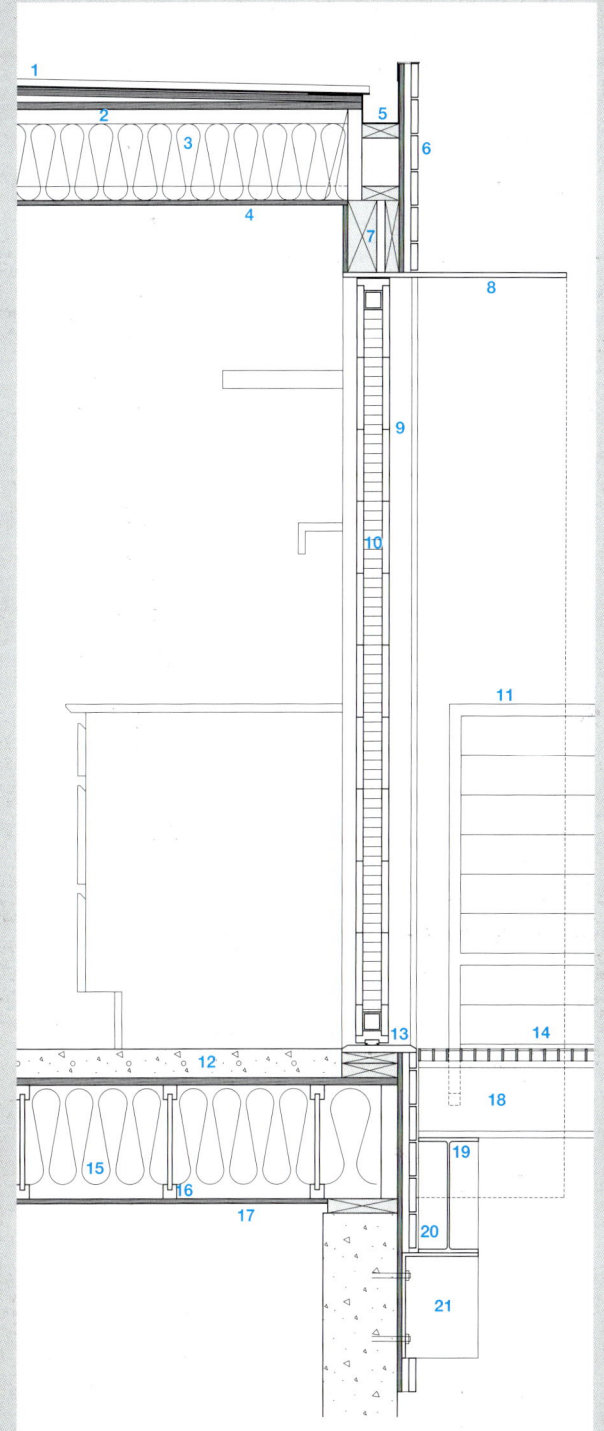

33.09
Front Door Detail
1:20
 1 Corrugated zincalume on waterproofing membrane on plywood
 2 Engineered timber roof joists
 3 Insulation
 4 Lite-ply ceiling
 5 Built-in zincalume gutter
 6 Rain screen comprised of cedar boards on timber battens on waterproofing membrane on plywood
 7 Timber beam
 8 Aluminium plate
 9 Door jamb
 10 Solid core door with interior steel tube frame clad with cedar boards and ipe timber on four sides
 11 Steel tube handrail with stainless steel cables
 12 Concrete floor with hydronic heating on plywood subfloor
 13 Ipe timber threshold
 14 Galvanized steel grating
 15 Insulation
 16 Engineered timber floor joists
 17 Exterior grade plywood
 18 Steel channel
 19 Steel beam
 20 Rain screen comprised of cedar boards on timber battens on waterproofing membrane on plywood
 21 Steel bracket
 22 Cast-in-place concrete wall
 23 Reinforced concrete slab
 24 Reinforced concrete footing

147

148

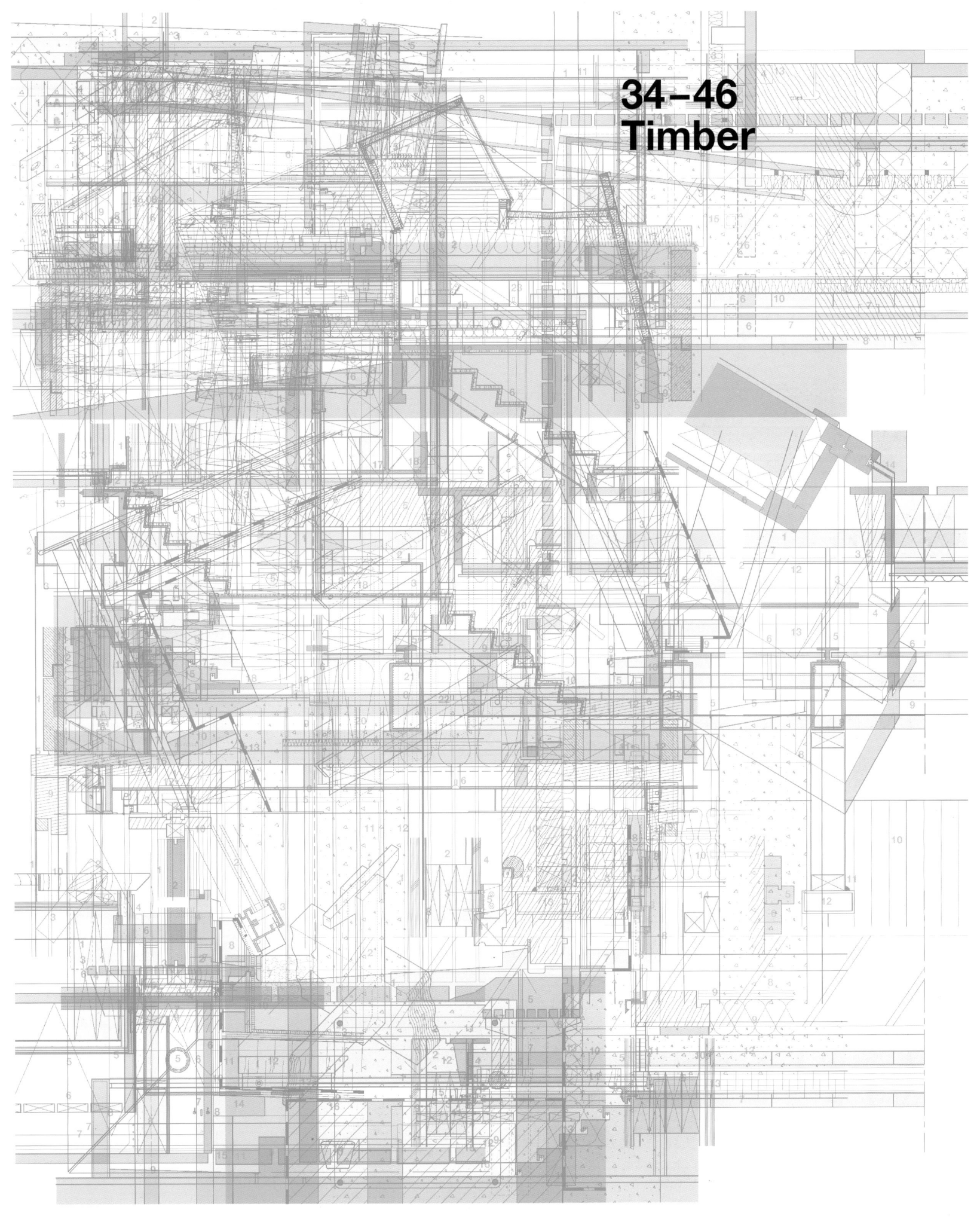

House in Oudenbourg
Oudenbourg, Belgium

Area
1,774 square metres (19,095 square feet)

Project Team
Roberto Cremascoli, Daniela Antonucci, Maurice Custers, Andrea Smaniotto, Ueli Krauss

Located in a small town not far from Ostend in a windswept landscape of flat plains and canals, this house involved the renovation and extension of an existing farm into living spaces and an art gallery. The three original farm buildings, arranged in a loose U-shape, are used as the fundamental starting point for the project. The addition is an L-shaped configuration which establishes a second U-shape in relation to the existing buildings. One existing structure, along with the extension, becomes the house, another the gallery and the third a garage and storage space. The 200 year old buildings were constructed in terracotta brick and tiles, and the refurbishment respects local building traditions which feature black mouldings and red-painted timber window frames.

The new volumes are seamlessly integrated using the same geometric section as the existing buildings, distinguishing themselves through contrasting materials and detail. The point of attachment between the old and new structures is resolved by a small entrance where curved glass acknowledges the transition. At the junction of the two wings, an oblique alcove window is grafted onto the structure – a place to sit and admire the landscape. To one side are bedrooms and bathrooms, while the other wing accommodates living, dining and kitchen spaces, as well as the primary circulation space. The facades are sheathed in western red cedar and a lead-covered roof makes it clear that the new forms are of their own time, as well as continuing the tradition of local craftsmanship. The patina and the slowly changing colours of the materials with the passage of time, help to integrate the new forms into the context of the historic building.

1 The new addition (right) employs the same geometric section as the existing buildings (left), however contrasting materials are used to distinguish old from new. One of the main features is an oblique window at the junction of the L-shaped extension, offering views out over the polder.
2 A view of the gallery which is located in one of the existing farm buildings, renovated to complement the historic architecture and the needs of the clients who have an extensive art collection. The simple white-painted, timber-floored spaces rely on the drama of the pitched-roofed spaces to create an appropriate space for viewing the art.

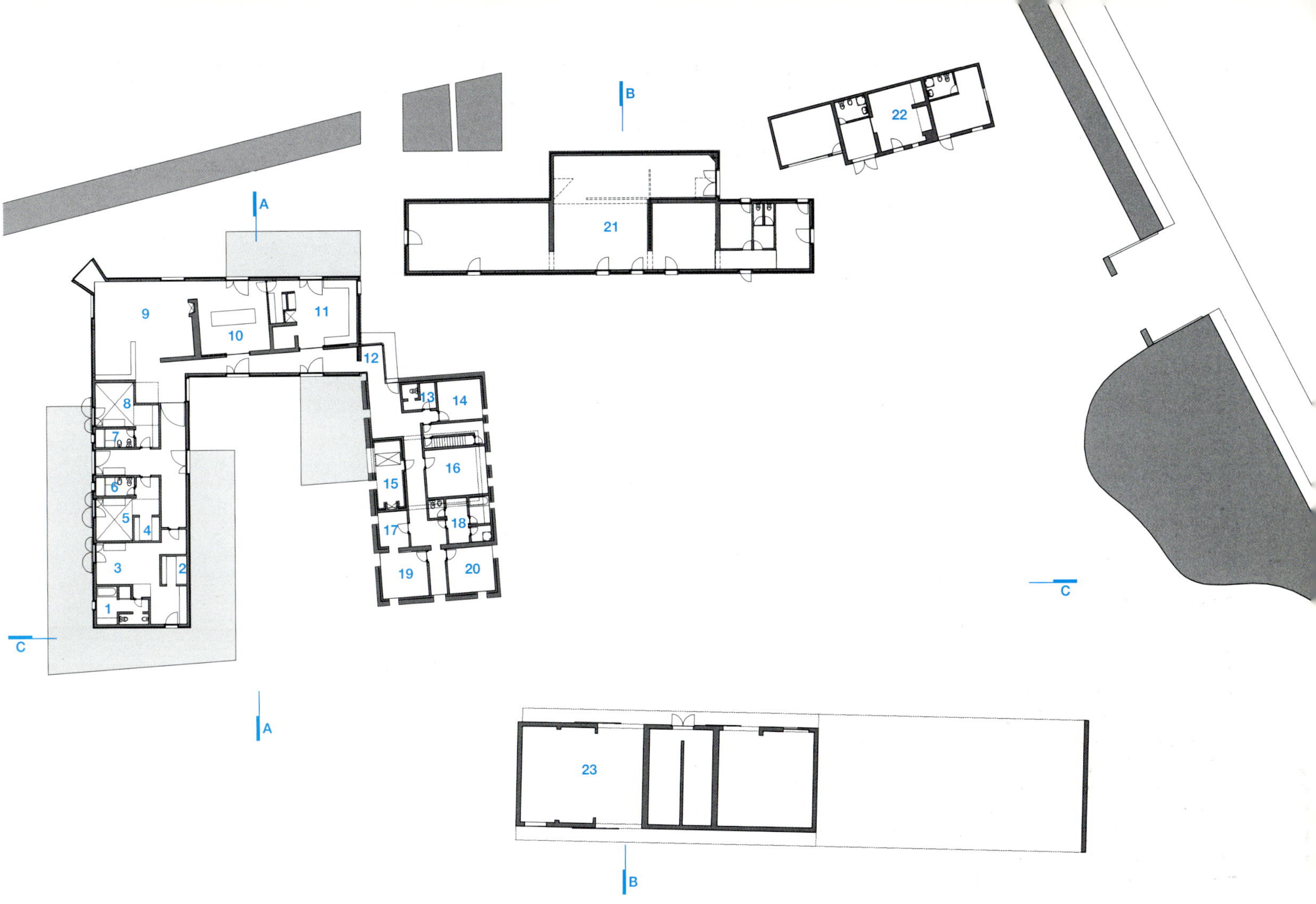

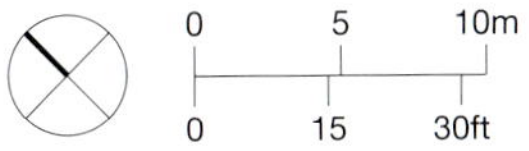

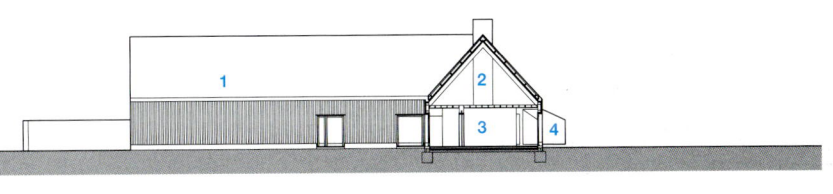

34.01
Ground Floor Plan
1:500

1 Bathroom
2 Dressing room
3 Bedroom
4 Dressing room
5 Bedroom
6 Bathroom
7 Bathroom
8 Bedroom
9 Living room

10 Dining room
11 Kitchen
12 Entrance
13 Locker room and
   WC
14 Laundry
15 Loggia
16 Office
17 Hobby room
18 Locker room and
   bathroom
19 Bedroom

20 Bedroom
21 Art gallery
22 Old house
23 Warehouse

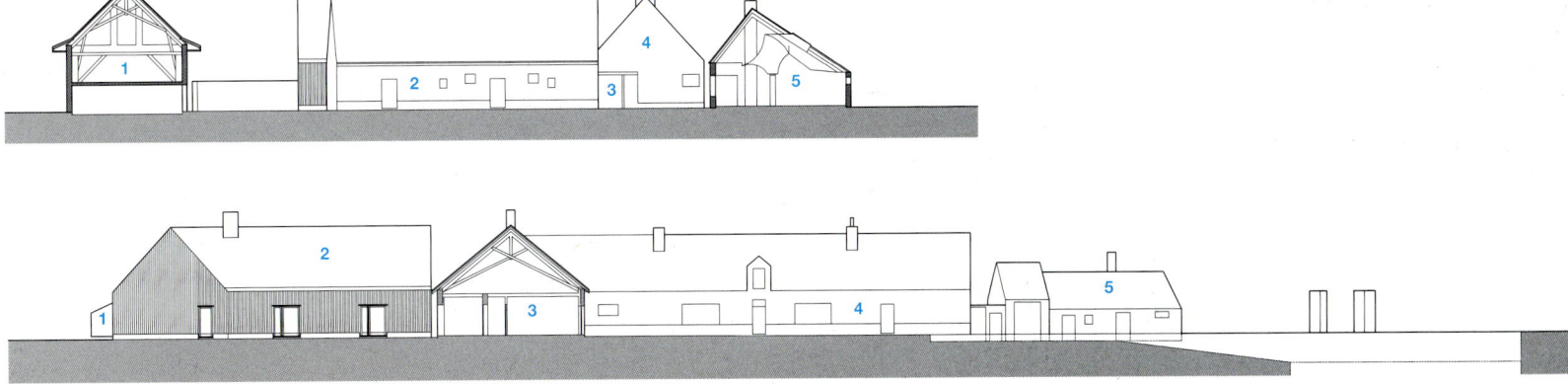

34.02
Section A–A
1:500
1 Bedroom wing
2 Chimney
3 Dining room
4 Oblique window

34.03
Section B–B
1:500
1 Warehouse
2 Guest wing of main
  house
3 Entrance
4 Extension
5 Art gallery

34.04
Section C–C
1:500
1 Oblique window
2 Extension
3 Guest wing
4 Art gallery
5 Old house

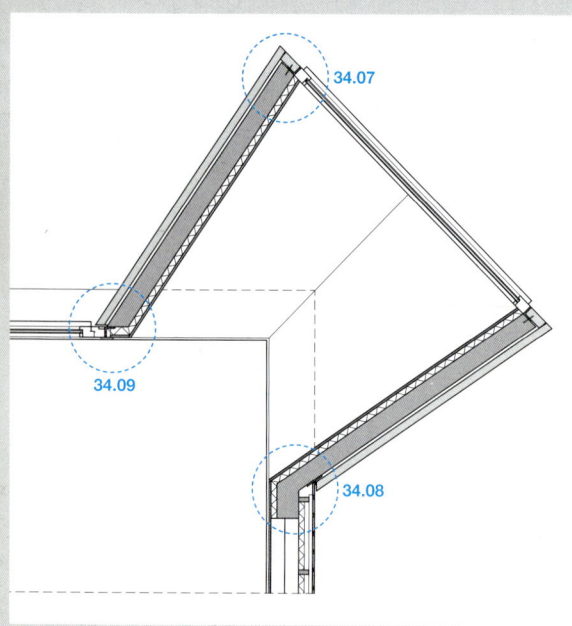

34.05
Oblique Window Plan Detail
1:50

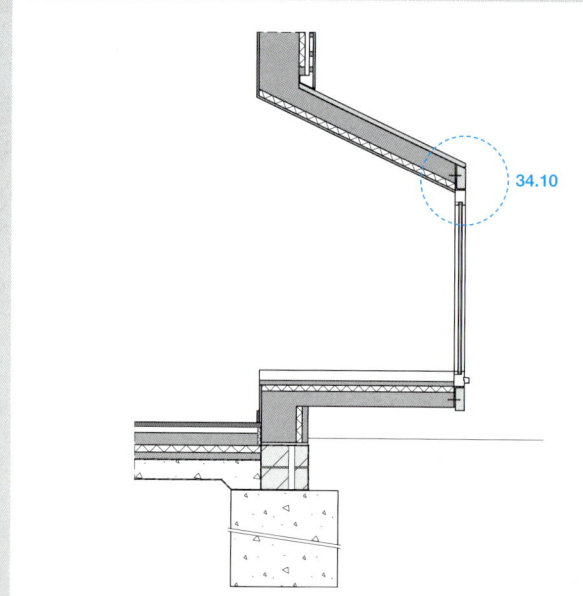

34.06
Oblique WIndow Section Detail
1:50

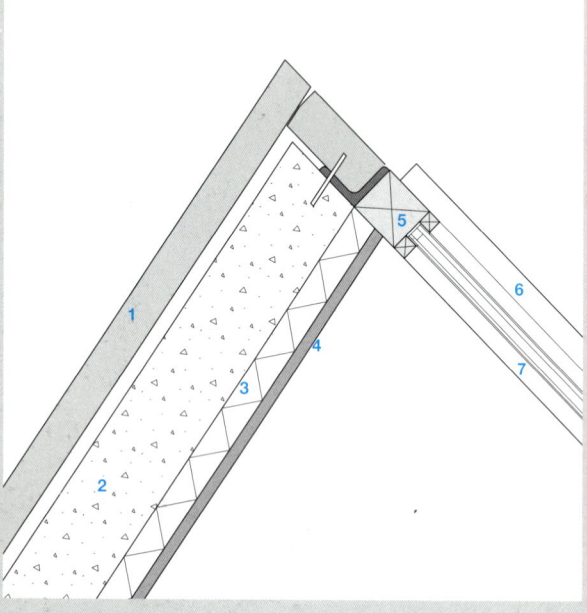

34.07
Window Detail 1
1:10
1 Stone cladding to exterior wall
2 Concrete wall
3 Insulation
4 Interior gypsum board wall
5 Timber frame
6 Exterior element of timber frame with drip groove
7 Double glazing

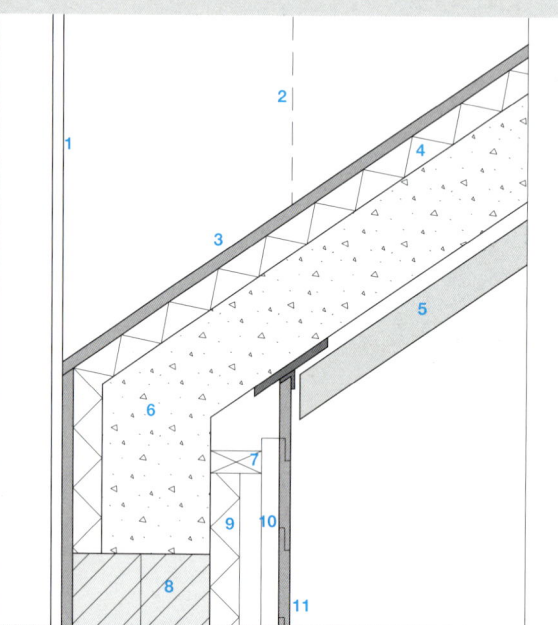

34.08
Window Detail 2
1:10
1 Leather cushion to window seat
2 Line of exterior wall beyond
3 Interior gypsum board wall
4 Insulation
5 Stone cladding
6 Concrete wall
7 Internal sub-structure to support exterior face of cladding
8 Masonry wall structure
9 Insulation
10 Internal sub-structure to support timber facade
11 Exterior timber facade

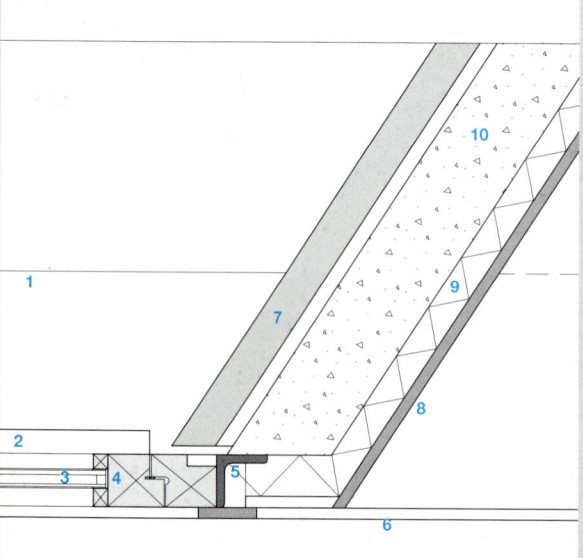

34.09
Window Detail 3
1:10
1 Window sill
2 Exterior element of timber frame with drip groove
3 Double glazing
4 Timber frame
5 Metal profile to support timber frame
6 Timber skirting board
7 Exterior stone cladding
8 Interior gypsum board wall
9 Insulation
10 Concrete wall

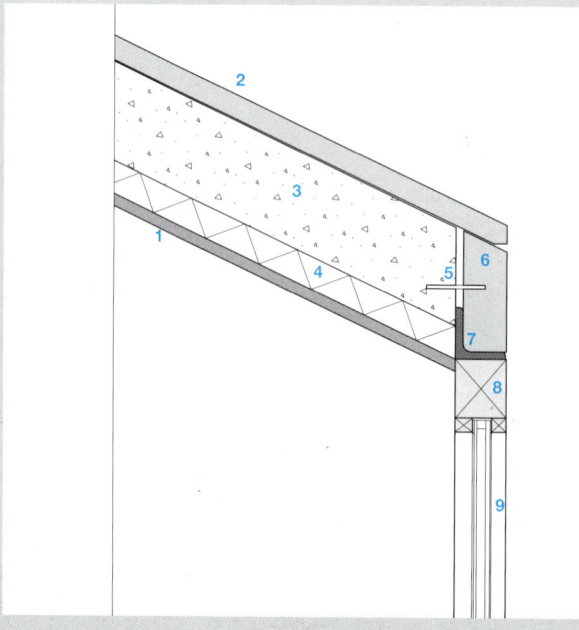

34.10
Window Detail 4
1:10
1 Interior gypsum board wall
2 External stone cladding
3 Concrete slab
4 Insulation
5 Metal fixing rod to exterior stone cladding
6 Exterior stone cladding
7 Metal profile to support timber frame
8 Timber frame
9 Double glazing

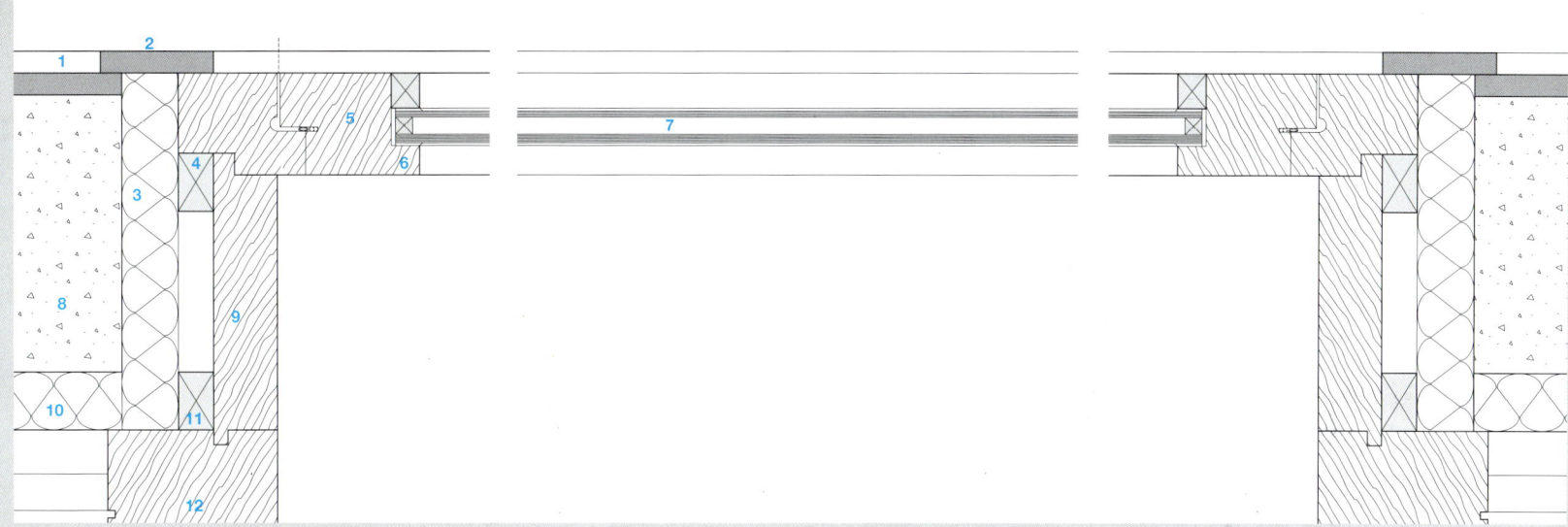

34.11
Typical Window Plan Detail
1:5

1 Timber skirting board
2 Timber frame as transition between timber window and stucco lining
3 Insulation and timber sub-structure to support window jamb and frame
4 Interior sub-structure to support exterior jamb and frame
5 Timber frame
6 Timber sill
7 Double glazing
8 Concrete wall
9 Timber window jamb
10 Insulation
11 Interior sub-structure to support timber jamb
12 Timber window jamb

34.12
Typical Door Section Detail
1:5

1 Timber clad facade
2 Internal sub-structure to support timber facade
3 Insulation
4 Stucco finish to interior wall
5 Timber lintel
6 Insulation and timber sub-structure to support timber lintel and frame
7 Interior timber frame to make the transition between timber window and stucco lining
8 Upper part of timber frame
9 Double glazing
10 Lower part of timber frame
11 Exterior element of timber frame with drip groove
12 Stone threshold
13 Waterproof membrane and insulation
14 Stone work to support sub-structure of timber frame
15 Waterproof membrane and mortar joint
16 Masonry structure

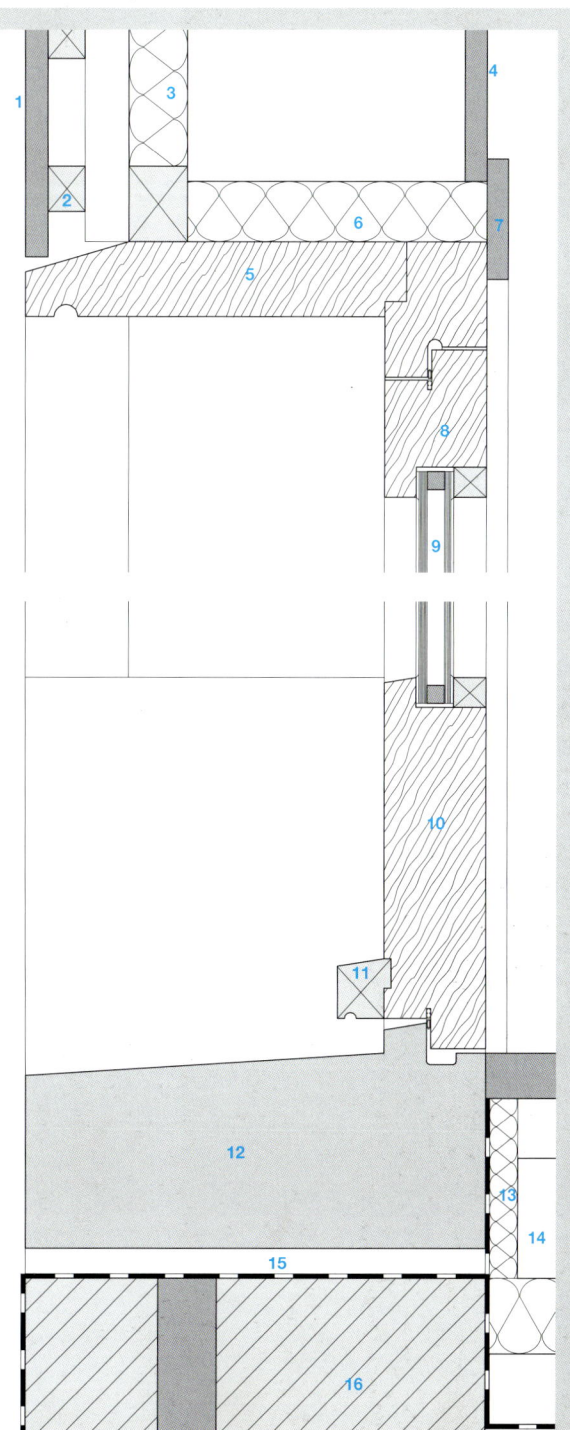

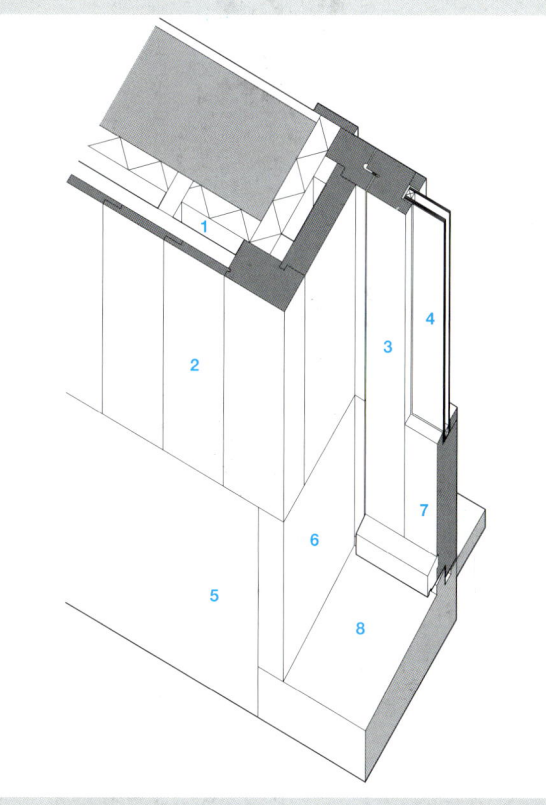

34.13
Axonometric Door Detail

1 Internal sub-structure to support timber facade with insulation in between
2 Timber-clad facade
3 Timber door frame
4 Double glazing assembly
5 Stone cladding
6 Stone cladding
7 Timber door frame
8 Stone threshold

Single Family House
Brixlegg, Tirol, Austria

Client
Antonius Lanzinger

Area
160 square metres (1,720 square feet)

Structural Engineer
Merz + Kaufmann + Partner

Located in the Inn River valley where historic castles and towers are a common sight, this modest timber house for the architect and his family nonetheless draws on a centuries-old tradition of vertical architecture. Spectacularly sited on a 36 degree slope with panoramic views of the Alps, the house at first appears to be dwarfed by the landscape. However, it is not reticence so much as empathy with the majesty of the mountains that creates a dialogue between the dwelling and its site. The four-storey structure rests on a six by eight metre (19 by 26 feet) concrete foundation, oriented so that living spaces enjoy the warmth of the sun. The inhabitants can also enjoy the sun and views from a roof terrace that spans the full width of the house.

The domestic programme is stacked up so that each level enjoys a separate function. In the concrete base are the entrance, auxilliary functions and recreation area; the ground floor accommodates the kitchen and dining areas as well as a five metre (16 feet) high living room and gallery; the second floor contains the children's rooms while the top floor accommodates the parent's bedroom and shower. A vertical backbone contains the stair and services installations, as well as energy efficient ceramic stoves on each level for heating. Environmental efficiency is also found in the insulating quality of the timber block construction which is so efficient that the originally designed inner layer of wood panelling was not needed. Exterior joints are fully exposed to the weather and demonstrate a high degree of craftmanship in the detailing of the house. Due to the type of construction, the structure has settled 16 centimetres (6 inches) in the first year – a planned effect for which the windows were specially designed.

1 Contemporary references to the fortified historic structures found in this area of the Tirol are reflected in the way that the openings in the timber facade are protected – in this case from the sun rather than from aggressors.
2 The tower is an economical form for the steeply sloping site, avoiding the excavation and fill that would be required for a more horizontal structure.
3 Detail view of the external timber cladding. Corner joints are expressive of the sophistication of the tradition of timber construction in this region.
4 The interior is almost totally clad in timber – walls, floors, ceilings, doors and stairs are left unpainted to reveal the nature of the wood.

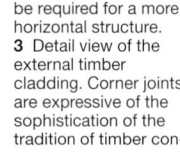
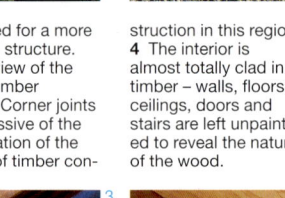

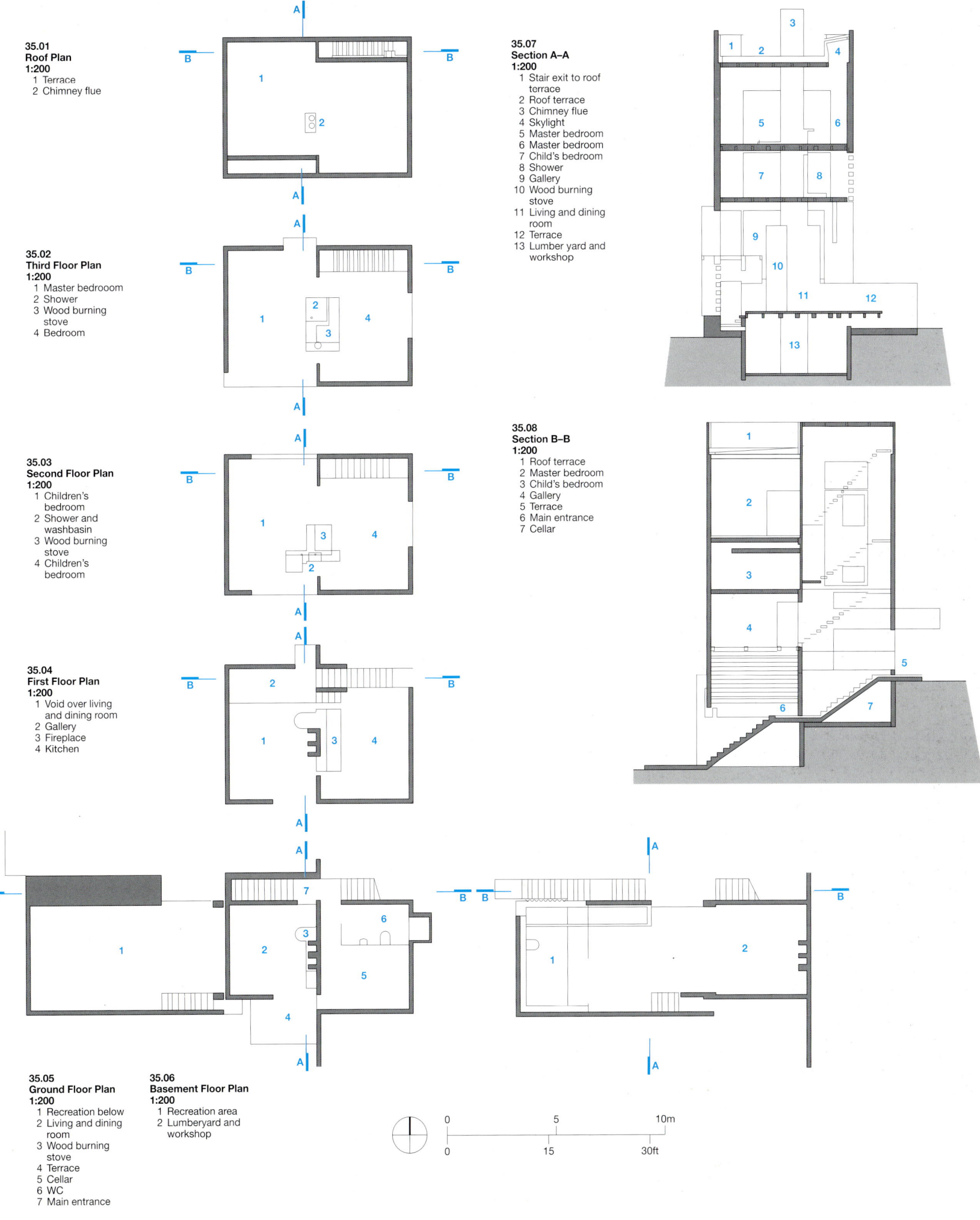

35.01
Roof Plan
1:200
1 Terrace
2 Chimney flue

35.02
Third Floor Plan
1:200
1 Master bedrooom
2 Shower
3 Wood burning stove
4 Bedroom

35.03
Second Floor Plan
1:200
1 Children's bedroom
2 Shower and washbasin
3 Wood burning stove
4 Children's bedroom

35.04
First Floor Plan
1:200
1 Void over living and dining room
2 Gallery
3 Fireplace
4 Kitchen

35.05
Ground Floor Plan
1:200
1 Recreation below
2 Living and dining room
3 Wood burning stove
4 Terrace
5 Cellar
6 WC
7 Main entrance

35.06
Basement Floor Plan
1:200
1 Recreation area
2 Lumberyard and workshop

35.07
Section A–A
1:200
1 Stair exit to roof terrace
2 Roof terrace
3 Chimney flue
4 Skylight
5 Master bedroom
6 Master bedroom
7 Child's bedroom
8 Shower
9 Gallery
10 Wood burning stove
11 Living and dining room
12 Terrace
13 Lumber yard and workshop

35.08
Section B–B
1:200
1 Roof terrace
2 Master bedroom
3 Child's bedroom
4 Gallery
5 Terrace
6 Main entrance
7 Cellar

0   5   10m

0   15   30ft

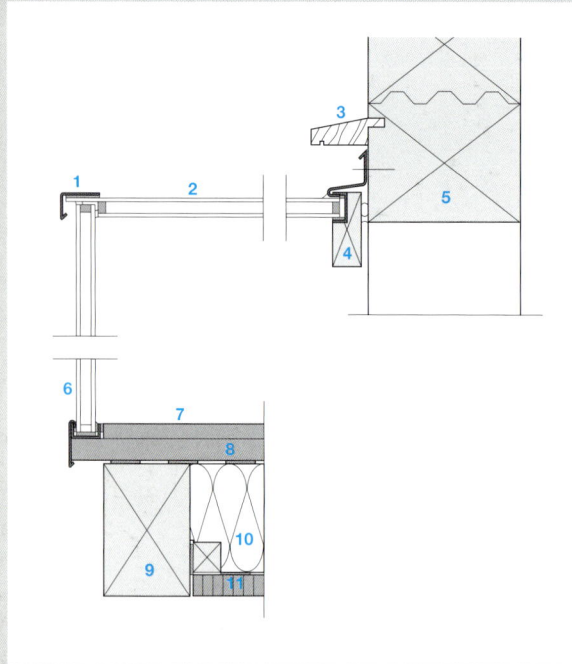

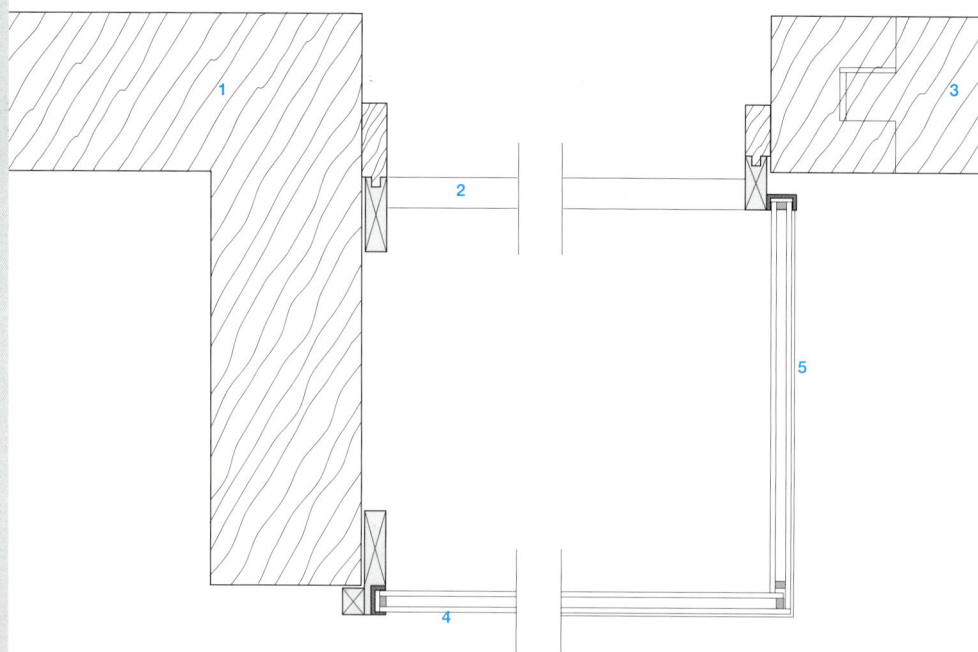

35.09
Corner Window Detail
1:10
 1 Flashing with lug pattern
 2 Fixed double glazing
 3 Weatherboard
 4 Timber window frame
 5 210 mm (8^{1}/$_{3}$ inch) thick timber block construction
 6 Fixed double glazing
 7 Parquet flooring to interior
 8 30 mm (1^{1}/$_{5}$ inch) thick three-ply laminated timber

sheeting
 9 120 x 180 mm (4^{3}/$_{4}$ x 7 inch) timber blocking
 10 Flax insulation
 11 30 mm (1^{1}/$_{5}$ inch) thick three-ply laminated timber

35.10
Corner Window Plan Detail
1:10
 1 210 mm (8^{1}/$_{3}$ inch) thick timber block construction
 2 Timber window frame
 3 210 mm (8^{1}/$_{3}$ inch) thick timber block construction
 4 Fixed double glazing
 5 Fixed double glazing

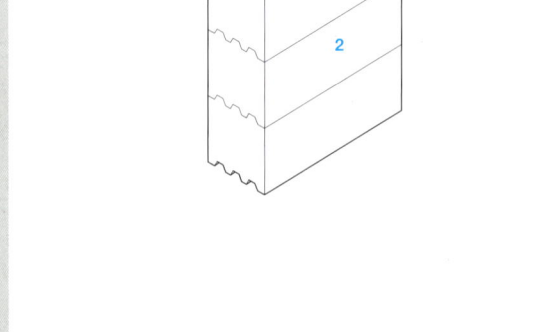

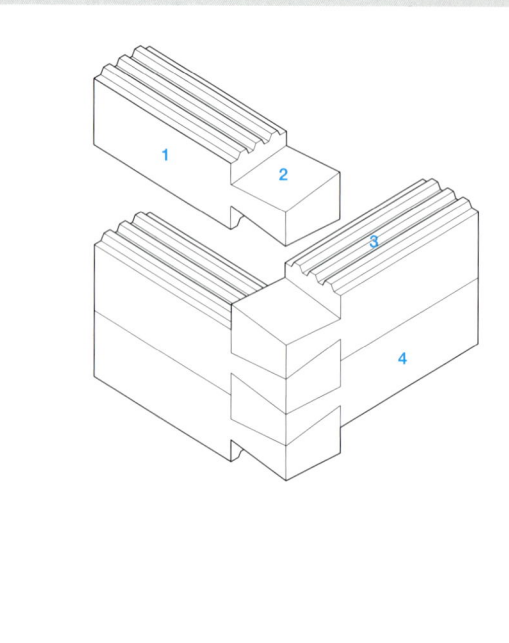

35.11
Timber Connection Detail 1
1:25
 1 Multi-ridged three-tooth comb connection joint between timber blocks
 2 210 mm (8^{1}/$_{3}$ inch) thick timber block construction

35.12
Timber Connection Detail 2
1:25
 1 210 mm (8^{1}/$_{3}$ inch) thick timber block construction
 2 Tyrolean lock corner joint
 3 Multi-ridged three-tooth comb connection joint between timber blocks
 4 210 mm (8^{1}/$_{3}$ inch) thick timber block construction

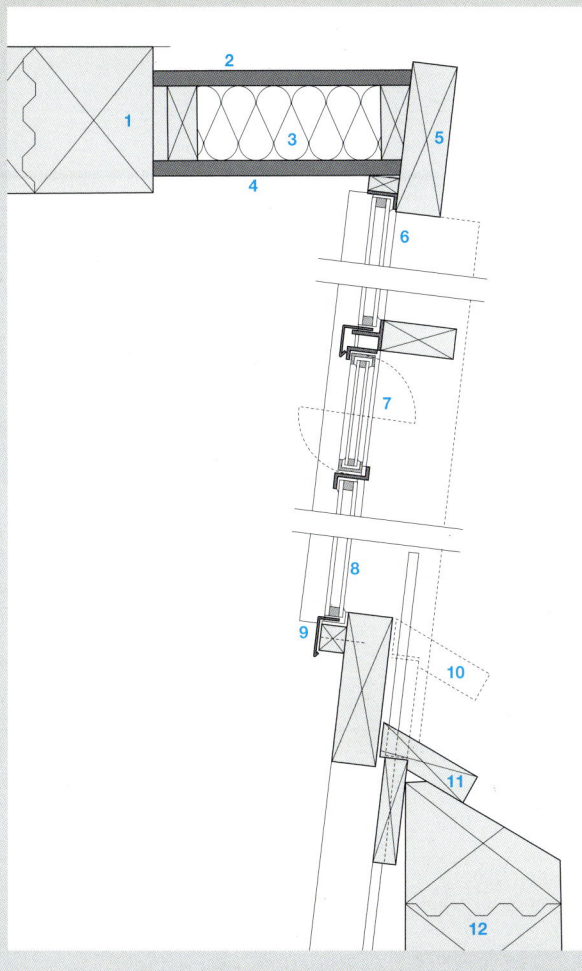

35.13
Raked Glazing Detail
1:10
 1 210 mm (8¹/₃ inch) thick timber block construction
 2 20 mm (³/₄ inch) thick plywood
 3 100 mm (4 inch) thick flax insulation
 4 20 mm (³/₄ inch) thick plywood
 5 Timber blocking
 6 Fixed double glazing
 7 Double-glazed louvred window
 8 Fixed double glazing
 9 Flashing with lug pattern
 10 Location of sill (11) after wall shrinkage
 11 Location of sill at installation
 12 210 mm (8¹/₃ inch) thick timber block construction

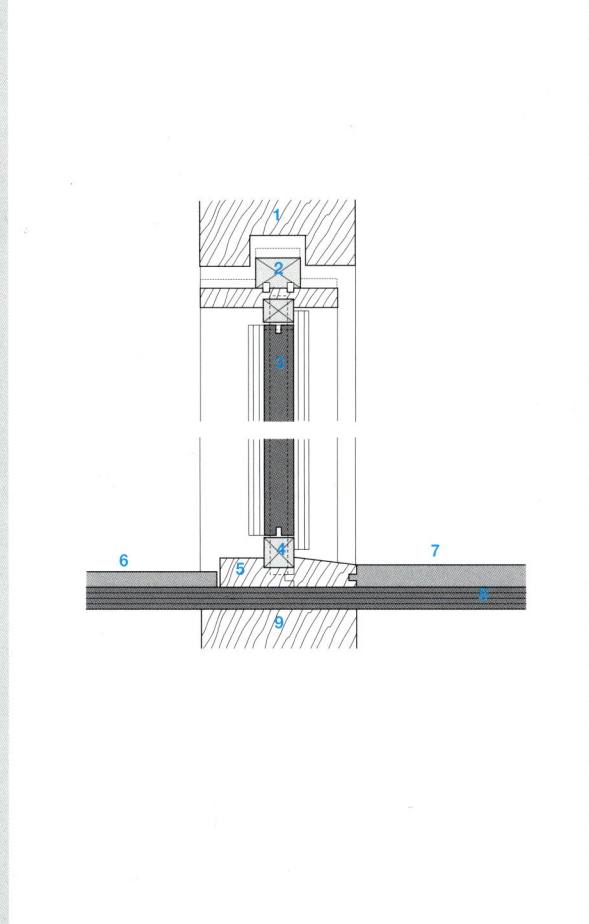

35.14
Door Detail
1:10
 1 210 mm (8¹/₃ inch) thick timber block construction
 2 Timber lintel
 3 Timber door leaf
 4 Door swing limiter
 5 Sill
 6 Parquet flooring to interior
 7 Sheet timber to exterior
 8 30 mm (1¹/₅ inch) thick three-ply laminated timber sheeting
 9 210 mm (8¹/₃ inch) thick timber block construction

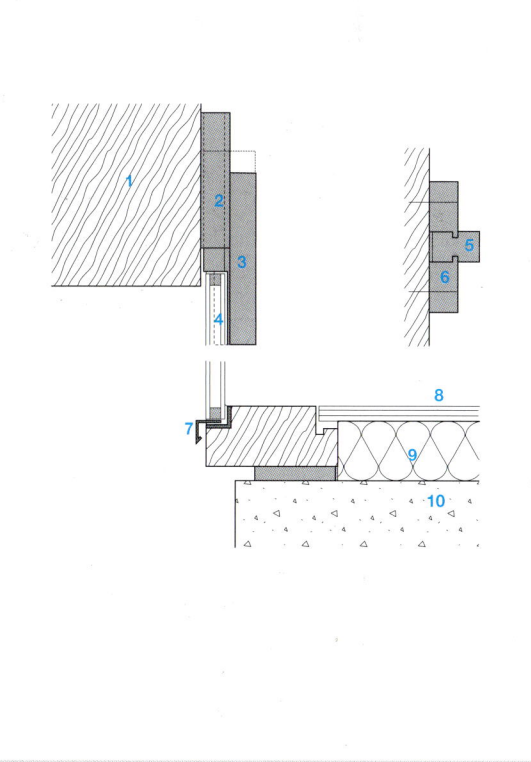

35.15
Fixed Glazing Detail
1:10
 1 210 mm (8¹/₃ inch) thick timber block construction
 2 Timber batten
 3 Timber batten
 4 Fixed double glazing
 5 Timber batten
 6 Timber batten
 7 Flashing with lug pattern
 8 Parquet flooring to interior
 9 Flax insulation
 10 Reinforced concrete foundation

**Convercey House
Grachaux, France**

Client
Mr and Mrs Convercey

Area
125 square metres (1,345 square feet)

Project Team
Bernard Quirot, Olivier Vichard, Alexandre Lenoble, Emmanuel Beaudoin

Structural Engineer
ADC Structure

Built for a landscape architect and his wife, this house is described by the architects as a machine to capture the landscape. It is a narrow, timber-clad rectilinear volume, stretched over the gently sloping landscape it frames. Elevated on pilotis, the primary objective of the house is to capture long views over the plain. Throughout the simple, open plan, the entire length of the house is visible, however the longitudinal dynamic is interrupted twice to define the main living spaces. In the dining corner, two large opposing windows create a transversal axis allowing the landscape to cross the house from east to west. The living room, the tallest space in the house, creates a vertical axis emphasized by a roof light and the verticality of the chimney.

The steel structure gives the silhouette of the house a simplicity and lightness. The house appears to touch the ground plane at only one point – the entrance – where the composition finds its equilibrium. In counterpoint, a delicate steel spiral stair giving access to the ground from the terrace, adds a sculptural touch. Above, what appears at first to be a single large volume is in fact two – one long narrow form containing the living spaces, and a shorter, wider volume housing two bedrooms. The interior is characterized by plain white-painted walls and timber floor boards, with horizontal and vertical notches and planes embedded in the main surfaces to create niches for storage heaters, a focus for the fireplace and places to display special objects, without interrupting the spatial fluidity of the house.

1 The house, a rectangular timber prism, barely appears to touch the ground. Held aloft on slender pilotis, the main structure only touches the site to create an entrance at the lower level, bringing people up into the kitchen area.
2 View from the west where a terrace runs the full width of the house, accessed from the living room. The bedroom wing to the rear of the house is just visible to the left, beyond the black steel spiral stair.
3 View of the north facade – the ground plane continues uninterrupted beneath the house.
4 Detail view of the timber clad house. Vertical cladding is interrupted only to insert typically vertical windows, or to create a frame, for example to the bedroom wing.
5 The living space is emphasized with extra verticality where a clerestory window allows daylight into the space.

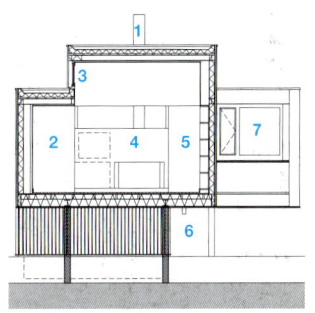

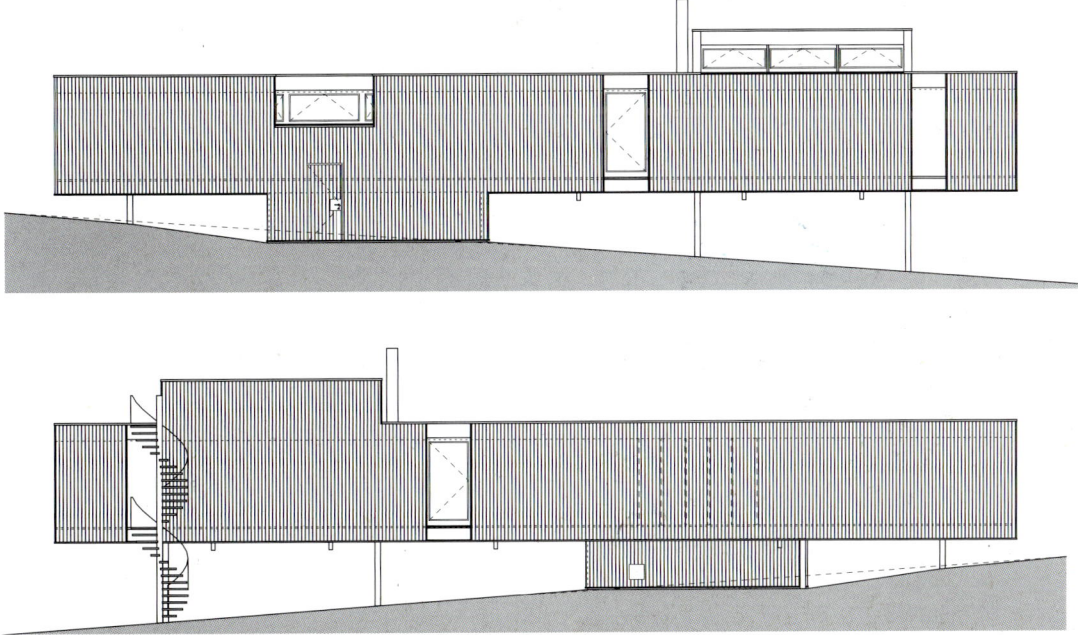

0   5   10m

0   15   30ft

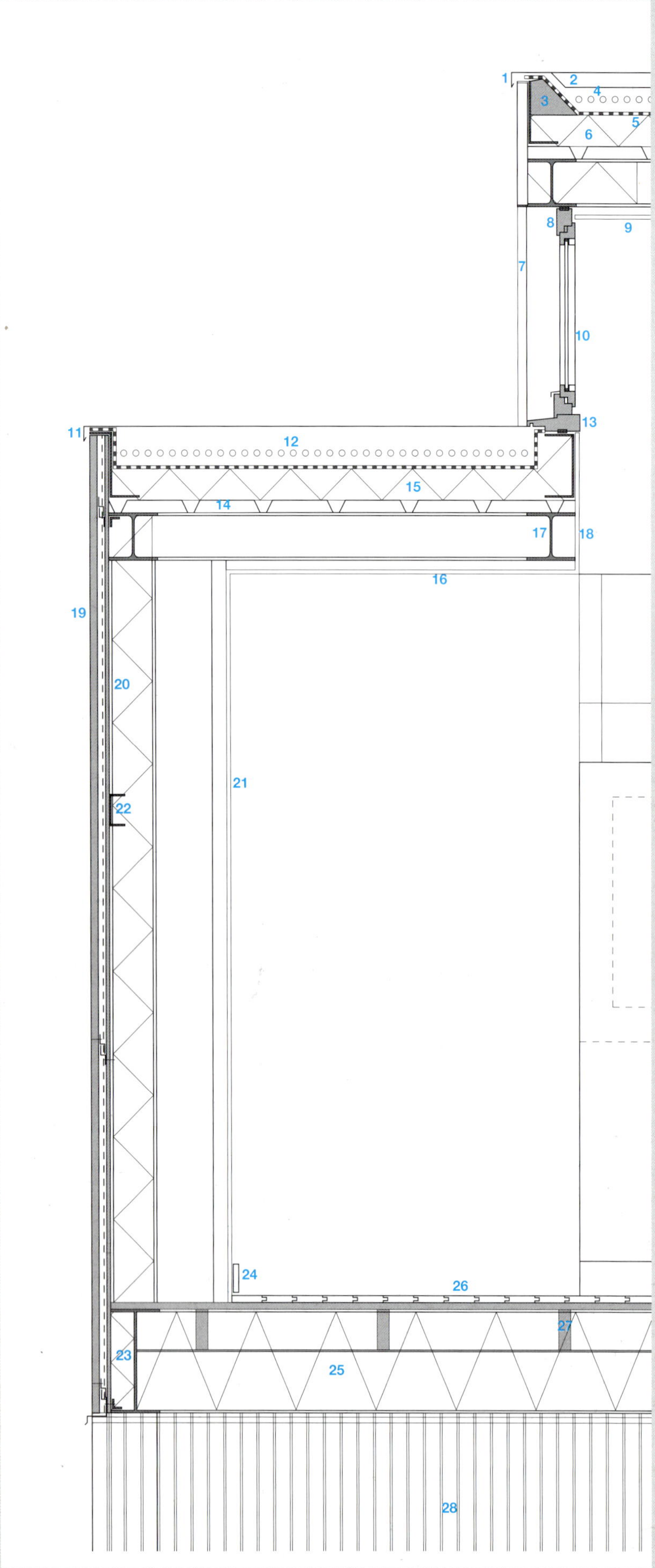

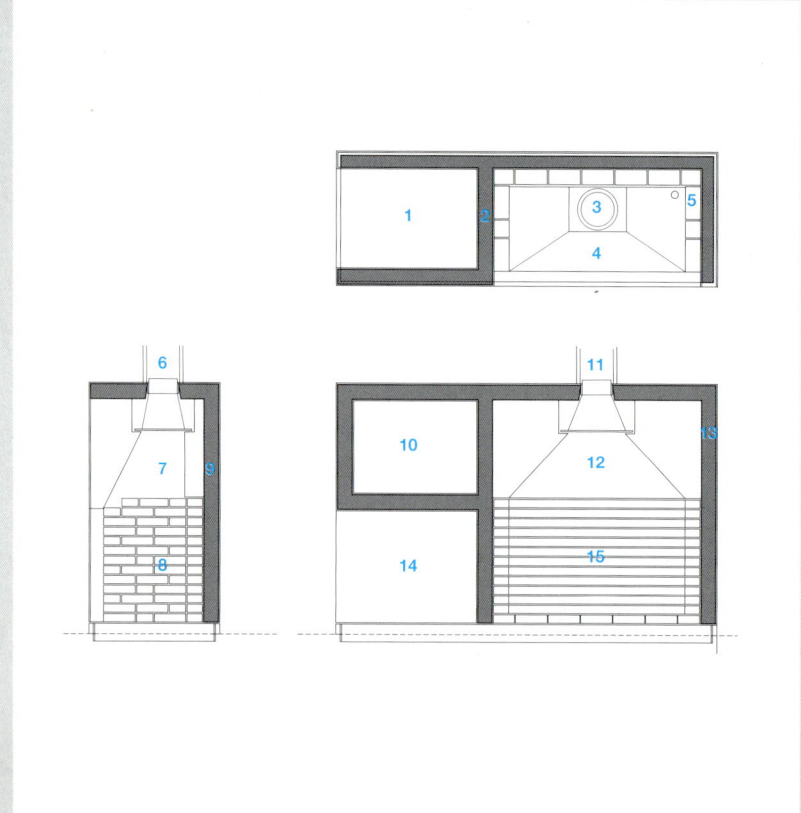

36.06
External Wall Detail
1:20
 1 Sheet aluminium covering
 2 Sheet aluminium covering
 3 Timber packing
 4 Gravel to roof surface
 5 Waterproofing membrane
 6 Rockwool thermal insulation
 7 Untreated larch cladding
 8 Exotic timber casement
 9 Plasterboard ceiling
10 Double glazing
11 Sheet aluminium covering to parapet
12 Gravel covering to roof
13 Timber window sill
14 Ribbed sheet steel roof structure
15 Rockwool thermal insulation
16 Plasterboard ceiling
17 160 mm (6¹/3 inch) steel I-beam
18 Plasterboard wall
19 Untreated larch cladding
20 Plywood with windproof paper lining
21 Plasterboard wall
22 100 mm (4 inch) steel U-beam
23 330 mm (13 inch) steel I-beam
24 Exotic timber skirting

25 Mineral wool insulation
26 Pine tongue and groove flooring
27 Timber joist
28 Untreated larch cladding

36.07
Chimney Detail
1:50
 1 Cement render to interior of log store
 2 Breeze block structure to fireplace, chimney and log store
 3 Chimney flue
 4 Argile bricks to interior of fireplace
 5 Argile bricks to interior of fireplace
 6 Chimney flue
 7 Concrete structure
 8 Argile bricks to interior of fireplace
 9 Breeze block structure to fireplace, chimney and log store
10 Cement render finish
11 Chimney flue
12 Concrete structure
13 Breeze block structure to fireplace, chimney and log store
14 Cement render finish
15 Argile bricks to interior of fireplace

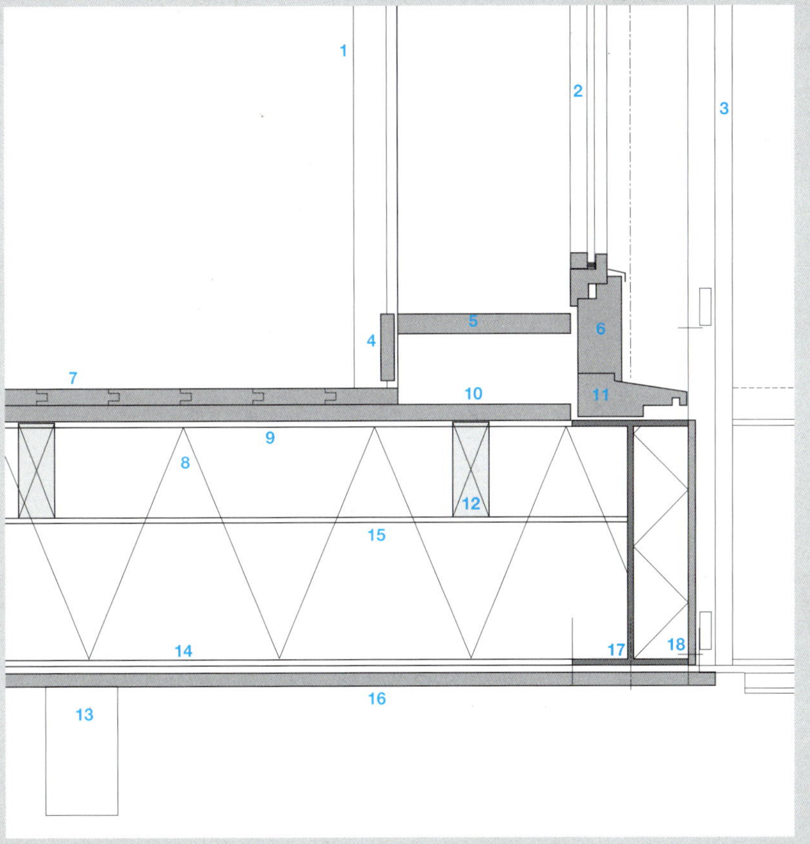

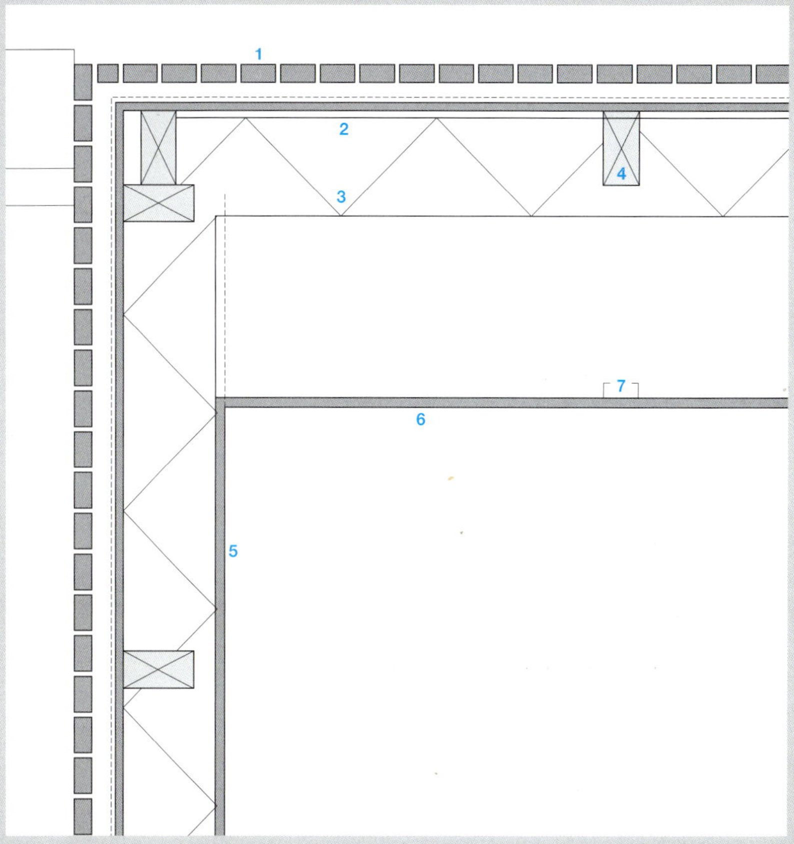

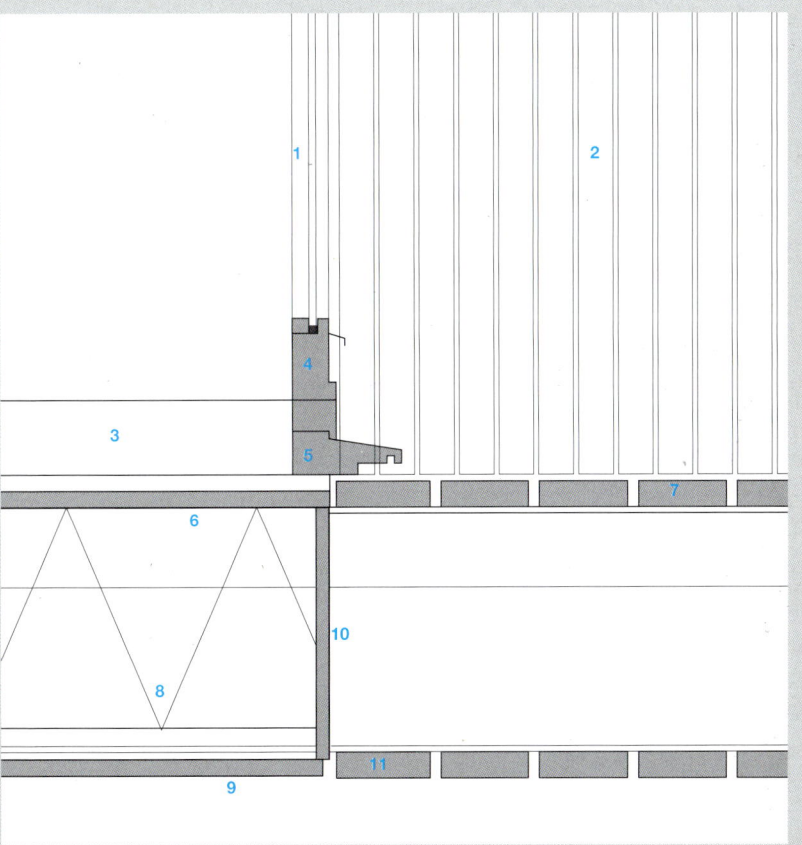

36.08
Floor and Wall Detail
1:10
  1 Plasterboard wall
  2 Double glazing
  3 Untreated larch
cladding
  4 Exotic timber
skirting
  5 Exotic timber
threshold
  6 Exotic timber
casement
  7 Pine tongue and
groove flooring
  8 Mineral wool
thermal insulation
  9 160 mm (6$\frac{1}{3}$ inch)
steel H-beam
10 Plywood floor
substrate
11 Window sill
12 Timber joist
13 Rain water down
pipe
14 330 mm (13 inch)
steel I-beam
15 Mineral wool
thermal insulation
16 Ribbed steel sheet
to underside of floor
17 330 mm (13 inch)
steel I-beam
18 Plywood filler

36.09
External Corner
Detail
1:10
  1 Untreated larch
cladding
  2 Plywood with
windproof paper lining
  3 Rock wool
insulation
  4 Timber stud
structure
  5 Plasterboard wall
lining
  6 Plasterboard wall
lining
  7 Metal C-section
plasterboard fixing

36.10
Internal and External
Floor Detail
1:10
  1 Double glazing
  2 Untreated larch
cladding
  3 Exotic timber
skirting
  4 Exotic timber
casement
  5 Window sill
  6 Plywood floor
substructure
  7 Open exotic timber
boards to deck
  8 Mineral wool
thermal insulation
  9 Ribbed sheet steel
to underside of floor
10 Plywood filler
11 Open exotic timber
boards to underside of
deck

Zig Zag Cabin
Wollombi, New South Wales,
Australia

Client
Ross Harley and Maria Fernanda
Cardoso

Area
25 square metres (270 square feet)

Project Team
S. Barnett, C. Morrison, T. Dwyer,
R. Langdon

Builder
Drew Heath

Conceived as a playful folly, this
'caravan without wheels' is an
amalgamation of bold colours and
geometric planes. The building is a
compact sleeping, sitting and cooking
shelter designed as a get-away for
Sydney based clients. Within its cubic
form, views of the bush are controlled
by the 'zigging and zagging' of the
window apertures. This creates long
and short views and breaks the
building up into a series of glass,
timber or fibre cement sheet panels.
At the lower level, windows provide
views of the earth and bush. The
vertical windows give a sectional view
of the trees and the top-level windows
look into the canopy.

   The cabin has two sleeping areas,
one on the ground level and one on a
mezzanine. A timber deck provides
outdoor living space and a rain water
collection tank behind the cabin
supplies fresh water. The hardwood
timber framing is clad in timber and
fibre cement sheeting, while the
interior is clad in masonite with a
timber floor and plywood joinery.
The form and colour palette is derived
from two references. One is the
iconic Schroder House (1924) by
Gerrit Rietveld in The Netherlands.
The influence is apparent in the
clever detailing, compact layout and
intersecting planes. The second
reference is the Australian bush. Using
a colour specifier to match colours
from the landscape, the building
enjoys a comfortable familiarity in
the bush setting. With its campsite
feel, the Zig Zag Cabin offers a
sensitive and intelligent alternative to
larger scale permanent structures in
the fragile bush environment.

1 Doors located at the
corner of the cabin
open up to reveal a
jigsaw-like interior
opening up onto a
simple but generous
timber deck.
2 The 'zig-zag' for
which the cabin is
named is apparent in
the layout of the fenes-
tration across and
around the facades.
3 Detail of the glazing
in which corner mul-
lions are eliminated in
order to capitalize on
carefully edited views
of the bushland
setting.
4 At the junction of the
horizontal and vertical
strips of glazing,
square windows open
to encourage cross
ventilation.
5 Inside, the cabin is
organized rationally
and intelligently.
Bedding, for example,
doubles as seating and
preparation surfaces.

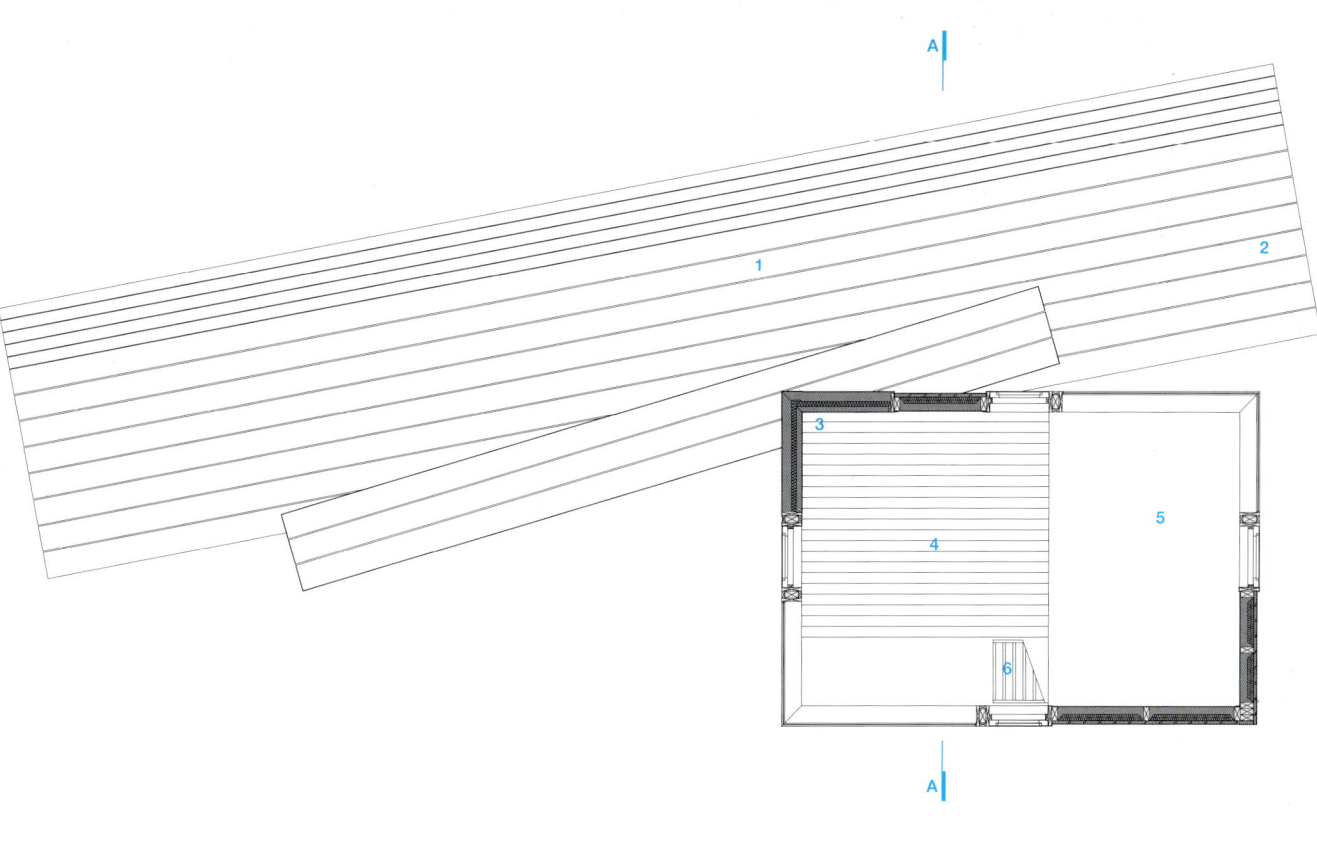

0   2.5   5m

0   7.5   15ft

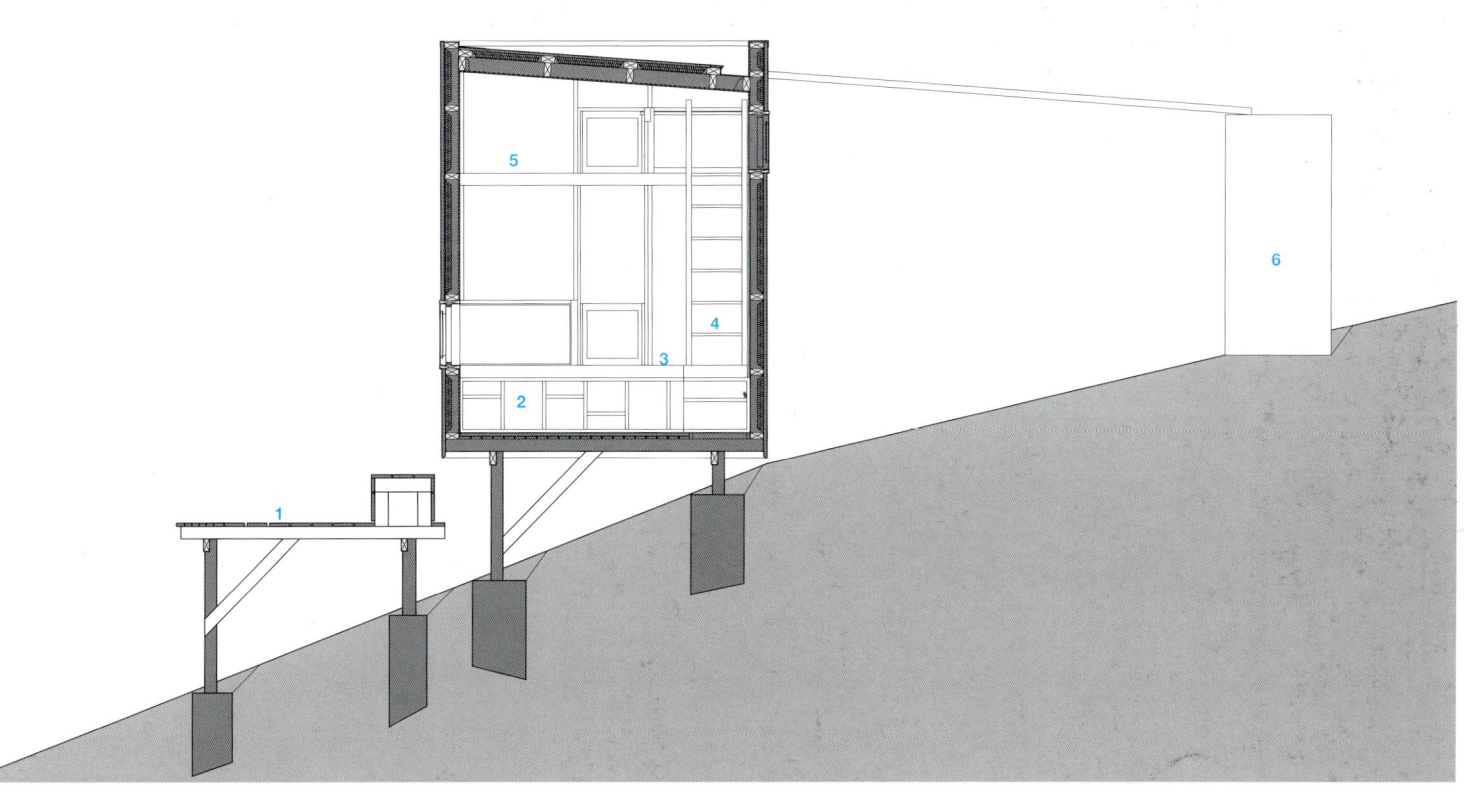

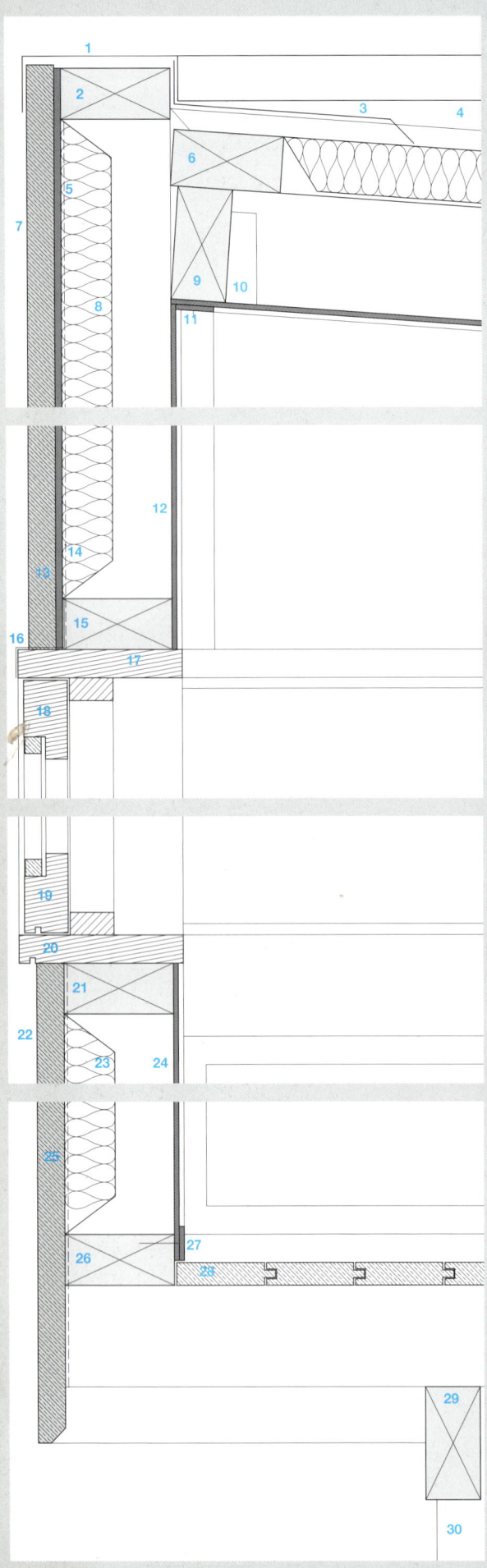

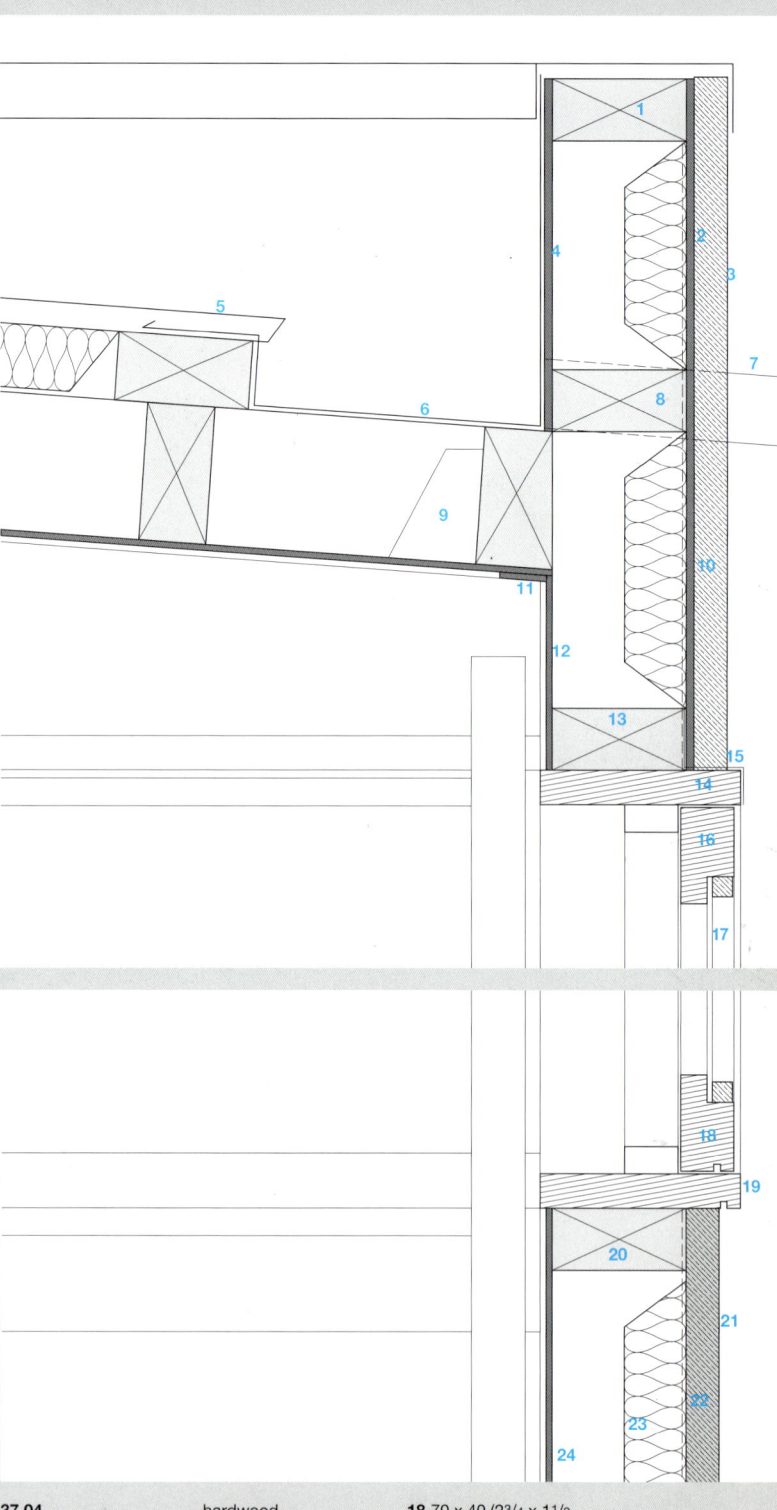

37.03
Roof, Wall and Floor Detail
1:5
1 Zincalume flashing
2 100 x 50 mm (4 x 2 inch) recycled hardwood
3 Zincalume flashing
4 18 mm (3/4 inch) Colorbond steel roof
5 Perforated sarking
6 100 x 50 mm (4 x 2 inch) recycled hardwood
7 25 mm (1 inch) rough sawn cypress shiplap boards
8 R1.5 insulation blanket
9 100 x 50 mm (4 x 2 inch) recycled hardwood
10 Joist hanger
11 30 x 4.5 mm (1 x 1/3 inch) masonite cover strips
12 4.5 mm (1/3 inch) masonite
13 6 mm (1/3 inch) compressed fibre cement sheet cladding
14 R1.5 insulation blanket
15 100 x 50 mm (4 x 2 inch) recycled hardwood
16 Zincalume flashing
17 150 x 25 mm (6 x 1 inch) hardwood
18 70 x 40 (23/4 x 11/2 inch) hardwood window frame
19 70 x 40 (23/4 x 11/2 inch) hardwood window frame
20 150 x 25 mm (6 x 1 inch) hardwood window sill
21 100 x 50 mm (4 x 2 inch) recycled hardwood
22 25 mm (1 inch) rough sawn cypress shiplap boards
23 R1.5 insulation blanket
24 4.5 mm (1/4 inch) masonite
25 25 mm (1 inch) rough sawn cypress shiplap boards
26 100 x 50 mm (4 x 2 inch) recycled hardwood
27 30 x 4.5 mm (11/4 x 1/4 inch) masonite cover strips
28 80 x 20 mm (31/4 x 3/4 inch) tongue and groove flooring
29 100 x 50 mm (4 x 2 inch) recycled hardwood
30 100 x 100 mm (4 x 4 inch) hardwood post

37.04
Roof Parapet and Window Detail
1:5
1 100 x 50 mm (4 x 2 inch) recycled hardwood
2 Perforated sarking
3 25 mm (1 inch) rough sawn cypress shiplap boards
4 4.5 mm (1/4 inch) masonite
5 18 mm (3/4 inch) Colorbond steel roof
6 Zincalume flashing
7 50 mm (2 inch) diameter zincalume downpipe
8 100 x 50 mm (4 x 2 inch) recycled hardwood
9 Joist hanger
10 6 mm (1/3 inch) compressed fibre cement sheet cladding
11 30 x 4.5 mm (1 x 1/3 inch) masonite cover strips
12 4.5 mm (1/4 inch) masonite
13 100 x 50 mm (4 x 2 inch) recycled hardwood
14 150 x 25 mm (6 x 1 inch) hardwood
15 Zincalume flashing
16 70 x 40 (23/4 x 11/2 inch) hardwood window frame
17 4 mm (1/5 inch) float glass
18 70 x 40 (23/4 x 11/2 inch) hardwood window frame
19 150 x 25 mm (6 x 1 inch) hardwood window sill
20 100 x 50 mm (4 x 2 inch) recycled hardwood
21 25 mm (1 inch) rough sawn cypress shiplap boards
22 Perforated sarking
23 R1.5 insulation blanket
24 4.5 mm (1/4 inch) masonite

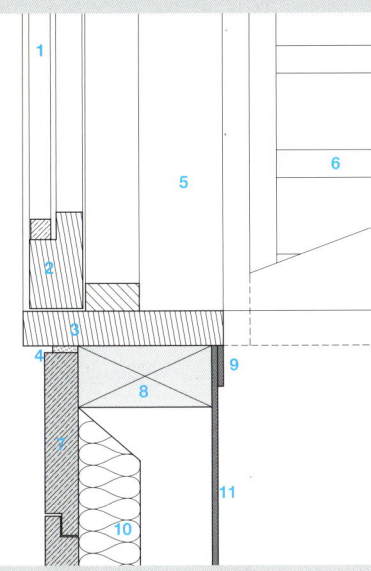

37.05
Window Detail 1
1:5
1 4 mm (1/4 inch) float glass
2 70 x 40 mm (3 x 1 1/2 inch) hardwood window frame
3 150 x 25 mm (6 x 1 inch) hardwood
4 Mastic joint
5 150 x 25 mm (6 x 1 inch) hardwood
6 Recycled timber ladder
7 25 mm (1 inch) rough sawn cypress shiplap boards
8 100 x 50 mm (4 x 2 inch) recycled hardwood
9 30 x 4.5 mm (11/4 x 1/4 inch) masonite cover strips
10 R1.5 insulation blanket
11 4.5 mm (1/4 inch) masonite

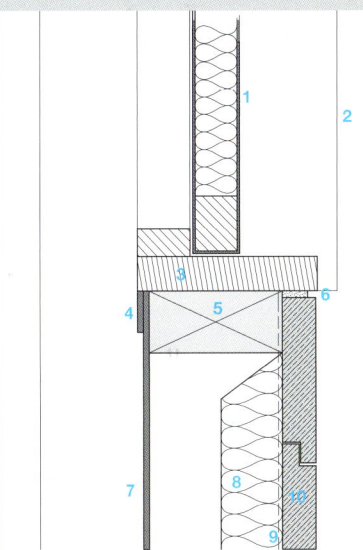

37.06
Wall Detail 1
1:5
1 35 mm (11/3 inch) hollow core door
2 150 x 25 mm (6 x 1 inch) hardwood
3 150 x 25 mm (6 x 1 inch) hardwood
4 30 x 4.5 mm (11/4 x 1/4 inch) masonite cover strips
5 100 x 50 mm (4 x 2 inch) recycled hardwood
6 Mastic joint
7 4.5 mm (1/4 inch) masonite
8 R1.5 insulation blanket
9 Perforated sarking
10 25 mm (1 inch) rough sawn cypress shiplap boards

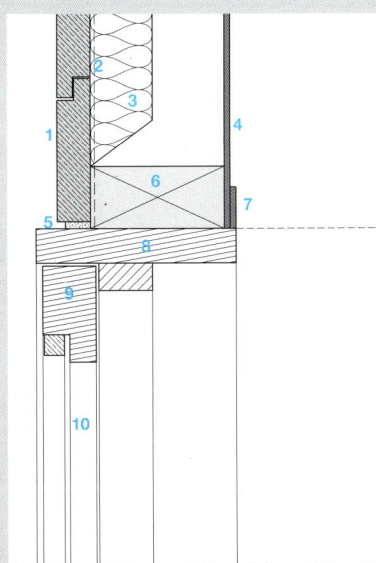

37.07
Window Detail 2
1:5
1 25 mm (1 inch) rough sawn cypress shiplap boards
2 Perforated sarking
3 R1.5 insulation blanket
4 4.5 mm (1/4 inch) masonite
5 Mastic joint
6 100 x 50 mm (4 x 2 inch) recycled hardwood
7 30 x 4.5 mm (11/4 x 1/4 inch) masonite cover strips
8 150 x 25 mm (6 x 1 inch) hardwood
9 70 x 40 mm (23/4 x 11/2 inch) hardwood window frame
10 4 mm (1/5 inch) float glass

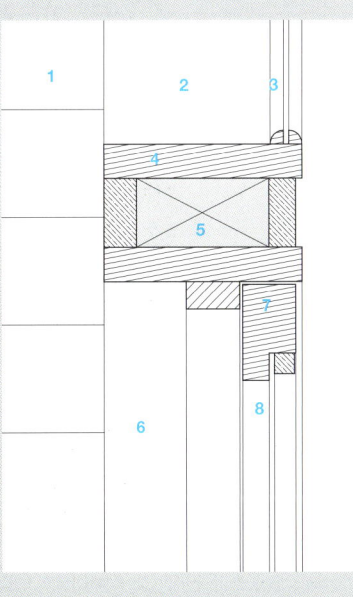

37.08
Wall Detail 2
1:5
1 80 x 20 mm (31/4 x 1/4 inch) tongue and groove flooring
2 150 x 25 mm (6 x 1 inch) hardwood sill below
3 4 mm (1/4 inch) float glass
4 150 x 25 mm (6 x 1 inch) hardwood
5 100 x 50 mm (4 x 2 inch) recycled hardwood
6 150 x 25 mm (6 x 1 inch) hardwood sill below
7 70 x 40 mm (3 x 1 1/2 inch) hardwood window frame
8 4 mm (1/4 inch) float glass

38
Edge Design Institute Ltd.

Suitcase House
Shuiguan, Badaling, China

Client
SOHO China Ltd.

Area
250 square metres (2,690 square feet)

Project Team
Gary Chang, Andrew Holt, Howard
Chang, Popeye Tsang, Yee Lee

Structural Engineer
Qin Min-De

Services Engineer
Beijing Century Co.

Local Architect
Beijing Century Architectural Design +
Planning Co. Ltd.

Main Contractor
China Construction 1st Division, 4th
Company, 3rd Housing Architecture
Construction Company

The Suitcase House is part of the
experimental development 'The
Commune by the Great Wall' near
Beijing. Twelve young Asian architects
were invited to design 11 houses and
a clubhouse at the foot of the Great
Wall. The Suitcase House attempts to
rethink the nature of privacy and
adaptability, and is a demonstration of
the desire for ultimate flexibility. Made
up of three strata, the middle layer is
a plane on which the majority of
domestic activities occur. This space
transforms itself according to the
nature of the activities and personal
preferences for enclosure with the
help of a number of mobile elements.

The bottom strata acts as a
container for dedicated spaces
including bedrooms, bathrooms and
kitchen as well as a meditation
chamber with glazed floor, music
room, library, study and sauna.
Compartments are concealed by a
landscape of pneumatically assisted
floor panels so that only the required
elements have a spatial presence.
To blur the boundaries between
exterior, interior and furniture, every
element is clad monochromatically in
timber. The steel structure is
supported on, and cantilevers out
from, a concrete base that houses
utilitarian facilities such as the pantry,
butler's quarters, boiler room and
the sauna.

1 The simple
rectilinear form masks
the ultimate flexibility
of the house in which
the inhabitants are
able to create spaces
and use facilities in a
completely personal
manner.
2 With all the panels
closed, the interior
appears as a simple
open plan space.
3 Sliding panels divide
the space from floor to
ceiling, while hinged
doors in the floor
reveal all manner of
services that can be
opened up or
concealed at will.
4 The pneumatically
assisted floor panels
reveal sunken bath-
rooms, as seen here,
as well as bedrooms
and a kitchen.

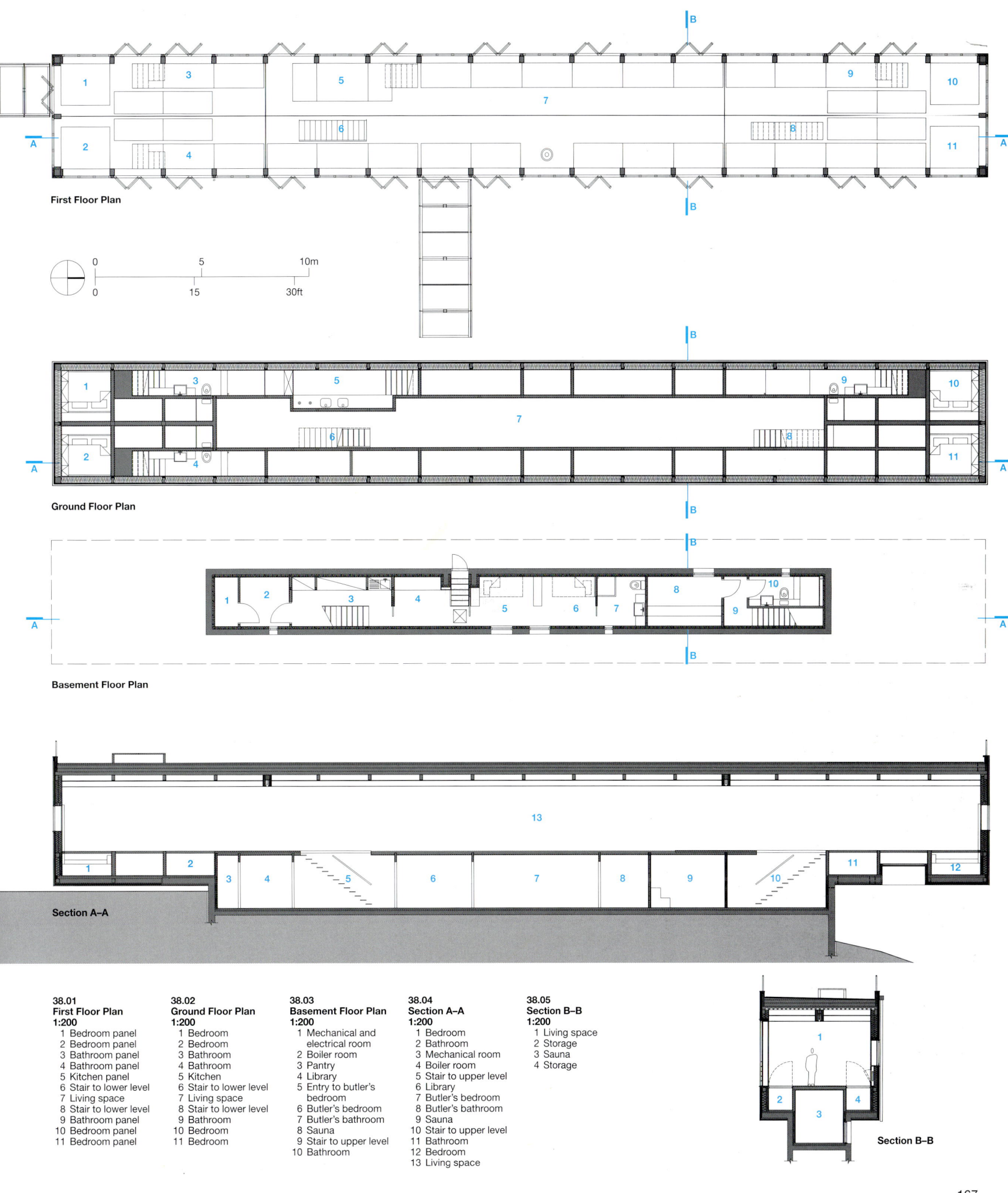

First Floor Plan

Ground Floor Plan

Basement Floor Plan

Section A–A

Section B–B

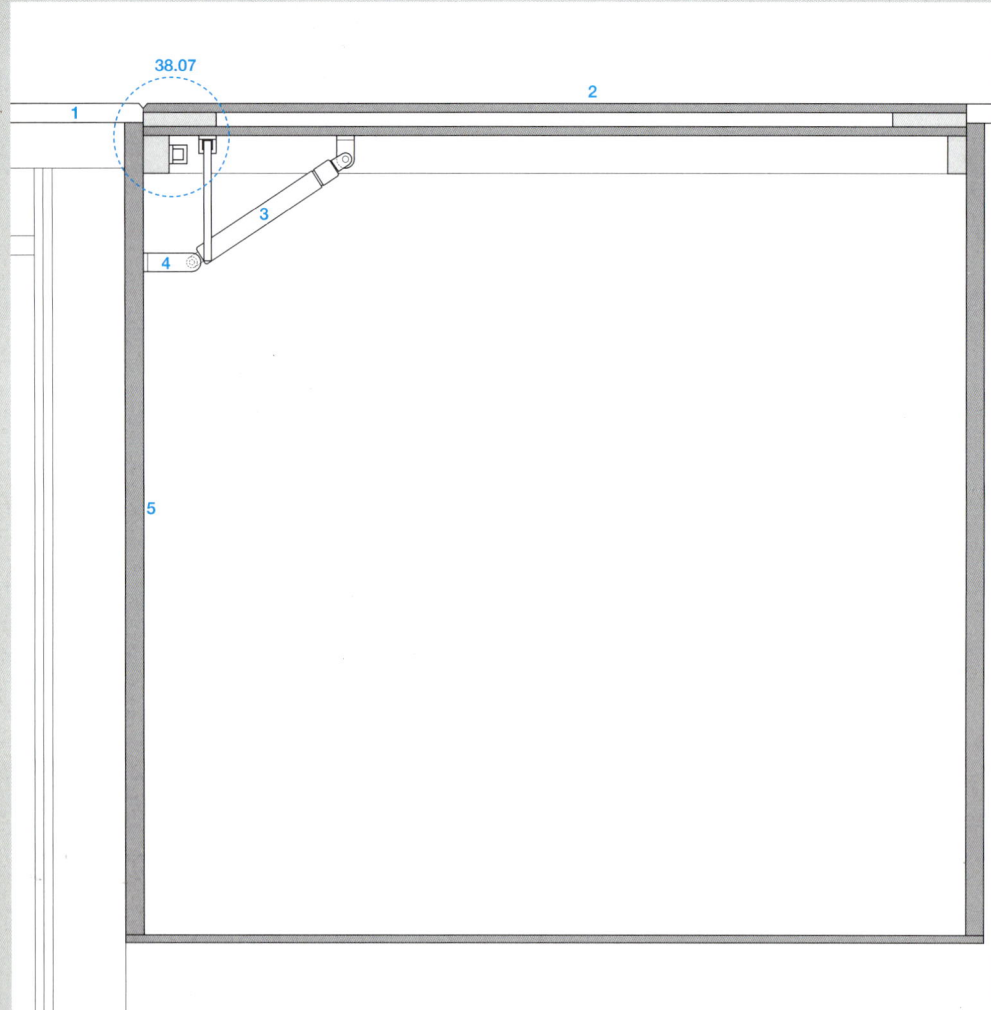

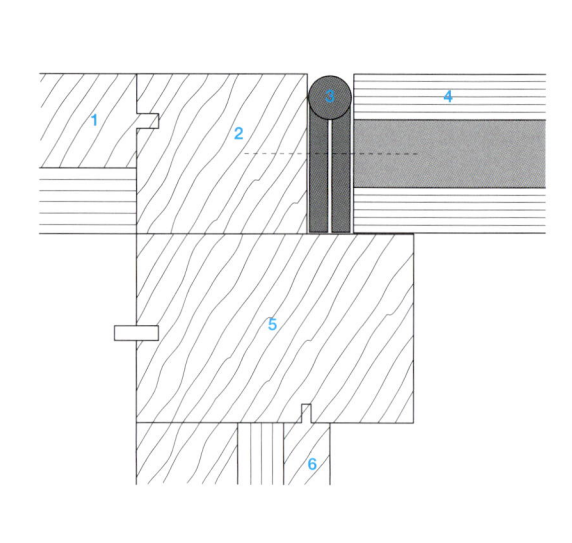

38.06
Pneumatic Floor
Panel Detail
1:10
1 Timber floor
2 Openable timber
floor panel
3 Gas spring
4 Metal bracket
5 Timber lined interior

38.07
Pneumatic Floor
Hinge Detail
1:2
1 Hardwood flooring
2 Hardwood block
3 Recessed hinge
4 Hardwood panel
5 Hardwood frame
6 Timber wall panel

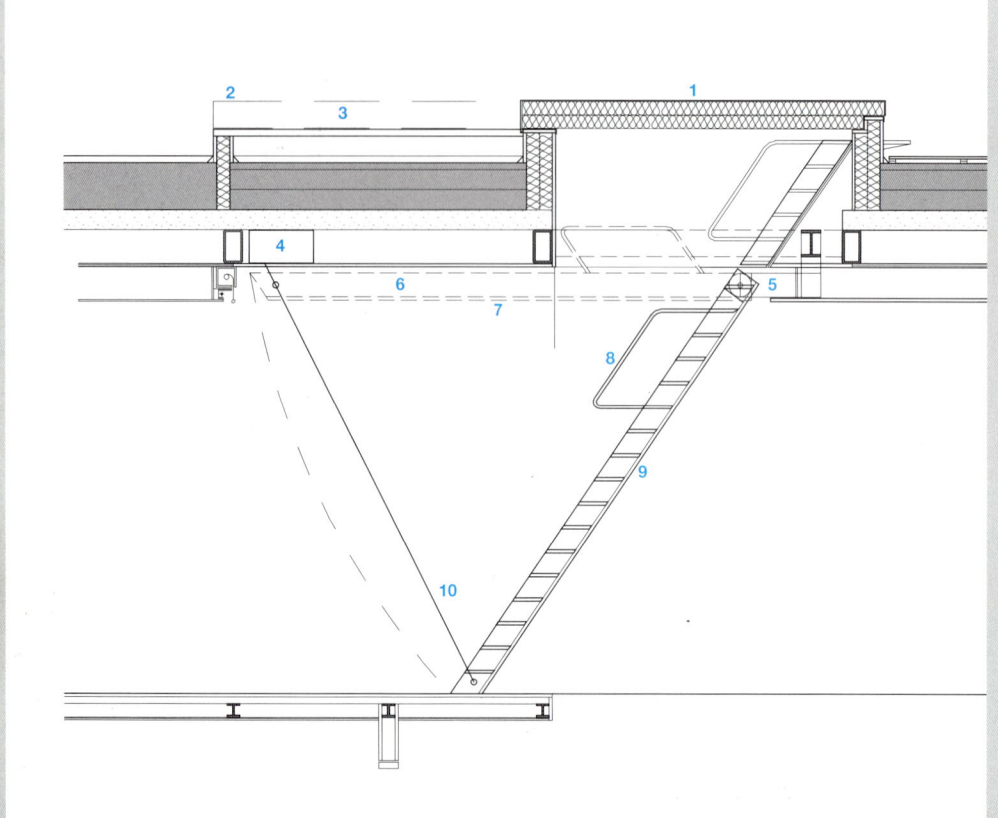

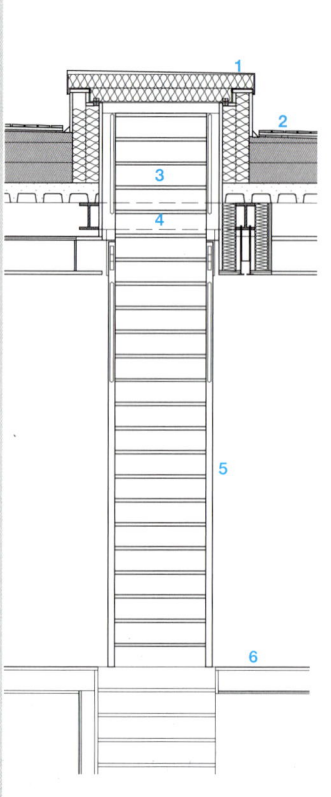

38.08
Roof Access
Longitudinal Section
1:50
1 Insulated sliding
roof hatch
2 Line of roof in open
position
3 Guide rail
4 Concealed electric
motor for raising and
lowering staircase
5 Pivot point
6 Plywood ceiling
7 Line of staircase in
raised position
8 Hand rail
9 Veneered plywood
backing to stair
10 Steel cable to raise
and lower stair

38.09
Roof Access Cross
Section
1:50
1 Electrically
operated insulated roof
hatch in closed
position
2 Timber roof deck
3 Fixed section of
staircase
4 Pivot point
5 Staircase in
lowered position
6 Interior timber floor

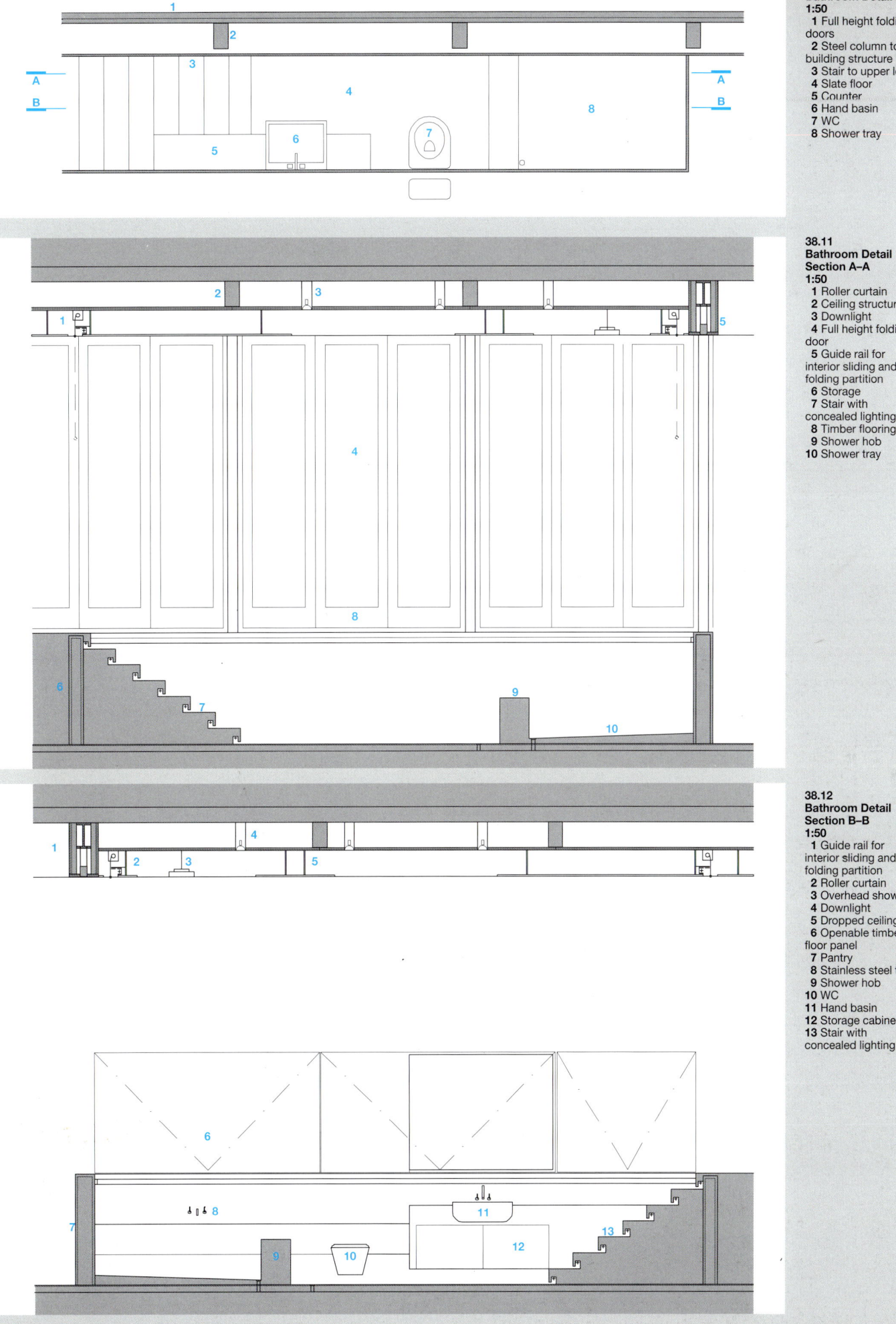

38.10
Bathroom Detail Plan
1:50
 1 Full height folding
doors
 2 Steel column to
building structure
 3 Stair to upper level
 4 Slate floor
 5 Counter
 6 Hand basin
 7 WC
 8 Shower tray

38.11
**Bathroom Detail
Section A–A**
1:50
 1 Roller curtain
 2 Ceiling structure
 3 Downlight
 4 Full height folding
door
 5 Guide rail for
interior sliding and
folding partition
 6 Storage
 7 Stair with
concealed lighting
 8 Timber flooring
 9 Shower hob
 10 Shower tray

38.12
**Bathroom Detail
Section B–B**
1:50
 1 Guide rail for
interior sliding and
folding partition
 2 Roller curtain
 3 Overhead shower
 4 Downlight
 5 Dropped ceiling
 6 Openable timber
floor panel
 7 Pantry
 8 Stainless steel taps
 9 Shower hob
 10 WC
 11 Hand basin
 12 Storage cabinet
 13 Stair with
concealed lighting

Jackson Family Retreat
Big Sur, California, USA

Area
232 square metres (2,500 square feet)

Project Team
Anne Fougeron, Michel Pierry, Anne
Tipp, Vivian Dwyer, Ethen Wood, Ryan
Murphy, Todd Aranaz

Structural Engineer
Endres Ware Consulting Engineers

Main Contractor
Thomas George Construction

Located in the Big Sur area of northern California, this weekend retreat is composed of four volumes, each from a different material, interconnected to create visually and spatially complex exterior and interior spaces. The main volume features a butterfly roof and glass corners that reach out to the sky. The roof sits delicately above a band of glass, connecting to the roof structure with thin steel rods. At the corners of the house, two-storey-high windows frame views of the redwoods and the sky. This volume is clad in standing seam copper. The second volume is a one-storey structure that houses the service functions and acts as a buffer from the road. This is clad in yellow Alaskan cedar turned in three directions to act as a rain screen and a fence.

The back of the house is comprised of a steel and glass volume, open to views of the creek. Finally the fourth volume, containing the staircase, and clad inside and out with grey stucco, is both the seismic structural brace for the house and a visual foil to the transparent volumes around it. On the ground floor, two bedrooms sandwich the two-storey communal living space, the fireplace, and the loft library. Tall windows in the bedrooms dissolve the corners of the spaces, bringing light and views into the bedroom and living spaces. On the second floor, the space is open with the library and communal sleeping room separated from the bedrooms below by glass panels. A combination of transparent glass and extruded channel glass reflects light, creating an ever-changing interior with a warm play of light and shadow throughout the day.

1 A view of the three main volumes – the grey stucco-clad stair volume on the left, the glazed living room extension opening onto a timber deck, and the copper-clad main volume with two-storey-high windows at the corners accommodate the main living spaces and bedrooms above.
2 At the rear of the house, a timber screen acts as a buffer from the adjacent approach road, while an elegant butterfly roof caps the composition.
3 The library on the first floor, overlooking the living spaces, features a dramatic exposed roof structure of timber beams and steel tension rods.
4 View of the living room with spectacular views of the canyon wall through the steel-framed, full height glazed walls and ceiling.

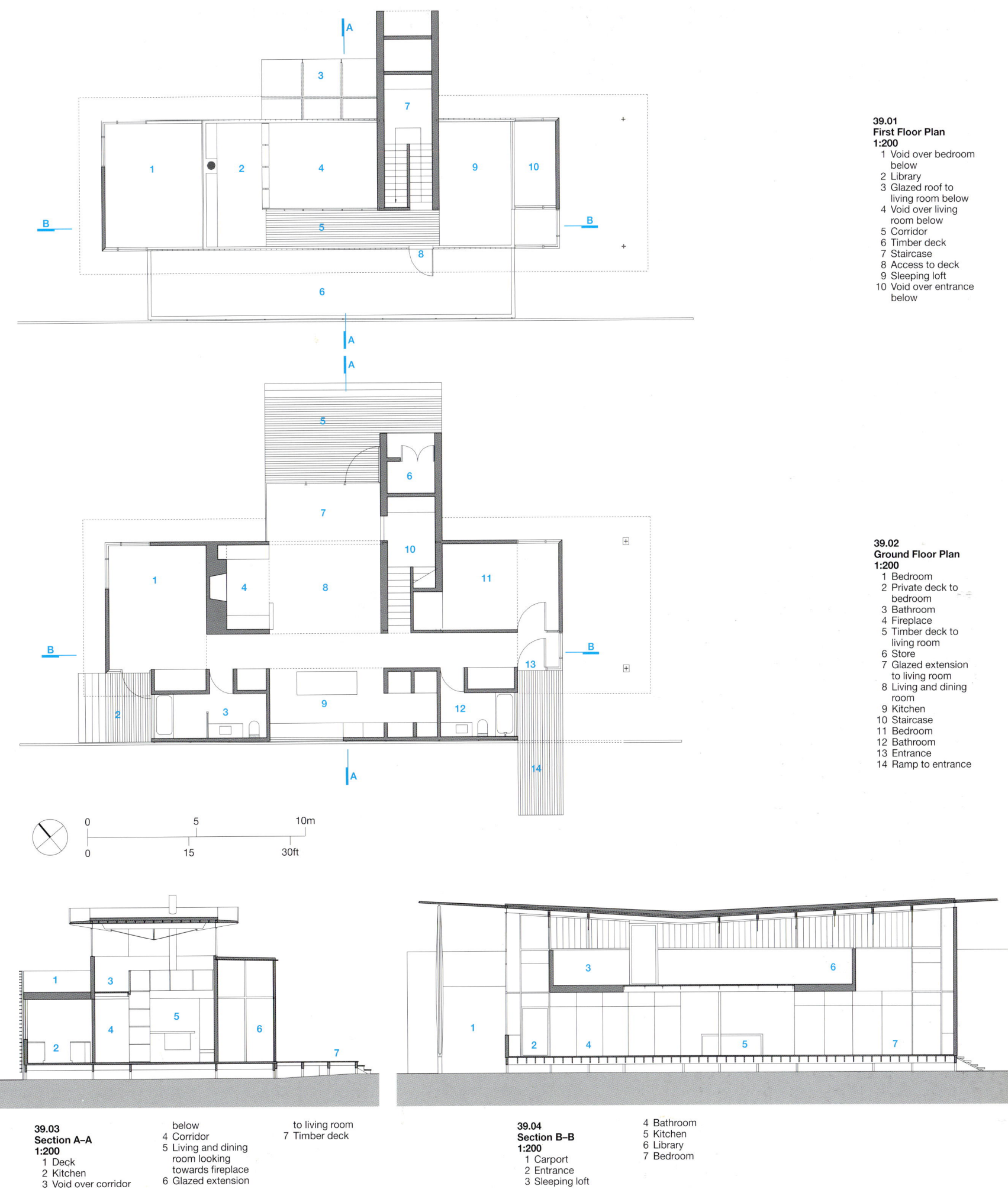

39.01
First Floor Plan
1:200
1 Void over bedroom below
2 Library
3 Glazed roof to living room below
4 Void over living room below
5 Corridor
6 Timber deck
7 Staircase
8 Access to deck
9 Sleeping loft
10 Void over entrance below

39.02
Ground Floor Plan
1:200
1 Bedroom
2 Private deck to bedroom
3 Bathroom
4 Fireplace
5 Timber deck to living room
6 Store
7 Glazed extension to living room
8 Living and dining room
9 Kitchen
10 Staircase
11 Bedroom
12 Bathroom
13 Entrance
14 Ramp to entrance

39.03
Section A–A
1:200
1 Deck
2 Kitchen
3 Void over corridor
  below
4 Corridor
5 Living and dining room looking towards fireplace
6 Glazed extension
  to living room
7 Timber deck

39.04
Section B–B
1:200
1 Carport
2 Entrance
3 Sleeping loft
4 Bathroom
5 Kitchen
6 Library
7 Bedroom

171

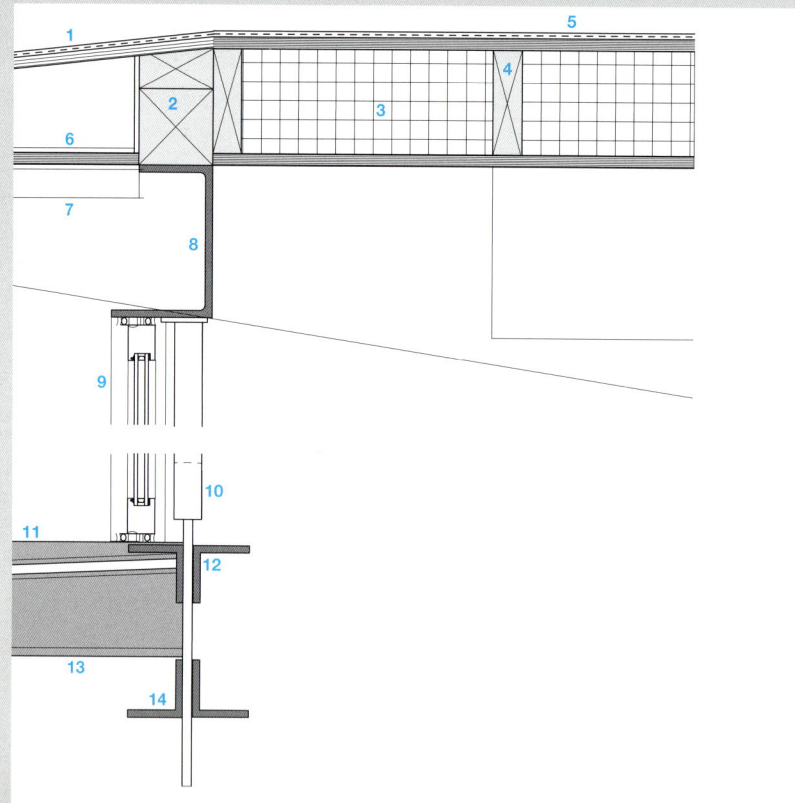

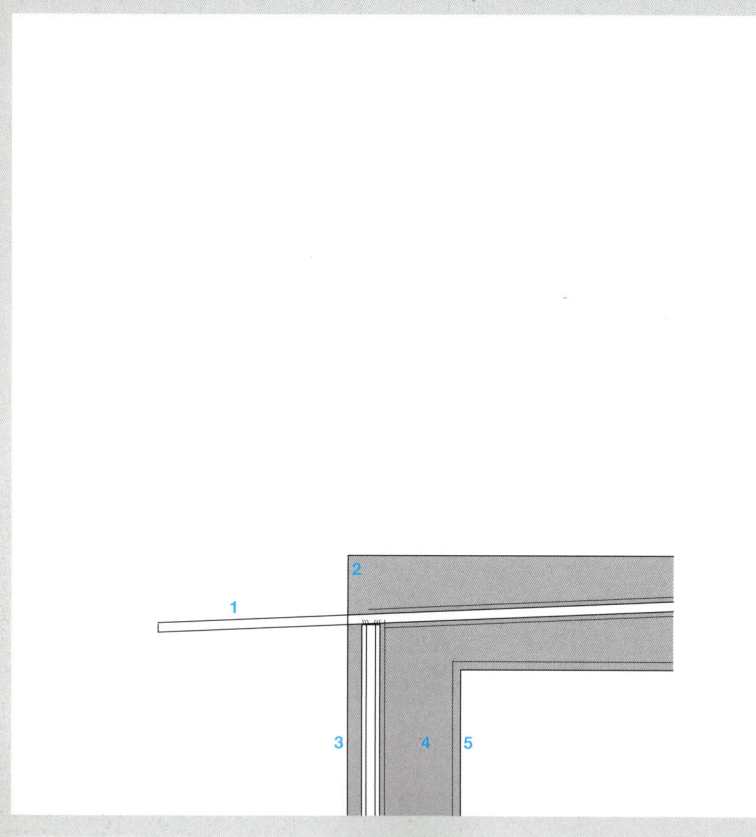

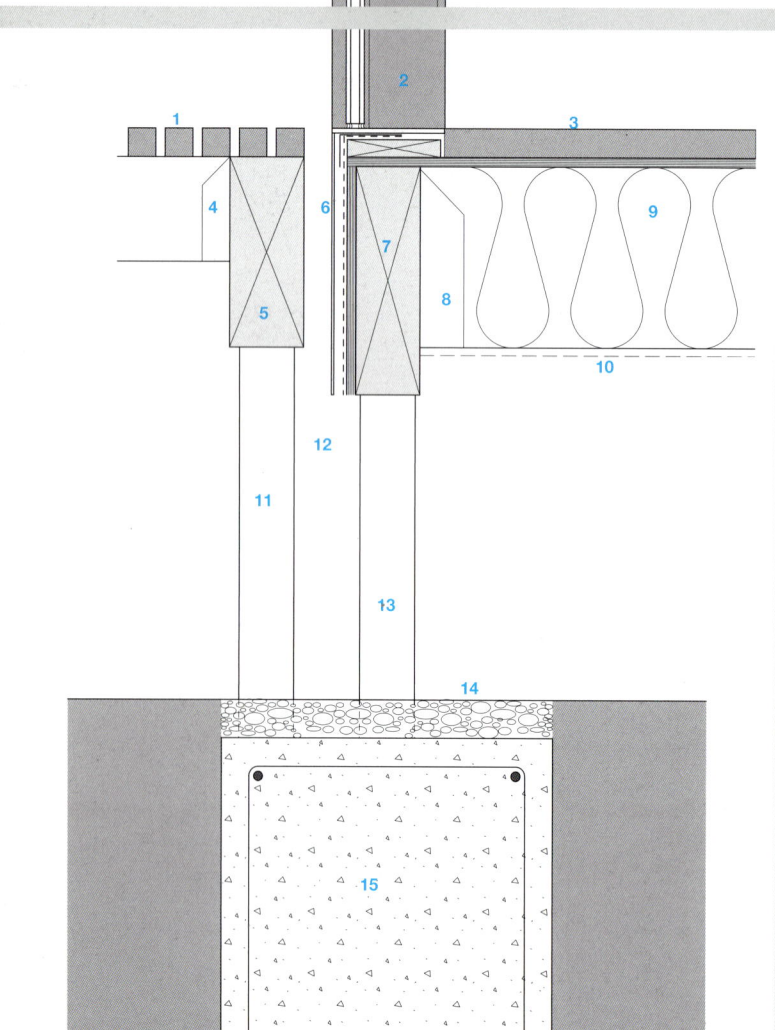

39.05
Wall Section Detail at Glass Box 1
1:10
  1 Insulated glass
  2 Steel section beyond
  3 Steel section beyond
  4 Steel section beyond
  5 Steel section beyond

39.06
Wall Section Detail at Glass Box 2
1:10
  1 Redwood decking
  2 Painted flat steel bar
  3 Concrete floor with radiant heating
  4 Joist hanger
  5 100 x 250 mm (4 x 10 inch) redwood timber beam
  6 Metal flashing
  7 100 x 300 mm (4 x 12 inch) glulam beam
  8 Joist hanger
  9 Batt insulation
  10 Fibreglass mesh
  11 76 mm (3 inch) steel pipe column
  12 Air space
  13 76 mm (3 inch) steel pipe column
  14 Granite rubble
  15 Reinforced concrete beam

39.07
Wall Section Detail at Glass Box 3
1:10
  1 Built-up roof
  2 100 x 100 mm (4 x 4 inch) header
  3 Rigid insulation
  4 50 x 150 mm (2 x 6 inch) stud
  5 Built-up roof
  6 50 mm (2 inch) diameter vent
  7 6 mm (1/4 inch) steel truss beyond
  8 Bent steel channel
  9 Insulated glass
  10 50 mm (2 inch) steel rod
  11 Steel T-section beyond
  12 Custom composite beam
  13 Steel T-section beyond
  14 Custom composite beam

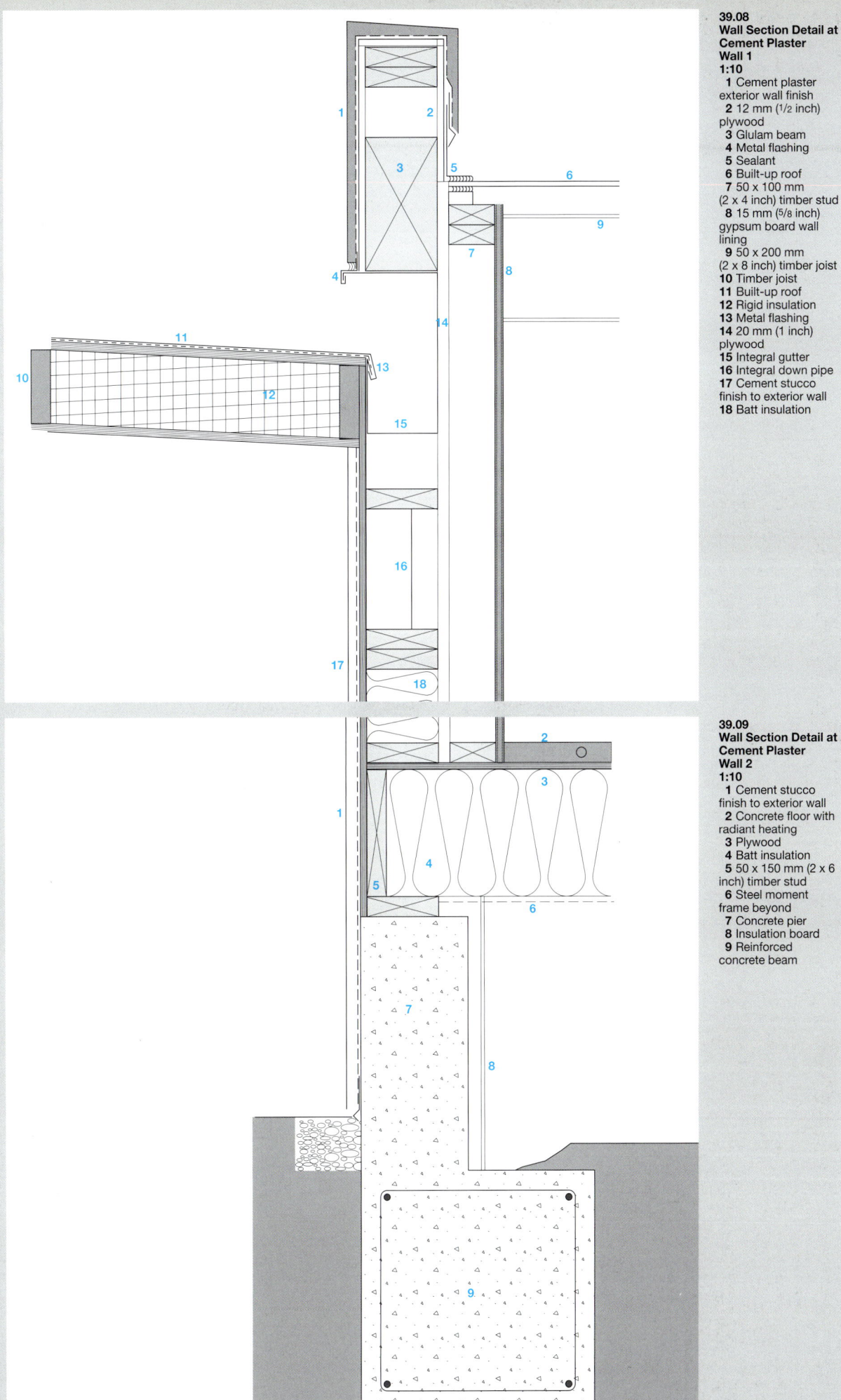

39.08
Wall Section Detail at Cement Plaster Wall 1
1:10
 1 Cement plaster exterior wall finish
 2 12 mm (1/2 inch) plywood
 3 Glulam beam
 4 Metal flashing
 5 Sealant
 6 Built-up roof
 7 50 x 100 mm (2 x 4 inch) timber stud
 8 15 mm (5/8 inch) gypsum board wall lining
 9 50 x 200 mm (2 x 8 inch) timber joist
 10 Timber joist
 11 Built-up roof
 12 Rigid insulation
 13 Metal flashing
 14 20 mm (1 inch) plywood
 15 Integral gutter
 16 Integral down pipe
 17 Cement stucco finish to exterior wall
 18 Batt insulation

39.09
Wall Section Detail at Cement Plaster Wall 2
1:10
 1 Cement stucco finish to exterior wall
 2 Concrete floor with radiant heating
 3 Plywood
 4 Batt insulation
 5 50 x 150 mm (2 x 6 inch) timber stud
 6 Steel moment frame beyond
 7 Concrete pier
 8 Insulation board
 9 Reinforced concrete beam

Bamboo Wall House
Badaling, Beijing, China

Client
SOHO China Ltd.

Area
716 square metres (7,707 square feet)

Structural Engineer
ARUP China

Landscape Design
Rocco Landscape Design

The Commune by the Great Wall is a private collection of contemporary architecture on a spectacular site near the Great Wall of China. The architect was inspired by the seamless nature of the Great Wall of China that forms one of the boundaries to the Commune site. The monolithic structure of the wall nonetheless sits delicately on a virtually unadulterated topography, so that any variations in height and direction are absorbed rather than flattened to accommodate the structure. Kuma takes the same approach, placing the house carefully over a dip in the ground and allowing the landscape to continue uninterrupted.

The residence is arranged over two levels, with living, dining, kitchen and four guestrooms on the upper level, and additional guest rooms and staff quarters below. The centrepiece of the house is a ceremonial space known as the Bamboo Lounge, reached via bridges across a reflecting pool and surrounded by a veil of bamboo. The use of bamboo as the primary building material arose from a keen desire to utilize local building methods to create a recognizably Chinese architectural language. Taking into account the inherent rawness of bamboo as a construction material, and the fact that it was not used locally for anything other than scaffolding, Kuma worked with the local builders to develop a simple method of construction that would enhance its natural qualities. Used throughout the house for flooring, walls, exterior cladding, sliding shutters and sun shades, bamboo here bridges the gap between the sophistication of the architecture and the robustness of the natural landscape.

1 Sittling lightly over a small dip in the natural topography, the bamboo facades further contribute to an impression of lightness and delicateness, in contrast with the drama of the forested mountains surrounding the site.
2 In the centre of the house, the Bamboo Lounge is sheltered by a ceiling of bamboo and surmounted by a glass roof to let in natural light and the changing moods of the sky above.
3 A simple bench in the Bamboo Lounge suggests the perfect place from which to contemplate dramatic views of the mountains, seen between and through veils of vertical bamboo curtains.
4 View of the kitchen and dining room (half a level below), separated by a simple screen of bamboo shafts.

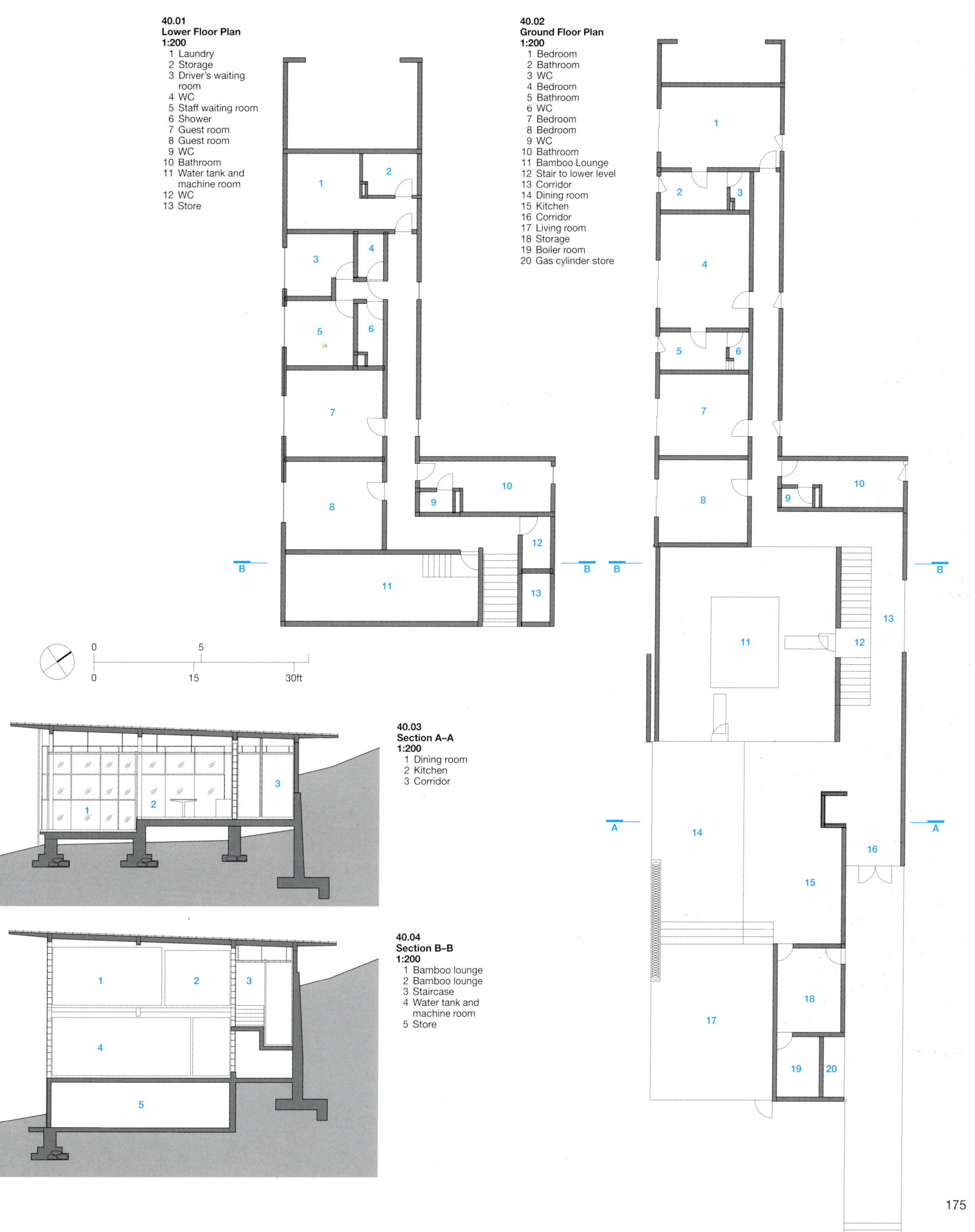

40.01
Lower Floor Plan
1:200
1 Laundry
2 Storage
3 Driver's waiting room
4 WC
5 Staff waiting room
6 Shower
7 Guest room
8 Guest room
9 WC
10 Bathroom
11 Water tank and machine room
12 WC
13 Store

40.02
Ground Floor Plan
1:200
1 Bedroom
2 Bathroom
3 WC
4 Bedroom
5 Bathroom
6 WC
7 Bedroom
8 Bedroom
9 WC
10 Bathroom
11 Bamboo Lounge
12 Stair to lower level
13 Corridor
14 Dining room
15 Kitchen
16 Corridor
17 Living room
18 Storage
19 Boiler room
20 Gas cylinder store

40.03
Section A–A
1:200
1 Dining room
2 Kitchen
3 Corridor

40.04
Section B–B
1:200
1 Bamboo lounge
2 Bamboo lounge
3 Staircase
4 Water tank and machine room
5 Store

0   5
0   15   30ft

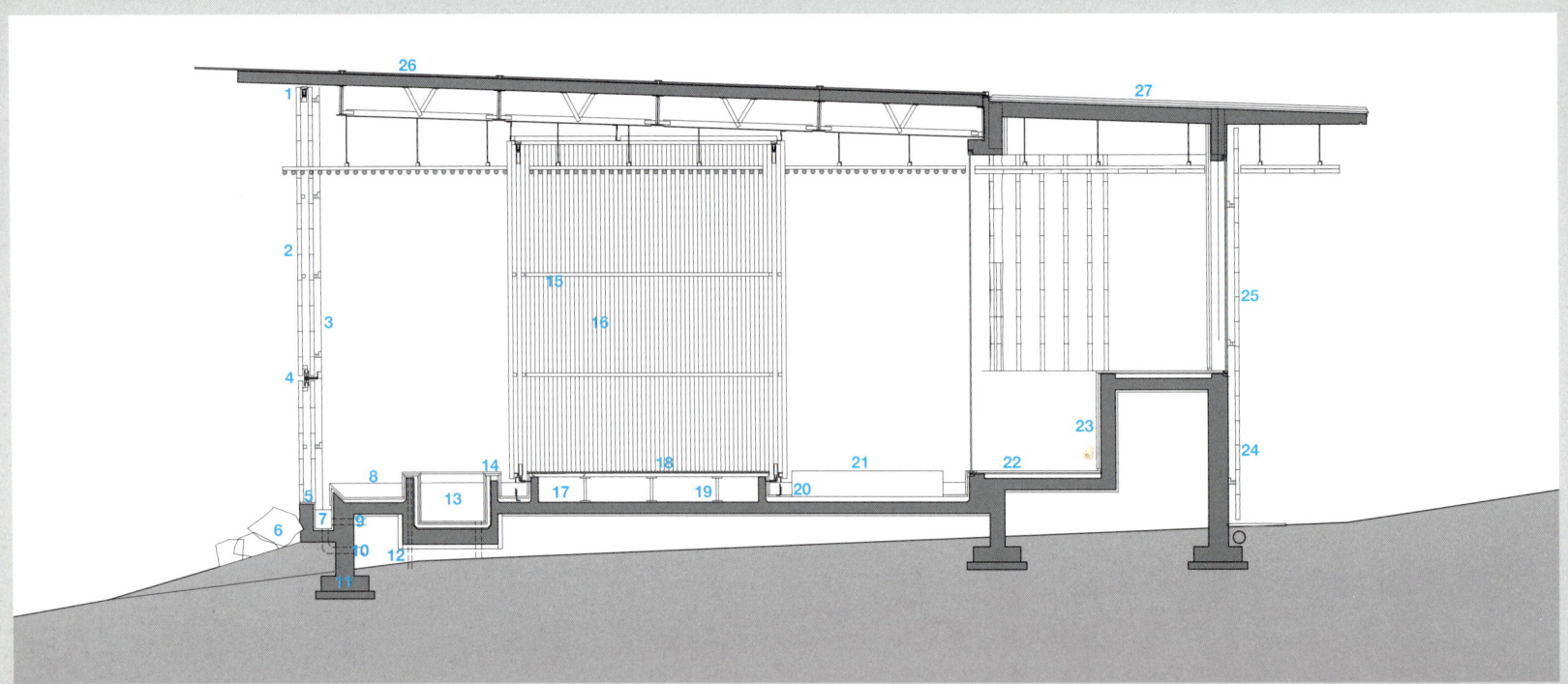

40.05
Detail Section Through Bamboo Lounge
1:100
1 Sliding rail for bamboo screen
2 Sliding bamboo partition with sliding top rail
3 Exposed fixed

bamboo wall on 45 x 45 mm (1³/₄ x 1³/₄ inch) timber furring strips
4 Black painted stainless steel guide rail
5 Black painted stainless steel guide rail
6 Exposed stone wall

7 Waterproof mortar to pool drain
8 Water surface
9 Service pipe
10 Drain pipe
11 Continuous footing over binding concrete and broken stone sub-surface
12 Service pipe
13 Bath with

underwater light, local slate finish to interior surface on mortar bed, mesh metal and asphalt waterproof membrane
14 Local slate bath surround on timber frame
15 45 x 45 mm (1³/₄ x 1³/₄ inch) timber furring

strips
16 Sliding bamboo partition
17 Lighting fixture
18 30 mm (1¹/₅ inch) diameter exposed bamboo flooring
19 Timber floor joists and raised floor structure over concrete slab sloped for

drainage over polysthylene foam insulation
20 Guide rail mounted on stainless steel plate
21 Granite stone on mortar setting bed over asphalt waterproof membrane
22 Local slate floor over structural

plywood base
23 Rice paper wall finish over plasterboard and polysthylene foam insulation
24 Exposed bamboo louvre wall over paint finished concrete wall
25 Exposed bamboo louvre wall over

tempered glass wall
26 Laminated tempered glass roof on structural steel frame
27 Fluorine resin treated metal roofing with standing seams over polysthylene insulation and asphalt waterproof membrane

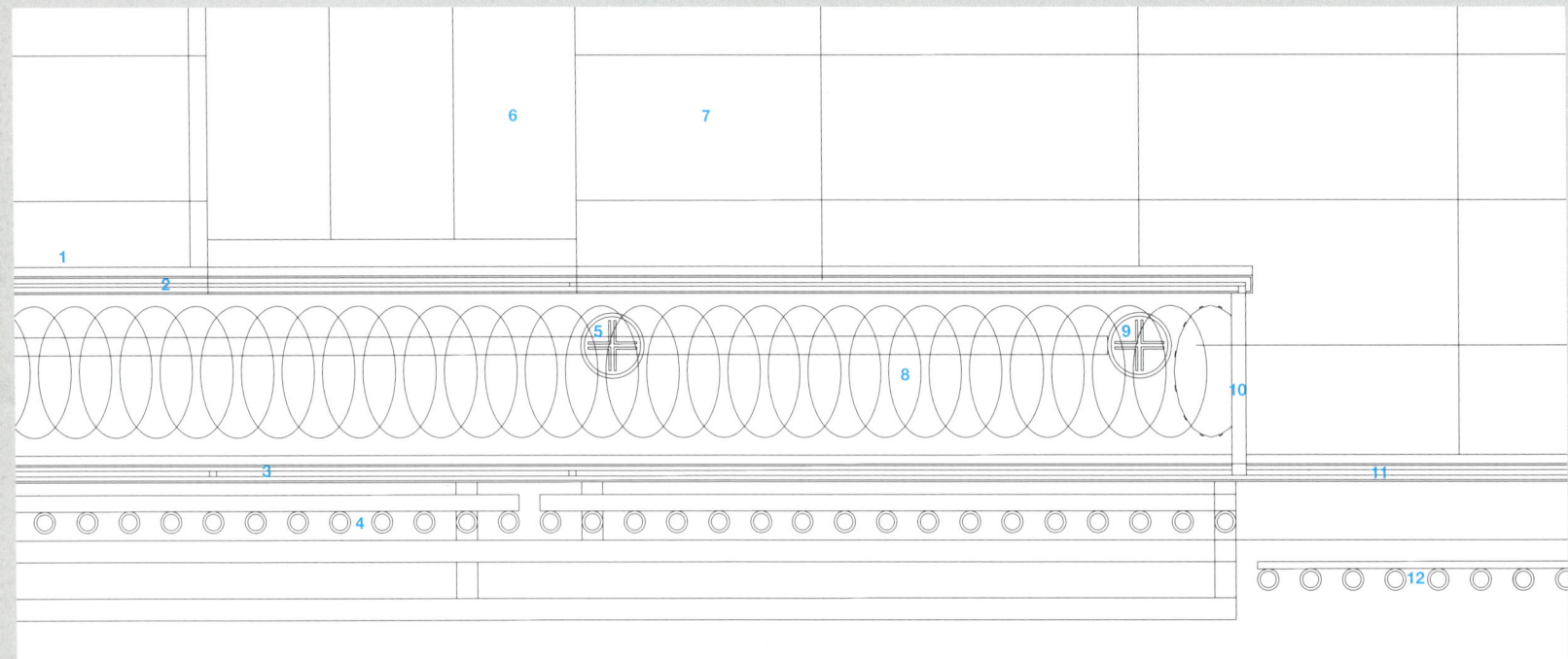

40.06
Bamboo Wall Detail
1:20
1 Water condensation drain
2 Tempered glass
3 Tempered glass
4 Exposed fixed bamboo louvre
5 Exposed bamboo column

6 Local slate floor finish over structural mortar
7 Local slate floor finish over structural mortar
8 Domestic duck feather down insulation
9 Exposed bamboo column

10 Structural plywood wrapped in rice paper
11 Tempered glass
12 Sliding bamboo partition

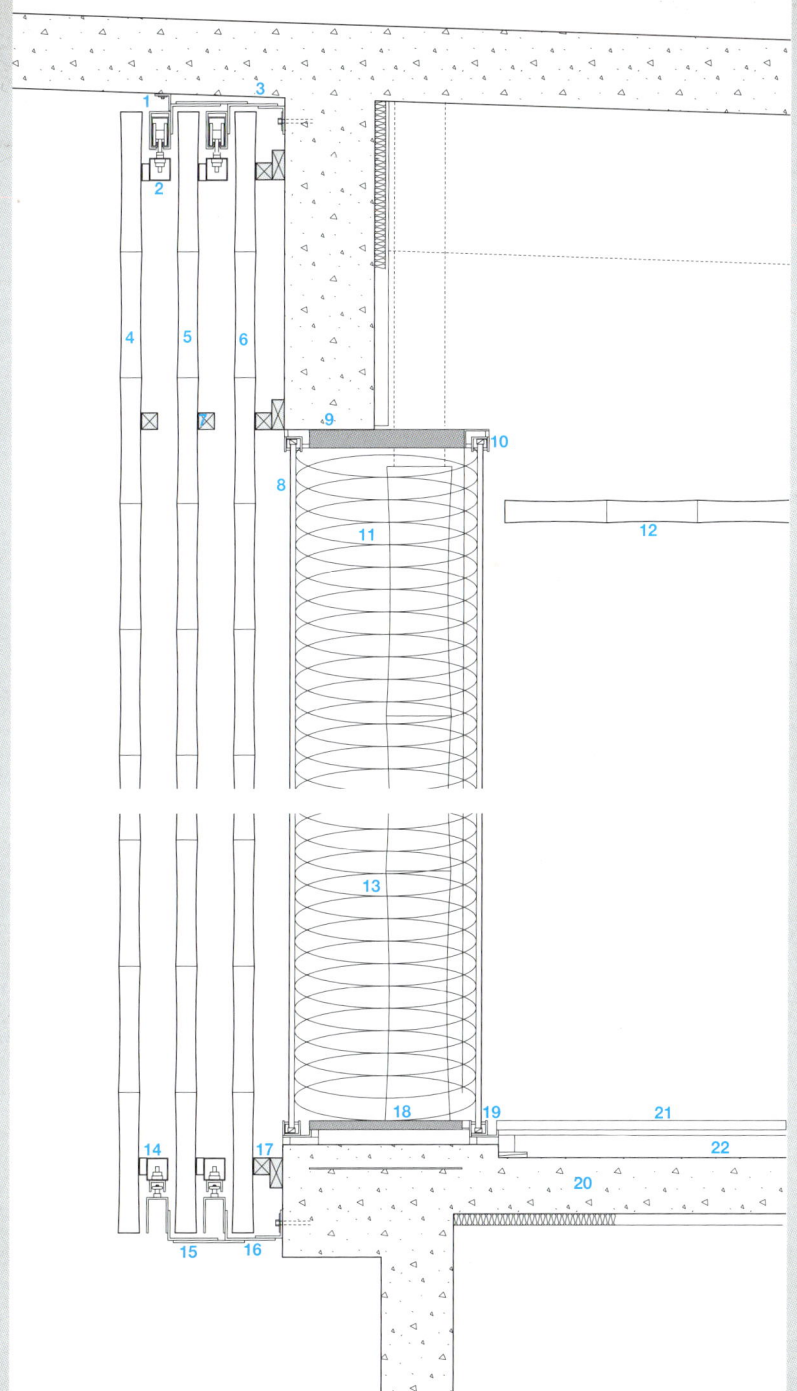

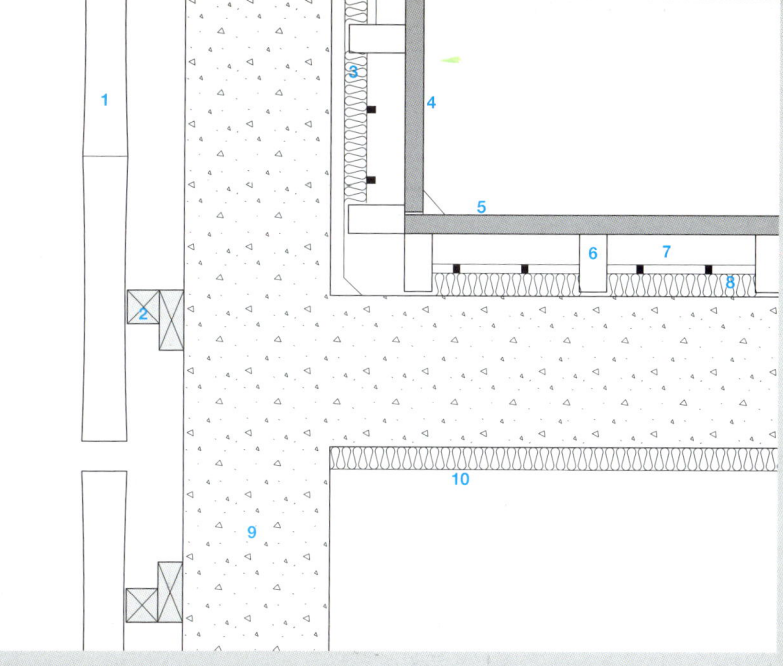

40.08
Bamboo Cladding
Detail
1:10
1 Fixed bamboo screen
2 45 x 45 mm (1³/₄ x 1³/₄ inch) timber furring strips with corrosion proof treatment
3 Insulation
4 Gypsum board with rice paper finish
5 Parquetry bamboo flooring
6 Concrete joist
7 Under floor heating on mortar bed
8 Insulation
9 Reinforced concrete structure
10 Rice paper ceiling finish

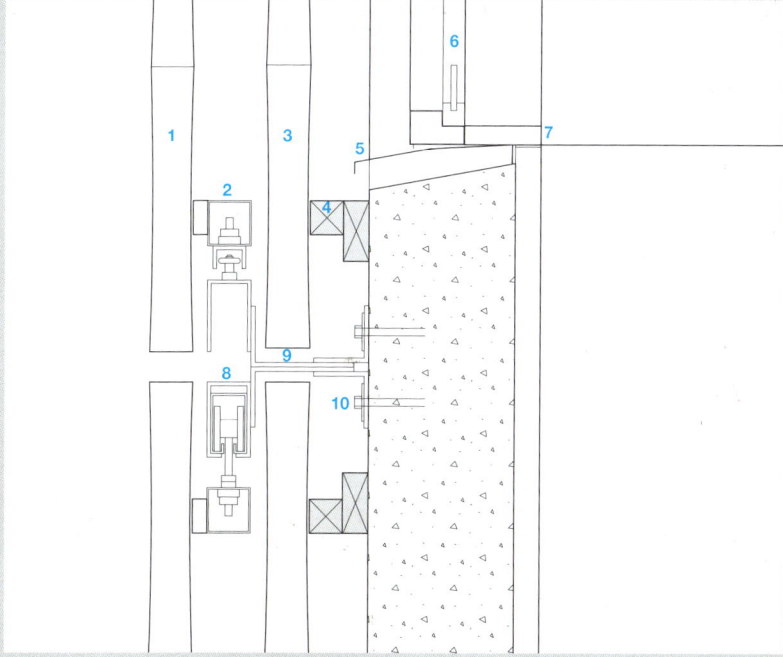

40.07
Bamboo Facade
Detail
1:20
1 Steel angle with paint finish
2 Stainless steel hanger rail with paint finish
3 Continuous steel angle with paint finish
4 Sliding bamboo partition
5 Sliding bamboo partition
6 Exposed fixed bamboo louvre
7 45 x 45 mm (1³/₄ x 1³/₄ inch) timber furring strips with corrosion proof treatment
8 Tempered glass
9 Structural plywood wrapped in rice paper
10 Stainless steel sash
11 Domestic duck feather and down
12 Ceiling
13 Exposed bamboo column

14 Stainless steel guide rail with paint finish
15 Steel flat bar with paint finish
16 Steel angle with paint finish
17 45 x 45 mm (1³/₄ x 1³/₄ inch) timber furring strips with corrosion proof treatment
18 Structural plywood wrapped in rice paper
19 Water condensation drain
20 Reinforced concrete floor
21 Slate stone floor on structural mortar
22 60 mm (2¹/₃ inch) clearance for floor heating

40.09
Window Detail
1:10
1 Sliding bamboo partition
2 Paint finished stainless steel guide rail
3 Fixed bamboo partition
4 45 x 45 mm (1³/₄ x 1³/₄ inch) timber furring strips with corrosion proof treatment
5 Window sill
6 Glazing assembly

7 Gypsum board with rice paper finish
8 Stainless steel hanger rail with paint finish
9 Steel angle with paint finish
10 75 x 75 mm (3 x 3 inch) continuous steel angle

Martín + Martín Arquitectos

La Vega House
Granada, Spain

Client
Eduardo Martín Martín, Olimpia
Gómez Rivero

Area
100 square metres (1,076 square feet)

Project Team
Eduardo Martín Martín, Luis Javier
Martín Martín

Builder
Gabriel Vallejo S.L.

The fertile plains known as Granada Vega that stretch out to the west of Granada have long supported the city through agriculture, and are protected as a site of historical significance. The new house is situated on the ruins of an old agricultural building and, according to local planning laws, was limited to the volume of the tobacco store it replaced. This limited the habitable space to 75 square metres (805 square feet) over a single storey. Charged with producing a house with no wasted space, without clutter and that is sympathetic to the local vernacular, the result is an elegant, symmetrical building that sits comfortably in the landscape.

To achieve this, all circulation space was eliminated and the available space was divided into three equal zones. The living space occupies the central zone. To the north-west end of the living room are the two bedrooms, while to the south-east, one side accommodates the bathroom and the other the kitchen and dining room. Each of these auxiliary spaces comes complete with generous storage, allowing the living area to remain clear of clutter. With the exception of one window, every opening on the exterior of the house is a door, making it possible to access the exterior directly from any room in the house. The structure is clad in black poplar, the same timber used for the original building, and left to age and fade naturally to a dull silver. The timber extends beyond the boundary of the building into a series of decks on the north-west and south-west edges, to provide a transition space between the privacy of the house and the open plain of the Vega.

1 A single large opening in the north-west facade opens onto an expansive deck. The remainder of the house is lit from above via a skylight protected by established trees.

2 During winter the deciduous trees allow light and warmth into the house.

3 and 4 The dark timber is left untreated and will fade to a silvery grey in time. The same material is used for the deck which appears to float in a number of staggered planes above the lawn.

5 The same timber is used on the interior, where a natural varnish gives it a warmth that complements the otherwise white finishes.

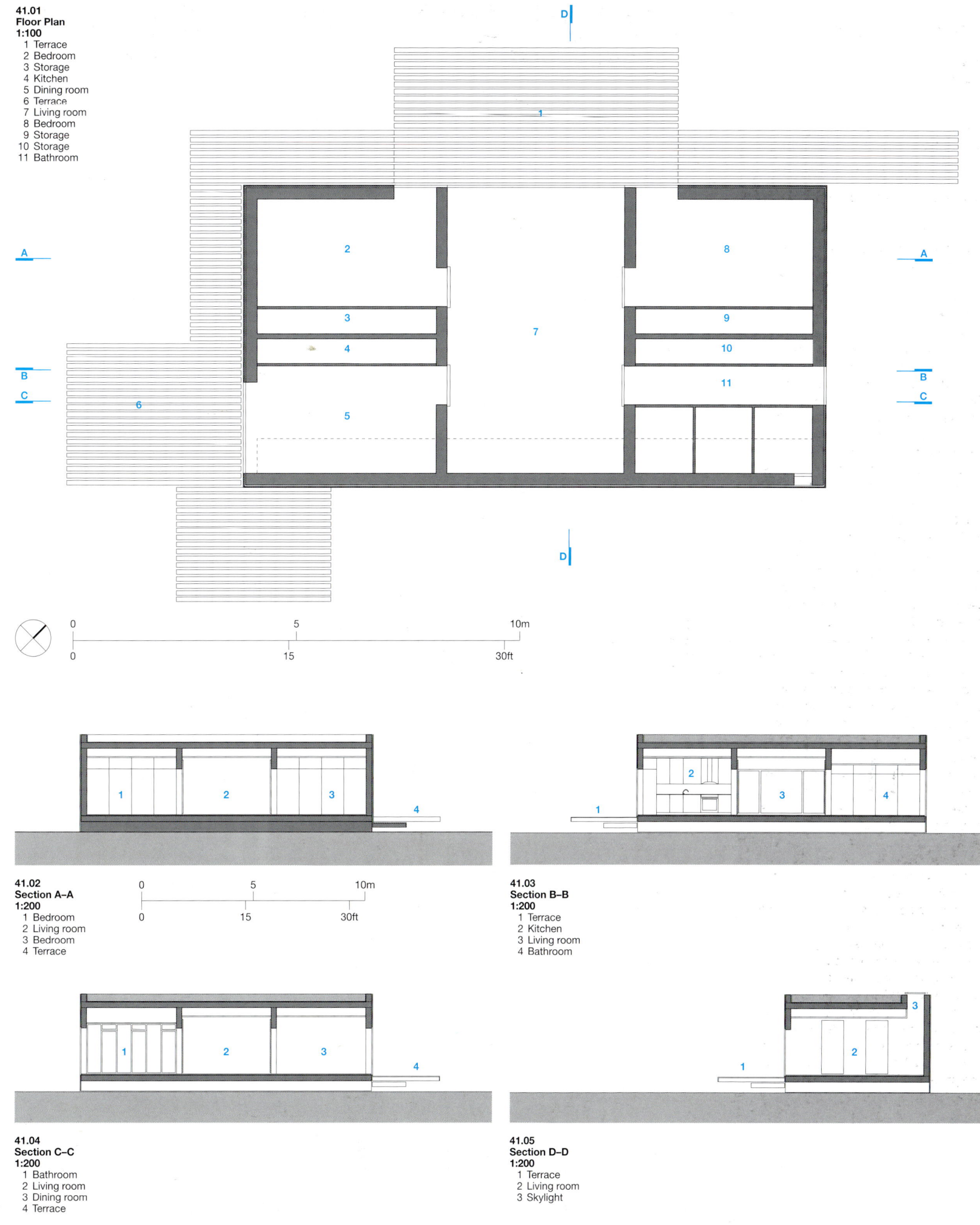

41.01
Floor Plan
1:100
1 Terrace
2 Bedroom
3 Storage
4 Kitchen
5 Dining room
6 Terrace
7 Living room
8 Bedroom
9 Storage
10 Storage
11 Bathroom

41.02
Section A–A
1:200
1 Bedroom
2 Living room
3 Bedroom
4 Terrace

41.03
Section B–B
1:200
1 Terrace
2 Kitchen
3 Living room
4 Bathroom

41.04
Section C–C
1:200
1 Bathroom
2 Living room
3 Dining room
4 Terrace

41.05
Section D–D
1:200
1 Terrace
2 Living room
3 Skylight

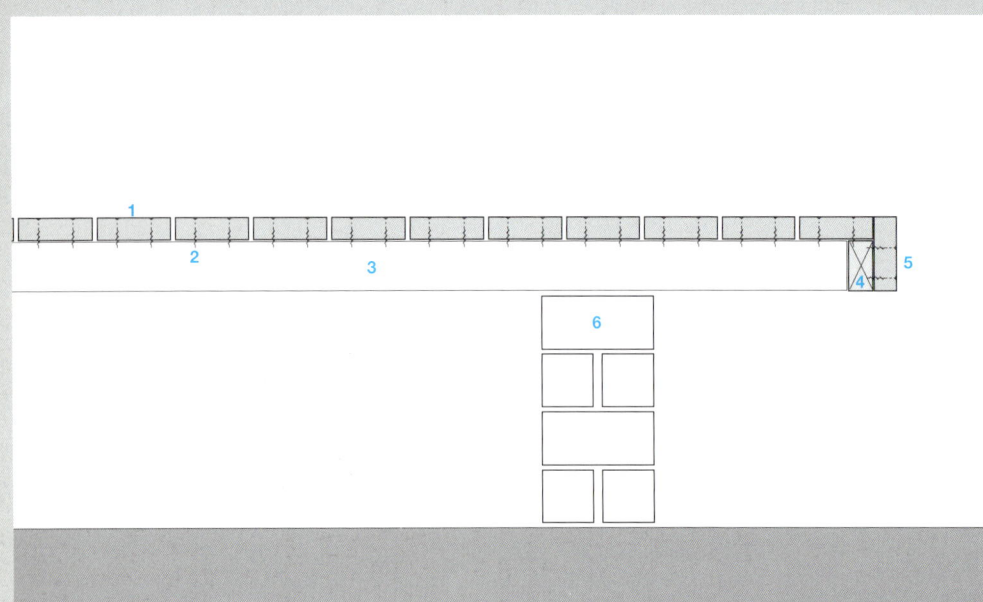

41.06
Terrace Detail
1:15
1 150 x 45 mm (6 x 1³/₄ inch) black poplar decking
2 60 mm (2¹/₃ inch) self-tapping screw
3 100 x 60 x 4 mm (4 x 2¹/₃ x ¹/₁₀ inch) steel beam
4 100 x 50 x 3 mm (4 x 2 x ¹/₁₀ inch) steel beam
5 Black poplar timber to edge of terrace
6 230 x 100 x 100 mm (9 x 4 x 4 inch) brick supporting pier

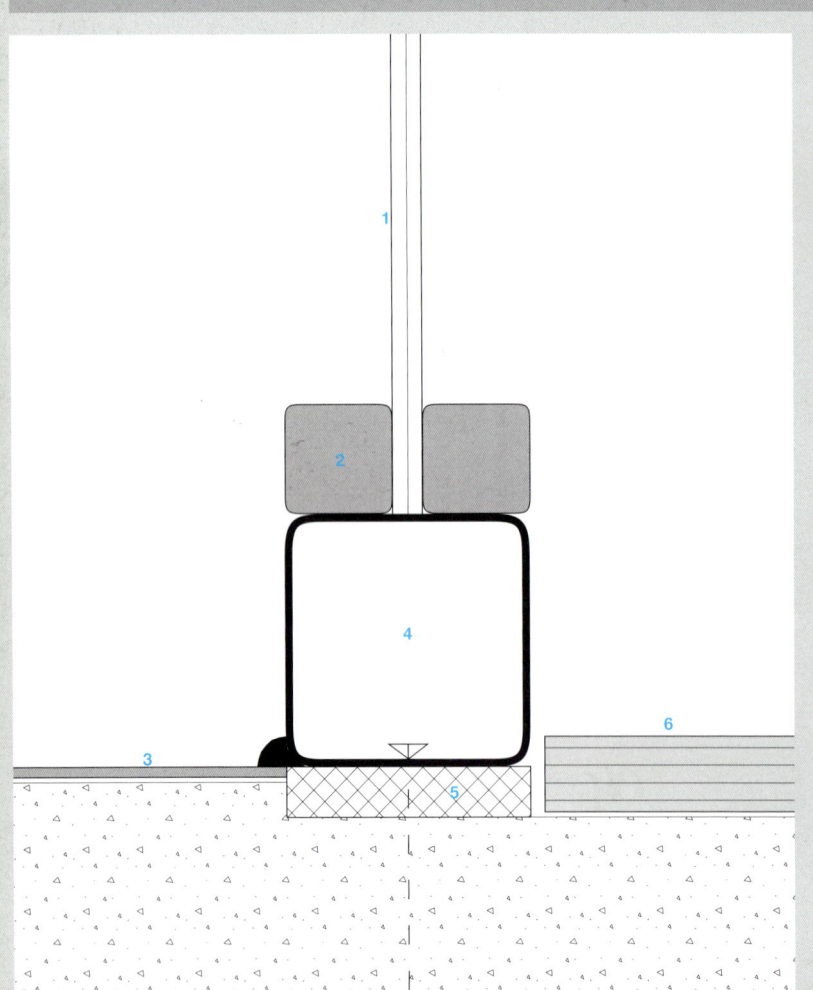

41.07
Glazing Detail
1:1.5
1 6 mm (¹/₁₀ inch) thick clear glazing
2 22 x 22 mm (⁴/₅ inch) steel bar
3 2 mm (¹/₁₂ inch) stainless steel slab
4 50 x 50 x 3 mm (2 x 2 x ¹/₁₂ inch) steel tube

5 50 x 10 mm (2 x ²/₅ inch) rubber
6 15 mm thick (³/₅ inch) mekoy timber parquetry

41.08
External Wall Detail
1:4
1 2 mm (¹/₁₂ inch) thick aluminium slab
2 25 mm (1 inch) thick fine mortar bed
3 230 x 100 x 100 mm (9 x 4 x 4 inch) brick
4 50 mm (2 inch)

thick insulation and 50 x 50 x 3 mm (2 x 2 x ¹/₁₂ inch) steel tube
5 40 mm (1¹/₂ inch) self-tapping screw
6 150 x 20 mm (6 x ³/₄ inch) black poplar cladding

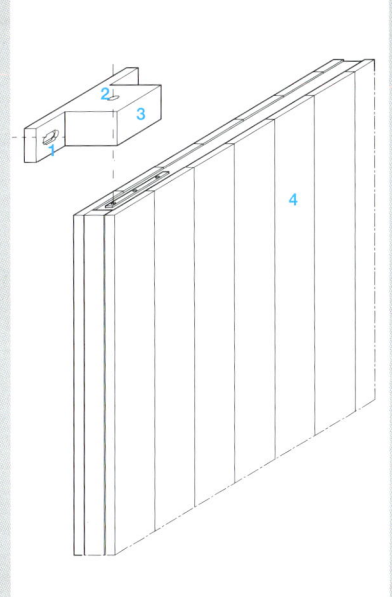

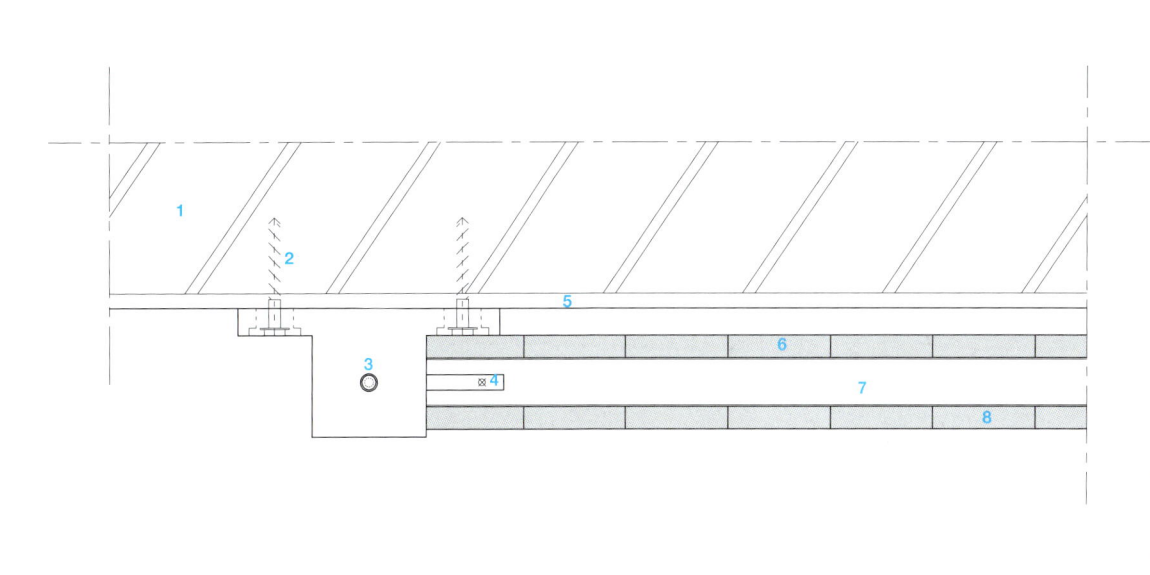

41.09
Interior Door Detail 1
1 Screw gap
2 Axis of hinge
3 Prefabricated
bronze hinge
mechanism
4 Mekoy-clad interior
door panel

41.10
Interior Door Detail 2
1:5
1 230 x 100 x 100
mm (9 x 4 x 4 inch)
brick
2 78 mm (3 inch) M14
screw
3 Prefabricated
bronze hinge element
4 3 mm ($^1/_{12}$ inch)
steel strip
5 10 mm ($^2/_5$ inch)
white plaster
6 15 mm thick ($^3/_5$
inch) mekoy timber
parquetry
7 Timber frame
8 15 mm thick ($^3/_5$
inch) mekoy timber
parquetry

41.11
Interior Door Detail 3
1:5
1 230 x 100 x 100
mm (9 x 4 x 4 inch)
brick
2 10 mm ($^2/_5$ inch)
white plaster
3 Layer of 70 x 15
mm ($2^3/_4$ x $^3/_5$ inch)
parquetry
4 Prefabricated
bronze hinge element
5 Layer of 70 x 15
mm ($2^3/_4$ x $^3/_5$ inch)
parquetry
6 Timber frame
7 Layer of 70 x 15
mm ($2^3/_4$ x $^3/_5$ inch)
parquetry

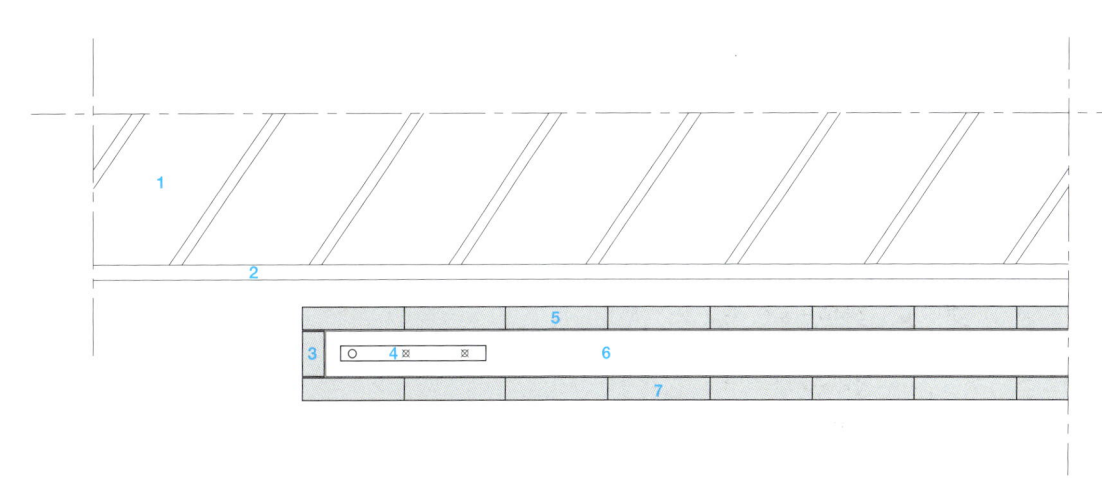

41.12
Interior Door Detail 4
1:5
1 230 x 100 x 100
mm (9 x 4 x 4 inch)
brick
2 10 mm ($^2/_5$ inch)
white plaster
3 Layer of 70 x 15
mm ($2^3/_4$ x $^3/_5$ inch)
parquetry
4 20 mm ($^3/_4$ inch)
diameter steel bar
5 Layer of 70 x 15
mm ($2^3/_4$ x $^3/_5$ inch)
parquetry
6 Timber frame
7 Layer of 70 x 15
mm ($2^3/_4$ x $^3/_5$ inch)
parquetry

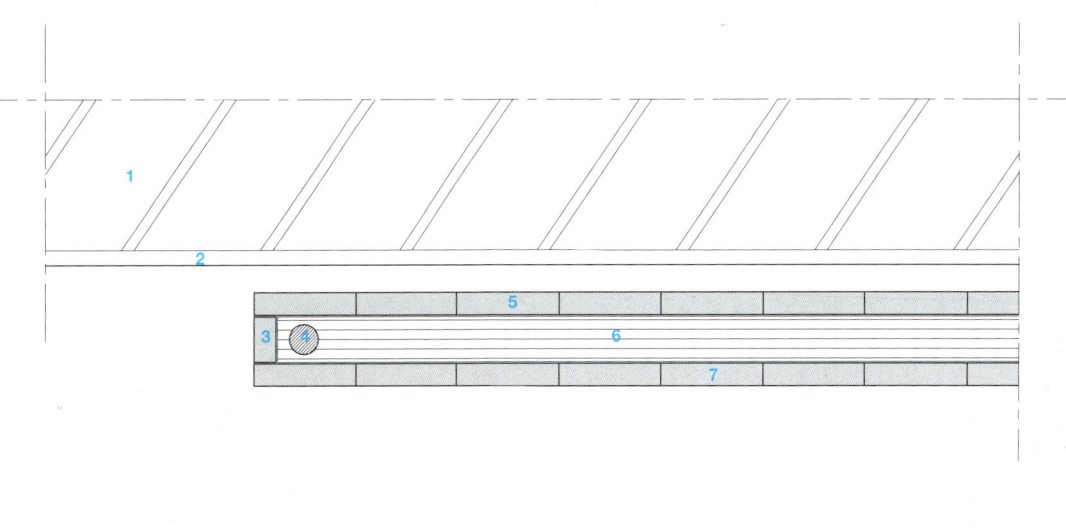

Agosta House
San Juan Island,
Washington, USA

Area
258 square metres (2,775 square feet)

Structural Engineer
Fast + Epp Structural Engineers

Builder
Ravenhill Construction

The Agosta House was designed for a couple relocating from Manhattan to San Juan Island, a small, largely rural location off the Pacific coast in Washington State. In addition to conventional domestic requirements, the programme includes an office, in which the couple intend to continue their professional work, and a garden enclosed within a tall fence to protect it from the wild deer. The site is largely covered by second-growth Douglas Fir forest, four hectares (ten acres) of which have been dedicated to a perpetual conservation easement. The house itself is situated on a grassed meadow, enclosed on three sides by the forest, but open to the north-west where it overlooks rolling fields below and, beyond, the Haro Strait and the gulf islands of British Columbia. The house is stretched across the ridge of the meadow dividing the site into an enclosed forecourt to the south-east, and an expansive panorama of picturesque fields and waterways to the northwest.

The sloped walls and roof of the battered building section respond to the gentle, but steady, slope of the site. The spatial organization of the house is the result of extruding this simple section and manipulating it either by erosion to create exterior in-between spaces which subdivide the house programmatically into general planning zones or by inserting non-structural bulkheads that organize the interior into finer spatial areas. The structure consists of a combination of exposed fir framing and conventional stud work clad in painted gypsum board founded on a concrete slab. The exterior is largely clad in light gauge galvanized sheet steel which not only protects the structure from the weather, but also addresses the possibility of wildfire in an area not well served by fire fighters.

1 A large timber fence to the south-east describes a protected courtyard within an extensive fir forest that surrounds the meadow on which the house sits.
2 The sloping roof responds to the fall of the site, while exposed timber elements reflect the local provenance of the construction materials.
3 Parts of the building are cut away to create intimate outdoor spaces protected by large roof overhangs.
4 The meadow continues right up to the house. Commanding views of the spectacular countryside are availble throughout the house.
5 The robust timber construction is left exposed where it contrasts with the pristine white-painted wall surfaces and large expanses of glass.

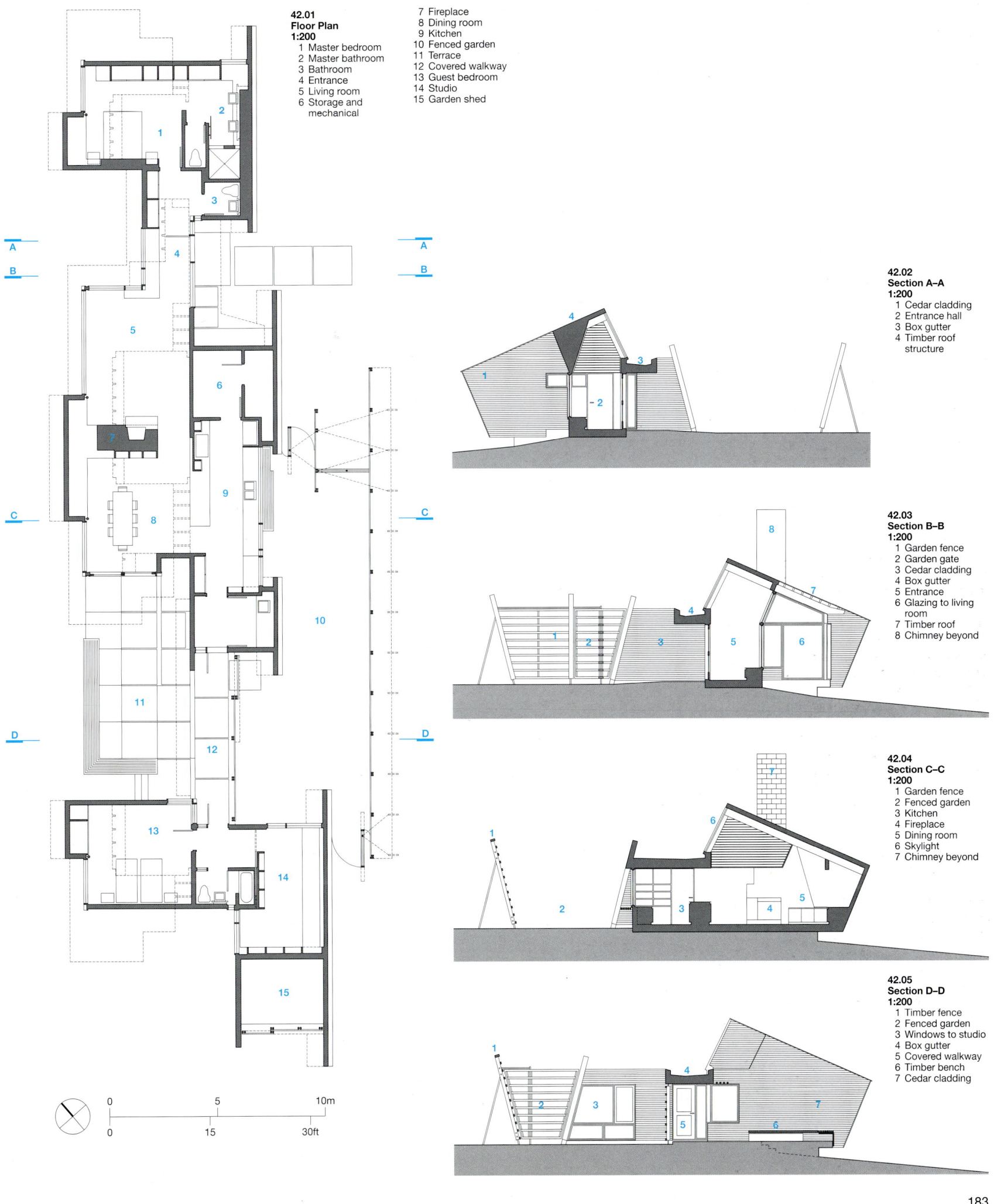

42.01
Floor Plan
1:200
1 Master bedroom
2 Master bathroom
3 Bathroom
4 Entrance
5 Living room
6 Storage and
  mechanical
7 Fireplace
8 Dining room
9 Kitchen
10 Fenced garden
11 Terrace
12 Covered walkway
13 Guest bedroom
14 Studio
15 Garden shed

42.02
Section A–A
1:200
1 Cedar cladding
2 Entrance hall
3 Box gutter
4 Timber roof
  structure

42.03
Section B–B
1:200
1 Garden fence
2 Garden gate
3 Cedar cladding
4 Box gutter
5 Entrance
6 Glazing to living
  room
7 Timber roof
8 Chimney beyond

42.04
Section C–C
1:200
1 Garden fence
2 Fenced garden
3 Kitchen
4 Fireplace
5 Dining room
6 Skylight
7 Chimney beyond

42.05
Section D–D
1:200
1 Timber fence
2 Fenced garden
3 Windows to studio
4 Box gutter
5 Covered walkway
6 Timber bench
7 Cedar cladding

0   5   10m
0   15   30ft

183

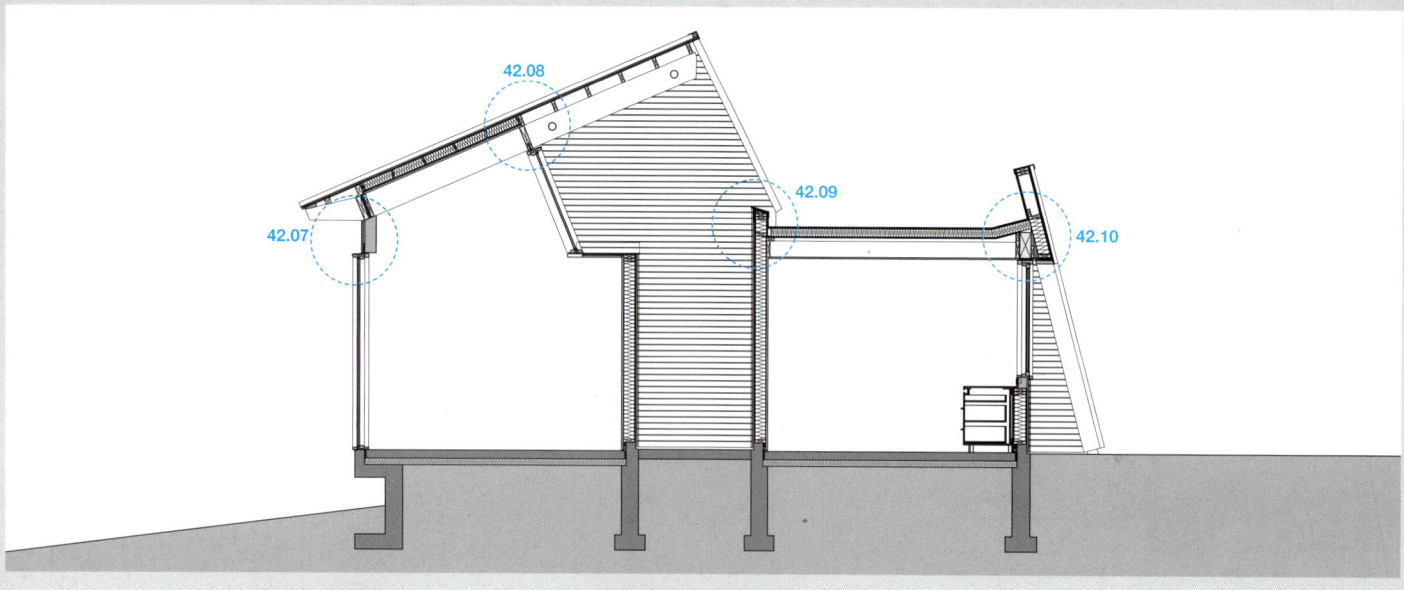

42.06
Sectional Detail
1:100

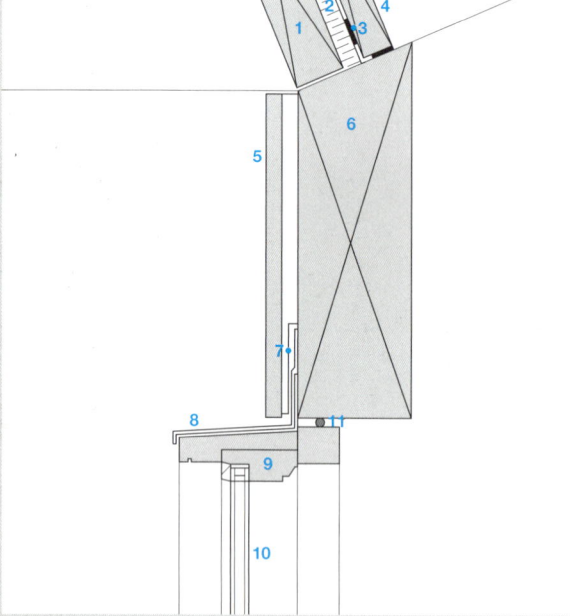

42.07
Eave and Window Detail
1:10
1 Timber blocking
2 Rigid insulation
3 Air vapour barrier
4 Timber blocking
5 Timber fascia
6 Timber beam
7 Membrane flashing
8 Galvanized sheet metal flashing
9 Timber window
10 Insulated double glazing
11 Sealant

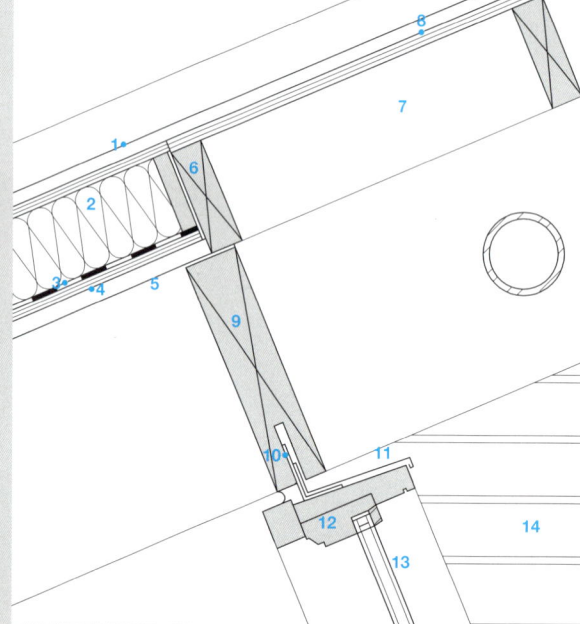

42.08
Roof and Skylight Detail
1:10
1 Galvanized sheet metal roofing
2 Batt insulation
3 Air vapour barrier
4 Plywood sheathing
5 Timber decking
6 Timber blocking
7 Void
8 Timber decking
9 Timber blocking
10 Membrane flashing
11 Galvanized sheet metal flashing
12 Timber window
13 Insulated double glazing
14 Cedar cladding

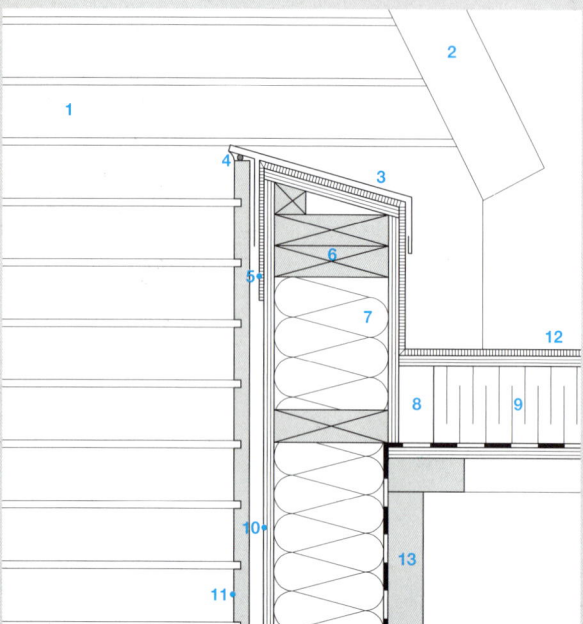

42.09
Roof Parapet Detail
1:10
1 Cedar cladding
2 Aluminium skylight framing
3 Galvanized sheet metal flashing
4 Sealant
5 Membrane flashing
6 Wood framing
7 Batt insulation
8 Timber framing
9 Rigid insulation
10 Plywood sheathing
11 Cedar cladding
12 Roofing membrane
13 Timber framing

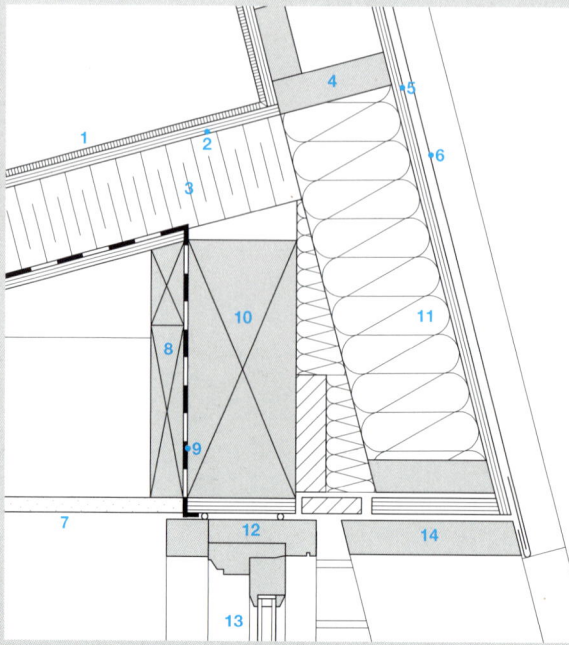

42.10
Roof and Window Detail
1:10
1 Roofing membrane
2 Plywood sheathing
3 Rigid insulation
4 Timber blocking
5 Plywood sheathing
6 Galvanized sheet metal roofing
7 Gypsum board ceiling
8 Timber blocking
9 Air vapour barrier
10 Timber beam
11 Batt insulation
12 Timber window frame
13 Insulated double glazing
14 Timber soffit

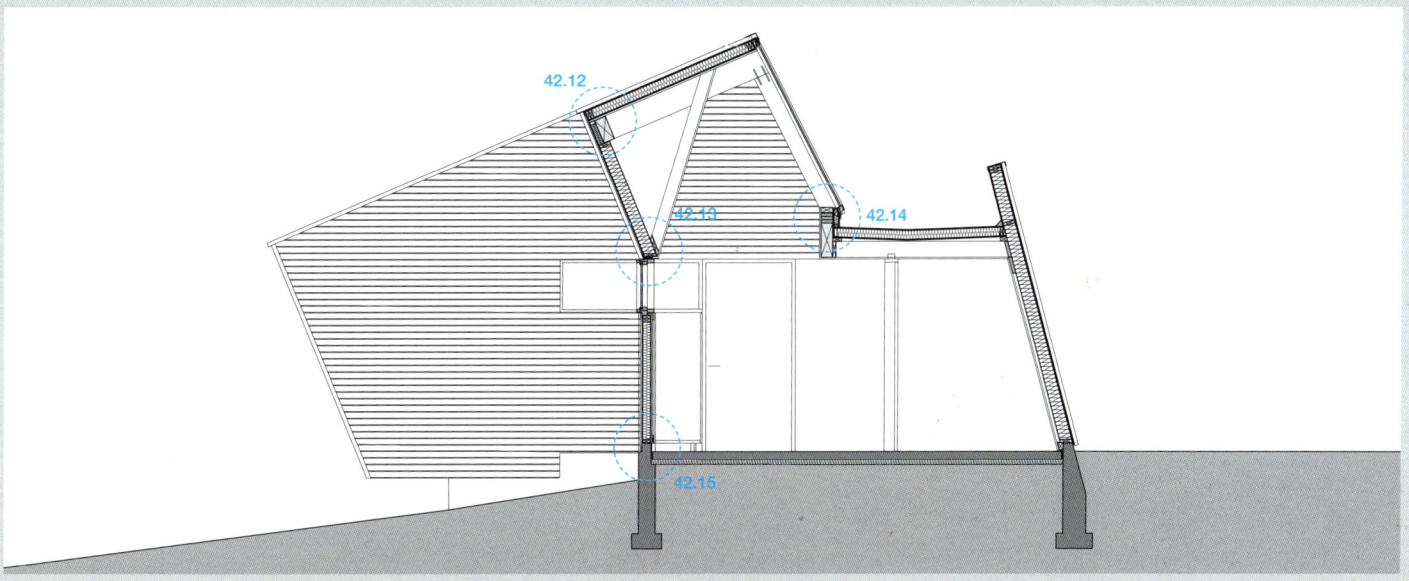

42.11
Sectional Detail
1:100

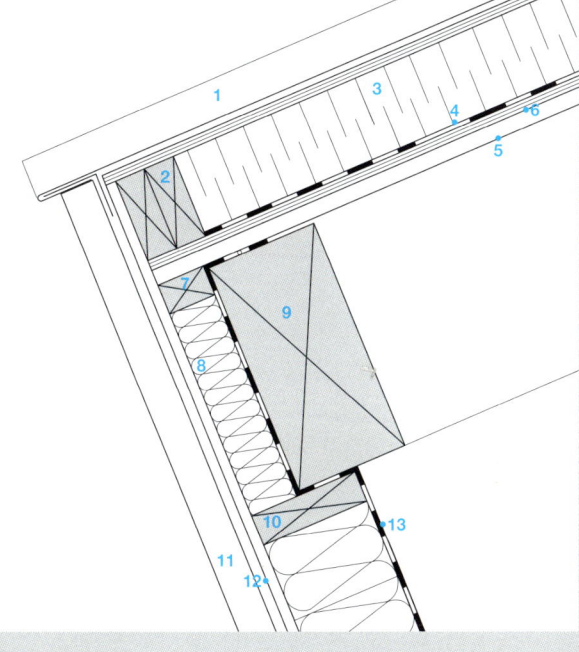

42.12
Roof and Wall Detail
1:10
1 Galvanized sheet
metal roofing
2 Timber blocking
3 Rigid insulation
4 Air vapour barrier
5 Exposed timber
decking
6 Plywood sheathing
7 Timber framing
8 Batt insulation
9 Timber beam
10 Timber framing
11 Galvanized sheet
metal cladding
12 Plywood sheathing
13 Air vapour barrier

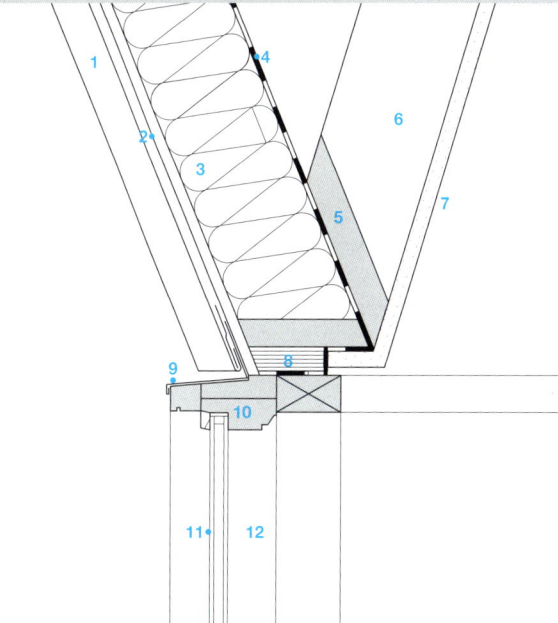

42.13
**Wall and Window
Detail**
1:10
1 Galvanized sheet
metal roofing
2 Plywood sheathing
3 Batt insulation
4 Air vapour barrier
5 Timber framing
6 Timber framing
7 Gypsum wall board
8 Plywood sheathing
9 Galvanized sheet
metal flashing
10 Timber window
11 Insulated double
glazing
12 Timber window

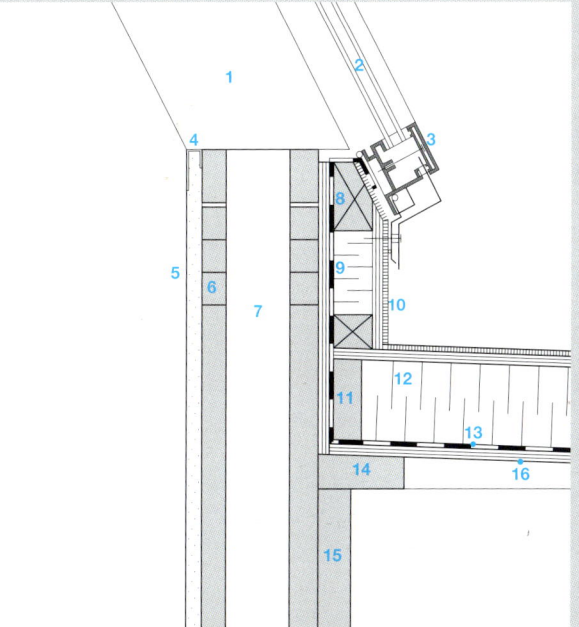

42.14
Skylight Detail
1:10
1 Timber framing
2 Insulated double
glazing
3 Aluminium skylight
framing
4 Gypsum wall board
trim
5 Gypsum wall board
6 Timber framing
7 Timber beam
8 Timber framing
9 Rigid insulation
10 Roofing membrane
11 Timber framing
12 Rigid insulation
13 Air vapour barrier
14 Timber framing
15 Timber framing
16 Plywood sheathing

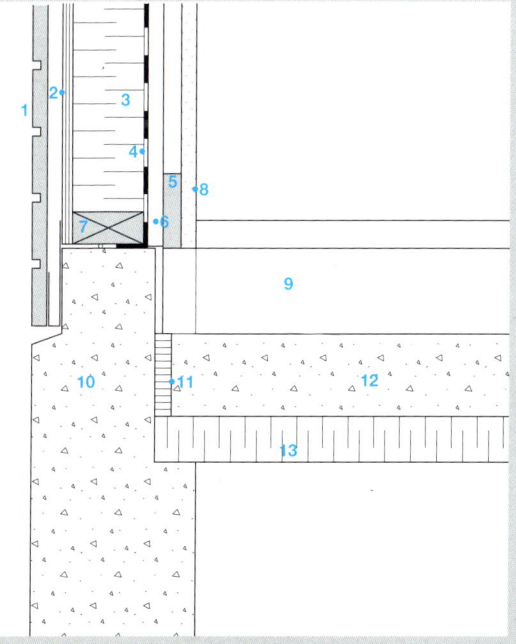

42.15
Wall and Floor Detail
1:10
1 Cedar cladding
2 Plywood sheathing
3 Batt insulation
4 Air vapour barrier
5 Timber blocking
6 Gypsum wall board
7 Timber framing
8 Timber millwork
9 Timber millwork
base
10 Concrete footing
11 Bond breaker
screed
12 Concrete slab
13 Rigid insulation

Verandah House
Sydney, NSW, Australia

Client
Laura and Terry Winder

Area
320 square metres (3,445 square feet)

Project Team
Peter Stutchbury, Sacha Zehnder

Structural Engineer
Professor Max Irvine

General Contractor
Pocklington and Thornton

The Verandah House is located on the edge of a valley, surrounded by a eucalypt forest. In winter the ground is damp and shaded, while in summer the only cooling breezes are at canopy level. The house is a response to site and environmental conditions – the building is lifted off the ground to avoid damp, gather sun and continue an uninterrupted ground plane below. A solid platform has been constructed adjacent to the forest, with a projecting elevated form above. The solid element below acts as a circulation core as well as providing sufficient thermal mass to generate warmth in winter and coolness in summer. The light-weight timber-framed pavilion above is the eponymous 'verandah', the iconic covered outdoor space of Australian architecture, here used as a living platform for all the activities of the house.

A living room takes advantage of the cool canopy of the forest at one end, with the kitchen and dining room at the other, sandwiching three bedrooms and a bathroom in between. On the lower level, a garage and guest accommodation are tucked away. Two staircases rise from ground level giving access to the lower level accommodation at one end and onto the landscaped ground plane at the other. Sun and light are pulled into the main spaces on the upper level via a 'corridor wall', introducing indirect light into the house. This avenue of space collects light, using large plywood blades to selectively reveal and conceal areas of the interior, therefore helping to manage the most difficult climatic challenges.

1 The verandah element is anchored to the ground with timber columns and diagonal steel bracing. Above, a light-weight corrugated steel roof with generous eaves protects the facades from the sun and rain.
2 A series of plywood blades angled along the north facade selectively allow sunlight into the living spaces. These are painted a grey-green to match the surrounding eucalyptus forest.
3 The interior is characterized by timber floors and joinery, with plywood blades running the length of the north facade and the ceiling.
4 Detail view of the blades, interspersed with slots of clear glazing. The angled geometry lends a dynamic repetition to the elongated form. Hardwood timber slats to the lower level enclosure encourage cooling breezes under and through the house.

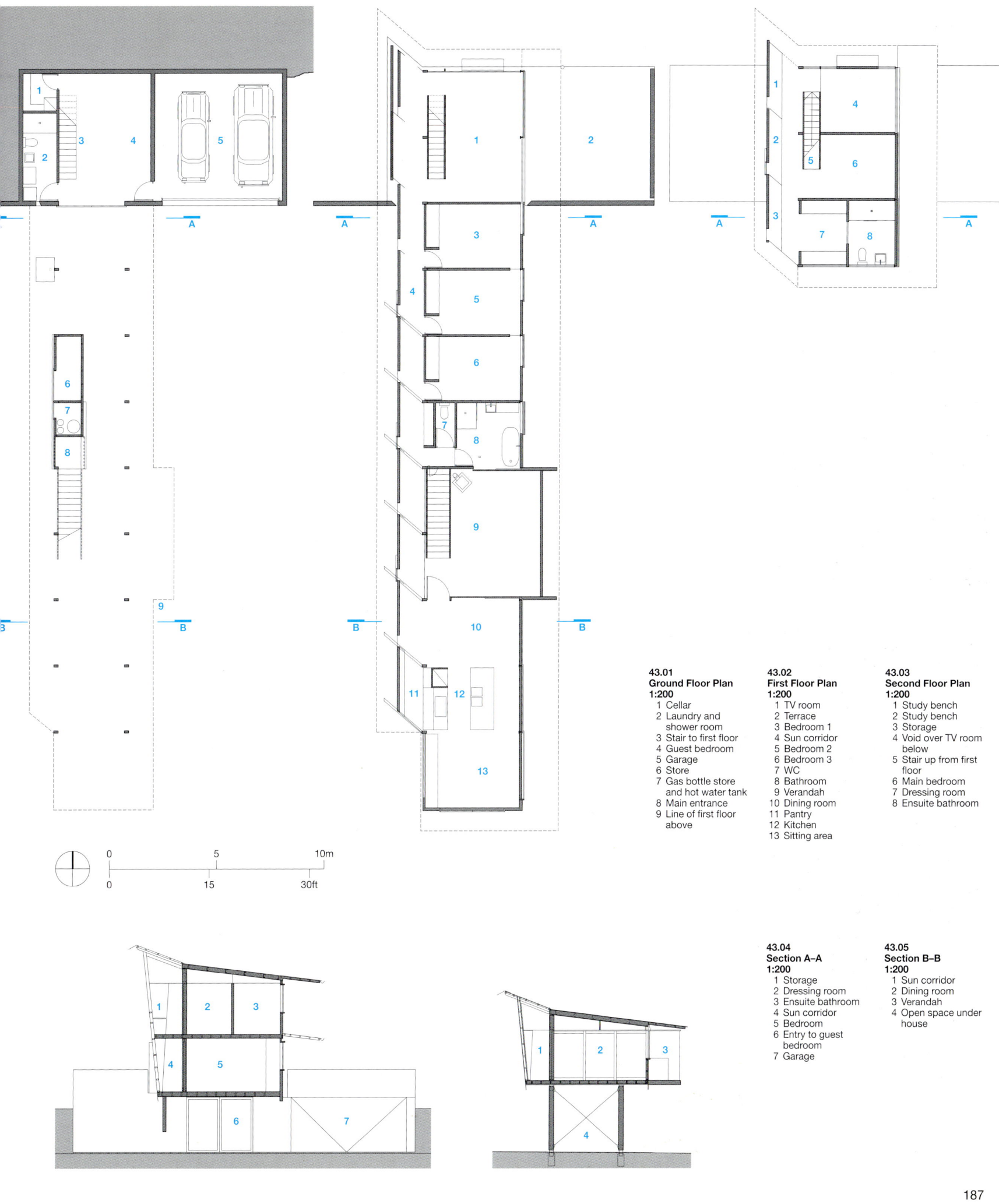

43.01
Ground Floor Plan
1:200
1 Cellar
2 Laundry and
  shower room
3 Stair to first floor
4 Guest bedroom
5 Garage
6 Store
7 Gas bottle store
  and hot water tank
8 Main entrance
9 Line of first floor
  above

43.02
First Floor Plan
1:200
1 TV room
2 Terrace
3 Bedroom 1
4 Sun corridor
5 Bedroom 2
6 Bedroom 3
7 WC
8 Bathroom
9 Verandah
10 Dining room
11 Pantry
12 Kitchen
13 Sitting area

43.03
Second Floor Plan
1:200
1 Study bench
2 Study bench
3 Storage
4 Void over TV room
  below
5 Stair up from first
  floor
6 Main bedroom
7 Dressing room
8 Ensuite bathroom

43.04
Section A–A
1:200
1 Storage
2 Dressing room
3 Ensuite bathroom
4 Sun corridor
5 Bedroom
6 Entry to guest
  bedroom
7 Garage

43.05
Section B–B
1:200
1 Sun corridor
2 Dining room
3 Verandah
4 Open space under
  house

0   5   10m
0   15   30ft

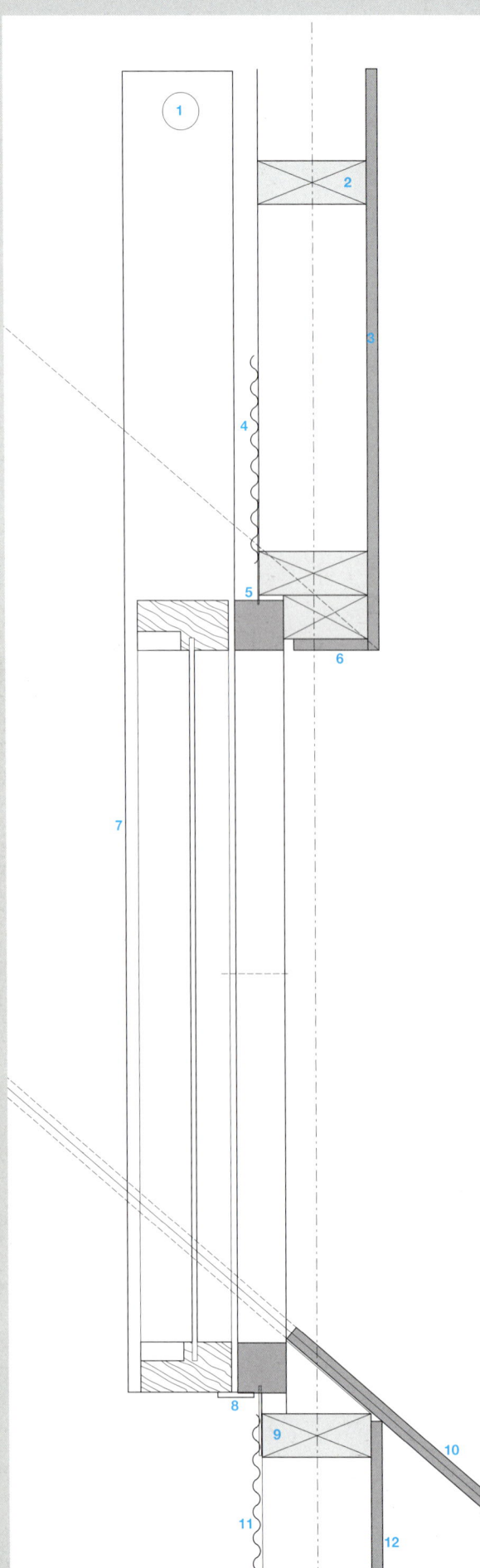

43.06
Sliding Window Plan Detail
1:5
1 Window stopper
2 Timber stud frame
3 Painted plasterboard to interior wall surface
4 Miniorb exterior cladding
5 Saw cut Colorbond flashing to window frame
6 Plasterboard to window corner
7 Hardwood sliding window frame
8 Galvanized flat bar
9 Timber stud frame wall
10 Painted plywood blade
11 Miniorb exterior cladding
12 Painted plasterboard to interior wall surface

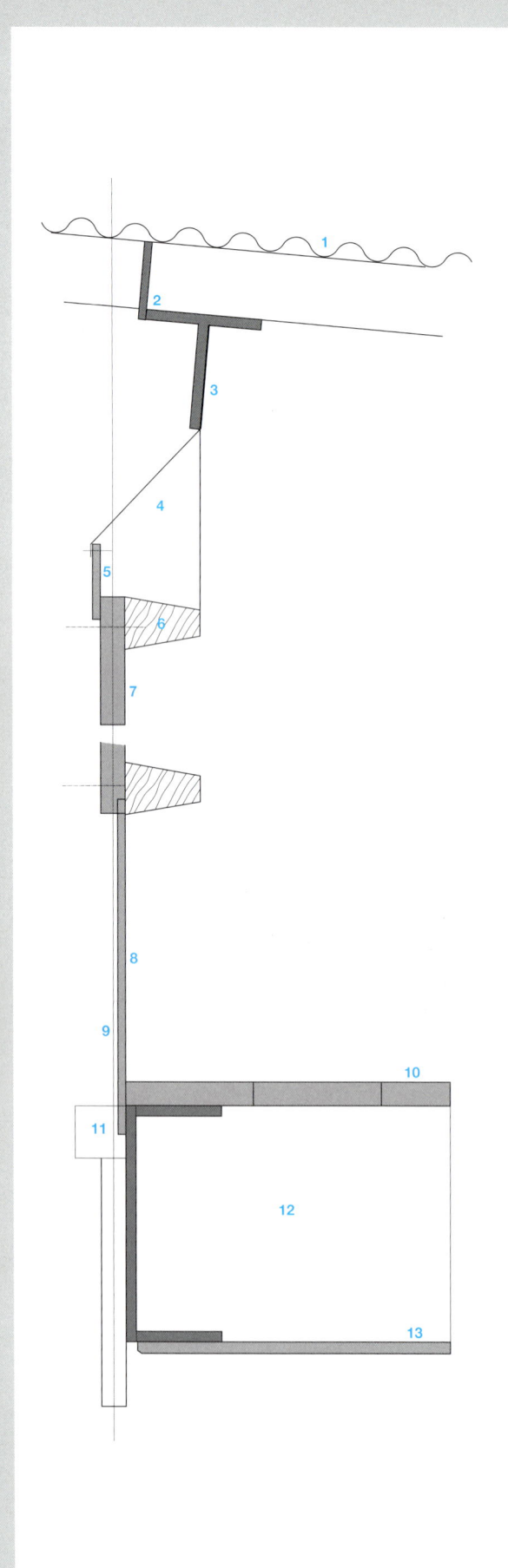

43.07
Detail Section at Exterior Plywood Bracing
1:5
1 Polycarbonate roof sheeting
2 Acrylic sheet between steel hollow section purlin fixed with silicone
3 Steel T-section
4 Colorbond flat sheet profile fixed to top of acrylic infill panel
5 Fixed acrylic panel
6 Hardwood batten fixed to compressed fibre cement sheet
7 Compressed fibre cement sheet to end bays
8 Rebated compressed fibre cement sheet to fixed glass
9 Sika flex behind glass
10 Timber tongue and groove flooring
11 Hardwood block to support glass above
12 Hyspan with insulation
13 9 mm (1/3 inch) structural plywood

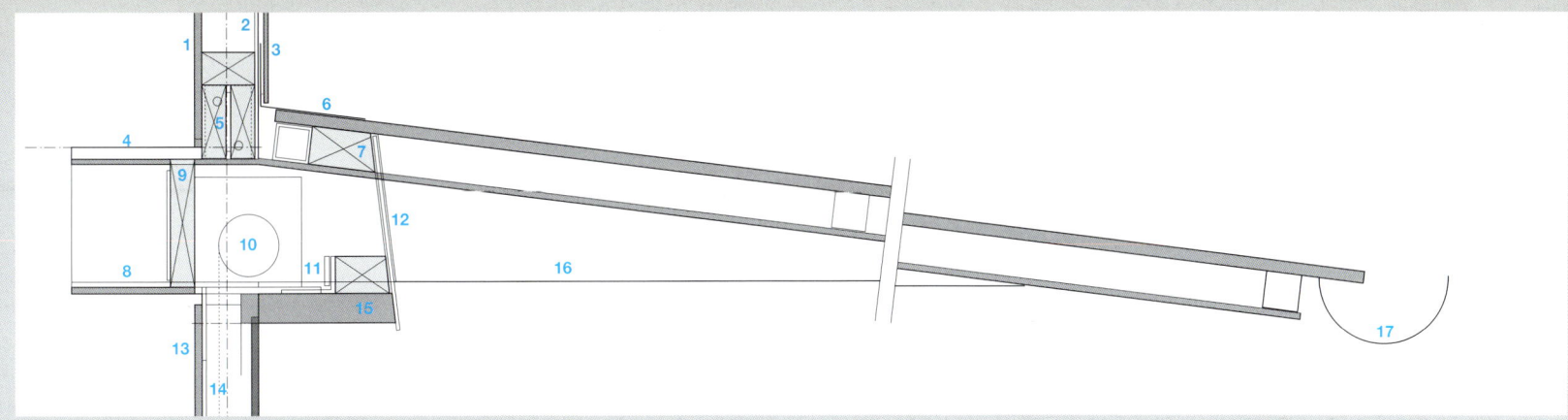

43.08
Eaves Detail
1:10
1 Plasterboard lining
2 Plywood lining
3 Miniorb exterior
cladding
4 Timber tongue and
groove flooring
5 Cleat to support
bridging under wall
6 Colorbond flashing
7 Removeable

blocking to allow
access to roller blind
8 Plywood lining
9 Timber joist
10 Recessed roller
blind cartridge
11 Angle to support
hardwood head with
glue and screw fixing
12 Access panel for
installation and repairs
to roller blind
13 Cleat welded to

floor beam bolted
through T-flange
14 T-column with
tapered hardwood on
either side
15 Hardwood head
16 T-section welded to
floor beam
17 Half-round
Colorbond gutter

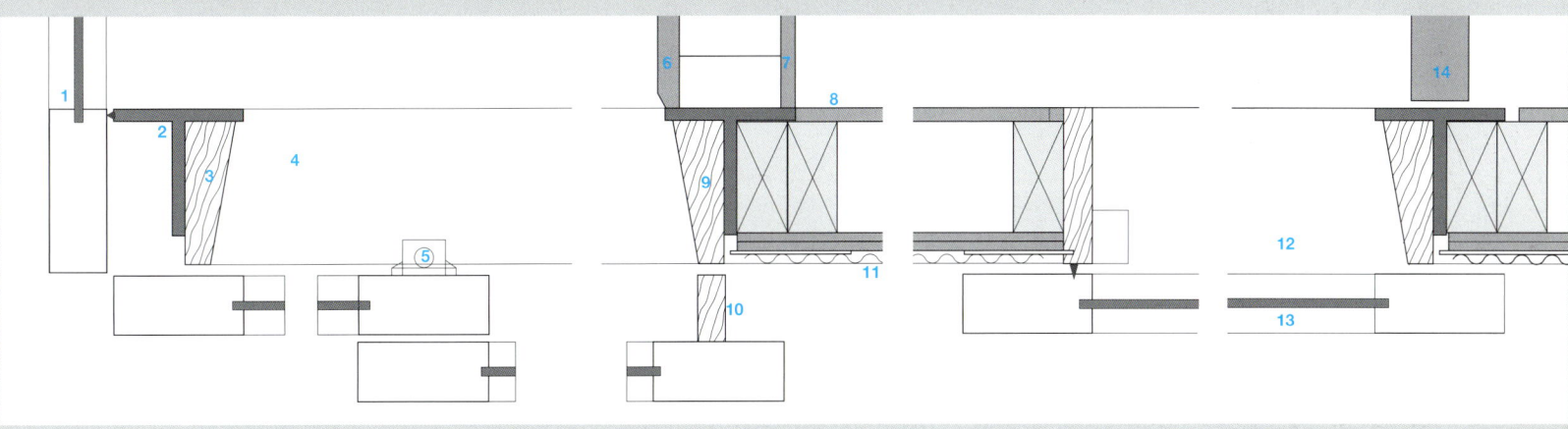

43.09
Interior Door Plan
Detail
1:5
1 Hardwood sliding
door with solid infill
2 Steel T-section
3 Hardwood reveal
4 Hardwood reveal
5 Mini push lock
mounted on bottom
rail locking into sill
6 Compressed fibre

cement sheet
bathroom lining
7 Plasterboard lining
8 Plasterboard lining
9 Hardwood reveal
10 Rubber stopper on
brass tracks
11 Miniorb with
flashing behind,
rebated into hard
wood mullion
12 Head alignment
13 Sliding window

14 Plywood pivot door

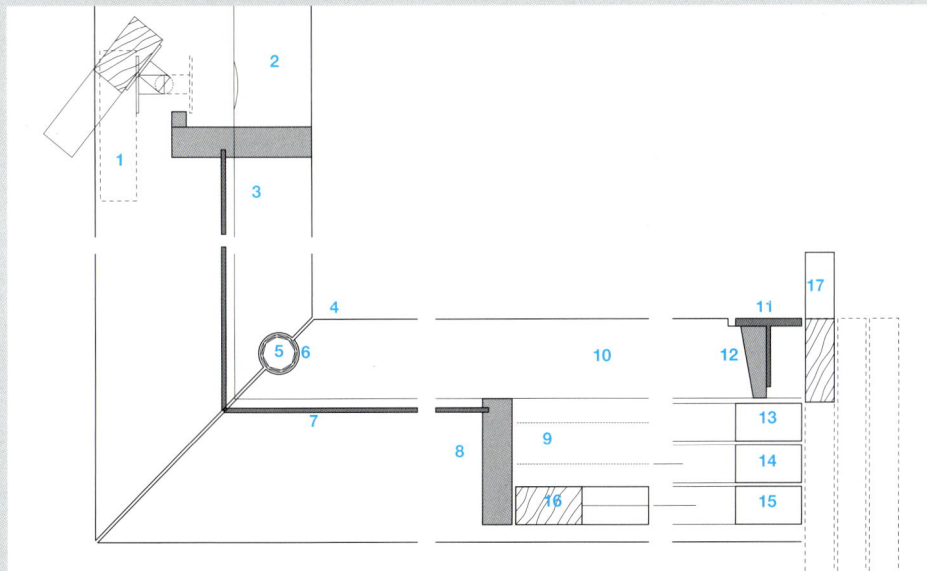

43.10
Corner Window Plan
Detail
1:10
1 Pivoting timber
framed window
2 Hardwood reveal
3 Window head
above
4 Hardwood reveal
with mitred corner
5 Circular hollow
section
6 Sikaflex join around
column
7 Fixed glass with
silicon joint to corner
8 Hardwood jamb
rebated for glazing
9 Brass sliding tracks
10 Hardwood sill
11 90 mm (3 1/2 inch)
T-section
12 Hardwood reveal
13 Sliding glass panel
14 Sliding glass panel
15 Sliding glass panel
16 Sliding glass panel
17 Sliding timber
framed door

**Gompertz Residence
Livingston, Montana, USA**

Client
Ron Gompertz

Area
167 square metres (1,800 square feet)

Project Team
Clark Stevens, Michael Rotondi,
Ben Ives, Dave Kitazaki, Kirby Smith,
Carrie Di Fiore, Eric Meglassen

Structural Engineer
MT Structural, Bozeman, Montana

Main Contractor
Ron Gompertz

The site consists of 5.6 hectares (14 acres) at the edge of the Absaroka Mountains. The house itself sits on the edge of the only sheltering feature in a valley famous for its storms and spectacular views on a bank of the now receded Yellowstone River. The owner wished to be able to climb up to experience the dramatic sky, rather than simply viewing it from the earth. In response, the design explores the potential of the region's grain silos. The View Silo, as the house is known, was designed to occupy the smallest footprint of earth and the narrowest sliver of sky. Entry is at the upper level, with two levels of sleeping spaces below, partially embedded in the earth.

Immediately above are located the work and living spaces. A mezzanine for cooking and eating is located within the tapering double-height volume. Above this, the stair tower is open to the sky and is terminated in a roof-top observatory, the slatted perimeter of which provides a filtered 360-degree view. The building is clad on the south and east walls with cedar slats over a waterproofing layer of brick-red asphalt roofing. Separated from the surface of the roofing by a gap so that all fasteners are invisible, the spacing of the slats varies to provide patterns of light and shade to openings behind the continuous surface. To protect openings from severe storms, the windows can be completely shuttered. When opened, the shutters provide a variety of sun shading appropriate to their orientation.

1 The house sits on a reinforced concrete base that rises out of the river bank, the timber-clad upper levels rising four storeys, culminating in a roof-top viewing terrace.
2 The weathered cedar slats are interrupted only to accommodate carefully placed openings in the form of windows, decks and bridges.
3 The gap between the timber slats varies to provide differentiations in the tone and texture of the facades and to protect openings behind from driving wind and rain.
4 Cedar wall and ceiling linings echo the language of the exterior. Simple white-painted walls and expansive windows give priority to the spectacular views.

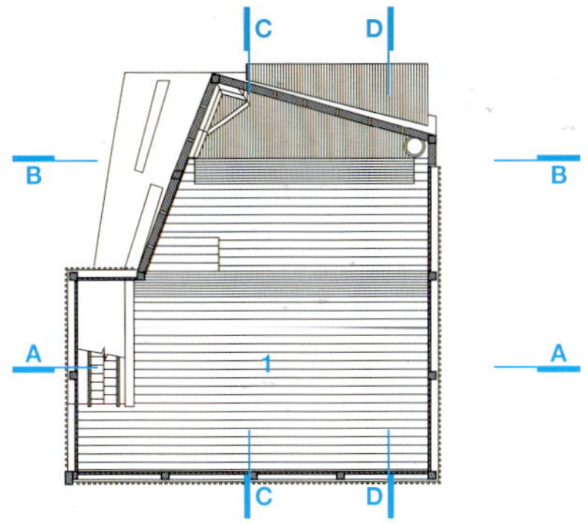

44.01
Roof Plan
1:200
1 Roof deck

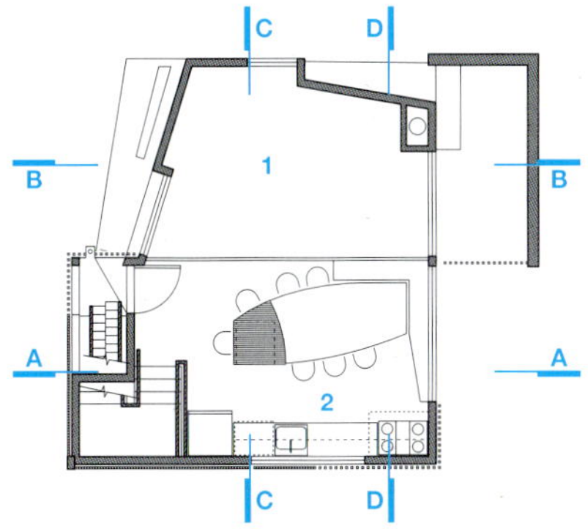

44.02
Second Floor Plan
1:200
1 Void over living
  room below
2 Kitchen

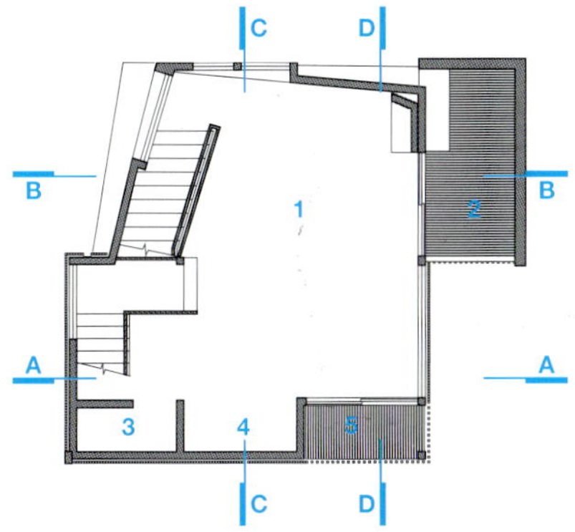

44.03
First Floor Plan
1:200
1 Living room
2 Porch 1
3 Store room
4 Study
5 Porch 2

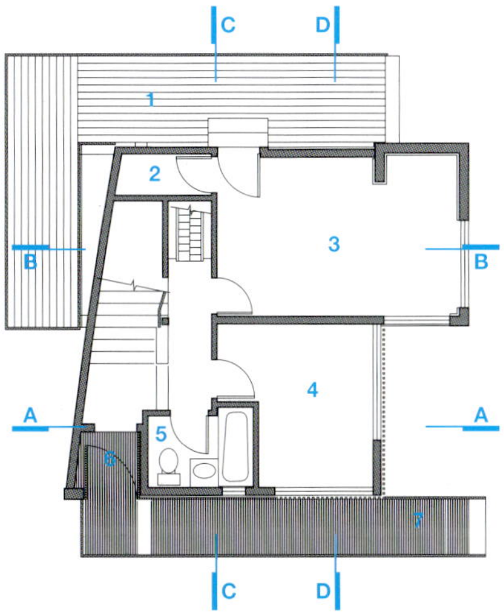

44.04
Ground Floor Plan
1:200
1 Balcony
2 Closet
3 Bedroom 1
4 Bedroom 2
5 Bathroom
6 Entry
7 Walkway

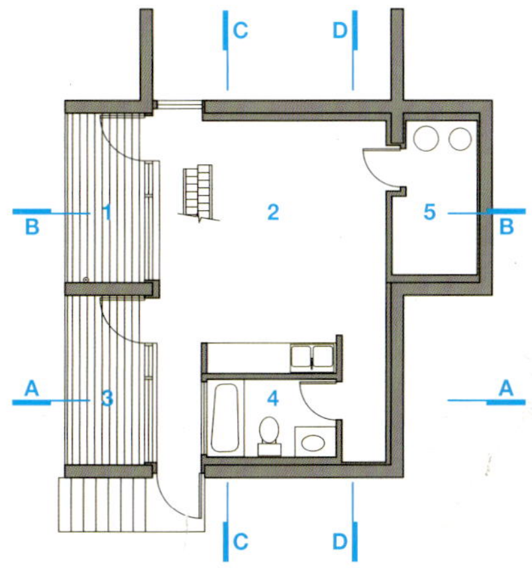

44.05
Basement Floor Plan
1:200
1 Deck
2 River room
3 Deck
4 Bathroom
5 Mechanical plant

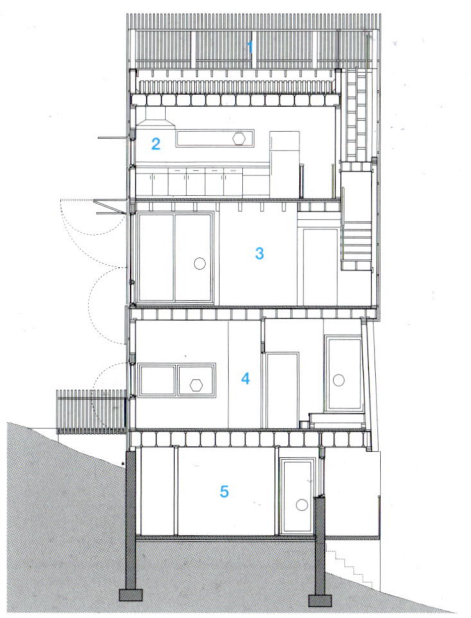

44.06
Section A–A
1:200
1 Roof deck
2 Kitchen
3 Living room
4 Bedroom
5 Bathroom

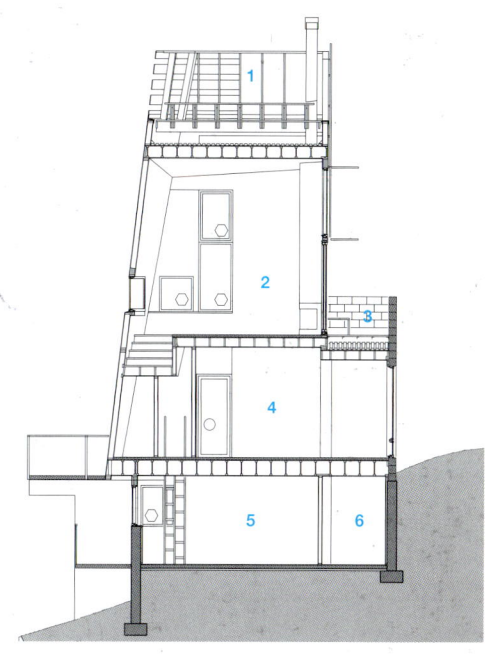

44.07
Section B–B
1:200
1 Roof deck
2 Living room
3 Porch 1
4 Bedroom
5 River room
6 Mechanical plant

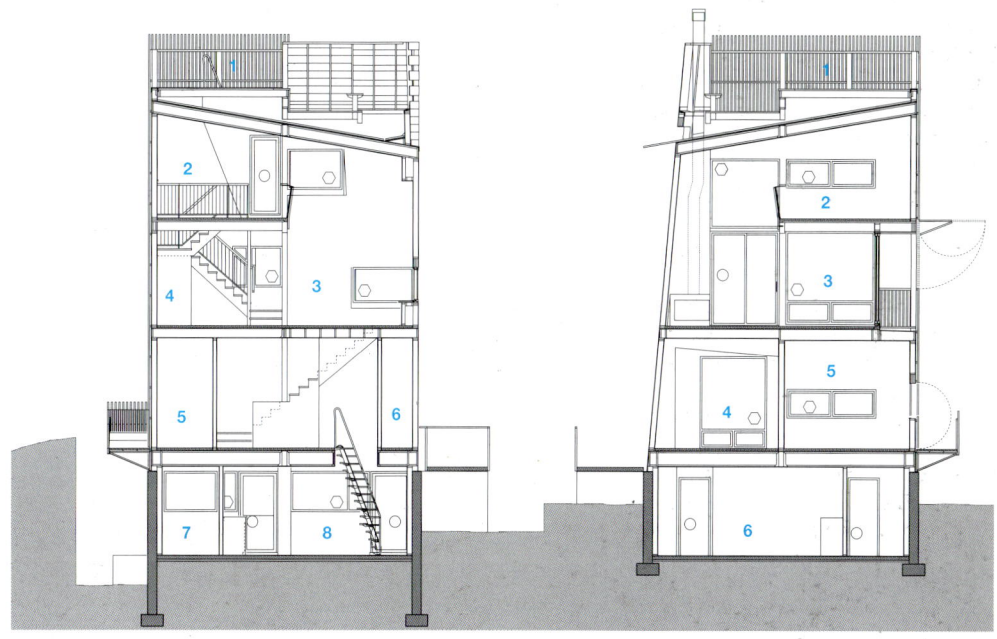

44.08
Section C–C
1:200
1 Roof deck
2 Kitchen
3 Living room
4 Study
5 Bathroom
6 Closet
7 Bathroom
8 River room

44.09
Section D–D
1:200
1 Roof deck
2 Kitchen
3 Living room
4 Bedroom 1
5 Bedroom 2
6 River room

0   5   10m

0   15   30ft

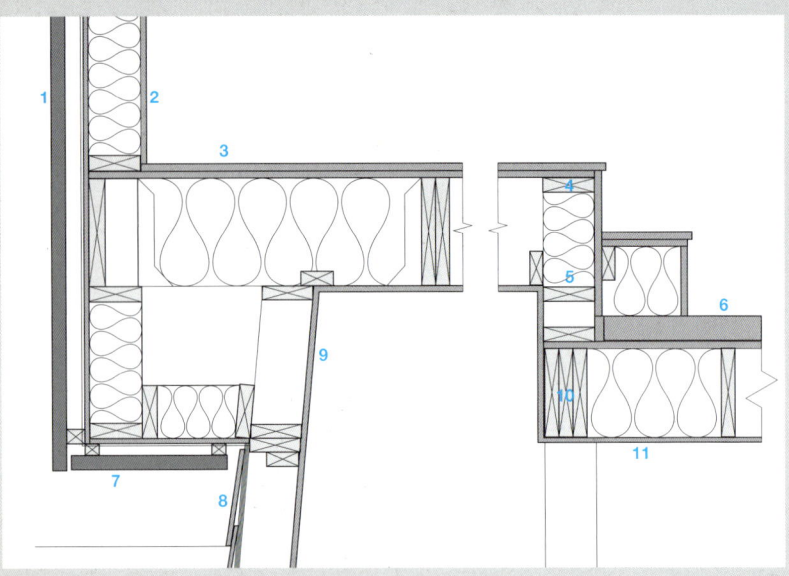

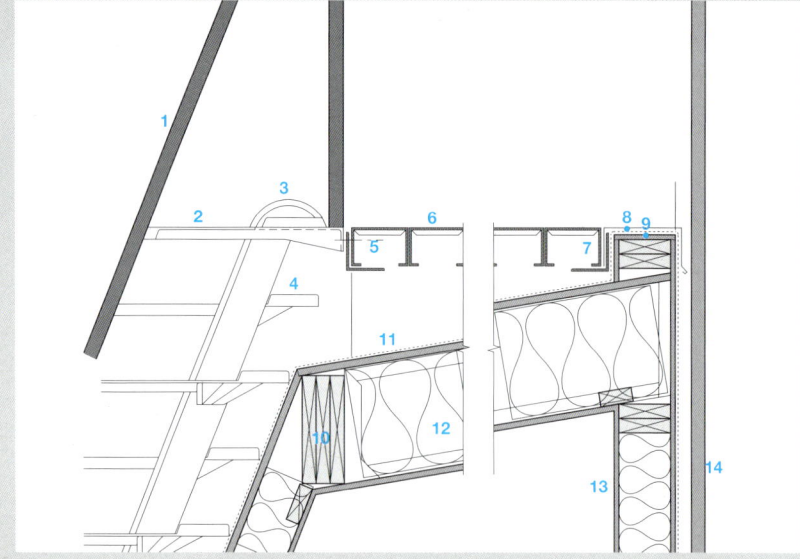

44.10
Stair Landing Detail
1:20
1 50 x 50 mm (2 x 2 inch) cedar slats
2 Interior wall lining
3 Maple flooring
4 Timber framing
5 Timber framing
6 Lightweight concrete topping slab with integrated radiant heating
7 50 x 50 mm (2 x 2 inch) cedar slats
8 Cedar cladding
9 Interior wall lining
10 Header beam
11 Interior wall board

44.11
Roof Deck Detail
1:20
1 Steel handrail
2 Custom steel alternating tread stair assembly
3 Steel stringer
4 Custom steel alternating tread stair assembly
5 100 x 100 mm (4 x 4 inch) steel grating support angles around perimeter of roof deck
6 100 x 150 mm (4 x 6 inch) steel grating
7 100 x 100 mm (4 x 4 inch) steel grating support angles around perimeter of roof deck
8 Pre-finished metal cap flashing
9 Continuous roll-on roofing, air barrier and plywood over 50 x 150 mm (2 x 6 inch) parapet
10 Three 50 x 300 mm (3 x 12 inch) beams
11 Continuous roll-on roofing, air barrier and plywood over 50 x 150 mm (2 x 6 inch) parapet
12 Batt insulation
13 Interior wall lining
14 Cedar slats

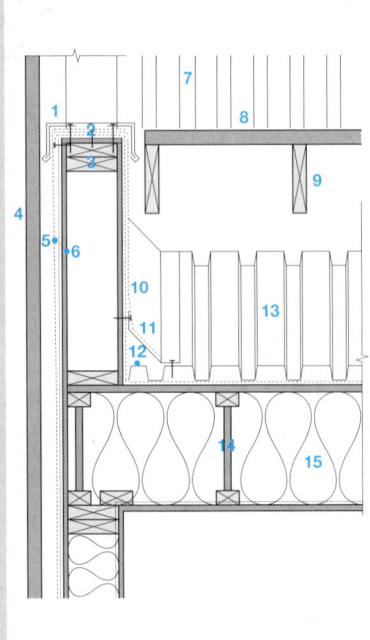

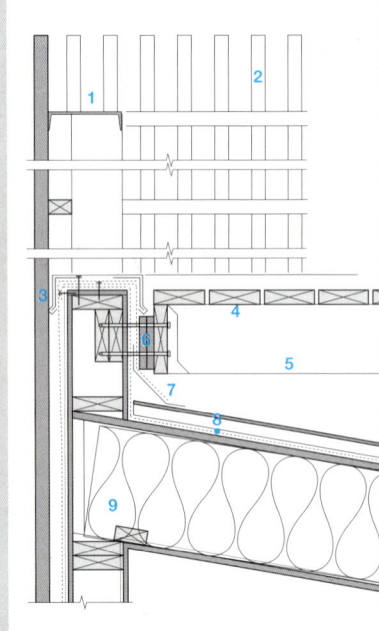

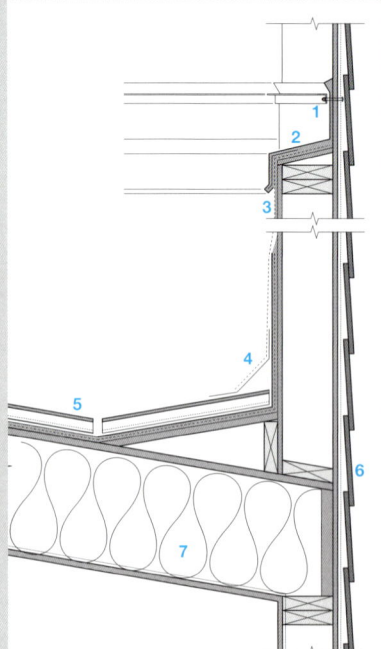

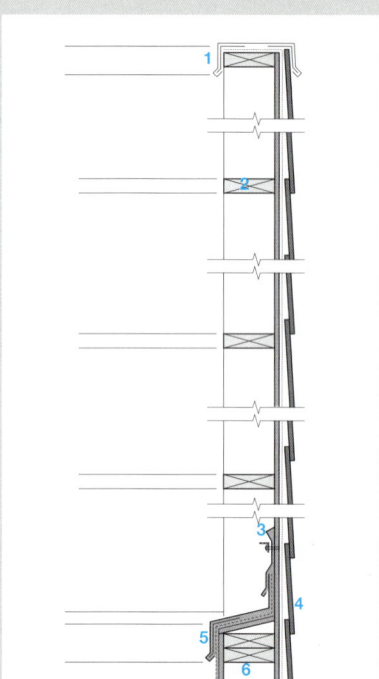

44.12
Parapet Detail 1
1:20
1 100 x 100 mm (4 x 4 inch) post beyond
2 Prefinished metal flashing clipped in continuous cleats
3 Double top plate to parapet
4 Cedar cladding
5 Continuous roll-on roofing, air barrier and plywood over parapet
6 Timber framing
7 Cedar rail beyond
8 Timber decking
9 Deck joists
10 Roll-on roofing overlapping cant strip
11 125 mm (5 inch) metal cant strip
12 Roll-on roofing underneath metal roofing over parapet
13 Metal roofing
14 Timber joists at 400 mm (16 inch) centres
15 Batt insulation over vapour barrier and dry wall lining

44.13
Parapet Detail 2
1:20
1 Continuous steel channel
2 Timber slats
3 Prefinished metal flashing on roll-on roofing
4 Timber decking at 12 mm (1/2 inch) spacings
5 Timber joists at 400 mm (16 inch) centres
6 Two layers of plywood spacers
glued and lag bolted to solid blocking into parapet
7 Prefinished metal cant
8 Metal roofing on roll-on roofing
9 Batt insulation over vapour barrier and dry wall lining

44.14
Roof Cricket Detail
1:20
1 Continuous galvanized metal clamp bar on top of caulked and sealed flashing
2 Prefinished metal flashing clipped in continuous metal cleat
3 Roll-on roofing over parapet above and over metal cant below
4 Prefinished metal cant strip
5 Metal roofing
6 Cedar cladding
7 Batt insulation over vapour barrier and dry wall lining

44.15
North Wall at Roof Deck Detail
1:20
1 Prefinished metal cap flashing clipped into continuous cleats on both sides
2 Blocking spaced to align with girts on west wall between studs
3 Flashing
4 Cedar cladding
5 Cap flashing
6 50 x 150 mm (2 x 6 inch) double top plate

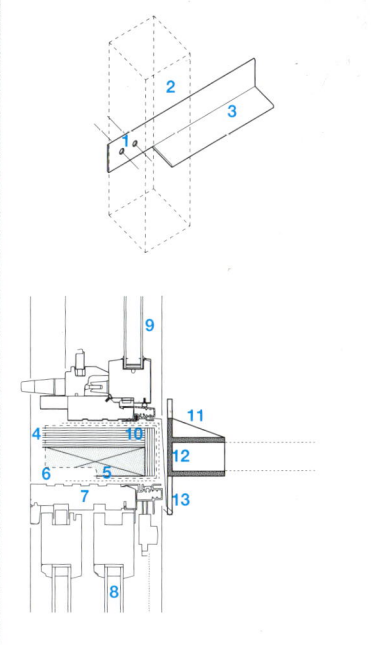

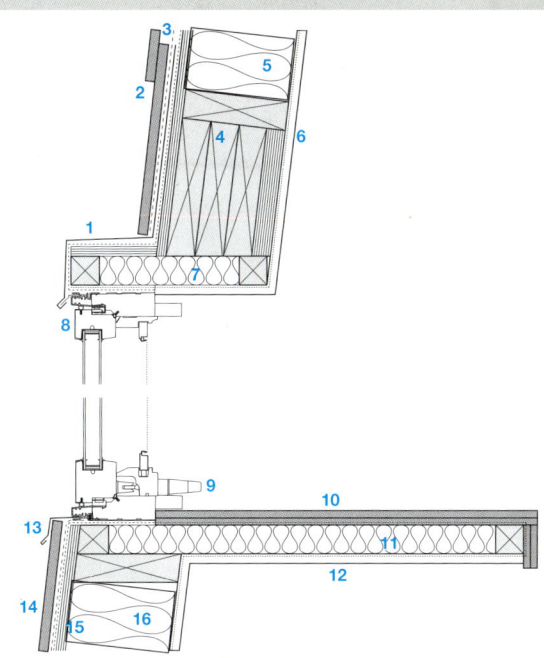

44.16
Sliding Door Head and Window Detail
1:20

1 Lag screws into 150 x 150 mm (6 x 6 inch) post
2 150 x 150 mm (6 x 6 inch) post
3 75 x 75 x 6 mm (3 x 3 x 1/4 inch) steel angle
4 75 x 75 x 6 mm (3 x 3 x 1/4 inch) steel angle mullion header
5 Notch 50 x 150 mm (2 x 6 inch) steel angle flush at bottom only
6 Vapour barrier wrapped around entire mullion
7 Shim as required
8 Sliding door aligned to inside face of dry wall finish
9 Window aligned to outside face of plywood
10 Two layers of 12 x 12 mm (1/2 x 1/2 inch) plywood
11 Custom steel bracket
12 Roll-on roofing wrapped around mullion
13 Prefinished metal flashing

44.17
Window Section Detail
1:20

1 Prefinished metal flashing sloped to drain
2 Cedar cladding
3 Cedar cladding
4 Structural window header
5 Rigid insulation
6 Interior wall lining
7 50 x 100 mm (2 x 4 inch) timber at 300 mm (12 inch) centres with 50 x 50 mm (2 x 2 inch) blocking in between 50 x 100 mm (2 x 4 inch) timbers at each end, and cavity filled with rigid insulation
8 Window head
9 Blind assembly
10 Hardwood window sill and trim, thickness and length as required over vapour barrier
11 Rigid insulation
12 Drywall to interior
13 Sill flashing

14 Cedar cladding
15 Vapour barrier
16 Insulation

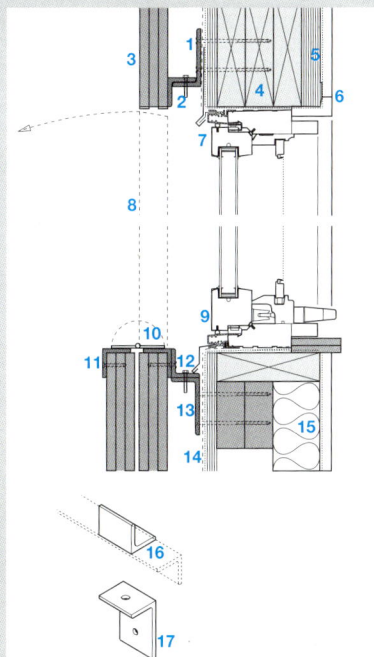

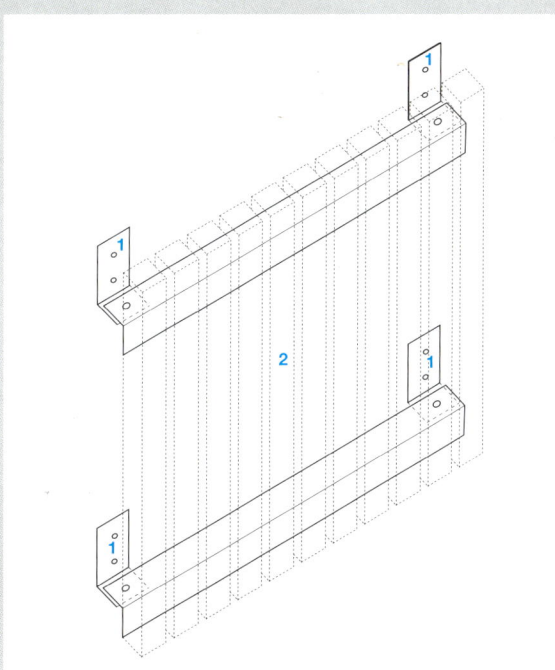

44.18
Typical WIndow Detail
1:20

1 Steel mounting brackets attached after roll-on roofing installed
2 Continuous steel angle pre-assembled to timber slats and steel bolt welded through angle
3 Cedar cladding
4 Structural window header
5 Rigid insulation
6 Interior wall lining
7 Heavy gauge prefinished metal flashing under roofing at head and over roofing at sill
8 Position of shutter at closed position
9 Heave gauge prefinished metal flashing under roofing at head and over roofing at sill
10 Continuous galvanized steel hinge
11 Continuous steel angle pre-assembled to timber slats and steel bolt welded through angle
12 Continuous steel angle pre-assembled to timber slats and steel bolt welded through angle
13 Steel angle mounting brackets at each end of window opening, attached after roll-on roofing is installed
14 Roll-on roofing
15 Vapour barrier and insulation
16 Continuous steel angle for mounting timber slats
17 Mounting bracket

44.19
Timber Slat Detail

1 Mounting brackets at 810 mm (32 inch) centres
2 Vertical timber slats

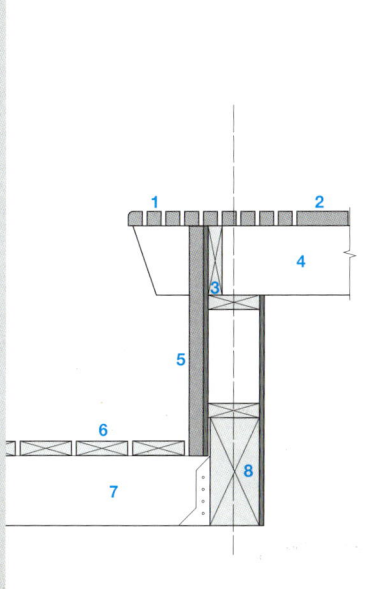

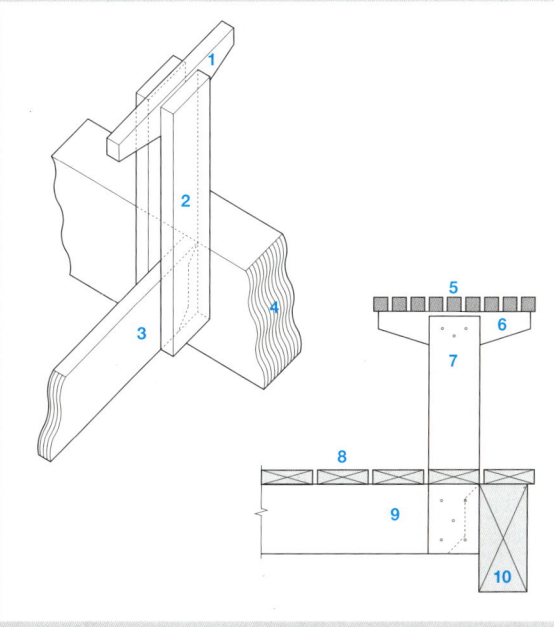

44.20
Bench Detail 1
1:20

1 Cedar slats at 12 mm (1/2 inch) spacing
2 40 x 150 (13/5 x 6 inch) timber decking with 12 mm (1/2 inch) spaces
3 Timber blocking in between deck joists
4 Timber joists at 400 mm (16 inch) centres, cantilevered 200 mm (8 inches) from the face of the framing
5 40 x 40 mm (13/5 x 13/5 inch) cedar slats on plywood studs placed directly under joists
6 40 x 150 mm (13/5 x 6 inch) timber decking
7 Timber joists
8 150 x 300 mm (6 x 12 inch) beam

44.21
Bench Detail 2
1:20

1 Shaped 50 x 100 mm (2 x 4 inch) timber
2 40 x 150 mm (13/5 x 6 inch) timber on each side of joist
3 Timber joists at 600 mm (2 foot) centres
4 150 x 300 mm (6 x 12 inch) timber beam
5 40 x 40 mm (13/5 x 13/5 inch) cedar slats at 12 mm (1/2 inch) spacing
6 Shaped 50 x 100 mm (2 x 4 inch) timber
7 40 x 150 mm (13/5 x 6 inch) timber on each side of joist
8 40 x 150 mm (13/5 x 6 inch) timber decking
9 Timber joists at 600 mm (2 foot) centres
10 150 x 300 mm (6 x 12 inch) timber beam

**Peninsula House
Victoria, Australia**

Area
210 square metres (2,260 square feet)

Project Team
Sean Godsell, Hayley Franklin

Structural Engineer
Felicetti Pty Ltd

General Contractor
Kane Constructions (Vic) Pty Ltd

This elegant timber house investigates the similarities between the enclosed verandah of traditional Japanese houses and the 'sun room' of the Australian house. An oxidized steel portal structure has been embedded into the side of a sand dune. This forms the 'exoskeleton' of the house upon which the weather controlling outer skin – operable timber shutters, glass roof and walls – are all mounted. The simple programme – a living and dining room, library and sleeping room – forms the 'endoskeleton'. The sleeping room is an inner area accessed by a private stair, while a double-height living volume at ground level opens directly onto the landscape, with an intimate guest room and library at the rear.

The notion of inner room (*moya*) enclosed verandah (*hisashi*) and fluid (aisle) space forms the basis of the design. The three primary spaces differ in dimension, volume and quality of light. The living room is very light, the bedroom is moderately light and the library is dark by comparison. The verandah has become further abstracted to form a protective outer layer. There is no distinction between the function of the roof and the function of the walls. The house itself is the nurturing inner room, protected from the elements by a coarse outer hide, principally expressed in the veil of closely spaced recycled eucalyptus battens. The interplay of the habitants between these two elements activates the simple form of the building via the opening and closing of the facade. This effect is further accentuated by the emptying and filling of the building with light, filtered through the timber screens, mapping the course of the day and the time of year in the shape and extent of the shadows cast by the screens.

1 A row of pneumatically operated timber panels open up from the verandah space onto a sheltered timber deck, enclosed by battered earth walls.

2 The seemingly fragile nature of the timber screen covering both the walls and the roof, protects what is essentially a glass box against the harsh marine climate.

3 A sliver of sky opens up between the walls of battens. While the screen acts as a privacy device and weather barrier, it also serves to connect the private domain to the landscape outside.

4 The progressive layering of space is apparent in the way the floor surfaces change from inside to outside – from the weathered timber deck to a concrete path to polished floorboards.

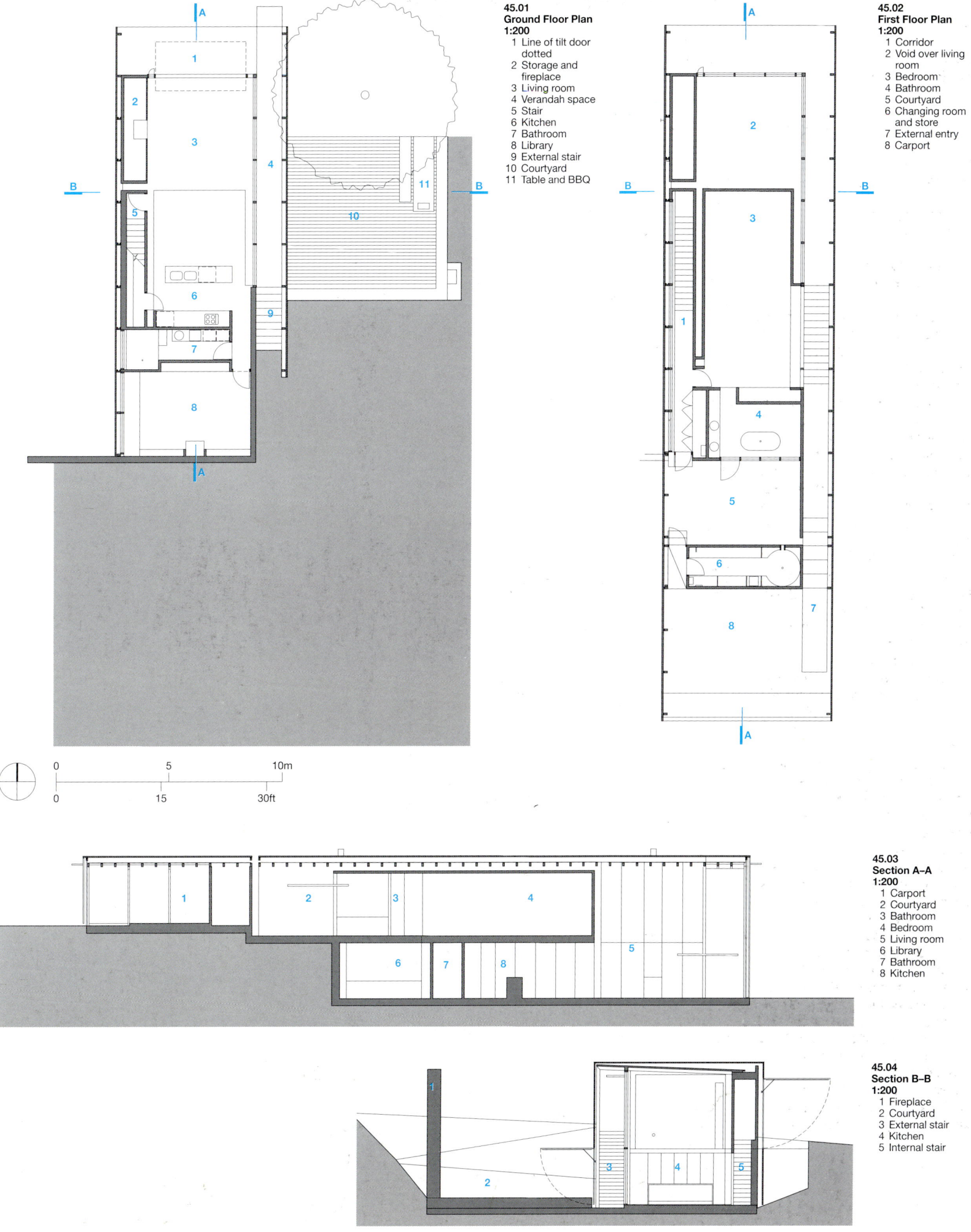

45.01
Ground Floor Plan
1:200
1 Line of tilt door dotted
2 Storage and fireplace
3 Living room
4 Verandah space
5 Stair
6 Kitchen
7 Bathroom
8 Library
9 External stair
10 Courtyard
11 Table and BBQ

45.02
First Floor Plan
1:200
1 Corridor
2 Void over living room
3 Bedroom
4 Bathroom
5 Courtyard
6 Changing room and store
7 External entry
8 Carport

0   5   10m

0   15   30ft

45.03
Section A–A
1:200
1 Carport
2 Courtyard
3 Bathroom
4 Bedroom
5 Living room
6 Library
7 Bathroom
8 Kitchen

45.04
Section B–B
1:200
1 Fireplace
2 Courtyard
3 External stair
4 Kitchen
5 Internal stair

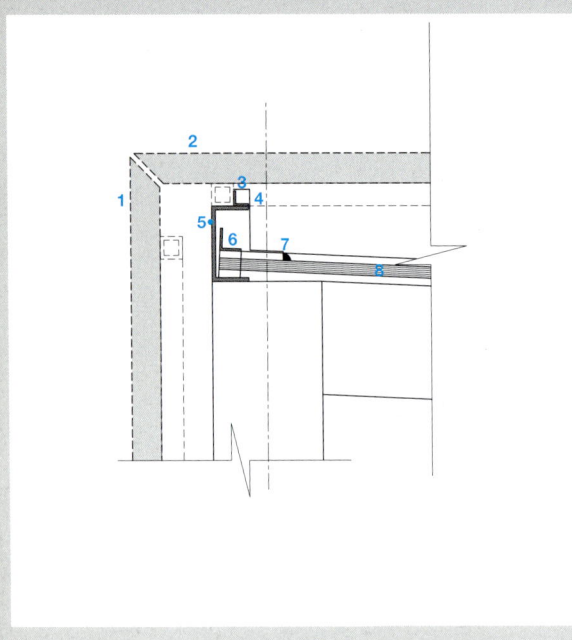

45.05
Timber Screen
Wall Detail
1:10
1 Timber screen
2 Timber screen
3 20 x 20 mm ($^3/_4$ x $^3/_4$ inch) mild steel angle
4 Zinc angle capping
5 100 x 50 (4 x 2 inch) mild steel pre-formed channel
6 20 x 20 mm ($^3/_4$ x $^3/_4$ inch) aluminium angle
7 Silicone
8 Glazing in aluminium channel

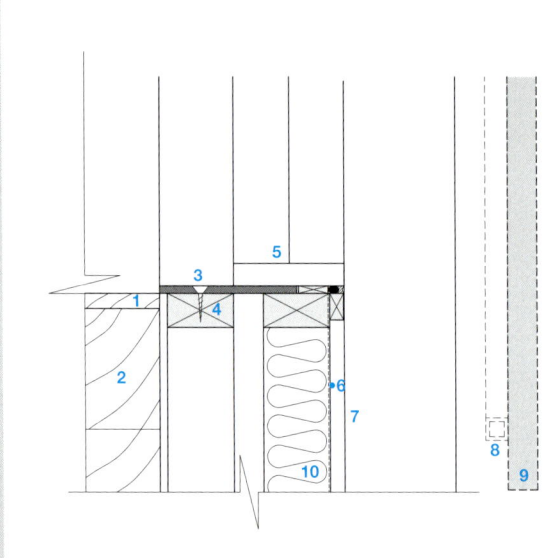

45.06
Wall Detail 1
1:10
1 Timber flooring
2 Timber stair riser
3 Mild steel plate countersunk and screw fixed to align with portal beyond
4 Nailing plate
5 Timber sill
6 Sarking (dotted)
7 Oxidized mild steel cladding on 19 mm ($^3/_4$ inch) battens at 600 mm (23$^1/_2$ inch) centres
8 30 x 30 mm (1$^1/_5$ x 1$^1/_5$ inch) square hollow section
9 Line of timber screen beyond
10 Insulation

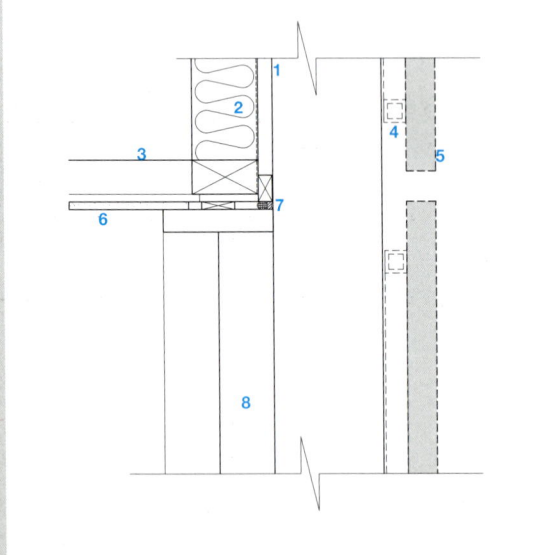

45.07
Wall Detail 2
1:10
1 Oxidized mild steel cladding
2 Insulation
3 32 Rondo screw up batten
4 30 x 30 mm (1$^1/_5$ x 1$^1/_5$ inch) square hollow section
5 Timber screen
6 Plasterboard
7 Clear silicone to polystyrene backing rod
8 150 x 75 mm (6 x 3 inch) pre-formed channel

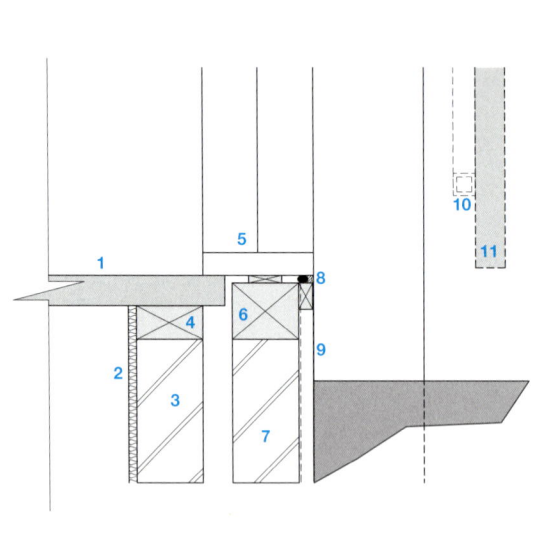

45.08
Wall and Desk Detail
1:10
1 Desk
2 12 mm ($^1/_2$ inch) MDF
3 Inner layer of structural masonry pier
4 Timber bearer plate
5 Timber window sill
6 Timber bearer plate
7 Outer layer of structural masonry pier
8 Silicone
9 1.6 mm ($^1/_{16}$ inch) mild steel on treated pine battens
10 30 x 30 mm (1$^1/_5$ x 1$^1/_5$ inch) square hollow section
11 Timber screen

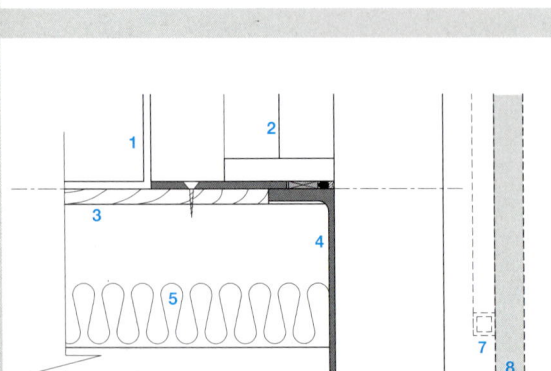

45.09
Wall Detail 3
1:10
1 Portal beyond
2 Timber-framed glazing
3 Timber floor boards
4 300 x 90 mm (11$^3/_4$ x 3$^1/_2$ inch) pre-formed channel
5 Insulation
6 Timber-framed glazing
7 30 x 30 mm (1$^1/_5$ x 1$^1/_5$ inch) square hollow section
8 Line of timber screen beyond

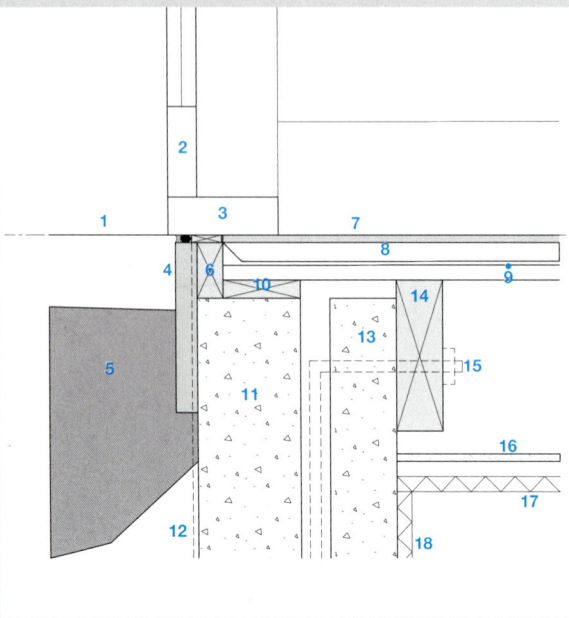

45.10
Floor Detail
1:10
1 8 mm ($^1/_3$ inch) mild steel portal beyond
2 Timber framed door
3 Timber door sill
4 20 mm ($^3/_4$ inch) unpainted cement render over tanking (dotted)
5 Finished ground level
6 Treated pine edge trim
7 Ceramic tiles on screed over tanking
8 Cement screed
9 18 mm ($^3/_4$ inch) wet area particleboard
10 Timber blocking
11 Masonry retaining wall
12 Tanking
13 Masonry wall
14 Timber floor joist
15 Hold-down bolt
16 Aluminium furring channel
17 Plasterboard
18 MDF

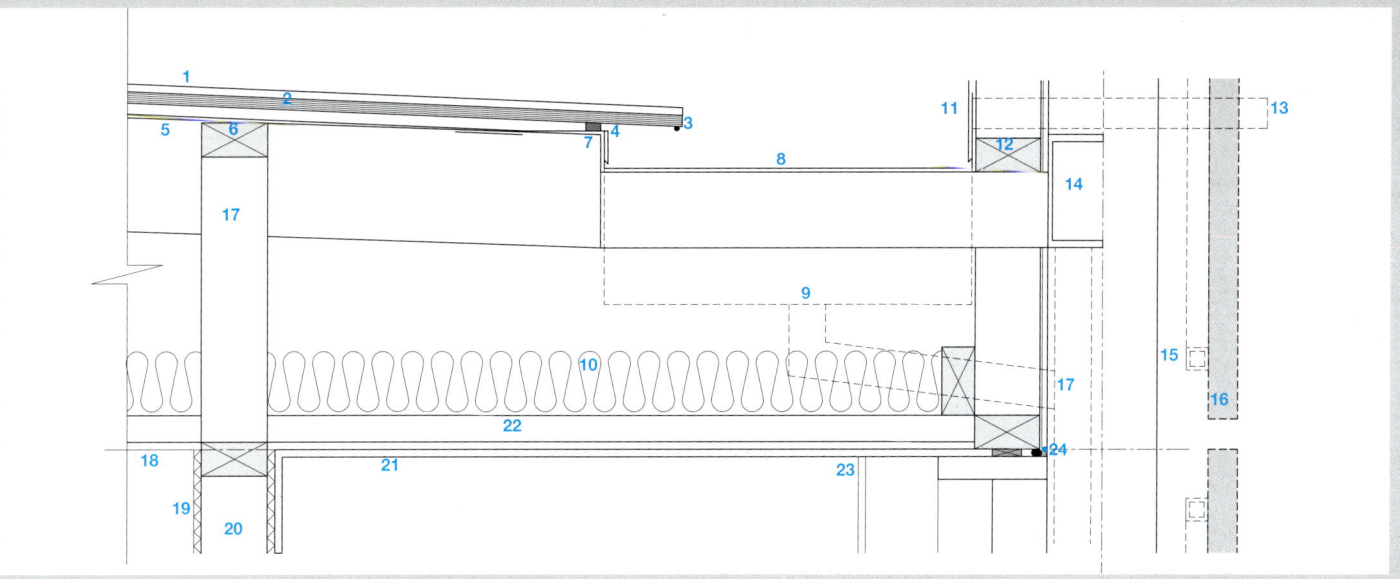

45.11
Roof and Gutter Detail
1:10
1 Aluminium channel
2 Glazing
3 Continuous silicone drip bead
4 Neoprene gasket
5 Timber rafter
6 Timber bearer
7 Timber batten
8 Stainless steel gutter
9 500 x 400 x 180 mm (19½ x 15¾ x 7 inch) stainless steel sump
10 Insulation
11 Flashing
12 Timber plate
13 32 mm (1¼ inch) diameter outlet
14 Channel
15 30 x 30 mm (⅕ x 1⅕ inch) square hollow section
16 Timber screen
17 Timber stud frame
18 Plasterboard
19 MDF
20 Timber stud frame
21 Plasterboard ceiling
22 32 Rondo batten
23 Steel portal
24 Silicone

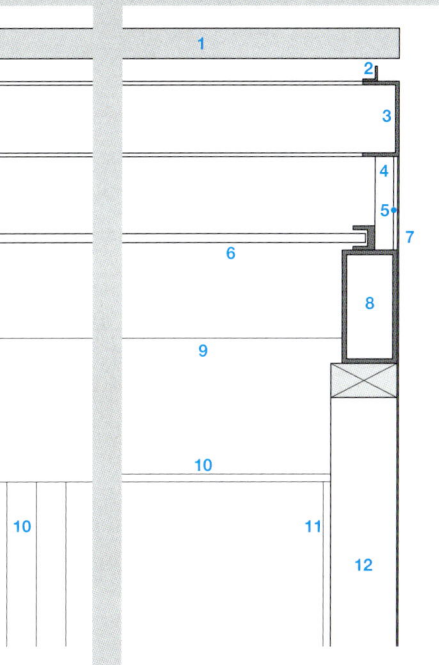

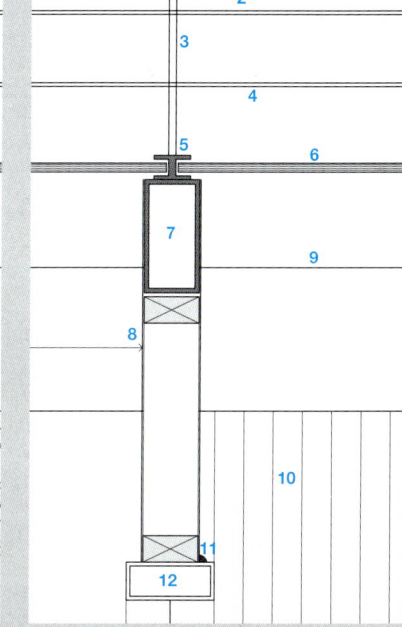

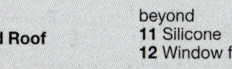

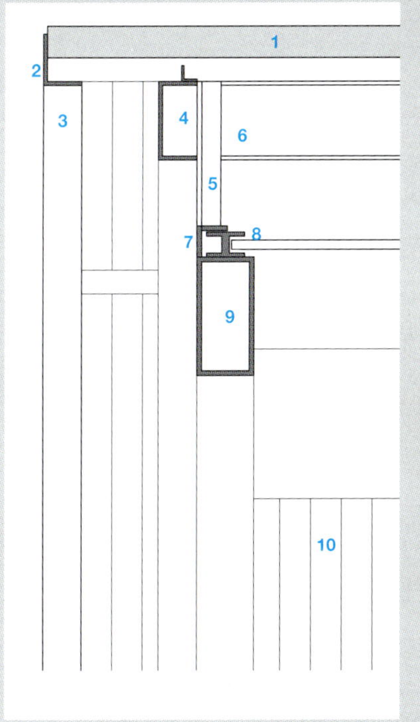

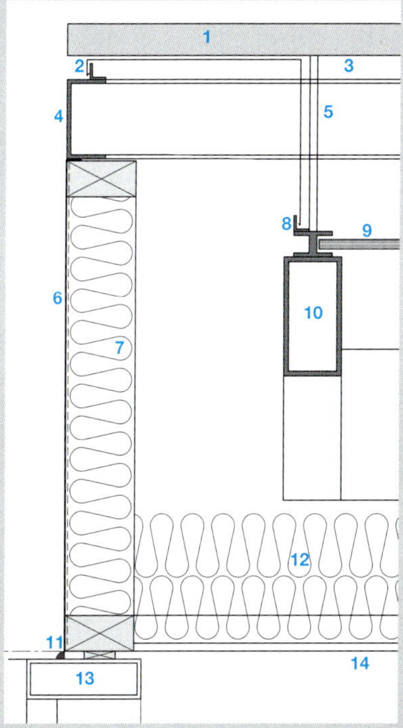

45.12
Wall and Glazing Detail 1
1:10
1 Timber screen
2 65 x 50 mm (2½ x 2 inch) mild steel angle
3 65 x 50 mm (2½ x 2 inch) mild steel angle
4 100 x 50 mm (4 x 2 inch) pre-formed channel
5 Plywood backing to 1.6 gauge mild steel fascia
6 20 x 20 mm (¾ x ¾ inch) mild steel rectangular hollow section at 450 mm (17¾ inch) centres
7 40 x 40 x 3 mm (1½ x 1½ x ¹⁄₁₀ inch) mild steel angle
8 Glazing in aluminium channel with separation strip between aluminium and steel
9 150 x 75 mm (6 x 3 inch) boxed section
10 Mild steel plate

45.13
Wall and Glazing Detail 2
1:10
1 Timber screen
2 20 x 20 mm (¾ x ¾ inch) mild steel angle
3 100 x 50 mm (4 x 2 inch) pre-formed channel
4 20 x 20 mm (¾ x ¾ inch) mild steel rectangular hollow section at 450 mm (17¾ inch) centres
5 Plywood backing to 1.6 gauge mild steel fascia
6 Glazing in aluminium channel with separation strip between aluminium and steel
7 Mild steel over sarking
8 150 x 75 mm (6 x 3 inch) boxed section
9 Mild steel plate
10 Mild steel plate
11 Mild steel plate
12 Timber stud

45.14
Wall and Roof Detail 1
1:10
1 Timber screen
2 Zinc angle capping
3 Capping
4 100 x 50 mm (4 x 2 inch) pre-formed channel
5 10 mm (⅓ inch) diameter threaded mild steel rod
6 Mild steel over sarking (dotted)
7 Insulation
8 40 x 40 mm (1½ x 1½ inch) continuous aluminium angle
9 Membrane roof over 12 WP PW set into glazing channel
10 150 x 75 mm (6 x 3 inch) boxed section
11 Silicone
12 Two layers of fibreglass insulation
13 Window frame
14 Plasterboard ceiling screwed in place with 'rondo' battens

45.15
Wall and Roof Detail 2
1:10
1 Timber screen
2 Capping
3 10 mm (⅓ inch) diameter threaded mild steel rod
4 20 x 20 mm (¾ x ¾ inch) mild steel rectangular hollow section at 450 mm (17¾ inch) centres
5 Glazing channel
6 Membrane roof over 12 WP PW set into glazing channel
7 150 x 75 mm (6 x 3 inch) boxed section
8 Mild steel plate
9 Mild steel plate
10 Timber screen beyond
11 Silicone
12 Window frame

Mustang Meadow
Colorado, USA

Client
Dennis Goggin

Area
317 square metres (3,415 square feet)

Project Team
Henry Smith-Miller, Ferda Kolatan,
Michael Johnston, Luben Dimcheff,
Twitee Vajrabhaya, Dannon
Canterbury

Structural Engineer
Buckhorn Geo Tech

Mechanical Engineer
Carstel Engineering

Landscape Architect
Quennell Rothschild and Partners

Main Contractor
Kent Building Company

The Mustang Meadow House is
situated on a remote mesa in the
Colorado Rocky Mountains. Located
on the wooded edge of a vast alluvial
meadow, the house enjoys
magnificant views of several million
acres of forest and mountains.
The project's formal origins lie in the
'long house' a Native American
communal dwelling – a large single
room dedicated to social gatherings,
sited according to local topography
and ritual. The house runs from east
to west, linking mountain to valley. It is
closed to the north in a manner
analogous to the forest edge, and
open to the south, the meadow.

The serpentine approach road leads
to the entrance in the opaque north
wall. Passing through an apparently
'broken' section, the hidden domestic
spaces are revealed. The building's
skin wraps and folds over the interior.
A large 'visor' shades the south-facing
spaces, qualifying the view while
offering protection from the
environment. Windows and doors are
set in the extruded fissures and folded
surfaces. The building's simple
section is broken to afford visual
access through the house. The interior
of plywood panelling and exterior
of plank siding, slip past glazed and
unglazed openings to reinforce the
presence of the site in the building.

1 Vertical timber
boards on the north
facade are interrupted
only by a few openings
and the canopied slot
where a stair leads up
to the main entrance.
2 Above the entrance,
an unglazed opening
provides a framed
outlook from a terrace
accessible from the
library on the first floor.
3 Inside, the plywood
lined, double-height
living space looks out
over the meadow,
overlooked by the
study and library
above.

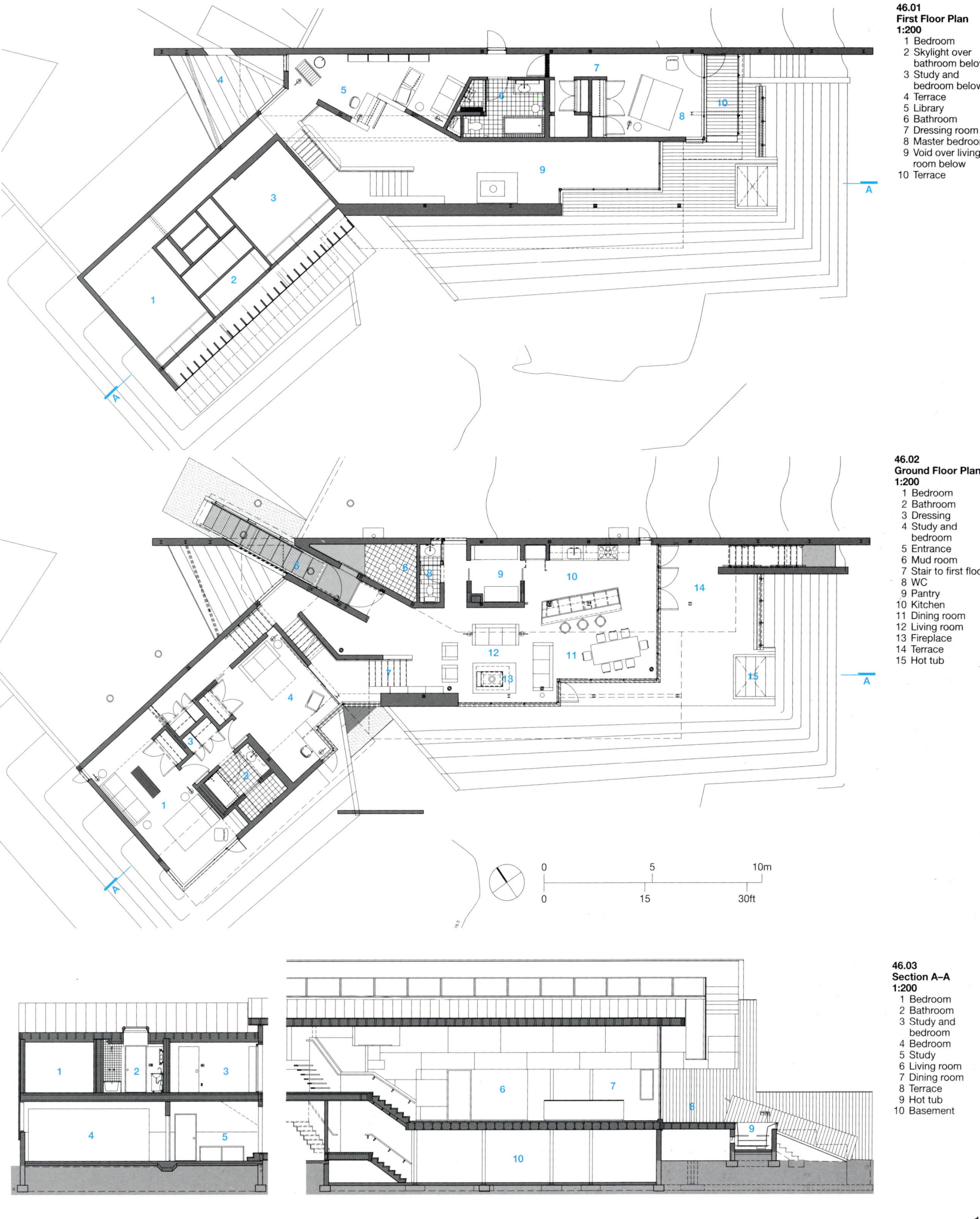

46.01
First Floor Plan
1:200
1 Bedroom
2 Skylight over bathroom below
3 Study and bedroom below
4 Terrace
5 Library
6 Bathroom
7 Dressing room
8 Master bedroom
9 Void over living room below
10 Terrace

46.01
First Floor Plan
1:200
1 Bedroom
2 Skylight over bathroom below
3 Study and bedroom below
4 Terrace
5 Library
6 Bathroom
7 Dressing room
8 Master bedroom
9 Void over living room below
10 Terrace

46.02
Ground Floor Plan
1:200
1 Bedroom
2 Bathroom
3 Dressing
4 Study and bedroom
5 Entrance
6 Mud room
7 Stair to first floor
8 WC
9 Pantry
10 Kitchen
11 Dining room
12 Living room
13 Fireplace
14 Terrace
15 Hot tub

46.03
Section A–A
1:200
1 Bedroom
2 Bathroom
3 Study and bedroom
4 Bedroom
5 Study
6 Living room
7 Dining room
8 Terrace
9 Hot tub
10 Basement

199

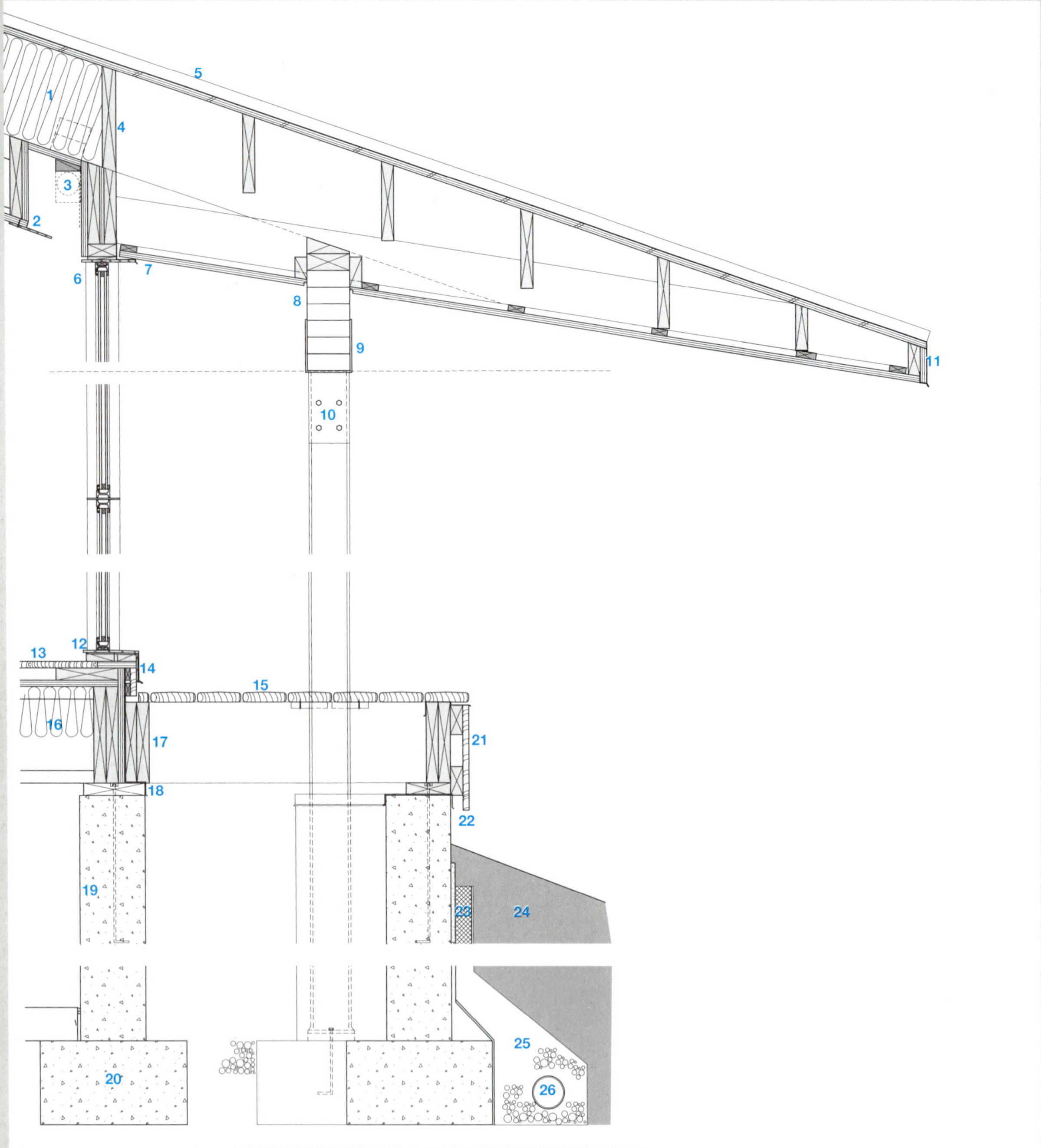

46.04
**Detail Building
Section**
1:20
1 Roof insulation
2 Shade cover
3 Roll-up shade
4 Tapered rafter
5 Roof sheathing
6 WIndow
7 Ceiling soffit lining
8 Glue laminated
beam
9 Custom steel
stirrup
10 Steel column
beyond
11 Fascia
12 Window sill
13 Hardwood floor
14 Sill cover plate
15 Timber decking
16 Floor insulation
17 40 x 250 mm ($1\frac{1}{2}$ x
10 inch) ledger
18 Flashing
19 Reinforced
concrete foundation
20 Reinforced
concrete footing
21 Fascia
22 Flashing
23 Rigid insulation
24 Earth berm
25 Gravel
26 Drain

46.05
Stair Plan
1:50
1 Gravel
2 Concrete pad
3 Stringer
4 Wire mesh guardrail
5 Stanchion
6 Tiling
7 Line of wall above
8 Stringer
9 Metal treads
10 Wall
11 Light fixture below
12 Door

46.06
Stair Section
1:50
1 Wire mesh guardrail
2 Handrail
3 Aluminium angle
4 Stringer
5 Metal tread
6 Metal balustrade
7 External concrete
wall

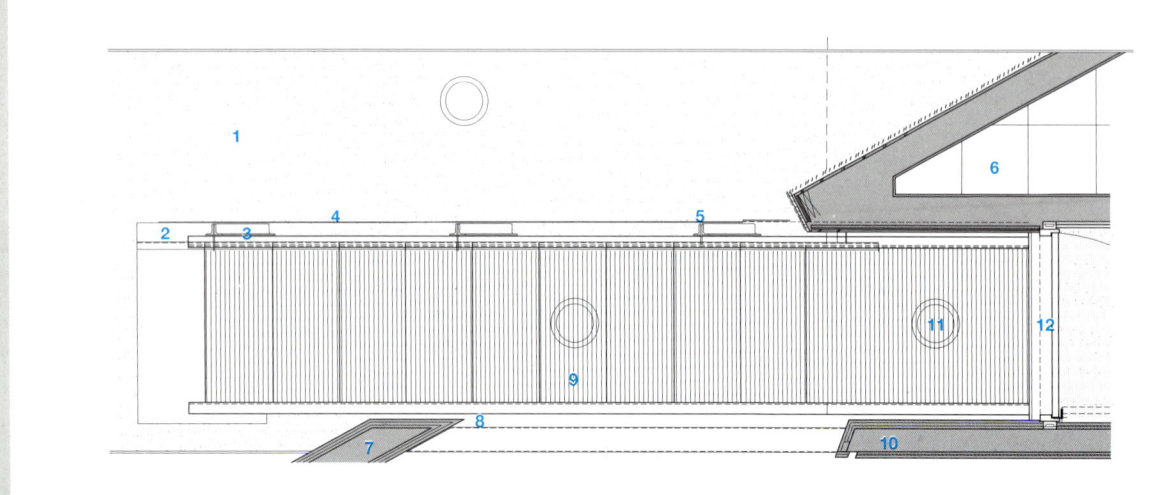

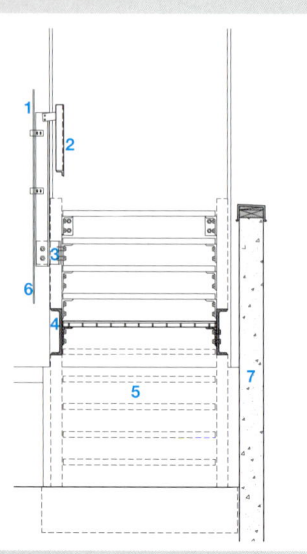

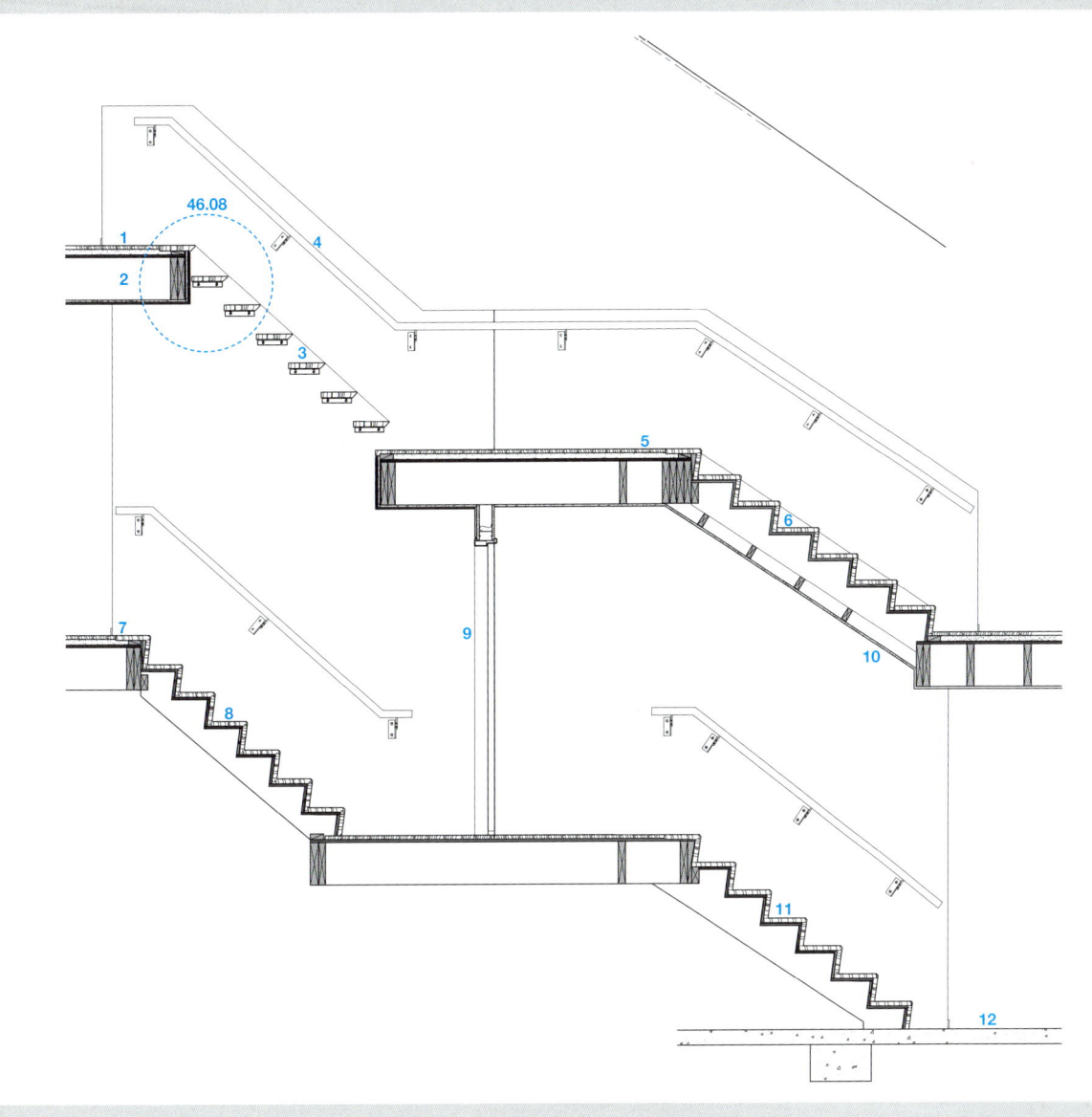

46.08

46.07
Stair Detail
1:50
1 Hardwood floor
2 50 x 250 mm (2 x 10 inch) timber framing
3 Timber stair with open risers
4 50 mm (2 inch) diameter round hardwood handrail to match hardwood flooring material
5 Top tread to match other stair treads
6 Timber treads and risers
7 Top tread to match other stair treads
8 Timber treads and risers
9 Door
10 Gypsum board ceiling
11 Timber treads and risers
12 Concrete floor

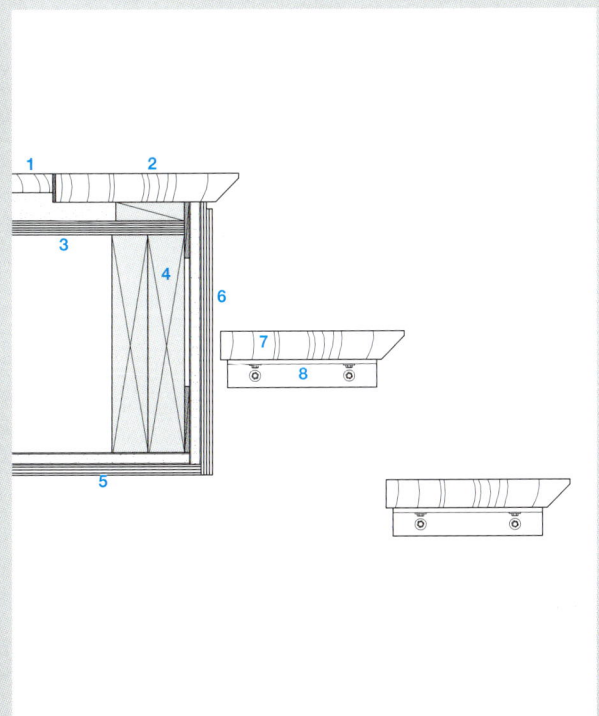

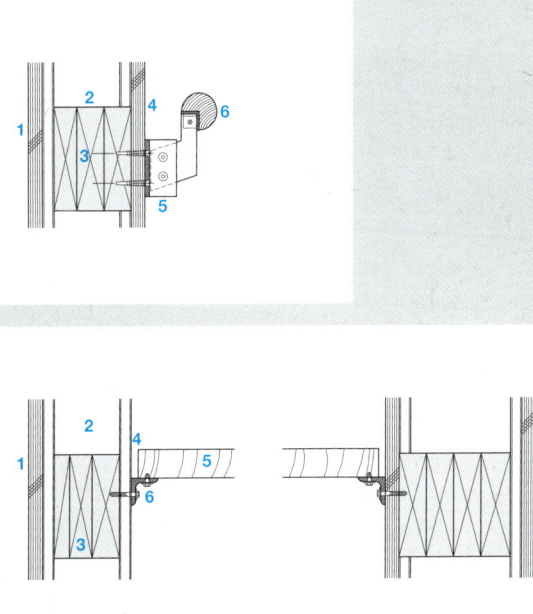

46.08
Stair Section Detail 1
1:10
1 Hardwood floor
2 Timber tread flush with floor
3 Plywood sub-floor
4 Timber framing
5 Plywood ceiling
6 Plywood fascia
7 Timber bevelled-edge tread
8 Aluminium angle fixed to wall to support tread

46.09
Stair Section Detail 2
1:10
1 Plywood wall cladding
2 Wall cavity
3 Timber framing
4 Plywood wall cladding
5 Aluminium angle fixed to wall
6 Hardwood handrail

46.10
Stair Section Detail 3
1:10
1 Plywood wall cladding
2 Wall cavity
3 Timber framing
4 Shadow gap between wall and tread
5 Timber tread
6 Aluminium angle

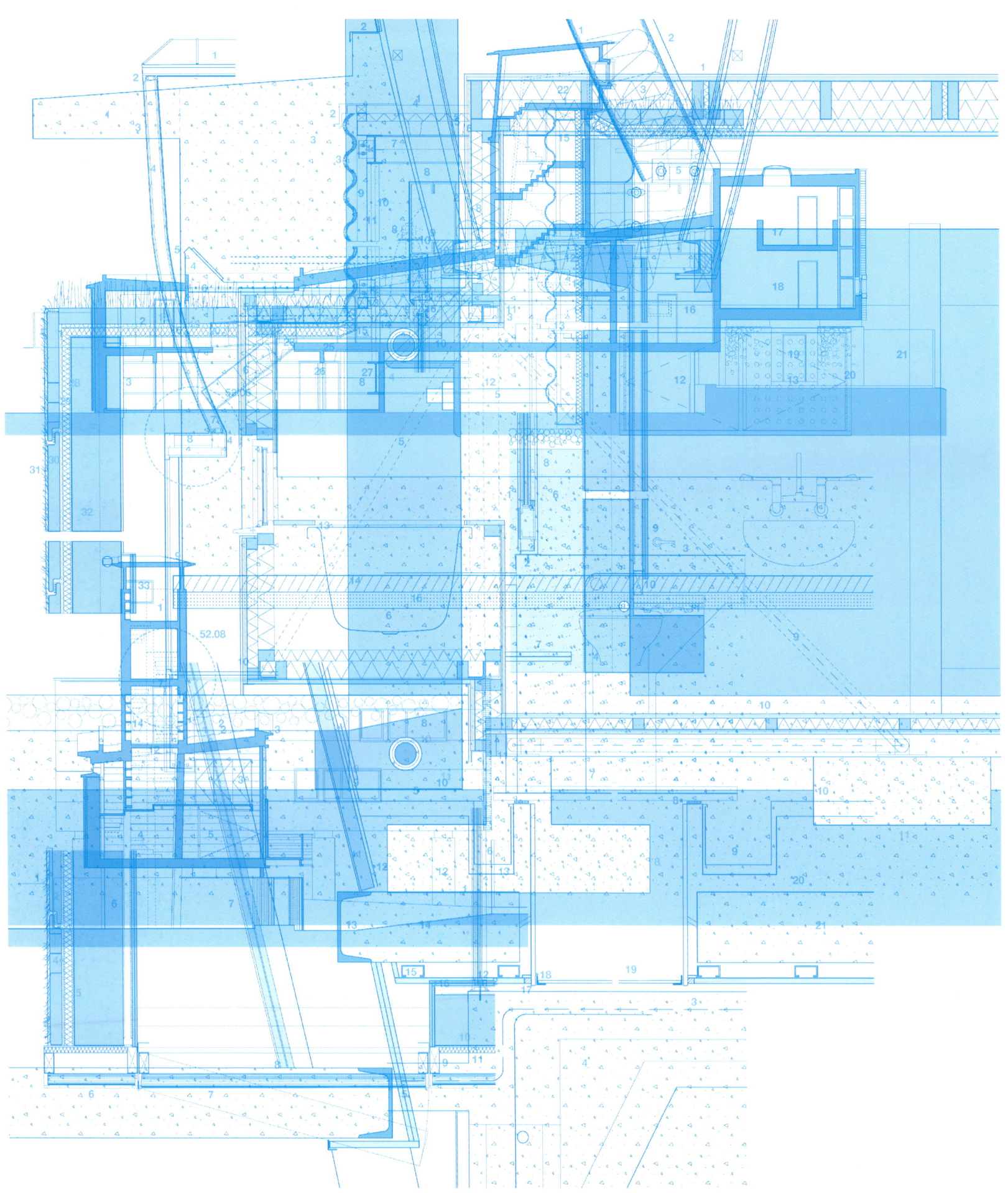

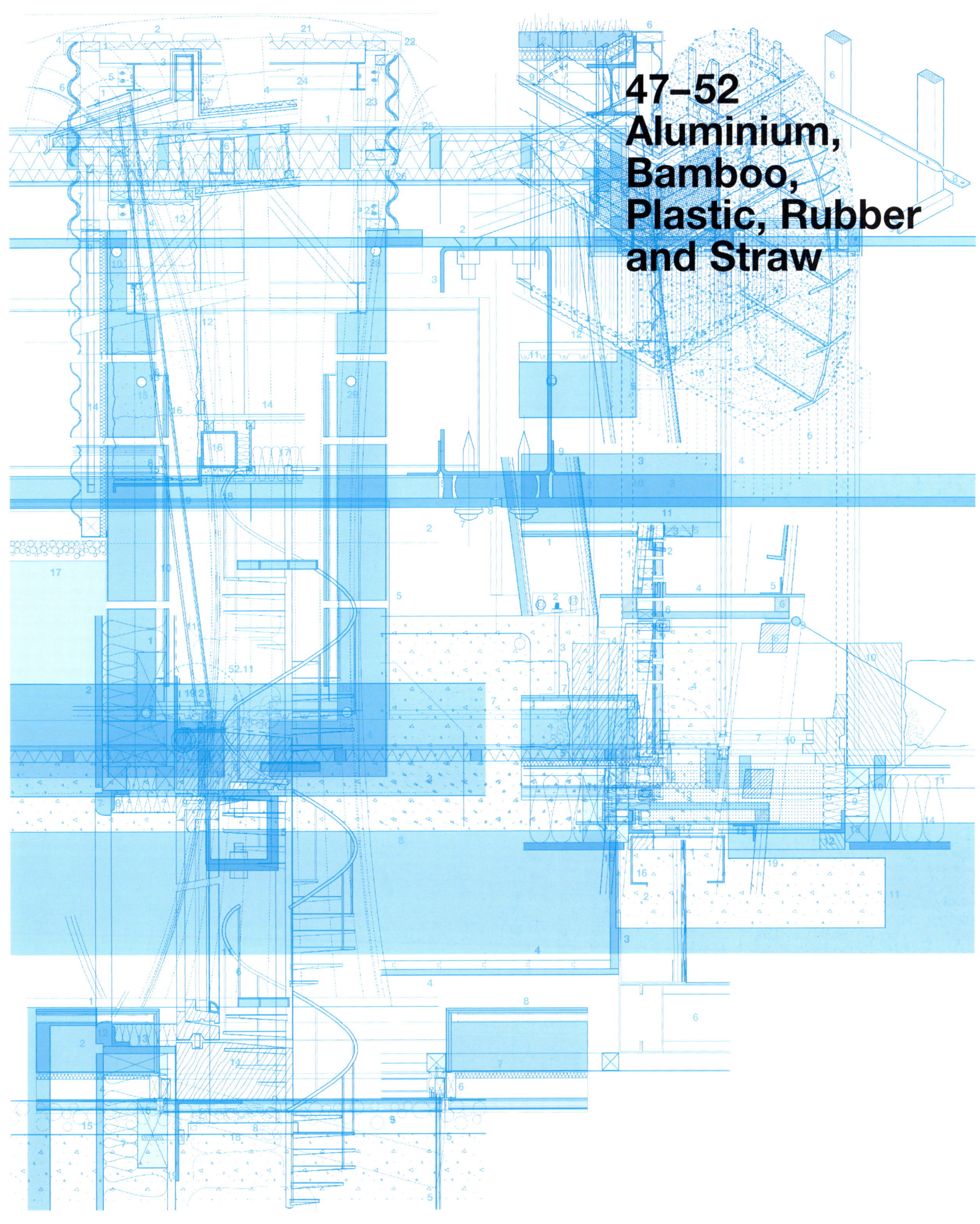

47–52
Aluminium,
Bamboo,
Plastic, Rubber
and Straw

Studio Gordillo
Madrid, Spain

Client
Luis Gordillo and Pilar Linares

Area
328 square metres (3,530 square feet)

Project Team
Iñaki Ábalos, Juan Herreros, Ángel
Jaramillo, Renata Sentkiewicz,
Auxiliadora Gálvez

Structural Engineer
Juan Gómez

Quantity Surveyor
José Torras

Landscape Architect
Fernando Valero

This light-filled artists' studio, located
in a Madrid suburb, is an adjunct to
an existing residence. Built as a
stand-alone structure, the studio is
arranged as a linear, semi-buried
volume with two light boxes projecting
from the roof. The primary facade
runs parallel to the east boundary, set
back from the street by five metres
(16 feet). The primary volume, behind
this facade, houses the main studio
along two-thirds of its length.
The other third houses the engravings
room, office, a kitchen and bathroom
on the upper floor, while storage
facilities and funds archive are
situated in the basement. The roof is
designed as an extension of the
garden. The two roof lights rise up
with north–south orientation to
illuminate the painting studio.

The substantial 328 square metre
(3,530 square foot) volume minimizes
its presence through the use of
translucent polycarbonate and dense
climbing plants. The former sets the
building apart from its neighbours
while creating a luminous and
practical environment for painting
as well as acting as a beacon at night.
The latter brings the building into a
harmonious relationship with the site,
enhanced by sliding panels that open
the workspace up to the garden.
As a result, the semi-buried interior
is constructed so that natural light is
modelled as a solid, expansive
material, satisfying not only the
specific demands of the workspace
but also creating a building that is
as austere as it is sensual.

1 From the street, the
building appears as a
single-height
polycarbonate volume,
extended upwards
with two light boxes to
fill the studio with
natural light.
2 The engraving
room, located in the
two-storey section to
the north, opens up via
sliding and hinged
panels to the garden.
3 At the edges of the
building, the materials
become softer to
create a transition
between artifact and
nature. Here, climbing
plants and brick
steps traverse a level
change.
4 At night, the
polycarbonate panels
act as a lantern throw-
ing soft light out into
the garden. Timber
decking and minimal
ground cover reinforce
the effect.
5 View of the main
studio where the light
boxes deliver luminous
natural light, enhanced
by white walls, white
structure and a pol-
ished concrete floor.

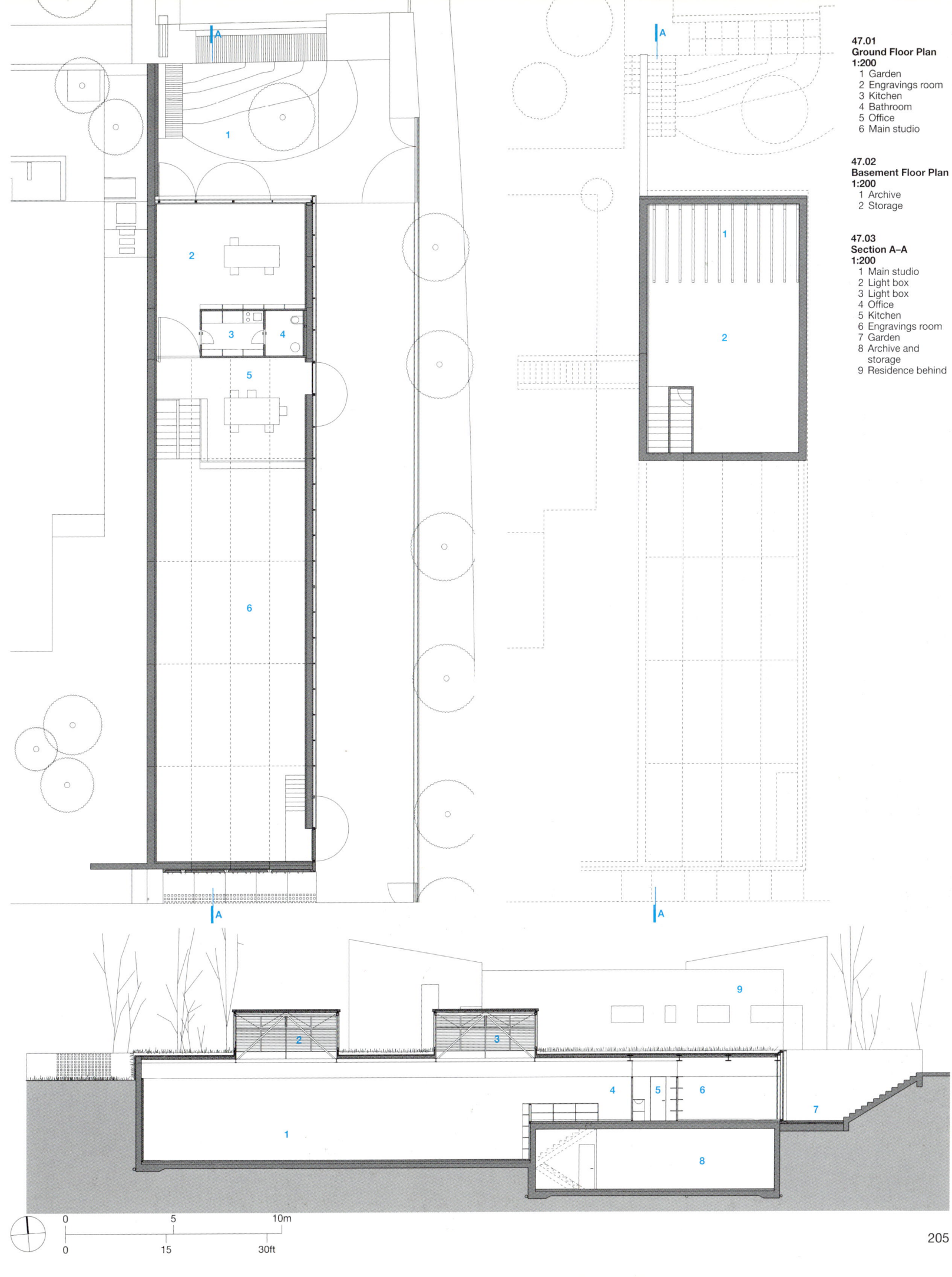

47.01
Ground Floor Plan
1:200
  1 Garden
  2 Engravings room
  3 Kitchen
  4 Bathroom
  5 Office
  6 Main studio

47.02
Basement Floor Plan
1:200
  1 Archive
  2 Storage

47.03
Section A–A
1:200
  1 Main studio
  2 Light box
  3 Light box
  4 Office
  5 Kitchen
  6 Engravings room
  7 Garden
  8 Archive and
     storage
  9 Residence behind

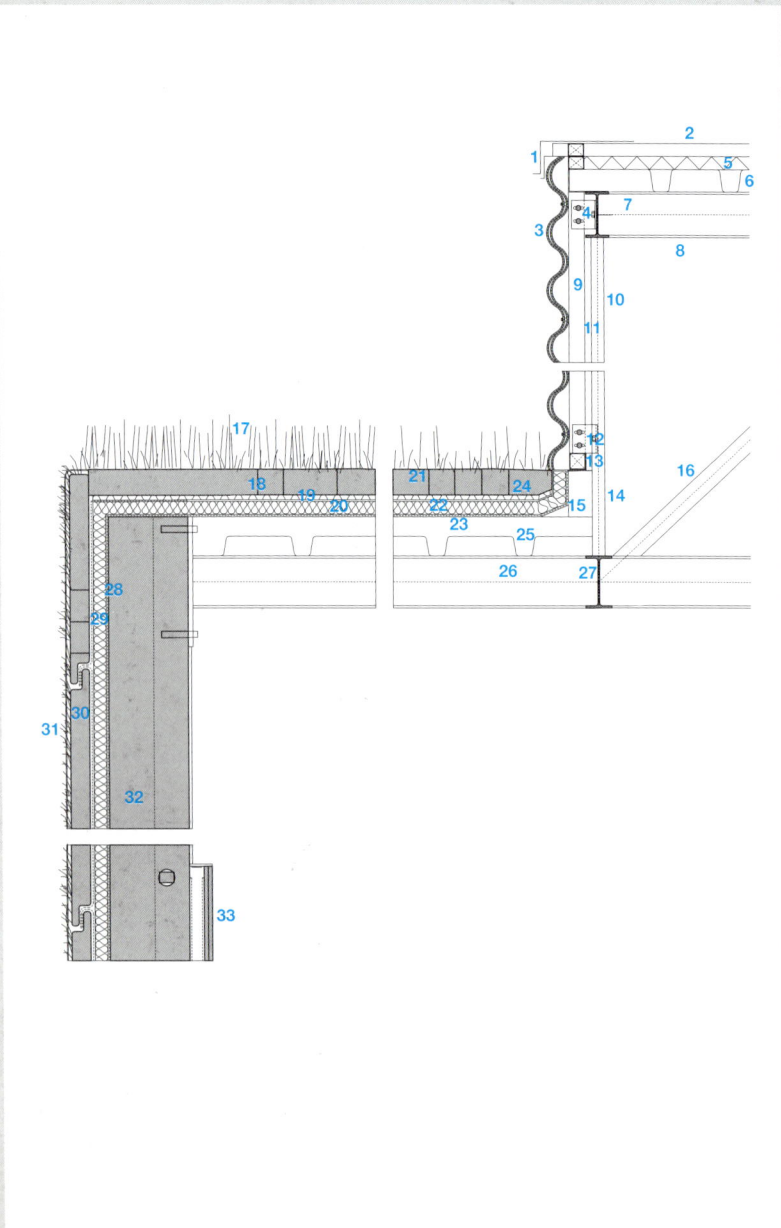

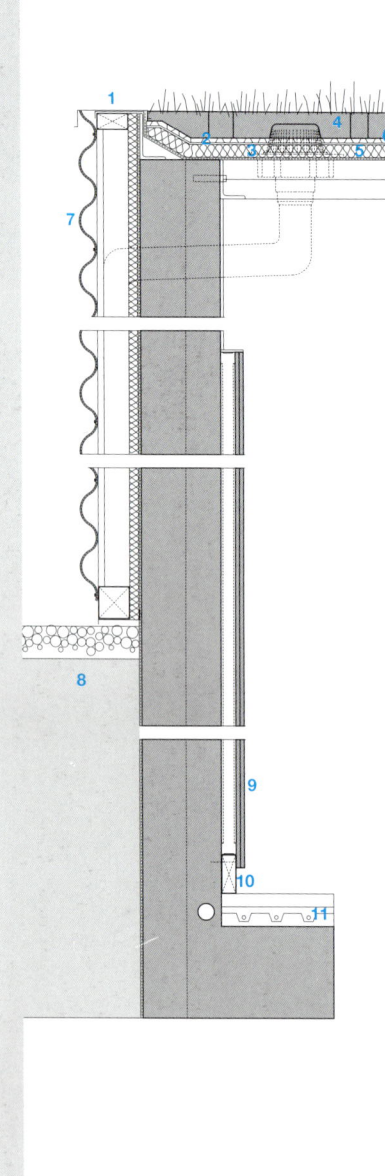

47.04
Light Box Detail
1:20
 1 Folded steel edge sheet
 2 Steel profile roof sheeting
 3 Corrugated polycarbonate sheeting
 4 Steel anchoring angle
 5 40 mm (1¹/2 inch) thick extruded polystyrene
 6 Bent sheet slab
 7 S-shape 160 gauge rolled steel
 8 S-shape 160 gauge rolled steel
 9 Rolled steel tube substructure
 10 S-shape 80 gauge rolled steel
 11 Rolled steel tube substructure
 12 Steel anchoring angle
 13 Rolled steel tube substructure
 14 S-shape 80 gauge rolled steel
 15 Support block
 16 S-shape 120 gauge rolled steel
 17 Vegetation planted on prepared roof surface
 18 Waterproofing membrane
 19 Separating layer of synthetic felt
 20 40 mm (1¹/2 inch) thick extruded polystyrene
 21 80 mm (3 inch) deep subsoil
 22 Separating layer of synthetic felt and rigid extruded polystyrene foam
 23 Waterproofing membrane
 24 Drain beyond
 25 Bent sheet slab under 60 mm (2¹/3 inch) concrete slab
 26 W-shape rolled steel belt
 27 Laminated steel I-beam
 28 S-shape 160 rolled steel
 29 Separating layer of synthetic felt and rigid extruded polystyrene foam

 30 40 mm (1¹/2 inch) thick extruded polystyrene
 31 Mesh base for vegetation
 32 Bearer wall of reinforced concrete
 33 Self supporting plasterboard partition

47.05
Wall and Roof Detail
1:20
 1 Drain beyond
 2 Waterproofing membrane
 3 40 mm (1¹/2 inch) thick extruded polystyrene
 4 80 mm (3 inch) deep subsoil
 5 Separating layer of synthetic felt
 6 Folded steel edge sheet
 7 Simple curved cellular polycarbonate plate
 8 Soil with drainage gravel over
 9 Self supporting partition
 10 Skirting block
 11 Polytherm floor heating

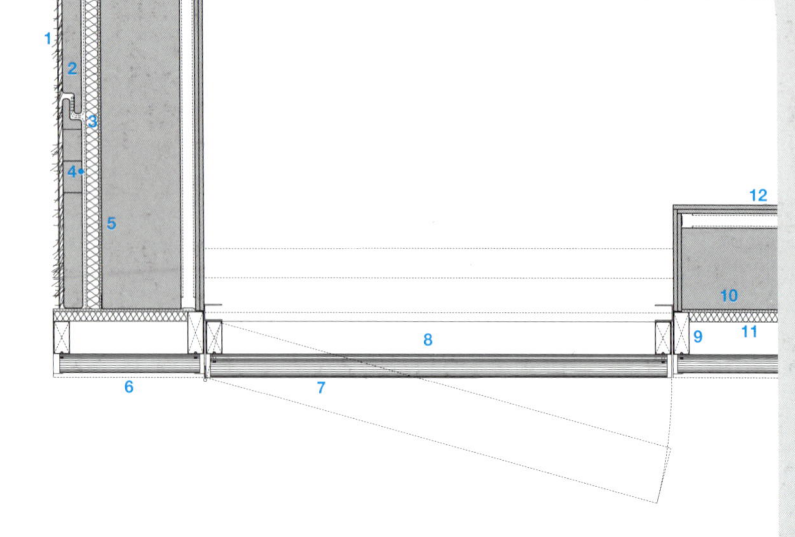

47.06
External Wall and Window Corner Detail 1:20
 1 Mesh base for vegetation
 2 Rigid reinforced polyethelene panel
 3 40 mm (1¹/2 inch) thick extruded polystyrene
 4 Separating layer of synthetic felt
 5 Waterproofing membrane
 6 Finishing sheet steel to external face
 7 Simple curved cellular polycarbonate panel
 8 Double curved cellular polycarbonate panel
 9 Rolled steel tube substructure
 10 Waterproofing membrane
 11 Separating layer of synthetic felt and rigid

extruded polystyrene
 12 Self supporting plasterboard partition

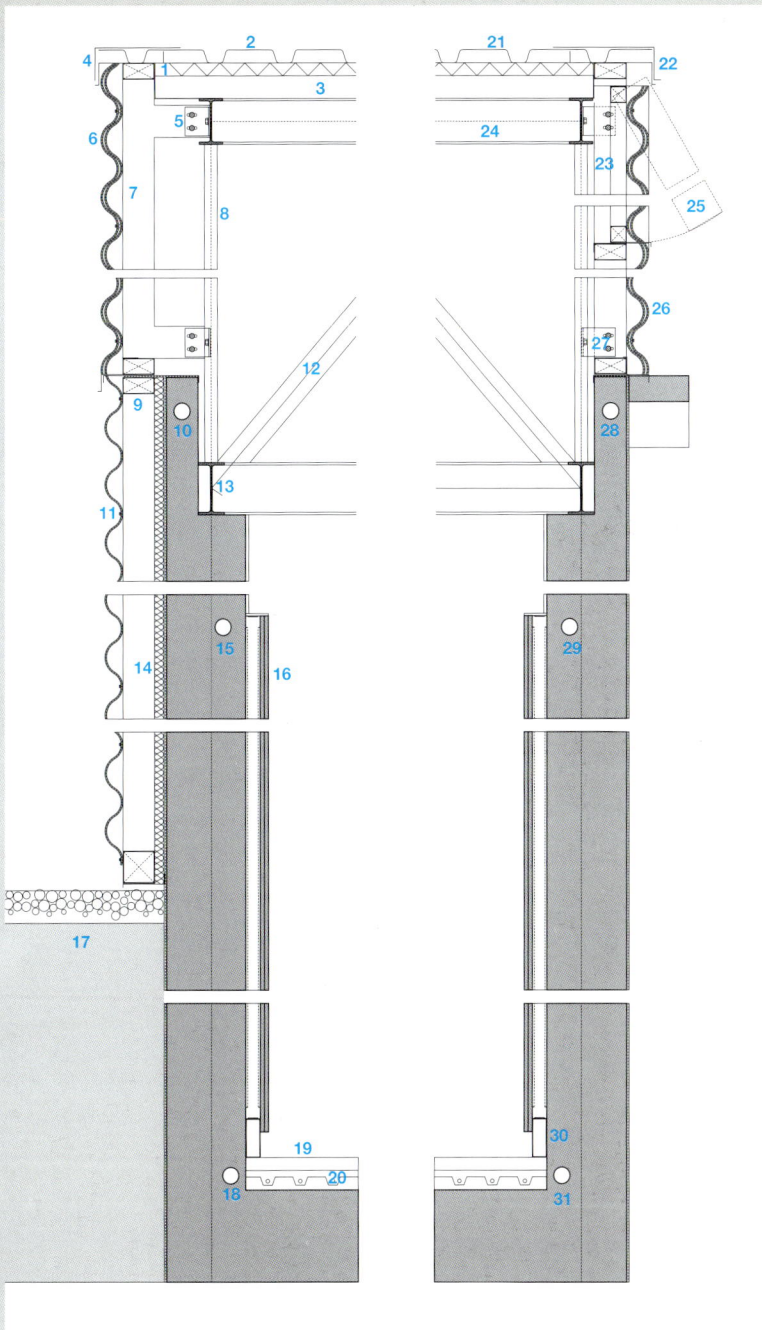

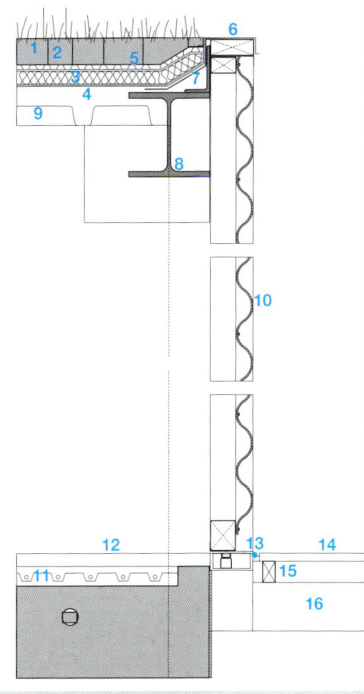

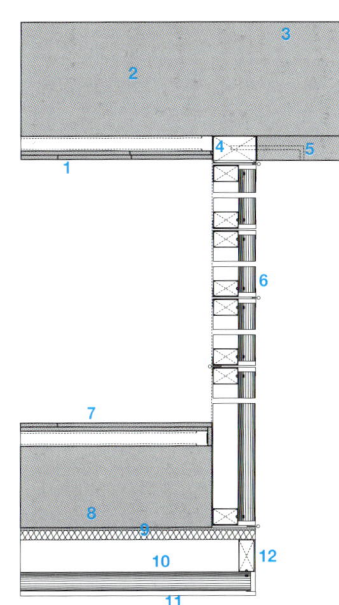

47.07
Light Box and
External Wall Detail
1:20
1 40 mm (1¹/2 inch)
thick extruded
polystyrene
2 Silver grey metallic
fretted sheeting
3 Bent steel slab
4 Folded steel lip
5 Anchoring angle
6 Double curved
cellular polycarbonate
panel
7 Laminated steel
tube substructure
8 S-shape 80 rolled
steel
9 Rolled steel tube
superstructure
10 Reinforced
concrete wall overlayer
11 Single curved
cellular polycarbonate
panel
12 S-shape 120 rolled
steel
13 S-shape 160 rolled
steel
14 Separating layer of
synthetic felt and rigid
extruded polystyrene
foam
15 Reinforced
concrete bearer wall
16 Self supporting
plasterboard partition
17 Soil with drainage
gravel over
18 Reinforced
concrete bearer wall
19 Terrazzo interior
paving
20 Polytherm floor
heating
21 Silver grey metallic
fretted sheeting
22 Steel lip
23 S-shape 160
laminated steel
24 S-shape 160
laminated steel
25 Operable hinged
ventilation panel
26 Double curved
cellular polycarbonate
panel
27 Anchoring angle
28 Reinforced
concrete wall overlayer
29 Reinforced
concrete bearer wall
30 Aluminium tube
skirting board
31 Reinforced
concrete floor

47.08
External Wall and
Roof Detail
1:20
1 80 mm (3 inch)
deep subsoil
2 Separating layer of
synthetic felt and
drainage
3 40 mm (1¹/2 inch)
thick extruded
polystyrene
4 Waterproofing
membrane
5 Drain
6 Bent finishing sheet
7 Support block
8 W-shape 260
gauge laminated steel
9 Bent sheet slab
with 60 mm (2¹/3 inch)
concrete
10 Double curved
cellular polycarbonate
panel
11 Polytherm floor
heating
12 Terrazzo interior
paving
13 Floor to wall silicon
joint
14 Resin treated
timber decking
15 Backing battens
16 Timber joist

47.09
Door Detail
1:20
1 Self supporting
plasterboard partition
2 Reinforced
concrete bearer wall
3 Reinforced
concrete wall overlayer
4 Rolled steel tube
superstructure
5 Canal for electrical
installation
6 Metal folding door
with double layer of
curved cellular
polycarbonate
panelling
7 Self suppporting
partition
8 Waterproofing
membrane
9 Separating layer of
synthetic felt
10 40 mm (1¹/2 inch)
thick extruded
polystyrene
11 Single curved
cellular polycarbonate
panel
12 Bent finishing sheet

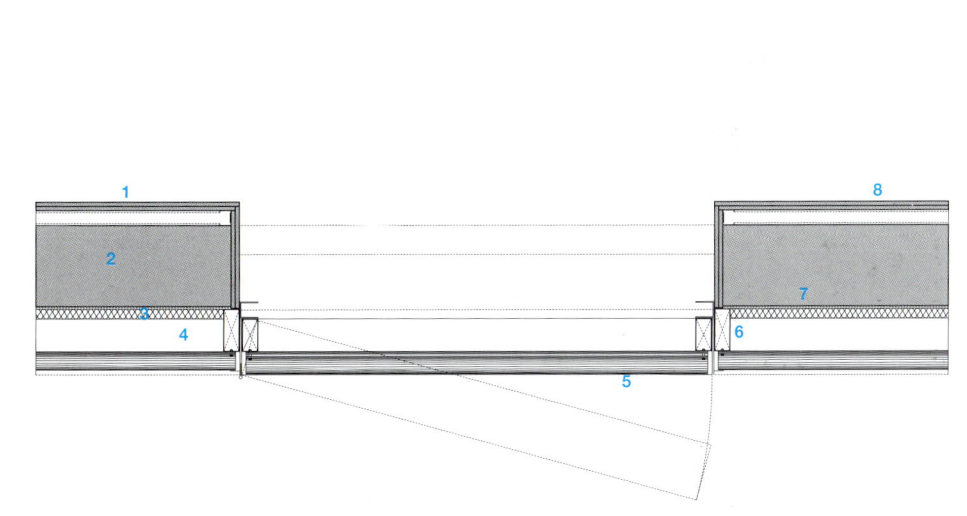

47.10
Window Detail
1:20
1 Self supporting
plasterboard partition
2 Reinforced
concrete bearer wall
3 Separating layer of
synthetic felt
4 40 mm (1¹/2 inch)
thick extruded
polystyrene
5 Curved cellular
polycarbonate opening
panel
6 Rolled steel tube
substructure
polycarbonate panel
7 Waterproofing
membrane
8 Self supporting
plasterboard partition

48
Kengo Kuma & Associates

Plastic House
Tokyo, Japan

Area
173 square metres (1,860 square feet)

Project Team
Kengo Kuma, Hiroshi Nakamura

Structural Engineer
Kajima Design

Main Contractor
Kajima Design

Mechanical Engineer
Koizumi Jyusan

Electrical Engineer
Tada Enterprise

Commissioned by a fashion photographer and his mother, a writer, this unusual house has been carved out of the dense urban fabric of Tokyo. Located on a typically confined, 151 square metre (1,625 square feet) site, the design breaks away from the concrete boxes so ubiquitously employed in Japanese cities in recent decades. Instead, plastic – recognized for its versatility, lightness and ability to be used in various levels of transparency and opacity – is used as the primary construction material. In doing so, plastic becomes the medium through which a reinterpretation of the traditional Japanese post and beam structure with its infill of translucent shoji screens is made.

A structural steel frame is concealed within an envelope of fibre-reinforced polyester wands and cavity walls of fibreglass panels attached to plastic studs with transparent plastic screws. An open ended box projects from the front facade creating a balcony to the bedroom and framing the stair tower on the roof. The space at the back of the house contains a plastic tatami platform which, via its translucency, admits light to the basement apartment. Inside, a white ground floor photo studio doubles as a living and dining room with glazed walls to the forecourt and rear garden. A staircase of plastic grid treads on the south wall connects all floors from the basement to the roof terrace, which serves as an outdoor studio as well as a space for entertaining.

1 Making the most of a narrow urban site, the house is arranged over three levels, crowned by a roof terrace. From the street, the most prominent feature is a large cantilevered box, fabricated from plastic sections which serves as a terrace to the bedroom as well as framing the stair tower to the roof terrace.
2 View of the kichen, dining and living areas on the ground floor. The lightweight furniture can be moved aside in order for the space to be used as a photographic studio. The steel-framed stair with plastic treads gives access to the bedrooms above and the apartment below.

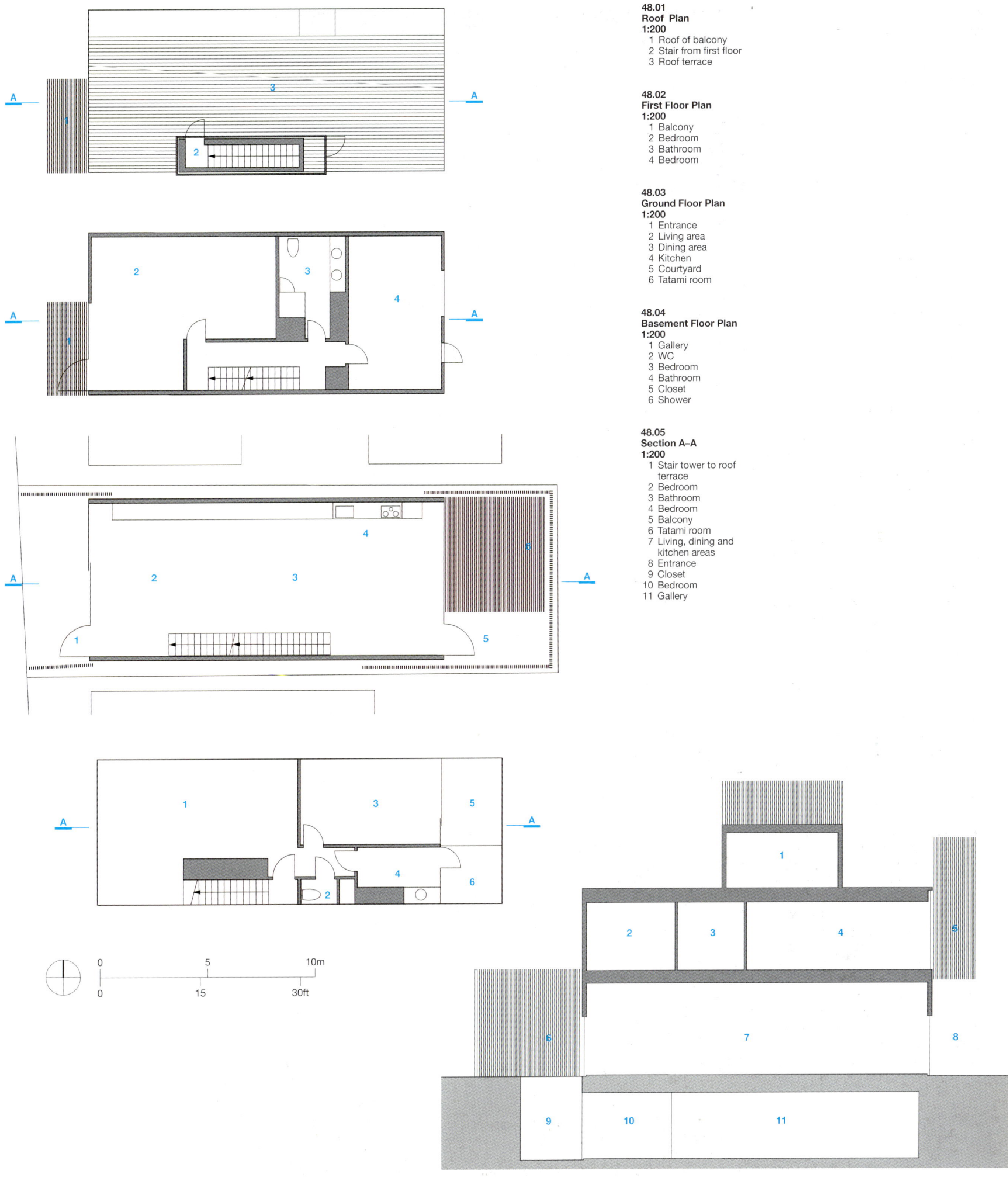

48.01
Roof Plan
1:200
1 Roof of balcony
2 Stair from first floor
3 Roof terrace

48.02
First Floor Plan
1:200
1 Balcony
2 Bedroom
3 Bathroom
4 Bedroom

48.03
Ground Floor Plan
1:200
1 Entrance
2 Living area
3 Dining area
4 Kitchen
5 Courtyard
6 Tatami room

48.04
Basement Floor Plan
1:200
1 Gallery
2 WC
3 Bedroom
4 Bathroom
5 Closet
6 Shower

48.05
Section A–A
1:200
1 Stair tower to roof
 terrace
2 Bedroom
3 Bathroom
4 Bedroom
5 Balcony
6 Tatami room
7 Living, dining and
 kitchen areas
8 Entrance
9 Closet
10 Bedroom
11 Gallery

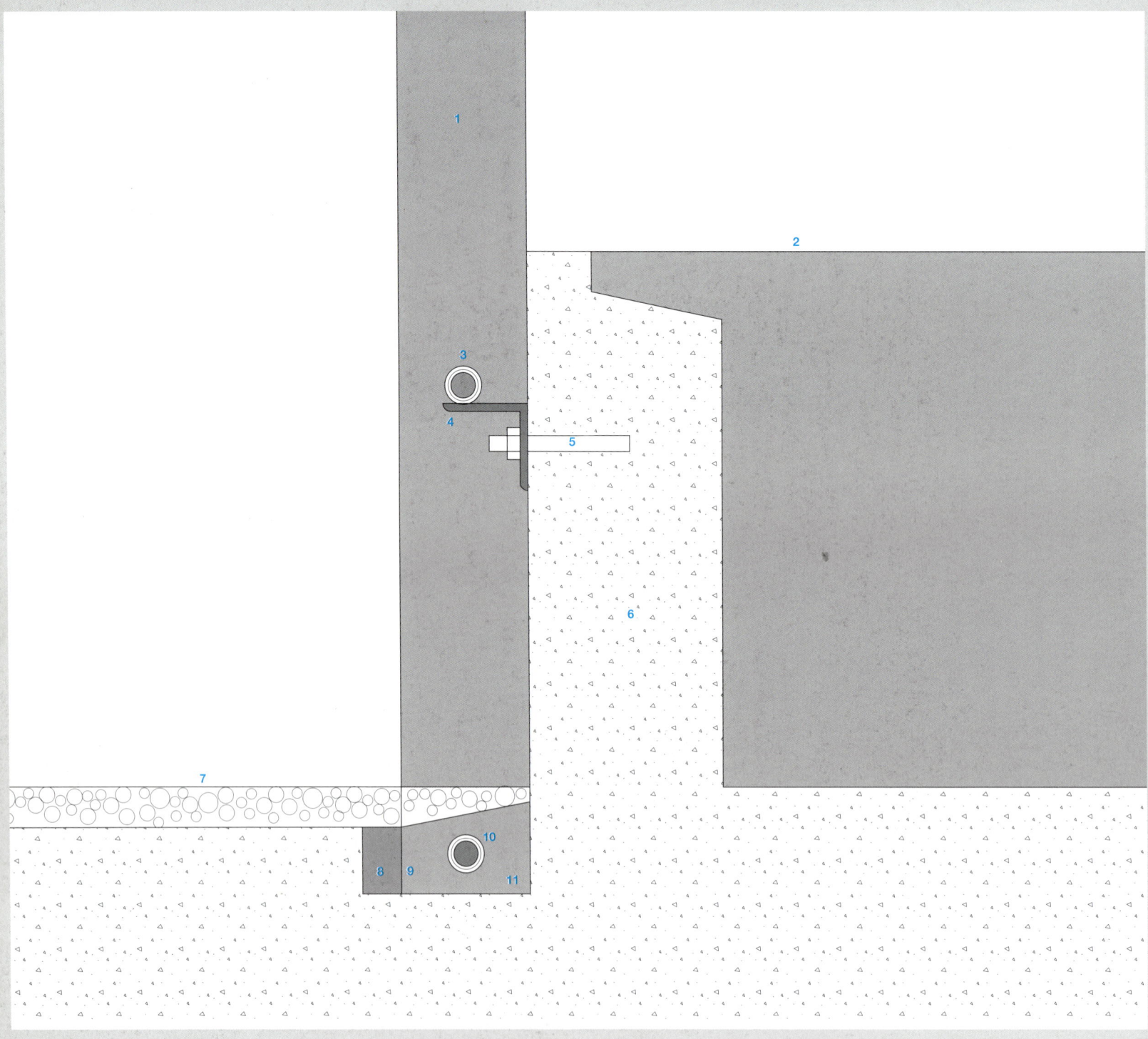

48.06
Section Detail at
Rear Garden
1:4
  1 100 x 22 x 5.5 mm
(4 x 7/8 x 1/5 inch) fibre
reinforced plastic
column
  2 Finished interior
floor level
  3 Steel bar hand rail
  4 65 x 65 mm (21/2 x
21/2 inch) metal angle
  5 Bolt fixing to hand
rail angle into
reinforced concrete

  6 Reinforced
concrete retaining wall
  7 Rubble to finished
ground level
  8 Steel plate
  9 Waterproofing layer
  10 Drain
  11 Mortar

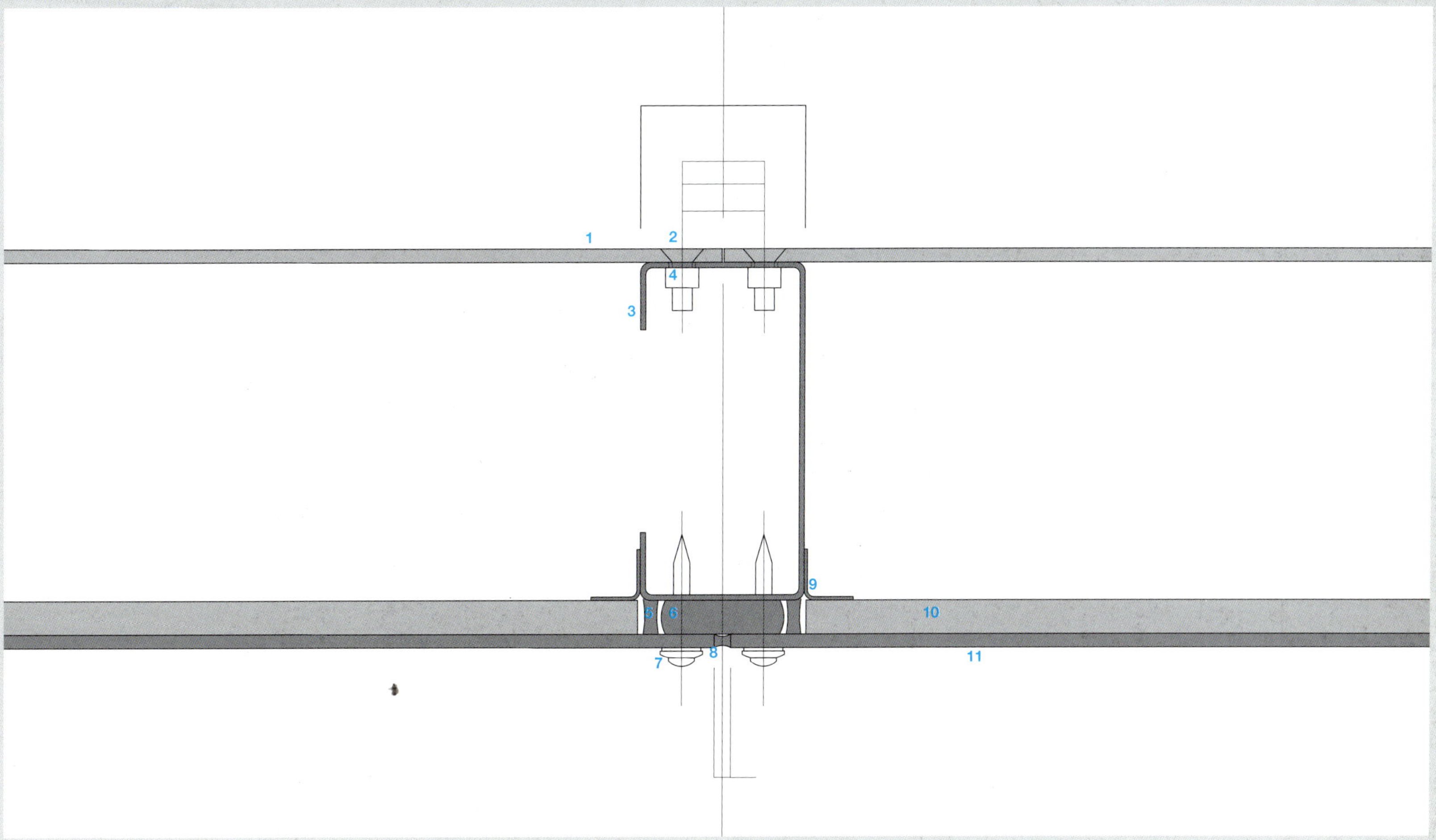

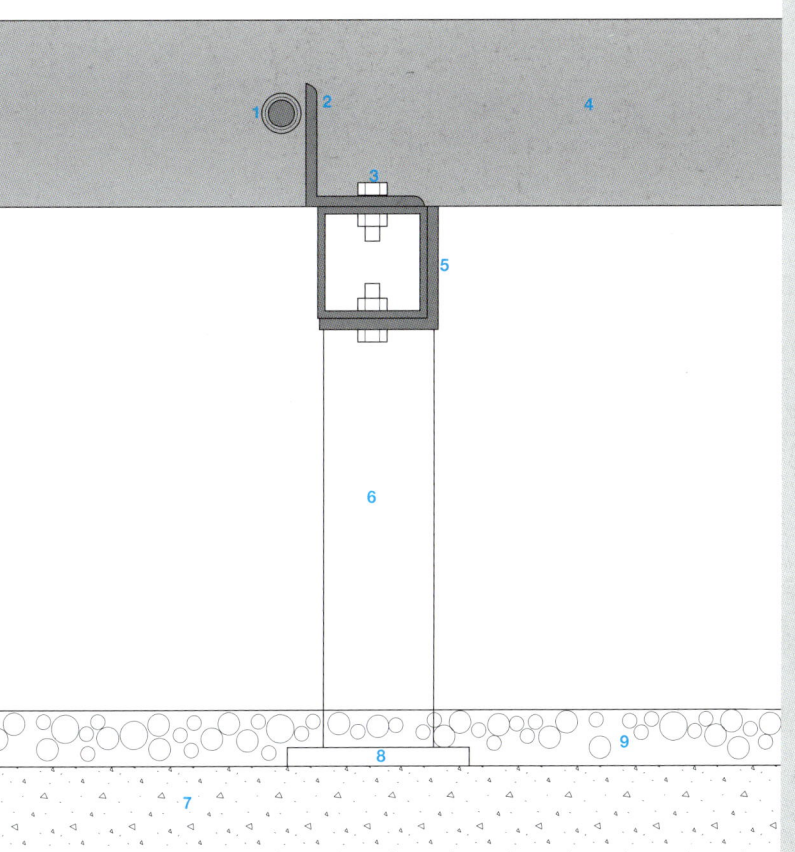

48.07
Fibre Reinforced
Plastic Exterior Wall
Detail
1:2
 1 Fibre reinforced
plastic with clear
polyeurethane coating
 2 Flat screws
 3 100 x 50 x 20 mm
(4 x 2 x 3/4 inch) steel
C-section with rust-
proof coating
 4 M4 turn nut
 5 Double sealant
 6 Butyle rubber
 7 Sealer washer with
M5 tapping sealant
 8 Modified silicon
sealant
 9 15 x 15 mm (3/10 x
3/10 inch) aluminium
angle
10 Translucent
insulation sheet
11 Fibre reinforced
plastic with clear
urethane coating

48.08
Section Detail at Rear
Garden
1:4
 1 Steel rod
balustrade
 2 65 x 65 mm (21/2 x
21/2 inch) metal angle
 3 Bolt fixing between
metal angle and
square hollow section
 4 Fibre reinforced
plastic beam
 5 60 x 60 x 4 mm
(21/3 x 21/3 x 1/8 inch)
fibre reinforced plastic
beam
 6 60 x 60 x 4 mm
(21/3 x 21/3 x 1/8 inch)
fibre reinforced plastic
column
 7 Reinforced
concrete slab
 8 Steel plate
 9 Rubble to finished
ground level

211

Masaki Endoh + Masahiro Ikeda

Natural Ellipse
Tokyo, Japan

Client
Horiike Katunori

Area
132 square metres (1,420 square feet)

Project Team
Masaki Endoh, Masahiro Ikeda,
Kenji Nawa

General Contractor
Ahagon-gumi Co. Ltd

This startlingly unique house is located in a densely populated area of Tokyo, famous for its shopping and night life. The architectural solution aims to safeguard the peace and quiet of the occupants amidst the noise and bright lights without cutting them off from the outside world. Inhabitants are allowed glimpses of the exterior through the few openings cut in apparently random fashion into the skin, though these have been carefully placed to frame particular views of neighbouring buildings. A secret terrace, open to the sky, is contained within (and concealed by) the convex walls of the deeply indented apex. Floored with glass, the terrace is also a skylight bringing natural light deep into the building via the stairwell.

The balloon-shaped volume is generated by 24 elliptical rings set vertically around a hollow elliptical core. The most prominent feature of the design is the Fibre-Reinforced Polymer (FRP) skin which wraps the entire building, barely allowing for the necessary openings to mediate between the interior and the exterior. The FRP skin is made up of unidirectional fibres embedded within a thin layer of light polymer matrix material. The fibres provide the strength and stiffness while the polymer matrix binds and protects the fibers from damage. The advantage of using FRP is that when subjected to loading or stress, it returns to its original shape – a major advantage in earthquake-prone Japan. The cage on which the FRP is stretched, is made of horizontal and vertical steel ribs. Internal materials and finishes are equally simple and austere: concrete slabs, simply painted, form the floors, ceilings are painted steel plate, and walls are of painted mineral board.

1 In the chaotic urban environment, the building appears as a serene insular form, revealing almost nothing of its interior arrangement.

2 The stretched polymer skin is punctured apparently at random with windows protected from the sun and prying eyes by white blinds.

3 The concave top of the structure incorporates a glass floor allowing light to filter down through the perforated steel staircase.

4 Every element in the building is resolutely white, creating an environment in which people become the only chromatic feature.

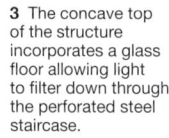

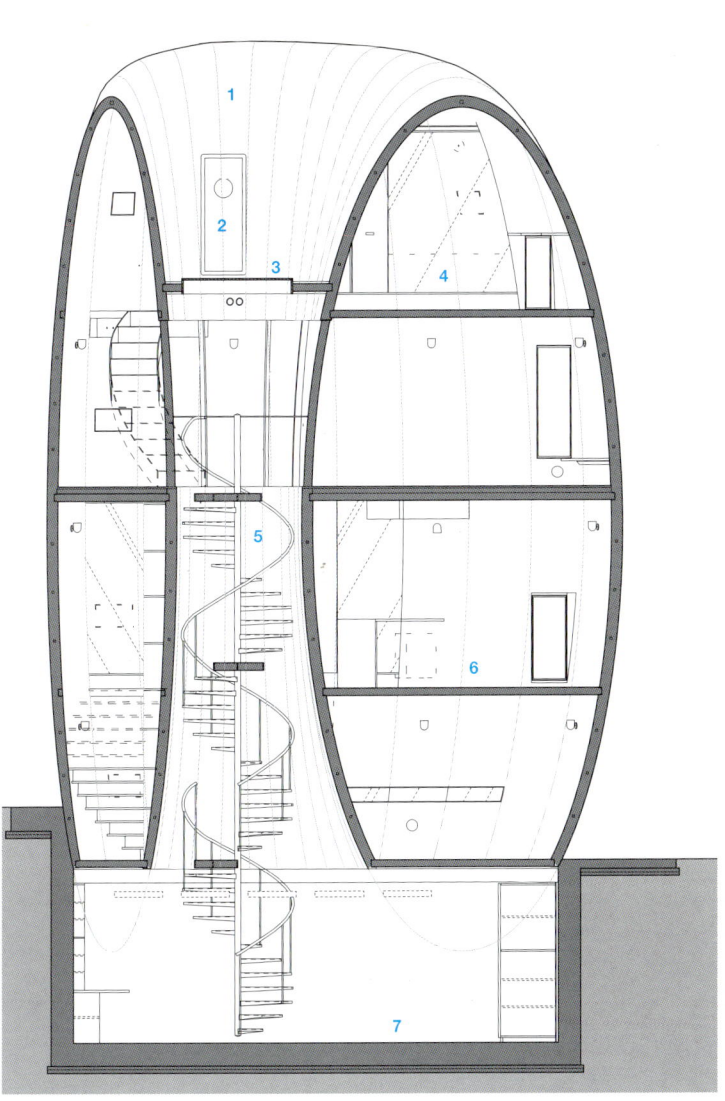

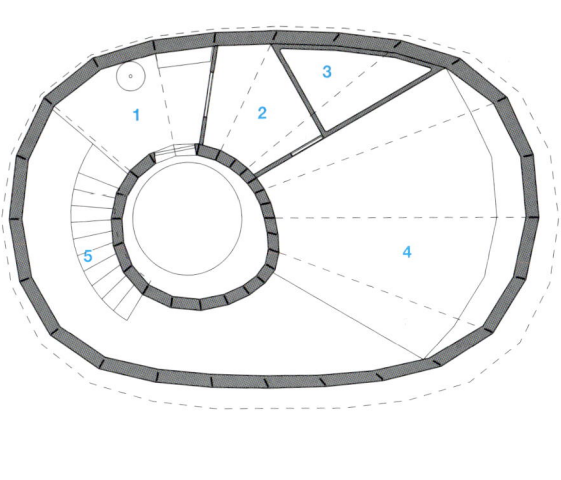

49.02
Third Floor Plan
1:100
1 WC
2 Bathroom
3 Bath tub
4 Bedroom
5 Stair up to roof
   terrace

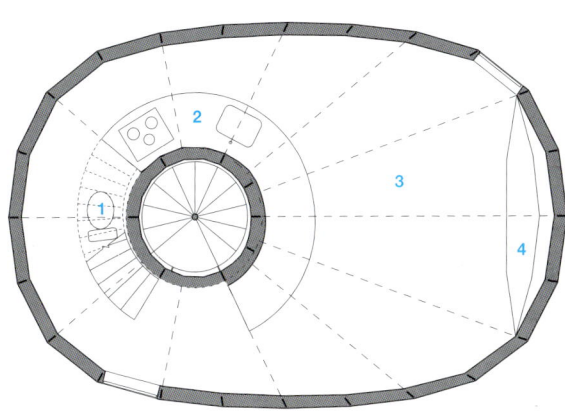

49.03
Second Floor Plan
1:100
1 WC
2 Kitchen
3 Living room
4 Storage rack

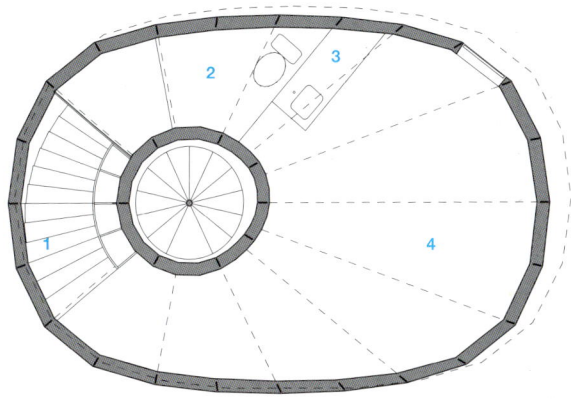

49.04
First Floor Plan
1:100
1 Stair
2 WC
3 Kitchen
4 Dining room

49.01
Sectional Detail
1:100
1 Non-inflammable
   FRP waterproofing
   with oil paint finish
2 Steel door with oil
   paint finish
3 10 mm (3/4 inch)
   thick tempered
   glass with shatter-
   prevention film
4 2 mm (1/8 inch)
   thick polyvinyl-
chloride sheet floor
system on
structural plywood
and 90 mm (3 1/2
inch) concrete slab
5 Structural steel
spiral stair
6 2 mm (1/8 inch)
thick polyvinyl-
chloride sheet floor
system on
structural plywood
and 90 mm (3 1/2
inch) concrete slab
7 2 mm (1/8 inch)
thick polyvinyl-
chloride sheet floor
system on
structural plywood
and 300 mm
(12 inch)
concrete slab

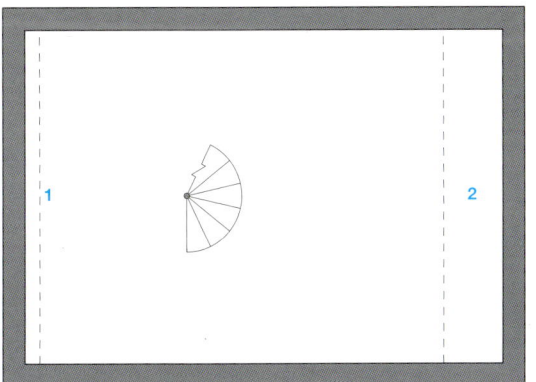

49.06
Basement Plan
1:100
1 Bookshelf to study
2 Closet

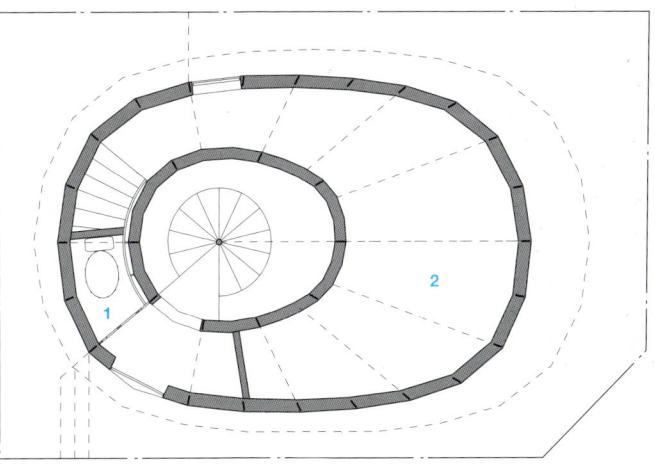

49.05
Ground Floor Plan
1:100
1 WC
2 Living room

| 0 | | 5 | | 10m |
| 0 | | 15 | | 30ft |

213

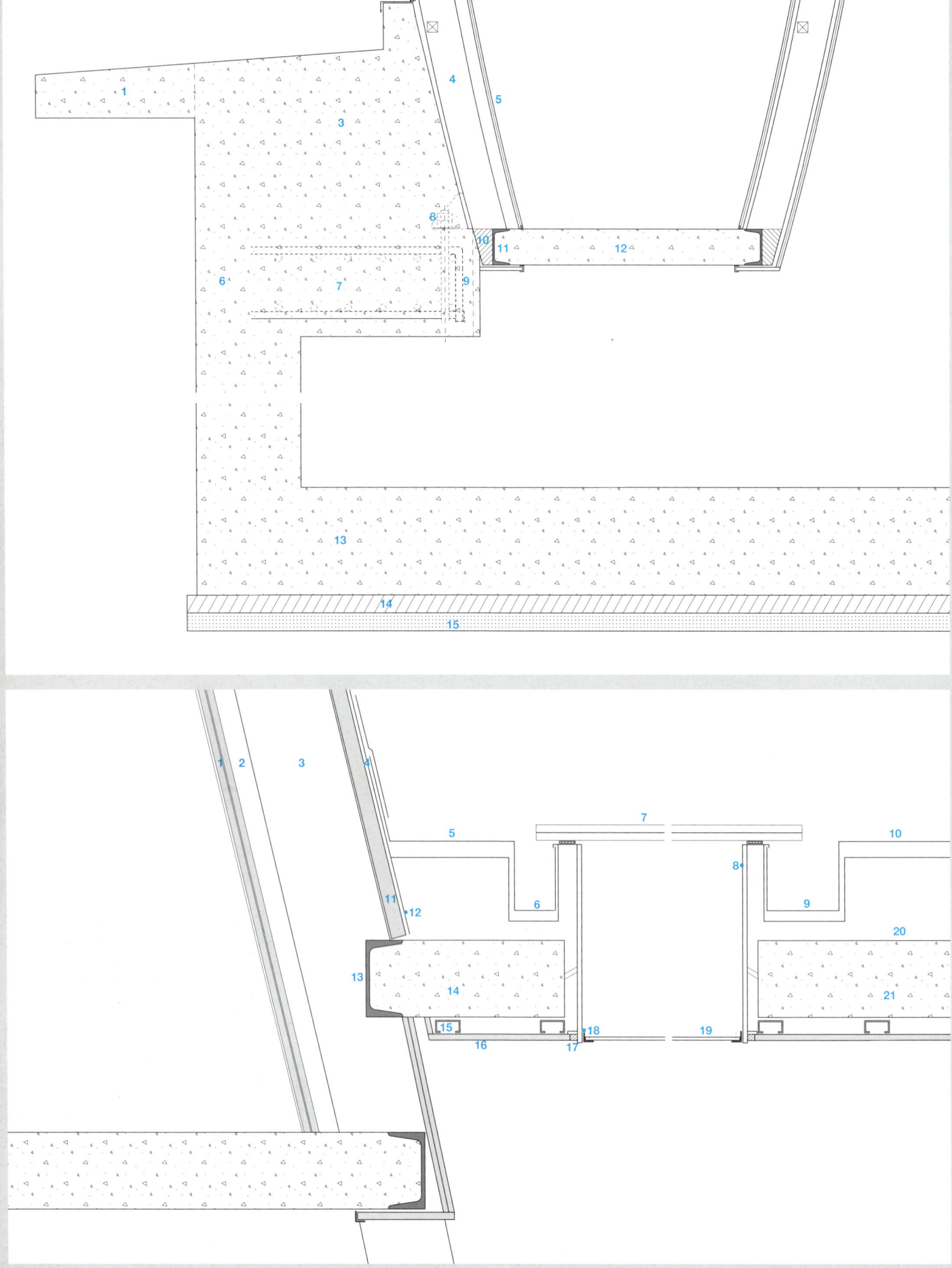

49.07
Joint Detail
1:20
1 Reinforced concrete
2 Sheet waterproofing
3 Reinforced concrete
4 22 x 100 mm (3/4 x 4 inch) flat bar column
5 Mineral board
6 Reinforced concrete
7 Reinforced concrete
8 A BL 2–M20
9 Reinforcing bar
10 Levelled concrete
11 Steel channel
12 Reinforced concrete
13 Reinforced concrete
14 Levelled concrete
15 Broken stone sub-layer

49.08
Skylight Detail
1:10
1 Mineral board with acrylic emulsion paint finish
2 Ventilation shaft
3 22 x 100 mm (3/4 x 4 inch) flat bar column
4 Non-inflammable fibre reinforced plastic waterproofing
5 Non-inflammable fibre reinforced plastic waterproofing
6 Guttering
7 15 mm (2/3 inch) tempered glass
8 Plasterboard with acrylic emulsion paint finish
9 Guttering
10 Sheet waterproofing
11 Mineral board
12 Non-inflammable fibre reinforced plastic waterproofing
13 Steel channel
14 150 mm (6 inch) thick reinforced concrete
15 Steel channel
16 Plasterboard with acrylic emulsion paint finish
17 Sealant
18 Steel angle
19 Acrylic plate
20 Heat insulating material
21 150 mm (6 inch) thick reinforced concrete

49.09
Stair Detail
1:50

1 Third floor: Ground floor + 7200 mm ($23\frac{2}{3}$ feet)
2 Second floor: Ground floor + 4990 mm ($16\frac{1}{3}$ feet)
3 First floor: Ground floor + 2250 mm ($7\frac{1}{3}$ feet)
4 Ground floor: Ground floor + 0 mm (0 feet)
5 Basement: Ground floor - 2400 mm ($7\frac{3}{4}$ feet)

49.10
Axonometric

1 30 x 30 mm ($1\frac{1}{5}$ x $1\frac{1}{5}$ inch) steel square
2 100 x 50 x 5 x 7.5 mm (4 x 2 x $\frac{1}{5}$ x $\frac{1}{3}$ inch) steel C-section
3 22 x 100 ($\frac{3}{4}$ x 4 inch) steel flat bar
4 100 x 100 x 6 x 8 mm (4 x 4 x $\frac{1}{4}$ x $\frac{1}{4}$ inch) steel H-section
5 100 x 50 x 5 x 7.5 mm (4 x 2 x $\frac{1}{5}$ x $\frac{1}{3}$ inch) steel C-section
6 300 mm ($11\frac{3}{4}$ inch) reinforced concrete

49.11
Window Detail
1:5

1 Non-inflammable fibre-reinforced plastic with wateproof oil paint finish
2 100 x 50 x 5 x 7.5 mm (4 x 2 x $\frac{1}{5}$ x $\frac{1}{3}$ inch) steel channel
3 30 x 30 mm ($1\frac{1}{4}$ x $1\frac{1}{4}$ inch) steel square section
4 3.2 mm ($\frac{1}{10}$ inch) steel angle
5 1.6 mm ($\frac{1}{20}$ inch) steel angle
6 Sealant
7 Steel U-section
8 Screen door frame
9 Stainless steel hinge
10 Screen door
11 3.2 mm ($\frac{1}{10}$ inch) steel angle
12 30 mm ($1\frac{1}{4}$ inch) steel door
13 Steel flat bar
14 3.2 mm ($\frac{1}{10}$ inch) steel angle
15 Non-inflammable fibre-reinforced plastic with wateproof oil paint finish
16 100 x 50 x 5 x 7.5 mm (4 x 2 x $\frac{1}{5}$ x $\frac{1}{3}$ inch) steel channel
17 Steel weld
18 1.6 mm ($\frac{1}{20}$ inch) steel plate
19 Cheese cloth puttied mineral board with acrylic emulsion paint finish

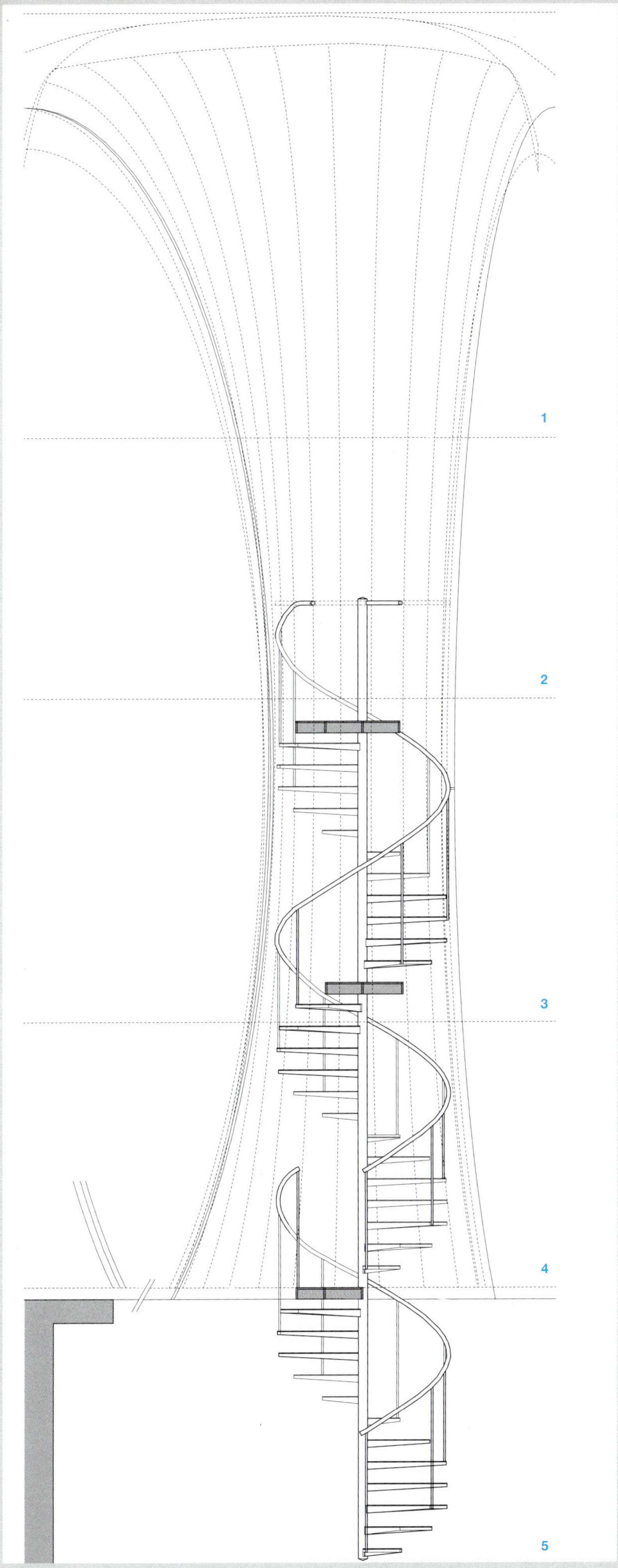

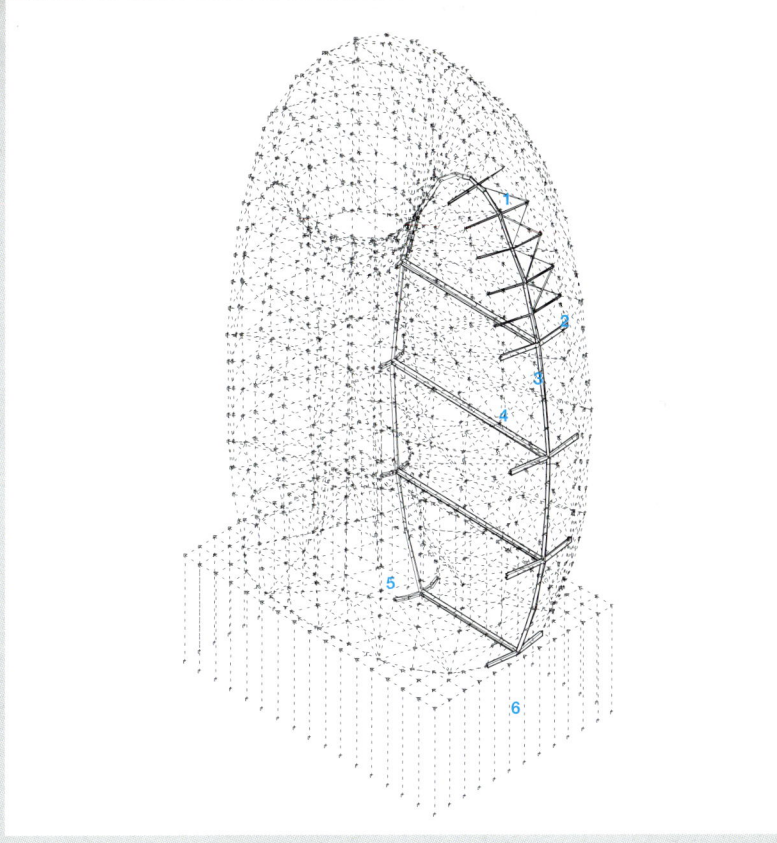

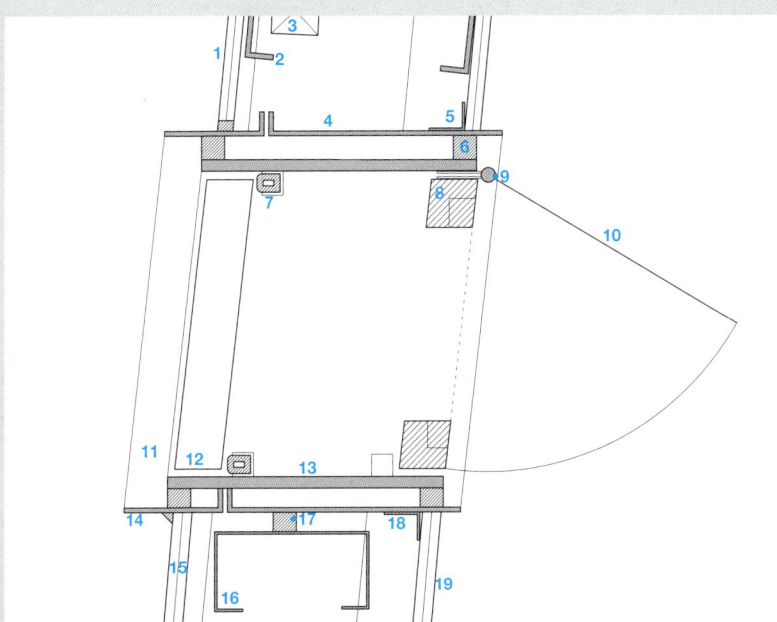

Stock Orchard Street House
London, England, UK

Client
Sarah Wigglesworth and Jeremy Till

Area
494 square metres (5,320 square feet)

Structural Engineer
Price and Meyers

Main Contractor
Koya Construction Limited

This residence and studio office in north London, provides a model of sustainable living in an urban setting. The building employs a number of innovative technologies based on principles of sustainable design, including a system of wall construction incorporating straw bales. The main floor is raised up on columns, with the garden and chickens occupying the undercroft. The bedroom wing is conceived as a warm haven, wrapped by a protective wall of straw. A five-storey tower of books rises through the roof, providing a lookout reading area overlooking the roof which is planted with a meadow of wild strawberries. The studio office fronts a railway line and is faced in sandbags for acoustic protection.

The design uses passive energy principles, with the heavily insulated straw bale wall wrapping around the north-east and north-west elevations, whilst the south-west facade is glazed to capture solar energy. The tower acts as a thermal flue, encouraging natural ventilation to cool the house in the summer. Materials have been chosen to limit their environmental impact. The north wall is made of straw bales, stacked between load-bearing timber ladders and protected by a transparent rain screen. Straw has the advantage of being extremely low cost, recyclable, highly insulative and has very low embodied energy. Other innovative materials include sandbags, a duvet type cladding and gabion walls filled with recycled concrete. Rainwater is collected to irrigate the roof meadow and feed toilets and washing machines, whilst a composting toilet ensures further water savings, all conforming to the environmental ethos of the design as a whole.

1 The separate elements of the domestic programme are expressed in the exterior. To the left, the straw bales clad the sleeping areas, the living room is raised above the ground on slender columns and to the right, the studio is clad in an innovative duvet-type material. Above the house, the library appears as a fortified tower.
2 Strong material contrast is used throughout the design. Here, the apparent softness of the sandbag wall sits above massive concrete-filled gabion supports.
3 The intriguing texture of the straw bales is revealed and protected by clear polycarbonate sheeting.
4 In contrast with the exterior, the interior features calm, neutral finishes including timber floors and doors, and white-painted walls.
5 The origin of the tower of books is suggested in the living space where a bookcase defined by a steel structure begins its rise towards the top of the house.

B
A
A
B

50.01
First Floor Plan
1:200

1 Bathroom
2 Upper part of courtyard
3 Dressing room
4 Bedroom
5 Deck
6 Kitchen
7 Larder
8 Living room
9 Living room with mezzanine gallery over
10 Balcony
11 Lobby
12 Dining and conference room
13 WCs
14 Kitchen
15 Stair to studio from entrance below
16 Studio

B
A
A
B

50.02
Ground Floor Plan
1:200

1 Utility room
2 Store
3 Store
4 Bedroom
5 Courtyard and pond
6 Study
7 Entrance hall
8 Bathroom
9 Porch
10 Undercroft
11 Base of tower
12 Cycle park
13 Gabion wall
14 Lobby to office
15 Entrance to office
16 Boundary between house and office
17 Courtyard
18 Retaining wall
19 Gabion wall
20 Office undercroft
21 Vehicle entrance
22 Entrance gate

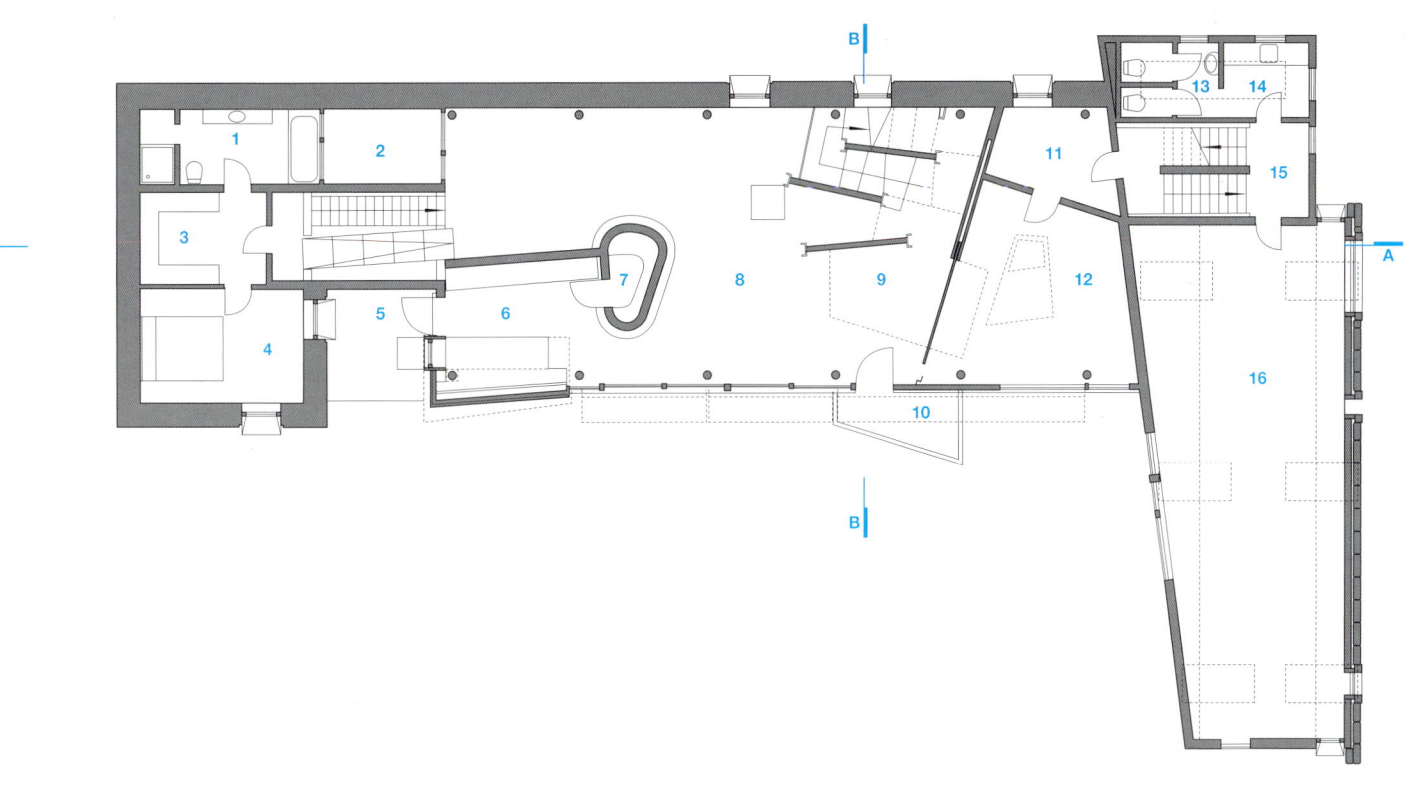

0
5
10m
0
15
30ft

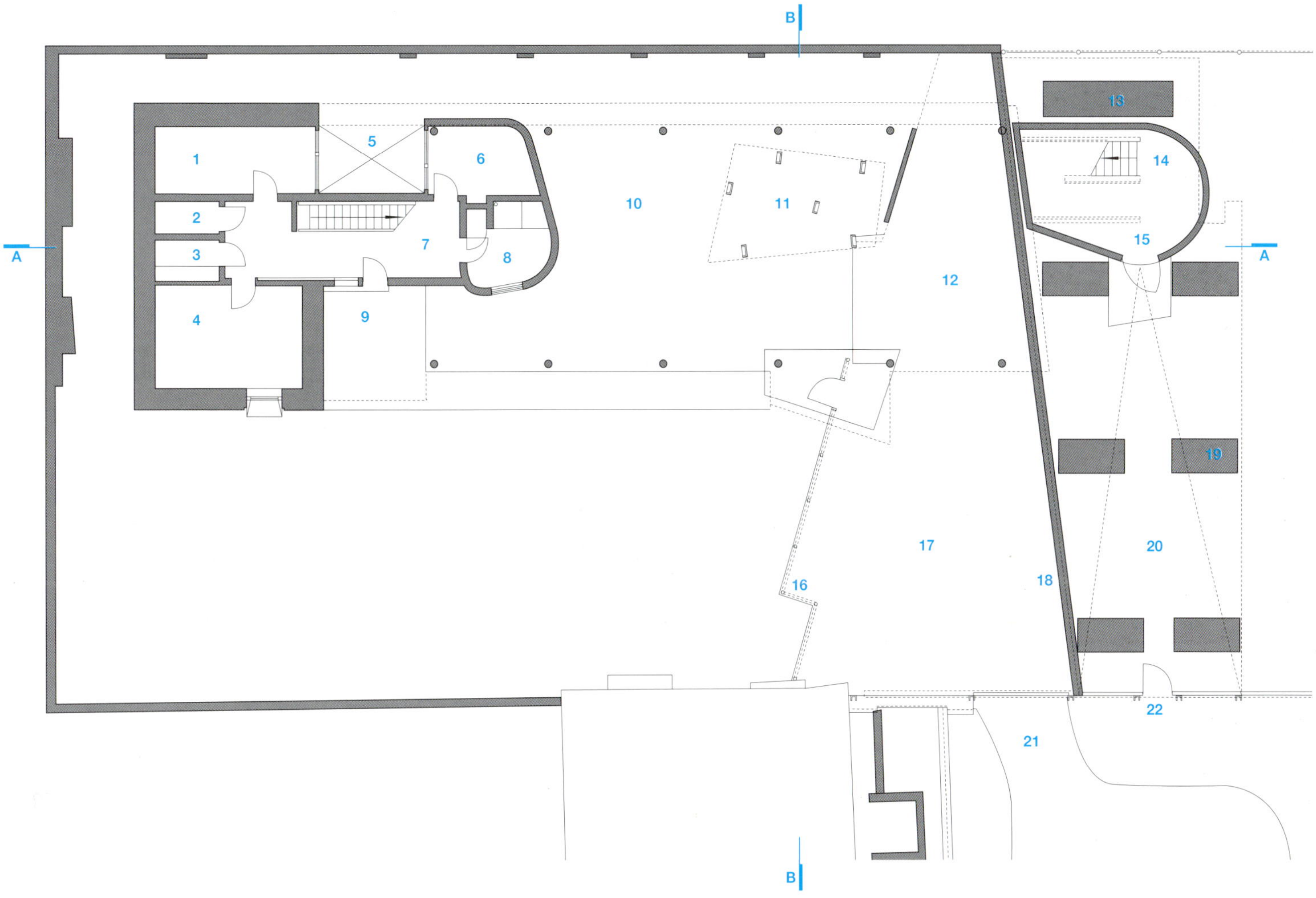

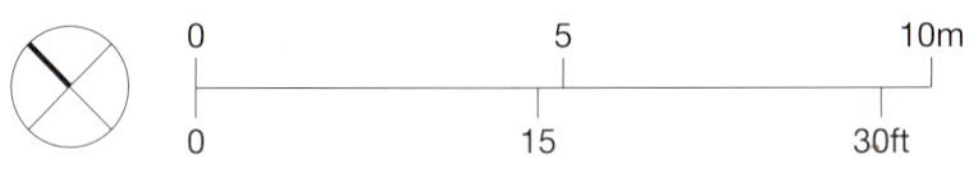

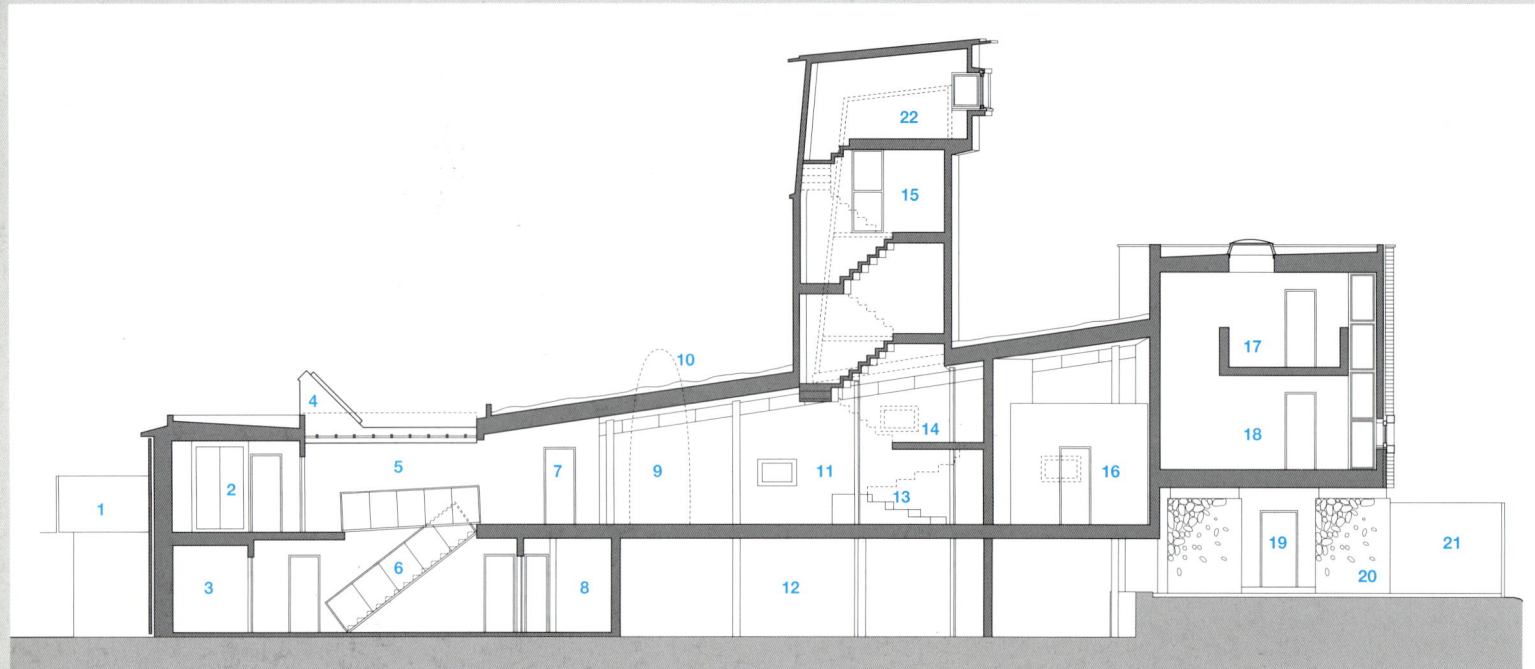

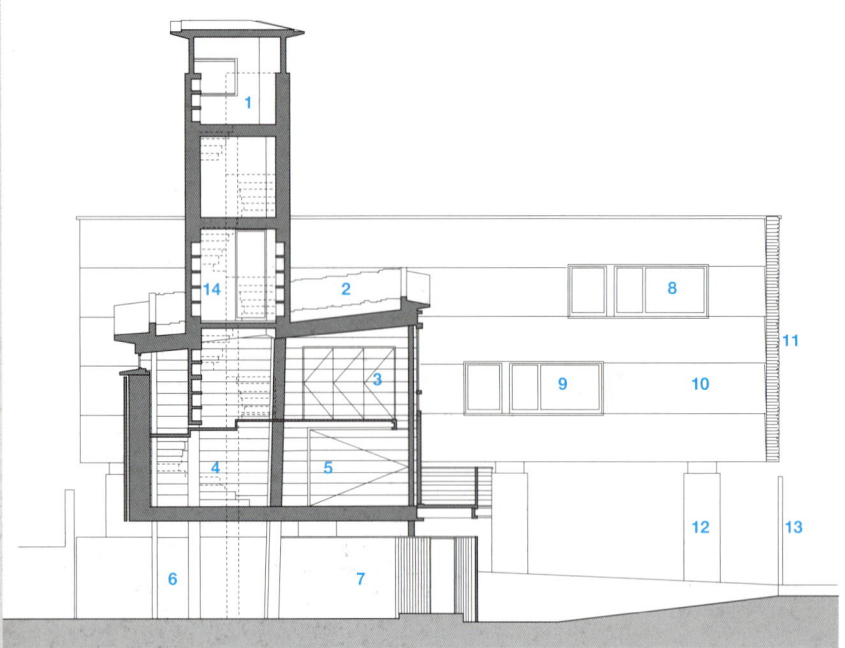

50.03
Section A–A
1:200

1 Wall to neighbouring properties
2 Dressing room
3 Store
4 Solar water heater
5 Bridge to bedroom
6 Staircase to main living level
7 Larder
8 Bathroom
9 Living room
10 Grass roof
11 Living room
12 Undercroft
13 Tower staircase
14 Mezzanine gallery
15 Library
16 Conference and dining room
17 Office mezzanine
18 Office (main level)
19 Office entrance
20 Gabion wall
21 Fence
22 Study

50.04
Section B–B
1:200

1 Study
2 Grass roof
3 Door from mezzanine to conference and dining room gallery
4 Tower staircase
5 Sliding door
6 Base of tower
7 Undercroft
8 Window to office
9 Window to office
10 Cladding to office
11 Sandbag wall
12 Gabion wall
13 Fence
14 Library

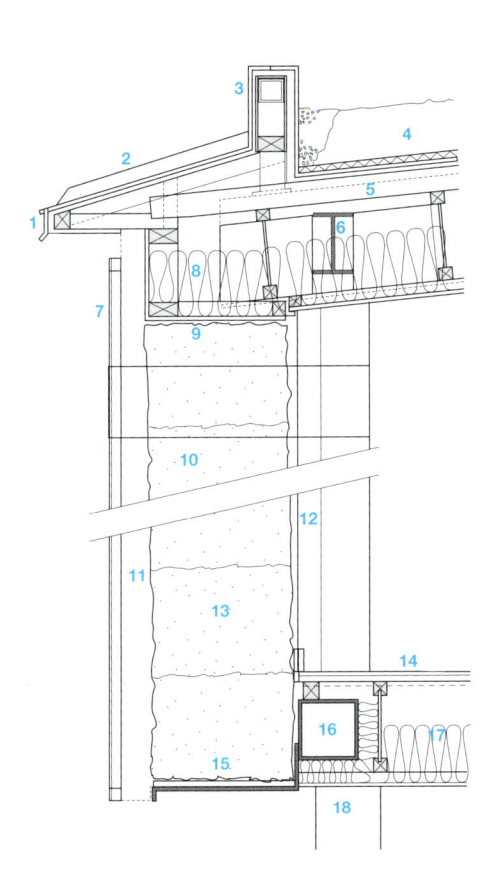

50.05
Wall Detail
1:20
 1 Zinc fascia and drip
 2 Zinc standing seam
 3 Zinc parapet upstand
 4 Green roof comprised of 150 mm (6 inch) low fertility soil on geotextile on welded EPDM waterproofing layer on 18 mm (3/4 inch) plywood deck
 5 Air gap
 6 Steel structure
 7 Corrugated steel or polycarbonate sheet according to area of roof
 8 200 mm (74/5 inch) thick insulation
 9 Timber head plate
 10 Straw bale
 11 100 mm (4 inch) air gap
 12 Lime render to face of bales
 13 Straw bale
 14 Timber floor comprised of 22 mm (9/10 inch) thick chipboard subfloor and 12 mm (1/2 inch) thick birch tongue and groove ply flooring panels
 15 Straw bales on 25 mm (1 inch) polystyrene insulation on steel bale tray
 16 Main steel floor structure
 17 Insulation
 18 Steel column

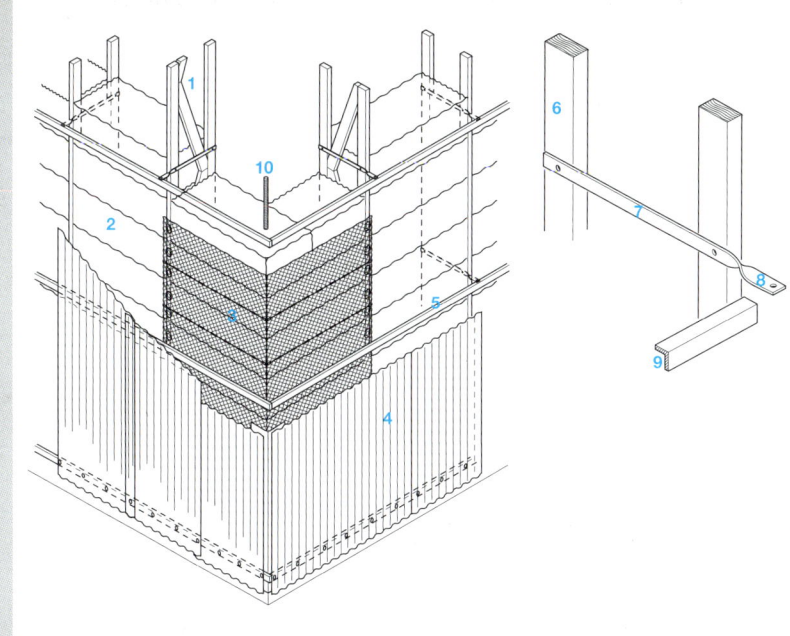

50.06
Straw Bale Wall Detail
 1 Timber ladder structure
 2 Straw bales
 3 Expanded metal latch stretched around corner to contain bales
 4 Corrugated steel or polycarbonate panel depending on position in wall
 5 Steel purlin
 6 Softwood ladder member
 7 Steel strap
 8 Turned end to accept purlin
 9 Steel purlin
 10 Reinforcing bar pinning bales together

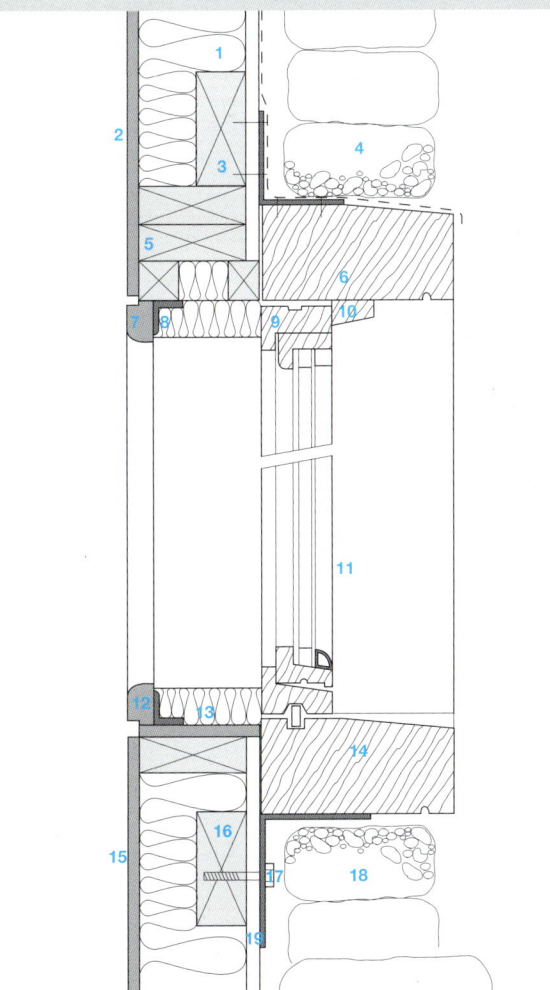

50.07
Glazing Detail
1:10
 1 Insulation
 2 Lime render
 3 Timber base plate
 4 Sandbags
 5 Timber head plate
 6 Railway sleeper forming window surround
 7 Timber architrave
 8 Angle for fixing timber trim
 9 Window frame
 10 Softwood beading
 11 Double-glazed opening light
 12 Timber trim frame
 13 Acoustic insulation lined with perforated board
 14 Railway sleeper forming window sill
 15 Lime render
 16 Timber plate for fixing bracket
 17 Steel angle bracket to support railway sleeper
 18 Sandbag
 19 9 mm (1/3 inch) panel vent

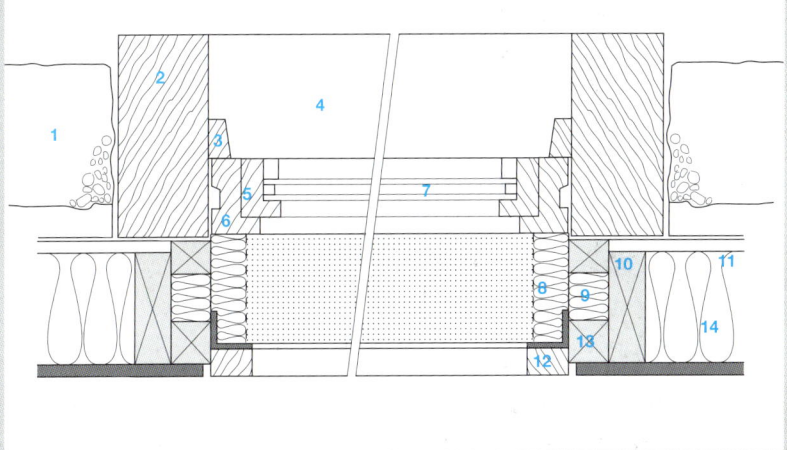

50.08
Glazing Detail
1:10
 1 Sandbag
 2 Railway sleeper forming window surround
 3 Softwood beading
 4 Railway sleeper forming window sill
 5 Double-glazed opening light
 6 Window frame
 7 Double glazing
 8 Acoustic insulation lined with perforated board
 9 Insulation
 10 Timber wall stud
 11 9 mm (1/3 inch) panel vent
 12 Timber architrave
 13 Softwood packing
 14 Insulation in studwork wall

51
Simon Conder Associates

Black Rubber Beach House
Dungeness, England, UK

Area
127 square metres (1,370 square feet)

Project Team
Simon Conder, Chris Neve

Structural Engineer
KLC Consulting Engineers

Contractor
Charlier Construction Ltd

This project demonstrates that the careful choice of materials combined with the innovatory use of new products can create domestic architecture of quality at very low cost. This scheme develops the tradition of ad hoc development in Dungeness in a way that responds to the drama and harshness of the landscape. The original fisherman's hut, built in the 1930s, has been stripped back to its timber frame, extended to the south and east to capture the views, and clad in Wisa-Spruce plywood. This also provides all the internal finishes, including walls, floors, ceilings, doors and joinery. External walls and roof are clad in black rubber, a technically sophisticated version of the felt and tar found on local buildings. The bath is cantilevered out over the beach, giving dramatic views to the sea.

Internally, priority has been given to the living areas – guests are accommodated in an iconic Airstream caravan parked next to the house. The project is the first to use EPDM (ethylene propylene diene monomer) rubber waterproofing to clad an entire building. The main advantages of the material are that it is water resistant yet vapour permeable, withstands extremes of temperature, is resistant to ozone and UV, presents no fire risk, and it is a natural product. By the same token, the plywood used for both the interior and exterior comes from managed forests in Finland. The constant coastal breeze, in combination with the black rubber, combines to provide an energy efficient environment. In summer, windows on opposing sides of the house are left open to provide cross ventilation. In the winter the black rubber acts as a heat sink so that the back-up heating system is minimized.

1 Black rubber, or EPDM (ethylene propylene diene monomer) characterizes the external appearance of the house, wrapping the walls and the roof to create a monolithic matt black form, interrupted only by a few windows and full-height doors, utilized to frame views of the landscape and the sea.
2 A south-east facing timber deck takes in views of the sea beyond the scrubland on which the house sits.
3 A whimsical addition to the tight domestic programme is a bath tub cantilevered out over the pebble beach with views of the sea.
4 View of the living space at dusk – all of the interior surfaces, including joinery, walls, floors and ceilings are clad in the same renewable source of spruce plywood.

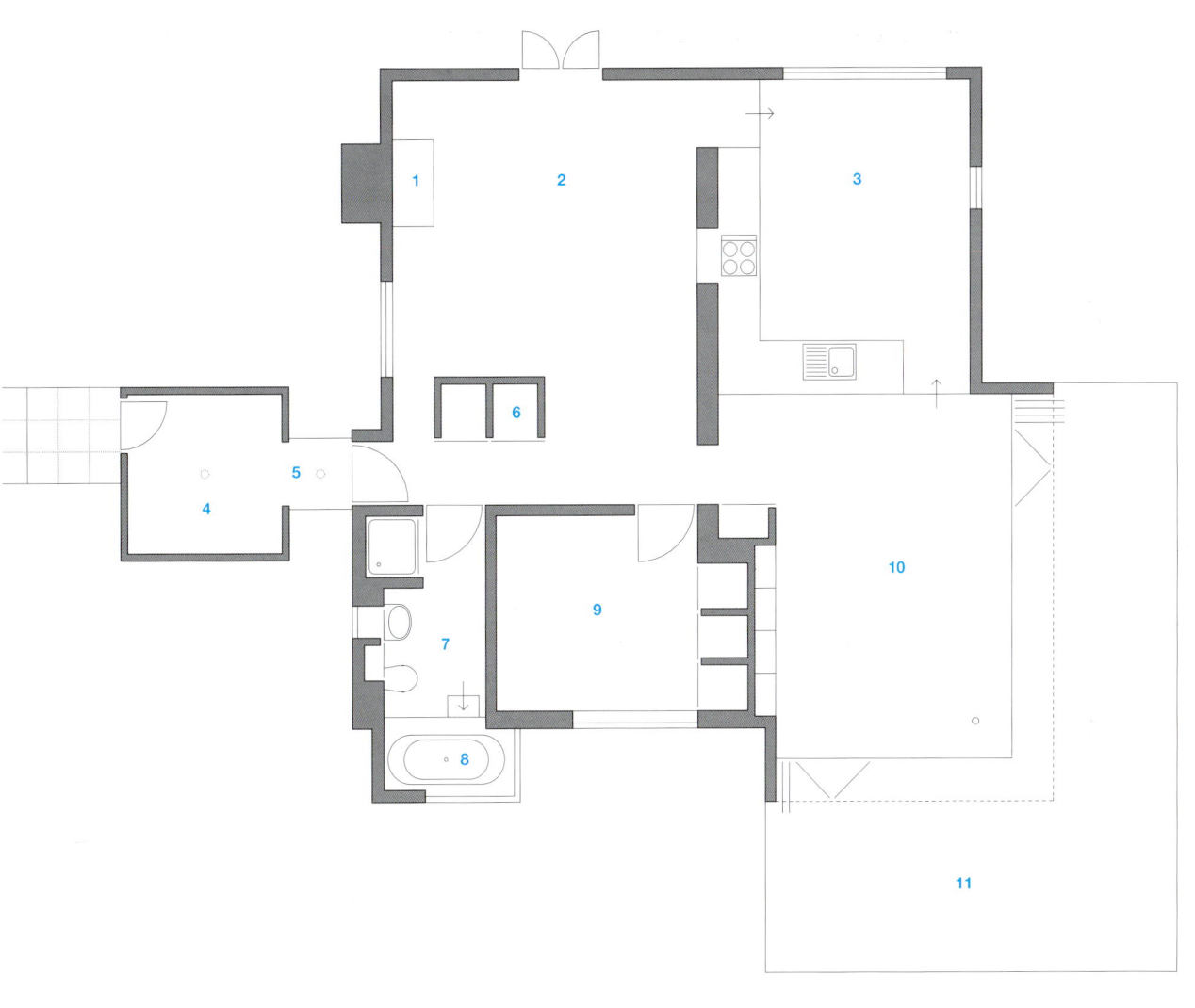

51.01
Floor Plan
1:100
1 Wood burning
   stove
2 Snug
3 Dining area and
   kitchen
4 Shed lobby
5 Glazed link
6 Storage
7 Bathroom
8 Cantilevered bath
9 Bedroom
10 Living area
11 Deck

0   5   10m

0   15   30ft

51.02
Axonometric
1 Entry lobby
2 Glazed link
3 Chimney
4 Cantilevered bath
   enclosure
5 Bedroom window
6 Black rubber
   membrane wall
   cladding
7 Folding, sliding,
   bottom running
   double-glazed
   door system
8 Timber deck

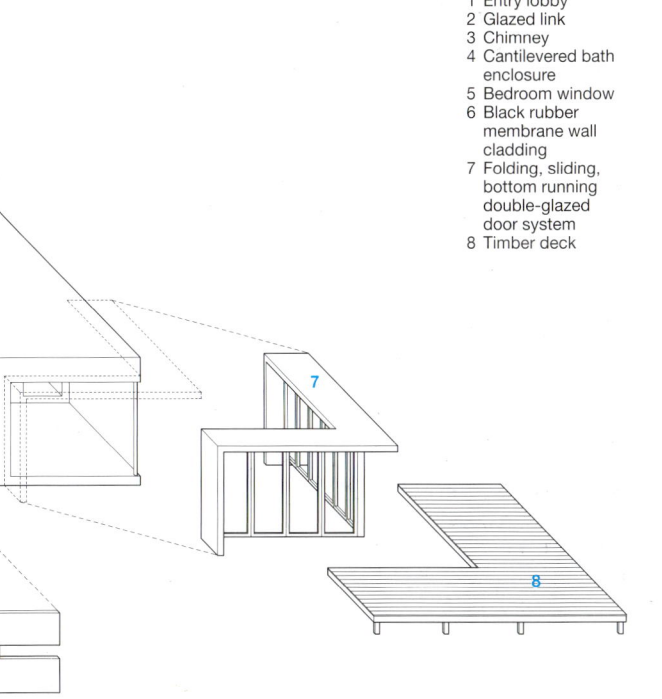

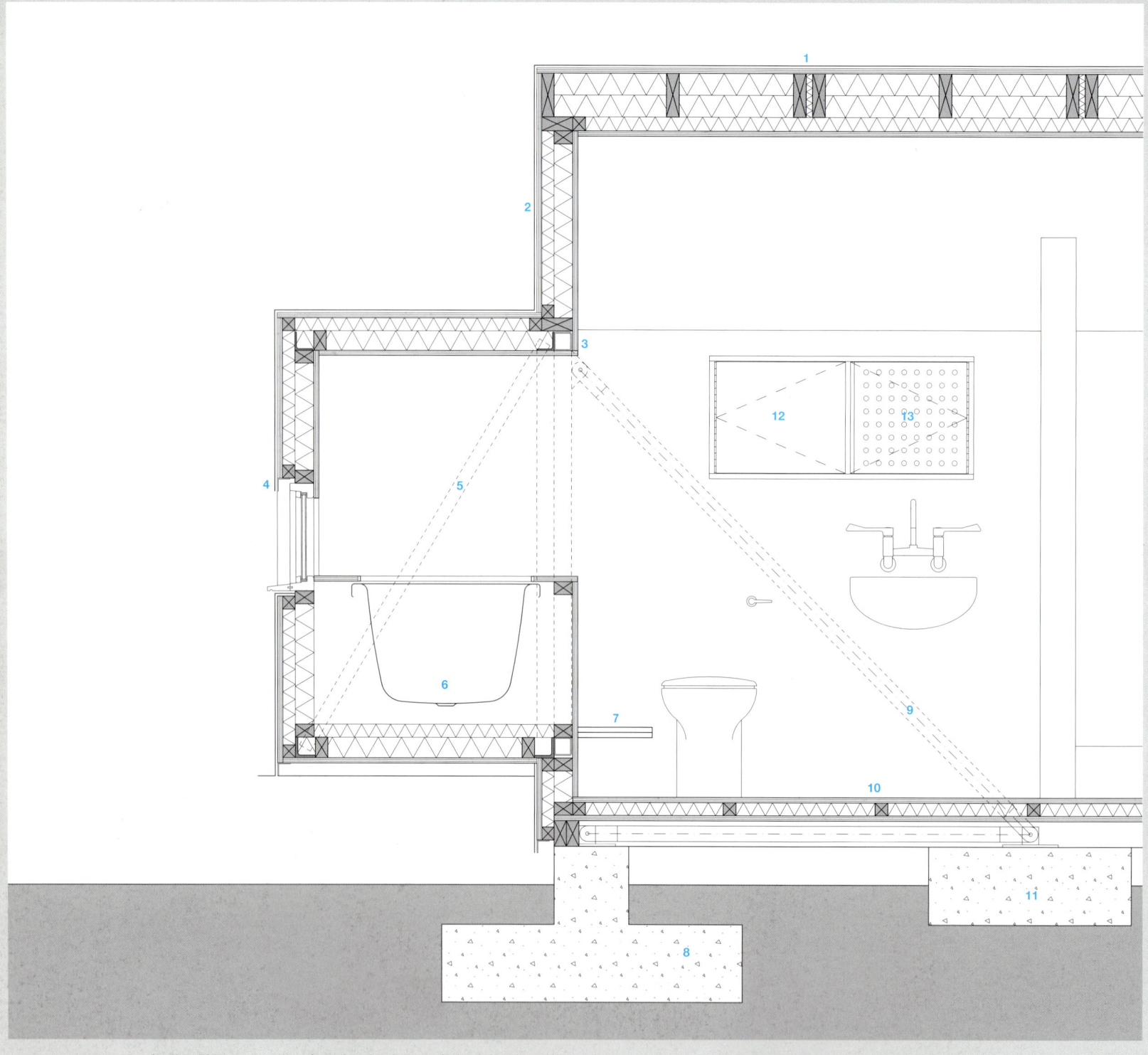

51.03
Detail Section 1
1:20

1 Pitched roof: 1.2mm (1/20 inch) EPDM black rubber membrane bonded to 18 mm (3/4 inch) spruce plywood; 150 x 50 mm (6 x 2 inch) softwood rafters interspersed with mineral wool insulation; 50 x 50 mm (2 x 2 inch) softwood battens interspersed with mineral wool insulation; radiant heating film – occasional back-up

heating; 500 gauge polythene vapour barrier; 18 mm (3/4 inch) spruce plywood with clear matt intumescent decoration to achieve class 1 flame resistance rating
2 Wall: 1.2 mm (1/20 inch) EPDM black rubber membrane bonded to 18 mm (3/4 inch) spruce plywood; 50 x 50 mm (2 x 2 inch) horizontal softwood battens interspersed with mineral wool insulation; 75 x 50 mm (3 x 2 inch) vertical

softwood studwork interspersed with mineral wool insulation; 500 gauge polythene vapour barrier; 18 mm (3/4 inch) spruce plywood with clear matt intumescent decoration to achieve class 1 flame resistance rating
3 70 x 70 x 4 mm (23/4 x 23/4 x 1/8 inch) galvanized square hollow section principle frame to cantilevered bath cubicle
4 40 x 40 x 2 mm

(11/2 x 11/2 x 1/14 inch) aluminium angle drip
5 70 x 70 x 6 mm (23/4 x 23/4 x 5/16 inch) galvanized rolled steel angle side panel frame to cantilevered bath cubicle with 50 x 5 mm (2 x 1/8 inch) galvanized mild steel flat diagonal
6 1700 x 750 x 430 mm (67 x 291/2 x 17 inch) double ended white enamelled steel bath
7 2 x 18 mm (1/14 x 3/4 inch) spruce plywood cantilevered bath step
8 New concrete edge

beam
9 60.3 x 4 mm (21/3 x 1/8 inch) galvanized circular hollow section with 60 x 10 mm (22/3 x 1/3 inch) galvanized mild steel flat welded to each end for bolted connections. (Diagonal bracing is duplicated within wall between bathroom and bedroom.)
10 Suspended floor: 18 mm (3/4 inch) spruce plywood; 1200 gauge polythene vapour barrier; 50 x 50 mm (2 x 2 inch) softwood battens

interspersed with extruded polystyrene insulation; 1200 gauge polythene vapour barrier; 18 mm (3/4 inch) spruce plywood; 100 x 50 mm (4 x 2 inch) softwood joists
11 Concrete counterweight to cantilevered bath cubicle
12 3 mm (1/7 inch) glass mirror with polished edges bonded to 18 mm (3/4 inch) spruce plywood hinged panel to cabinet
13 18 mm (3/4 inch)

spruce plywood perforated hinged panel screening window – 20 mm (3/4 inch) diameter holes drilled in a 50 mm (2 inch) grid

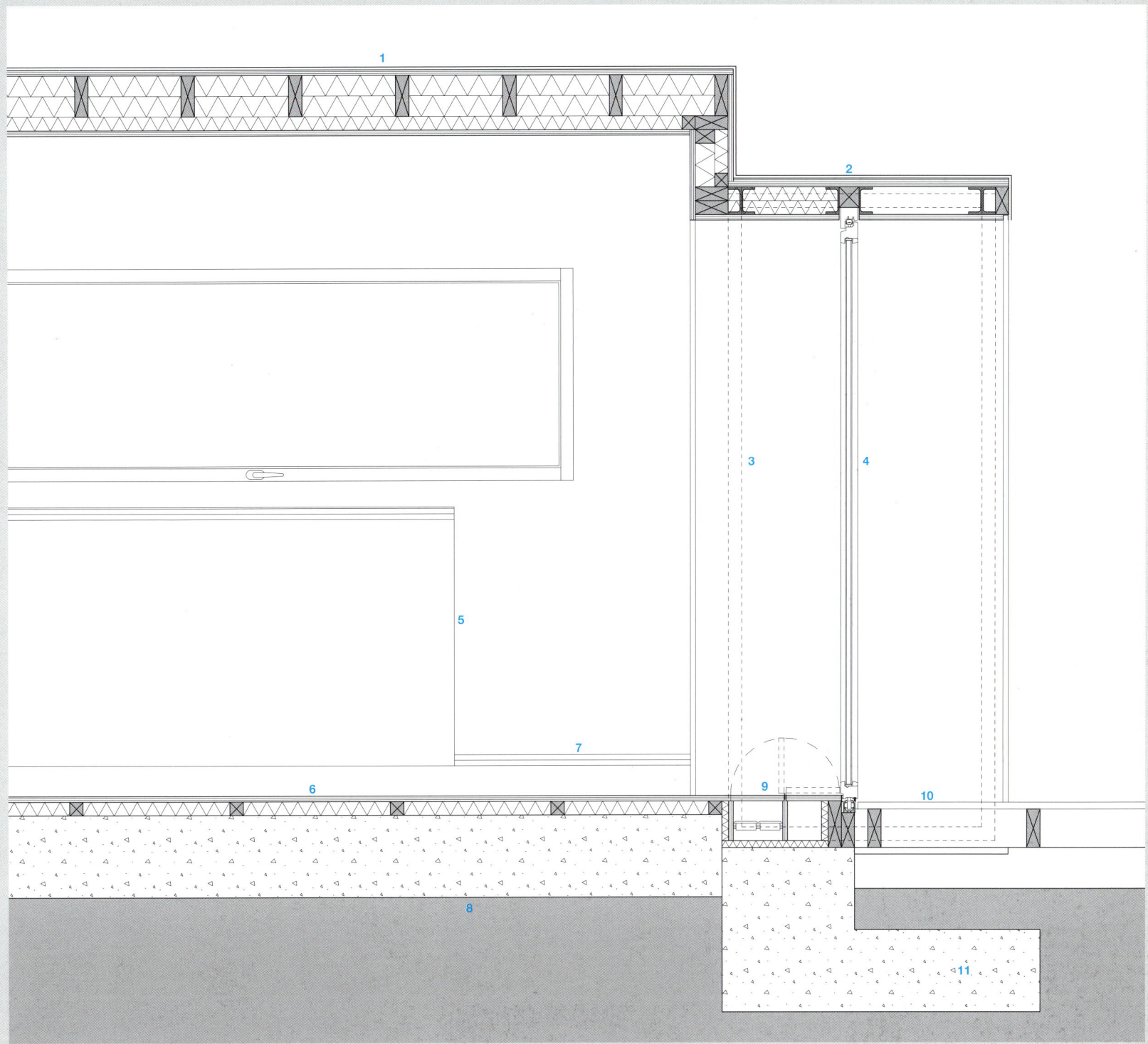

51.04
Detail Section 2
1:20

1 Flat roof: 1.2 mm (1/20 inch) EPDM black rubber membrane bonded to 18mm (4/5 inch) spruce plywood; 150 x 50 mm (6 x 2 inch) softwood joists interspersed with mineral wool insulation; 50 x 50 mm (2 x 2 inch) softwood battens interspersed with mineral wool insulation; radiant heating film – occasional back-up heating; 500 gauge polythene vapour barrier; 18 mm (3/4 inch) spruce plywood with clear matt intumescent decoration to achieve class 1 flame resistance rating

2 Canopy: 1.2 mm (1/20 inch) EPDM black rubber membrane bonded to 12 and 18 mm (1/2 and 3/4 inch) spruce plywood; 100 x 50 mm (4 x 2 inch) galvanized parallel flange channel frame sandwiching 80 x 75 mm (31/16 x 3 inch) softwood to take folding sliding glazed door system head track; 500 gauge polythene vapour barrier; 18 mm (3/4 inch) spruce plywood with clear matt intumescent decoration to achieve class 1 flame resistance rating

3 100 x 50 mm (4 x 2 inch) galvanized parallel flange channel side panel frame to canopy

4 Folding, sliding, bottom running double-glazed door system with clear toughened sealed units – inner pane of Pilkington K glass

5 18 mm (3/4 inch) spruce plywood kitchen units

6 Solid floor: 18 mm (3/4 inch) spruce plywood; 1200 gauge polythene vapour barrier; 50 x 50 mm (2 x 2 inch) softwood battens interspersed with extruded polystyrene insulation; 1200 gauge polythene vapour barrier

7 18 mm (3/4 inch) spruce plywood raised service floor to aid plumbing runs

8 Original concrete raft slab

9 18 mm (3/4 inch) spruce plywood hinged panel with cable notch to hidden electrical sockets

10 90 x 25 mm (31/2 x 1 inch) hardwood decking with 10 mm (2/5 inch) gaps set at 20 mm (4/5 inch) below internal floor level

11 New concrete with Fibrin X-T and plasticiser

Turbulence House
Abiqui, New Mexico, USA

Client
Richard Tuttle and Mei-mei
Berssenbrugge

Area
84 square metres (900 square feet)

Project Team
Steven Holl, Anderson Lee, Richard
Tobias, Arnault Biou, Matt Johnson

Structural Engineer
Delapp Engineering

Located adjacent to a series of adobe courtyard houses built by the artist Richard Tuttle, this intriguing house is situated on the top of a windy desert mesa. Its form, conceptualized as the tip of an iceberg indicating a much larger form below, allows turbulent wind to blow through the centre of the aluminium-clad form. The expressive facade was manufactured by a sheet metal fabrication company that utilizes digital definition combined with craftsmanship to produce highly intricate metal shapes and forms. The stressed skin and aluminium rib construction was digitally prefabricated, then bolted together on site. The sizes of the panels were governed by the inside dimensions of a generic 12 metre (40 foot) container, thus limiting the panel size to 2.4 metre (8 foot) wide modules.

A total of 31 metal panels, each with a unique shape, were fabricated to form the entire shell of the house. Computer generated templates were created to ensure the absolute minimum amount of aluminium was wasted in the production of the exterior panels, and prefabrication off-site ensured minimal on-site construction waste and fast assembly. The aluminium is naturally finished with flat lock seams – the light colour helping to reduce the cooling load. Two skylights at the northern and southern ends of the building allow for unwanted hot air to escape. To assist the passive environmental strategy, photovoltaic roof panels generate sufficient electricity to cover all of the domestic requirements, and a cistern on the south side of the house collects storm water which is recycled for site irrigation.

1 Sited in a windy desert environment, the 'hull' of the structure bends and undulates to allow turbulent winds to blow around and, indeed, through the house.
2 A detail view of the east facade reveals the central open space and the living room with black steel stair beyond.
3 Interior walls and ceilings are white-painted plaster, countered by a polished concrete floor and light-weight black-painted steel staircase.

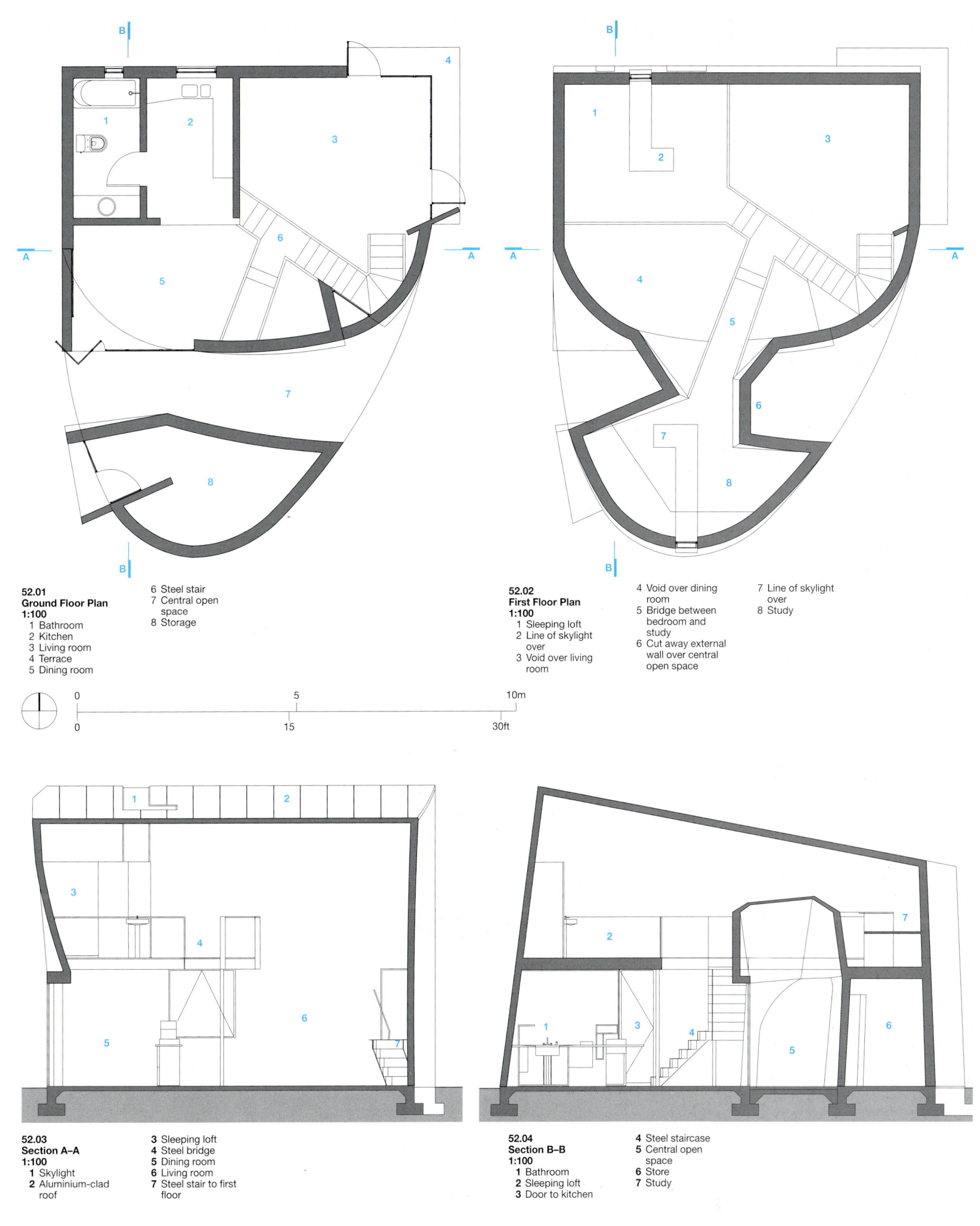

52.01
Ground Floor Plan
1:100
1 Bathroom
2 Kitchen
3 Living room
4 Terrace
5 Dining room
6 Steel stair
7 Central open space
8 Storage

52.02
First Floor Plan
1:100
1 Sleeping loft
2 Line of skylight over
3 Void over living room
4 Void over dining room
5 Bridge between bedroom and study
6 Cut away external wall over central open space
7 Line of skylight over
8 Study

52.03
Section A–A
1:100
1 Skylight
2 Aluminium-clad roof
3 Sleeping loft
4 Steel bridge
5 Dining room
6 Living room
7 Steel stair to first floor

52.04
Section B–B
1:100
1 Bathroom
2 Sleeping loft
3 Door to kitchen
4 Steel staircase
5 Central open space
6 Store
7 Study

0   5   10m
0   15   30ft

225

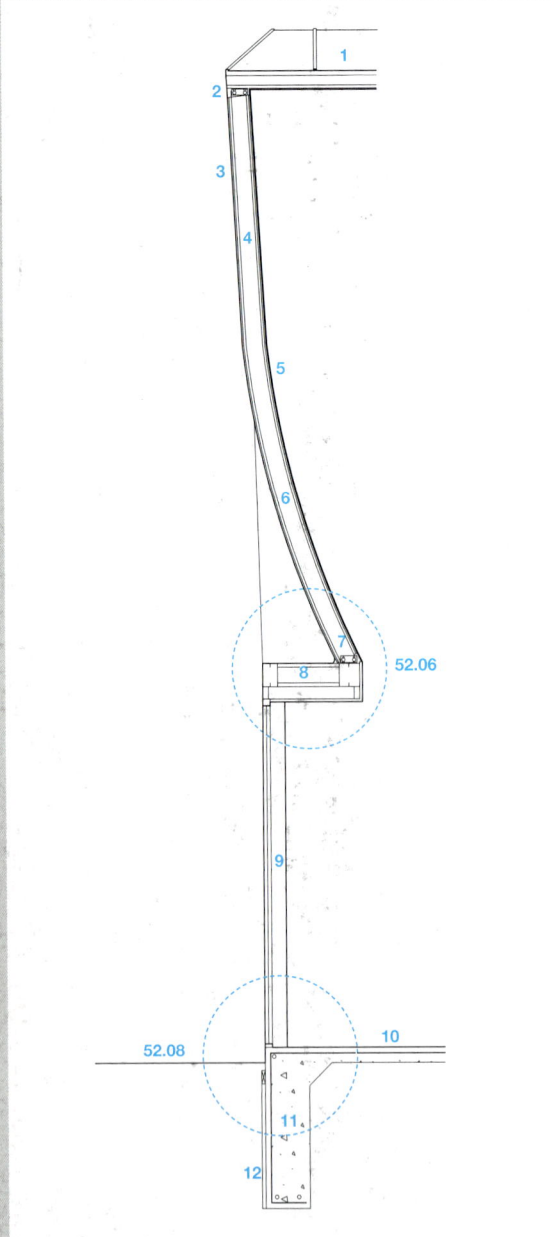

52.06

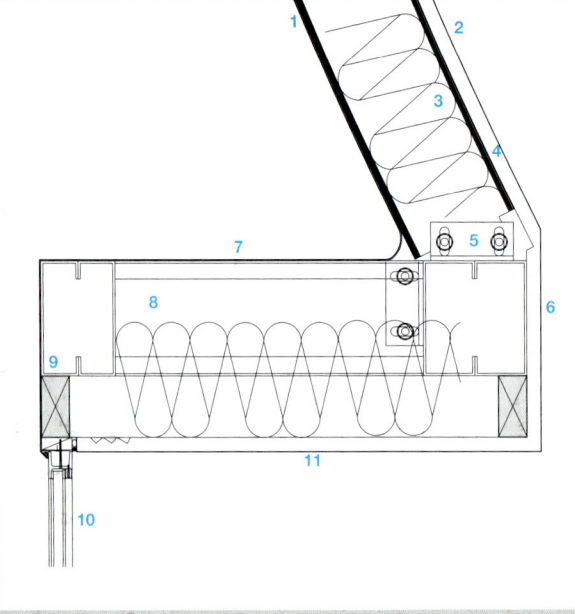

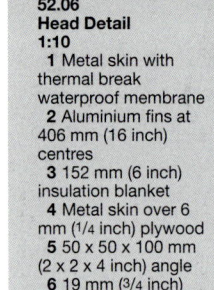

52.06
Head Detail
1:10
 1 Metal skin with
thermal break
waterproof membrane
 2 Aluminium fins at
406 mm (16 inch)
centres
 3 152 mm (6 inch)
insulation blanket
 4 Metal skin over 6
mm (1/4 inch) plywood
 5 50 x 50 x 100 mm
(2 x 2 x 4 inch) angle
 6 19 mm (3/4 inch)
plywood
 7 Metal skin
 8 C-purlins
 9 Steel C-section
 10 Aluminium-framed
glazing
 11 Ceiling lining

52.07
Sill Detail 1
1:10
 1 Glazed door in
aluminium window
system
 2 Aluminium nosing
 3 Reinforced
concrete floor
 4 Reinforced turn
down slab
 5 Rigid insulation

52.05
External Wall Detail
1:50
 1 304 x 50 x 406 mm
(12 x 2 x 16 inch)
galvanized angle at
610 mm (24 inch)
centres
 2 50 x 50 x 100 mm
(2 x 2 x 4 inch) angle
 3 Metal skin with
waterproof membrane
 4 Thermal break layer
 5 6 mm (1/4 inch)
plywood
 6 Aluminium fins at
406 mm (16 inch)
centres
 7 50 x 50 x 100 mm

(2 x 2 x 4 inch) angle
 8 C-purlins
 9 Clear-glazed
window
 10 Underfloor heating
over reinforced
concrete slab floor
 11 Reinforced
concrete footing
 12 Rigid insulation

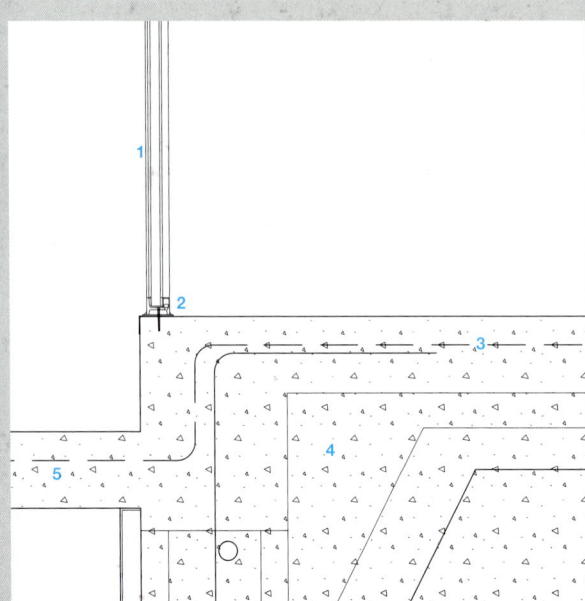

52.08
Sill Detail 2
1:10
 1 Steel frame door
with 12 mm (1/2 inch)
glazing
 2 Aluminium
threshold set in mastic
 3 Radiant floor
heating
 4 Reinforced
concrete foundation
 5 Reinforced
concrete floor slab

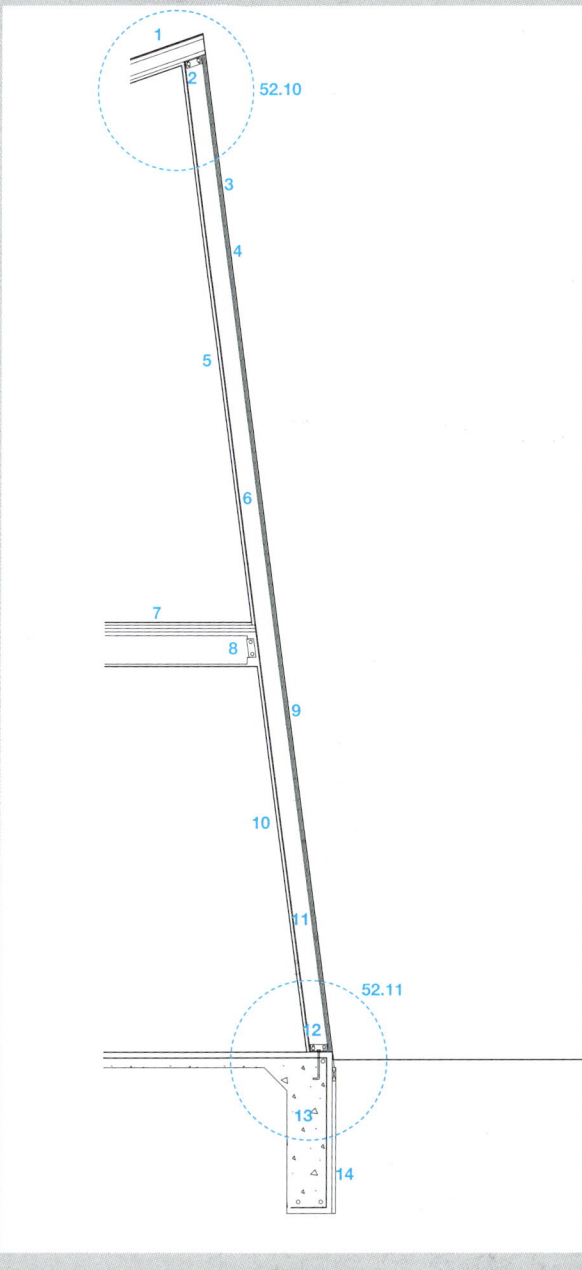

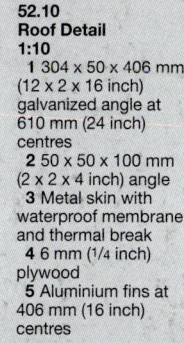

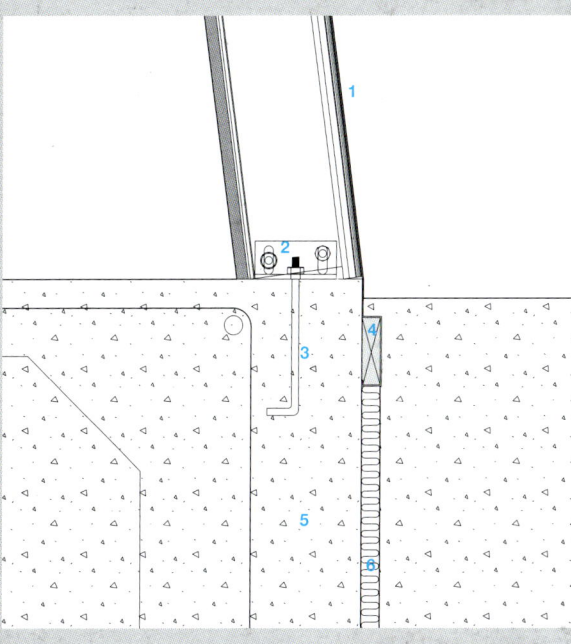

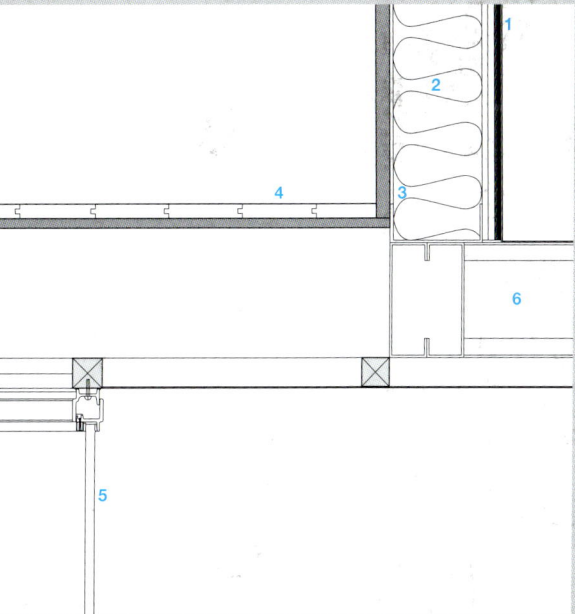

52.10
Roof Detail
1:10
 1 304 x 50 x 406 mm (12 x 2 x 16 inch) galvanized angle at 610 mm (24 inch) centres
 2 50 x 50 x 100 mm (2 x 2 x 4 inch) angle
 3 Metal skin with waterproof membrane and thermal break
 4 6 mm (1/4 inch) plywood
 5 Aluminium fins at 406 mm (16 inch) centres

52.11
Sill Detail 3
1:10
 1 Metal skin with waterproof membrane and thermal break
 2 50 x 50 x 100 mm (2 x 2 x 4 inch) angle
 3 Anchor bolt
 4 30 x 100 mm (1 1/5 x 4 inch) timber blocking
 5 Reinforced concrete turn down slab
 6 Rigid insulation

52.09
Wall Detail
1:50
 1 Galvanized flange bolted to roof structure
 2 50 x 50 x 100 mm (2 x 2 x 4 inch) angle
 3 Metal skin with waterproof membrane
 4 Thermal break layer
 5 6 mm (1/4 inch) plywood
 6 Aluminium fins at 406 mm (16 inch) centres
 7 Bamboo flooring over plywood subfloor
 8 Galvanized aluminium flange rim joint
 9 Metal skin with waterproof membrane over thermal break layer
 10 6 mm (1/4 inch) plywood
 11 Aluminium fins at 406 mm (16 inch) centres
 12 50 x 50 x 100 mm (2 x 2 x 4 inch) angle
 13 Reinforced concrete footing and floor slab
 14 Rigid insulation

52.12
Head Detail
1:10
 1 Metal skin with thermal break and waterproof membrane
 2 150 mm (6 inch) blanket insulation
 3 6 mm (1/4 inch) plywood
 4 Bamboo flooring over plywood subfloor
 5 Clear glazing
 6 C-purlins

Directories
of Details and
Architects

Directory of Details

Australia

Drew Heath Architect
7/67 Boronia Road
Bellevue Hill
Sydney
New South Wales 2023
Australia
E: drewheath@ozemail.com.au
T: +61 414 491 270
[37] Zig Zag Cabin, Wollombi, New
South Wales, Australia (2003), 162

Ian Moore Architects
44 McLachlan Avenue
Rushcutters Bay
Sydney
NSW 2011
Australia
E: mail@ianmoorearchitects.com
T: +61 2 9380 4099
F: +61 2 9380 4302
W: www.ianmoorearchitects.com
[11] Rose House, Kiama, New South
Wales, Australia (2001), 52

Sean Godsell
Level 1, 49 Exhibition Street
Melbourne
Victoria 3000
Australia
E: godsell@netspace.net.au
T: +61 3 9654 2677
F: +61 3 9654 3877
W: www.seangodsell.com
[45] Peninsula House, Victoria,
Australia (2002), 194

Stutchbury and Pape
Unit 5, 364 Barrenjoey Road
Newport
NSW 2106
Australia
E: snpala@ozemail.com.au
T: +61 2 9979 5030
F: +61 2 9979 5367
[43] Verandah House, Sydney, New
South Wales, Australia (2004), 186

Troppo Architects
6 Stack Street
Freemantle
Western Australia 6160
Australia
E: perth@troppoarchitects.com.au
T: +61 8 9336 4533
F: +61 8 9336 6609
W: www.troppoarchitects.com.au
[30] Rozak House, Lake Bennett,
Northern Territory, Australia (2001),
132

Austria

Architect Antonius Lanzinger
Maria Theresien Strasse 9
A-6020 Innsbruck
Austria
E: a.lanzinger@gmx.at
T: +43 51257 3198
[35] Single Family House, Brixlegg,
Tirol, Austria (2002), 154

Baumschlager & Eberle
Lindauer Strasse 31
A-6911 Lochau
Austria
E: office@baumschlager-eberle.com
T: +43 (0)5574 430 79
F: +43 (0)5574 430 79-30
W: www.baumschlager-eberle.com
[02] Flatz House, Schaan,
Liechtenstein (2002), 14

Georg Driendl
Mariahferstr. 9
A-1060 Vienna
Austria
E: architekt@driendl.at
T: +43 1 585 1868
F: +43 1 585 1868
W: www.driendl.at
[04] Solar Tube, Vienna, Austria
(2001), 22

China

EDGE Design Institute Ltd.
Suite 1604, Eastern Harbour Centre
28 Hoi Chak Street, Quarry Bay
Hong Kong
China
E: edgeltd@netvigator.com
T: +852 2802 6212
F: +852 2802 6213
W: www.edgedesign.com.hk
[38] Suitcase House, Shuiguan,
Badaling, China (2002), 166

MADA s.p.a.m.
No.2, Lane 134, Xinle Road
Xuhui District
Shanghai 200031
China
E: office@madaspam.com
T: +86 21 5404 1166
F: +86 21 621 77437
W: www.madaspam.com
[20] Father's House, Lantian, China
(2005), 90

France

Bernard Quirot and Olivier Vichard
4 rue de la Préfecture
25000 Besançon
France
E: quirot.vichard@wanadoo.fr
T: +33 3 81 81 31 31
F: +33 3 81 61 98 94
W: www.quirot-vichard.com
[36] Convercey House, Grachaux,
France (2001), 158

Marin & Trottin
8 rue Montcalm
Paris 75018
France
E: mt.peripheriques@club-internet.fr
T: +33 1 44 92 05 01
F: +33 1 44 92 05 14
[28] Artifice/MR House, Pompone,
France (2002), 124

Germany

Brückner + Brückner Architekten
Büro Würzburg
Veitshöchheimer Str. 14
97080 Würzburg
Germany
E: mail@architektenbrueckner.de
T: +49 931 575 47
F: +49 931 575 48
[16] House in the Landscape,
Bärnau, Germany (2002), 74

Léon Wohlhage Wernik Architekten
Leibnizstrasse 65
10629 Berlin
Germany
E: post@leonwohlhagewernik.de
T: +49 (30) 327 60 00
F: +49 (30) 327 60 060
W: www.leonwohlhagewernik.de
[07] House Voss, Münsterland,
Germany (2000), 34

Werner Sobek
Albstr. 14
70597 Stuttgart
Germany
E: mail@wsi-stuttgart.com
T: +49 711 767500
F: +49 711 7675044
W: www.wernersobek.com
[32] House R128, Stuttgart,
Germany (2000), 140

Japan

**Atelier Bow-Wow + Tokyo Institute
of Technology Tsukamoto Lab**
Negishi Building, 2nd Floor
2-23-8 Higashi Shibuya
Tokyo 150-0011
Japan
E: info@bow-wow.jp
T: +81 3 5774 6508
F: +81 3 5774 6508
W: www.bow-wow.jp
[31] Gae House, Tokyo, Japan
(2003), 136

Kazuyo Sejima & Associates
7-A Shinagawa-Soko
2-2-35 Higashi-Shinagawa
Shinagawa-ku
Tokyo 140
Japan
E: sanaa@sanaa.co.jp
T: +81 3 3450 1754
F: +81 3 3450 1757
W: http://sanaa.co.jp
[12] Small House, Tokyo, Japan
(2000), 56

Kei'ichi Irie + Power Unit Studio
#2107, 12-1 Sarugako-cho
Shibuya-ku
Tokyo 150-0033
Japan
E: info@pus.jp
T: +81 3 3461 9827
F: +81 3 3461 9829
W: www.pus.jp
[06] Y House, Chita, Aichi, Japan
(2003), 30

Kengo Kuma & Associates
2-24-8 Minami Aoyama
Minato-ku
Tokyo 107-0062
Japan
E: ikeguchi@kkaa.co.jp
T: +81 3 3401 7721
F: +81 3 3401 7778
W: www.kkaa.co.jp
[40] Bamboo Wall House, Badaling,
China (2002), 174
[48] Plastic House, Tokyo, Japan
(2002), 208

Masaki Endoh + Masahiro Ikeda
2-13-8 Honmachi
Shibuya-Ku
Tokyo 151 0071
Japan
E: edh-endoh@mvi.biglobe.ne.jp
T: +81 3 3377 6293
F: +81 3 3377 6293
[49] Natural Ellipse, Tokyo, Japan
(2002), 212

Japan (continued)

Shigeru Ban Architects
5-2-4 Matsubara Ban Bldg 1Fl
Setagaya
Tokyo 156
Japan
E: tokyo@shigerubanarchitects.com
T: +81 3 3324 6760
F: +81 3 3324 6789
W: www.shigerubanarchitects.com
**[14] Picture Window House,
Shizuoka, Japan (2002), 64**

Shuhei Endo
Domus AOI 5F
5-15-11 Nishitenma
Kita-ku
Osaka
Japan
E: endo@paramodern.com
T: +81 6 6312 7455
F: +81 6 6312 7456
W: www.paramodern.com
**[29] Springtecture B, Biwa-Cho,
Shiga Prefecture, Japan (2002), 128**

Tadao Ando
5-23 Toyosaki 2-Chome Kita-ku
Osaka 531-0072
Japan
E: taaa@mx6.nisiq.net
T: +81 6 6375 1148
F: +81 6 6374 6240
**[09] 4 x 4 House, Kobe, Hyogo,
Japan (2004), 42**

Portugal

Álvaro Siza Vieira
Rua Do Aleixo, 53-2
4150-043 Porto
Portugal
E: siza@mail.telepac.pt
T: +351 22 616 72 70
F: +351 22 616 72 79
W: www.alvarosiza.com
**[34] House in Oudenbourg,
Oudenbueg, Belgium (2002), 150**

Spain

Ábalos + Herreros
C / Gran Via
16 3C
Madrid 28013
Spain
E: studio@abalos-herreros.com
T: +34 91 5234 404
F: +34 91 5234 553
W: www.abalos-herreros.com
**[47] Studio Gordillo, Madrid, Spain
(2002), 204**

Alberto Campo Baeza
Almirante 9
28004 Madrid
Spain
E: estudio@campobaeza.com
T: +34 91 5217061
F: +34 91 7010695
W: www.campobaeza.com
**[01] De Blas House, Madrid, Spain
(2000), 10**

Aranda Pigem Vilalta
Passeig de Blay, 34
17800 Olot
Girona
Spain
E: rcr@rcrarquitectes.es
T: +34 972 269 105
F: +34 972 267558
W: www.rcrarquitectes.es
**[10] M-Lidia House, Girona, Spain
(2003), 48**
**[23] Bellows House, Girona, Spain
(2003), 104**

Carlos Ferrater
Balmes, 145 Bajos
08008 Barcelona
Spain
E: carlos@ferrater.com
T: +34 93 238 51 36
F: +34 93 416 1306
W: www.ferrater.com
**[18] Tagomago House, Ibiza, Spain
(2001), 82**

Martín + Martín Arquitectos
Mesones 37, 2
18001 Granada
Spain
E: emartinmartin@coagranada.org
T: +34 958 265 469
F: +34 958 529 008
**[41] La Vega House
Granada, Spain (2001), 178**

The Netherlands

**Kruunenberg Van der Erve
Architecten**
Conradstraat 8C
1018 NG Amsterdam
The Netherlands
E: info@kvde.nl
T: +31 20 320 8486
W: www.kvde.nl
**[13] Laminata, House of Glass,
Leerdam, The Netherlands
(2001), 60**

UK

Adjaye Associates
23–28 Penn Street
London N1 5DL
UK
E: info@adjaye.com
T: +44 20 77 39 4969
F: +44 20 77 39 3484
W: www.adjaye.com
**[17] Dirty House, London, UK
(2002), 78**

John Pawson
Unit B, 70-78 York Way
London N1 9AG
UK
E: email@johnpawson.co.uk
T: +44 20 7837 2929
F: +44 20 7837 4949
W: www.johnpawson.com
**[19] Tetsuka House, Tokyo, Japan
(2002), 86**

Sarah Wigglesworth Architects
9/10 Stock Orchard Street
London N7 9RW
UK
E: mail@swarch.co.uk
T: +44 20 7607 9200
F: +44 20 7607 5800
W: www.swarch.co.uk
**[50] Stock Orchard Street House,
London, UK (2001), 216**

Simon Conder Associates
Nile Street Studios
8 Nile Street
London N1 7RF
UK
E: sca@simonconder.co.uk
T: +44 20 7251 2144
F: +44 20 7251 2145
W: www.simonconder.co.uk
**[51] Black Rubber Beach House,
Dungeness, England, UK (2003), 220**

USA

Architecture Research Office (ARO)
180 Varick Street
10th Floor
New York
NY 10014
USA
E: mvoorhees@aro.net
T: +1 212 675 1870
F: +1 212 675 1645
W: www.aro.net
[24] Colorado House, Telluride, Colorado, USA (2000), 108

Carlos Zapata Studio
444 Broadway, 3rd Floor
New York
NY 10013
USA
E: mkoff@wood-zapata.com
T: +1 212 966 9292
F: +1 212 966 9242
W: http://wood-zapata.com
[15] Private House, Quito, Ecuador (2002), 68

Fougeron Architecture
720 York Street #107
San Francisco
CA 94110
USA
E: anne@fougeron.com
T: +1 415 641 5744
F: +1 415 282 6434
W: http://fougeron.com
[39] Jackson Family Retreat, Big Sur, California, USA (2005), 170

Jim Jennings Architecture
49 Rodgers Alley
San Francisco
CA 94103
USA
E: office@jimjenningsarchitecture.com
T: +1 415 551 0827
F: +1 415 551 0829
W: www.jimjenningsarchitecture.com
[05] Visiting Artists' House, Geyserville, California, USA (2002), 26

Julie Snow Architects
2400 Rand Tower
527 Marquette Ave
Minneapolis
MN 55402
USA
E: mail@juliesnowarchitects.com
T: +1 612 359 9430
F: +1 612 359 9530
W: www.juliesnowarchitects.com
[25] Koehler House, New Brunswick, Canada (2000), 112

Lorcan O'Herlihy Architects
5709 Mesmer Avenue
Culver City
CA 90230
USA
E: loh@loharchitects.com
T: +1 310 398 0394
F: +1 310 398 2675
W: www.loharchitects.com
[26] Vertical House, Los Angeles, California, USA (2003), 116

Mack Scogin Merrill Elam Architects
111 John Wesley Dobbs Avenue, NE
Atlanta
GA 30303
USA
E: office@msmearch.com
T: +1 404 525 6869
F: +1 404 525 7061
W: www.msmearch.com
[27] Mountain Tree House, Dillard, Georgia, USA (2001), 120

Olson Sundberg Kundig Allen Architects
159 South Jackson Street, 6th Floor
Seattle
WA 98104
USA
E: new_inquiry@olsonsundberg.com
T: +1 206 624 5670
F: +1 206 624 3730
W: www.olsonsundberg.com
[21] Chicken Point Cabin, Chicken Point, Idaho, USA (2003), 94

Patkau Architects
1564 West 6th Avenue
Vancouver BC
Canada V6J 1R2
E: info@patkau.ca
T: +1 604 683 7633
F: +1 604 6837634
W: www.patkau.ca
[42] Agosta House, San Juan Island, Washington, USA (2000), 182

Pugh + Scarpa
2525 Michigan Avenue, Building F1
Santa Monica
CA 90404
USA
E: info@pugh-scarpa.com
T: +1 310 828 0226
F: +1 310 453 9606
W: www.pugh-scarpa.com
[08] Solar Umbrella, Los Angeles, California, USA, 38

RoTo Architects
600 Moulton Avenue, No. 405
Los Angeles
CA 90031
USA
E: roto@rotoark.com
T: +1 323 226 1112
F: +1 323 226 1105
W: www.rotoark.com
[44] Gompertz Residence, Livingston, Montana, USA (2001), 190

Smith-Miller + Hawkinson Architects
305 Canal Street
New York
NY 10013
USA
E: contact@smharch.com
T: +1 212 966 3875
F: +1 212 966 3877
W: www.smharch.com
[46] Mustang Meadow, Colorado, USA (2001), 198

Steven Holl Architects
450 West 31st Street, 11th Floor
New York
NY 10001
USA
E: mail@stevenholl.com
T: +1 212 629 7262
F: +1 212 629 7312
W: www.stevenholl.com
[52] Turbulence House, Abiqui, New Mexico, USA (2005), 224

Studio Daniel Libeskind
2 Rector Street
New York
NY 10006
USA
E: info@daniel-libeskind.com
T: +1 212 497 9100
F: +1 212 285 2130
W: www.daniel-libeskind.com
[03] Studio Weil, Port d'Andratz, Mallorca, Spain (2003), 18

Will Bruder Architects
111 West Monroe, Suite 444
Phoenix
AZ 85003
USA
E: studio@willbruder.com
T: +1 602 324 6000
F: +1 602 324 6001
W: www.willbruder.com
[22] Sky Arc House, Marin County, California, USA (2001), 98

WPA Inc.
911 Western Avenue, Suite 380
Seattle
WA 98104
USA
E: apellecchia@wpastudio.com
T: +1 206.233.0550
F: +1 206.233.0663
W: wpastudio.com
[33] Villa Lucy, Port Townsend, Washington, USA (2004), 144

Index

Picture Credits

All architectural drawings are supplied courtesy of the architects

Photographic credits:

Acknowledgments

Thanks above all to the architects who submitted material for this book. Their time, effort and patience is very much appreciated. Special thanks to Hamish Muir, the designer of this book – a kindred soul, talented designer and resolver of many graphic challenges. Sincere thanks to Philip Cooper at Laurence King with whom it is a true pleasure to work. Also to Emily Asquith for her always good-humoured editorial input. To Sophia Gibb for her indomitable dedication in researching the pictures, often in the face of daunting challenges. To Greg Gibbon and Justin Fletcher for tackling the drawings in this volume and to Vic Brand for his invaluable technical expertise. And finally to Vishwa Kaushal for his support, friendship and generosity.

The attached CD can be read on both Windows and Macintosh computers. All the material on the CD is copyright protected and is for private use only. All drawings in the book and on the CD were specially created for this publication and are based on the architects' original designs.

The CD includes files for all of the drawings included in the book, with the exception of the drawings for Studio Weil. The drawings for each building are contained in a numbered folder. They are supplied in two versions: the files with the suffix '.eps' are 'vector' EPS files and can be opened using general graphics programmes such as Illustrator; all the files with the suffix '.dwg' are generic CAD format files and can be opened in a variety of CAD programmes.

Each file is numbered according to its original location in the book: project number, followed by drawing number(s), followed by the scale. Hence '01_01_200.eps' is the eps version of the first drawing in the first project and has a scale of 1:200. In some cases, there are several drawings within the same file, so '01_04-05_200.eps' contains drawings 4 and 5 from project 1, all at a scale of 1:200.

The generic '.dwg' file format does not support 'solid fill' utilized by many architectural CAD programs. All the information is embedded within the file and can be reinstated within supporting CAD programs. Select the polygon required and change the 'Attributes' to 'Solid', the colour information should be automatically retrieved. To reinstate the 'Walls'; select all objects within the 'Walls' layer/class and amend their 'Attributes' to 'Solid'.